Communications
in Computer and Information Science   1439

More information about this series at http://www.springer.com/series/7899

Ana C. R. Paiva · Ana Rosa Cavalli ·
Paula Ventura Martins ·
Ricardo Perez-Castillo (Eds.)

Quality of Information and Communications Technology

14th International Conference, QUATIC 2021
Algarve, Portugal, September 8–11, 2021
Proceedings

 Springer

Editors
Ana C. R. Paiva 🆔
Faculty of Engineering of the University
of Porto
Porto, Portugal

Paula Ventura Martins 🆔
University of Algarve
Faro, Portugal

Ana Rosa Cavalli 🆔
Institut Polytechnique de Paris
Paris, France

Ricardo Perez-Castillo 🆔
University of Castila-La Mancha
Ciudad Real, Ciudad Real, Spain

ISSN 1865-0929   ISSN 1865-0937   (electronic)
Communications in Computer and Information Science
ISBN 978-3-030-85346-4   ISBN 978-3-030-85347-1   (eBook)
https://doi.org/10.1007/978-3-030-85347-1

This Springer imprint is published by the registered company Springer Nature Switzerland AG
The registered company address is: Gewerbestrasse 11, 6330 Cham, Switzerland

Preface

The International Conference on the Quality of Information and Communications Technology (QUATIC) serves as a forum for disseminating advanced methods, techniques, and tools for supporting quality approaches to ICT engineering and management. Practitioners and researchers are encouraged to exchange ideas and approaches on how to adopt a quality culture in ICT process and product improvement and to provide practical studies in varying contexts.

QUATIC 2021 was led by Ana C. R. Paiva (Faculty of Engineering of the University of Porto) and Ana R. Cavalli (Institut Polytechnique Paris/Telecom Sud-Paris) as program chairs. The organizing chair of this 14th edition of QUATIC was Paula Ventura Martins (University of Algarve) and the event was locally organized along with Marielba Zacarias and João Dias at the University of Algarve. QUATIC 2021 was planned to be held during September 8–11, 2021 in Faro, Algarve, Portugal. Unfortunately, due to the effects of the COVID-19 pandemic, QUATIC 2021 was conducted as a fully online conference.

This volume is a collection of high-quality peer-reviewed research papers from all over the world. QUATIC 2021 attracted a good number of submissions from different areas spanning several thematic tracks, proposed in the call for papers, in various cutting-edge technologies of specialized focus, organized and chaired by eminent experts of each field. The following nine thematic tracks correspond to QUATIC 2021 sessions:

- ICT Verification and Validation (Francesca Lonetti, ISTI-CNR, Italy)
- Software Evolution (Nicolas Anquetil, Inria and ULille-1, France)
- Process Modeling, Improvement, and Assessment (Karol Frühauf, Infogem AG, Switzerland)
- Quality Aspects in Quantum Computing (Manuel Serrano, UCLM, Spain)
- Safety, Security, and Privacy (Valentina Casola, University of Napoli Federico II, Italy)
- Quality Aspects in Machine Learning, AI, and Data Analytics (Shuo Wang, University of Birmingham, UK)
- Evidence-Based Software Quality Engineering (Fernando Brito e Abreu, ISCTE, Portugal)
- Quality in Cyber-physical Systems (Shaukat Ali, Simula Research Laboratory, Norway)
- Software Quality Education and Training (Claudia Werner, UFRJ, Brazil, and Káthia Marçal de Oliveira, Polytechnic University of Hauts-de-France, France)

Due to the exigent review process, no papers were accepted for the following three tracks:

- ICT Requirements Engineering (Luiz Marcio Cysneiros, York University, Canada and Vera Werneck, State University of Rio de Janeiro, Brazil)

- Model-driven Engineering (Antonio Cicchetti, Mälardalen University, Sweden)
- SEDES - Doctoral Symposium (Miguel Goulão, NOVA School of Science and Technology, Portugal)

Technical Review Summary

The Technical Program Committee of QUATIC 2021 was made up of 171 international academic and industrial domain experts, from organizations in 29 different countries on 5 continents. Based on a rigorous peer-review process by the Technical Program Committee members along with external experts as reviewers, the best quality papers were identified for presentation and publication.

The review was carried out in a double-blind process, with a minimum of three reviews per submission. Submitted papers came from more than 45 countries and accepted papers originated from 26 countries. Out of the submission pool of 98 papers, 30 (30.6%) were accepted as full papers for inclusion in the proceedings and 9 (9.2%) as short papers.

Invited Talk

QUATIC 2021 was fortunate to have three invited talks presented by outstanding keynote speakers.

The first keynote was by Martin Shepperd. Martin Shepperd received a PhD in computer science from the Open University in 1991 for his work in measurement theory and its application to empirical software engineering. He is professor of Software Technology and Modelling at Brunel University London, UK. Previously he has worked as a software developer for HSBC and also as COPUS Fellow in the Parliamentary Office of Science and Technology. He has published more than 180 refereed papers and three books in the areas of software engineering and machine learning. He is a fellow of the British Computer Society.

The second keynote speaker was Manuel Wimmer. Manuel Wimmer is a full professor and head of the Institute for Business Informatics – Software Engineering at the Johannes Kepler University, Linz, Austria. He received his Ph.D. and Habilitation from TU Wien, Austria. He has been a research associate at the University of Malaga, Spain, a visiting professor at the University of Marburg, Germany, as well as at TU Munich, Germany, and an assistant professor at the Business Informatics Group (BIG), TU Wien, Austria. Currently, he is also leading the Christian Doppler Laboratory on Model-Integrated Smart Production (CDL-MINT). He is co-author of the book Model-driven Software Engineering in Practice (Morgan & Claypool, second edition, 2017).

The third talk was given by Jaime Jorge. Jaime Jorge (industry keynote) is the CEO and co-founder of Codacy, one of the best-known platforms for software quality standardization around the world. Jaime has an MSc in Software Engineering from IST and was previously an associate researcher in L2F/INESC-ID in Lisbon, Portugal.

September 2021

Ana C. R. Paiva
Ana Rosa Cavalli
Paula Ventura Martins
Ricardo Pérez-Castillo

Acknowledgments

As proceedings editors, we wish to thank all the people and organizations that directly or indirectly supported this event. Thanks to the thematic track and PhD symposium chairs and all other members of the Technical Program Committee for their many contributions and reviews that guaranteed the overall quality of the QUATIC 2021 conference.

Thanks to our colleagues from the University of Algarve for all the organizational details required for hosting the conference, despite the fact that the constraints and difficulties associated with the COVID-19 pandemic obliged us to do it fully online. Thanks to our colleagues that participated at different levels in the organization of the conference. Thanks to the QUATIC's Steering Committee members for their guidance and support throughout all this process.

Also, a special thanks to all the organizations involved in this conference, including our promoters (IPQ and CS03), supporters (UAlgarve, Brunel University, ISCTE-IUL, IST-UL, UCLM, FCT-UNL, FE-UP, UMinho, CNR, and UCoimbra), sponsor (ACM), and partners (NEEI/UALG and APQ).

Last but not least, special thanks to all the authors and participants at the conference. Without their efforts, there would be no conference or proceedings. Thank you for contributing to the critical mass of researchers that keep this conference alive for what we expect to be many years to come.

Organization

Program Committee Chairs

Ana C. R. Paiva	Universidade do Porto, Portugal
Ana Rosa Cavalli	Institut Polytechnique Paris/Telecom SudParis, France

Thematic Track Chairs

ICT Verification and Validation

Francesca Lonetti   National Research Council (CNR), Italy

Process Modeling, Improvement, and Assessment

Karol Frühauf   INFOGEM AG, Switzerland

Software Evolution

Nicolas Anquetil   Inria and University of Lille 1, France

Evidence-based Software Quality Engineering

Fernando Brito e Abreu   Instituto Universitário de Lisboa, Portugal

Safety, Security, and Privacy

Valentina Casola   University of Napoli Federico II, Italy

Quality Aspects in Quantum Computing

Manuel Serrano   University of Castilla-La Mancha, Spain

Quality Aspects in Machine Learning, AI, and Data Analytics

Shuo Wang   University of Birmingham, UK

Model-driven Engineering

Antonio Cicchetti   Mälardalen University, Sweden

Software Quality Education and Training

Claudia Werner	Universidade Federal do Rio de Janeiro, Brazil
Káthia Marçal de Oliveira	Polytechnic University of Hauts-de-France, France

ICT Requirements Engineering

Luiz Marcio Cysneiros	York University, Canada
Vera Werneck	State University of Rio de Janeiro, Brazil

PhD Symposium (SEDES)

Miguel Goulão	Universidade Nova de Lisboa, Portugal

Program Committee

Abdelhak-Djamel Seriai	LIRMM/University of Montpellier, France
Aitor Arrieta	Mondragon Goi Eskola Politeknikoa, Spain
Alessandra Bagnato	Softeam, France
Alessandra De Benedictis	University of Naples Federico II, Italy
Alessio Gambi	Passau University, Germany
Alessio Merlo	University of Genoa, Italy
Alexandros Chatzigeorgiou	University of Macedonia, Macedonia
Alin Stefanescu	University of Bucharest, Romania
Ambrosio Toval	University of Murcia, Spain
Andrea Janes	Free University of Bolzano, Italy
Andreas Nehfort	Nehfort IT-Consulting KG, Austria
Andreas Ulrich	Siemens AG, Germany
Andreas Wortmann	University of Stuttgart, Germany
Antonia Bertolino	ISTI-CNR, Italy
Antonino Sabetta	SAP Labs, Germany
Antonio Vallecillo	Universidad de Málaga, Spain
Antonio Cicchetti	Mälardalen University, Sweden
Apostolos Ampatzoglou	University of Macedonia, Greece
Barbara Gallina	Mälardalen University, Sweden
Bartosz Walter	PCSS/PPoz, Poland
Beatriz Marín	Universidad Diego Portales, Chile
Benoit Combemale	University of Rennes 1 and Inria, France
Breno Miranda	Universidade Federal de Pernambuco, Brazil
Christelle Urtado	LGI2P - IMT Mines Ales, France
Christian Esposito	University of Naples Federico II, Italy
Christopher Fuhrman	École de technologie supérieure, Canada
Chun Wai Chiu	University of Birmingham, UK
Claudia Raibulet	University of Milano-Bicocca, Italy
Dan Berry	University of Waterloo, Canada
Edgardo Montes de Oca	Montimage, France
Eduardo Spinosa	Federal University of Paraná, Brazil
Elena Navarro	University of Castilla-La Mancha, Spain
Emilio Insfran	Universitat Politècnica de València, Spain
Eric Yu	University of Toronto, Canada
Erkuden Rios	Tecnalia, Spain
Eugene Syriani	University of Montreal, Canada

Eva Navarro-Lopez	University of Wolverhampton, UK
Fabio Palomba	University of Salerno, Italy
Ferdinand Gramsamer	Infogem AG, Switzerland
Fernando Brito e Abreu	Instituto Universitário de Lisboa, Portugal
Francesca Lonetti	CNR-ISTI, Italy
Francisco Gortázar	University Rey Juan Carlos, Spain
Frank Phillipson	TNO, The Netherlands
Gabriel Alberto García-Mireles	Universidad de Sonora, Mexico
Gerhard Fessler	Steinbeis-Beratungszentrum Prozesse, Exzellenz und CMMI (PEC), Germany
Geylani Kardas	Ege University, Turkey
Gordana Rakic	University of Novi Sad, Serbia
Grischa Liebel	Reykjavik University, Iceland
Guido Peterssen	Alhambra IT, Spain
Guilherme Travassos	COPPE/UFRJ, Brazil
Gustavo Rossi	Universidad Nacional de La Plata, Argentina
Hakan Erdogmus	CMU, USA
Helge Pfeiffer	IT University of Copenhagen, Denmark
Hong Zhu	Oxford Brookes University, UK
Honghui Du	University of Leicester, UK
Hyunsook Do	University of North Texas, USA
Ignacio García	University of Castilla-La Mancha, Spain
Isabel Sofia Sousa Brito	Instituto Politécnico de Beja, Portugal
J. Andres Diaz-Pace	UNICEN University, Argentina
Jaelson Castro	Universidade Federal de Pernambuco, Brazil
Javier Troya	University of Malaga, Spain
Jeffrey Carver	University of Alabama, USA
Jennifer Pérez	Universidad Politécnica de Madrid, Spain
Jesús Morán	University of Oviedo, Spain
Jingyue Li	Norwegian University of Science and Technology, Norway
Joachim Denil	University of Antwerp, Belgium
Joao Fernandes	University of Porto, Portugal
Joao Gama	University of Porto, Portugal
João Faria	FEUP/INESC TEC, Portugal
Johnny Marques	Instituto Tecnológico de Aeronáutica, Brazil
Jordi Tura Brugués	Leiden University, The Netherlands
Jorge Casillas	University of Granada, Spain
Jose Hevia	Alhambra IT, Spain
Jose Antonio Cruz-Lemus	University of Castilla-La Mancha, Spain
Jose Luis de la Vara	University of Castilla-La Mancha, Spain
Juan Manuel Vara	University Rey Juan Carlos, Spain
Juan Manuel Murillo Rodríguez	University of Extremadura, Spain
Juan Pablo Carvallo	Universidad del Azuay, Equador

Julio Cesar Leite	PUC-Rio, Brazil
Juncal Alonso	Tecnalia, Spain
Karol Fruehauf	INFOGEM AG, Switzerland
Krzysztof Wnuk	BTH, Sweden
Leandro Minku	University of Birmingham, UK
Leire Orue-Echevarria	Tecnalia, Spain
Lidia Lopez	Universitat Politècnica de Catalunya, Spain
Liyan Song	Southern University of Science and Technology, China
Loli Burgueño	Open University of Catalonia, Spain
Ludovico Iovino	Gran Sasso Science Institute, Italy
Luigi Lavazza	Università degli Studi dell'Insubria, Italy
Luis Olsina	National University of La Pampa, Argentina
Luiz Marcio Cysneiros	York University, Canada
M.J. Escalona	University of Seville, Spain
Macario Polo	University of Castilla-La Mancha, Spain
Magne Jorgensen	Simula Metropolitan Center for Digital Engineering, Norway
Man Zhang	Kristiania University College, Norway
Manuel Wimmer	Johannes Kepler University Linz, Austria
Manuel Serrano	University of Castilla-La Mancha, Spain
Marcela Ruiz	Zurich University of Applied Sciences, Switzerland
Marcos Didonet Del Fabro	Universidade Federal do Paraná, Brazil
Maria Lencastre	Universidade de Pernambuco, Brazil
Maria Teresa Baldassarre	University of Bari, Italy
Mario Piattini	University of Castilla-La Mancha, Spain
Martin Höst	Lund University, Sweden
Massimiliano Rak	University of Campania, Italy
Maurizio Leotta	Università di Genova, Italy
Michael Felderer	University of Innsbruck, Austria
Miguel Goulão	Universidade Nova de Lisboa, Portugal
Miguel Ehécatl Morales Trujillo	University of Canterbury, New Zealand
Moharram Challenger	University of Antwerp, Belgium
Moises Rodríguez	AQCLab, Spain
Nelly Condori-Fernández	Universidade da Coruña, Spain
Nicolas Anquetil	University of Lille, France
Oscar Pastor Lopez	Universitat Politècnica de València, Spain
Oum-El-Kheir Aktouf	LCIS Grenoble INP, France
Paolo Arcaini	National Institute of Informatics, Japan
Patrizio Pelliccione	Gran Sasso Science Institute, Italy, and Chalmers University of Technology and University of Gothenburg, Sweden
Rafael Capilla	Universidad Rey Juan Carlos, Spain
Ralf Kneuper	IU Internationale Hochschule, Germany
Ricardo Pérez-Castillo	University of Castilla-La Mancha, Spain
Robert Clarisó	Universitat Oberta de Catalunya, Spain

Roberto Pietrantuono	University of Naples Federico II, Italy
Roberto Nardone	Mediterranean University of Reggio Calabria, Italy
Rui Abreu	INESC-ID/University of Porto, Portugal
Sandro Morasca	Università degli Studi dell'Insubria, Italy
Shaukat Ali	Simula Research Laboratory, Norway
Sigrid Eldh	Ericsson AB, Sweden
Sotirios Liaskos	University of York, UK
Stefan Wagner	University of Stuttgart, Germany
Steve Counsell	Brunel University, UK
Tao Yue	Nanjing University of Aeronautics and Astronautics, China
Tao Chen	Loughborough University, UK
Timo Kehrer	Humboldt-Universität zu Berlin, Germany
Torsten Bandyszak	The Ruhr Institute for Software Technology, Germany
Tracy Hall	Lancaster University, UK
Tullio Vardanega	University of Padua, Italy
Umberto Villano	University of Sannio, Italy
Valentina Casola	University of Naples Federico II, Italy
Vânia Neves	UFF, Brazil
Vasco Amaral	Universidade NOVA de Lisboa, Portugal
Vera Werneck	Rio de Janeiro State University, Brazil
Wasif Afzal	Mälardalen University, Sweden
Wissam Mallouli	Montimage, France
Xiaofen Lu	Southern University of Science and Technology, China
Xiaofeng Wang	Free University of Bozen-Bolzano, Italy
Yania Crespo	University of Valladolid, Spain
Yun Yang	Yunnan University, China
Yunwen Lei	University of Birmingham, UK
Yuwei Guo	China

Additional Reviewers

Changwu Huang	Rui He
Denis Pinheiro	Salvatore Barone
Guoming Long	Shulei Liu
Heleno Campos	Yu Zhang
Liu Zhening	Yunce Zhao
Qing Bao	

Organizing Chair

Paula Ventura Martins   Universidade do Algarve, Portugal

Local Co-chairs

Marielba Zacarias	Universidade do Algarve, Portugal
João Dias	Universidade do Algarve, Portugal

Proceedings Chair

Ricardo Perez del Castillo   Universidad de Castilla-La-Mancha, Spain

Publicity Chair

Américo Rio   ISCTE-IUL/UNL, Portugal

Web Chair

José Pereira dos Reis   ISCTE-IUL, Portugal

Sponsors Chair

Margarida Madeira   Universidade do Algarve, Portugal

Industrial Day Co-chairs

Vanessa Nascimento   Algarve Tech Hub, Portugal
Hugo Barros   CRIA/Universidade do Algarve, Portugal

Contributing Organizations

Promoters

Comissão Sectorial
para as *Tecnologias da*
CS/03 *Informação e Comunicações*

Instituto Português
da Qualidade

Supporters

UNIVERSIDADE DE COIMBRA

Partners

Contents

Quality Aspects in Machine Learning, AI and Data Analytics

Evidence-Based Software Quality Engineering

Quality in Cyber-physical Systems

Software Quality Education and Training

ICT Verification and Validation

Reducing Flakiness in End-to-End Test Suites: An Experience Report

Dario Olianas[1]([⊠])⬤, Maurizio Leotta[1]⬤, Filippo Ricca[1]⬤, and Luca Villa[2]

[1] Dipartimento di Informatica, Bioingegneria,
Robotica e Ingegneria dei Sistemi (DIBRIS), Università di Genova, Genoa, Italy
dario.olianas@dibris.unige.it,
{maurizio.leotta,filippo.ricca}@unige.it
[2] IRCCS Istituto Giannina Gaslini, Clinica Pediatrica e Reumatologia,
PRINTO, Genoa, Italy
lucavilla@gaslini.org

Abstract. End-to-end (E2E) testing, a technique employed to assure quality of web applications, is cost-effective only if the test suite is not flaky. Flaky test scripts produce non-deterministic results that undermine testers' trust and thus the usefulness of the entire test suite.

Recently, we were involved in the refactoring of an existing automated flaky E2E test suite for a large Web application. In this paper, we report on our experience. During the refactoring, we have computed the effort made and formalized the procedure we followed in algorithmic way so that our experience can also be of help to other developers/testers. Our procedure allowed to reduce the flakiness to virtually zero w.r.t. the original flaky test suite. Moreover, as a positive side effect, the execution time of the test suite has been reduced by of the 57%.

Keywords: E2E testing · Flakiness · Empirical study

1 Introduction

Recently, many companies are gearing up to have automated test suites capable of quickly detecting bugs during software evolution. In fact, if implemented correctly, the automated test suites are able to bring many benefits to companies, such as better quality software and cost reduction [6,16]. However, these benefits can only be achieved if the automated test suite is reliable and has no flakiness problems.

A test script is *flaky* when may non-deterministically pass or fail on the same version of the Application Under Test (AUT), i.e. leading to different results in different runs on the same AUT without any change in both the app and test code [5,22]. The flakiness problem is very insidious for companies because: (1) it makes lose confidence in the results of the execution of the test suites with false alarms, (2) it increases deployment/release times, and generally, (3) it increases development costs [22]. Many big companies, such as Google, Facebook and Microsoft are facing this problem [22] and unfortunately effective solutions that

© Springer Nature Switzerland AG 2021
A. C. R. Paiva et al. (Eds.): QUATIC 2021, CCIS 1439, pp. 3–17, 2021.
https://doi.org/10.1007/978-3-030-85347-1_1

4   D. Olianas et al.

allow to reveal and resolve the flakiness do not exist yet. Most of the proposed methods depend on test repetition, i.e. a test script is applied to the same AUT for a given number of times, if the results are different, then the test is marked as flaky [13].

Recently the authors were involved in the refactoring of an existing automated End-to-End (E2E) test suite concerning a large multi-page Web application for paediatric rheumatology patients management. The partner organization is PRINTO, a not for profit, non governmental, international research medical network with the goal to foster, facilitate and coordinate the development of clinical studies in children with paediatric rheumatic diseases. The testsuite was developed in Java language using the Selenium WebDriver [19] and TestNG [2] frameworks and had relevant flakiness problems that created continuous false alarms.

To face and limit the flakiness problem, we considered tools and best practices available in the state-of-the-art literature, utilizing also the experience gained from our past scientific [7,10,12,21] and industrial [8,9] collaborations in developing E2E test suites for web applications. After a thorough analysis of the problem, we used a well-defined manual procedure based mainly on substitution rules of thread-sleep commands located in test scripts with a better alternative, WebDriverWait commands, based on a polling mechanism built into Selenium able to wait for an element to appear or exist, and to wait for some sort of change in a web page. We have quantified the effort made and formalized the procedure in algorithmic way so that our experience can also be of help to other developers/testers.

This paper is organized as follows: Sect. 2 describes the PRINTO web app and the test suite we refactored. Section 3 sketches the approach we used to limit the flakiness problem present in the original test suite. Section 4 reports the data on the reduction of flakiness compared to the original test suite. Section 5 presents lessons learnt and gives future extensions. Finally, Sect. 6 summarizes related works and Sect. 7 concludes the paper.

2 The PRINTO Web App and the Associated E2E Test Suite

2.1 The PRINTO Web Application

The Paediatric Rheumatology INternational Trials Organisation (PRINTO) is an academic international research network with the goal to facilitate and coordinate multi-centre international clinical trials and registries in children with paediatric rheumatic diseases and autoinflammatory diseases. Having the need to collect clinical information worldwide, PRINTO has developed and maintained during the years a large multi-page web application (www.printo.it) to achieve its goal. The PRINTO web application is used by more than 500 centers worldwide with about 1500 members today and it provides several functionalities to collect information for clinical trials, disease registries, safety registries and clinical consensus processes. It was developed on the server side in PHP language (approximately 100k LOCs[1]) and on the client side in HTML and JavaScript (for the latter, approximately 2k LOCs).

---

[1] Computed using Locmetrics (https://www.cheonghyun.com/blog/120).

2.2   Original PRINTO's E2E Test Suite

The original E2E test suite we refactored is a Java test suite that relies on Selenium WebDriver [19] to interact with the application's pages. The test suite has been built with Maven, and it uses the testing framework TestNG [2]. It uses the GeckoDriver implementation for the browser Mozilla Firefox and is designed following the Page Object model [1], i.e., a model where Object Oriented classes serves as interfaces to Web pages. It contains 11707 LOCs, namely 5523 in the page objects and 6184 in the test scripts. It is composed by 169 independent test scripts that can be executed in any order. The independence of test scripts has been obtained by the accurate use of Setup and Teardown TestNG methods, respectively, methods that are executed before a test script (or a test class) to set up the initial state, and after a test script (or test class) to undo the test script actions with the goal of resetting the initial state of the application. The original test suite contains 82 of such methods, also known as *test fixtures*, for a total of 251 methods (test scripts plus test fixtures). Both test scripts and test fixtures can be executed multiple times in a single run of the test suite. The test fixtures are executed several times according to the specific TestNG method (for example, a BeforeMethod method is executed for each test script it belongs to its test class) while test scripts, that are in several cases parameterized, are executed multiple times, depending on the number of different values passed to them. In total, 551 methods are executed for each execution of the testuite (of which 334 test fixtures).

Statistics on the Test Suite Execution. The original test suite was heavily affected by the flakiness problem. To quantify the problem, we executed the original test suite in a controlled environment (i.e., without modifying the test suite and system under test during runs) for 100 times and obtained that, on 55100 total method executions (counting both test fixtures and test scripts), 54699 (**99.27%**) passed, 44 (**0.08%** failed) and 357 (**0.65%**) were skipped. In TestNG, a test script is skipped when its corresponding Before method fails: because of that, flakiness is still more problematic when it happens in a Before method, since it will prevent other test scripts to be executed. The above reported number of false alarms may seem negligible with respect to the total number of test methods executions, but if we count every execution of the test suite in which at least one method failed, we have 18 failures out of 100 executions, giving a flakiness score for the test suite of **18%**. Since the original test suite runs every night, approximately means a false failure report every 5 days. Looking at the finer grained results, we realized that flakiness is quite localized: out of 251 test methods, only 26 failed at least one time during the 100 executions. For these methods, we have computed the flakiness scores as: number of times the method failed divided by number of times the method passed. The maximum flakiness score was 3.09% for two methods (i.e., the most flaky). Finally, concerning execution times, the original test suite required on average 81 min to run (value calculated by averaging the 82 runs that were not affected by flakiness over a total of 100).

3   Overview of the Approach for Reducing Flakiness

As a first step to discover the reasons for the flakiness of the test suite, we have analyzed in detail the code of the test scripts and the page objects that compose it. The first thing we noticed was the presence of thread sleeps positioned both in the code of the page objects and in that of the test scripts. Thread sleeps, i.e., function calls that pause the execution of a test script for a given time, are usually employed by developers for managing *asynchronous calls*. In the context of web applications, asynchronous calls happen whenever there is an interaction with a page that requires some data to be retrieved from the web server. However, this solution has two disadvantages, indeed thread sleeps: a) are inefficient, especially in large test suites, because they always wait the same amount of time, defined a priori by the developer, even when the page finishes to load more quickly and, b) are often one of the reasons of flakiness, as testified for example in Luo et al. [13] and Ricca and Stocco papers [17]. The problem is that thread sleeps often handle asynchronous calls 'badly', without properly waiting for the web server response, thus leading to flakiness. From several years now the Selenium testing framework has provided a smarter mechanism for managing asynchronous calls, called explicit wait. Technically speaking, an explicit wait is a Java object of class WebDriverWait, that can be used in combination with an ExpectedCondition, that is a function that informs the explicit wait about which condition must be verified to stop waiting. From the Selenium documentation[2] we can identify six main categories of expected conditions:

- expected conditions checking the visibility of an element
- expected conditions checking the clickability of an element
- expected conditions checking the presence of an element
- expected conditions checking the number of elements
- expected conditions checking the page's URL
- expected conditions for text comparison
- expected conditions checking DOM attributes

Explicit waits are more efficient w.r.t. thread sleeps because they stop waiting when the element in question is ready for the specific interaction, and if we consider all the test scripts in a large test suite the usage of explicit waits can lead to great time savings. Moreover, explicit waits are more flexible and more reliable, because they allow to check for complex conditions to be verified: for example, if we have a text in a page that can be dynamically updated via AJAX, it would be difficult to check it using thread sleeps, but with the textToBe expected condition offered by explicit waits this control becomes feasible.

As already mentioned, the original test suite was implemented using thread sleeps. After a first analysis, we realized that they were set incorrectly: some

---

[2] Documentation for the ExpectedConditions class
https://www.selenium.dev/selenium/docs/api/java/org/openqa/selenium/support/ui/ExpectedConditions.html.

were missing in some points and some had too short or too long waiting times. The presence of these thread sleeps could be one of the reasons for the flakiness and also could explain the very long execution times with respect to the number and length of executed test scripts. So, we decided to modify the existing test suite with a two-steps approach. First, by adding or modifying the thread sleeps in all the points where failures occurred. As a result, we were able to reduce flakiness, but at a cost of an increased total execution time: from 81 min to 128 min. Second, we decided to refactor this time-consuming version of the test suite by changing every thread sleep (both those already present in the original test suite and those introduced by us to limit flakiness) with explicit wait, relying on a phased approach to make sure we do not introduce novel regressions (i.e. some tests that previously worked fine start to fail or to be flaky) during the refactoring.

3.1 Test Suite Refactoring

In this subsection, we will describe the refactoring procedure we used for PRINTO test suite. Since the flakiness problem is, by definition, non-deterministic, the procedure is based on heuristics and follows a step-by-step approach to detect possible regressions as soon as possible (i.e., immediately after their introduction). In our case, we have a regression when a refactored test script that previously passed starts to fail, also in non-deterministic way; in this last case, it means that our refactoring worsened flakiness rather than improving it. The procedure **RemoveSleep** is described in Algorithm 1, and it can be summarized as follows: for each thread sleep in the test suite, we replace it with the appropriate explicit wait (**NewExplicitWait**), then, we select a test script that calls the method containing the introduced explicit wait (most likely a page object method, since thread sleeps have been mainly inserted in page object methods) and execute it $K = 3$ times (**Validate**). If it passes K times, we consider the next thread sleep, otherwise we try to fix the test script using different strategies (**FixExplicitWait**). In the worst case, i.e., if all fixing attempts fail, we give up and restore the original thread sleep: in our case, this happened only four times on 196 thread sleeps. The choice of using a single test script to validate an explicit wait is mainly motivated by time-saving requirements. A completely safe solution would be to run every test script calling the PO method where the introduced explicit wait is used, but this would enormously increase the required time. So, to compensate for the adopted simplification, every $W = 15$ thread sleeps replaced, we execute the whole test suite $H = 3$ times to check that the inserted explicit waits do not introduce novel regressions: this check can help us to find previously undetected regressions. When this happen, we troubleshoot the regression by applying **FixExplicitWait** to the points of failure. The selection of 15 (W) as the number of changes before re-executing the entire test suite for three times (H) is part of our heuristics. We selected that number since it appears to be a reasonable trade off between (a) the number of modifications: increasing this number can make difficult to understand the cause of a possible regression and (b) the time required to execute the test suite: executing it too often could slow down too much the refactoring process.

Algorithm 1: replacing all thread sleeps in a test suite with explicit waits

---

// **RemoveSleep** procedure for replacing all thread sleeps in a test suite with explicit waits

Input   : T – a test suite with thread sleeps
Output: T_E – the same test suite but with explicit waits instead of thread sleeps

```
 1  RemoveSleep(T):
 2  │   foreach thread sleep TS in T do
 3  │   │   WPI ← web page interaction after TS
 4  │   │   EW ← NewExplicitWait(WPI)
 5  │   │   if not Validate(EW) then
 6  │   │   │   POF ← point of failure (failed WebDriver interaction of the test case t
    │   │   │        executed in Validate)
 7  │   │   │   if POF == WPI then
 8  │   │   │   │   fixed ← FixExplicitWait(EW)
 9  │   │   │   │   if not fixed then  remove explicit wait EW and restore thread sleep TS
10  │   │   │
11  │   │   │   else
12  │   │   │   │   newEW ← NewExplicitWait(POF)
13  │   │   │   │   if not Validate(newEW) then
14  │   │   │   │   │   fixed ← FixExplicitWait(newEW)
15  │   │   │   │   │   if not fixed then
16  │   │   │   │   │   │   remove explicit wait newEW
17  │   │   │   │   │   │   fixed ← FixExplicitWait(EW)
18  │   │   │   │   │   │   if not fixed then  remove explicit wait EW and restore thread
    │   │   │   │   │   │        sleep TS
```

// **NewExplicitWait** subprocedure for inserting new explicit wait

Input   : WPI – a WebDriver interaction with the web page, e.g. click, sendKeys or getText
Output: EW – the newly inserted explicit wait

```
19  NewExplicitWait(WPI):
20  │   if a thread sleep is present before WPI then  remove thread sleep from the test suite
21  │   if WPI is a read access then  insert EW with expected condition that checks if the
    │        element is visible
22  │   else if WPI is a write access then  insert EW with expected condition that checks if
    │        the element is clickable
23  │   return EW
```

// **Validate** subprocedure for validation of a newly inserted explicit wait

Input   : EW – an explicit wait
Output: res – result of validation

```
24  Validate(EW):
25  │   t ← a test script that calls, directly or indirectly, the method where EW is
26  │   run t K times
27  │   if all executions of t passed then return true
28  │   else return false
```

// **FixExplicitWait** subprocedure for fixing a failing explicit wait

Input   : EW – an explicit wait
Output: res – result of fix procedure

```
29  FixExplicitWait(EW):
30  │   ECs ← list of N expected conditions most suitable for the type of access after EW
31  │   foreach EC in ECs do
32  │   │   replace the expected condition used in EW with EC
33  │   │   if Validate(EW) then return true
34  │   restore original EW
35  │   WPIs ← web page interactions after EW in the execution flow of the test script
36  │   foreach WPI in WPIs do
37  │   │   currentEW ← NewExplicitWait(WPI)
38  │   │   if validate(currentEW) then return true
39  │   │   else remove currentEW
40  │   return false
```

Table 1. Statistics for single thread sleep replacement and for whole page object refactoring

	Max (minutes)	Min (minutes)	Average (minutes)	Std dev (minutes)
Single thread sleep replacement	8	2	9.52	4.47
Whole page object refactoring	330	5	40.54	53.11

3.2 Statistics on the Test Suite Refactoring Costs

One of the authors manually applied the procedure shown in Algorithm 1 and annotated the times needed to substitute the thread sleeps and troubleshoot regressions (if any). The total time required to replace all thread sleeps with explicit waits plus test scripts re-executions (i.e., executing $K = 3$ times the impacted test scripts) was 31 h. The time for executing the whole test suite (three times every 15 modifications), to check for any final regression, was 36.2 h, and the time required to troubleshoot regressions in total was 5.7 h, for a total time of the entire refactoring of 73 h. We applied the procedure on 196 thread sleeps: 187 were located in page objects and 9 directly in test scripts. We replaced 192 thread sleeps out of 196: in only 4 cases the application of the procedure did not allow us to eliminate them. Table 1, reports minimum, maximum and average time for replacing a single thread sleep and for replacing all thread sleeps in a page object, along with their standard deviation.

The time for replacing and validating each thread sleep is on average 9.5 min, with a standard deviation of 4.47 min. Obviously, more 'problematic' thread sleeps required more time: as an example, the maximum time employed to replace a single thread sleep was 28 min. For what concerns page objects, the average refactoring time is 40 min, with a standard deviation of 53 min. The high standard deviation is due to the fact that page objects in the PRINTO test suite have a great variability in size: some of them expose only a couple of methods, while some others are pretty large. Moreover, some page object methods contain only a few thread sleeps while other many.

3.3 Details on the Kind of Explicit Waits Inserted and Corresponding Costs

By applying the procedure, we were able to remove 192 thread sleeps out of 196. Of the 192 replaced thread sleeps, 177 have been replaced with an explicit wait that uses the expected condition *elementToBeClickable*, 11 with the expected condition *visibilityOf* and four with the expected condition *presenceOfElement-Located*.

When applying the sub-procedure **NewExplicitWait** in Algorithm 1, we employed the expected conditions *visibilityOf* and *elementToBeClickable* as default choices respectively for read accesses and write accesses. This means that only in four cases those expected conditions were not sufficient, and we needed to employ a different one, i.e., *presenceOfElementLocated*. In total, we had to apply the **FixExplicitWait** sub-procedure 10 times: we changed the expected condition with *presenceOfElementLocated* four times; we added another explicit wait in a different point of the page objects' code two times; we removed the explicit wait and restored the thread sleep four times. The average time it took to replace these thread sleeps was much longer than the others (20.3 min vs. 8.9 min).

4   Quantifying the Obtained Improvements

In this section, we describe the improvements of the refactored test suite with respect to the previous versions. Before applying the procedure to replace thread sleeps with explicit waits, we tried to reduce flakiness by adding thread sleeps in points where failures were more frequent. After applying the procedure to replace thread sleeps with explicit waits, we ran the test suites 100 times to quantify the obtained improvements, both on flakiness reduction and on execution time reduction. We executed the test suites on a Debian GNU/Linux 10 virtual machine with 6 GB of RAM assigned, hosted on a Windows 10 Pro laptop with 16 GB of RAM and Intel Core i3 10110U CPU with four logical cores (two physical). To avoid interferences, no other applications were running on the host system and on the virtual machine. The test suite has been executed using Jenkins[3], a popular continuous integration tool used by PRINTO to run the test suite. The system under test, instead, is deployed on a cloud solution. We decided to provide results on flakiness reduction at two levels of granularity, respectively at test method granularity and at test suite execution granularity.

4.1   Test Method Granularity Analysis

In Table 2, the column *Total test methods executions* reports the total number of executed test methods obtained running the three test suites 100 times, including test fixtures and multiple executions of the same test script with different

Table 2. Validation results at test method granularity

	Test methods executions	Passed	Failed	Skipped
Original test suite	55100	54699 (99.270%)	44 (0.080%)	357 (0.650%)
Refactored test suite with thread sleep	55100	55099 (99.998%)	1 (0.002%)	0 (0.000%)
Refactored test suite with explicit waits	55100	55092 (99.990%)	8 (0.010%)	0 (0.000%)

---

[3] Jenkins website https://www.jenkins.io/.

parameters. The other columns report respectively: number and percentage of methods passed, failed and skipped.

For the original version of the test suite, on 55100 total method executions 44 failed and 357 were skipped. The high number of skipped test is due to the fact that some of the flaky test methods were setup methods, executed before other test methods of their classes: as a consequence, when a setup method fails, the whole test class is skipped.

In the thread sleep-based refactored version of the test suite, we can see that only one test script failed on 100 executions. This is the best result we obtained from a flakiness-reduction point of view, but on the other hand the execution time increased from an average of 81 min to an average of 128 min.

In the final version of the test suite (the one with explicit waits), we can see that, on 55100 test methods executions, eight failed against only one for the refactored version with thread sleeps (in both cases we have no test scripts skipped). This would seem to suggest that the version with all the thread sleeps is more reliable, but, however, it is important to note that the eight test scripts that failed in the last version of the test suite happened during the same execution (the ninth execution in time order). Since these failures never happened again in the subsequent 91 executions, we assume that they were not caused by defects of the test suite, but probably by network problems (or other server-side problems).

4.2   Test Suite Granularity Analysis

Table 3 reports the flakiness results at test suite execution granularity. The column *Total test suite executions* reports the number of times each test suite was executed, the column *Flaky executions* reports the number of executions in which at least one test method failed and the column *Flakiness score* reports the percentage of flaky executions.

Table 3. Validation results at whole test suite execution granularity

	Total test suite execution	Flaky test suite execution	Flakiness score
Original test suite	100	18	18%
Refactored test suite with thread sleep	100	1	1%
Refactored test suite with explicit waits	100	1	1%

This table shows results more interesting from a tester's perspective since reports the probability of having a false alarm after executing the test suite. We can note that the scores of the full thread sleep version and of the explicit wait version are comparable.

4.3 Execution Time

Considering the execution time of the three test suites, we can note that the explicit wait based test suite is much faster. In fact, for the explicit wait version we obtained an average execution time of the whole test suite of 35 min, reducing the execution time of 57% with respect to the original, flaky test suite (that required 81 min) and of 72% with respect to the second version of the test suite, with all the required thread sleeps, that required 128 min.

5 Discussions, Lessons Learnt, and Future Extensions

In this section, we discuss the obtained results, lessons learnt and possible future extensions of this work.

5.1 Following a Precise Procedure Is Extremely Important

We learnt that removing flakiness in a E2E test suite is a hard task. Indeed, the non-deterministic behavior of test scripts makes difficult to understand if a change in the code has positive effects or if, on the contrary, the flakiness is getting worse. During this experience we understood that it is not possible to deal with the flakiness problem without following a precise procedure. For this reason, we defined the procedure described in Algorithm 1. We believe that a well defined procedure helps to minimize subjectivity during refactoring in order to guide programmers with little experience of Selenium WebDriver. Moreover, we learnt that it is fundamental make few changes at a time and rerun the test suite very often. This is because if flakiness occurs after a long series of changes, finding the cause is extremely difficult.

5.2 Conservative Solutions Are Too Time-Consuming

A specificity of our procedure is that we use a single test script to validate newly inserted explicit waits. Usually, if the test suite is designed following the page object pattern, a page object method will be used by more than one test script, and so will be any explicit wait inside the method. To be completely sure to not introduce regressions at each insertion of an explicit wait, we should execute multiple times every test script who uses it. However, we learnt that this is prohibitive from the point of view of execution time, so we opted for a time-saving heuristics: running a single test script at each change and then, to find possible undetected regressions, running the whole test suite after a predetermined number of changes.

5.3 It Is Hard to Be Too Prescriptive

We learnt that a procedure is useful but it has to be flexible. Indeed, our procedure leaves some degrees of freedom to the developer when it comes to select expected conditions. In sub-procedure **NewExplicitWait**, the developer is asked to choose "an expected condition that checks if the element is visible" or "an expected condition that checks if the element is clickable", but the precise choice of the expected condition is left to the developer. Also in sub-procedure **FixExplicitWait** the developer is just asked to list the k most suitable expected conditions for the WebDriver interaction under analysis. This is due to the fact that the precise expected condition to use strictly depends on the characteristics of both the test suite and the application under test. For example, if the test suite adopts the Page Factory pattern [11], the category of expected conditions that take a WebElement as argument, instead of a locator, should be used.

5.4   Thread Sleeps Substitution Can be Automated

This work was very important for understanding that thread sleeps replacement (Algorithm 1) can be automated, at least partially. Perhaps this is the most important lesson we learnt. This insight is supported by the data shown in Sect. 3.3, where it is clear that in many cases the thread sleeps have been replaced using the simpler heuristics and the re-execution of the test suite was not always necessary. It is clear that, sub-procedure **NewExplicitWait** (insertion of a new explicit wait) and sub-procedure **Validate** (validation of a newly inserted explicit wait) are the easiest procedures to automate. For sub-procedure **NewExplicitWait**, we just need to specify an expected condition to be used for the two type of considered web page interactions (i.e., read and write). Sub-procedure **Validate** is pretty straightforward too, since the list of tests that use the explicit wait under validation can be easily extracted from the test suite's code by means of static analysis techniques. Eventually, the implemented tool should be able to: refactoring the test scripts (i.e., substituting thread sleeps with explicit waits), execute the modified test scripts and collect the results showing statistics about flakiness. Clearly automating the procedure completely is much more challenging, in particular it is difficult to mechanize sub-procedure **FixExplicitWait** which is the part where human intervention is most needed. However, it is important to highlight that even the basic implementation of this tool should be able to automate a relevant portion of the refactorings (i.e., 182 out of 196 thread sleep replacements), significantly reducing the time and cost of the entire work.

5.5   Manual Intervention Is Needed

As we have already said, the application of the procedure did not allow us to replace all the thread sleeps. In four cases the procedure left the thread sleeps. This is a consequence of our heuristic which does not require the developer executing the refactoring to inspect the DOM of the web pages but relies mainly on the access done by the test scripts to the web pages. We are aware that this choice can be limiting in certain specific cases, however it works very often because web page inspection, we learnt, is rarely necessary. In retrospect, we investigated why the procedure didn't work in these four cases. In all cases, the problem was due to page elements dynamically loaded via JavaScript: the thread sleep originally inserted allows to complete the loading of the required content, while the explicit waits did not. In one case, we have that a test script compiles a form and sends it to the server. It inserts in the form wrong values, and checks if the web application detects the problem and replies with an error message. The form includes a field with auto-completion and a client-side script is in charge of checking the correctness of the inserted value. With the original thread sleep (inserted just before interacting with the submission button), the client-side check has enough time to complete its execution and shows the expected error. When we applied the procedure, we replaced the thread sleep with an explicit wait that waits for the submission button to be clickable. In this way the sequence of actions is performed correctly, but the client-side validation is skipped because does not have enough time to check the correctness of the inserted value. Thus, the web application responds with a different error from server side and this makes the test script fail. We manually fixed this explicit wait by changing the waited object to the first element that pops up in the auto-completing field: this gives the client-side check enough time to complete its execution and show the client side error. In cases like these it is very difficult (if not impossible) to automate the refactoring and therefore the manual intervention is necessary.

6 Related Work

Since the problem of flakiness is often faced in practice by practitioners, there are many works in the scientific literature that consider it.

Among these works we find some that try to understand the reasons of the flakiness and characterize the main causes by means of surveys with professional developers (e.g., [5,13]) or analyzing open source code (e.g., [13,18]). Our experience confirm the results by Eck et al. [5] and Luo et al. [13] on the high diffusion of the *Async category* as main reason of flakiness problems, that happens when a test script performs asynchronous calls without waiting properly the result. Indeed, in our test suite almost all flakiness problems fell into this category. Other works, on the other hand, confirm our choice to replace thread sleeps with explicit waits to alleviate the problem of flakiness as well as reduce execution times. Among these, we find for example the paper by Ahmad et al. [3] where they came to the conclusion that some test smells (e.g., inserting thread sleeps and having dependent test scripts) are the main reasons for test scripts flakiness. This choice of substituting thread sleeps with explicit waits is instead contradicted by Presler-Marshall et al. [15]. In a work similar to ours, carried out by students on a large electronic health record system, the authors came to the conclusion that thread waits give the lowest flakiness, while explicit waits giving the highest.

Finally, there are also many works with a different goal from ours that propose techniques and tools to detect the root cause of a specific case of flaky test script [14] or others that detect flaky test scripts in a test suite [4] or others that deal with fixing them [20]. The latter paper presents iFixFlakies, a framework for automatically fixing order-dependent test scripts. The framework is based on the idea that test suites already have helper tests whose code can help fix this particular category of flakiness-prone test suites. Compared to iFixFlakies, our strategy is simpler but in some ways more general as it applies to different types of flakiness and not to only order-dependent test scripts.

Before embarking on our refactoring work we considered the existing literature. Unfortunately, it is not always easy to use the proposed techniques due to unsatisfied requirements and constraints. For example, we considered DeFlaker [4] but it relies heavily on Java AST analysis, which makes it inapplicable to web applications written in PHP, such as PRINTO application.

7 Conclusions and Future Work

In this paper, we have described our refactoring experience of an existing automated E2E Selenium WebDriver test suite concerning a large multi-page Web application for paediatric rheumatology patients management. The main goal of refactoring was to limit flakiness as much as possible.

As a result, we devised and formalized a repeatable procedure which does not require the analysis of the DOM to be used in cases of flaky test suites. Furthermore, we have quantified the effort it takes to replace thread sleeps—often a cause of flakiness—with more performing WebDriverWaits. The adoption of WebDriverWaits also allowed to reduce the execution time of the test suite, 57% w.r.t. the original flaky test suite and of the 72% w.r.t. the flakiness-equivalent version based on the usage of thread sleeps (this version was created during the refactoring process).

As a future work, in addition to proving the generalizability and effectiveness of the proposed procedure using other test suites, we also intend to investigate the feasibility of developing an automatic tool capable of automating much of the work of replacing thread sleeps.

Acknowledgement. This work was carried out in the context of a collaboration between DIBRIS (University of Genova) and PRINTO (Gaslini Hospital). We want to show our gratitude to Dr. Nicolino Ruperto, Senior scientist of PRINTO for the support provided.

References

1. Page Object Model. https://www.selenium.dev/documentation/en/guidelines_ and_recommendations/page_object_models/
2. Testng testing framework (2021). https://testng.org/doc/. Accessed 08 Apr 2021
3. Ahmad, A., Leifler, O., Sandahl, K.: Empirical analysis of factors and their effect on test flakiness - practitioners' perceptions. arXiv:1906.00673 (2019)
4. Bell, J., Legunsen, O., Hilton, M., Eloussi, L., Yung, T., Marinov, D.: DeFlaker: automatically detecting flaky tests. In: 2018 IEEE/ACM 40th International Conference on Software Engineering (ICSE), pp. 433–444 (2018). https://doi.org/10.1145/3180155.3180164

5. Eck, M., Palomba, F., Castelluccio, M., Bacchelli, A.: Understanding flaky tests: the developer's perspective. In: Proceedings of the 2019 27th ACM Joint Meeting on European Software Engineering Conference and Symposium on the Foundations of Software Engineering, ESEC/FSE 2019, pp. 830–840. Association for Computing Machinery, New York (2019). https://doi.org/10.1145/3338906.3338945

6. Garousi, V., Felderer, M.: Developing, verifying, and maintaining high-quality automated test scripts. IEEE Softw. **33**, 68–75 (2016)

7. Leotta, M., Biagiola, M., Ricca, F., Ceccato, M., Tonella, P.: A family of experiments to assess the impact of page object pattern in web test suite development. In: Proceedings of 13th IEEE International Conference on Software Testing, Verification and Validation (ICST 2020), pp. 263–273. IEEE (2020). https://doi.org/10.1109/ICST46399.2020.00035

8. Leotta, M., Clerissi, D., Ricca, F., Spadaro, C.: Comparing the maintainability of selenium webdriver test suites employing different locators: a case study. In: Proceedings of 1st International Workshop on Joining AcadeMiA and Industry Contributions to testing Automation (ISSTA 2013 Workshops), pp. 53–58. ACM (2013). https://doi.org/10.1145/2489280.2489284

9. Leotta, M., Clerissi, D., Ricca, F., Spadaro, C.: Improving test suites maintainability with the page object pattern: an industrial case study. In: Proceedings of 6th International Conference on Software Testing, Verification and Validation Workshops (ICST 2013 Workshops), pp. 108–113. IEEE (2013). https://doi.org/10.1109/ICSTW.2013.19

10. Leotta, M., Clerissi, D., Ricca, F., Tonella, P.: Capture-replay vs. programmable web testing: an empirical assessment during test case evolution. In: Proceedings of 20th Working Conference on Reverse Engineering (WCRE 2013), pp. 272–281. IEEE (2013). https://doi.org/10.1109/WCRE.2013.6671302

11. Leotta, M., Clerissi, D., Ricca, F., Tonella, P.: Approaches and tools for automated end-to-end web testing. Adv. Comput. **101**, 193–237 (2016). https://doi.org/10.1016/bs.adcom.2015.11.007

12. Leotta, M., Stocco, A., Ricca, F., Tonella, P.: PESTO: automated migration of DOM-based web tests towards the visual approach. J. Softw. Test. Verif. Reliabil. (STVR) **28**(4), e1665 (2018). https://doi.org/10.1002/stvr.1665

13. Luo, Q., Hariri, F., Eloussi, L., Marinov, D.: An empirical analysis of flaky tests. In: Proceedings of the 22Nd ACM SIGSOFT International Symposium on Foundations of Software Engineering, FSE 2014, pp. 643–653. ACM (2014). https://doi.org/10.1145/2635868.2635920

14. Moran, J., Augusto Alonso, C., Bertolino, A., de la Riva, C., Tuya, J.: FlakyLoc: flakiness localization for reliable test suites in web applications. J. Web Eng. (2020). https://doi.org/10.13052/jwe1540-9589.1927

15. Presler-Marshall, K., Horton, E., Heckman, S., Stolee, K.T.: Wait wait. No, tell me: analyzing selenium configuration effects on test flakiness. In: Proceedings of the 14th International Workshop on Automation of Software Test, AST 2019, pp. 7–13. IEEE Press (2019). https://doi.org/10.1109/AST.2019.000-1

16. Rafi, D., Moses, K., Petersen, K., Mäntylä, M.: Benefits and limitations of automated software testing: systematic literature review and practitioner survey, pp. 36–42 (2012). https://doi.org/10.1109/IWAST.2012.6228988

17. Ricca, F., Stocco, A.: Web test automation: insights from the grey literature. In: Bureš, T., et al. (eds.) SOFSEM 2021. LNCS, vol. 12607, pp. 472–485. Springer, Cham (2021). https://doi.org/10.1007/978-3-030-67731-2_35

18. Romano, A., Song, Z., Grandhi, S., Yang, W., Wang, W.: An empirical analysis of UI-based flaky tests. arXiv:2103.02669 (2021)

19. SeleniumHQ web browser automation (2021). https://www.selenium.dev/. Accessed 08 Apr 2021
20. Shi, A., Lam, W., Oei, R., Xie, T., Marinov, D.: iFixFlakies: a framework for automatically fixing order-dependent flaky tests. In: Proceedings of the 2019 27th ACM Joint Meeting on European Software Engineering Conference and Symposium on the Foundations of Software Engineering, ESEC/FSE 2019, pp. 545–555. Association for Computing Machinery, New York (2019). https://doi.org/10.1145/3338906.3338925
21. Stocco, A., Leotta, M., Ricca, F., Tonella, P.: APOGEN: automatic page object generator for web testing. Softw. Qual. J. (SQJ) 25(3), 1007–1039 (2017). https://doi.org/10.1007/s11219-016-9331-9
22. Zolfaghari, B., Parizi, R.M., Srivastava, G., Hailemariam, Y.: Root causing, detecting, and fixing flaky tests: state of the art and future roadmap. Softw.: Pract. Exp. 51, 851–867 (2020)

Mutation Subsumption as Relative Incorrectness

Besma Khaireddine[1], Amani Ayad[2], Imen Marsit[3], and Ali Mili[4(✉)]

[1] University of Tunis El Manar, Tunis, Tunisia
[2] SUNY Farmingdale, Farmingdale, NY, USA
`ayada@farmingdale.edu`
[3] University of Sousse, Sousse, Tunisia
[4] New Jersey Institute of Technology, Newark, NJ, USA
`mili@njit.edu`

Abstract. This paper attempts to link two lines of research that have proceeded independently so far: Mutant subsumption, which is used to identify redundant mutants; and Relative correctness, which is used to define and analyze software faults. We say that a mutant M' of a program P subsumes a mutant M of P if and only if any test datum that kills M kills M'. On the other hand, we say that a program P' is more-correct than a program P with respect to a specification R if and only if whenever program P behaves correctly with respect to R on some input datum, so does program P'. We highlight the relationships between these two concepts and consider some potential synergies between these two research directions.

Keywords: Mutant equivalence · Mutant subsumption · Relative correctness · Differentiator sets · Competence domains

1 Subsumption and Relative Correctness

Mutation testing is the art of generating versions of a base program using syntactic change operators, and analyzing the semantic impacts of these changes [3,4]; mutation testing can be used in the analysis and design of test suites.

Mutants are useful in testing only to the extent that syntactic differences between the base program and mutants (or among mutants) yield semantically different behaviors; better mutants are mutants that exhibit a different behavior from the base program for a larger set of input data. As a consequence, researchers have been interested in the concept of *mutant subsumption*, which provides that a mutant M' subsumes a mutant M if and only if any input datum for which M yields a different outcome from the base program (say P), M' will necessarily yield a different outcome from P as well [9,12,13]; it is possible to define a strict version of this ordering when there is at least one input datum for which M' exhibits a different behavior from P but M does not. A set of mutants can be used to evaluate a test suite or to design a test suite: a test suite

A. C. R. Paiva et al. (Eds.): QUATIC 2021, CCIS 1439, pp. 18–28, 2021.
https://doi.org/10.1007/978-3-030-85347-1_2

is adequate if it can detect all the non-equivalent mutants of a program P. For the sake of efficiency, we are interested in minimal mutant sets, i.e. mutant sets such that any proper subset is less effective at evaluating test suites than the original set. Mutant subsumption is useful in the derivation of minimal mutant sets because whenever a mutant M' subsumes a mutant M then the singleton $\{M'\}$ is as effective as the set $\{M, M'\}$ since any test suite that detects M detects M'.

Independently of this line of research, a study of relative correctness in [5,6] introduces an ordering between programs which characterize the property of a program P' to be *more-correct* than a program P with respect to a specification R; this concept was introduced as a basis for defining faults in programs, and was later used to model various software engineering processes.

In this paper we argue that there are significant similarities between the concept of subsumption between two mutants with respect to a base program and the concept of relative correctness between two programs with respect to a specification. In particular, we find that relative correctness can be determined by comparing *competence domains* of programs with respect to a specification; whereas subsumption can be determined by comparing *differentiator sets* of mutants with respect to a base program [16,19,20]. Interestingly, competence domains and differentiator sets tend to be complementary. The main motivation of this paper is to highlight relationships between these two concepts, and to explore whether, how and to what extent the highlighted relationships between these two concepts can be used synergetically to share insights and possibly advance the state of the art in both research directions.

In Sect. 2 we review the main definitions pertaining to mutant subsumption, due to [9,12,13] and in Sect. 3 we introduce the mathematics of relative correctness, due to [5,6,15]. In Sect. 4 we revisit the definitions of mutant subsumption using the mathematics of relative correctness, and in Sect. 5 we explore potential applications of the new model to mutation testing. We conclude in Sect. 6 with a summary, assessment, and future prospects.

2   Mutant Subsumption

In this section, we adhere closely to the definitions of [9,12,13], though we formulate them in our own notations. We consider a state space S defined by C-like variable declarations and we let P be a program on space S; the *function* of program P, which (by abuse of notation) we also denote by P, is the set of pairs (s, s') such that if execution of P starts in state s then it terminatres normally in state s'.

Definition 2.1. True Subsumption. *Let M and M' be two mutants of a program P on space S. We say that M' subsumes M with respect to P if and only if the following conditions are satisfied:*

$$\forall s \in S : M(s) \neq P(s) \Rightarrow M'(s) \neq P(s)$$
$$\exists s \in S : M(s) = P(s) \wedge M'(s) \neq P(s).$$

This relation is abbreviated as: $M' >_P M$. Because it is impossible in practice to verify the subsumption relation between two mutants, Kurtz et al. [12] introduce the property of *dynamic subsumption*.

Definition 2.2. Dynamic Subsumption. *Let M and M' be two mutants of a program P on space S. We say that M' dynamically subsumes M with respect to P for test suite $T \subseteq S$ if and only if the following conditions are satisfied:*

$$\forall s \in T : M(s) \neq P(s) \Rightarrow M'(s) \neq P(s)$$
$$\exists s \in T : M(s) = P(s) \wedge M'(s) \neq P(s).$$

This relation is abbreviated as: $M' >_P^T M$. True subsumption is just a special case of dynamic subsumption for the case when $T = S$. Kurtz et al. [12] also introduce the concept of *static subsumption*, but this concept does not represent a different relation between P, M and M'; rather, it represents a different way to check subsumption properties (through static analysis of P, M and M' rather than through testing).

3   Absolute Correctness and Relative Correctness

3.1   Absolute and Relative Correctness

We consider a program P on space S and a relation R on S; the following definition, due to Mills et al. [17] gives a set theoretic formula for the correctness of program P with respect to specification R.

Definition 3.1. *A program P on space S is said to be* correct *with respect to specification R if and only if $dom(R \cap P) = dom(R)$.*

This definition is equivalent, modulo differences of notation, to the traditional definitions of (total) correctness [7,8,10,14]. The domain of $(R \cap P)$ is referred to as the *competence domain* of P with respect to R. This definition is illustrated in Fig. 1: Program P is correct with respect to R because for all the elements in the domain of R ($\{1,2\}$), P is is defined (terminates normally) and returns an output (2 for input 1, 3 for input 2) among those ($\{0,1,2\}$ for input 1, $\{1,2,3\}$ for input 2) that R mandates.

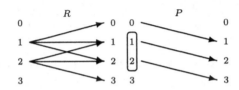

Fig. 1. Program P is correct with respect to R

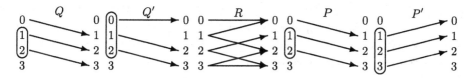

Fig. 2. Preserving correctness $(dom(R \cap P) \subseteq dom(R \cap P'))$ vs. preserving correct behavior $((R \cap Q) \subseteq (R \cap Q'))$

3.2 Relative Correctness

Definition 3.2. *A program P' is said to be more-correct (respectively, strictly more-correct) than P with respect to R if and only if $dom(R \cap P') \supseteq dom(R \cap P)$, denoted by $P' \sqsupseteq_R P$ (respectively $dom(R \cap P') \supset dom(R \cap P)$, denoted by $P' \sqsupset_R P$).*

To contrast correctness with relative correctness, we may refer to the former as absolute correctness. As defined, relative correctness has the following properties:

- It is reflexive and transitive; but it is not antisymmetric, since two programs may be mutually more-correct yet still distinct.
- It culminates in absolute correctness, in the sense that an absolutely correct program is more-correct than (or as correct as) any candidate program.
- It logically implies (but is not equivalent to) higher reliability.

Figure 2 shows two examples of relative correctness relationships: specification R is in the middle; to the right, Q' is more-correct than Q with respect to R by virtue of duplicating the correct behavior of Q; on the right, P' is more-correct than P with respect to R by virtue of a different correct behavior; this is possible because R is non-deterministic, hence correct behavior is not unique.

3.3 A Relative Correctness Graph

As an illustrative example, we consider the following specification on space S of natural numbers:

$$R = \{(s, s')| -1 \leq s \leq 1 \wedge s' = s^3 - s\}.$$

We consider the following candidate programs; alongside each program, we show its competence domain (obtained by computing the term $R \cap P$ then its domain). Figure 3 shows the relative correctness relations between these programs, which are a mere reflection of the inclusion relations between their competence domains.

p0: {s = s*s*s-s+1;}.
    Its competence domain is: $CD_0 = \{\}$.

p1: $\{$s = s*s*s;$\}$.
   Its competence domain is: $CD_1 = \{0\}$.
p2: $\{$s = s*s*s+1;$\}$.
   Its competence domain is: $CD_2 = \{-1\}$.
p3: $\{$s = s*s*s-1;$\}$.
   Its competence domain is: $CD_3 = \{1\}$.
p4: $\{$s = s*s*s+s*s;$\}$.
   Its competence domain is: $CD_4 = \{0, -1\}$.
p5: $\{$s = s*s*s+s*s-2*s;$\}$.
   Its competence domain is: $CD_5 = \{0, 1\}$.
p6: $\{$s = s*s*s+s*s-s-1;$\}$.
   Its competence domain is: $CD_6 = \{-1, 1\}$.
p7: $\{$s = 4*s*s*s-4*s;$\}$.
   Its competence domain is: $CD_7 = \{-1, 0, 1\}$.
p8: $\{$s = 3*s*s*s-3*s;$\}$.
   Its competence domain is: $CD_8 = \{-1, 0, 1\}$.
p9: $\{$s = 2*s*s*s-2*s;$\}$.
   Its competence domain is: $CD_9 = \{-1, 0, 1\}$.

Whereas absolute correctness divides candidate programs into two classes (correct vs. incorrect), relative correctness ranks candidate programs on a partial ordering, whose maximal elements are absolutely correct.

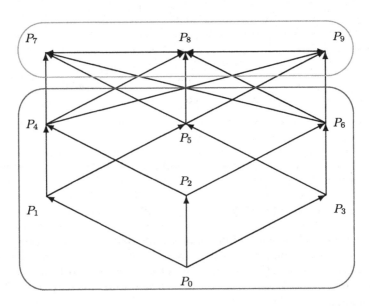

Fig. 3. Relative correctness ordering (in black) vs. absolute correctness partitioning (green vs. red) (Color figure online)

4 Subsumption as Relative Incorrectness

The relationship between relative correctness and mutant subsumption is captured in the following Propositions.

Proposition 4.1. *We consider a program P on space S and two mutants M and M' of P. M' subsumes (in the sense of true subsumption) M with respect to P if and only if M is strictly more-correct than M' with respect to specification P. This is written as:*

$$(M' >_P M) \Leftrightarrow (M \sqsupset_P M').$$

Proof: We proceed by equivalence:

$M' >_P M$
$\Leftrightarrow$ {Definition 2.1}
$\quad \forall s \in S : M(s) \neq P(s) \Rightarrow M'(s) \neq P(s)$
$\quad \wedge \exists s \in S : M(s) = P(s) \wedge M'(s) \neq P(s).$
$\Leftrightarrow$ {Reformulating the first clause}
$\quad \forall s \in S : M'(s) = P(s) \Rightarrow M(s) = P(s)$
$\quad \wedge \exists s \in S : M(s) = P(s) \wedge M'(s) \neq P(s).$
$\Leftrightarrow$ {Interpreting the first clause}
$\quad dom(M' \cap P) \subseteq dom(M \cap P) \wedge \exists s \in S : M(s) = P(s) \wedge M'(s) \neq P(s).$
$\Leftrightarrow$ {Interpreting the second clause}
$\quad dom(M' \cap P) \subseteq dom(M \cap P) \wedge \exists s \in S : s \in dom(M \cap P) \wedge s \notin dom(M' \cap P).$
$\Leftrightarrow$ {Interpreting the conjunction}
$\quad dom(M' \cap P) \subset dom(M \cap P)$
$\Leftrightarrow$ {Definition 3.2}
$\quad M \sqsupset_P M'.$

qed

Intuitively, this Proposition makes perfect sense: since mutants are supposed to be distinct from the base program, the less correct they are the better they are. The relative correctness graph given in Sect. 3.3 can be seen as the inverse of mutant subsumption graphs discussed in [9, 12, 13].

Proposition 4.2. *We consider a program P on space S, a subset T of S, and two mutants M and M' of P. M' subsumes (in the sense of dynamic subsumption) M with respect to P for set T if and only if M is strictly more-correct than M' with respect to specification $_{T\backslash}P$, the pre-restriction of P to T. This is written as:*

$$(M' >_P^T M) \Leftrightarrow (M \sqsupset_{_{T\backslash}P} M').$$

Proof: The proof of this proposition is the same as that of Proposition 4.1, and relies on the simple identity that $(s \in T \wedge s \in dom(M \cap P))$ is equivalent to $(s \in dom(M \cap_{T\backslash} P))$.   **qed**

For the remainder of this paper we only talk about true subsumption; dynamic subsumption is the same as true subsumption, but for a different program P' whose function is the pre-restriction of P to test suite T.

The best case scenario from the standpoint of correctness with respect to some specification is absolute correctness; not surprisingly, it is the worst case scenario from the standpoint of mutation, as confirmed by the following simple Proposition.

Proposition 4.3. *Let P be a program on space S and let M be a mutant of P. M is absolutely correct with respect to P if and only if $P \subseteq M$.*

Proof: *Proof of Necessity:* By Definition 3.1, $dom(M \cap P) = dom(P)$; this in conjunction with the set theoretic identity $(M \cap P) \subseteq P$, and the fact that both $(M \cap P)$ and P are functions yields (per [2]) $(M \cap P) = P$; this yields, by set theory, $P \subseteq M$.

Proof of Sufficiency. From $P \subseteq M$ we infer $(M \cap P) = P$, whence $dom(M \cap P) = dom(P)$.   **qed**

The least useful mutants are equivalent mutants, i.e. mutants that satisfy the equation $M = P$. This proposition provides the condition $P \subseteq M$, which means that M behaves the same way as P on the domain of P, but may have behavior outside the domain of P; hence while the condition $P \subseteq M$ is weaker than the condition $P = M$, it does mean that M is equivalent to P for the inputs that matter, namely inputs in $dom(P)$.

5   Implications

Whereas relative correctness between two programs is determined by comparing their competence domains, we argue that true subsumption between two mutants is determined by comparing their *differentiator sets* [16,19,20], which we define below.

Definition 5.1. *Given a program P on space S and a mutant M of P, the differentiator set of M with respect to P is the set denoted by $\delta_P(M)$ and defined by:*

$$\delta_P(M) = \overline{dom(M \cap P)}.$$

The interest of this definition stems readily from the following Proposition.

Proposition 5.2. *Given a program P on space S and two mutants M and M' of P, M' subsumes M (in the sense of true subsumption) if and only if:*

$$\delta_P(M) \subset \delta_P(M').$$

Proof: The first clause of Definition 2.1 can be interpreted as: $\delta_P(M) \subseteq \delta_P(M')$, and the second clause as: $\exists s : s \notin \delta_P(M) \wedge s \in \delta_P(M')$.   **qed**

Whereas subsumption is defined between individual mutants, we can generalize it as a property between two sets of mutants, by generalizing the concept of differentiator set.

Definition 5.3. *Given a program P on space S and a set of mutants of P,* $m = \{M_1, M_2, ..M_k\}$, *the* differentiator set *of m is the union of the differentiator sets of all the elements of m:*

$$\delta_P(m) = \bigcup_{M_i \in m} \delta_P(M_i).$$

Using differentiator sets of mutant sets enables us to identify redundancies (and opportunities to get rid of redundant mutants, and minimize mutant sets) between sets of mutants even when there are no subsumption relations between individual mutants; this is illustrated in the example below. But first, we define subsumption between sets of mutants.

Definition 5.4. *Given a program P on space S and two sets of mutants m and* m', *we say that* m' subsumes m *if and only if:* $\delta_P(m) \subseteq \delta_P(m')$.

Note that we use reflexive inclusion $\subseteq$ rather than strict inclusion ($\subset$) as it is simpler (weaker condition) and better (if two sets of mutants have the same differentiator set, we can eliminate one set and keep the other). For illustration, we consider the following program P on space S defined by a single variable s of type integer:

$$P : \{s = \mathtt{pow(s, 4)} + 2 * \mathtt{pow(s, 2)}; \}$$

the following test suite $T = \{-3, -2, -1, 1, 2, 3\}$, and we consider the following mutants:

- M1: `{s=2*pow(s,4)-11*pow(s,2)+36}`.
- M2: `{s=2*pow(s,4)-8*pow(s,2)+9}`.
- M3: `{s=2*pow(s,4)-3*pow(s,2)+4}`.
- M4: `{s=pow(s,4)+pow(s,3)-4*pow(s,2)+11*s-6}`.
- M5: `{s=pow(s,4)+pow(s,3)+8*pow(s,2)-11*s+6}`.

Note that our focus in this study is purely semantic, i.e. we are interested to analyze the semantic relationships between programs and mutants; hence we are not concerned about what mutation operators generate M_i's from P; we are only interested in the semantic relations between them. Table 1 shows the competence domains and the differentiator sets of mutants M_1 .. M_5 with respect to $_{T \backslash} P$; the competence domain of each mutant M_i with respect to P is obtained by computing the intersection $(M_i \cap P)$ then taking its domain; the differentiator set is the complement of the competence domain. Figure 4 shows the differentiator sets of mutants M_1 .. M_5 with respect to $_{T \backslash} P$. Using the terminology of [12], we find that all mutants M_1 through M_5 are killable by test suite T, since their differentiator sets are non-empty.

According to this table, there are no subsumption relations between mutants M_1, M_2, M_3, M_4, and M_5 since there are no inclusion relations between the

Table 1. Competence domains and differentiator sets

Mutant	Competence domain with respect to $_T\backslash P$	Differentiator set with respect to $_T\backslash P$
M_1	$\{-2, -3, 2, 3\}$	$\{-1, 1\}$
M_2	$\{-1, -3, 1, 3\}$	$\{-2, 2\}$
M_3	$\{-1, -2, 1, 2\}$	$\{-3, 3\}$
M_4	$\{1, 2, 3\}$	$\{-1, -2, -3\}$
M_5	$\{-1, -2, -3\}$	$\{1, 2, 3\}$

differentiator sets of the mutants; hence if we limit ourselves to individual subsumption relations, we see no opportunity to reduce the set of mutants

$$m = \{M_1, M_2, M_3, M_4, M_5\}.$$

But if we consider sets of mutants rather than individual mutants, we may be able to reduce the set of mutants without loss; the concept of minimal set of mutants, due to [12], is supposed to achieve this goal. Given a set m of non-equivalent mutants of a base program P, a subset m' of m is said to be a *minimal set of mutants* if and only if:

– The differentiator set of m' is the same as that of m.
– No proper subset of m' has the same differentiator set as m.

On the basis of this definition, we find that both:

$m_1' = \{M_1, M_2, M_3\}$,
$m_2' = \{M_4, M_5\}$,

are minimals set of mutants.

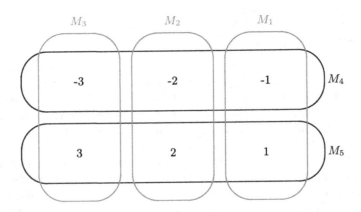

Fig. 4. Mutants and differentiator sets

6   Conclusion

6.1   Summary and Assessment

In this paper we highlight a duality between the concept of mutant subsumption introduced in mutation testing [9,12,13] and the concept of relative correctness introduced in the study of faults [5,6]. Given that mutations are representations of (artificial simulations of) faults [1,11,18], it is hardly surprising that similar concepts are used to model them. Still it is instructive to see that relative correctness can be determined by comparing competence domains whereas mutant subsumption can be determined by comparing differentiator sets; these two sets are complements of each other, which makes sense since subsumption and relative correctness aim to represent opposite properties: semantic difference vs. correctness (semantic compliance). Highlighting the analogy between these two concepts and the related research efforts enables us to exchange results and insights between these two research directions which have so far proceeded independently; in this paper we have barely started to explore potential synergies, but we anticipate that much remains to be investigated.

Even though the property of subsumption is originally applied to individual mutants, we find that when we apply it to sets of mutants we find greater opportunities for minimizing mutant sets.

6.2   Prospects

We envision several possible venues for exploring the impact of this duality between mutant subsumption and relative correctness of candidate programs; these are considered for future investigation.

Beyond the mechanics of analyzing and exploiting subsumption relationships between mutants or sets of mutants, we raise the problem of cost-effectiveness: If we are interested to minimize the number of mutants, an intuitive approach would be to highlight equivalence relations between mutants, and select one mutant from each equivalence class. On the other hand, it is clear that subsumption relations hold between equivalence classes, in the sense that if M' subsumes M then any member of the equivalence class of M' subsumes any member of the equivalence class of M. Hence the difference between minimizing the number of mutants by the criterion of equivalence and minimizing the number of mutants by the criterion of subsumption amounts to the difference between the number of equivalence classes and the number of maximal nodes in the subsumption graphs. Whether this difference justifies the extra complexity and uncertainty involved in using subsumption remains an open problem. Also, it may be useful to apply the criterion of equivalence first, then apply the criterion of subsumption between provably non-equivalent mutants.

Acknowledgement. This work is partially supported by NSF under grant number DGE1565478.

References

1. Andrews, J.H., Briand, L.C., Labiche, Y.: Is mutation an appropriate tool for testing experiments? In: Proceedings of ICSE (2005)
2. Brink, C., Kahl, W., Schmidt, G.: Relational Methods in Computer Science. Advances in Computer Science, Springer Verlag, Berlin (1997). https://doi.org/10.1007/978-3-7091-6510-2
3. Budd, T.A., DeMillo, R.A., Lipton, R.J., Sayward, F.: Theoretical and empirical studies on using program mutation to test the functional correctness of programs. In: Proceedings of 7th ACM SIGPLAN-SIGACT Symposium on Principles of Programming Languages, POPL 1980, pp. 220–233, January 1980
4. DeMillo, R.A., Lipton, R.J., Sayward, F.G.: Hints on test data selection: help for the practicing programmer. IEEE Comput. **11**(4), 34–41 (1978)
5. Desharnais, J., Diallo, N., Ghardallou, W., Frias, M.F., Jaoua, A., Mili, A.: Relational mathematics for relative correctness. In: Kahl, W., Winter, M., Oliveira, J.N. (eds.) RAMICS 2015. LNCS, vol. 9348, pp. 191–208. Springer, Cham (2015). https://doi.org/10.1007/978-3-319-24704-5_12
6. Desharnais, J., Diallo, N., Ghardallou, W., Mili, A.: Projecting programs on specifications: definitions and implications. Sci. Comput. Program. **138**, 26–48 (2017)
7. Dijkstra, E.W.: A Discipline of Programming. Prentice Hall, Hoboken (1976)
8. Gries, D.: The Science of Programming. Springer, Heidelberg (1981). https://doi.org/10.1007/978-1-4612-5983-1
9. Guimaraes, M.A., Fernandes, L., Riberio, M., d'Amorim, M., Gheyi, R.: Optimizing mutation testing by discovering dynamic mutant subsumption relations. In: Proceedings of 13th International Conference on Software Testing, Validation and Verification (2020)
10. Hehner, E.C.R.: A Practical Theory of Programming. Prentice Hall, Hoboken (1992)
11. Just, R., Jalali, D., Inozemtseva, L., Ernst, M.D., Holmes, R., Fraser, G.: Are mutants a valid substitute for real faults in software testing? In: Proceedings of FSE (2014)
12. Kurtz, B., Amman, P., Delamaro, M.E., Offutt, J., Deng, L.: Mutant subsumption graphs. In: Proceedings of 7th International Conference on Software Testing, Validation and Verification Workshops (2014)
13. Kurtz, B., Ammann, P., Offutt, J.: Static analysis of mutant subsumption. In: Proceedings of IEEE 8th International Conference on Software Testing, Verification and Validation Workshops (2015)
14. Manna, Z.: A Mathematical Theory of Computation. McGraw-Hill, New York (1974)
15. Mili, A., Frias, M.F., Jaoua, A.: On faults and faulty programs. In: Höfner, P., Jipsen, P., Kahl, W., Müller, M.E. (eds.) RAMICS 2014. LNCS, vol. 8428, pp. 191–207. Springer, Cham (2014). https://doi.org/10.1007/978-3-319-06251-8_12
16. Mili, A.: Differentiators and detectors. Inf. Process. Lett. **169**, 106111 (2021)
17. Mills, H.D., Basili, V.R., Gannon, J.D., Hamlet, D.R.: Structured Programming: A Mathematical Approach. Allyn and Bacon, Boston (1986)
18. Namin, A.S., Kakarla, S.: The use of mutation in testing experiments and its sensitivity to external threats. In: Proceedings of ISSTA (2011)
19. Shin, D., Bae, D.H.: A theoretical framework for understanding mutation-based testing methods. In: Proceedings of ICST 2016, Chicago, IL, April 2016
20. Shin, D., Yoo, S., Bae, D.-H.: A theoretical and empirical study of diversity-aware mutation adequacy criterion. IEEE TSE **44**(10), 914–931 (2018)

What We Talk About When We Talk About Software Test Flakiness

Morena Barboni[1](✉) ⓘ, Antonia Bertolino[2] ⓘ, and Guglielmo De Angelis[1] ⓘ

[1] IASI-CNR, Rome, Italy
{morena.barboni,guglielmo.deangelis}@iasi.cnr.it
[2] ISTI-CNR, Pisa, Italy
antonia.bertolino@isti.cnr.it

Abstract. Software test flakiness is drawing increasing interest among both academic researchers and practitioners. In this work we report our findings from a scoping review of white and grey literature, highlighting variations across flaky tests key concepts. Our study clearly indicates the need of a unifying definition as well as of a more comprehensive analysis for establishing a conceptual map that can better guide future research.

Keywords: Flaky tests · Flakiness · Software testing · Scoping review

1 Introduction

In recent years research aiming at understanding and mitigating the problem of test flakiness has boomed, also pushed by alarms raised by big companies as Google [29], Facebook [27] or Apple [17], among others, on the extent and cost of this phenomenon.

However, in the fast rising of articles addressing the theme, researchers provide different characterizations and modelings of the involved aspects and connected techniques. Terms such as *flaky* or *intermittent* or *non-deterministic* are used by some as synonyms, by others to identify differing test behaviors. Some works study in depth the causes of flakiness and introduce more specific test characterizations. However, as it is inevitable when many authors work in concurrence, a same concept is introduced in more articles using differing terms.

Lack of a shared terminology and of an agreed conceptual scheme may be confounding and may also waste effort in re-inventing existing knowledge. For instance, already in the 90's Carver and Tai [6] warned that multiple executions of a concurrent program under a same test input might produce different results, if the underlying sequence of synchronization events is not specified. This sounds to us closely related with those flaky test categories commonly classified as due to concurrency or asynchronous wait [26], but to the best of our knowledge no recent article has ever acknowledged the evident connection. On the other hand,

Work supported by the Italian MIUR PRIN 2017 Project: SISMA (Contract 201752ENYB), and partially by the Italian Research Group: INdAM-GNCS.

© Springer Nature Switzerland AG 2021
A. C. R. Paiva et al. (Eds.): QUATIC 2021, CCIS 1439, pp. 29–39, 2021.
https://doi.org/10.1007/978-3-030-85347-1_3

our analysis of the literature also emphasizes how the same term of a "flaky test" can refer to situations that require different treatments, e.g., in some cases fixing the test code, in other ones refining the test environment configuration. For all such reasons, we think that putting order in the fuzz around test flakiness can be helpful to better guide future research efforts.

In this short paper we highlight the problem of inconsistent terminology based on a scoping review of literature [3,30] (Sect. 2), and move some first steps towards proposing a unifying definition and vocabulary for test flakiness (Sect. 3), which will be the aim of our future work (Sect. 4).

2   Scoping Review of White and Grey Literature

This study aims to examine definitions and key concepts related to software testing flakiness. For this purpose we borrow from medical research the recently introduced approach of a *scoping review* [3,30]. Similarly to systematic review, which is a better known methodology in software engineering [16], a scoping review must apply a defined and repeatable search protocol. However, scoping studies[1] do not address the lengthy synthesis stage, aiming rather at a fast descriptive appraisal of broad questions, often as a precursor to deeper systematic reviews. As our goal was to highlight variations behind definitions of flaky tests, our search methodology relied on two pragmatic criteria: *i)* it should cover both white and grey literature, as the phenomenon of flakiness has raised great interest from both academic researchers and practitioners; and *ii)* for the sake of timeliness, we established well-delimited boundaries to our search (explained below). While these limitations may hinder comprehensiveness, nevertheless our results were already sufficient to find inconsistencies, as we discuss later in this section.

Search Methodology: The entries from the white literature have been retrieved by consulting three among the most relevant Academic Digital Libraries in Software Engineering, namely: Scopus, ACM Digital Library, IEEE eXplore. For the analysis of the grey literature, we rely on articles posted on Medium.com, a well-known online publishing platform hosting many informal technology blogs that are frequently written/followed by Software companies and practitioners.

We launched an automated search on the white literature sources by querying: title, abstract and keywords; matching with: "Flaky test" OR "Flakiness", and selecting those *English papers* published until Feb. 2021 (date of the query). From the collected entries, it appears evident that before Luo et al.'s paper [26], there were only few works explicitly referring to software testing "flakiness".

Then, the same query string has been run on Google Search but limiting the search space to Medium.com and by considering the top-ten returned *English articles* written until Apr. 2021 (date of the query).

---

[1] A useful comparison between systematic reviews, scoping reviews and other review types is available from https://guides.temple.edu/systematicreviews.

Even though we did not include a formal snowballing process, during the analysis of the collected entries, two blog posts, namely [12] and [29], stood out as playing a seminal role, and therefore we decided to also include them among the grey literature entries.

Overview of Findings: Interestingly, our preliminary analysis of the collected entries revealed quite different implications and perspective on how literature conceives flaky tests. Indeed there are works that explicitly refer to their randomised nature: *"Flaky tests are software tests that exhibit a seemingly random outcome (pass or fail) despite exercising unchanged code"* [10], but also others that definitively reject such vision: *"They are sometimes referred to as random failures, but in reality, it's often less about actual randomness than very reproducible edge cases that happen in a seemingly random fashion"* [41].

In addition, along with definitions that exclude any evolution exclusively referring to the software under test (SUT) as in [10] above, others also cover testing configurations or the execution environment: *"A flaky test is a test that can be failing or passing with no changes in the application or infrastructure"* [40].

Finally, most works depict flakiness as an undesired behavior of test programs, but few others highlight how it may lead developers to disclose potential bugs not revealed otherwise: *"Part of the test or production code has a nondeterministic outcome"* [31].

For lack of space, the complete list of the collected definitions is made available online [4].

3   Commonalities in Test Flakiness Concepts

Based on the outcome of our scoping review, in the following subsections we aim to bring some order to flaky test-related concepts (Sect. 3.1) and classifications (Sect. 3.2), taking a first step towards the identification of a more consistent vocabulary.

3.1   Definitions of Flaky Test Concepts

Table 1 shows a synthesis of the terminology actively used by both academics and practitioners. This summary was derived after a careful sampling and analysis of concepts related to the behavior of test outcomes. The most recurring definition of **Flaky Test** from the literature is (1) *"a test that exhibits a non-deterministic behavior"*. This suggests that any test showing both pass and failure outcomes upon multiple repeated executions is usually marked as flaky. Conversely, **Not Flaky** tests are defined by Lam et al. [22] as tests that either always pass or always fail in a deterministic manner, whereby tests that always exhibit a failure outcome can be further classified as **Consistently Failing Tests** [42]. The most common synonym for flaky test is **Non-Deterministic Test** [12]. However, we observed that considering *"flaky"* and *"non-deterministic"* as interchangeable terms can be a source of confusion. In fact, as we discuss in Sect. 3.2, the term Non-Deterministic is also used for designating a very specific subclass of flaky

Table 1. Definitions of flaky test concepts

Term	Definition	Source(s)
Non-flaky	A test that either always passes or always fails	[22]
Flaky	(1) A test that exhibits a non-deterministic behavior	[17, 25, 27, 31, 34, 37, 39, 45]
	(2) A test that provides different results inconsistently	[41]
	(3) A test that fails intermittently	[10, 26, 46]
	(4) A test that fails randomly	[7]
	(5) A test that exhibits pass and failure outcomes despite exercising *unchanged code*	[2, 5, 9, 10, 19, 24, 26, 29, 32, 33, 35, 36, 44]
	(6) A test that exhibits pass and failure outcomes although *neither the code nor the test has changed*	[11, 15, 21, 49]
	(7) A *regression* test that exhibits pass and failure outcomes *although neither the code nor the test has changed*	[13]
	(8) A test that exhibits pass and failure outcomes *although neither the code nor the test infrastructure has changed*	[40]
	(9) A test that exhibits pass and failure outcomes although *neither the code nor the configuration has changed*	[18]
	(10) A test that exhibits pass and failure outcomes although *the code, the inputs and the configuration have not changed*	[43]
	(11) A test that exhibits pass and failure outcomes although *the SW, the HW and the TW have not changed*	[42]
	(12) A test that exhibits pass and failure outcomes while exercising a *potentially changed version of the code*	[20, 23, 26, 38]
	(13) A test that exhibits pass and failure outcomes in *apparently identical test scenarios*	[28]
	(14) A test that exhibits pass and failure outcomes although *neither the test code nor the configuration parameters has changed*	[48]
	(15) A test that exhibits pass and failure outcomes while exercising a *potentially changed version of the code* and a *potentially evolved test environment*	[22]
Non-deterministic	A test exhibits both pass and failure outcomes without any noticeable change in the code, tests, or environment	[12]
Latent flaky	A test that is not currently flaky, but that could become so due to a latent source(s) of flakiness	[33]
Intermittently failing	A test that exhibits pass and failure outcomes while there has been a potential evolution in the SW, the HW or the TW	[42]
Consistently failing	A test that exhibits a consistent failure outcome	[42]

tests. On several occasions, flaky tests are also referred to as (3) "*tests that fail intermittently*". Although the manifestation of intermittent outcomes can accurately depict the behavior of flaky tests, Strandberg et al. [42] explicitly differentiate **Intermittently Failing Tests** from the former. We also observed flaky tests being described as (4) "*tests that fail randomly*". However, as specified by Stosik [41], this definition is imprecise because the randomness of flaky tests is only apparent. Indeed, the (2) "inconsistent behavior" of a flaky test is often caused by a well-defined, reproducible set of conditions. Even though commonly accepted, definitions (1–3) do not provide any insight relative to the context in which the test exhibits an inconsistent behavior. In particular, it is unclear whether the flakiness is associated to problems in the test code, in the SUT, or to any other environmental factor. Moreover, they do not specify explicitly whether any element, such as the SUT or the test code, underwent any type of modification across different test re-runs.

Several works extend these generic definitions with additional details. In particular, definitions (5–11) agree upon the fact that flaky tests *"exhibit both pass and failure outcomes despite exercising unchanged code"*. The fact that a given test can return non-deterministic outcomes for the same code version was identified as one of the main obstacles for regression testing activities. Whenever a developer updates the code, the tests are re-run to ensure that said changes do not break existing functionalities. A regression test failure normally indicates the (re)introduction of a bug that impacts previously working software. However, a test that non-deterministically passes and fails for the same code version provides misleading signals to the developer, who might waste considerable time and effort in debugging the code under test. While definition (5) only makes assumptions related to the SUT, definitions (6–11) provide further constraints as to what constitutes a flaky test. In particular, definitions (6) and (7) require both the SUT and the test code to be unchanged, although the latter explicitly identifies a flaky test as a type of regression test. Other authors require the test environment (8), the configuration (9, 10) and the inputs (10) to stay the same upon multiple test executions. The definition (11) proposed by Strandberg et al. [42] specifies that a flaky test yields differing verdicts when *"nothing in the SW, HW or TW has been changed."*. This vision of flakiness stems from the analysis of test intermittence in industrial Embedded Systems (ES), which comprise hardware (HW), software (SW), and testware (TW). The TW includes both software and hardware components, such as test libraries and the physical environment on which the tests are executed. This definition implies that flaky test verdicts are not caused by modifications to the aforementioned Embedded System components. Instead, flakiness can be due to "hidden" state or environment changes that might have occurred since the previous test run.

The vision of test flakiness described in definitions (12–15) is quite different, in that they do not require the immutability of the code under test. In particular, definition (12) explicitly admits changes to the code under test among multiple test re-runs. Definitions (13, 14) require the same test scenarios, and the same test and configuration respectively, but they do not explicitly ask for unchanged software. Lastly, definition (15) admits *"a potentially changed version of the code and a potentially evolved test environment"*. We observed that the idea of test flakiness emerging from definitions (12–15) is partly reflected by Strandberg et al.'s [42] definition of Intermittently Failing Test for the Embedded Systems domain. As introduced earlier, the authors provide a separate definition for Intermittently Failing Tests, in that Flaky Tests as defined in (11) can be rarely observed in practice. Indeed, industrial ES undergo rapid and frequent changes during their development process. Conversely, an **Intermittently Failing Test** provides different verdicts over time, but it *"allows changes in the SW or HW of the ES under test, as well as in the TW used for testing"*. Definition

(15) used in more traditional software systems is particularly in line with this vision of test intermittence, as it also admits changes in the code and test environment. To complete this preliminary categorization, we also report the concept of **Latent Flaky Test** proposed by Parry et al. [33]. A Flaky Test is said to be latent if it contains a source of flakiness that has not yet manifested. The concept of latent flakiness brings further attention to the problem of exposing test flakiness as soon as possible, so as to improve the reliability of the test suite.

3.2   Classification of Flaky Tests

As for different types of flakiness, many works broadly split flaky tests into two groups based on the underlying source of flakiness (Table 2). The dashed line denotes the separation of different classifications of flaky tests that we encountered during our research. **Order-Dependent (OD)** tests are usually described as tests that *"can pass or fail based on the order in which they are run"*. The unreliability of OD test verdicts is generally caused by their reliance on some environment state that has been improperly (re)set by another test execution. Although the research community seems to agree on the concept of OD test, a minority of works [20,22] further extend definition (1), specifying that OD tests actually exhibit deterministic behavior. In other words, an OD test either always passes or always fails for each order of tests, and there exist at least two orders for which it provides different verdicts. The flaky tests that do not match this requirement are commonly identified as **Non Order-Dependent (NOD)**. A typical example would be a test that uses the result of an asynchronous call without waiting for it to be ready. Based on the availability of the requested resource, the test can non-deterministically pass (or fail) regardless of its execution order. The possible root causes of flakiness for a NOD test are plentiful, but discussing them is out of scope for this work, as they have already been broadly investigated and analyzed in the literature [1,10,18,26,42,44,49]. During our research, we also encountered the term **Non-Deterministic (ND)** being used for identifying a test that *"passes or fails with no changes to test execution order"*. Therefore, using "flaky" and "non-deterministic" interchangeably might be confusing in certain contexts, as OD tests can be flaky whilst providing a deterministic outcome for a specific order. Conversely, NOD tests always show a non-deterministic outcome regardless of the order in which they are run(1). Lam et al. [22] provide a more specific definition of NOD tests (2), hinting at an underlying order-dependency. Depending on the failure rate associated to each order, they classify a NOD test as either a NDOI or a NDOD, which we discuss later.

Classification of OD Tests. According to several works [23,38], there exist two different types (see Table 2) of OD flaky tests: Victim (OD-Vic) and Brittle (OD-Brit). The difference between the two lies in the behavior of the OD test when run in isolation from the test suite. If an OD test *"consistently passes when run by itself, but fails when run in combination with some other test(s)"*, then it is marked as a **Victim**. Indeed, it suffers the consequences of executing other

Table 2. Classification of flaky tests

Order-dependent tests		
Term	Definition	Source(s)
OD	(1) A test that can pass or fail based on the order in which it is run	[2, 10, 14, 21, 23, 26, 36, 38, 47]
	(2) A test that can *deterministically* pass or fail based on the order in which it is run	[20, 22]
Victim	OD test that always passes when run in isolation from other tests	[23, 38]
Brittle	OD test that consistently fails when run in isolation from other tests	[23, 38]
Non order-dependent tests		
Term	Definition	Source(s)
NOD	(1) A test that non-deterministically passes and fails regardless of its execution order	[2, 20]
	(2) A test that non-deterministically passes and fails for at least one execution order	[22]
ND	A test that non-deterministically passes or fails with no changes to test execution order or implementation of test dependencies	[23]
NDOD	NOD test where at least one order's failure rate significantly differs from other orders' failure rates	[22]
NDOI	NOD tests where all failure rates do not significantly differ	[22]
ID	A test whose outcome depends on the implementation of a non-deterministic specification	[23]
Smelly	A test that might be flaky due to the presence of a test smell (i.e. a bad testing practice)	[1, 2, 42]

tests (i.e., polluters) that modify the test environment state without cleaning it up. On the other hand, a **Brittle** *"fails when run in isolation but passes when run with some other test(s)"*. The flakiness of a Brittle comes from its reliance on some state that should be set up by other tests. When this precondition is missing, the Brittle exhibits a failing behavior. Table 3 illustrates additional definitions for tests that, although not flaky, play an important role in the behavior of OD tests. As introduced earlier, a **Polluter** (or *State-Polluting* test) is (1) *"a test that pollutes (i.e. modifies) the state shared across tests"*. Gyori et al. [14] specify that if a test makes assumptions about the shared location, the resulting dependency can affect the reliability of its outcome. Shi et al. [38] provide

Table 3. Classification of order-dependent related tests

Term	Definition	Source(s)
Polluter	(1) A test that pollutes (i.e. modifies) the shared state	[14]
	(2) A test that pollutes the state on which a Victim depends	[38]
Helper	A test whose logic (re)sets the state required for an Order-Dependent test to pass	[38]
Cleaner	A test order that resets the state polluted by a polluter	[38]
State-Setter	A test order that sets up the state for a brittle	[38]

a consistent definition (2), although they clarify that a Polluter can comprise multiple tests, as long as their combination causes a Victim to fail consistently. It is worth noting that both definitions suggest that a Polluter always causes its Victim to fail, raising a *"false alarm"*. While this is the most common scenario [47], a polluter might also generate a state in which an OD test accidentally passes, masking a real fault in the code under test. Such failures are sometimes referred to as *missed alarms* [47] or *silent horrors* [45]. Shi et al. [38] also provide a definition for **Helpers**. These are commonly run in between OD tests to ensure that the state is properly cleaned or set up before their execution. In particular, the **Cleaners** reset the state previously modified by a Polluter, so that subsequent OD tests are not negatively affected by the dependency. Conversely, **State-Setters** implement logic that purposefully sets up the state required for a Brittle to pass.

Classification of NOD Tests. As introduced earlier, a NOD test inconsistently passes and fails even for the same execution order. Given the erratic and usually infrequent manifestation of NOD flakiness, these tests are generally harder to identify and debug. Indeed, the inconsistency of the test outcomes is not simply attributable to the presence of a test order dependence. However, a recent work of Lam et al. [22] questions the adequacy of this definition, specifying that NOD flakiness can sometimes be affected by the execution order. As a result of this observation, the authors further refine the definition of a NOD tests, specifying that it (2) *"fails non-deterministically for at least one order (failure rate is neither 0% nor 100%)"*. Depending on the failure rate associated to each execution order, a NOD test can be further classified into two groups. **Non-Deterministic Order-Dependent** (NDOD) show a significantly higher failure rate for at least one execution order. Since there exists an order for which the flakiness is much more likely to manifest, NDOD tests are characterized by an underlying order dependence. NDOD tests should not be confused with OD tests, because the latter always behave in a deterministic manner. On the other hand, **Non-Deterministic Order-Independent** (NDOI) tests are characterized by a similar failure rate for each possible execution order, thus they are more in line with the general idea of non order-dependent test. Again, this underlines the fact that Non-Deterministic tests and Flaky Tests should not be used as synonyms. Although NOD tests can be further classified according to the root causes of their flakiness, here we just focus on two further definitions that might generate confusion among researchers and practitioners. An **Implementation Dependent** (ID) test is defined by Lam et al. [23] as *"a test whose outcome depends on the implementation of a non-deterministic specification"*. Therefore it can be identified as a NOD test whose flakiness is caused by wrong assumptions about the SUT, which unexpectedly behaves in inconsistent manners. Lastly, a **Smelly Test** is not necessarily flaky. The term *"smelly"* is commonly used for identifying any kind of a poorly designed test. We can depict a *test smell* as an anti-pattern that decreases the quality of the test suite and/or the code under test. The effects of a test smell can range from poor test code understandability up to pontentially missing severe bugs into the SUT. Several works [1, 2, 42] identify the presence of a test smell as a potential cause for test flakiness as well. In particular, Alshammari et al. [2] report specific classes of smells that can be commonly found in flaky tests. For instance, the *Mistery Guest* smell can be found in a test whose execution relies on some external resources. The underlying dependency can cause the test to exhibit a non-deterministic behavior, in that the availability of such resources can change over time.

4   Conclusions and Future Work

Motivated by the lack of a consistent vocabulary, we undertook a pragmatic scoping review of white and grey literature, based on which we reported a first analysis of definitions relative to flakiness concepts, as well as a first classification of flaky test types. This study provides a preliminary assessment of key concepts and evidences the need of establishing an agreed terminology, perhaps after having conducted a more extensive synthesis of current knowledge. We think that the study of causes and remedies to test flakiness must also link to other related research topics, such as the already mentioned early literature on replaying of concurrent tests [6] or even the several studies about the nature of bugs [8].

References

1. Ahmad, A., Leifler, O., Sandahl, K.: Empirical analysis of factors and their effect on test flakiness-practitioners' perceptions. arXiv preprint arXiv:1906.00673 (2019)
2. Alshammari, A., Morris, C., Hilton, M., Bell, J.: FlakeFlagger: predicting flakiness without rerunning tests. In: Proceedings of ICSE Art. Ev. Track. IEEE (2021)
3. Arksey, H., O'Malley, L.: Scoping studies: towards a methodological framework. Int. J. Soc. Res. Methodol. **8**(1), 19–32 (2005)
4. Barboni, M., Bertolino, A., De Angelis, G.: Supplemental material: what we talk about when we talk about software test flakiness (2021)
5. Bell, J., Legunsen, O., Hilton, M., Eloussi, L., Yung, T., Marinov, D.: DeFlaker: automatically detecting flaky tests. In: Proceedings of ICSE, pp. 433–444. ACM (2018)

6. Carver, R.H., Tai, K.C.: Replay and testing for concurrent programs. IEEE Softw. **8**(2), 66–74 (1991)
7. Champier, C.: Flaky tests caused by a production bug: fix the flakiness, not the bug, February 2019. medium.com
8. Cotroneo, D., Grottke, M., Natella, R., Pietrantuono, R., Trivedi, K.S.: Fault triggers in open-source software: an experience report. In: Proceedings of ISSRE, pp. 178–187. IEEE (2013)
9. Dutta, S., Shi, A., Choudhary, R., Zhang, Z., Jain, A., Misailovic, S.: Detecting flaky tests in probabilistic and machine learning applications. In: Proceedings of ISSTA, pp. 211–224. ACM (2020)
10. Eck, M., Palomba, F., Castelluccio, M., Bacchelli, A.: Understanding flaky tests: the developer's perspective. In: Proceedings of ESEC/FSE, pp. 830–840. ACM (2019)
11. Eloussi, L.: Flaky tests (and how to avoid them), September 2016. medium.com
12. Fowler, M.: Eradicating non-determinism in tests, April 2011
13. Groce, A., Holmes, J.: Practical automatic lightweight nondeterminism and flaky test detection and debugging for Python. In: Proceedings of QRS, pp. 188–195. IEEE (2020)
14. Gyori, A., Shi, A., Hariri, F., Marinov, D.: Reliable testing: detecting state-polluting tests to prevent test dependency. In: Proceedings of ISSTA, pp. 223–233. ACM (2015)
15. King, T.M., Santiago, D., Phillips, J., Clarke, P.J.: Towards a Bayesian network model for predicting flaky automated tests. In: Proceedings of QRS-C, pp. 100–107. IEEE (2018)
16. Kitchenham, B.: Procedures for performing systematic reviews. Keele UK Keele Univ. **33**(2004), 1–26 (2004)
17. Kowalczyk, E., Nair, K., Gao, Z., Silberstein, L., Long, T., Memon, A.: Modeling and ranking flaky tests at Apple. In: Proceedings of ICSE-SEIP, pp. 110–119. ACM (2020)
18. Lam, W., Godefroid, P., Nath, S., Santhiar, A., Thummalapenta, S.: Root causing flaky tests in a large-scale industrial setting. In: Proceedings of ISSTA, pp. 101–111. ACM (2019)
19. Lam, W., Muşlu, K., Sajnani, H., Thummalapenta, S.: A study on the lifecycle of flaky tests. In: Proceedings of ICSE, pp. 1471–1482. ACM (2020)
20. Lam, W., Oei, R., Shi, A., Marinov, D., Xie, T.: iDFlakies: a framework for detecting and partially classifying flaky tests. In: Proceedings of ICST, pp. 312–322. IEEE (2019)
21. Lam, W., Shi, A., Oei, R., Zhang, S., Ernst, M.D., Xie, T.: Dependent-test-aware regression testing techniques. In: Proceedings of ISSTA, pp. 298–311. ACM (2020)
22. Lam, W., Winter, S., Astorga, A., Stodden, V., Marinov, D.: Understanding reproducibility and characteristics of flaky tests through test reruns in Java projects. In: Proceedings of ISSRE, pp. 403–413. IEEE (2020)
23. Lam, W., Winter, S., Wei, A., Xie, T., Marinov, D., Bell, J.: A large-scale longitudinal study of flaky tests. Proc. ACM Program. Lang. **4**(OOPSLA), 1–29 (2020)
24. Lee, B.: We have a flaky test problem, November 2019. medium.com
25. Liviu, S.: A machine learning solution for detecting and mitigating flaky tests, October 2019. medium.com
26. Luo, Q., Hariri, F., Eloussi, L., Marinov, D.: An empirical analysis of flaky tests. In: Proceedings of FSE, pp. 643–653. ACM (2014)
27. Machalica, M., Samylkin, A., Porth, M., Chandra, S.: Predictive test selection. In: Proceedings of ICSE-SEIP, pp. 91–100. IEEE (2019)

28. Malm, J., Causevic, A., Lisper, B., Eldh, S.: Automated analysis of flakiness-mitigating delays. In: Proceedings of AST, pp. 81–84. IEEE (2020)
29. Micco, J.: Flaky tests at Google and how we mitigate them, May 2016D
30. Munn, Z., Peters, M.D., Stern, C., Tufanaru, C., McArthur, A., Aromataris, E.: Systematic review or scoping review? Guidance for authors when choosing between a systematic or scoping review approach. BMC Med. Res. Methodol. **18**(1), 1–7 (2018)
31. Otrebski, K.: Flaky tests, April 2018. medium.com
32. Palmer, J.: Test flakiness - methods for identifying and dealing with flaky tests, November 2019. medium.com
33. Parry, O., Kapfhammer, G.M., Hilton, M., McMinn, P.: Flake it'till you make it: using automated repair to induce and fix latent test flakiness. In: Proceedings of ICSE Workshops, pp. 11–12. ACM (2020)
34. Presler-Marshall, K., Horton, E., Heckman, S., Stolee, K.: Wait, wait. No, tell me. Analyzing selenium configuration effects on test flakiness. In: Proceedings of Wksp AST, pp. 7–13. IEEE (2019)
35. Rahman, M.T., Rigby, P.C.: The impact of failing, flaky, and high failure tests on the number of crash reports associated with Firefox builds. In: Proceedings of ESEC/FSE, pp. 857–862. ACM (2018)
36. Shi, A., Bell, J., Marinov, D.: Mitigating the effects of flaky tests on mutation testing. In: Proceedings of ISSTA, pp. 112–122. ACM (2019)
37. Shi, A., Gyori, A., Legunsen, O., Marinov, D.: Detecting assumptions on deterministic implementations of non-deterministic specifications. In: Proceedings of ICST, pp. 80–90. IEEE (2016)
38. Shi, A., Lam, W., Oei, R., Xie, T., Marinov, D.: iFixFlakies: a framework for automatically fixing order-dependent flaky tests. In: Proceedings of ESEC/FSE, pp. 545–555. ACM (2019)
39. Silva, D., Teixeira, L., d'Amorim, M.: Shake it! Detecting flaky tests caused by concurrency with Shaker. In: Proceedings of ICSME, pp. 301–311. IEEE (2020)
40. Słapiński, M.: What is flakiness and how we deal with it, February 2020. medium.com
41. Stosik, D.: Dealing with flaky tests, November 2019. medium.com
42. Strandberg, P.E., Ostrand, T.J., Weyuker, E.J., Afzal, W., Sundmark, D.: Intermittently failing tests in the embedded systems domain. In: Proceedings of ISSTA, pp. 337–348. ACM (2020)
43. Terragni, V., Salza, P., Ferrucci, F.: A container-based infrastructure for fuzzy-driven root causing of flaky tests. In: Proceedings of ICSE-NIER, pp. 69–72. IEEE (2020)
44. Thorve, S., Sreshtha, C., Meng, N.: An empirical study of flaky tests in android apps. In: Proceedings of ICSME, pp. 534–538. IEEE (2018)
45. Vahabzadeh, A., Fard, A.M., Mesbah, A.: An empirical study of bugs in test code. In: Proceedings of ICSME, pp. 101–110. IEEE (2015)
46. Waterloo, M., Person, S., Elbaum, S.: Test analysis: searching for faults in tests (N). In: Proceedings of ASE. IEEE, November 2015
47. Zhang, S., et al.: Empirically revisiting the test independence assumption. In: Proceedings of ISSTA, pp. 385–396. ACM (2014)
48. Ziftci, C., Cavalcanti, D.: De-Flake your tests: automatically locating root causes of flaky tests in code at Google. In: Proceedings of ICSME, pp. 736–745. IEEE (2020)
49. Zolfaghari, B., Parizi, R.M., Srivastava, G., Hailemariam, Y.: Root causing, detecting, and fixing flaky tests: state of the art and future roadmap. Softw.: Pract. Exp. **51**, 851–867 (2020)

Looking for the Needle in the Haystack: End-to-end Tests in Open Source Projects

Francisco Gortázar(✉) ⓘ, Michel Maes-Bermejoⓘ, Micael Galegoⓘ,
and Jorge Contreras Padilla

Universidad Rey Juan Carlos, Móstoles, Madrid, Spain
{francisco.gortazar,michel.maes,micael.gallego}@urjc.es,
j.contrerasp@alumnos.urjc.es
https://www.urjc.es/

Abstract. There's a common agreement in the industry that integration and end-to-end (e2e) tests are a challenge for many teams wanting to enable frequent deployments while at the same time guaranteeing quality. What this means for the research community is that there are open research problems that might be interesting to solve. However, little effort is put by academia on these integration and e2e tests. Truth is that all datasets available for research in software testing are focused on unit tests.

In this paper we propose an approach to build datasets of e2e tests from active open source projects. The approach is based on mining open source repositories from GitHub, in order to find those projects containing e2e tests. We defined 12 different criteria to find those tests. We investigate which of the 12 criteria are more reliable for detecting this kind of tests by manually analyzing the results of these criteria on 100 projects from GitHub. Then we performed a search on 1,800 projects (900 Java-specific, and 900 not constrained to Java), and used the three most promising criteria to detect e2e tests within all of them. Our results show that it is easier to detect this kind of tests in Java projects than on projects using other programming languages. Also, more than 500 projects were reported as having e2e tests. We hypothesize that good e2e test datasets could be built out of these results.

Keywords: Testing · End-to-end tests · Integration tests

1 Introduction

There's a common agreement in the industry [6] that integration and end-to-end tests (e2e tests for short in the rest of the paper) are a challenge for many

This work has been supported by the Government of Spain through project "BugBirth" (RTI2018-101963-B-100), the Regional Government of Madrid (CM) through project Cloud4BigData (S2013/ICE-2894) cofunded by FSE & FEDER and the European Commission through European Project H2020 822717: MICADO.

© Springer Nature Switzerland AG 2021
A. C. R. Paiva et al. (Eds.): QUATIC 2021, CCIS 1439, pp. 40–48, 2021.
https://doi.org/10.1007/978-3-030-85347-1_4

teams wanting to enable frequent deployments while at the same time guaranteeing quality. What this means for the research community is that there are open research problems that might be interesting to solve. However, little effort is put on these integration and e2e tests. Truth is that all datasets available for research in software testing, are focused on unit tests. Therefore, all the solutions published for the different problems in software testing research (Test Case Prioritization, Test Case Minimization, Test Case Selection, Bug localization, to name a few) might be fundamentally biased. How do we know that solutions for unit tests will work successfully for e2e tests? It could be the case that solutions that consider, for instance, test case running times, provide better results.

Research datasets for software testing research, consider usually open source projects, which are more easily available. However, tests in those datasets are mostly unit tests, for several reasons. First, most open source projects considered do not contain integration or end-to-end (e2e) tests, as they are programming libraries that do not expose an API over the network. Second, e2e tests are difficult to run, as they usually require to start the whole project and its dependencies before e2e tests can be actually run. Finally, e2e tests are in many cases difficult to detect. How to pick up projects that really contain e2e tests? This work proposes an approach to detect, by inspecting projects from GitHub, which of those projects are promising candidates that might contain e2e tests.

Building a dataset of e2e tests is a huge task that requires fulfilling several steps, one at a time:

- Mining project repositories for e2e tests. This task is the purpose of this paper, and its objective is to find open source projects that contain e2e test cases by means of using heuristics based on e2e test best practices and common approaches in the industry. At the end of this step, a list E of open source projects with e2e tests is identified.
- Collecting e2e test runs. The purpose of this task is to find regressions from actual runs of the e2e tests of the project. Either the project's continuous integration information, if publicly available, is used, or researchers will have to run the e2e tests by themselves on each commit. At the end of this step, a list of runs of the e2e tests R at different commits with their associated data (logs, test results, etc.) are available.
- Mining runs of e2e tests mapping failures to fixes. The purpose of this step is to detect e2e test case failures, determining if those are regressions, and mapping the failure with the fixing commit. At the end of this step, a list of regressions R is available, with its associated data (commit on which the regression was detected by an e2e test case, fixing commit, etc.)

Any of those steps require a considerable effort. This paper focuses on detecting open source projects in GitHub which contain integration or e2e tests. This is a mandatory first step in order to be able to build dataset of e2e tests that can be used by the research community.

The rest of the paper is structured as follows: Sect. 2 discusses existing datasets of tests. Section 3 introduces the methodology followed in our study.

Results are discussed in Sect. 4. Finally, Sect. 5 concludes the paper and provides future research directions.

2   Related Work

In a previous work [8], authors used three applications from the students of the subject *Development of Web Applications* from the Software Engineering degree at Rey Juan Carlos University to build a dataset of e2e tests. These projects have been built as complete and functional applications, getting as close as possible to how an application would be developed in the industry. All the applications consist on a backend written in Java using the Spring framework, and a frontend, and the three of them require a MySQL database to store contents. Authors then injected regression bugs into the three applications in a controlled way, imitating the way developers work in many cases on a project: each bug was introduced during the development of a feature in a separate branch of the project. Therefore, all the bugs are properly identified, and thus making possible to use it in many research works. However, the dataset was quite limited, as it provided only 6 bugs.

Other datasets all consider exclusively unit tests. Bugs.jar [7] is a large-scale dataset for research in automated debugging, patching, and testing of Java programs. It contains a total of 1,158 bugs and patches from 8 large open source Java projects.

The iBugs [2] project provides a repository of real bugs in Java projects. It contains 364 bugs, of which there is only one test that reveals the bug, and it includes mechanisms to get the corrected version of the bug, as well as its previous version for comparison. The dataset tools also allows the execution of the tests in both versions.

Defects4J [4] is an extensible framework which provides real bugs to enable reproducible studies. This framework contains 835 real bugs from 17 real-world open source projects written in Java. Each bug included in their dataset contains information about the commit where the bug is fixed (which includes at least one test that reveals the bug), plus a failed commit to compare them. All bugs have their origin in the source code, are reproducible (both their failed and fixed versions) and the fix-commit does not include changes unrelated to the fix. The most recent version of the dataset includes a docker image to ease working with it.

BugsJS [3] is the first large benchmark of 453 real manually selected and validated JavaScript bugs from 10 popular server-side programs. Like Defects4J, it facilitates the reproducibility of the execution of the tests, specifically reproducing the environment from a Docker image.

Due to the increasing use of Python, datasets of this language have emerged for research. One of the most recent and relevant is BugsInPy [9]. This dataset is inspired by Defects4J and according to the authors follows a similar structure, including 493 bugs in 17 Python projects.

Another Python dataset, specifically oriented to research in Data Science is Boa Meets Python [1], which gathers 1,558 Python projects available in GitHub, all of them focused on solving Data Science tasks like machine learning.

A more recent dataset is ManySStuBs4J [5], in which the authors provide 153,652 single statement bug-fix changes mined from 1,000 popular open-source Java projects. Although oriented to research on program repair, many studies use it to train bug detection models, research about the authorship of commits or the time it takes for a bug to be fixed.

3   Methodology

For our aim of being able to detect promising project candidates that might contain e2e test, we first deeply investigated some projects containing e2e tests, in order to come up with some criteria that might work in detecting them (i.e., criteria that, when applied to this list of projects would detect at least one of the projects in the list). Then, we validated the criteria in a set of 100 projects from GitHub. We applied each criterion to the 100 projects. The criterion can provide a positive (the project satisfies the criterion, and might contain e2e tests under such criterion) or a negative (that specific criterion is not satisfied). Then we inspected each of the 100 projects, and confronted our findings with those of the proposed criteria, by marking the result provided by each criterion for a specific project as true positive (the criterion was positive, and there were tests), true negative (the criterion was negative and there weren't tests), false positive (the criterion was positive, and there weren't tests), and false negative (the criterion was negative and there were tests). With this information, we pruned the original criteria and chose the four criteria that were the most promising on the set of 100 projects (i.e., those that provided more true positives, as we are interested in finding e2e tests).

The specific steps of our methodology are as follows:

- Selecting some open source projects with e2e tests.
- Studying the selected projects in order to: a) check whether they actually included e2e tests; b) write down any relevant information about the tests (location and test case names.)
- Based on information about the test collected in the previous step, preparing a set of criteria that can identify at least one of the selected projects.
- Select 100 popular GitHub projects
- Check every criterion on each of the projects, recording whether the criterion was positive or negative.
- Manually check every positive (i.e., a criterion that was successful) to discard false positives.
- Pruning the set of criteria, selecting only those that are actually effective.
- Running the selected criteria over two different queries: 900 popular java projects, and 900 popular projects on any language.

For the first step, one of the authors, with more experience in developing, maintaining and running e2e tests and their infrastructure (including continuous integration systems), selected some open source projects, programmed in different programming languages, that according to their nature might have e2e tests. These projects were further analyzed by the rest of the authors. For each project, authors reported if there were e2e tests, and their location (folder and test case names). This labeling is shown in Table 1.

Table 1. Projects analyzed in step 1.

Project	Language	Findings
Redis	C	Integration folder
RabbitMQ	Erlang	Not found
Envoy	C++	Integration folder, Azure pipeline (CI)
Traefik	Go	Integration folder
Redmine	Ruby	Integration and system folders, Jenkinsfile (CI)
Ingress-nginx	Go	E2e folder, github actions
Vuejs	Javascript	E2e, circle-ci
Angular	Javascript	Integration and e2e folders
Kafka	Java	Docker and $end_{to_e}nd$ folders
Camel	Java	itest folder
Cassandra	Java	Distributed folder, Jenkinsfile
Consul	Go	Integration folder
Flink	Java	End-to-end folder
Vscode	Javascript	Integration folder
Grafana	Javascript	e2e folder
Express	Javascript	Acceptance folder

It is common practice that e2e tests are kept separated from unit tests, and run at different moments during the software development lifecycle. For instance, unit tests are usually run on each build in a continuous integration (CI) system, whereas e2e tests might only be run on specific events, like a merge into the main branch, or a pull request, as they usually require deploying the application before actually running the tests. We planned to use this common practice of keeping unit and e2e tests separated to figure out ways in which e2e tests could be identified. After a detailed inspection of the selected projects, a set of 12 criteria for detecting e2e tests was agreed by the authors. This agreement took place as follows: the three authors proposed one or more criteria for each of the projects that might work well in identifying the e2e tests for the given project. Then, two of the authors with more experience, decided which of those criteria made sense. Reasons for excluding a criteria included specificity (a criterion too specific to work as a general rule), and difficulty in assessing if the criteria is satisfied. Both authors reviewing the criteria voted to include or exclude a criterion. When there was agreement, the criterion was kept or removed, when there wasn't, the senior researcher decided whether to keep or remove the criterion. The final list of criteria is as follows:

- Integration: An *integration* folder into a *test* folder. Precisely, we search for a folder named integration within a folder named test.
- System: A *system* folder into a *test* folder. Precisely, we search for a folder named system within a folder named test.
- E2e: An *e2e* folder.
- Itest: An *itest* folder
- Acceptance: An *acceptance* folder
- Distributed: A *distributed* folder
- End-to-end: An *end-to-end* folder
- Docker: A *docker* folder
- Swagger: Presence of Swagger files
- Test name: Test case file names starting or ending in *IT*, or test case file names containing *e2e*, *system* or *rest-assured*
- Dependencies: The following dependencies on pom.xml/build.xml files: selenium-java, rest-assured
- CI: Presence of the following files denoting configuration of CI systems: Jenkinsfile, .travis-ci.yml, .circle-ci, .github/workflows/pipeline.yml, .azure-pipelines/pipelines.yml, .gitlab-ci.yml

On our second stage, we selected 100 projects from GitHub. The projects were selected according to the following criteria: any language and at least 500 stars in GitHub and at least 300 forks and created before 2015 and active with pushes after January 2020 and not archived and public. From the returned list we selected the first 100. After collecting the projects, the 12 criteria were applied to each project, noting which of them were bringing a positive (the criteria is satisfied, thus possible presence of e2e tests). Then we did a manual check of each of the projects bringing at least a positive in one of the criteria to discard false positives. Based on our findings, we then selected the three most effective criteria: those providing more true positives. Specifically, the selected criteria were: *integration*, *e2e*, and *test name*.

Finally, on our third stage consisted on applying the three criteria selected from the previous stage on two different sets. A set of 900 popular and active projects from GitHub, and a set of 900 popular and active Java projects from GitHub. Notice that for the first set of 900 projects, no language constraint was enforced. The set contains projects on different languages, including Java. For the project selection we used the same query as for the 100 selection, but selected the first 900 projects. In the specific case of Java projects, we added to the query the Java language, and again we selected the first 900 projects. We applied each criterion to the 1,800 projects and noted which were positive on which criteria.

4   Results

Our results are discussed in two stages. First, we report results for the 100 projects inspected manually. Then, we describe results for the 1,800 projects automatically assessed with the three selected criteria.

For the 100 projects obtained from GitHub, the results are shown in Table 2. The *Automatic* column shows the number of e2e tests reported automatically by each criterion. The *Manual* column shows those reported by the criterion for which the manual inspection determined it was a true positive. Finally, the row *Total* reflects the number of projects where at least one criterion reported a positive. According to the results, the best criterion (the one with more true positives) is *integration*. Other criteria with true positives are far from this one, like *e2e, docker, test name*. Some criteria were not useful in detecting e2e tests, such as *acceptance, distributed, end-to-end-test swagger, dependencies* or *ci-files*. Note that these criteria were selected because they appeared in some projects as a feasible way of detecting e2e tests in those projects.

The effectiveness of these criteria is limited, as all of them are below a 50% confidence. From the total 62 positives, only 13 were actual e2e test, that is, only 20.9% of the positives were true positives and corresponded to e2e tests.

Table 2. Preliminary experiment results with 100 Java projects

Approach	Occurrences	
	Automatic	Manual
integration	29	11
system	46	1
e2e	10	3
itest	25	1
acceptance	2	0
distributed	6	0
end-to-end-test	0	0
docker	17	2
swagger	3	0
test name	65	2
dependencies	3	0
ci-files	3	0
Total	62	13

For our final experimentation, we applied the best three criteria (*integration, e2e,* and *test name*) to two different sets of 900 projects: one agnostic of the programming language, and the other one based in Java. Table 3 shows the results for the 900 Java projects. In total 344 projects were reported as having e2e tests at least by one criterion. The largest number of positives (298) is reported by the *integration* criterion, with more than twice positives than the second one in the ranking (*test name*). The other criterion was only triggered by 45 (*e2e*) projects.

Table 3. Experiment results with 900 Java projects for the three selected criteria

Approach	Occurrences
integration	298
e2e	45
test name	121
Total	344

Table 4 shows the results for the three selected criteria on a set of 900 projects from different programming languages. When languages other than Java are selected, the number of positives decreases. In total, 270 projects had at least one positive. Again, the criterion with more positives is *integration*, although in this case the number of positives is slightly smaller (237). The second criterion in the ranking is again *test name* (76 positives), but in this case, followed closely by *e2e* with 69 positives.

Table 4. Experiment results with 900 projects (multi language)

Approach	Occurrences
integration	237
e2e	69
test name	76
Total	270

It is worth noting that these 1,800 projects were not validated manually. Hence, actual numbers might be considerably smaller. If the confidence reported for the preliminary experiment with 100 projects holds, that would mean that out of 270 positives for the multi-language experiment, around 54 would correspond to projects with actual e2e tests. For Java projects, this number would be almost 70. Despite the low confidence of the criteria, these numbers might be enough to find sufficient e2e tests to build a proper dataset of this kind of tests.

5   Conclusions

We investigated the presence of e2e tests in open source projects in GitHub, with the aim of building a dataset of e2e tests from real tests in active projects. Specifically, we envisioned 12 criteria that could reveal e2e tests in projects. In a preliminary experiment with 100 projects, we pruned the list and selected the three most promising criteria. Then we performed two analysis: one on a set of 900 Java project, and another one on a set of 900 projects from different languages.

According to the selected criteria, 344 and 270 projects contained e2e tests (at least one criterion was positive for that project). These numbers are big enough to ensure many tens of projects will actually contain e2e tests. In a future research we will validate these 614 projects and include those with real e2e tests into a dataset. This dataset will be made available to researchers on software testing.

References

1. Biswas, S., Islam, M.J., Huang, Y., Rajan, H.: Boa meets python: a boa dataset of data science software in python language. In: 2019 IEEE/ACM 16th International Conference on Mining Software Repositories (MSR), pp. 577–581. IEEE (2019)
2. Dallmeier, V., Zimmermann, T.: Extraction of bug localization benchmarks from history. In: Proceedings of the Twenty-second IEEE/ACM International Conference on Automated Software Engineering, ASE 2007, pp. 433–436. ACM, New York (2007). https://doi.org/10.1145/1321631.1321702. http://doi.acm.org/10.1145/1321631.1321702
3. Gyimesi, P., Vancsics, B., Stocco, A., Mazinanian, D., Árpád Beszédes, Ferenc, R., Mesbah, A.: BugsJS: a benchmark of javascript bugs. In: Proceedings of 12th IEEE International Conference on Software Testing, Verification and Validation (ICST) (2019)
4. Just, R., Jalali, D., Ernst, M.D.: Defects4J: a database of existing faults to enable controlled testing studies for java programs. In: Proceedings of the 2014 International Symposium on Software Testing and Analysis, ISSTA 2014, pp. 437–440. ACM, New York (2014). https://doi.org/10.1145/2610384.2628055. http://doi.acm.org/10.1145/2610384.2628055
5. Karampatsis, R.M., Sutton, C.: How often do single-statement bugs occur? The manysstubs4j dataset. In: Proceedings of the 17th International Conference on Mining Software Repositories, pp. 573–577 (2020)
6. Memon, A., et al.: Taming google-scale continuous testing. In: Proceedings of the 39th International Conference on Software Engineering: Software Engineering in Practice Track, ICSE-SEIP 2017, pp. 233–242. IEEE Press, Piscataway (2017). https://doi.org/10.1109/ICSE-SEIP.2017.16
7. Saha, R., Lyu, Y., Lam, W., Yoshida, H., Prasad, M.: Bugs. jar: a large-scale, diverse dataset of real-world java bugs. In: 2018 IEEE/ACM 15th International Conference on Mining Software Repositories (MSR), pp. 10–13. IEEE (2018)
8. Soto-Sánchez, Ó., Maes-Bermejo, M., Gallego, M., Gortázar, F.: A dataset of regressions in web applications detected by end-to-end tests. In: Shepperd, M., Brito e Abreu, F., Rodrigues da Silva, A., Pérez-Castillo, R. (eds.) QUATIC 2020. CCIS, vol. 1266, pp. 439–448. Springer, Cham (2020). https://doi.org/10.1007/978-3-030-58793-2_35
9. Widyasari, R., et al.: BugsInPy: a database of existing bugs in python programs to enable controlled testing and debugging studies. In: Proceedings of the 28th ACM Joint Meeting on European Software Engineering Conference and Symposium on the Foundations of Software Engineering, ESEC/FSE 2020, pp. 1556–1560. Association for Computing Machinery, New York (2020). https://doi.org/10.1145/3368089.3417943

Evaluating Sensor Interaction Failures in Mobile Applications

Euler Horta Marinho[1,2]([✉]) [ID], João P. Diniz[1] [ID], Fischer Ferreira[1] [ID],
and Eduardo Figueiredo[1]([✉]) [ID]

[1] Computer Science Department, Federal University of Minas Gerais,
Belo Horizonte, MG, Brazil
{eulerhm,jpaulo,fischerjf,figueiredo}@dcc.ufmg.br
[2] Computer and Systems Department, Federal University of Ouro Preto,
João Monlevade, MG, Brazil
euler@ufop.edu.br

Abstract. Mobile devices have a rich set of small-scale sensors which improve the functionalities possibilities. The growing use of mobile applications has aroused the interest of researchers in testing mobile applications. However, sensor interaction failures are a challenging and still a little-explored aspect of research. Unexpected behavior because the sensor interactions can introduce failures that manifest themselves in specific sensor configurations. Sensor interaction failures can compromise the mobile application's quality and harm the user's experience. We propose an approach for extending test suites of mobile applications in order to evaluate the sensor interactions aspects of mobile applications. We used eight sensors to verify the occurrence of sensor interaction failures. We generated all configurations considering the sensors enabled or disabled. We observed that some pairs of sensors cause failures in some applications including those not so obvious.

Keywords: Mobile application testing · Software failures · Sensor interactions

1 Introduction

Mobile devices have a rich set of small-scale microelectromechanical sensors which improve the functionalities possibilities as illustrated in specific application domains such as context-aware mobile applications [13]. Mobile applications are context-aware in a unique way since they can integrate data from multiple sensors [19,20]. Furthermore, the user interaction with device settings can enable or disable some sensors increasing the space of the test inputs.

The growing use of mobile applications has aroused the interest of researchers in testing mobile applications as evidenced by several works [10,15,16,21,24,27]. However, sensor interaction failures are a challenging and a still little-explored aspect of research. Applications can present unexpected behaviors because the

A. C. R. Paiva et al. (Eds.): QUATIC 2021, CCIS 1439, pp. 49–63, 2021.
https://doi.org/10.1007/978-3-030-85347-1_5

sensor interactions can introduce failures that manifest themselves in specific sensor configurations. Sensor interaction failures can compromise the mobile application's quality and harm the user's experience. The literature presents some works in this direction [4,12]. However, we lack work to evaluate sensor interaction failures in real mobile applications and verify which sensors are most related to failures. Testers may neglect to test mobile applications considering the interaction of sensors due to a lack of knowledge of such failures. However, sensor interaction failures may occur in the productive use of the mobile application but may be imperceptible in the testing phase.

Feature interaction has been widely discussed in the configurable software systems domain [2,7,14,18,22,23]. Initially, the feature interaction problem was observed in the telecommunications domain [3]. Feature interactions occur when features influence the behavior of other features. In this work, we look at sensor interactions through an approach to turn sensors enabled or disabled.

We propose an approach for extending test suites of mobile applications in order to evaluate the sensor interaction aspects of mobile applications. For the sake of simplicity, we use the term "sensor" in the same sense as in the taxonomy of Luo et al. [13] that consider hardware resources, such as Camera, Wi-Fi, and Bluetooth, as sensors. Besides, we included devices settings that can influence the behavior of sensors. For the sake of simplicity, we will refer to them also as sensors. Therefore, we used eight sensors to verify the occurrence of sensor interaction failures. We generated all combinations (2^8) considering the sensors enabled or disabled. For each of the 256 configurations, we run the test suite of 10 Android applications. Our study was designed to address the following research questions:

RQ1: Do sensor interactions cause failures in mobile applications?
RQ2: What are the sensor interactions most likely to cause a failure?

Surprisingly, we can find sensor interaction failures that we were not aware of before. We observed that some pairs of sensors cause failures in some applications. Moreover, the sensors used by the application must be identified in a more systematic way, since this use can be indirect. For instance, the camera can use location data for image tagging. Researchers can benefit from our analysis and replicate our study for other mobile applications technologies besides Android. Testers can, through our results, see the importance of considering sensor interaction when implementing their test suites.

The remainder of this paper is organized as follows. Section 2 describes a motivating example. Section 3 describes the study design. Section 4 discusses our achieved results. Section 5 presents the limitations of this work. Section 6 discusses some related work. Finally, Sect. 7 concludes this study and points directions for future work.

2   Motivating Example

In this session, we show an example of how the combination of mobile sensors, Android device settings, and application configurations may lead to an unexpected failure of the application. Traccar Client[1] is an open source application available to download at Google Play Store. In summary, it is a GPS Tracker, which communicates with its own application server. Traccar Client has a configuration called Accuracy, which can be set to three values: High, Medium, or Low. To achieve the Accuracy High, it is necessary that the GPS, Wi-Fi, Mobile data, and Bluetooth sensors are enabled on the smartphone.

According the the issue #390, opened at the Traccar issue manager at GitHub[2], it can be seen that, even if the four sensors are enabled, the application stops changing location when its Accuracy is set do Medium. However, works again for the other two possible values, i.e., High and Low. It is worth to mention that the referred issue was registered in 2019 and remains "Open" until this paper submission time[3].

3   Study Design

This section presents the steps of our study. Figure 1 illustrates an overview of these steps. Firstly, we conduct an application selection, and we define a configuration set considering the target sensors. Second, we perform an extension of test suites, aiming to control the test executions. Third, we executed the extended test suites using each configuration. Finally, we conduct analysis of the generated test reports.

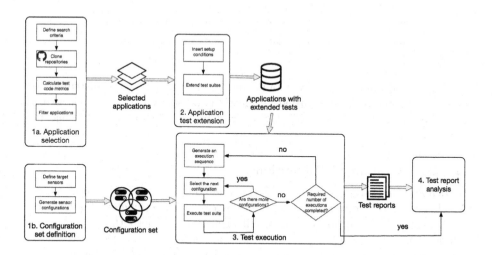

Fig. 1. The steps of the study.

---

[1] https://www.traccar.org.

[2] https://github.com/traccar/traccar-client-android/issues/390.

[3] Apr 20, 2021.

3.1   Application Selection

We selected Android applications from public Github repositories. Initially, we defined the search criteria to include repositories with at least 100 stars, whose programming languages were Java or Kotlin, and with last commit on or after January 1, 2017. We cloned the initial 1,000 repositories of the search. One of the identified repositories[4] contains a curated list of Kotlin applications. It was analyzed apart, resulting in 123 additional repositories. For obtaining an initial comprehension of the test suites, we use the `cloc` tool[5] to get the test code size of each project with instrumented tests[6]. In order to reduce the complexity of the executions, we filter the applications with test code between 450 LOC and 3,000 LOC. Additionally, we use the Manifest file of the apps to find the sensor related tags of Table 1. Finally, we select all the applications whose Manifest files have at least one of those tags.

Table 1. Sensor related tags.

Sensor	Tag	Value
Bluetooth	uses-feature	android.hardware.bluetooth
Bluetooth	uses_permission	bluetooth
Location	uses-permission	access_fine_location
Location	uses-feature	android.hardware.location
Wi-Fi, Mobile data	uses-permission	internet
Camera	uses-feature	android.hardware.camera
Others	uses-feature	android.hardware.sensor.*

The filtered applications were built and the test suites of the instrumented tests were executed. We discarded applications presenting build or test execution issues not easily solvable. Table 2 shows some characteristics of the selected applications.

3.2   Configuration Set Definition

We defined the target sensors to be evaluated in the study: usual sensors (Accelerometer, Barometer, Camera, Gyroscope, Magnetometer, Microphone, and Proximity), Location, Wi-Fi, Mobile Data, and Bluetooth. Moreover, we included three device settings: Auto Rotation, Battery Saver, Do not Disturb. Auto Rotation uses a synthetic sensor named Rotation Vector[7]. Battery Saver limits the operation of background functionalities[8]. Do not Disturb can mute

[4] https://github.com/androiddevnotes/awesome-android-kotlin-apps.
[5] https://github.com/AlDanial/cloc.
[6] A kind of test that runs on devices or emulators: https://developer.android.com/studio/test.
[7] https://developer.android.com/guide/topics/sensors/sensors_position.
[8] https://developer.android.com/about/versions/pie/power.

Table 2. Characteristics of the selected applications.

Application	Test LOC	# Test cases	Sensors	Last commit
AnkiDroid	2,770	164	Wi-Fi, Mobile Data, Camera	Mar 15, 2021
CovidNow	540	21	Wi-Fi, Mobile Data	Aug 14, 2020
iosched	473	9	Wi-Fi, Mobile Data, Location	Jun 25, 2020
lockwise-android	1,184	38	Wi-Fi, Mobile Data	Dec 10, 2020
nl-covid19	1,114	20	Wi-Fi, Mobile Data, Bluetooth	Mar 15, 2021
openScale	1,451	14	Bluetooth, Location	Mar 9, 2021
owntracks	889	27	Wi-Fi, Mobile Data, Location	Mar 15, 2021
pocketHub	1,663	107	Wi-Fi, Mobile Data	Apr 11, 2020
SpaceXFollower	940	30	Wi-Fi, Mobile Data	Feb 27, 2021
vocable-android	499	14	Camera	Oct 28, 2020

sound, stop vibration, and block notifications[9]. As we can see in Table 2, part of the target sensors were identified from the sensors of the selected applications. We considered the Camera as a usual sensor.

A configuration is a 8-tuple of pairs $(sensor\_name, state)$ where $state$ can be $True$ or $False$ depending on whether $sensor\_name$ is enabled or disabled. For the eight sensors, we generated all configurations ($2^8 = 256$). A file with the configuration set is used as input for the test execution.

3.3 Application Test Extension

We extended the test suites of each application in order to enable or disable sensors. We adopt a strategy using the control of buttons in Quick Settings[10] shown in Fig. 2. We can see the buttons associated to the target sensors. The button **Sensors Off** is activated by means of a developer option[11]. This button enables or disables all usual sensors.

We implemented this strategy as a class with a setup method using the UIAutomator testing framework[12]. We extended each test class with the referred class. Besides, we modified the build scripts in order to use the Android Test Orchestrator[13], a tool that helps minimize possible shared states and isolate the crashes.

3.4 Test Execution

We implemented the algorithm described in Fig. 3 for test execution management as a Python script. We executed tests in Android 10 using two smartphones: a

---

[9] https://support.google.com/android/answer/9069335?hl=en.
[10] https://support.google.com/android/answer/9083864?hl=en.
[11] https://source.android.com/devices/sensors/sensors-off.
[12] https://developer.android.com/training/testing/ui-automator.
[13] https://developer.android.com/training/testing/junit-runner.

Fig. 2. Android quick settings.

Samsung Galaxy M30 with 4 GB RAM and a Samsung Galaxy S10 with 8 GB RAM.

We use multiple executions (line 3) because this is a known approach used to detect the existence of flaky tests [28]. The configuration set (allConfigurations) is shuffled (line 4), aiming to deal with the effect of ordering dependencies between tests, a possible source of this kind of test [8].

3.5 Test Report Analysis

We analyze each test report in order to identify the tests with failures. We implemented Python scripts for extracting the test names and recording this information along with the respective configurations. Therefore, for each failure, we identify the name of the test, the description of the failure, and the configuration related to the failure.

For each Android application, we use a Python implementation[14] of the Apriori algorithm [1] to perform a frequent itemset mining analysis on the occurrences of all configurations that led a test case to fail. A frequent itemset is defined as a set of items that occur together in at least a Support threshold value of all transactions available. The Support of an itemset is defined as the proportion of transactions in the data set which contain the itemset [9]. In this work, each item is a sensor state, enabled or disabled, and we set the Support to 0.1 (10%).

---

[14] http://rasbt.github.io/mlxtend/user_guide/frequent_patterns/apriori/.

Algorithm Test execution manager

Input: Application *app* with extended tests
Output: Test reports
1: *maxExecutions* ← 3
2: *exec* ← 1
3: **while** *exec* ≤ *maxExecutions* **do**
4:     shuffle(allConfigurations)
5:     **for all** *c* ∈ *allConfigurations* **do**
6:         Execute the test suite of application *app* with configuration c
7:     **end for**
8:     *exec* ← *exec* + 1
9: **end while**

Fig. 3. Test execution manager.

The lower value for support allowed us to do a more in-depth analysis, as can be seen in Sect. 4.2.

4 Results and Discussion

This section presents data from test reports and the discussion of the results according to the research questions. In Sect. 4.1, we address the first research question whereas in Sect. 4.2, we answer the second research question.

4.1 RQ1. Do Sensor Interactions Cause Failures in Mobile Application?

We tabulated the test report data aiming to summarize the amount of occurrences of each failure. Along the test executions, we observed that test suites can reveal multiple failures. For each failure, we identify the configuration used during test execution.

Table 3 presents the failure occurrences by execution amount. Among parentheses, we mentioned the number of configurations followed by the failure identifier. The number of one-occurrence failures varied between 2 and 11. Two applications (CovidNow and vocable-android) exhibited about 50% of this kind of failure. The other applications had between 1% and 29% of failures with relation to the number of test cases. Two-occurrence failures varied between 1 and 7. One application (vocable-android) had 50% of this kind of failure. The other applications had between 3% and 20% of failures. Three-occurrence failures varied between 1 and 7. One application (vocable-android) exhibited 50% of this kind of failure. The other applications had between 7% and 20% of failures. Furthermore, openScale application does not exhibit failures.

We argue that failures manifested only in one or two executions can be related to flaky tests or adverse conditions related to test infrastructure. Almost all configurations were associated to some failure. For instance, we can see that Anki-Android, iosched, and pocketHub applications had failures only in one execution.

Table 3. Failure occurrences by execution amount.

	Application	Occurrences	Percentage
1 execution	Anki-Android	4 ($3A_1$, $1A_2$)	1%
	CovidNow	33 ($3B_1$, $10B_2$, $2B_3$, $2B_4$, $2B_5$, $2B_6$, $2B_7$, $2B_8$, $3B_9$, $2B_{10}$, $3B_{11}$)	52%
	iosched	10 ($5C_1$, $5C_1$)	22%
	lockwise-android	95 ($84D_1$, $1D_2$, $2D_3$, $1D_4$, $1D_5$, $1D_6$, $1D_7$, $1D_8$, $1D_9$, $1D_{10}$, $1D_{11}$)	29%
	nl-covid19	74 ($2E_1$, $3E_2$, $2E_3$, $3E_4$, $64E_5$)	25%
	owntracks	42 ($35F_1$, $6F_3$, $1F_4$)	11%
	pockethub	22 ($19G_1$, $2G_2$, $1G_3$)	3%
	SpaceXFollower	188 ($71H_1$, $89H_2$, $28H_3$)	10%
	vocable-android	213 ($19I_1$, $19I_2$, $19I_3$, $39I_4$, $39I_5$, $39I_6$, $39I_7$)	50%
2 executions	lockwise-android	11 ($11D_4$)	3%
	nl-covid19	176 ($35E_1$, $53E_2$, $35E_3$, $53E_4$)	20%
	owntracks	46 ($24F_1$, $22F_2$)	7%
	SpaceXFollower	51 ($17H_1$, $32H_2$, $1H_3$, $1H_4$)	13%
	vocable-android	354 ($62I_1$, $62I_2$, $62I_3$, $42I_4$, $42I_5$, $42I_6$, $42I_7$)	50%
3 executions	CovidNow	128 ($64B_1$, $64B_2$)	10%
	nl-covid19	454 ($91E_1$, $136E_2$, $91E_3$, $136E_4$)	20%
	owntracks	305 ($71F_1$, $234F_2$)	7%
	SpaceXFollower	444 ($75H_1$, $60H_2$, $54H_3$, $255H_4$)	13%
	vocable-android	681 ($111I_1$, $111I_2$, $111I_3$, $87I_4$, $87I_5$, $87I_6$)	50%

On the other hand, lockwise-android had failures in one and two executions. Failures H_4 in SpaceXFollower and F_2 in owntracks occurred with an excessive number of configurations. Therefore, as we can see that three-occurrence failures are not so common, this highlights the need of developers and testers to take care of sensor interactions.

4.2   RQ2. What Are the Sensor Interactions Most Likely to Cause a Failure?

In order to explore the sensor interactions causing failures, we proceed with the analysis of the results of the frequent item set mining procedure. The procedure was focused only on applications with failures in three executions. Therefore, we selected data from five applications: CovidNow, nl-covid19, owntracks, SpaceX-Follower, and vocable-android. From the analysis, we can observe that sensor pairs have more influence on failures compared to other combinations, since their support is more prominent. For instance, in combinations of size greater than three, the range of the support was less than 0.3.

Table 4 shows, for each application, the sensor pairs and the support reached. The name of the sensor is preceded by the exclamation mark when the sensor is disabled. As we can see, the sensor pairs are related to sensors used by applications, according to the fourth column of Table 2. It is important to note, that vocable-android had failures associated to location, since the device camera can use location sensor to record location tags[15].

Table 4. Sensor pairs.

Application	Sensor pairs	Support
CovidNow	$\langle !mobiledata, !wifi \rangle$	1.0
nl-covid19	$\langle wifi, !bluetooth \rangle$	0.8
owntracks	$\langle !location, !wifi \rangle$	0.4
SpaceXFollower	$\langle !mobiledata, !wifi \rangle$	0.5
vocable-android	$\langle location, !sensors \rangle$	0.7

Figure 4 presents heat maps with the supports of sensor pairs for each application. In CovidNow, failures are more associated to wifi and mobiledata combined with other sensors. In nl-covid19, they are more associated to wifi and bluetooth combined with other sensors, followed by location. In owntracks, failures are more associated to location and wifi, followed by mobiledata, bluetooth and usual sensors. In SpaceXFollower, they are more related to wifi and mobiledata, followed by other sensors. In vocable-android, failures are more related to location and sensors.

Our findings highlight that some sensors can be used indirectly by some applications, as the case of vocable-android with location sensor involved in failures. However, the use of sensors in applications can be more intricate. Such case happens with owntracks. As we mentioned, in this application, usual sensors were involved in failures. A probable cause is due to the use of the Fused Location Provider API[16] that uses usual sensors such as Accelerometer and Gyroscope to improve indoor tracking. Moreover, recent versions of Android are able to use Bluetooth to enhance location services[17].

5 Threats to Validity

We carefully designed and conducted our study (cf. Sects. 3 and 4). However, some threats to validity may have harmed our study results and discussions. During the study conduction, we considered certain threats are obstacles we should

---

[15] https://developer.android.com/reference/androidx/exifinterface/media/ExifInterface.

[16] https://developers.google.com/location-context/fused-location-provider.

[17] https://support.google.com/nexus/answer/3467281?hl=en.

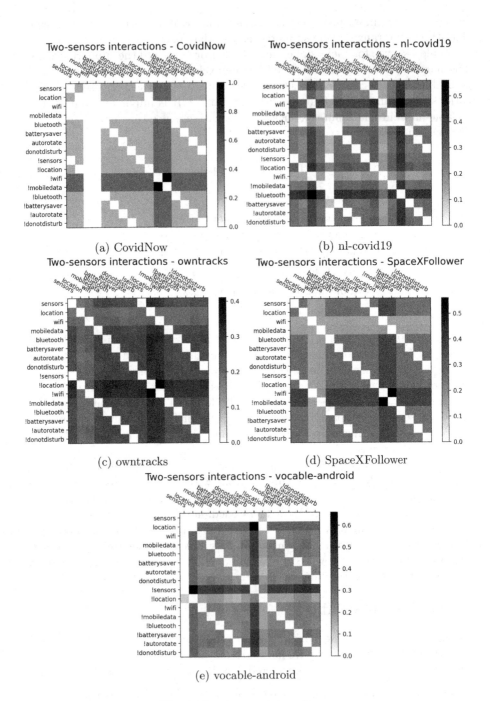

(a) CovidNow

(b) nl-covid19

(c) owntracks

(d) SpaceXFollower

(e) vocable-android

Fig. 4. Two-sensors interactions.

address minimally. We discuss below some major threats and their respective treatments. We divided into construct, internal, and external threats to validity below.

Construct Validity: There are two threats to construct validity. The first is related to the implementation of our approach to extend test suites and control the sensor states (enabled/disabled). To mitigate this threat, the implemented code was carefully inspected and validated by all authors of this study. Moreover, we conduct essays to evaluate the suitable behavior of the implemented code. The second is the fact that we adopt a simplistic treatment for analysing the found failures. We do not conduct a deep investigation for understanding the cause of these failures, in other words, the probable software defects. However, since we only selected applications without build or test execution issues, we believed this threat was mitigated.

Internal Validity: There are four major threats to the internal validity of our study. First, we discarded from our study the Android applications in which the test suite failed before submitting the systems to 256 configurations. Second, the downloaded systems could contain setup errors causing failures to run the test suite. To mitigate the effect of using systems in which the test suite fails for any configuration, we ensure that the Android applications do not have any setup errors. Third, to minimize faults occurring because of our instrumentation for faulty configurations, we set the sensor status manually and ran the tests that identified faults. Finally, we restricted our study to run each test suite three times for our system set for each 256 configurations. We empirically analyzed the number of times viable to run the suite for the Android applications set. Some systems took too long, for instance, test execution for pocketHub spent 4 days to complete 107 test cases for each 256 configurations. Therefore, we have empirically chosen three times to run the test suite in different configurations. This limitation was needed because it tested all test cases for the 256 different configurations for some subject systems. This time constraint may affect our findings since flaky tests can occur in other executions. However, according to our evaluations (Sect. 4), we observed three separate runs were sufficient to find the flaky tests.

External Validity: First, we have performed our study with 10 Android applications. As one could expect, our Android applications may not represent the characteristics of all Android applications systems. To mitigate the effect of the Android applications' representativeness chosen to compose our study, we are confident that we selected systems from various domains, longevity, sizes, and test suite sizes (between 450 and 3,000 LOC). Nevertheless, our Android applications set allowed us to achieve some preliminary insights on mobile applications' sensor interaction failures. Second, we have restricted our analysis to mobile applications developed in the JAVA and KOTLIN programming languages. We cannot generalize to other programming languages and frameworks such as Flutter and React Native. This limitation may affect the generalization of our results. We invite researchers to replicate our work in other technologies and frameworks and validate our study findings. Third, our analysis focuses on sensor interactions, but we may have chosen systems that do not use any sensors. To minimize this threat, we use the Manifest file of the apps to find the sensor related. We discarded Android applications that had no indication of using sensors indicated in the Manifest file. Finally, a threat to our study is the quality of the test suite in the selected applications. All of our analysis is conditioned on the test suite's ability to reveal failures. To mitigate the incomplete test suite's effect, we limited our analysis to applications with a test suite size of at least 450 LOC.

6   Related Work

This section discusses the related work, focusing on papers proposing or evaluating approaches to support tests of mobile applications.

Some relevant works [12, 25, 26] investigated the problem of testing a large set of configurations in mobile applications. For instance, Lu et al. [12] proposed the preference-wise testing of applications to improve the efficacy of existing testing approaches by considering the effects of user preferences. They argue that the proposed approach can reduce test cost because it executes test cases only under relevant preference combinations. Unlike Lu's work, our study does not aim to reduce test cost, but it investigates all combinations of sensors to identify interaction failures.

Other studies [4, 6, 11] have also highlighted the problem of hidden failures in mobile applications due to the large set of possible configurations, including hardware and software options. For instance, Ceccato and his colleagues [4] presented an in-vivo study about testing of mobile applications. They relied on feature models to handle the representation of the configuration space and, then, analyzed combinations of features, such as operating systems and supported camera devices. Similarly to their work, we also investigate the combinations of features and their impact on failures. However, we focus on enabling and disabling sensors instead of hardware and software variations.

We can note an increasing number of studies focusing on Android fragmentation/compatibility issues [11, 25, 26]. This is a broader research theme mainly targeting the quality evaluation of Android applications. Our study treat one dimension of device configurations, since other dimensions are present, such as screen sizes, camera qualities etc. Wei et al. [26] highlight the relevance of sensors behavior in device-specific issues arising from the interaction with Android APIs, as in the case of the proximity sensor.

7   Conclusion

In this work, we propose an approach for extending test suites aiming to evaluate the sensor interactions aspects of mobile applications. We used eight sensors to verify the occurrence of sensor interaction failures. For each of the 256 possible combinations (2^8), we run the test suites of 10 real Android applications of different domains, complexity, and size.

We observed that some pair of sensors are related to sensor interaction failures. However, the sensors used by the analysed applications cannot always be directly inferred. In our study, we faced challenge factors as test execution issues (e.g., flaky tests) and possible adverse conditions related to test infrastructure.

As future work, we will expand our analysis to construct a dataset of mobile applications with sensor interaction failures. As a part of this effort, we plan to validate these failures along the application developers and to explore the software defects [5] that cause such failures. We aiming to improve the detection of sensors used by the applications, possibly by using static and dynamic analysis strategies. Another point of investigation are test patterns [17], in other words, testing strategies, to deal with sensor interactions. The artifacts used in this study are available in a Github repository[18].

Acknowledgements. This research was partially supported by Brazilian funding agencies: CNPq, CAPES, and FAPEMIG.

References

1. Agrawal, R., Srikant, R., et al.: Fast algorithms for mining association rules. In: Proceedings of 20th International Conference on Very Large Data Bases, VLDB, vol. 1215, pp. 487–499. Citeseer (1994)
2. Apel, S., Speidel, H., Wendler, P., Rhein, A.V., Beyer, D.: Detection of feature interactions using feature-aware verification. In: Proceedings of the 26th International Conference on Automated Software Engineering (ASE), pp. 372–375 (2011)
3. Bowen, T.F., Dworack, F., Chow, C., Griffeth, N., Herman, G.E., Lin, Y.J.: The feature interaction problem in telecommunications systems. In: Proceedings of the 7th International Conference on Software Engineering for Telecommunication Switching Systems (SETSS), pp. 59–62 (1989)
4. Ceccato, M., Gazzola, L., Kifetew, F.M., Mariani, L., Orrú, M., Tonella, P.: Toward in-vivo testing of mobile applications. In: 2019 IEEE International Symposium on Software Reliability Engineering Workshops (ISSREW), pp. 137–143. IEEE (2019)
5. Esteves, G., Figueiredo, E., Veloso, A., Viggiato, M., Ziviani, N.: Understanding machine learning software defect predictions. Autom. Softw. Eng. **27**(3), 369–392 (2020). https://doi.org/10.1007/s10515-020-00277-4
6. Farooq, U., Zhao, Z.: RuntimeDroid: restarting-free runtime change handling for Android apps. In: Proceedings of the 16th Annual International Conference on Mobile Systems, Applications, and Services, pp. 110–122 (2018)
7. Ferreira, F., Vale, G., Diniz, J.P., Figueiredo, E.: Evaluating T-wise testing strategies in a community-wide dataset of configurable software systems. J. Syst. Softw. **179**, 110990 (2021)
8. Gambi, A., Bell, J., Zeller, A.: Practical test dependency detection. In: Proceedings of the IEEE International Conference on Software Testing, Verification, and Validation (ICST), pp. 1–11 (2018)

---

[18] https://github.com/quatic2021-sensorinterpaper/artifacts.

9. Hornik, K., Grün, B., Hahsler, M.: arules-a computational environment for mining association rules and frequent item sets. J. Stat. Softw. **14**(15), 1–25 (2005)
10. Kong, P., Li, L., Gao, J., Liu, K., Bissyandé, T.F., Klein, J.: Automated testing of Android apps: a systematic literature review. IEEE Trans. Reliabil. **68**(1), 45–66 (2018)
11. Kowalczyk, E., Cohen, M.B., Memon, A.M.: Configurations in Android testing: they matter. In: Proceedings of the 1st International Workshop on Advances in Mobile App Analysis, pp. 1–6 (2018)
12. Lu, Y., Pan, M., Zhai, J., Zhang, T., Li, X.: Preference-wise testing for Android applications. In: Proceedings of the 2019 27th ACM Joint Meeting on European Software Engineering Conference and Symposium on the Foundations of Software Engineering, pp. 268–278 (2019)
13. Luo, C., Goncalves, J., Velloso, E., Kostakos, V.: A survey of context simulation for testing mobile context-aware applications. ACM Comput. Surv. (CSUR) **53**(1), 1–39 (2020)
14. Machado, I., McGregor, J., Cavalcanti, Y., Almeida, E.: On strategies for testing software product lines: a systematic literature review. Inf. Softw. Technol. (IST) **56**, 1183–1199 (2014)
15. Marinho, E.H., Figueiredo, E.: PLATOOL: a functional test generation tool for mobile applications. In: Proceedings of the 34th Brazilian Symposium on Software Engineering, Tools Track, SBES 2020, pp. 548–553 (2020)
16. Mendez-Porras, A., Quesada-Lopez, C., Jenkins, M.: Automated testing of mobile applications: a systematic map and review. In: Proceedings of the Ibero-American Conference on Software Engineering (CIbSE), pp. 195–208 (2015)
17. Morgado, I.C., Paiva, A.C.: The impact tool for Android testing. Proc. ACM Hum.-Comput. Interact. **3**(EICS), 1–23 (2019)
18. Nguyen, S., Nguyen, H., Tran, N., Tran, H., Nguyen, T.: Feature-interaction Aware configuration prioritization for configurable code. In: Proceedings of the 34th IEEE/ACM International Conference on Automated Software Engineering (ASE), pp. 489–501 (2019)
19. Oliveira, J., Viggiato, M., Santos, M., Figueiredo, E., Marques-Neto, H.: An empirical study on the impact of Android code smells on resource usage. In: Proceedings of the International Conference on Software Engineering and Knowledge Engineering (SEKE), pp. 314–313 (2018)
20. Rubinov, K., Baresi, L.: What are we missing when testing our Android apps? Computer **51**(4), 60–68 (2018)
21. Sahinoglu, M., Inckin, K., Aktas, M.S.: Mobile application verification: a systematic mapping study. In: Proceedings of the International Conference on Computational Science and Its Applications (ICCSA), pp. 147–163 (2015)
22. Siegmund, N., et al.: Predicting performance via automated feature-interaction detection. In: Proceedings of the 34th International Conference on Software Engineering (ICSE), pp. 167–177 (2012)
23. Soares, L.R., Schobbens, P., do Carmo Machado, I., de Almeida, E.S.: Feature interaction in software product line engineering: a systematic mapping study. Inf. Softw. Technol. (IST) **98**, 44–58 (2018)
24. Tramontana, P., Amalfitano, D., Amatucci, N., Fasolino, A.R.: Automated functional testing of mobile applications: a systematic mapping study. Softw. Qual. J. **27**(1), 149–201 (2019). https://doi.org/10.1007/s11219-018-9418-6
25. Vilkomir, S.: Multi-device coverage testing of mobile applications. Softw. Qual. J. **26**(2), 197–215 (2018). https://doi.org/10.1007/s11219-017-9357-7

26. Wei, L., Liu, Y., Cheung, S.C., Huang, H., Lu, X., Liu, X.: Understanding and detecting fragmentation-induced compatibility issues for Android apps. IEEE Trans. Softw. Eng. **46**(11), 1176–1199 (2018)
27. Zein, S., Salleh, N., Grundy, J.: A systematic mapping study of mobile application testing techniques. J. Syst. Softw. **117**, 334–356 (2016)
28. Zolfaghari, B., Parizi, R.M., Srivastava, G., Haleimariam, Y.: Root causing, detecting, and fixing flaky tests: state of the art and future roadmap. Softw. Pract. Exp. **51**(5), 1–17 (2020)

Software Evolution

Software Evolution

Feature-Oriented Clone and Pull for Distributed Development and Evolution

Daniel Hinterreiter[1], Lukas Linsbauer[3], Herbert Prähofer[2], and Paul Grünbacher[1(✉)]

[1] Christian Doppler Laboratory MEVSS, Institute of Software Systems Engineering, Johannes Kepler University, Linz, Austria
`paul.gruenbacher@jku.at`
[2] Institute of System Software, Johannes Kepler University, Linz, Austria
[3] Institute of Software Engineering and Automotive Informatics, Technische Universität Braunschweig, Braunschweig, Germany

Abstract. Product line engineering aims at quickly delivering individual solutions to customers by customizing and evolving products based on a common platform. Engineers commonly follow a distributed and feature-oriented process, supported by version control systems, to track implementation-level changes. For instance, feature branches are widely used to add new or modify existing features. However, when merging back features to the product line, the information how features map to code is usually lost. Furthermore, the granularity of merging is limited to branches, making it hard to transfer individual features from one product to another. This paper thus presents feature-oriented clone and pull operations for the distributed development and evolution of product lines, which are implemented in the FORCE[2] platform. Our evaluation uses the ArgoUML product line to assess the correctness and performance of our approach. The results show that the feature-oriented operations work with high precision and recall for different cases of feature interactions. The performance measurements demonstrate that the clone and pull operations can be integrated in typical workflows of engineers.

Keywords: Feature-oriented development · Distributed development · Variation control systems · Software product lines

1 Introduction

Software product line engineering is widely used to provide individual solutions to customers. Engineers often follow a feature-oriented approach when developing customer-specific systems. They customize and evolve product lines in different concurrent projects to quickly deliver solutions, e.g., by creating new features or by selectively reusing and adapting existing features. Supporting such a distributed and feature-oriented process is challenging. Version control systems

© Springer Nature Switzerland AG 2021
A. C. R. Paiva et al. (Eds.): QUATIC 2021, CCIS 1439, pp. 67–81, 2021.
https://doi.org/10.1007/978-3-030-85347-1_6

like Git are widely used to track fine-grained, implementation-level changes to product lines and products. Feature branches are a common mechanism to add new or modify existing features. Pull requests are then used to integrate changes of engineers into the platform in a controlled fashion. However, this approach has two problems [7]: *(i)* the mapping of features to code is commonly lost after integrating and merging a feature branch. As a consequence, the feature becomes mandatory and cannot be used to systematically create variants. *(ii)* The granularity of integration is limited to branches, i.e., there is no support for merging only selected features from a branch.

This paper thus presents feature-oriented operations for distributed development. Our approach builds on our earlier work on variation control systems [7], feature-to-artifact mappings [2], and workflows for feature-oriented development [5]. In particular, we have realized and evaluated feature-oriented *clone* and *pull* operations for our FORCE^2 platform: cloning allows to create a new product line based on an existing one by including only the features needed for a specific development task. In distinction to existing version control systems such as Git, it composes only the features needed for a specific purpose. Pulling allows transferring feature implementations between individual products or product lines, thus supporting feature-level code reuse. For example, pulling can be used to transfer a feature from a cloned product line back to its origin product line to make it generally available. In distinction to Git, this means that also fine-grained variants can be handled, i.e., variability is preserved by managing traces to artifacts implementing the features.

2   Distributed Feature-Oriented Workflow

We illustrate typical workflows motivating our approach based on the ArgoUML system (argouml.org) and use the ArgoUML variants used in Martinez et al.'s [8] feature location benchmark study to explain scenarios for the distributed operations contributed by our paper. Figure 1 presents an overview: the scenario starts with the ArgoUML product line *ORIGIN* containing the mandatory features *Base, Diagrams,* and *Class*, which represent the common code of all ArgoUML variants, as well as the optional features *Activity* and *Logging*. The cross-cutting feature *Logging* interacts with the feature *Activity*, i.e., some code is only present if both features are enabled.

In our scenario, an engineer decides to start a new development task based on the *ORIGIN* product line using the feature-based *clone* operation. He chooses to include only the mandatory features and the feature *Logging* from *ORIGIN*, thus excluding the optional feature *Activity*. The result of the *clone* operation is the product line *CLONE A* with the features *Base, Diagrams, Class,* and *Logging*. The engineer extends *CLONE A* with a new feature *Sequence* for modeling sequence diagrams and first adds it to the feature model (step 2). He then performs a *checkout* for this task to create a product variant *P1*, which contains the source code of all mandatory and a new optional feature *Sequence* in the feature model. After developing the feature (step 4), the engineer *commits* the

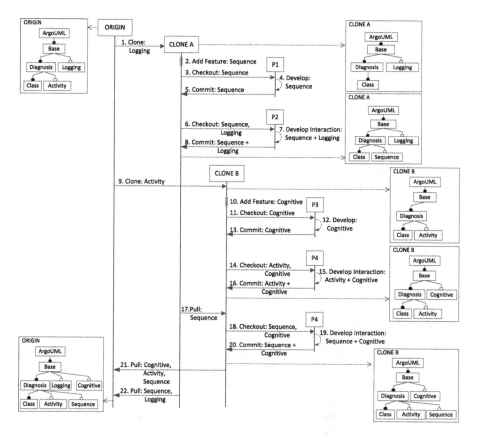

Fig. 1. A scenario illustrating feature-oriented operations in a distributed workflow.

new source code to the repository, which is thereby also automatically mapped to the feature *Sequence*. The engineer further decides to also develop the code handling the interaction [13] of the features *Sequence* and *Logging*. This is done by checking out and composing a product variant for this task, which contains the features *Sequence* and *Logging*. The engineer then adds the code ensuring the joint operation of the two features, and then commits the changes (steps 6–8), thereby mapping the feature interaction code to both features.

Independently of these tasks another engineer derives a product line variant *CLONE B* from *ORIGIN* (step 9). She includes *Activity* but decides to exclude *Logging*. The engineer then develops the feature *Cognitive* and commits it to the repository (steps 10–13). She also adds code handling the interaction of the features *Activity* and *Cognitive* (steps 14–16). The engineer then notices that the feature *Sequence* in *CLONE A* is useful for her own task. Therefore, she *pulls* the feature and the source code mapped to it from *CLONE A* (step 17). She then commits these changes to the local repository. However, as *CLONE A* not yet includes the feature *Cognitive*, she needs to add code to cover the interaction. She thus checks out a product variant containing both features (step 18), develops the required interaction code for *Sequence* and *Cognitive* (step 19), and commits it to the repository (step 20).

Finally, the engineer maintaining the product line *ORIGIN* decides to integrate all features developed in the product line *CLONE B*. For that purpose, he pulls the features *Sequence*, *Activity* and *Cognitive* (step 21), thereby also retrieving the code needed for the interaction of these features. However, the feature interaction code of *Sequence* and *Logging* is still missing, as *CLONE B* did not yet contain the feature *Logging*. *CLONE A*, however, for which the feature *Sequence* was originally developed, contains the feature *Logging* and thus also the interaction code. Therefore, the engineers fetches the feature interaction code for *Sequence* and *Logging* by pulling it from *CLONE A* (step 22). In this scenario, code for the interaction of the features *Cognitive* and *Logging* might still be missing, requiring the engineer of *ORIGIN* to develop and commit it as described for other cases.

3   Feature-Oriented Clone and Pull Operations

The scenario demonstrates the need for clone and pull operations to support distributed feature-oriented development. However, in contrast to existing version control systems such as Git our operations are feature-oriented and allow engineers to clone or pull a single feature, a set of features, or a (partial) configuration as needed for their development tasks.

This section describes the two feature-oriented operations `clone` and `pull`. Our approach uses a product line platform comprising a *repository* with the *features* of the product line, *constraints* among features in the form of a *feature model*, *fragments* of implementation artifacts, as well as *mappings* between features and fragments in the form of *presence conditions* (cf. [1,4,7,11]). In the following we assume a product line *PL* with a set of features *F*. The presence conditions are Boolean formulas in disjunctive normal form (DNF) with features as literals. A DNF formula is a disjunction of clauses. Every clause is a conjunction of features and can be interpreted as a feature interaction, i.e., fragments that map to such a condition implement the interaction of the involved features. An example is the presence condition (*Activity* ∧ *Logging*) ∨ (*Sequence* ∧ *Logging*). Fragments related to this condition implement the interaction of the features *Activity* and *Logging* as well as *Sequence* and *Logging* and are included in any product variant that contains this combination of features. Another example is *Activity* ∧ ¬*Cognitive*. Artifact fragments with this mapping are included in any product variant containing the feature *Activity* but not the feature *Cognitive*. Many presence conditions, however, consist of a single variable, meaning that the associated code fragment belongs to one feature only (e.g., *Activity*).

Clone. The feature-oriented `clone` operation is used to derive a new product line from an existing one. While the clone operation in Git copies the entire repository, our feature-oriented `clone` creates a more specific product line excluding optional features and their implementation, if they are not needed for a specific development task. It also adapts and pre-configures the feature model, i.e., it removes deselected features while selected features become mandatory or remain variable. The cloned platform then serves as foundation for further development, i.e., adding new or modifying existing features. If further features from the original platform or features implemented in other platforms are required, they can be pulled at any time. The `clone` operation is based on the *subset* operation $PL' = subset(PL, C)$. It receives as input a product line PL and a partial configuration C and creates another product line $PL' \subseteq PL$, i.e., the features and supported product variants of PL' are a subset of the features and supported product variants of PL.

A feature configuration is a set of positive or negative features. A partial feature configuration is a feature configuration with some selected (value *true*) or deselected (value *false*) features. However, features may also remain variable (value *undecided*). Thus, a partial feature configuration for a clone operation can be defined by the user from the set of features F as follows: A user can *(i)* decide to keep a feature f variable; *(ii)* set a feature f to true and thus make it mandatory; *(iii)* set a feature f to false and thus exclude it from the partial configuration. That means, all features with a value assigned in C are no longer variable in the target product line, i.e., they are either removed (value *false*) or become mandatory (value *true*), in which case they could optionally be merged with their parent feature. Moreover, a partial feature configuration must be *consistent* such that all the feature constraints are fulfilled. For example, if a feature from an XOR-group is set to true to become mandatory, all other features in the XOR-group can no longer be selected and are set to false. However, if a feature in an XOR-group is selected but kept variable, other features in the group can still be set as variable or be deselected.

Artifact Fragments and Mappings. The cloned subset product line PL' contains only the mappings and related artifacts fragment from the original product line, whose presence conditions are still satisfiable given the partial feature configuration C, i.e., only code fragments with satisfiable presence conditions are included. In particular, features set to true or false may render presence conditions unsatisfiable. However, features which are still variable remain in the DNF clauses as feature variables. Finally, the resulting presence conditions are trimmed such that DNF clauses no longer satisfiable are removed from the presence conditions. For example, consider a product line PL with the optional features *Activity, Sequence, Logging,* and *Cognitive* (cf. Fig. 1). Assume the product line contains a mapping m_1 with condition *Activity*, a mapping m_2 with condition *Activity* $\land \neg Cognitive$ and a mapping m_3 with condition (*Activity* $\land$ *Logging*) $\lor$ (*Sequence* $\land$ *Logging*). When creating a clone by selecting the features *Activity* and *Sequence* but excluding the features *Logging* and *Cognitive*, i.e., `clone`$(PL, \{\neg Logging, \neg Cognitive\})$, the condition (*Activity* $\land$ *Logging*) $\lor$ (*Sequence* $\land$ *Logging*) is not satisfiable anymore and the mapping m_3 and its associated code fragments are thus not included. The condition *Activity* $\land \neg Cognitive$ of mapping m_2 on the other hand becomes *Activity*, which is still satisfiable, meaning that its code fragments are included. The condition *Activity* of m_1 (which is not modified) is also satisfiable, i.e., m_1 and its code fragments are therefore also included.

Pull. The feature-oriented `pull` operation allows transferring one or more features between related product line platforms. In contrast to a Git pull, which always pulls an entire platform, our feature-oriented `pull` only fetches the selected set of features and associated artifacts. Besides performance benefits, this allows getting specific features from a product line without bothering about other features, for which different versions may already exist in the target platform. The `pull` operation is based on the previously explained *subset* operation, followed by the *merge* operation. Thus, it also relies on a partial feature configuration C representing the set of features to pull. However, in contrast to `clone`, the partial configuration is built depending on the feature $f \in F$ or subset of features $F' \subseteq F$ the user selects for pulling. When a user specifies a feature $f \in F$: *(i)* the specified feature f remains variable (i.e., is NOT set to true as it would then become mandatory in the target platform), *(ii)* all interactions of the selected feature with other features already in the target platform will also be pulled, and *(iii)* all other features are deselected (i.e., set to false) in the partial feature configuration used in the subset operation. Note that case (ii) guarantees that also feature interactions of the selected feature, which are needed in the target platform, are pulled. The approach naturally expands when several features are selected for pulling.

The *merge* operation then integrates the transferred subset product line into the target product line. $PL' = merge(PL_{pull}, PL_{target})$ receives two product lines PL_{pull} and PL_{target} as input and merges them to produce another product line PL'. Merging two product lines means merging their feature models as well as their artifact fragments and mappings. Feature models are merged by making as few changes as possible in the target platform and leaving the fundamental decisions about the intended feature model structure deliberately to the engineer: when a pulled feature is already contained in the target platform, it is added as a new revision. When a feature is already contained in the target platform, but in a different position in the feature model, the engineer is notified and the feature remains at its original position in the target model. In case the pulled feature does not yet exist in the target feature model, it is inserted as the feature which is the next common ancestor in both models. In both cases, it is up to the engineer to confirm the final position of the feature in the target model and update constraints accordingly [2]. The `pull` operation then adds the set of mappings and related artifact fragments to the target platform.

The state of the platform repository depends on whether the `pull` was complete or incomplete. In a *complete* pull no further interaction of an engineer is required to generate a semantically and syntactically correct product line variant. A pull is complete if the origin platform contains a superset of the features and their revisions in the target platform. This means that the origin platform contains all features and feature revisions also contained in the target platform, also including the required code for all feature interactions. Recall case (ii) of building the partial feature configuration for the `pull`: feature interaction code is also transferred to the target platform, thus making it complete. A pull is *incomplete* if certain artifact fragments and their mappings are missing. This usually happens if the target platform repository contains features not contained in the origin repository. This means that interaction code needed for the combined use of features is missing. There are different ways to address this problem as illustrated from a developer perspective in the scenario in Sect. 2. An engineer can checkout a variant containing the feature combinations and then implement the missing or adapt the conflicting glue code such that these feature will work together. Afterwards, the glue code can be committed to the repository. Alternatively, the engineer can pull feature interaction code from another repository already containing both features and thus their corresponding glue code.

4   Evaluation

Our evaluation pursues two research questions:

RQ1. Correctness – Do the feature-oriented operations provide correct results? We showed that both `clone` and `pull` rely on the `subset` operation. The clone operation is realized by pulling the selected features into an empty repository. Our evaluation thus investigates the correctness of pulling code in different scenarios and for different cases of feature interactions. As discussed a pull is complete if the origin platform contains a superset of the features in the target platform. In this case no further interaction of an engineer is required to generate a semantically and syntactically correct product line variant. Otherwise, the pull is regarded as incomplete and closer inspections are required to assess correctness. Section 4.2 summarizes the different cases we explored.

RQ2. Performance – Does the execution time of the feature-oriented operations allow their use in engineering workflows? We evaluated the run-time performance of the `pull` operation for different numbers of feature-to-code mappings and artifact fragments.

4.1   Method

Figure 2 gives an overview of the research method we used for our evaluation. We used the well-known ArgoUML system for evaluating our approach and adopted the ArgoUML benchmark suite [8] for our experiments. The benchmark suite allowed us to generate all 256 variants of ArgoUML based on its eight optional features. We first created FORCE[2] platforms and repositories for all ArgoUML variants based on a script containing a series of commit operations. The order of the commits mimics the evolution from a small variant containing just the base feature to larger variants containing all of the available features. The correctness of the commit operation was evaluated already in earlier work [6].

The evaluation then continued with both a manual procedure regarding RQ1 and an automated procedure regarding both RQ1 and RQ2. Our first research question investigates whether the feature-to-artifact mappings of the

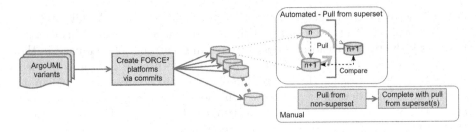

Fig. 2. Research method.

platform repository created via pull operations are equal to the mappings created via the commit operations. For the manual part we executed 15 scenarios of pulling feature sets of different sizes to cover different cases of incomplete pulls (cf. Sect. 4.2). We manually inspected and compared these cases based on our ArgoUML baseline. For the automated part, we developed a script creating new FORCE^2 platforms and repositories based on existing ones and then incrementally extended them using pull operations. In particular, for this part of the evaluation we pulled features from a FORCE^2 platform containing a superset of the features of the platform (pull case I in Sect. 4.2). This process was done for all FORCE^2 platforms, i.e., all ArgoUML variants.

Specifically, our script starts with a repository only containing the mandatory features of ArgoUML. Hence, with respect to this basic platform, all other ArgoUML variants represent supersets, meaning that pulling features would be possible from any platform. However, the script incrementally increases the number of platform features with one new feature per pull. Hence, we pull a single optional feature from a repository containing exactly this feature in addition to the common features in the platforms. We repeat this process for each variant containing a single optional feature, always starting with a repository only containing the base features. After the first iteration, the script starts with the repositories containing the newly pulled optional feature, copies them and continues with pulling another optional feature from a superset platform. The resulting projects can then be compared to their baseline FORCE^2 project variants to answer RQ1.

We use precision and recall to measure the correctness of the automated part: *Precision* is the number of matching feature mappings contained in both the origin and the target repository divided by the overall number of mappings in the target repository. *Recall* is the number of matching feature mappings contained in both the origin and the target repository divided by the overall number of mappings in the origin repository.

4.2   Pull Cases

As already mentioned pulls can have different outcomes with respect to their completeness, so different cases need to be distinguished: in case of tightly coupled features we can expect interactions between them. For instance, crosscutting features often require certain interaction code to work correctly with other features. Examples are the ArgoUML features *Logging* and *Cognitive*. No interactions are expected if features do no exchange data or functionally rely on each other. However, even in this case interactions may be discovered in the code, e.g., related to the configuration, initialization or declaration of features, as such source code often depends on the presence of certain features. If such interactions can not be pulled from the origin repository, glue code may need to be developed. However, often the feature interaction code is already contained in the origin platform repository as we will show. Specifically, we distinguished the following four cases in our evaluation:

I. Pulling features from a superset. In this case a feature (or set of features) is pulled from an origin platform repository containing a superset of the features in the target platform. As all potential interactions are already included in the target platform a complete pull is possible. We covered this case with the automated evaluation procedure (cf. Sect. 4.1), i.e., we created repositories by incrementally pulling features from superset repositories and compared the resulting repository with the one created with the commit operations.

II. Pulling independent features from a non-superset. Pulling features from an origin that contains features which are not a superset of the features in the target platform will often result in missing feature interaction code. In this case the pull can still succeed completely if the pulled features are truly independent from any features in the target platform. We did not assess this pull case in our evaluation as there are no truly independent features in the ArgoUML data set.

III. Pulling interacting features from a non-superset. If a target platform contains features not contained in the origin platform and one or more interacting features are pulled from an origin, the target platform will miss glue code needed for the joint operation of the features. An engineer then needs to implement the glue code ensuring their correct interaction. There are many possibilities with respect to the kinds of artifacts that might be missing as we will discuss later. To cover this pull case we manually selected eight variants (cf. Table 1) and pulled certain features from an origin to a target platform. When selecting variants we excluded trivial variants (e.g., target repositories with only base features) and included different sizes of repositories and pull feature sets. The goal of this evaluation was to verify that the only missing elements in the repository are the ones representing the feature interactions.

IV. Pulling features from multiple non-supersets. As just described, pulling crosscutting features leads to missing interaction code with existing features in the target platform. However, an alternative to developing the missing interaction code is to pull it from a platform already containing the code. A prerequisite is that the involved features in the origin and target platform share the same revision. Note that pulling the interaction code also works for different revisions, but requires merging of the revisions to solve potential issues. The features in the ArgoUML case study do not have revisions and thus pulling missing feature interactions works without further involvement from an engineer. For the

Table 1. Pull Case III – We confirmed the missing feature interaction code via inspection when pulling features from a repository for the following scenarios.

Origin	Target	Pulled	Missing feature interaction code
B, UC	B, ST, cog	UC	No Interaction
B, SQ	B, ST, cog	SQ	SQ-cog
B, SQ, cog	B, ST, UC, log	SQ	SQ-log
B, DP	B, cog	DP	DP-cog
B, DP, CL, cog	B, AC, UC, cog, log	DP, CL	DP-log, CL-log, UC-DP
B, AC, SQ	B, cog, log	AC, SQ	AC-log, SQ-cog, SQ-log
B, AC, UC, CL	B, ST, DP, SQ, log, cog	AC, CL	AC-log, AC-ST, UC-SQ, CL-SQ, CL-log, CL-SQ-log
B, log	B, AC	log	AC-log

Features. B = Base+Class diagram, ST = State diagram, SQ = Sequence diagram, UC = Use Case diagram, CL = Collaboration diagram, DP = Deployment diagram, AC = Activity diagram, log = Logging, cog = Cognitive

evaluation of this case we thus selected 7 scenarios (cf. Table 2) for which feature interactions exist that require the implementation of glue code or pulling of interactions from other repositories. We reused the selected variants from the previous evaluation step and only excluded one variant with no interaction present. We pulled the missing interactions from another repository and again checked if the repository contains all required elements after the pull. Obviously, directly pulling the features from the more complete repository would be more efficient. However, we wanted to demonstrate that pulling different parts of a feature and feature interactions from different repositories works correctly.

5   Results

We summarize and discuss the main results of our evaluation:

RQ1: Correctness. We can report interesting results for the different cases.

I. Pulling features from a superset. The automated part of our evaluation showed very high values for precision (0.987) and recall (0.966). While these numbers are very good it is interesting to find out what prevented perfect values for the pull operation. Upon closer inspection of selected repositories we learned that the small problems are not caused by the pull operation itself but are already rooted in the commit operation of the variation control system. Specifically, the diffing and merging algorithms of ECCO already introduce these slight imperfections. As a consequence, in some rare cases no presence condition was assigned to artifact mappings. This happened when for artifact fragments with an already assigned valid condition a contradicting condition for the supposedly same artifact fragments was found in a later commit. This minor problem can be fixed by

Table 2. Pull Case IV – We checked for the following cases that no code is missing when pulling missing interaction code from multiple repositories.

Origin 1	Origin 2	Origin 3	Target	Pull from 1	Pull from 2	Pull from 3
B, SQ	B, SQ, cog	B, SQ, ST	B, ST, cog	SQ	SQ, cog	SQ, ST
B, SQ, cog	B, ST, SQ, log	–	B, ST, UC, log	SQ	SQ, log	–
B, DP	B, DP, cog	–	B, cog	DP	DP, cog	–
B, DP, CL, cog	B, DP, UC, log	B, CL, AC, log	B, AC, UC, cog, log	DP, cog	DP, log	CL, AC, cog
B, AC, SQ	B, AC, LC, cog	B, SQ, log, cog	B, CL, log	AC, SQ	AC, SQ, log, cog	
B, AC, UC, CL	B, AC, SQ, ST, UC, DP, log, cog	–	B, ST, DP, SQ, log, cog	AC, CL	AC, ST, UC, SQ, CL, log	–
B, log	B, AC, log, cog	–	B, AC	log	AC, log	–

Features. B = Base+Class diagram, ST = State diagram, SQ = Sequence diagram, UC = Use Case diagram, CL = Collaboration diagram, DP = Deployment diagram, AC = Activity diagram, log = Logging, cog = Cognitive

improving the comparison and matching algorithm in ECCO or by using coding conventions to avoid problematic program structures.

II. Pulling interacting features from a non-superset: The results for the first part of the manual evaluation case are presented in Table 1. The first column *Origin* lists the features present in the platform from where a feature was pulled. The second column *Target* shows the features which were already present in the platform. The third column lists the features pulled from origin. The fourth column presents the expected missing mappings. All test scenarios met the expectations with respect to the missing mappings and corresponding artifact fragments. However, as in case I, we discovered some unexpected missing mappings, which are caused by the matching algorithm or artifact plugin of ECCO. The missing elements are mostly related to initialization and declaration aspects, or user interface elements changing slightly depending on the features present. Again, such problems could be fixed by improving the source code structure or by improving the mapping precision.

III. Pulling features from multiple non-supersets: Table 2 presents the results of the second part of our manual evaluation. Specifically, the columns *Origin 1–3* list the features contained in the different platforms from which features were pulled. The column *Target* lists the features contained in the target platform before executing the pulls. The three right columns describe the features pulled from the different origin platforms: *Pull from 1* presents the features which are originally of interest to be reused in the target platform and pulled from *Origin 1* while *Pull from 2* and *Pull from 3* are the feature combinations pulled to retrieve the missing interactions from *Origin 2* and *Origin 3*, respectively.

Again, all results were correct, meaning that after all pulls no artifacts or traces were missing, and no unnecessary elements were transferred.

RQ2: Performance. During the automated execution of our pull operation, we measured the run time for the execution of each pull and also logged the number of mappings and artifacts involved. These measurements were executed on a Windows 10 system, with an Intel Core i9-9900K 3.6 GHz, 32 GB RAM using Hotspot Java VM 1.8 inside an Eclipse IDE. The results of the run time measurement of more than 1000 pulls show that the run time lies between about 8 and 14 s. There is a high correlation of the run time and number of mappings involved in the pull operation with a Spearman rank correlation coefficient of 0.86. We also analyzed the distribution showing the number of artifact fragments pulled from the origin platform for all pulls. Numbers mostly vary between 1000 and 4000 artifact fragments, while some outliers have more than 14000 artifacts. However, the number of artifact fragments did not have a noticeable influence on the run time of the pull operation.

Threats to Validity. FORCE^2 utilizes ECCO as a variation control system. One might argue that the generated FORCE^2 platforms can not be used as a baseline for checking the correctness of the pull operation. However, existing research [9] already demonstrated that ECCO extracted the location of features, i.e., feature-to-artifact mappings, for ArgoUML variants with high precision. We did not evaluate and investigate the ECCO commit and checkout operations as part of this paper, as positive evaluation results are already reported in existing research [6]. Additionally, there might be a bias due to using ArgoUML, which consists primarily of Java source code. We did not investigate the potential influence of other artifact types. Furthermore, the ArgoUML software product line was originally extracted from ArgoUML for a feature location benchmark [8]. ArgoUML was not developed as an SPL from the beginning. Therefore, the extracted feature locations, which might have an influence on feature-to-code mapping results, could be inaccurate. However, as discussed above, ECCO has been evaluated for different types of artifacts. Furthermore, the quality of the pull operation is independent of the plugins used by ECCO to support different languages. In terms of performance one might argue that ArgoUML is not comparable with an industry-size case study. However, ArgoUML is a complex system (120 KLoC) and the performance results show that the feature-oriented operations can be integrated in the daily workflows of developers.

Discussion. As demonstrated in this section, we achieved very high *correctness* values, close to 1.0 for both precision and recall for the feature-oriented pull operation. The minor problems we discovered were caused by the mappings automatically extracted by the variation control system, which depend on the used diffing and matching algorithms as well as the reader for the specific artifact types. An example of a program structure causing problems is a highly fragmented if-elseif cascade mapping to many different features. Due to its structure it can be problematic to maintain correct mappings during evolution. One way to address the problem is replacing the if-elseif cascade with a switch-statement providing a clearer and more uniform structure. Another approach to eliminate this uncertainty is an improved matching algorithm. However, this problem is not subject to the distributed operation but caused by ECCO's commit operation and the reader used for the specific artifact type (in this case Java code) and thus out of the scope of this paper.

Proving *usefulness* usually is much more difficult than proving correctness. However, in this case, we argue that the usefulness of feature-oriented distributed development operations is already evident in everyday practice. The success of distributed version control systems such as Git and platforms such as GitHub, which were adopted by open source projects as well as large corporations, is evidence of the demand for support of distributed development. The fact that many popular branching models for Git use feature branches shows that developers try to find ways to introduce feature-oriented development into their workflows even with lack of dedicated tool support (which our work provides). Another piece of evidence for the usefulness and applicability of distributed feature-oriented development is related research on extracting features from forks [13]. Such work shows that current development practices already map well to feature-oriented development paradigms, despite a lack of tool support. Using feature-oriented distributed operations in the first place would make the retroactive extraction of features from forks (resulting from conventional distributed operations) obsolete.

6 Related Work

Clone-and-Own Reuse. Several approaches provide support for creating and managing clones in product line engineering. Rubin et al. [10] present an operator framework covering atomic operations for managing cloned variants. For instance, they provide operations for checking dependencies between features, distinct implementations of similar features, and conflicting features.

Variation Control Systems. The variation control system ECCO [6] is a key component of the FORCE^2 platform. A similar approach is SuperMod [11], which provides feature-oriented support in the area of model-driven software product line engineering. SuperMod also provides a collaborative development environment and support for merging and solving conflicts. Similar to our approach, SuperMod also provides a pull operation, which allows to pull evolved product lines from a remote repository. However, the distributed operations of Super-Mod are not feature-aware, i.e., one cannot limit the features transferred and thus always transfers the entire repository.

Feature Interactions. Interactions between software features have been investigated in multiple communities. For instance, Zave [12] reported on the problem of feature interactions in continuously evolving systems. Dependencies and interactions between features can be inferred from the hierarchical feature models representing commonalities and variability of a system but they also exist as cross-tree relations in the feature tree. Ferber et al. have shown that such dependencies are often difficult to represent in feature models [3]. This gap has been addressed by Feichtinger et al. who present an approach combining feature-to-code mappings, static code analysis, and a variation control system to identify inconsistencies between features and the code implementing them [2].

7 Conclusions and Future Work

We presented an approach supporting distributed development with feature-oriented operations for clone and pull. While current version control systems support cloning of entire repositories, the distribution operations presented in this paper support handling variants at the level of features. Our approach is implemented in the FORCE^2 approach and relies on a variation control system. It expands our approach towards a distributed platform for managing development in multiple distributed product lines, which is highly important in software ecosystems. Our evaluation demonstrates high precision and recall of the feature-oriented pull operation for transferring features and corresponding artifacts between platforms. We also looked at specific pull cases to confirm the behaviour for cases of interacting features. Furthermore, our performance evaluation demonstrates that the operations are fast enough to be integrated in the development workflows of engineers.

Acknowledgements. The financial support by the Austrian Federal Ministry for Digital and Economic Affairs, the National Foundation for Research, Technology and Development, and KEBA AG is gratefully acknowledged.

References

1. Czarnecki, K., Grünbacher, P., Rabiser, R., Schmid, K., Wasowski, A.: Cool features and tough decisions: a comparison of variability modeling approaches. In: Proceedings of the 6th International Workshop on Variability Modeling of Software-Intensive Systems, pp. 173–182 (2012)
2. Feichtinger, K., Hinterreiter, D., Linsbauer, L., Prähofer, H., Grünbacher, P.: Guiding feature model evolution by lifting code-level dependencies. J. Comput. Lang. (2021)
3. Ferber, S., Haag, J., Savolainen, J.: Feature interaction and dependencies: modeling features for reengineering a legacy product line. In: Chastek, G.J. (ed.) SPLC 2002. LNCS, vol. 2379, pp. 235–256. Springer, Heidelberg (2002). https://doi.org/10.1007/3-540-45652-X_15
4. Hinterreiter, D., Linsbauer, L., Feichtinger, K., Prähofer, H., Grünbacher, P.: Supporting feature-oriented evolution in industrial automation product lines. Concurr. Eng. Res. Appl. **28**, 265–279 (2020)
5. Hinterreiter, D., Linsbauer, L., Reisinger, F., Prähofer, H., Grünbacher, P., Egyed, A.: Feature-oriented evolution of automation software systems in industrial software ecosystems. In: Proceedings of the 23rd IEEE International Conference on Emerging Technologies and Factory Automation, pp. 107–114 (2018)
6. Linsbauer, L., Lopez-Herrejon, R.E., Egyed, A.: Variability extraction and modeling for product variants. Softw. Syst. Model. **16**(4), 1179–1199 (2016). https://doi.org/10.1007/s10270-015-0512-y

7. Linsbauer, L., Schwägerl, F., Berger, T., Grünbacher, P.: Concepts of variation control systems. J. Syst. Softw. **171**, 110796 (2021)
8. Martinez, J., et al.: Feature location benchmark with ArgoUML SPL. In: Proceedings of the 22nd International Systems and Software Product Line Conference, pp. 257–263 (2018)
9. Michelon, G.K., Linsbauer, L., Assunção, W.K.G., Egyed, A.: Comparison-based feature location in ArgoUML variants. In: Proceedings of the 23rd International Systems and Software Product Line Conference, pp. 93–97 (2019)
10. Rubin, J., Czarnecki, K., Chechik, M.: Managing cloned variants: a framework and experience. In: Proceeding of the 17th International Software Product Line Conference, pp. 101–110 (2013)
11. Schwägerl, F., Westfechtel, B.: Integrated revision and variation control for evolving model-driven software product lines. Softw. Syst. Model. **18**(6), 3373–3420 (2019). https://doi.org/10.1007/s10270-019-00722-3
12. Zave, P.: Feature interactions and formal specifications in telecommunications. Computer **26**(8), 20–28 (1993)
13. Zhou, S., Vasilescu, B., Kästner, C.: What the fork: a study of inefficient and efficient forking practices in social coding. In: Proceedings of the 27th ACM Joint Meeting on European Software Engineering Conference and Symposium on the Foundations of Software Engineering, pp. 350–361 (2019)

Detecting Sudden Variations in Web Apps Code Smells' Density: A Longitudinal Study

Américo Rio[1,2(✉)] [iD] and Fernando Brito e Abreu[1] [iD]

[1] Instituto Universitário de Lisboa (ISCTE-IUL), ISTAR, Lisboa, Portugal
{jaasr,fba}@iscte-iul.pt
[2] NOVAIMS, Universidade Nova de Lisboa, Lisboa, Portugal
americo.rio@novaims.unl.pt
https://www.iscte-iul.pt, https://www.novaims.unl.pt/

Abstract. Code smells are considered potentially harmful to software maintenance. Their introduction is dependent on the production of new code or the addition of smelly code produced by another team. Code smells survive until being refactored or the code where they stand is removed. Under normal conditions, we expect code smells density to be relatively stable throughout time. Anomalous (sudden) increases in this density are expected to hurt maintenance costs and the other way round. In the case of sudden increases, especially in pre-release tests in an automation server pipeline, detecting those outlier situations can trigger refactoring actions before releasing the new version.

This paper presents a longitudinal study on the sudden variations in the introduction and removal of 18 server code smells on 8 PHP web apps, across several years. The study regards web applications but can be generalized to other domains, using other CS and tools. We propose a standardized detection criterion for this kind of code smell anomalies. Besides providing a retrospective view of the code smell evolution phenomenon, our detection approach, which is particularly amenable to graphical monitoring, can make software project managers aware of the need for enforcing refactoring actions.

Keywords: PHP · Code smells · Web apps · Sudden variations · Anomaly detection · Outliers

1 Introduction

1.1 Motivation

A major manifestation of maintenance issues is the existence of code smells [10], since they are seen as potential catalysts of software evolution costs, due to increased defect incidence, poorer code comprehension, and longer times to release. A code smell (CS) may be something like a long method, or many parameters in a method. Java desktop applications have been particularly analyzed

© Springer Nature Switzerland AG 2021
A. C. R. Paiva et al. (Eds.): QUATIC 2021, CCIS 1439, pp. 82–96, 2021.
https://doi.org/10.1007/978-3-030-85347-1_7

regarding this aspect [21,25]. The Software Engineering community has proposed several techniques and tools, both for CS detection and refactoring, but several problems remain such as detection subjectivity [5] and, low coverage of existing CS catalogs and programming languages [22,28].

While looking for the CS phenomenon on a quantitative basis, we should not analyze the raw number of existing (or removed) CS, because that number will largely depend on system size. Some measure of CS density (the number of CS divided by a size measure) should be used instead, like for instance in [8,17]. For a reasonably large project, maintained by a large team, developing code as usual, we expect to observe an inertia effect, i.e. that CS density is relatively stable throughout time. However, there are moments in the history of a project where that density may have sudden variations.

CS sudden variations are relevant to understand the story of a project, can be used as an explanatory factor (e.g. for consequent variations in reported issues and maintenance effort) and, justify the relevance of refactoring actions. Software managers should: (i) be aware if CS are under control (i.e. if CS infection is not going wild) and, if not, (ii) prioritize refactoring of detected CS. A solution to prevent the first problem is proposed in this paper for PHP web apps. A solution to the second can be found in [9] in the context of Java systems.

Web apps are different from desktop and mobile apps. The latter run on the OS, while the former run both on a browser and a server, and thus have server-side programming and client/browser-side programming, that run in two separate environments. Thus, they encompass a heterogeneity of target platforms, programming, and content formatting languages. Due to this difference and diversity, it is necessary to perform similar and different studies (from the applications that run directly in the OS), regarding their specificity. In the study, we focus on web applications using the PHP programming language, currently reported to hold 79% of the market share in that sector [27]. We considered as many years as possible for each web app, summing up a total of 441 versions.

1.2   Research Questions

During data collection for another study [23], we noticed that sudden variations in CS density, in both directions (steep increase or steep decrease), occur in some versions (also called releases) of the target web apps. These anomalous situations deserve our attention, either for recovering the story of a project or, if used just-in-time (e.g., integrated into a pre-release tests battery), to provide awareness to decision-makers that something unusual is taking place for good or bad. In this paper we aim at providing an answer to the following research questions in the context of web apps using PHP as the server language:

RQ1 – How to detect sudden variations in the evolution of code smells?
RQ2 – When are the sudden variations in changes of code smells in a new version considered too high? or When are there too many code smells?

To answer these research questions, we perform a longitudinal study with 8 web applications and 18 server-side CS. This paper is structured as follows:

Sect. 2 introduces the study design; Sect. 3 describes the results of data analysis, while Sect. 4 discusses the findings and identifies validity threats; Sect. 5 overviews the related work on longitudinal studies on CS and in web apps; finally, Sect. 6 outlines the major conclusions and outlines future work.

2   Study Design

2.1   Applications Sample

The criteria for selecting the sample of PHP web apps were the following:

Inclusion criteria: code availability (open source); complete or self-contained applications, taken from the *GitHub* top listings; programmed with an object-oriented programming (OOP) style; covering a long period (at least 5 years)

Exclusion criteria: libraries; frameworks or applications used to build other applications; web apps built using a framework.

We excluded frameworks and libraries because we want to study typical web apps. We excluded web apps built with frameworks because we want to analyze app code and not the framework code itself, thus aiming for comparability among apps. Probably, apps made with frameworks would deserve a separate study. Another reason is that we have apps with a long history, and many started when modern frameworks were not available. Some apps that we had as candidates failed the requisite of being OOP. PHP allows for a procedural development paradigm, but the detected CS are OOP in nature. Table 1 shows the sample of apps used, including some metrics.

Table 1. Characterization of the target web apps (* on last version)

Name	Purpose	#Versions(period)	Last version	LOC*	#Classes*
PhpMyAdmin	Database administration tool	181 (09/2008-09/2019)	4.9.1	301748	1174
DokuWiki	Wiki solution	40 (07/2005-01/2019)	04-22b	271514	402
OpenCart	Shopping cart solution	28 (04/2013-04/2019)	3.0.3.2	206253	955
PhpBB	Forum/bulletin board solution	50 (04/2012-01/2018)	3.2.2	341159	1330
PhpPgAdmin	Database administration tool	29 (02/2002-09/2019)	7.12.0	71210	54
MediaWiki	Wiki solution	145 (12/2003-10/2019)	1.33.1	754941	2479
PrestaShop	Shopping cart solution	74 (06/2011–08/2019)	1.7.6.1	516737	2597
Vanilla	Forum/bulletin board solution	75 (06/2010–10/2019	3.3	193435	533

For each app we collected as many versions as possible. Sometimes we could not get the whole lifecycle either because not all versions were available online or did not match the OOP criterion in the earlier versions. The LOC (Lines Of Code) and "number of Classes" are size metrics from the last version and were measured by the *PHPLOC* tool.

2.2   CS Sample

We used *PHPMD*, an open-source tool that detects CS in PHP. *PHPMD* was the base for many other PHP CS detection tools existing today, and we can automatize it via the command line. Although the tool supports more CS, we chose the maximum number of highly cited ones in the literature for other languages, leaving us with the 18 CS which are briefly characterized in Table 2. For comparability among apps, the thresholds are the same among apps, and the default ones used in *PHPMD*, witch in turn came from *PMD*, and are generally accepted from the references in the literature [4,16]. For individual app evaluation these could be optimized [13].

Table 2. Characterization of the target code smells

Code smell name	Code smell description	Threshold
CyclomaticComplexity	Determined by the number of decision points in a method plus one for the method entry	10
NPathComplexity	Number of acyclic execution paths through that method	200
ExcessiveMethodLength	(Long method) the method is doing too much	100
ExcessiveClassLength	(Long Class) class does too much	1000
ExcessiveParameterList	Method with too long parameter list	10
ExcessivePublicCount	A large number of public methods and attributes declared in a class	45
TooManyFields	Class with too many fields	15
TooManyMethods	Class with too many methods	25
TooManyPublicMethods	Class with too many public methods	10
ExcessiveClassComplexity	Excessive Sum of complexities of all methods in a class	50
NumberOfChildren	Class with an excessive number of children	15
DepthOfInheritance	Class with many parents	6
CouplingBetweenObjects	Class with too many dependencies	13
DevelopmentCodeFragment	Development Code ex: var_dump(), print_r() etc.	1
UnusedPrivateField	A private field is declared and/or assigned a value, but not used	1
UnusedLocalVariable	A local variable is declared and/or assigned, but not used	1
UnusedPrivateMethod	A private method is declared but is unused	1
UnusedFormalParameter	Unused parameters in methods/constructors that are not used	1

2.3 Data Collection and Preparation

In the data collection and preparation phase, we downloaded the source code of all versions of the selected web applications, in ZIP format, from *GitHub*, *Source-Forge*, and application site (when not available), except the alpha, beta, release candidates, and corrections for old versions. We created a database table with the application versions, later exported to a CVS file, containing the timestamps for each downloaded version. Using *PHPMD*, we extract the CS, file and line locations, dates, and other CS indicators from every version, and store them in a database. For the applications, we excluded some directories that were not part of the applications (vendor, libraries, images, etc.). The data at this point was stored by version/smell. We then exported the results to CVS format, in preparation for the data analysis phase. We used the *PHPLOC* tool to extract several code metrics from the source code of each version of each app. The collected dataset is available *here*, in csv format, for replication purposes.

3 Results and Data Analysis

3.1 Evolution of the Number of CS per Version

Figure 1 presents the evolution of CS by version. Software delivery occurs at unequally spaced moments in time, that we usually call "versions", or "releases". The visualization in Fig. 1 allows identifying the versions where a major refactoring occurred. For example, in *PhpMyAdmin*, from a graph of survival of code smells not shown here (space constrictions), versions 4.6, 4.7 and 4.8 seem to have a lot of refactoring. We drilled down this behavior in the code of version 4.8 because a lot of smells were introduced in this version, and a lot were removed. By code inspection we found that during that refactoring some files changed their names, so the smell appears in another file. In other words, a rename in a file or class causes the fake conclusion that some existing smells were removed while new ones were created. To block this fake effect, we should observe the evolution of the total number of occurrences for each CS, by version. We observed these phenomena in the record of each CS, in our data. If we observe Fig. 2, we do not understand if the smells are all new or came from renaming operations but observing the total number of CS in Fig. 3 we have a different perspective. We also pinpoint that for 2 of the applications, *Vanilla* and *MediaWiki*, the number of CS increases steadily during the life of the application. The "ExcessiveMethodLength" (aka *Long Method*) CS is one of the more recurrent. However, the "complexity" smells play an important part in the total computation, and also in some applications, the "unused" group of smells.

3.2 Anomalies in CS Evolution

During data analysis, we found versions where refactoring on file names and location in folders occurred, but CS prevailed in a different file/folder. So, is it

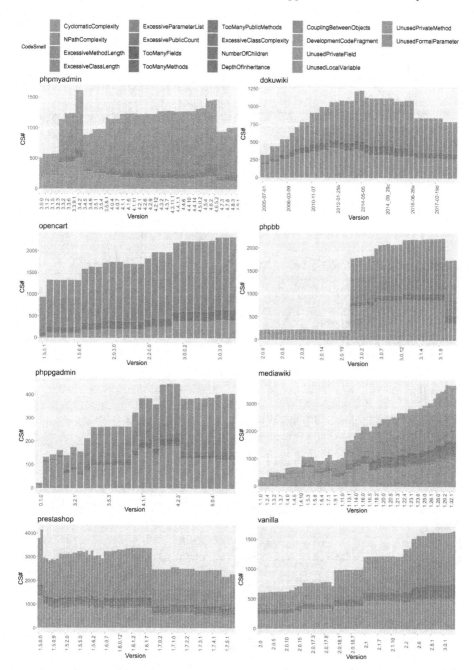

Fig. 1. Evolution of the total number of each code smell by app and version

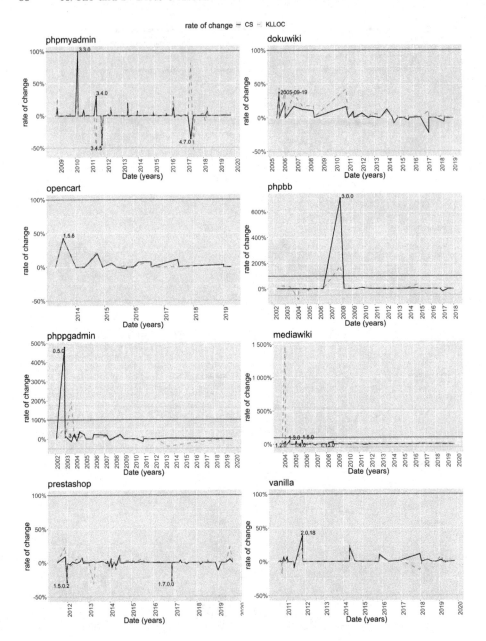

Fig. 2. CS and *KLLOC* rate of change evolution

possible to check those versions for anomalies (sudden variations) in the number/intensity of CS?

In Fig. 2, we can see the relative change of CS from the previous version (black), and the relative change in *KLLOC* (thousands of logical lines of code) from the previous version (blue/dashed). *KLOC* (thousands of lines of code) is a well know measure, although here we used the logical lines of code. The relative change in the number of CS is given by:

$$\Delta cs = \frac{cs_i - cs_{i-1}}{cs_{i-1}} = \frac{cs_i}{cs_{i-1}} - 1 \tag{1}$$

where Δ is the rate of change, cs_i is the number of CS in the current version and cs_{i-1} is the number of CS in the previous version. The same is calculated for the size, i.e. the Logical Lines of Code (LLOC).

The sudden variations occur when there is a large increase in the number of CS and the size does not grow accordingly. It is also possible to get the version in which a lot of CS were removed by refactoring. For comparability sake, we use CS density or ρcs = number of CS/LLOC. We can now calculate the rate of change of the CS density, which we calculate in the same way as referred before for the CS number:

$$\Delta \rho cs = \frac{\rho cs_i - \rho cs_{i-1}}{\rho cs_{i-1}} = \frac{\rho cs_i}{\rho cs_{i-1}} - 1 \tag{2}$$

where $\Delta \rho cs$ is the rate of change of density of CS, ρcs_i is the density of CS in the current version and ρcs_{i-1} is the density of CS in the previous version. Figure 3 presents the evolution of CS density, making it easy to pinpoint the peaks, labeled according to the corresponding version.

In the graphs per application, we use lines representing thresholds, signaling the increase of 50% and 100% and the reduction of 50% in the rate of change in the density of CS. The thresholds can be changed according to application, team, quality, and company, if applicable.

In Table 3 we can observe the variance of *CS by KLLOC*, as well as the *Cyclomatic Complexity by LLOC* (aka Cyclomatic Complexity Density) from the current and previous versions, a long used objective metric for maintainability prediction [11].

Table 3. Metrics for the outliers

App	Version	Date	CS	LLOC	CS/kLLOC	var(CS/kLLOC)	CC/LLOC	CC/LLOC previous
phpmyadmin	3.3.0	2010-03-07	1145	130863	8.75	0.55	0.129	0.095
phpmyadmin	3.4.0	2011-05-11	1617	57338	28.20	2.02	0.425	0.137
phpmyadmin	4.7.1	2017-05-26	948	56192	16.87	1.11	0.391	0.321
phpbb	2.0.7	2004-03-13	226	12511	18.06	4.88	0.436	0.073
phpbb	3.0.0	2007-12-12	1781	32291	55.15	1.90	0.547	0.462
phppgadmin	5.1.0	2013-04-14	402	37098	10.84	0.71	0.152	0.095

4 Discussion

4.1 Introduction

We could find CS sudden variations in 4 web apps (*PhpMyAdmin, PhpBB, PhpP-gAdmin* and *MediaWiki*). For example, *PhpMyAdmin* has 3 of these anomalies,

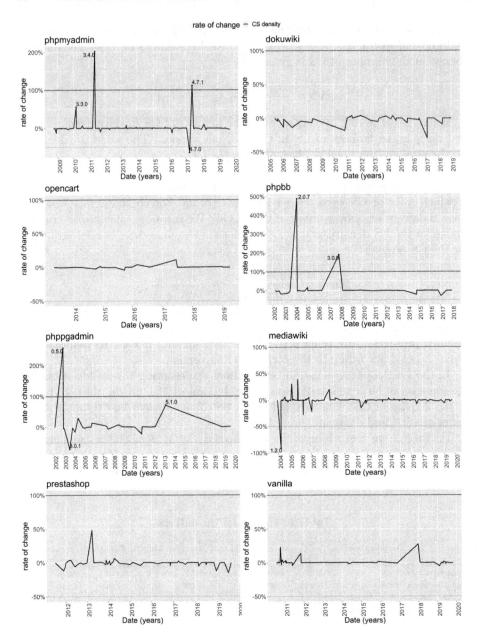

Fig. 3. CS density rate of change evolution

where CS rose abnormally without a correspondent rise in the app size. This can point to problems in those versions. We also spot a decrease anomaly, in version 4.7. By reading the code we confirmed that refactoring was then applied considerably, which is in line with the changes observed in Fig. 2. The other 4 apps (*DokuWiki, OpenCart, PrestaShop* and *Vanilla*) are not exactly stable but do not have anomalies crossing the warning threshold. This somewhat simple method to implement - measuring $\Delta\rho$cs - is able to detect the anomalies/sudden variations in the CS density.

4.2   Answers to Research Questions

RQ1 – How to detect sudden variations in the evolution of code smells? - As shown in Figs. 2 and 3 it is possible to detect these CS anomalies or peaks. We can analyze the rate of change (current version vs previous version) on the CS intensity alone (Eq. 1) or their relative rate of change by size (density), given by Eq. 2, which will be a more comparable metric across versions of the same application and even among applications.

RQ2 – When are the sudden variations of code smells in a new version considered too high? - or *When are there too many code smells?* Similar to limits in control charts, where you have limits equal to 3 times the variance, in this case we have to define thresholds, that can be chosen among development teams. We believe that a threshold of 50% will be sufficient to rise maintainability alerts. Knowing that we can never remove all the CS from an application, a 50% increase would raise a yellow flag, and a 100% increase would raise a red flag (stop immediately). Looking at Table 3 we can see that peaks also affect the *cyclomatic complexity per LLOC*, which it turn affects maintainability [11].

4.3   Applicability

Ideally, the removal of CS can be done in a "Total Quality" manner, where the developer is responsible to avoid the introduction of CS in the code, but often this is not possible. CS density thresholds detection can be integrated into an automation server tool such as *Jenkins*, that runs a battery of tests before a release - comparing it with the previous released version. If a threshold is reached, the release could be put on hold for some refactoring to be performed. This would act as a safeguard with the other tests in the test battery. Since *Jenkins* already has support for *PHPMD* in PHP projects, it is feasible to add our approach to the pipeline. The value of the threshold should be decided by each development team, depending on the development circumstances and requirements.

4.4   Comparison to Other Techniques

We also tried other methods, and among them, to apply SPC (Statistical Process Control) techniques with 2 or 3 standard deviations as limits, but we could not get limits due to the nature of the evolution (for long periods the value of number of CS was the same, then this value sudden increases). The main problem was that the standard deviation is 0 or close to 0. Another problem that arises with methods that use the average, for example [7], is that you have to know all the history of the project, while in the method shown here, the computation at each point in time is just based on data collected from the previous and current versions.

4.5   Threats to Validity

Threats to construct validity concern the statistical relation between the theory and the observation, in our case the measurements and treatment to the data. We detected the CS using *PHPMD*, where we detected 18 smells. We could expand this study to consider even more CS, and compare the detection with other tools for PHP. However, some of them are based in *PHPMD*.

Threats to internal validity concern external factors we did not consider that could affect the variables and the relations being investigated. We can say that *PHPMD* allows to change the thresholds of the of the CS detection, but we worked with the default values for comparing between applications. These values can, however, be questioned for different applications.

Threats to conclusion validity concern the relation between the treatment and the outcome. One can argue that CS are often considered by absolute number or normalized by *LOC* or *LLOC*. However, our experiments have shown that the normalization by *LLOC* describes the peaks better.

Threats to external validity concern the generalization of results. We recognize that having just 8 web applications may not be enough for generalization sake.

5   Related Work

Much literature in software evolution has been published in the last decades, but few on web apps.

Longitudinal on CS: In [17] are described different phases in the evolution of CS and reported that components infected with CS have a higher change frequency. Later, [19] results indicate: CS lifespan is close to 50% of the lifespan of the systems. In [6] it is reported that a large percentage of CS was introduced in the creation of class/methods, but very few CS are removed. Later, [26] sustains that most CS are introduced when artifacts are created and not because of their evolution. In [20] the authors claim that the latest versions of the observed application have more CS/design issues than the oldest ones. They also note that the first version of the software is cleaner. In [8] the authors found that TD (Technical Debt) increases for most observed systems. However, TD normalized to the size of the system decreases over time in most systems. In [12], the authors conclude that CS can remain in the application code for years before removal, and CS detected and prioritized by linters, disappear from code before other CS. Recently [7] find that the number of TD items introduced through new code is a stable metric, although it presents some spikes; and also that the number of commits is not strongly correlated to the number of introduced TD items.

Non-longitudinal in Web Apps: These studies include [24], which found that for JS applications, and for the time before a fault occurrence, files without CS have hazard rates 65% lower than files with CS. As an extension to the previous paper, [14] show the results: files without CS have hazard rates of at least 33% lower than files with CS. In [2] study with PHP TD, which includes CS, they find that, on average, the number of times that a file with high TD is modified is 1.9 times more than the number of times a file with low TD is changed. In terms of the number of lines, the same ratio is 2.4. In [3] the authors find: complex and large classes and methods are frequently committed in PHP files; smelly files are more prone to change than non-smelly files. Studies in Java [18] report similar findings to the last two studies.

Longitudinal with PHP, without CS: Studies of this type include [15], where authors study 5 PHP web apps, and some aspects of their history, like unused code, removal of functions, use of libraries, stability of interfaces, migration to OOP, and complexity evolution. They found these systems undergo systematic maintenance. Later in [1], they expanded the study to analyze 30 PHP projects extracting their metrics, and found that not all of Lehman's laws of software evolution were confirmed in web applications.

Longitudinal with Fluctuations in CS: The only study we found regarding this aspect, which indeed is the most related to our work, is an already referred recent study [7], about the fluctuation in the evolution of technical dept (which includes CS). Their authors propose to divide applications into *stable* and *sensitive* (if they have spikes). To perform this classification, they use SMF (Software Metrics Fluctuation), which is defined as the average deviation from successive version pairs.

Related Work Discussion: The method described in [7] should prove effective for detecting anomalies or outliers in a continuous growing metric, or a metric that varies around a average value (fluctuates), with variations different from 0, witch was not the case with CS evolution with these apps. Another difference is that you have to known the history of the project.

6   Conclusions and Future Work

We studied the evolution and sudden variations of 18 CS in 8 widely used PHP web apps, across many years. It is important for PHP project managers to have an evolutionary perspective on the CS in an application, to decide on the allocation of resources to mitigate their maintainability effects. We observed sudden variations in CS occurrence in specific versions, whose root causes deserve investigation and are important for project managers to understand, especially for long-lived projects where managers' turnover inevitably happens.

In this paper we proposed a normalized technique that is simple to implement, for detecting those sudden variations in specific versions during the evolution of web apps, allowing us to unveil the CS story of a development project and make managers aware of the need for enforcing regular refactoring practices.

This technique can also be useful in an automation server pipeline, to add in the quality certification before the release. Our main goal was to achieve a simple technique that prevents a given version of software to be released with an extraordinary increase in CS, which later will be costly to maintainability. We used web applications in our study, but we think this method can be generalized to other domains or types of apps.

Regarding future work, we would like to increase the number of applications and CS studied, with more computing power. The obvious way forward here, is comparing PHP to Java since many more longitudinal studies on CS exist for the latter.

Acknowledgments. This work was partially supported by the Portuguese Foundation for Science and Technology (FCT) projects UIDB/04466/2020 e UIDP/04466/2020.

References

1. Amanatidis, T., Chatzigeorgiou, A.: Studying the evolution of PHP web applications. Inf. Softw. Technol. **72**(April), 48–67 (2016). https://doi.org/10.1016/j.infsof.2015.11.009
2. Amanatidis, T., Chatzigeorgiou, A., Ampatzoglou, A.: The relation between technical debt and corrective maintenance in PHP web applications. Inf. Softw. Technol. **90**, 70–74 (2017). https://doi.org/10.1016/j.infsof.2017.05.004
3. Bessghaier, N., Ouni, A., Mkaouer, M.W.: On the diffusion and impact of code smells in web applications. In: Wang, Q., Xia, Y., Seshadri, S., Zhang, L.-J. (eds.) SCC 2020. LNCS, vol. 12409, pp. 67–84. Springer, Cham (2020). https://doi.org/10.1007/978-3-030-59592-0_5
4. Bieman, J.M., Kang, B.K.: Cohesion and reuse in an object-oriented system. SIGSOFT Softw. Eng. Notes **20**(SI), 259–262 (1995). https://doi.org/10.1145/223427.211856
5. Bryton, S., Brito e Abreu, F., Monteiro, M.: Reducing subjectivity in code smells detection: experimenting with the long method. In: 7th International Conference on the Quality of Information and Communications Technology (QUATIC 2010), pp. 337–342. IEEE (2010)
6. Chatzigeorgiou, A., Manakos, A.: Investigating the evolution of code smells in object-oriented systems. Innov. Syst. Softw. Eng. **10**(1), 3–18 (2013). https://doi.org/10.1007/s11334-013-0205-z
7. Digkas, G., Ampatzoglou, A., Chatzigeorgiou, A., Avgeriou, P.: On the temporality of introducing code technical debt. In: Shepperd, M., Brito e Abreu, F., Rodrigues da Silva, A., Pérez-Castillo, R. (eds.) QUATIC 2020. CCIS, vol. 1266, pp. 68–82. Springer, Cham (2020). https://doi.org/10.1007/978-3-030-58793-2_6
8. Digkas, G., Lungu, M., Chatzigeorgiou, A., Avgeriou, P.: The evolution of technical debt in the apache ecosystem. In: Lopes, A., de Lemos, R. (eds.) ECSA 2017. LNCS, vol. 10475, pp. 51–66. Springer, Cham (2017). https://doi.org/10.1007/978-3-319-65831-5_4
9. Fontana, F.A., Ferme, V., Zanoni, M., Roveda, R.: Towards a prioritization of code debt: a code smell intensity index. In: 7th International Workshop on Managing Technical Debt (MTD 2015), pp. 16–24. IEEE (2015)

10. Fowler, M.: Refactoring: Improving the Design of Existing Code. Addison-Wesley, Boston (1999)
11. Gill, G.K., Kemerer, C.F.: Cyclomatic complexity density and software maintenance productivity. Trans. Softw. Eng. **17**(12), 1284 (1991)
12. Habchi, S., Rouvoy, R., Moha, N.: On the survival of android code smells in the wild. In: 6th International Conference on Mobile Software Engineering and Systems (MOBILESoft 2019), pp. 87–98. IEEE, May 2019. https://doi.org/10.1109/MOBILESoft.2019.00022
13. Herbold, S., Grabowski, J., Waack, S.: Calculation and optimization of thresholds for sets of software metrics. Empir. Softw. Eng. **16**(6), 812–841 (2011). https://doi.org/10.1007/s10664-011-9162-z
14. Johannes, D., Khomh, F., Antoniol, G.: A large-scale empirical study of code smells in JavaScript projects. Softw. Qual. J. **27**(3), 1271–1314 (2019). https://doi.org/10.1007/s11219-019-09442-9
15. Kyriakakis, P., Chatzigeorgiou, A.: Maintenance patterns of large-scale PHP web applications. In: 30th International Conference on Software Maintenance and Evolution (ICSME 2014), pp. 381–390 (2014). https://doi.org/10.1109/ICSME.2014.60
16. Lanza, M., Marinescu, R.: Object-Oriented Metrics in Practice. Springer, Heidelberg (2007)
17. Olbrich, S., Cruzes, D.S., Basili, V., Zazworka, N.: The evolution and impact of code smells: a case study of two open source systems. In: 3rd International Symposium on Empirical Software Engineering and Measurement (ESEM 2009), pp. 390–400. IEEE (2009). https://doi.org/10.1109/ESEM.2009.5314231
18. Palomba, F., Bavota, G., Penta, M.D., Fasano, F., Oliveto, R., Lucia, A.D.: On the diffuseness and the impact on maintainability of code smells: a large scale empirical investigation. Empir. Softw. Eng. **23**(3), 1188–1221 (2017). https://doi.org/10.1007/s10664-017-9535-z
19. Peters, R., Zaidman, A.: Evaluating the lifespan of code smells using software repository mining. In: European Conference on Software Maintenance and Reengineering (CSMR 2012), pp. 411–416. IEEE (2012). https://doi.org/10.1109/CSMR.2012.79
20. Rani, A., Chhabra, J.K.: Evolution of code smells over multiple versions of softwares: an empirical investigation. In: 2nd International Conference for Convergence in Technology (I2CT 2017), vol. 2017-January, pp. 1093–1098. IEEE, December 2017. https://doi.org/10.1109/I2CT.2017.8226297
21. Rasool, G., Arshad, Z.: A review of code smell mining techniques. J. Softw. Evol. Process **27**(11), 867–895 (2015). https://doi.org/10.1002/smr.1737
22. Pereira dos Reis, J., Brito e Abreu, F., de Figueiredo Carneiro, G., Anslow, C.: Code smells detection and visualization: a systematic literature review. Arch. Comput. Methods Eng. (2021). https://doi.org/10.1007/s11831-021-09566-x
23. Rio, A., Brito e Abreu, F.: Code smells survival analysis in web apps. In: Piattini, M., Rupino da Cunha, P., García Rodríguez de Guzmán, I., Pérez-Castillo, R. (eds.) QUATIC 2019. CCIS, vol. 1010, pp. 263–271. Springer, Cham (2019). https://doi.org/10.1007/978-3-030-29238-6_19
24. Saboury, A., Musavi, P., Khomh, F., Antoniol, G.: An empirical study of code smells in JavaScript projects. In: 24th International Conference on Software Analysis, Evolution, and Reengineering (SANER 2017), pp. 294–305. IEEE, March 2017. https://doi.org/10.1109/SANER.2017.7884630

25. Singh, S., Kaur, S.: A systematic literature review: refactoring for disclosing code smells in object oriented software. Ain Shams Eng. J. **9**(4), 2129–2151 (2018). https://doi.org/10.1016/j.asej.2017.03.002

26. Tufano, M., et al.: When and why your code starts to smell bad (and whether the smells go away). Trans. Softw. Eng. **43**(11), 1063–1088 (2017). https://doi.org/10.1109/TSE.2017.2653105

27. W3techs.com: Usage Statistics and Market Share of Server-side Programming Languages for Websites, January 2021. https://w3techs.com/technologies/overview/programming_language

28. Zhang, M., Hall, T., Baddoo, N.: Code bad smells: a review of current knowledge. J. Softw. Maintenance Evol. **23**(3), 179–202 (2011). https://doi.org/10.1002/smr.521

Risk and Complexity Assessment on the Context of Language Migration

Santiago Bragagnolo[1,2(✉)], Abderrahmane Seriai[1], Stéphane Ducasse[2], and Mustapha Derras[1]

[1] Berger-Levrault, Montpellier, France
{santiago.bragagnolo,abderrahmane.seriai,
mustapha.derras}@berger-levrault.com
[2] Université de Lille, CNRS, Inria, Centrale Lille, UMR 9189 – CRIStAL,
Lille, France
stephane.ducasse@inria.fr

Abstract. Language Migration is a highly risky and complex process. Many authors have provided different ways to tackle down the problem, but it still not completely resolved, even-more it is considered almost impossible on many circumstances. Despite the approaches and solutions available, no work has been done on measuring the risks and complexity of a migration process based on the technological gap. In this article we contribute a first iteration on Language Migration complexity metrics, we apply and interpret metrics on an industrial project. We end the article with a discussion and proposing future works.

Keywords: Migration · Challenges · Risk · Assessment · Metrics

1 Introduction

With the fast evolution of programming languages and frameworks, companies must evolve their systems. This evolution may imply the full migration of their applications to new technological environments. Our work takes place in collaboration with Berger-Levrault, a major IT company selling information systems developed in Microsoft Access among others. Microsoft Access is ageing and not able to respond to the architectural needs of modern times, threatening the continuity of these information systems and pushing them into the classification of Legacy Systems.

To respond to the process of obsolescence, as explained by [5], we are working on a **software evolution** process of modernization by migration of Microsoft Access applications (source application) to a web architecture (target application). The technological choice of the target web architecture is Angular for the front-end and microservices for the back-end, in alignment with the migration policy of the company.

According to [5] a generic iterative migration responds to the iterative application following process steps: (i) Plan (ii) Understand system (iii) Understand

© Springer Nature Switzerland AG 2021
A. C. R. Paiva et al. (Eds.): QUATIC 2021, CCIS 1439, pp. 97–110, 2021.
https://doi.org/10.1007/978-3-030-85347-1_8

destination (iv) transform knowledge (v) Produce Destination. Our article aims to help to *plan* by measuring the potential complexity of the *transform knowledge* phase, by measuring the distance in between the origin system and the destination system.

Modernization is a risky and complex case of software evolution that could be near to impossible or just not worthy in certain circumstances. This complex and risky nature is not only due to the quality of the source project (as many other articles already spotted [1,17]), but also due to the gap in between the origin and destination technologies. Much has been told about the impact of cohesion and coupling to the decomposability of software, and how this decomposability is key for iterative processes of migration [2,8,10,15,21,25], but to the best of our knowledge there are not works on the measure of the technological gap, despite the conscious acknowledgement on the literature [22] of the correlation between the difficulty of a migration and the difference between origin and target technological platforms.

Following we explain the context and highlight the challenges of our migration project (Sect. 2). We introduce our different counters and highlight their relationship with the complexity of the process of migration on different levels in our particular setup (Sect. 3). We extract the proposed metrics on an industrial project, and propose an interpretation of the extracted numbers (Sect. 4). After interpretation, we discuss the flaws of this kind of metrics and what it still to be done for having a functional set of gap metrics useful to predict complexity (Sect. 5) We finish the article with a preview of future works (Sect. 6) and a conclusion (Sect. 7).

2 Challenges

The migration of Microsoft Access applications to a web technology is a difficult task. Indeed, it requires working on several levels of abstraction, namely: the architectural level and the source code level. In this section we present, in a non-exhaustive way, the difficulties inherent in the process of migrating VBA applications to a web technology.

It is important to remark that these challenges are not solved yet, but exposed to give context to the metrics. The metrics should contribute to the measurement of these challenges.

2.1 Software Architecture Challenges

Moving from a Centralized/Standalone Application to a Distributed Application. Microsoft Access is a development environment used to create database based applications. It comes with a programming language called Visual Basic For Application (VBA) and various libraries. This language and the libraries are used in a programming environment called Microsoft Visual Basic, which also comes with Microsoft Access. Microsoft Access applications are so-called "standalone" applications, i.e. they are developed to be deployed centrally, although they have the ability to interact with remote data servers. Furthermore, a standalone application can access the resources of its deployment environment (user computer), such as the operating system used, the file system, printers, etc. In contrast, a distributed application rarely access users resources but network resources, assuming the existence of a network and shared resources. [20] is a good example of how radical may be this kind of modification. The difference between this two environments makes many original development assumptions to not be valid any more, requiring to be adapted or completely redeveloped during a migration process. Further, in this article (Sect. 3), we propose the paradigmatic change and the dependencies counters which measure the amount of entities that are related with this aspect.

Moving from a Monolithic Application to a Microservice Application. A monolithic application is often described as a single-tier system in which the user interface, business logic and data layer are combined into a single application. Microservices is one of the latest trends in software development that has emerged from service-oriented architecture styles. Microservices are expected to be specialized on specific concerns, small, highly cohesive, loosely coupled services, each independently deployable and communicating with communication mechanisms (such as REST or a message bus like RabbitMQ). In addition, there is a lot of microservices architectures and existing approaches for this kind of migration, that are not addressed in this paper, since we have not yet made the decision of which specific composition and migration approach to take. The contrast between this two architectures is dramatic. The original source code has been developed with the assumption of local synchronized execution with low-level shared resources (as memory and stack), while the destination proposes full distribution as assumption, requiring to be adapted or completely redeveloped during a migration process. Alongside it also requires the production of configuration files that allow to find a service composition that produces an equivalent work to the original software. [10,25] have exposed with detail the case serving monolithic applications as web pages or services, identifying the multiple challenges that come from such a modernization. Further, in this article (Sect. 3), we propose the paradigmatic change and the dependencies counters which measure the amount of entities that are also related with this aspect.

Moving from a Desktop Application GUI to a Web Application GUI. Graphical user interfaces for Microsoft Access applications are developed using Microsoft Office GUI components. These components generally use the libraries provided by the Microsoft Windows operating system. Even when the GUI can be highly customized, it is no wonder that most of these applications respond to the unified aesthetics of the operative system, using not only the same look and feel, but the same navigation metaphor (from pop-up and dialogue windows to modal and non-modal sub windows). However, the GUIs of a web application typically use HTML and CSS (or derivations) used to customize the look-and-feel of the web page. The originality of aesthetics is encouraged and welcomed, as part of the company identity. Along with that, navigation methods such as pop-up and dialogues are not welcomed and even banned by many web browsers. These two paradigms are completely different. Thus, a mapping work is necessary in order to be able to transform the VBA graphical interfaces into web interfaces. All of these differences together mean that the migration of graphical constructs, both visual and behavioural [23] are developed with assumptions that are not valid on the destination platform, and may require to be adapted or completely redeveloped during a migration process. [7,12,13,18,19] and many others have contributed in identifying the challenges and validation opportunities of GUI migration. Because of lack of time for further experiments we do not provide metrics for this challenge in this article.

2.2   Source Code Difficulties

VBA/Macro Code to Typescript/Java. VBA (Visual Basic for Applications) is a language similar to Visual Basic that requires a host application to run (Access in our case). Microsoft Access projects provide two kinds of source code: The "macros" language – a specific user-friendly language for Microsoft Access– and VBA, a language inspired by Visual Basic, adapted for use in the Microsoft Office context, and Microsoft Access. It is an interpreted language, and developed to run in the context of a database. Furthermore, VBA does not support namespaces nor packages, meaning that all the module functions and classes defined in a project are visible within the project. By other hand, TypeScript is a statically typed programming language that transpiles to JavaScript code. TypeScript allows for development in both the procedural and object-oriented paradigms. Regardless to support for both procedural and object-oriented, an Angular application (the technological target for the GUI), is expected to be written by using mainly object-oriented and component-oriented code. Java is an object-oriented programming language used to develop mainly object-oriented and component oriented software. Both languages are file-oriented, and require the usage of namespaces or packages and importing for visibility. All this code must be generated by instrumentation of algorithms as type inference. Also, the clustering of functions into classes is compulsory in java and mostly desirable in the context of an Angular project [15,26]. The difference between grammatical constructs, the existence of namespaces and the file oriented source code are really challenging chasms to cross, and in many cases leading to problems as the impossibility of expressing important semantic on the destination target or requiring to adapt the semantic into concepts that may lead to ambiguity or in extreme cases requiring the redevelopment of a component during a migration process [22].

Moving the Internal Structural Representation from VBA to Angular. As an extension of the language difference, the graphical constructs are designed and developed differently. In Microsoft Access the development of graphical interfaces is done using a wizard (drag and drop). This drag and drop adds graphical controls to the built GUI. Each of these controls and the form itself can be bound to a database table directly. However, GUI development in Angular is done using the Angular templating language. This language mixes HTML, HTML code generation directives and directives for linking to GUI behavioural code. Angular manual encourage the developers to use interface objects for storing the data produced by the user interaction, and use this objects afterwords as data transfer objects. Therefore, this migration implies the production of state-holding objects, the production of database CRUD code, and to produce calls to remote services thus none of these calls or objects exists in the origin system. [18,23] have discussed on challenges related with the structural representation of the GUI. [11] also has discussed the user interaction impact over a software adaptation that can shed light also to the potential risks on invalidating the assumptions that were followed during the development of the original software.

3   Metrics

The various difficulties related to the migration of VBA applications (source of the migration) to a web architecture (target of the migration) highlight the incompatibilities that exist between VBA and its paradigm as well as web applications and their paradigm. In this section, we present a set of metrics that measure these incompatibilities and try to quantify the different gaps between source and destination technologies, in an intent to measure the inherent risks to the semi-automatic migration process. These metrics are the result of our experiences as well as our readings in the literature.

3.1   Risks Related to the Relevance of the Source Code Analysis

Parsers has been used largely in the migration and reverse-engineering literature, as we have seen in different works as [3,6,8,13,23,24] and many others. We know also from other studies that Microsoft access projects are complex to analyse [4]. Often, to count with a parser able to parse all possible program on a language is key for the automatic and semi-automatic approaches.

A parser is a program that analyses a string written according to the rules of a formal grammar and produces some kind of output. Among the set of tools we have developed to work with Microsoft Access projects, we have a VBA parser that takes as input a source code and produces a so-called Abstract Syntax Tree (AST). Our parser is based on the grammar of the VBA language as described in the Microsoft Access documentation. For ensuring the completeness we created tests for each of the grammar cases proposed by the documentation. We test also our tool by parsing the Microsoft Northwind Traders[1] example project, covering the full extension of the program.

Risk. Despite our efforts to ensure completeness, we found that at least in one of the companies projects, our parser fails to produce an AST in %30 of the modules/class modules, due to unexpected usage of different grammatical constructions. The lack of documentation coverage of these grammatical formulas

---

[1] https://docs.microsoft.com/en-us/powerapps/maker/canvas-apps/northwind-install.

threatens the validity of our semantic analysis since we have to interpret ourselves what these grammatical composition means, opening the door to ambiguity and misinterpretation. The measuring of this risk contributes to the understanding of the *source code related challenges*, depicted in Subsect. 2.2.

Parsing Error Counter. In order to quantify the parsing errors, we use the following Parsing error counter metric In the context of interpreting VBA source code with our parser, we have defined the "SyntaxError" counter. This gives us the amount of parsing errors due to a syntax error (especially those mentioned in the previous paragraph). The higher the value of this counter, the more complex the migration will be.

3.2   The Risks of Language Translation

Programming languages often respond to specific formal grammar, that define the limits and possibilities of a language. These grammatical constructions allow expressing semantics that respond to a proposed programming paradigm. Many approaches to software migration are based on the interpretation of the semantics of the different source artefacts (contained in the language/application to be migrated) and the expression of an equivalent semantic in the target language/paradigm. Many times the grammatical constructions and or the paradigmatic concepts are incompatible, leading to the inability to express an equivalent semantic.

The Risks of Mapping Entities from One Formal Grammar to Another. One of the most important steps in a migration process is the transformation of grammatical entities from the source language to their equivalents in the target language. This consists in associating each element of the source language dataset with one or more elements of the target language dataset. This task is not trivial, because it is possible to have elements of the source language dataset that have no equivalents in the target language.

Risk. The lack of equivalent grammatical entity causes loss of semantics during the transformation.[22]. VBA is a language that has a particularly rich grammar. Thus, the same semantics can be expressed in several ways, this is even true when it comes to information flow control or error handling. Therefore, we find it important to map the elements of the VBA dataset that do not have equivalents in the destination environment and to count them when analysing the code of VBA applications. The measuring of this risk contributes to (i) the understanding of the *VBA/Macro code to Typescript/Java related challenges*, since the lack of equivalence implies, depicted in Subsect. 2.2, and (ii) the complexity of error management, what gives insight of the complexity of the *architectural challenges depicted* in Subsect. 2.1.

Incompatible Grammatical Construct Counter. Different languages provide different ways to control the flow of execution of a program. Control flow management includes normally conditional branching (such as if, else if and switch), loops (such as for, while and repeat) and error management (such as try/catch). There are other less popular and harder to predict such as conditional and unconditional jumps (also known as go-to statements). There are many VBA grammatical entities that are used for error handling and control flow and for which we do not have an equivalent in Typescript/Java, we mention: Resume Label, Resume Empty, Error Resume Next, OnError GoTo, Resume Next, Property, PropertyAccessors. This grammatical entity counter counts the amount of appearances of these entities in a given source code. The higher the value of these counters, the more complex the migration.

The Risks of Paradigm Shift. A programming paradigm is a way of approaching computer programming and conceiving problem solutions and their formulation in an appropriate programming language. It thus provides (and determines) the developer's understanding of the execution of his programme. For example, in object-oriented programming, developers may conceive the program as a collection of interacting objects, while in functional programming a program may be seen as a sequence of stateless function evaluations. VBA proposes a hybrid paradigm programming language that aims the development of information technology systems focused on human-machine interaction with direct impact on an integrated database, we find many concepts that do not exist in the paradigms of our target languages.

Risk. While VBA allows the usage of functions and procedures, all our destination require the code to be expressed in object oriented fashion. This requires the identification of concerns, and clusterization of variables and functions into potential classes. This kind of problem does not have automatic solutions, since most of the approaches are based on heuristics and multiple results are possible, exposing seriously the consistency of the produced code [15,16,26]. Furthermore, VBA includes many first-class citizen that do not exist in the target environments such as Tables Queries and Macros. Each of these cases are mean to be transformed into something else, risking the loss of semantics and of consistency.[22]. The measuring of this risk contributes to understand (i) the complexity of the *VBA/Macro code to Typescript/Java* related challenge, depicted in Subsect. 2.2, and (ii) the complexity of *Moving from a monolithic application to a microservices-based application,* depicted in Subsect. 2.1.

Counter for Incompatible Entities. Among the all the first class citizens of VBA language, we find the followings that have no equivalent on our target platforms: Modules, Tables, Queries, Macros. For measuring the paradigm shift complexity we opt for counting the amount of entities belonging to these categories. The higher the value of this counter, the more complex the migration.

3.3   The Risks of Using Libraries as Dependencies

A VBA project interacts with other projects or libraries. These are called dependencies. They can be of three types: (i) "BuiltInDependency": dependencies that are part of Microsoft Access (standard) (ii) "BinaryDependency": dependencies provided by a third party or by Berger-Levrault (iii) "MicrosoftAccess Dependency": dependencies developed in Microsoft Access Each kind of dependencies is different, and may not have an equivalent on the target technology. These dependencies need to be taken into account in our migration process.

Risk. There are many risks associated with dependencies update or migration [9]. In this article we consider the fact that in different runtime and languages there is a high probability that the same library is not going to be available, [8]. Therefore, each library used by the program, is likely to be changed. The measuring of this risk contributes to understand the general complexity, since affect *all the proposed challenges* depicted in Sect. 2.

Dependency Counter. In the context of interpreting VBA source code with our parser, we have defined a counter for each type of dependency. The higher the value of these counters, the more complex the migration.

4   The eGRC Use Case

eGRC is an extremely complex project. Indeed, we have seen that it contains all the types of risks that were mentioned in the previous sections. Therefore, in order to get a clear picture of the proportion of these risks in the eGRC project, we have activated all the metrics mentioned above in our VBA code parser. To understand these metrics, we provide graphs that explain the proportion of risks in eGRC and its sub-projects. As a demographic, eGRC counts with *900.000 LoC* distributed in between *1232 widgets*, *564 reports*, *271 function-modules*, *491 class-modules* and *18 macros*. These different modules are implemented by using a total of *21 libraries*, *1172 queries* and *1437 tables*. This project has in charge a heavy load of business rules since it is in charge of the management of several public services such as electoral planning, civil status and cemetery management.

4.1   The Pareto Chart

As largely explained on books as [14], the purpose of the Pareto chart is to identify important individuals in a sample of data. The diagram follows the Pareto principle (also known as the 80-20 principle), which is an empirical phenomenon found in some fields: about 80% of the effects are the product of 20% of the causes. The Pareto chart consists of two graphs: a histogram of frequencies on the measured variable (grouped by project complexity in our case), where the individual values are represented in descending order by bars, and an accumulation line. In our case, we want to identify the 20% of eGRC sub-projects that cover the 80% of the risks. This will help us to focus only on the important sub-projects. For this reason, we have decided to use the Pareto chart.

4.2   Study of the Complexity of Syntactic Errors

The objective is to show the coverage of our parser by making explicit the grammatical entities that are not recognized by our code analysis tool. The histogram shows the number of syntactic errors for each of the eGRC sub-projects. Example: The magact sub-project has just over 85 syntax errors. The accumulation line shows us the percentage of the cumulative frequency. Example: If we solve the syntax problems in the magact sub-project, we will cover 15% of the total number of syntax errors in the eGRC project, and if we solve the syntax problems in both the magact and magelereu sub-projects, we will cover just over 30% of the total number of syntax errors in the eGRC project. To get 80% coverage we need to solve the syntax problems in the first 7 sub-projects (Fig. 1).

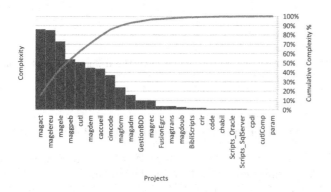

Fig. 1. Study of the complexity of syntactic errors.

4.3   Study of the Complexity Related to the Differences in the Source (VBA) and Target (Typescript/Java) Grammar

The objective is to show the degree of mismatch between the grammar of VBA and Typescript/Java. This consists of counting the number of grammatical elements in the source language (VBA) that have no equivalent in the target languages (Typescript/Java). The histogram shows us the number of occurrences of grammatical elements for which we have no equivalent in each of the eGRC sub-projects. Example: The magact sub-project has just over 9000 occurrences of grammatical elements with no Typescript/Java equivalent. The accumulation line shows us the cumulative frequency percentages. Example: if we solve the equivalence problems in the magact sub-project, we will cover 28% of the total number of elements without Typescript/Java equivalents in the eGRC project, and if we solve the problems of elements without equivalents in both the magact, and cimcode sub-projects, we will cover a little more than 45% of the total number of elements without Typescript/Java equivalents in the eGRC project. In order to achieve 80% coverage, we need to solve the problems of grammatical elements without equivalents in the first 6 sub-projects (Fig. 2).

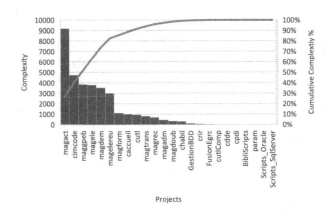

Fig. 2. Study of the complexity related to the differences in the source.

4.4   Study of the Complexity Related to the Paradigm Shift

As mentioned in a previous section, many of the notions related to the hybrid paradigm of VBA have no equivalent in the object and component oriented paradigm: Modules, Tables, Queries, Macros, etc. The objective is to show the degree of mismatch between the VBA and Typescript/Java paradigms. This consists of counting the number of paradigm elements in the source language (VBA) that do not have equivalents in the target languages (Typescript/Java). The histogram shows us the number of occurrences of paradigm elements for which we have no equivalents in each of the eGRC sub-projects. Example: the magact sub-project has just over 650 occurrences of paradigm elements without Typescript/Java equivalents. The accumulation line shows us the cumulative frequency percentages. Example: if we solve the equivalence problems in the magele sub-project, we will cover more than 25% of the total number of elements without Typescript/Java equivalents in the eGRC project, and if we solve the problems of elements without equivalents in both the magele, and magelereu sub-projects, we will cover a little more than 40% of the total number of elements without Typescript/Java equivalents in the eGRC project. In order to achieve 80% coverage, we need to solve the problems of paradigm elements without equivalents in the first 8 sub-projects (Fig. 3).

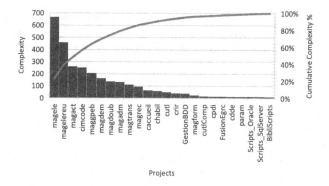

Fig. 3. Study of the complexity related to the paradigm shift.

4.5   Study of the Complexity of the Use of Dependencies

The objective is to show the degree of use of dependencies in each of the eGRC sub-projects. The histogram shows the number of occurrences of dependencies in each of the eGRC sub-projects. Example: The magact sub-project has 17 occurrences of dependencies. The accumulation line shows us the percentage of the cumulative frequency. Example: If we solve the dependencies in the magact, magelereu, magform, maggpeg subprojects, we will only cover 30% of the total number of occurrences of dependencies in the eGRC project. All dependencies must be handled in the same way, this can be very time-consuming (Fig. 4).

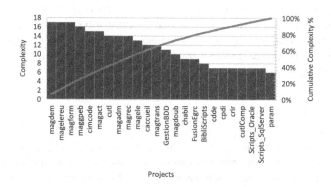

Fig. 4. Study of the complexity of the use of dependencies.

5   Discussion

The metrics we proposed are based on our understanding of the problems encountered in the literature, and some found in our own migrating experience. Regardless the link with previous empirical experiments, our work still shallow, since all the proposed metrics measure complexity in **Nominal Scale** units. Validability and Reliability have not being tested nor enhanced, the experiments using our metrics still few, and our work on the generalization of these metrics still far.

Nominal Scale metrics are useful to understand how many entities do we have in a continuum. This is useful to get an idea of how many of these entities we are bound to find but nothing more. More work is required to be able to establish the contribution of each of these variables to the complexity of the migration.

Validability and Reliability are two of the most important fundamental aspects of measurement [14], and there are required to be measured, validated and empirically proofed. While validability can be enhanced and validated by more exact means, the reliability of the metric requires empirical validation, what implies the requirement of statistical samples on the usage of such metrics.

Uses nevertheless, we have put to work these counters already to be able to select elements from many experiments still to be done. The required expertise to respond to a survey on the utility our context is quite unique.

Our metrics work has been already leveraged by our selves on the detection of projects and files that are more likely to be interesting for the study of layer violation on Microsoft Access elements.

6   Future Work

From this point we plan to wide-up the measurement of complexity to other dimensions of migration such as architectural migration complexity, or the third-party migration complexity. We expect also to work on the unification of the measurement units and on the empirical analysis of the reliability of the metrics in the context of an industrial migration.

7   Conclusion

In this article we contribute a first iteration on Language Migration complexity metrics. We also contribute the interpretation and study the application of such metrics on our current migration project for obtaining a general overview. We contribute also our first use case of these metrics, what is our first step into the iterative enhancement. We discuss on the scales, and our lack of studies on validability and reliability, remarking their importance. We conclude that our metrics give a some understanding of the potential risks during the effort measurement of a migration, but this understanding still fuzzy. More work must be done in the refinement of the proposed metrics to make them useful.

References

1. Adjoyan, S., Seriai, A.D., Shatnawi, A.: Service identification based on quality metrics object-oriented legacy system migration towards SOA. In: SEKE: Software Engineering and Knowledge Engineering, pp. 1–6. Knowledge Systems Institute Graduate School (2014)
2. Ahmad, A., Babar, M.A.: A framework for architecture-driven migration of legacy systems to cloud-enabled software. In: Proceedings of the WICSA 2014 Companion Volume, WICSA 2014 Companion. Association for Computing Machinery, New York (2014). ISBN 9781450325233
3. Angulo, G., Martín, D.S., Santos, B., Ferrari, F.C., de Camargo, V.V.: An approach for creating KDM2PSM transformation engines in ADM context: the RUTE-K2J case. In: Proceedings of the VII Brazilian Symposium on Software Components, Architectures, and Reuse, SBCARS 2018, pp. 92–101. Association for Computing Machinery, New York (2018). ISBN 9781450365543
4. Bragagnolo, S., Anquetil, N., Ducasse, S., Abderrahmane, S., Derras, M.: Analysing Microsoft access projects: building a model in a partially observable domain. In: Ben Sassi, S., Ducasse, S., Mili, H. (eds.) ICSR 2020. LNCS, vol. 12541, pp. 152–169. Springer, Cham (2020). https://doi.org/10.1007/978-3-030-64694-3_10
5. Bragagnolo, S., Anquetil, N., Ducasse, S., Seriai, A., Derras, M.: Software migration: a theoretical framework (a grounded theory approach on systematic literature review). Empirical Softw. Eng. (2021)
6. Bragagnolo, S., Rocha, H., Denker, M., Ducasse, S.: Ethereum query language. In: 1st International Workshop on Emerging Trends in Software Engineering for Blockchain (WETSEB), pp. 1–8, May 2018
7. Bragagnolo, S., Verhaeghe, B., Seriai, A., Derras, M., Etien, A.: Challenges for layout validation: lessons learned. In: Shepperd, M., Brito e Abreu, F., Rodrigues da Silva, A., Pérez-Castillo, R. (eds.) QUATIC 2020. CCIS, vol. 1266, pp. 107–119. Springer, Cham (2020). https://doi.org/10.1007/978-3-030-58793-2_9
8. Brant, J., Roberts, D., Plendl, B., Prince, J.: Extreme maintenance: transforming Delphi into C#. In: ICSM 2010 (2010)
9. Cossette, B.E., Walker, R.J.: Seeking the ground truth: a retroactive study on the evolution and migration of software libraries. In: Proceedings of the ACM SIG-SOFT 20th International Symposium on the Foundations of Software Engineering, FSE 2012, pp. 55:1–55:11. ACM, New York (2012). ISBN 978-1-4503-1614-9
10. De Lucia, A., Francese, R., Scanniello, G., Tortora, G.: Developing legacy system migration methods and tools for technology transfer. Softw. Pract. Exp. 38(13), 1333–1364 (2008)
11. DeLine, R., Zelesnik, G., Shaw, M.: Lessons on converting batch systems to support interaction: experience report. In: Proceedings of the 19th International Conference on Software Engineering, ICSE 1997, pp. 195–204. Association for Computing Machinery, New York (1997). ISBN 0897919149
12. Di Santo, G., Zimeo, E.: Reversing GUIs to XIML descriptions for the adaptation to heterogeneous devices. In: Proceedings of the 2007 ACM Symposium on Applied Computing, SAC 2007, pp. 1456–1460. Association for Computing Machinery, New York (2007). ISBN 1595934804
13. Garcés, K., et al.: White-box modernization of legacy applications: the oracle forms case study. Comput. Standards Interfaces 57, 110–122 (2017)
14. Kan, S.H.: Metrics and Models in Software Quality Engineering. O'Reilly (2006)

15. Kontogiannis, K., Martin, J., Wong, K., Gregory, R., Müller, H., Mylopoulos, J.: Code migration through transformations: an experience report. In: Proceedings of the 1998 Conference of the Centre for Advanced Studies on Collaborative Research, CASCON 1998, p. 13. IBM Press (1998)
16. Martin, J., Muller, H.A.: C to Java migration experiences. In: Proceedings of the Sixth European Conference on Software Maintenance and Reengineering, pp. 143–153. IEEE (2002)
17. Mateus, B.G., Martinez, M., Kolski, C.: An experience-based recommendation system to support migrations of Android applications from Java to Kotlin (2021)
18. Moore, Rugaber, Seaver: Knowledge-based user interface migration. In: Proceedings 1994 International Conference on Software Maintenance, pp. 72–79, IEEE Computer Society Press (1994). ISBN 978-0-8186-6330-7
19. Moore, M.M.: Rule-based detection for reverse engineering user interfaces. In: Proceedings of WCRE 1996: 4th Working Conference on Reverse Engineering, pp. 42–48. IEEE (1996)
20. de Souza, P., McNair, A., Jahnke, J.H.: Network-centric migration of embedded control software: a case study. In: Proceedings of the 2003 Conference of the Centre for Advanced Studies on Collaborative Research, pp. 54–65 (2003)
21. Su, X., Yang, X., Li, J., Wu, D.: Parallel iterative reengineering model of legacy systems. In: 2009 IEEE International Conference on Systems, Man and Cybernetics, pp. 4054–4058. IEEE (2009)
22. Terekhov, A.A., Verhoef, C.: The realities of language conversions. IEEE Softw. 17(6), 111–124 (2000). ISSN 0740-7459
23. Verhaeghe, B., et al.: GUI migration using MDE from GWT to Angular 6: an industrial case. In: 2019 IEEE 26th International Conference on Software Analysis. Evolution and Reengineering (SANER 2019), Hangzhou, China, pp. 579–583 (2019)
24. Williams, J.R., Paige, R.F., Polack, F.A.C.: Searching for model migration strategies. In: Proceedings of the 6th International Workshop on Models and Evolution, ME 2012, pp. 39–44. Association for Computing Machinery, New York (2012). ISBN 9781450317986
25. Zhang, Z., Yang, H.: Incubating services in legacy systems for architectural migration. In: 11th Asia-Pacific Software Engineering Conference, pp. 196–203. IEEE (2004)
26. Zou, Y., Kontogiannis, K.: A framework for migrating procedural code to object-oriented platforms. In: Proceedings Eighth Asia-Pacific Software Engineering Conference, pp. 390–399. IEEE (2001)

Automatically Assessing Complexity of Contributions to Git Repositories

Rolf-Helge Pfeiffer[(✉)]

IT University of Copenhagen, Rued Langgaards Vej 7, Copenhagen, Denmark
`ropf@itu.dk`

Abstract. Lehman's second law of software evolution suggests that under certain conditions software *"becomes more difficult to evolve"*. Similarly, Technical Debt (TD) is often considered as technical compromises that render future changes of software more costly. But how does one actually assess if modifying software becomes more difficult or costly? So far research studied this question indirectly by assessing internal structural complexity of successive software versions arguing that increasing internal complexity renders evolution tasks more difficult and costly too. Our goal is to assess complexity of evolution tasks *directly*. Therefore, we present an algorithm and tool that allows to automatically assess Contribution Complexity (CC), which is the complexity of a contribution respecting difficulty of integration work. Our initial evaluation suggests that our proposed algorithm and readily available tool are suitable to automatically assess complexity of contributions to software in `Git` repositories and the results of applying it on 8 686 contributions to two open-source systems indicate that evolution tasks actually become slightly more difficult.

1 Introduction

Software is usually evolving to adapt to changing environments or requirements, to correct errors, to address *"problems ... that are not carried out adequately during ... development"* [18], etc. Software is said to become increasingly difficult to evolve over time unless it is continuously refactored to decrease internal complexity. For example, Lehman's second law of software evolution says: *"As [software] is changed its complexity increases and [it] becomes more difficult to evolve unless work is done to maintain or reduce the complexity."* [14] Similarly, the term *technical debt* is used to describe software constructs that render future contributions increasingly complex. For example, the participants of Dagstuhl Seminar 16162 agreed to define TD as: *"a collection of design or implementation constructs that are expedient in the short term, but set up a technical context that can make future changes more costly or impossible."* [3].

But how does one actually assess if software *"becomes more difficult to evolve"* or if *"future changes [are] more costly"*? Either human developers possess a skill allowing them to assess if modifying existing software becomes more difficult,

© Springer Nature Switzerland AG 2021
A. C. R. Paiva et al. (Eds.): QUATIC 2021, CCIS 1439, pp. 111–124, 2021.
https://doi.org/10.1007/978-3-030-85347-1_9

managers unearth such knowledge from business/process data, or such assessments are conducted indirectly by assessing complexity of successive versions of software. For example, researchers apply various complexity metrics, such as, size in LOC, cyclomatic (McCabe) complexity [16], coupling of functions or modules [12] to assess change of internal complexity of software over time and argue by induction that more complex systems are more complex to evolve. Using these metrics researchers invalidate Lehman's second law, see [10] for an overview or, e.g., [2].

To the best of our knowledge, there is no research or tool available that allows to directly and automatically assesses if the actual *work of evolving* a software system is getting more difficult/complex. In this paper we present an algorithm that allows to directly asses if evolution work becomes more complex and thereby more costly. Our Contribution Complexity (CC) algorithm computes a score that indicates mainly how difficult it is to integrate work (a set of commits) into an existing software system. The CC score is computed on basic size-based and entropy-based metrics on commit and file level, i.e., number of modified lines/files, degree of scattered work across files/methods, etc. Together with this paper, we publish a tool (https://pypi.org/project/contribution-complexity/) that implements the proposed algorithm. The tool can be used by practitioners to enhance CI/CD chains and by researchers to study software evolution and TD.

The contributions of this paper are *a)* presentation of an algorithm to automatically assess CC of contributions to `Git` repositories (Sect. 3), *b)* implementation of that algorithm in a readily installable open-source tool, *c)* initial evaluation of the CC demonstrating its suitability for the task (Sect. 4), and *d)* together with initial results of applying CC to two open-source database systems (Sect. 4.2), we provide a corresponding dataset containing CC scores together with the tool.

2   Background, Terminology, and Motivation

In this section we explain the terminology that we use in the remainder of the paper and motivate our CC score. In this and the following sections we refer to examples from development of the graph database `Gaffer`, which is created mainly by the British Government Communications Headquarters (GCHQ). More details about `Gaffer` and why it appears in this paper follow in Sect. 4.

Terminology: Work in software projects is often organized via issue trackers, e.g., Atlassian's `Jira` (https://www.atlassian.com/software/jira) or Github's integrated issue tracker, and work on files is handled via VCS like `Git`.

Tickets in issue trackers describe work, such as, perfective or adaptive maintenance task, new features, etc. Tickets may be resolved without any *contribution* to the developed software. For instance, unwanted features or not reproducible bugs are marked accordingly and respective tickets are closed without modification of the software. Other tickets get resolved by implementing a required change via one or more commits to a VCS repository. Commonly, a commit refers

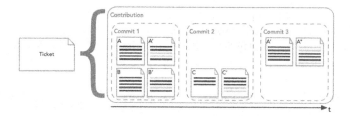

Fig. 1. A contribution resolving a ticket. The contribution consists of three commits with in total four modifications (file changes) over time.

to a corresponding ticket via a ticket identifier in the commit message, i.e., multiple commits can refer to one ticket. To present a clean development history (https://git-scm.com/book/en/v2/Git-Tools-Rewriting-History) multiple commits are sometimes *squashed* into a single commit when merging branches. Consequently, there exists a one to many relation between tickets and commits.

Each commit consists of zero or more file *modifications* where conflict-free merges contain zero modifications. The term *modification* is synonymous to a change of a file, see Spadini et al. [20]. *Modifications* can be considered as edit deltas even though `Git` stores commits as snapshots of entire files. Most `Git` tools present *modifications* as deltas or patches too, see e.g., commit ee3e2a in the `Gaffer` repository on Github. Modifications carry information about the kind of change that was applied. For example, `Git` records if a file is *added, deleted, modified, copied,* or *renamed.*

In this paper, we call one or more commits to a `Git` repository, which consist of one or more *modifications* a *contribution*. Contributions, contain the *work* that eventually resolves tickets. Figure 1 shows a conceptual illustration of *tickets, contributions, commits,* and *modifications,* where two file *modifications* (A to A′ and B to B′) form commit 1, commits 2 and 3 are formed by one file *modification* respectively, and the three commits form a *contribution* that resolves a *ticket*.

Complexity: This work is based on two conceptions of *complexity*. Basili [4], describes *complexity* as the difficulty a developer faces when performing tasks like coding, debugging, or modifying software. Clearly, different kinds of work on existing software are differently complex. For example, implementing a new feature in an object-oriented system via inheritance and conformance to interface specifications is less complex than implementing a feature for which existing abstractions have to be refactored or a patch has to be woven into existing classes and methods. This varying cognitive complexity of tasks is described by Dörner via the "... *existence of many independent variables in a given system. The more variables and the greater their interdependence, the greater that system's complexity. Great complexity places high demands on a planner's capacities to gather information, integrate findings, and design effective actions.*" [6] The exemplary extension of an object-oriented system via inheritance deals with a low amount of independent variables (conformance to class interfaces and interface specifications provide a low number of integration points) compared to a higher amount of strongly interdependent variables when integrating scattered changes during refactoring of existing abstractions.

We believe that besides the inherent complexity of a contribution (conceptual difficulty of realizing it), the complexity of *integration work* (scattered changes to integrate a solution into an environment) characterizes to a large degree the complexity of a contribution. We call the *complexity* of a *contribution* respecting the work of integrating it into existing software Contribution Complexity (CC).

Motivational Example: Before formally defining CC in the next section, we illustrate it on three examples from the `Gaffer` project:

Ticket gh-1808 describes a bug which prevents release of a package to the Maven Central package store.

Ticket gh-2228 specifies that copyright headers in all code files need to be updated to point to the correct time range.

Ticket gh-190 asks to refactor `Gaffer`'s storage engine to be better encapsulated and more descriptive.

`Gaffer`'s `Git` repository contains a single commit (31e23a) that refers to ticket gh-1808, another commit (ee3e2a) that refers to ticket gh-2228, and 21 commits that refer to ticket gh-190. Of the 21 commits, 17 contain modifications and 4 are empty merge commits. Due to constrained space, we refer to the online representations of the respective contributions (https://github.com/gchq/Gaffer/commits). The bug fix that resolves ticket gh-1808 excludes a conflicting dependency from a file with project meta-information (`pom.xml`). The contribution is of low complexity since it consists only of six contiguous lines, which are added in a single commit to a single file. More complex than this minuscule contribution is the update of all copyright headers (ticket gh-2228 with commit ee3e2a). Even though conceptually only four digits need to change, they are changed across 1 975 code files replacing 1 977 lines with a new line. Note, `Git` operates with lines as smallest unit of change. Even changing one character of a line in a file, first deletes that entire line and subsequently adds its new version.

Certainly the most complex contribution of the three examples, is the refactoring of `Gaffer`'s storage engine (ticket gh-190). Over multiple commits multiple hundreds of lines in dozens of files are modified and the changes are scattered within files and across methods, see e.g., commit 2874da.

These three examples shall illustrate that traditional complexity metrics, such as, size of change in LOC/number of files or change of McCabe complexity alone are not suitable to assess CC. For example, size-wise the largest contribution (modifying 1 977 lines in 1 975 files) updates the copyright headers, see commit ee3e2a. Contrary, only some dozens of files with some hundreds of lines are modified to refactor the storage engine. However, these changes are scattered within files and across methods (high entropy). When considering *complexity* as the difficulty of performing tasks like coding or software modification [4], then only the high entropy of the modifications in refactoring of the storage engine suggests higher complexity than the size-wise bigger copyright header update. Furthermore, complexity measures like McCabe complexity would not yield insightful results for the three examples. Either it is not applicable to relevant artifacts (McCabe complexity of a `pom.xml` file?), not all relevant changes are analyzed by it (update of copyright headers), or it 'overlooks' complexity caused by distributed nature of changes.

To overcome these restrictions of traditional complexity metrics when assessing complexity of contributions, we develop an algorithm that should mimic human intuitions as presented above. We implement it in a tool and we call both the algorithm in the next section and the tool uniformly Contribution Complexity (CC).

3   Computing Contribution Complexity

In this section we describe how to compute a discrete Contribution Complexity (CC) score ($c_{contrib}$) for a set of commits using basic metrics on *modification, commit,* and *contribution* level. A priori, we decided that a CC score should map a contribution to the discrete values *low, moderate, medium, elevated,* or *high.* To facilitate presentation, we use the following notation: $\mathbb{C}$ denotes the set of all commits of a contribution and $\mathbb{M}$ denotes the set of all modifications of all commits of a contribution. The CC score is computed in two stages. First, a set of metrics is applied to modifications, whose results are aggregated and subsequently merged with the results of metrics computed for commits. Our presentation follows these two stages.

Per modification ($m \in \mathbb{M}$), i.e., per modified file in a commit, the following basic metrics are computed:

Number of lines added ($m_{l+}(mod)$) The total number of lines added to the file in this modification.

Number of lines removed ($m_{l-}(mod)$) The total number of lines removed from the file in this modification.

Number of hunks ($m_h(mod)$) The total number of blocks that are modified contiguously. For example, A$'$ in Fig. 1 contains two hunks and C$'$ contains one hunk. The number of hunks indicates how scattered a change is and thereby how difficult is it to integrate it into the file.

Number of modified methods ($m_{mth}(mod)$) In case a modified file contains programming language source code, the number of modified methods (or functions) is counted. For non-programming language artifacts the metric evaluates to zero. Similar to $m_h(mod)$, the rationale is that work with changes scattered over multiple methods is more difficult. Note, since our tool depends internally on pydriller (https://pydriller.readthedocs.io/) which uses the lizard (https://github.com/terryyin/lizard) tool to parse source code, the number of methods can only be non-zero for the 16 languages that are currently supported by `lizard`.

Modification kind ($m_{mk}(mod)$) This metric returns the kind of file modification in `Git` terms, i.e., one of the values *added, deleted, modified, copied,* or *renamed.*

Before the final CC score is computed, a separate *modification complexity* score (c_{mod}) is computed for each modification (*mod*) separately. It is defined as the arithmetic mean of the lines added complexity (c_{l+}), the lines removed complexity (c_{l-}), the hunk complexity (c_h), and the method complexity (c_{mth}), see Eq. 1. In case a file is *deleted* or *copied* in a commit, its *modification complexity* is *low*, since there is no 'real' work behind all the removed or newly added lines.

$$c_{mod} = \begin{cases} low & \text{if } m_{mk}(mod) = deleted|added \\ \frac{1}{4} \times (c_{l+}(m_{l+}(mod)) + c_{l-}(m_{l-}(mod)) + c_h(m_h(mod)) + c_{mth}(m_{mth}(mod))) & \text{if } otherwise \end{cases}$$
(1)

The lines added and the lines removed complexity (c_{l+} and c_{l-} respectively) are computed via the same model as in Eq. 2, i.e., $c_{l+}(l) = c_{l-}(l)$, and only the former is presented here. The hunk and the method modified complexity (c_h and c_{mth}) are both computed via the mapping in Eq. 3, i.e., $c_h(n) = c_{mth}(n)$, and only $c_h(n)$ is presented here. Note, that we assume that the complexity values *low* to *high* are equivalent to the numerical values 1 to 5, so that we can use them in calculations.

$$c_{l+}(l) = \begin{cases} low & \text{if } 0 \leq l \leq 15 \\ moderate & \text{if } 15 < l \leq 30 \\ medium & \text{if } 30 < l \leq 60 \\ elevated & \text{if } 60 < l \leq 90 \\ high & \text{if } l > 90 \end{cases} \quad (2) \qquad c_h(n) = \begin{cases} low & \text{if } 0 \leq n \leq 2 \\ moderate & \text{if } 2 < n \leq 5 \\ medium & \text{if } 5 < n \leq 7 \\ elevated & \text{if } 7 < n \leq 9 \\ high & \text{if } n > 9 \end{cases} \quad (3)$$

Rationale for the Modification Complexity Models: The line modification complexity models (c_{l+} and c_{l-}) are adapted from Visser et al. [22], where the authors argue that maintainable methods shall contain less than 15 LOC and higher values render a method progressively more complex. We re-use their thresholds only extending them by a fifth level for *high* complexity. The hunk and method complexity model (c_h and c_{mth}) are based on Miller [17] who argues that human short-term memory usually deals well with is 7 ± 2 entities. Visser et al. use similar thresholds [22], e.g., for assessing complexity of method signatures.

All modification complexities c_{mod} contribute to the CC score ($c_{contrib}$) not individually but in aggregated form. First, the frequencies of all modification complexity
values are collected into a set of pairs ($\mathbb{K} = hist\left([c_{mod}(m) : m \in \mathbb{M}]\right)$). For example, $\mathbb{K} = \{(low, 12), (moderate, 14), (medium, 5), (elevated, 3), (high, 0)\}$ would mean that a contribution consists of 12 modifications with *low* complexity, 14 with *moderate* complexity, etc. The modification complexity frequencies are aggregated into a single value $c_{\forall mod}$ as a weighed average of all the frequency pairs $c_{\forall mod} = \frac{1}{5} \times \sum_{(i,j) \in \mathbb{K}} i^i \times j$. The exponential weights (i^i) are inspired by using Fibonacci numbers for time estimation [21]. We use exponentials to express that it is way harder to work on high complexity modifications than low complexity modifications.

To compute the overall CC score, the following metrics are computed over all commits ($c \in \mathbb{C}$), i.e., for the entire contribution:

Number of modified files in commit $(m_{|f|}(c))$ The total number of files that were either *added, deleted, modified, copied,* or *renamed* in a commit.

Number of lines in commit $(m_{|l|})$ The sum of all added and removed lines in all modifications of a commit.

The CC score $(c_{contrib})$ is defined as the arithmetic mean of the modified files complexity $(c_{|f|})$, changed lines per file complexity $(c_{l/f})$, modification kind complexity (c_{mk}), and the overall modification complexity $(c_{\forall m})$, see Eq. 4. There, n_{files} is the total number of modified files in all commits $(n_{files} = \sum_{n_f \in \{m_{|f|}(c):c \in \mathbb{C}\}} n_f)$, n_{lines} is the total number of modified lines in all commits $(n_{lines} = \sum_{n_l \in \{m_{|l|}(c):c \in \mathbb{C}\}} n_l)$, and the cardinality of all work kinds $(n_{mk} = |\{m_{mk}(m) : m \in \mathbb{M}\}|)$ encodes the variety of work in a contribution. n_{mk} ranges from 1 to 5 denoting, e.g., if files were only added or only modified $(n_{mk} = 1)$ or if files were added, deleted, renamed, copied, and modified $(n_{mk} = 5)$.

$$c_{contrib} = \tfrac{1}{4} \times c_{|f|}(n_{files}) + c_{l/f}\left(\tfrac{n_{lines}}{n_{files}}\right) + c_{mk}(n_{mk}) + c_{\forall m}(c_{\forall mod}) \quad (4)$$

The modified files complexity model $(c_{|f|})$ and the changed lines per file complexity $(c_{l/f})$ use the same thresholds as the line modification complexity models c_{l+} and c_{l-}, see Eq. 2, and are therefore omitted here. The modification kind complexity (c_{mk}), and the overall modification complexity $(c_{\forall m})$ are computed via the mappings in Eq. 5 and Eq. 6 below.

$$c_{mk}(n) = \begin{cases} low & \text{if } n = 1 \\ moderate & \text{if } n = 2 \\ medium & \text{if } n = 3 \\ elevated & \text{if } n = 4 \\ high & \text{if } n = 5 \end{cases} \quad (5) \qquad c_{\forall m}(n) = \begin{cases} low & \text{if } 0 \le n \le 195 \\ moderate & \text{if } 195 < n \le 390 \\ medium & \text{if } 390 < n \le 781 \\ elevated & \text{if } 781 < n \le 1562 \\ high & \text{if } n > 1562 \end{cases} \quad (6)$$

Computation Example: For brevity, we illustrate calculation of CC on a small contribution to `Gaffer`. Consider ticket gh-2304, which reports a bug on lost status information when certain exceptions are caught and re-raised. The contribution resolving the issue consists of a single commit (291111) that modifies two files, i.e., $n_{files} = 2$. In both files, in total 29 lines are modified $(n_{lines} = 29)$. In the first file 5 lines of a method are replaced by two new lines in one hunk, i.e., $m_{l+}(mod) = 2$, $m_{l-}(mod) = 5$, $m_h(mod) = 1$, and $m_{mth}(mod) = 1$. In the second file 20 lines of a method, and two new import lines are newly added over three hunks, i.e., $m_{l+}(mod) = 22$, $m_{l-}(mod) = 0$, $m_h(mod) = 3$, and $m_{mth}(mod) = 1$. That is, we have one modification (c_{mod_1}) of *low* and another one (c_{mod_2}) of *moderate* modification complexity, see below.

$$c_{mod\_1} = \frac{c_{l+}(2) + c_{l-}(5)) + c_h(1) + c_{mth}(1)}{4} = \frac{1+1+1+1}{4} = \frac{4}{4} = 1 = low$$

$$c_{mod\_2} = \frac{c_{l+}(22) + c_{l-}(0)) + c_h(3) + c_{mth}(1)}{4} = \frac{2+1+2+1}{4} = \frac{6}{4} = 1.5 = moderate \qquad (7)$$

$$\mathbb{K} = [(low, 1), (moderate, 1), (medium, 0), (elevated, 0), (high, 0)]$$

$$c_{\forall mod} = \frac{\sum_{(i,j) \in \mathbb{K}} i^i \times j}{5} = \frac{1^1 \times 1 + 2^2 \times 1 + 3^3 \times 0 + 4^4 \times 0 + 5^5 \times 0}{5} = \frac{5}{5} = 1 = low$$

Since both files exist before the contribution the only modification kind is *modified*, i.e., $n_{mk} = 1$. That leads to a contribution of *low* CC via the final $c_{contrib}$ formula.

$$c_{contrib} = \frac{c_{|f|}(2) + c_{l/f}\left(\frac{29}{2}\right) + c_{mk}(1) + c_{\forall m}(1)}{4} = \frac{4}{4} = \underline{\underline{\textbf{low}}} \tag{8}$$

4   Evaluation

In this section, we evaluate to which degree the CC scores that our tool computes are aligned with human assessment of complexity of selected contributions and we provide results of an initial experiment of distribution of CC scores of all contributions to two open-source case systems.

Case Systems: To evaluate our CC score and for initial experimentation, we need software projects as cases that have publicly available Git repositories and issue trackers so that we can compute CC scores of actual contributions. Furthermore, these cases should be of a certain size and age so that contributions of various complexities exist. Due to our work for the Research Center for Government IT at IT University of Copenhagen, we are interested in studying software that is developed and deployed at public agencies. To identify possible case systems, we manually search Github's list of public agencies that use the platform for development (https://government.github.com/community). There, we identify Gaffer (https://gchq.github.io/gaffer-doc) as a suitable case. It is a graph database, that is created mainly by the British signals intelligence agency GCHQ. A first version of it was open-sourced in 2015 (with 125 releases since then), and the project's issue tracker is available on Github (https://github.com/gchq/Gaffer/issues). Since we cannot identify a software project from the same domain on the mentioned list, we choose Apache Cassandra (https://cassandra.apache.org) as a second case. It is an open-source, distributed, wide-column store, NoSQL DBMS that was originally developed by Facebook [13]. It was open-sourced in 2008 (with 265 releases since then). The project uses Jira (https://issues.apache.org/jira/projects/CASSANDRA) as issue tracker. Both systems are written mainly in Java, are licensed under Apache License 2.0, and their sources are available as Git repositories (https://github.com/gchq/Gaffer, https://github.com/apache/cassandra.

Even though, Gaffer (version 1.9.1) and Cassandra (version 3.9) consist of approximately the same amount of files (2 294 and 2 316 respectively), Cassandra is circa twice as large as Gaffer (588 017 lines with 424 733 LOC versus 291 071 lines with 199 816 LOC). Statistics are generated with the Succinct Code Counter tool (version 2.13.0) https://github.com/boyter/scc.

Dataset Creation: With two Python scripts, we export all tickets, ticket identification keys, ticket resolution dates, etc., from the respective issue trackers. Using our tool, we compute a mapping from ticket identifiers to commits. The mapping is created by matching ticket identifiers via regular expressions in commit messages. For example, the regular expression for Gaffer is

(Gh |gh-)<issue_key>(|$) and for Cassandra it is CASSANDRA-<issue_key>(|$), where <issue_key> is an integer in both cases. We identify these regular expressions by brief manual inspection of the commit histories, and via the contribution guidelines of the respective project. The resulting dataset with all tickets and corresponding contributions contains 2 403 tickets for Gaffer, of which 2 300 are resolved and 820 of these are resolved with contribution, i.e., with at least one commit attached to the respective ticket. For Cassandra, the dataset includes 16 485 tickets, of which 14 158 are resolved, and 7 866 are resolved with contribution. We let our CC tool compute the a CC score for each resolved ticket with contribution from both projects. The resulting datasets are stored as CSV files and are available online (https://raw.githubusercontent.com/HelgeCPH/ contribution-complexity/master/data/cassandra_contrib_compl.csv, https://git hub.com/HelgeCPH/contribution-complexity/blob/master/data/gaffer_contrib_ compl.csv).

For the manual evaluation, see Sect. 4.1, we sample 25 contributions (five from each possible CC score) from Cassandra and 23 for Gaffer (five from each CC score except for *high*, where there are only three contributions). The author of this paper manually classifies the CC scores for each of these 48 contributions, that consist in total of 247 commits. Thereafter, we compare our manually classified CC scores with those created by the tool. The protocols, for this step are available online too (https://github.com/HelgeCPH/contribution-complexity/ blob/master/data/cas_evaluation_tab.md, https://github.com/HelgeCPH/contr ibution-complexity/blob/master/data/gaf_evaluation_tab.md).

Note, the entire experiment setup with dataset creation and data reproduction is automatically reproducible via a Shell script in the experiment directory in the CC tool's repository. We provide a replicable environment specification for a virtual machine on DigitalOcean via a Vagrant file.

4.1 Manual Evaluation Results

In 36 cases (75%) our manual classification is equal to the tool's CC score. For the remaining 25% of the cases, most often (8 cases ≈17%) our assessment is one level higher than the score computed by the tool and in 4 cases (≈8%) the tool's assessment is one level higher than our classification. Discrepancies between our classification and tool's score is actually most frequent around the two scores *moderate* and *medium*. In six cases (12.5%) we assigned a *moderate* CC and the tool a *medium* score or vice versa. The second most frequent discrepancy is between *medium* and *elevated* scores (in 3 cases ≈6%).

That is, our classification differs from the tool's assessment always only by one level and in most cases on those centered around *medium* contribution complexity. Our experience during manual classification, was also that we found it hardest to distinguish complexities on closely related levels. That is, we found coarse-grained assessment into three levels (*low*, *medium*, and *high*) more easy than deciding between more fine-grained five levels of CC.

Threats to Validity: The manual classification of the CC score would likely have been more accurate if performed by developers from the Gaffer and

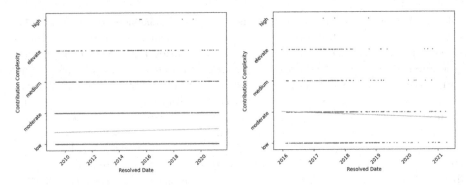

Fig. 2. Development of complexities (CC) of all contributions of Apache `Cassandra` (left) and `Gaffer` (right), with linear regression model (yellow line). (Color figure online)

`Cassandra` projects. Since we do neither know the design or architecture of the systems our assessments are prone to be too high. We try to mitigate this risk by carefully examining each contribution and the corresponding modifications. Our classification might be biased since the author performing it also developed and implemented the CC score. We tried to minimize this risk by running the manual classification first 10 days after the last modification to the CC score, which should be sufficient with regards to memory retention [15].

Here, we evaluate if CC scores correspond to human assessment of complexity of contributions. We do not evaluate to which degree the CC metric assesses the actual complexity of contributions. Even though not a software quality metric, a thorough and more rigid evaluation of the CC metric along the lines of the validation criteria of IEEE 1061 Standard for a Software Quality Metrics Methodology [1], should complement the provided initial evaluation in future.

4.2   Contribution Complexities of Two Open-Source Systems

Figure 2 illustrates the distribution of CC scores over time. Each blue dot is a resolved ticket with contribution (ticket closing times on x-axis). Obviously, the different complexity levels are not equally distributed. Table 1 shows the frequencies of the various complexity levels per system. For `Cassandra`, the amount of contributions with a *low* CC is highest. 67.0% of all contributions possess that complexity and frequencies decrease for higher CC scores. Only five contributions (0.1%) are of *high* CC. For `Gaffer` *moderately* complex contributions are most frequent (44.3%) followed by *low* complexity contributions (35.5%) and from *medium* to *high* frequencies decrease, though with higher ratios compared to `Cassandra`.

The yellow lines in Fig. 2 are linear regression models that should provide an impression of development of CC over time, i.e., if software *"becomes more difficult to evolve"*. For `Cassandra` it suggests that contributions become more complex, whereas for `Gaffer` it suggest the opposite. To accommodate for the

Table 1. Absolute and relative (rounded) frequencies of contribution complexity scores.

	Low	Moderate	Medium	Elevated	High
`Gaffer`	291 35.5%	363 44.3%	91 11.1%	72 8.8%	3 0.4%
`Cassandra`	5 273 67.0%	2 055 26.1%	363 4.6%	170 2.2%	5 0.1%

impact of location of the contributions with *high* CC on the regression models, we also compare the first full year of contributions with the last full year of contributions per system. In 2016, `Gaffer` has 194 contributions with avg. CC 1.91 (*std* 0.91) and median CC *moderate* versus 37 contributions with avg. CC 2.08 (*std* 0.83) and median CC *moderate* in 2020. In 2010, `Cassandra` has 606 contributions with average CC 1.51 (*std* 0.74) and median CC *low* versus 461 contributions with avg. CC 1.59 (*std* 0.73) and median CC *low* in 2020. These numbers suggest, that there is actually a slight increase in CC for less work in both systems.

5 Related Work and Discussion

There exists a plethora of software complexity metrics, see e.g., Zuse's overview [23] over many of them. Usually, these assess internal structural complexity of *programs*, e.g., how many branch points there are [16], how difficult programs are to understand [19], how well structured they are [12], their size [9], etc. Based on these metrics, higher level models are developed, such as, the SIG Maintainability Model (SIG-MM) [8], which combines multiple such complexity metrics to compute a maintainability score for software.

The Contribution Complexity score described in this paper is different to, e.g., the SIG-MM in that it is not constrained to analyzing complexity of source code artifacts. In essence, it is an aggregate of multiple basic size- and frequency-based metrics (number of changed lines per modification/commits, number of hunks per modifications, number of changed files per commits, etc.), which yields useful results for any textual artifacts including configuration files, build scripts, schema files, documentation, etc. The contributions to `Gaffer` and `Cassandra` that we studied (Sect. 4.1) contain modifications of such files. However, computation of CC (Sect. 3) is inspired by SIG-MM [8,22] in that results of basic metrics are aggregated and mapped to a single score.

By counting frequencies of hunks, of changed methods per modification, and number of changed files per commit, our CC includes a measure of entropy. This is similar to Hassan's Code Change Models [7] that consider scattered changes across files to be highly entropic. Hassan equates high entropy changes with *complexity* and our work follows the same reasoning. However, Hassan operates only on the level of file changes. Our approach is more fine-grained since it includes, e.g., number of hunks and number of changed methods. Unlike Hassan, who aims to predict faults from patterns of frequently changing files, we are interested in the complexity of contributions to enable research of software evolution. Also

Hindle et al. [11] compute complexity of changes, i.e., of commits instead of entire systems or modules. They compute the complexity of source code patches (modifications in our terminology) based on indentation-levels of code, which they demonstrate to be similarly expressive as, e.g., McCabe complexity. Our work is similar to Hindle et al. in that we provide a language agnostic and simple –in the sense of underlying basic metrics– solution that operates mostly on syntactic properties of modifications. However, in case a modification's source code is in a supported programming language, our solution incorporates the number of changed methods too.

The Delta Maintainability Model (DMM) by di Biase et al. [5] assesses how much a commit in-/decreases the *maintainability* of a software system, which is based on multiple structural complexity metrics, such as, McCabe complexity, coupling, size, etc., The DMM can be considered an adaptation of SIG-MM [8] to commit level instead of system level. Our CC score is different than both whitespace-complexity [11] and DMM [5] since both of them are concerned about assessing the internal structural complexity of commits. By including entropy measures (number of hunks, changed method/files) our CC score captures complexity of integration work too. Also, Hassan and di Biase et al. study only certain kinds of changes *"Feature Introduction modifications"* and bug fixes, requests for enhancement, and improvements respectively. We consider our CC score more universal since it is applicable to any kind of change including work on documentation, tests, etc., which all are part of the initial experiment in Sect. 4.2.

Unfortunately, CC scores of different systems are currently not directly comparable since our algorithm consumes absolute numbers, see Sect. 3. The main reason for not relying on normalized values yet, is that the absolute numbers of files/methods that would serve as denominator in normalization are not fixed per contribution. They can change with every single modification. Hassan suggests to resort on the number of recently changed files as denominator instead. We consider such time-/period-based normalization future work. Another concern about our CC tool might be that the thresholds of the complexity classification models (c_*) that map input values to discrete scores (Sect. 3) appear arbitrary and do not fit across domains. To mitigate this risk, all these functions are user configurable in the tool and we present in this paper the default models. Similarly, weights of certain aggregation functions may be adapted in the tool.

Implications for Practitioners: Next to this paper, we provide a readily installable open-source tool (usable as Python library and CLI tool), which can be integrated into development processes, e.g., in CI/CD chains, to automatically assess and report on development of CC of contributions to `Git` repositories. That would not only allow for more accurate assessment of which work tasks (tickets) are most difficult to work on and thereby guide potential refactorings but it would also allow to gradually adjust time and effort estimations when planning new tasks that are similar to resolved ones.

Note however, that our tool analyses local `Git` repositories only. It does not have any dependency to platforms like Github of Gitlab and can therefore not assess richer knowledge that might be present there. For example, Github tracks related commits of remote repositories, which cannot be assessed by our tool unless explicitly merged with the respective repository.

Implications for Researchers: With our work it is now possible to study for example Lehman's second law of software evolution [14] or implications of TD [3] *directly*. Previous work, see e.g., [10], studied development of certain internal complexity metrics on successive versions of entire systems or modules and thereby invalidated Lehman's second law of software evolution. But our results for `Gaffer` and `Cassandra` (Sect. 4.2) suggest a slight increase in difficulty of evolving software, i.e., they support Lehman's second law. It would be interesting to replicate previous studies and compare indirect complexity metrics with CC over time to understand if previous results are only due to indirect assessment of complexity.

6   Conclusions

Our goal with this work is to create, implement, and evaluate an algorithm and tool to automatically assesses complexity of contributing a change into an existing software system. We present the Contribution Complexity (CC) algorithm (Sect. 3) and we provide a readily installable tool for it. To evaluate our CC algorithm and tool, we compare the tool computed CC scores of 48 randomly sampled contributions from two open-source systems (`Gaffer` and `Cassandra`) with manually assessed CC scores of the same contributions (Sect. 4). Our results show that in 75% of the cases the automatic assessment matches the human assessment and we interpret the remaining cases to be due to the tool's superiority when assessing finer-grained complexity differences.

To illustrate applicability of our solution, we present an initial empirical analysis of 8 686 contributions from two open-source systems. Our results show that the average CC scores of both systems are slightly increasing with decreasing contribution frequency, which might hint at, that Lehman's second law of software evolution is not invalid when complexity of evolution tasks is directly assessed instead of indirectly as in previous work.

In future work we plan to extend the study of in-/decrease of difficulty of evolution tasks with the help of our CC to identify root causes of TD. Furthermore, we plan to conceptually extend CC to better distinguish inherent complexity of a contribution versus complexity of integration work.

References

1. IEEE Standard for a Software Quality Metrics Methodology. Technical report (1998)
2. Amanatidis, T., Chatzigeorgiou, A.: Studying the evolution of PHP web applications. Inf. Softw. Technol. **72**, 48–67 (2016)
3. Avgeriou, P., Kruchten, P., Ozkaya, I., Seaman, C.: Managing technical debt in software engineering (dagstuhl seminar 16162). In: Dagstuhl Reports, vol. 6. Schloss Dagstuhl-Leibniz-Zentrum fuer Informatik (2016)

4. Basili, V.R.: Qualitative software complexity models: a summary. Tutorial on models and methods for software management and engineering (1980)
5. di Biase, M., Rastogi, A., Bruntink, M., van Deursen, A.: The delta maintainability model: measuring maintainability of fine-grained code changes. In: 2019 IEEE/ACM International Conference on Technical Debt (TechDebt), pp. 113–122. IEEE (2019)
6. Dörner, D.: The Logic of Failure: Recognizing and Avoiding Error in Complex Situations. Merloyd Lawrence Book, Basic Books (1997)
7. Hassan, A.E.: Predicting faults using the complexity of code changes. In: 2009 IEEE 31st International Conference on Software Engineering, pp. 78–88. IEEE (2009)
8. Heitlager, I., Kuipers, T., Visser, J.: A practical model for measuring maintainability. In: 6th International Conference on the Quality of Information and Communications Technology (QUATIC 2007), pp. 30–39. IEEE (2007)
9. Herraiz, I., Hassan, A.E.: Beyond lines of code: do we need more complexity metrics? Making Software: What Really Works, and Why We Believe It, pp. 125–141 (2010)
10. Herraiz, I., Rodriguez, D., Robles, G., Gonzalez-Barahona, J.M.: The evolution of the laws of software evolution: a discussion based on a systematic literature review. ACM Comput. Surv. (CSUR) **46**(2), 1–28 (2013)
11. Hindle, A., Godfrey, M.W., Holt, R.C.: Reading beside the lines: indentation as a proxy for complexity metric. In: 2008 16th IEEE International Conference on Program Comprehension, pp. 133–142. IEEE (2008)
12. Hitz, M., Montazeri, B.: Measuring coupling and cohesion in object-oriented systems. Citeseer (1995)
13. Lakshman, A., Malik, P.: Cassandra: a decentralized structured storage system. ACM SIGOPS Oper. Syst. Rev. **44**(2), 35–40 (2010)
14. Lehman, M.M., Fernández-Ramil, J.C.: Rules and tools for software evolution planning and management. Softw. Evol. Feedback 539–560 (2006)
15. Loftus, G.R.: Evaluating forgetting curves. J. Exp. Psychol. Learn. Mem. Cogn. **11**(2), 397 (1985)
16. McCabe, T.J.: A complexity measure. IEEE Trans. Softw. Eng. **4**, 308–320 (1976)
17. Miller, G.A.: The magical number seven, plus or minus two: some limits on our capacity for processing information. Psychol. Rev. **63**(2), 81 (1956)
18. Rios, N., de Mendonça Neto, M.G., Spínola, R.O.: A tertiary study on technical debt: types, management strategies, research trends, and base information for practitioners. Inf. Softw. Technol. **102**, 117–145 (2018)
19. Shao, J., Wang, Y.: A new measure of software complexity based on cognitive weights. Can. J. Electr. Comput. Eng. **28**(2), 69–74 (2003)
20. Spadini, D., Aniche, M., Bacchelli, A.: Pydriller: python framework for mining software repositories. In: Proceedings of the 2018 26th ACM Joint Meeting on European Software Engineering Conference and Symposium on the Foundations of Software Engineering, pp. 908–911 (2018)
21. Tamrakar, R., Jørgensen, M.: Does the use of Fibonacci numbers in planning poker affect effort estimates? (2012)
22. Visser, J., Rigal, S., van der Leek, R., van Eck, P., Wijnholds, G.: Building Maintainable Software, Java Edition: Ten Guidelines for Future-Proof Code. 1st edn. O'Reilly Media Inc. (2016)
23. Zuse, H.: Software Complexity: Measures and Methods, vol. 4. Walter de Gruyter GmbH & Co KG (1991)

Process Modeling, Improvement and Assessment

Scrum for Safety: Agile Development in Safety-Critical Software Systems

Riccardo Carbone[ID], Salvatore Barone[(✉)][ID], Mario Barbareschi[ID], and Valentina Casola[ID]

Department of Electrical Engineering and Information Technologies, University of Naples Federico II, Via Claudio, 21, 80125 Naples, Italy
ric.carbone@studenti.unina.it, {salvatore.barone, mario.barbareschi,valentina.casola}@unina.it

Abstract. The adoption of agile methodologies in all domains of software development is a desired goal. Unfortunately, many obstacles have been meet in the past for a full adoption in secure and safe systems, where different standards and operational constraints apply. In this paper we propose a novel agile methodology to be applied in the development of safety critical systems. In particular, we developed an extension of the well-known Scrum methodology and discussed the complete workflow. We finally validated the applicability of the methodology over a real case study from the railway domain.

Keywords: Agile software development · Agile processes · Software development · Safety-critical software systems

1 Introduction

The adoption of agile methodologies has been introduced in different domains to improve the management of software development life-cycle, and to considerably reduce the time to market. In spite of its advantages, it still encounters obstacles when referring to secure and safe systems, where the adoption of automatic tools to design, develop, test and continuously integrate components is conflicting with the need of coping with strict standards that mainly refer to traditional waterfall models.

Indeed, some pioneering works concerning the adoption of agile methods in the safety-critical domain concluded, hastily, that the former and the latter are incompatible [4,15]. Nevertheless, more recent results questioned this conclusion, identifying four main challenges inherently arising while adopting agile methods in the safety-critical context, i.e.: (i) documentation, since it is not essential in agile software development; (ii) requirements, since traditional safety-critical development processes discourage requirement changes [25]; (iii) project life-cycle, since safety-critical projects are developed neither iteratively nor incrementally [12], and (iv) testing, which, in the safety-critical context, is done only at final stages of the development [18].

© Springer Nature Switzerland AG 2021
A. C. R. Paiva et al. (Eds.): QUATIC 2021, CCIS 1439, pp. 127–140, 2021.
https://doi.org/10.1007/978-3-030-85347-1_10

As for the adoption of agile methodologies in the development of secure systems, authors in [3] introduced a novel methodology to extend the DevOps approach towards systems secure systems. They mainly implemented an automated security-by-design approach that can be easily mapped with the well-known Scrum methodology.

In this paper, we propose an extension of the Scrum agile methodology, namely Scrum for Safety (S4S), to guide and help research & development groups involved in the design and development of safe solutions in the railway domain. In this domain, the software development is not linear as expected, yet the output of a regular mediation between multiple stakeholders, heterogeneous complex technologies and mandatory regulations to be satisfied. Therefore, an agile-based process instead of a classical waterfall has been developed.

The reminder of this paper is structured as follows. In Sect. 2 we review the current state of the art. In Sect. 3 we present our novel proposal for the adoption of Scrum in the development of safe software. In Sect. 4 we illustrate the applicability of our methodology over a real case-study from the railway domain. Finally, in Sect. 5 we will discuss some conclusions and future work.

2   Related Works

With regards to the obstacles identified in the scientific literature, documentation is considered one of the major obstacles hindering the adoption of agile methods in the safety-critical context [19,21,29]. Indeed, regulatory agencies responsible for inspecting of software do not agree to less documentation of software requirements and design [31], as the limited focus on documentation makes cumbersome to determine the quality of systems [32]. The scientific literature, however, empirically proved that the documentation is not a problem, since agile processes strive to deliver what is requested by the customer, which includes documentation to prove the safety in the case of safety-critical software [11,19]. In addition, in order to keep the documentation at a minimum, the purpose of the documentation itself must be taken into account, determining which knowledge needs to be expressed [14,21].

Testing is yet another aspect that seriously limits the adoption of agile methods in the safety critical context, since incorporating verification techniques is challenging, and these activities are work intensive [26]. Indeed, while test-driven development is widely used in the agile community [24], in safety-critical software development, instead, testing is done only in the final phases [18]. Moreover, some standards, such as the CENELEC EN50128 [7], mandate that the testers must be responsible for specifying the test and that developers and testers must be separate persons [17]. This is in contrast with test-driven development, which require developers to write the tests themselves. The scientific literature reports examples of safety-critical software development in which test-first processes have been implemented successfully [9,13]. In [30], for instance, authors proposed a test-aware development process: test developers are involved in the development of requirements, in order to ensure that the latter are testable at the needed level. This allows mitigating the risk of requirement changes due to untestable requirements being identified only during the testing phase of a program.

Over time, the experiences of individual work groups flowed into more articulate and better formalized methodologies, such as R-Scrum [10] and Safe-Scrum [16]. The latter represents the result of a theoretical work in which Scrum has been brought into compliance with various standards in the critical systems world, including the IEC 61508 [8] and the CENELEC EN 50128. Recently, this agile development methodology has been profitably used in a variety of contexts, including military [2,20], railway [23] and aerospace [28]. However, we consider still insufficient the current empirical evidence on agile benefits in critical contexts. Therefore, in this paper, we describe our novel methodology, showing its impact on a complex case study in the railway environment.

3 Scrum for Safety

Scrum for Safety (S4S) aims to guide and help research & development groups involved in the exploration of effective, efficient and safe solutions in the railway domain. Nevertheless, it can be adopted in every domain in which safety must be taken into account. Indeed, in the R&D context, software development is not a linear and graceful activity, rather the output of a regular mediation between multiple actors, various complex technologies and strict regulations to satisfy. Therefore, an agile-based process allows engineers to rapidly explore and validate every single possibility before taking any crucial decision.

In this Section, we provide the reader with full details concerning our proposed methodology, including its principles, roles and workflow.

3.1 Principles

S4S embraces all the agile core principles and Scrum values [27], yet extends them with some new objectives, which are derived from critical software requirements. Results of this extension are the following eight principles, which constitutes the main base of the development process:

1. *Cover all the alternatives before making some decision*: all architectural or detailed design decisions must be preceded by an in-depth evaluation of all possible options. Valuable solutions could be cut-off if one restricts and focus its attention on a single alternative;
2. *Experiment and fail frequently*: the best way to evaluate the effect of a single design choice is to try it, and potentially fail. System modeling and simulation are good tools, but research groups have also to implement and test their solutions on target architectures and operative conditions to prove their real effectiveness;
3. *Deliver software continuously to the users*: as soon as the research started to produce partially implemented software architectures, principal financiers have to begin a review of the achieved results. This is one of the core values of agile where the stakeholders have a central role in the development process [1];

4. *Integrate software continuously with other actors*: large and complex projects are frequently broken into small and much more controllable ones. In that case, coordination and periodic integration activities between the various research groups could anticipate a great number of subsequent incompatibilities among the developed subsystems;

5. *Continuously V&V (Verify and Validate)*: in order to release software in critical environments, where a single failure could potentially cause loss of human lives, environmental pollution or huge economic losses, each developed subsystem must be meticulously verified and validated. Verification & Validation (V&V) are two core activities for Software Quality Assurance (SQA): they must be done to increase our trust that the developed product satisfies its specification, and it is adequate to resolve the original research purpose. Furthermore, V&V activities have to be applied continuously, possibly when the research work reaches a new development step, in order to rapidly identify and manage deviations that could affect critical properties, such as security and safety;

6. *Make your work traceable*: a trace of all the done work for the currently developed software must be always present and available to researchers. In that way, all the principal design decision and software architecture are visible, and they determine the basis for the subsequent work. Moreover, it constitutes the only way to prove to an independent *Assessor* how the risks related to software functionalities were identified and mitigated. Otherwise, it is impossible to observe and appreciate the fundamental design choices for the final product;

7. *Let your approach be risk-based*: finding, covering and monitoring risks related to software functionalities constitutes a vital activity for critical software. A risk-based approach is much more effective than a "no one", since it explicitly identifies and addresses all the software failures which could cause tangible damages to people or to the environment;

8. *Don't break or lose the already achieved quality*: as the work proceeds, and the SQA techniques improve its internal and external quality, it becomes essential to preserve it. In particular, new requested changes to the software must not conflict or undermine the already done risk management activities and software implemented functions.

3.2   Roles and Workflow

Principal roles and workflow of S4S take into account the requirements described in the CENELEC EN50126 [5], EN50128 [7], EN50129 [6] standards.

Roles. Table 1 reports the professional figures described in CENELEC standards. It is pretty noticeable that the Scrum basic roles of *Product Owner*, *Scrum Master* and *Development Team* [27] fit perfectly with figures related to software development, i.e. *Requirements Managers*, *Designers* and *Implementers*, while others not frequently mentioned roles – like *Managers* – correspond for responsibilities to *Project Managers*.

Despite this evident matching, the Scrum framework does not provide any professional independent figure related to the SQA process [27]. Therefore, since the central role that SQA has for critical software, *Verifiers*, *Validators* and *Assessors* roles have to introduced, in order to be able to check for software technical quality, and its adequacy to the original problem. In particular, S4S extends the set of Scrum roles with these figures, which are strictly related to critical software development, while adapting their activity in an agile perspective. Thus, as we will observe after, V&V and Assessment activities are potentially executed after the end of each Sprint, providing rapid identification of possibly compliance and safety issues.

Another fundamental point regards the independence of *Integrators* and *Testers* from software implementation. Although in the CENELEC standards domain, tests written by programmers could be accepted by the *Verifier* whether they are adequate and completely specified [7], verification independence is considered crucial for safety-critical products. Therefore, S4S prescribes that during each Sprint, the same person can not cover both development and verification activities. In that way, developers will not influence testers or integrators judgment.

Workflow. The S4S workflow is constructed on the Scrum key concepts of iterative development and time-boxed sprints [27]. Moreover, it enriches the single iteration with a set of activities that empower researchers with fine-grained control on quality of developed software. Indeed, Scrum is a general framework that was born to be adapted to the specific needs of a single user [27].

Many techniques have been discovered and analyzed in literature during the last years to make an agile process much safer. Two noticeable works are Safe-Scrum [16,22,23,29] and R-Scrum [10], from which we started to reach the more depth concept of safe-sprint depicted in Fig. 1.

In S4S, the starting point of all successive Safe-Sprints is not an isolated and self-contained Product-Backlog, rather a strongly linked one to the parent project. The software product constitutes, in fact, only a single part of a large industrial railway project, which inherits from the latter a set of well-defined functional and non-functional responsibilities. Making the Backlog stories traceable to the global *System Requirements Specification* and the *Hazard Analysis Report* becomes the only way to prove how those responsibilities were designed and implemented. Therefore, researchers, as in Safe-Scrum, have to distinguish user stories related to safety concerns and maintain two traceability matrices. The first one must show how each requirement was divided into a set of user stories and how they were implemented. The second, instead, serves to prove that all identified safety stories cover all the most crucial and not negligible hazards. Only once the research team has produced a strongly linked backlog, Safe-Sprints can be planned and implemented.

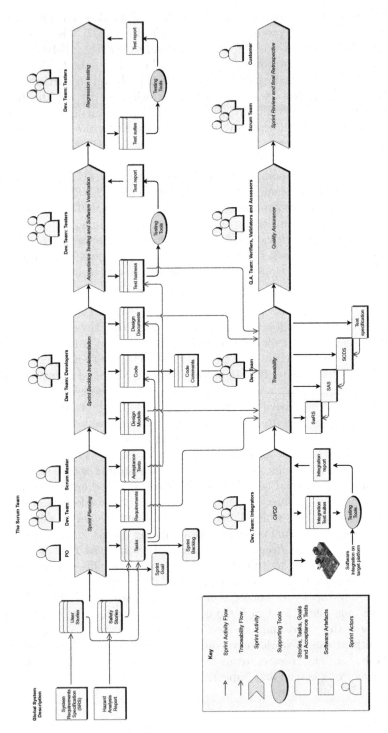

Fig. 1. S4S workflow

Table 1. CENELEC standards defined roles

Role	Responsibilities
Project Manager	Creating the development team; Defining the project scheduling and milestones; Overseeing the respect of the defined schedules; Monitoring the quality of the produced software
Requirements Manager	Managing the requirements engineering process; Specify the software requirements
Designer	Select the design principles, techniques and tools; Specify the software architecture
Implementer	Transform the software design in code; Applying a coding standard; Maintain the codebase under version control; Integrate the software with the target hardware
Configuration Manager	Managing all the defined software configurations
Tester	Managing the software testing process; Select the testing techniques and tools; Communicate any observed deviation of software from its specification to the "Change Management Body"
Integrator	Managing the software integration process; Specify a set of test suites for each integration activity; Communicate any observed deviation of software from its specification to the "Change Management Body"
Verifier	Overseeing the software verification process; Check the adequacy of the testing and integration processes to the verification objectives; Guarantee the independence of the verification process; Communicate any observed deviation of software from its specification to the "Change Management Body"
Validator	Validate the software requirements specification; Check the compliance of the development process with the CENELEC standards; Check the correctness and consistency of the verification process; Check the existence and correctness of a unique trace between the requirements and the software implementation; Check that all the hazard are classified, identified and correctly mitigated; Communicate any identified problem to the "Change Management Body"
Assessor	Check the conformity of the developed software and the adopted development process with the CENELEC standards; Verifying the adequacy of the V&V; Verifying the organization personnel competence; Verifying the correctness of the software quality assurance process adopted; Verifying the correctness of the configuration management process adopted; Check that all the hazard are classified, identified and correctly mitigated

As depicted in the Fig. 1, researchers have to begin with *Sprint Planning*. Here, the objective remains the same as in Scrum, i.e. to select a group of manageable and most important user stories (the Sprint Goal), and refine them into a set of more detailed tasks, distributed across the development team (Sprint Backlog) [27].

Planning is then followed by the *Sprint Implementation* phase, which represents the research practical part beginning. During that phase, the team must experiment and fail to explore and try all the available design alternatives. Researchers have to evaluate every single valuable solution, otherwise, they could discard a more efficient one. Moreover, every single task derived from a single user story and related design, implementation and testing artifacts must be linked together. This third trace is essential, since it actually enables in-depth inspections on how single user stories were implemented and verified.

Another remarkable aspect during the *Sprint Implementation* phase is to make the subsequent testing and verification activities independent from all the design consideration. In S4S, we prescribe that during a Safe-Sprint, people can not cover both development and testing activities. Therefore, the team splits into two groups, the first one formed by developers and the second with testers and integrators, preventing potential verification conflicts. This division spans until all testing and integration stages end.

After that, the two presented groups will work in parallel, so when the implementation is finished, verification of the newly implemented features could begin. Here, the *Acceptance Testing and Software Verification* phase take place: testers check whether all the selected user stories are correctly implemented and software behaviors as expected. Other techniques, such as static analysis and formal methods, may be employed by testers if they retain it useful. Nevertheless, for Safety Integrity Level (SIL) 3 & 4 software systems, combining testing with one of these techniques is strictly required.

After user stories were accepted and tested, a typical Scrum Sprint generally ends. However, for critical software research projects, there are other fundamental needed steps.

Firstly, although user stories added to the Sprint Goal have been tracked and verified, there is no confirmation that they did not adversely impact the already available features and covered hazards. Thus, a subsequent *Regression Testing* step becomes vital in order to preserve the already achieved technical quality. That activity, differently from the expectations, is straightforward to realize into the context of an iterative development process. Indeed, already planned tests may be reused without the need of producing new code. Furthermore, integrators have to realize a complete stage of *Continuous Integration and Deployment (CI/CD)* to check that software preserves its quality on the selected target architectures.

The second step is to provide a *Taceability* phase during which all the Development Team contributes to update the software specification documents with the newly discovered observations. Indeed, the research purpose is not to produce a vendible product, but guidelines to construct it. In that way, documents could be employed multiple times to create an engineered version of the final product and prove its functional safety. By default, S4S adopts the set of documents described in the CENELEC standards for railway signaling. Anyway, needed documents can be adapted depending on the developed product.

Finally, there is a last essential phase of *Quality Assurance*, which implements the Continuous V&V concept described in the literature. Letting an independent group of *Verifiers, Validator,* and *Assessors,* to check the produced increment against the software requirements specification, and the applicable standards allows to identify and rapidly correct any critical violation. Ideally, the output of each Sprint could be potentially released to the final user. However, the reality is quite different. In most cases, research groups are small, and SQA experts, if available, can review the work on a timeline of months, not weeks. Therefore, in S4S this phase could be also planned after a group of Sprints, and possibly exploiting automatic SQA tools and external experts, if any.

After the Quality Assurance phase ends, the Safe-Sprint terminates with the Scrum known activities of *Review* and *Retrospective.*

4   A Case Study

In order to evaluate the impact of S4S, observing its main effects on a very highly complex research product with changeable requirements, we adopted our proposed methodology in the context of a real-world safety-critical product, owned by one of the most important Italian company in the railway domain. Concerning complexity, the software exhibits some technical difficulties due to the presence of (i) SIL 4 safety functions, (ii) constrained embedded targets and (iii) many different deployment platforms. For what pertains to changes in requirements, the entire project is continuously subjected to the vast plethora of platform technologies, and requirements imposed from research groups developing other crucial parts of the global system.

In order to address these challenges, we did ten Safe-Sprints, completing 38 user stories from a Product Backlog of 126 (30%). This allowed us to get some important considerations, which we briefly report in the following.

The first consideration pertains to Sprint duration. We deemed a time interval between either 3 or 4 weeks to be a good thread-off between achieved software quality and frequent releases. This choice correlates to the scheduling of activities pertaining Sprints of 3 weeks, which is the following:

1. in the first week, we define and implement the Sprint Backlog, including the code for successive testing activities;
2. the second week is split in two parts: (i) in the first part, we execute the developed tests for every user story and do non-regression checks. Here, we used to employ an automatic testing framework to speed up the entire process; (ii) in the last part, we update software requirements and architecture with all the captured observations in order to be ready for the Quality Assurance phase;
3. during the third week, we release the product to our customer experts in order to check its quality with V&V activities. However, if they are not available,

we will use only automatic tools to check and extract quality metrics from code. We, then, review all the done work with our final customer, updating the Product Backlog with all feedback and finally proceed with the Sprint Retrospective. Here, we discuss how to pass-over some obstacles appeared during the development.

Sprints of 4 weeks are almost the same and imply only a longer time for SQA.

As one could observe, we typically spend two or three weeks to guarantee that potential hazards are adequately covered, and that software performs as expected without dangerous side-effects. Automatic tools could help to reduce this time, but quality assurance investments must not be eliminated or shrank. Otherwise, we risk to adversely impact product safety. Thus, the S4S adoption had the first effect to lay down Sprint duration, due to risk-related reasons.

The second consideration pertains to sustainable documentation. S4S, in fact, revisits the purpose and the use of software specifications by stopping to consider them as a driver of the development process, rather documentation is one of its main outputs. Moving away from this classical document-driven philosophy substantially reduced the quantity of documentation rework, since theoretic and unproved decisions do not need to be documented. Therefore, although formal specifications had an intrinsic long time to be written, the process avoids investing time on not yet verified solutions.

The third observation focuses on tests: by continuously testing the product, avoiding relegating the verification only at the last part of the development cycle, S4S allows to rapidly discover errors, and to correct them before their fixing-cost would explode. Moreover, by investing efforts in automatic tools and testing framework, tests written for a certain user story can be reused to check for non-regressions. Thus, we consider continuous testing as one of the main benefits of the iterative development, which our process inherits and enforces with independent testing activities. In Table 2 and Table 3 we report the percentages of testable and completely covered requirements as the achieved results for code lines and branches. Please kindly note that, although the actual coverage percentage has to be increased to become acceptable, the adoption of an iterative approach ensures that coverage increases as far as new users stories, functionalities and tests are defined and implemented in successive sprints.

Table 2. Software requirements coverage data

	Total number of requirements	Totale number of testable requirements
Value	94	63
% of coverage	32,98% (31/94)	49,21% (31/63)
% of fully covered	19,15% (18/94)	28,57% (18/63)
% of partially covered	13,83% (13/94)	20,63% (13/63)

Table 3. Code coverage data extracted with gcov

Software components	Line coverage		Functions		Branches	
COMP.A	76,8%	383/505	75,0%	45/60	46,3%	174/384
COMP.B	71,4%	65/91	75,0%	6/8	32,8%	19/56
COMP.C	84,4%	81/96	100,0%	4/4	58,2%	33/55
COMP.D	48,8%	184/377	46,2%	12/26	41,1%	60/146
COMP.E	0,0%	0/10	0,0%	0/2	–	0/0
COMP.F	92,5%	74/80	100,0%	6/6	78,7%	37/47
COMP.G	30,5%	102/334	33,3%	7/21	76,3%	45/59
Total	**59,54%**	**889/1493**	**62,99%**	**80/127**	**49,26%**	**368/747**

The last remarkable point concerns requirements change. As mentioned, software requirements may be subject to changes due to our customer, platform technologies and other research groups. As for the first ones, they typically start introducing new requirements as soon as their comprehension of software improves. As for the seconds, they follow the floating market trends, which must be taken into account during the long development time characterizing critical software. As for research groups, they eventually introduce new requirements in order to accommodate their specific product functions.

In this situation, even inside a strongly regulated environment, the agile core mindset of S4S demonstrated to remain an effective tool for uncertain problem solution. Thanks to frequent reviews and releases, our customer and other involved teams became an integrative part of the development workflow, contributing to stabilizing software requirements. Also, by not planning all future sprints, we always reserved the possibility to accept some new features and technological changes, absorbing market trends. However, for each change, we had to pay a cost to update our formal specifications, which had to reflect the research state of work, in order to enable successive quality assurance activities.

In conclusion, we could state that the S4S iterative development is not less safe than the classical V-model, since:

1. CENELEC documentation, required to prove the safety of the final product, is equally produced. Indeed, not specifying unverified solutions only reduces rework activities;
2. Continuous V&V and Traceability activities incrementally increase the team trust in achieved product quality. Indeed, people become much more reactive in discovering bugs and critical violation of applicable standards;
3. Requirements change is accepted and taken into account by (i) directly involving customers and other teams in the development process and (ii) experiment frequently with new technologies.

5 Conclusion

In this paper, we proposed an extension of the Scrum agile methodology, namely S4S, suitable to guide and help the design and development of software components in safety-critical domains, in particular, in the railway domain. We discussed S4S in full details, including its principles, roles and workflow. Furthermore, in order to evaluate the methodology, we report a case-study on a real, highly complex safety-critical research product with changeable requirements, which represents a typical situation for research groups.

The reported case study highlighted that S4S (i) enables iterative and evolutive development of safety-critical software, even if architecture and/or requirements need to be refined, (ii) allows documentation to be produced – and kept updated – as an output of the entire process, and (iii) makes the entire process much more safe and reactive w.r.t human errors.

Therefore, from these conclusions, we could state that the agile mindset remains effective in a critical context if it embraces all its values in terms of quality. Nevertheless, this paper only constitutes a starting point: we are bound to apply S4S in other different critical research projects, even those involving third-party and/or legacy software components, in order to add new tools and techniques that would increase its current efficiency and safety.

References

1. Beck, K., et al.: Manifesto for agile software development (2001). http://www.agilemanifesto.org/
2. Benedicenti, L., et al.: Applying scrum to the army: a case study. In: Proceedings of the 38th International Conference on Software Engineering Companion, pp. 725–727 (2016). https://doi.org/10.1145/2889160.2892652
3. Casola, V., Benedictis, A.D., Rak, M., Villano, U.: A novel security-by-design methodology: modeling and assessing security by SLAs with a quantitative approach. J. Syst. Softw. **163**, 110537 (2020). https://doi.org/10.1016/j.jss.2020.110537
4. Cawley, O., Wang, X., Richardson, I.: Lean/Agile software development methodologies in regulated environments – state of the art. In: Abrahamsson, P., Oza, N. (eds.) LESS 2010. LNBIP, vol. 65, pp. 31–36. Springer, Heidelberg (2010). https://doi.org/10.1007/978-3-642-16416-3_4
5. Européen de normalisation en électronique et en électrotechnique (CENELEC), C.: Railway applications the specification and demonstration of reliability, availability, maintainability and safety (rams). Standard, Comité européen de normalisation en électronique et en électrotechnique (CENELEC) (1999)
6. Européen de normalisation en électronique et en électrotechnique (CENELEC), C.: Railway application - communications, signaling and processing systems - safety related electronic systems for signaling. Standard, Comité européen de normalisation en électronique et en électrotechnique (CENELEC) (2003)
7. Européen de normalisation en électronique et en électrotechnique (CENELEC), C.: Railway applications - communication, signalling and processing systems - software for railway control and protection systems. Standard, Comité européen de normalisation en électronique et en électrotechnique (CENELEC) (2011)

8. International Electrotechnical Commision: Functional safety of electrical/electronic/programmable electronic safety-related systems. Standard, International Electrotechnical Commision (2010)
9. Drobka, J., Noftz, D., Raghu, R.: Piloting XP on four mission-critical projects. IEEE Softw. **21**(6), 70–75 (2004). https://doi.org/10.1109/MS.2004.47
10. Fitzgerald, B., Stol, K., O'Sullivan, R., O'Brien, D.: Scaling agile methods to regulated environments: an industry case study. In: 2013 35th International Conference on Software Engineering (ICSE), pp. 863–872 (2013). https://doi.org/10.1109/ICSE.2013.6606635
11. Gary, K., et al.: Agile methods for open source safety-critical software. Softw. Pract. Exp. **41**(9), 945–962 (2011). https://doi.org/10.1002/spe.1075
12. Ge, X., Paige, R.F., McDermid, J.A.: An iterative approach for development of safety-critical software and safety arguments. In: 2010 Agile Conference, pp. 35–43. IEEE (2010). https://doi.org/10.1109/AGILE.2010.10
13. Górski, J., Łukasiewicz, K.: Towards agile development of critical software. In: Gorbenko, A., Romanovsky, A., Kharchenko, V. (eds.) SERENE 2013. LNCS, vol. 8166, pp. 48–55. Springer, Heidelberg (2013). https://doi.org/10.1007/978-3-642-40894-6_4
14. Grenning, J.: Launching extreme programming at a process-intensive company. IEEE Softw. **18**(6), 27–33 (2001). https://doi.org/10.1109/52.965799
15. Hajou, A., Batenburg, R., Jansen, S.: How the pharmaceutical industry and agile software development methods conflict: a systematic literature review. In: 2014 14th International Conference on Computational Science and Its Applications, pp. 40–48. IEEE (2014). https://doi.org/10.1109/ICCSA.2014.19
16. Hanssen, G., Stålhane, T., Myklebust, T.: SafeScrum® - Agile Development of Safety-Critical Software. Springer, Heidelberg (2018). https://doi.org/10.1007/978-3-319-99334-8
17. Jonsson, H., Larsson, S., Punnekkat, S.: Agile practices in regulated railway software development. In: 2012 IEEE 23rd International Symposium on Software Reliability Engineering Workshops, pp. 355–360. IEEE (2012). https://doi.org/10.1109/ISSREW.2012.80
18. McCaffery, F., Trektere, K., Ozcan-Top, O.: Agile – is it suitable for medical device software development? In: Clarke, P.M., O'Connor, R.V., Rout, T., Dorling, A. (eds.) SPICE 2016. CCIS, vol. 609, pp. 417–422. Springer, Cham (2016). https://doi.org/10.1007/978-3-319-38980-6_30
19. McHugh, M., McCaffery, F., Casey, V.: Barriers to adopting agile practices when developing medical device software. In: Mas, A., Mesquida, A., Rout, T., O'Connor, R.V., Dorling, A. (eds.) SPICE 2012. CCIS, vol. 290, pp. 141–147. Springer, Heidelberg (2012). https://doi.org/10.1007/978-3-642-30439-2_13
20. Messina, A., Fiore, F., Ruggiero, M., Ciancarini, P., Russo, D.: A new agile paradigm for mission-critical software development. CrossTalk **29**(6), 25–30 (2016)
21. Misra, S.C., Kumar, V., Kumar, U.: Identifying some critical changes required in adopting agile practices in traditional software development projects. Int. J. Qual. Reliabil. Manage. (2010). https://doi.org/10.1108/02656711011035147
22. Myklebust, T., Stålhane, T., Hanssen, G.: Important considerations when applying other models than the waterfall/V-model when developing software according to IEC 61508 or EN 50128. Technical report, Norwegian University of Science and Technology and SINTEF Digital/Software Engineering, Safety and Security, August 2015. https://doi.org/10.13140/RG.2.1.4739.2480

23. Myklebust, T., Stålhane, T., Lyngby, N.: Application of an agile development process for EN50128/railway conformant software. In: Safety and Reliability of Complex Engineered Systems, September 2015. https://doi.org/10.1201/b19094-529
24. Nerur, S., Mahapatra, R., Mangalaraj, G.: Challenges of migrating to agile methodologies. Commun. ACM **48**(5), 72–78 (2005). https://doi.org/10.1145/1060710.1060712
25. Notander, J.P., Runeson, P., Höst, M.: A model-based framework for flexible safety-critical software development: a design study. In: Proceedings of the 28th Annual ACM Symposium on Applied Computing, pp. 1137–1144 (2013). https://doi.org/10.1145/2480362.2480575
26. Paige, R.F., Charalambous, R., Ge, X., Brooke, P.J.: Towards agile engineering of high-integrity systems. In: Harrison, M.D., Sujan, M.-A. (eds.) SAFECOMP 2008. LNCS, vol. 5219, pp. 30–43. Springer, Heidelberg (2008). https://doi.org/10.1007/978-3-540-87698-4_6
27. Rubin, K.S.: Essential Scrum: A Practical Guide to the Most Popular Agile Process. 1st edn. Addison-Wesley Professional (2012)
28. Smith, J., Bradbury, J., Hayes, W., Deadrick, W.: Agile approach to assuring the safety-critical embedded software for NASA's orion spacecraft. In: 2019 IEEE Aerospace Conference, pp. 1–10. IEEE (2019). https://doi.org/10.1109/AERO.2019.8742095
29. Stålhanea, T., Myklebustb, T., Hanssenb, G.: The application of safe scrum to IEC 61508 certifiable software, pp. 6052–6061. Curran, Associates, Inc. (2012)
30. VanderLeest, S.H., Buter, A.: Escape the waterfall: agile for aerospace. In: 2009 IEEE/AIAA 28th Digital Avionics Systems Conference, pp. 6-D. IEEE (2009). https://doi.org/10.1109/DASC.2009.5347438
31. Vogel, D.: Agile methods: most are not ready for prime time in medical device software design and development. DesignFax Online 2006 (2006)
32. Wolff, S.: Scrum goes formal: agile methods for safety-critical systems. In: 2012 First International Workshop on Formal Methods in Software Engineering: Rigorous and Agile Approaches (formsera), pp. 23–29. IEEE (2012). https://doi.org/10.1109/FormSERA.2012.6229784

Empirical Evaluation of Agile Teamwork

Paolo Ciancarini[1,2]([✉]) [ID], Marcello Missiroli[1] [ID], and Sofia Zani[1] [ID]

[1] University of Bologna, Bologna, Italy
`paolo.ciancarini@unibo.it`
[2] Innopolis University, Innopolis, Russia

Abstract. During the fall 2020 we observed and tracked several student teams working remotely and independently to develop a non-trivial software product as the capstone project for a course of Software Engineering in our university. The teams used an integrated open-source development environment that we designed to be useful to support and measure Agile development efforts, storing all artifacts and logging productivity and interaction data. Moreover, teams were required to use the Essence visual language during the retrospectives in order to analyze and improve their Scrum-like process. The tools used by the teams were used to store and collect several process data, that post-mortem were also integrated by the answers given by the students to some questionnaires. This paper proposes an empirical evaluation of the process followed by the teams, using a teamwork quality model and an Agile maturity model. The two models highlight different facets of the teamwork. We have studied and compared the development and interaction activities of the teams, and found a correlation between the results of the two models.

Keywords: Agile · Essence · Teamwork quality

1 Introduction

Traditionally, undergraduate student projects are either personal or group-based. It is possible to assign a project to a whole class seen as a unique group, but it requires a quite complex organization [2,32].

In Software Engineering courses, student projects are usually team-based; the evaluation of the result is often based on the quality of the process enacted by the team, including the quality of the teamwork [21].

If there are several teams developing independently and in parallel, the task of the instructors is complex, because they need to track and compare the progress of all the teams. This problem is well known, and in literature some tool-based solutions have been proposed, see for instance TeamScope [10].

During the fall 2020 we observed and tracked 21 student teams working remotely and independently to develop a non-trivial software product as the capstone project for our course of Software Engineering at the University of Bologna. The teams used the Compositional Agile System (CAS for short), an

© Springer Nature Switzerland AG 2021
A. C. R. Paiva et al. (Eds.): QUATIC 2021, CCIS 1439, pp. 141–155, 2021.
https://doi.org/10.1007/978-3-030-85347-1_11

integrated open-source development environment we built and useful to support and measure team-based Agile development efforts [4]. The Agile Manifesto minimized the importance of both processes and tools, in fact the first of the four Agile values says: *"(...we have come to value...) Individuals and interactions over processes and tools"*. The issue of effective interactions is especially important for a successful teamwork [18]. However most Agile developments in COVID-19 pandemic required the usage of tools to organize remote work and to support interactions of team members, who all worked at home. It was also important to stress the process rules - we used Scrum - as a way of making the teams more cohesive and self-organizing.

In order to support the teamwork, the teams practiced some team building activities before and during the project. In fact, we devoted some care to the topic of team building, as there was no chance of face-to-face, colocated collaboration due to the pandemic sanitary rules applied in our country. We have chosen to train students to the Scrum process model using a serious game called Scrumble[1], that could be played remotely and self-evaluated by the students. Moreover, teams were required to use the Essence visual language during the retrospectives in order to analyze and improve their Scrum-like process [9]. We hoped that the use of Essence cards could support the recording of retrospective analysis. In fact, each retrospective had to prepare an Essence-based report discussing eventual problems met during the sprint and which remedies should be introduced in the next sprint.

This paper proposes an empirical evaluation of the process followed by the teams, using a teamwork quality model and an Agile maturity model. The two models highlight different facets of the teamwork. We discuss the development and interaction activities of the teams and study the correlation between the results of the two models.

The structure of this paper is the following: in Sect. 2 we summarize some works related to our approach; in Sect. 3 we present the experiment we set up with our students, describing the most important activities and tools used; in Sect. 4 we give an overview of the results we obtained; finally, in Sect. 5 we draw our conclusions and describe some future plans.

2   Related Works

The problem of evaluation is central in education, and in case of problem-based learning (PBL) it is particularly challenging, as it requires the integration of several different dimensions.

Agile teamwork is especially complex to evaluate, as there are several possible viewpoints and approaches. For example, Poženel [22] and Wedemann evaluated teamwork interactions [30], whereas Mahnic [16] and Baham [1] evaluated the students' perceptions when using Agile practices and tools. Scott [26] and Lang [13], instead, focused on the evaluation of Scrum learning outcomes related to

---

[1] See http://scrumble.pyxis-tech.com/.

different learning styles of students. Surprisingly, not much research exists on software process quality education, one of the few exceptions is [14]. Sussy and others present a study on the Team Software Process enacted by graduate students [29]. Instead, here we focus on undergraduates using Agile practices and Scrum.

In 2008 Dingsøyr et al. [6] wrote that Scrum was not enough studied: it was already popular in companies, but not used in university course. Since then, studies have progressed, and some focus on the approach to Agile practices in an educational context.

Kropp and Meier [12] described a course organization and some tools similar to our case. There are important differences though, such as the intensive use of Essence cards [9] and the evaluation of both process and product. Another recent paper with an approach similar to ours is [23], which exploited a number of tools for Agile collaboration and surveyed students by questionnaires. Two important differences are that we insisted that students should use only open source tools, and use Essence to guide their retrospectives.

Retrospectives are in fact a crucial practice in Agile developments and team building. Recently, Steghöfer et al. [27] completely re-imagined their course in order to teach Agile methods - and Scrum in particular - introducing student reflection in the evaluation process. Their practice has been followed by others, such as [17] and ourselves.

Traditionally, Agile developers have frowned upon tools usage [11], and though the tendency has changed through the years [5], the current pandemic crisis has been the real game-changer. Currently, most development happens remotely, even at the educational level, and required us to use a tool-intensive approach. Previous studies pioneered remote development: [25], which describes and evaluates a virtual Scrum environment, [19], that outlines a distributed Scrum activity involving students of two different universities located in two continents, and more.

3   Methods

The Software Engineering course offered at our university is based on about 75 h of theory lectures and 150 h of project work for third year Computer Science students. The theory lectures are devoted to presenting the basics of software process models, especially Agile including some practices like test driven programming or pair/mob programming. We devote time to explain and demonstrate examples of user stories, design patterns, architecture diagrams in UML, estimation techniques of development efforts, and software quality metrics.

This year we had more than 100 students, who self organized in 21 teams. They all worked remotely, as the department rooms and laboratories were off limits for sanitary reasons.

3.1 The Project Work

The students' project work has been organized in phases as shown in Fig. 1.

Fig. 1. Work phases illustration.

1. Students profiled themselves by filling personal cards using Trello, describing their previous programming experiences and their specific knowledge and skills in software development. Trello is not open source, and was chosen because it was quite popular among students, and easy to use online.
2. Using Microsoft Teams students were able to dialog and freely move cards forming groups of five or six people. This was also the time where Scrum Masters where chosen. Usually SM where chosen either because they volunteered declaring to be less able as programmers, or because they declared a strong interest in leading the team.
3. The first meeting of each group was devoted to a specific team building activity: playing remotely (mandatory, given the pandemic) a game of Scrumble to learn with a gamified approach the Scrum process model[2]. The game was useful to improve the self confidence of Scrum Masters and clarify roles and responsibilities; at the end of this activity each team had a retrospective meeting for self evaluating its own performance using a Goal-Question-Metric approach suggested by the instructors.

   This game and the subsequent Goal-Question-Metric (GQM) self-evaluation were useful to the teams for familiarizing with Scrum and discuss some critical issues, like technical debt.
4. The first sprint started when the POs introduced software requirements. Moreover, in order to inspire the teams POs gave them access to the codebase of a previous project with similar software requirements. The code base had been developed by a single student as his graduation project. Teams were allowed to reuse this code, but only two decided to reuse and extend it. The initial product backlog was formulated by the teams using a standard user story template (*As a User I need this Goal for this Motivation*). Each team built its own product backlog containing its own user stories.
5. Project work was organized over three week sprints. Three sprint were carried out by all teams, but they had the chance to add additional sprints. At the end of the work, the teams released their final software product version and a document called "Final team report", which summarized artifacts and process documentation produced during each sprint.

---

[2] Game manual and materials are freely available at http://scrumble.pyxis-tech.com/.

Each sprint devoted some time to a retrospective, that the team's Scrum Master coordinated referring to the Essence cards for Agile[3].

The product to develop was a Twitter client, enriched with features for data analytics: the product should be able to capture large sets of geolocalizable tweets and: a) put them on a map b) create a word cloud with their contents c) create a temporal diagram to show the distribution of collected tweets across time, and so on. The main use cases were: a) using Twitter in an emergency, like an earthquake, to collect help messages; b) using tweets to track the movements and collect the picture of a group of travelers in a city or across a region; c) using tweets for simple diachronic sentiment analysis. The teams were instructed to create independently their own user stories, so each product backlog was different. Also, the teams were free to use any technology they prefered. Most of them used Javascript with some framework, like Vue. The other teams used Java.

Each team had to develop the software product using the open source services included in the development environment hosted by a university server, and to adopt some Agile best practices and a Scrum-like process. Teams were encouraged to gather together periodically, in daily Scrum meetings, but most teams usually performed bi-weekly meetings. Moreover they practiced pair or mob programming to increase collective code ownership.

In the beginning of the sprint each team gathered together in a sprint planning meeting using an audio and/or video calling app (either MS Teams or Discord). Each team planned independently their sprint backlog, namely the selection of user stories, from their own product backlog. Each user story was decomposed in tasks and had a story point effort estimate given by the team. The process of effort estimation was performed by Planning poker.

During the sprint, each member with the assignment to complete an user story had to update its state in Taiga virtual kanban. When an user story was put in "done" status Taiga updated the sprint burn down chart.

Each personal IDE had to be instrumented with a plug-in able to log and track productivity counting keystrokes, modified lines of code, and actions on the main tools like Taiga, GitLab, and SonarQube. The plug-in was open source but not available for commercial IDEs, so several teams replaced it with Wakatime, with the difference that it tracked working hours.

The codebase had to be organized with version control inside a GitLab repository.

Source code quality had to be checked by SonarQube, which produced a report with quality ratings for each test.

Team textual communication had to be managed with Mattermost.

In the end of the sprint each team gathered together in sprint review and sprint retrospective meetings.

They stored in Taiga Wiki the following artifacts: demo video of software increment with last functionalities implemented, SonarQube report of the final release, team diary, Essence cards arrangement produced during each sprint retrospective, UML diagrams.

---

[3] https://www.scruminc.com/better-scrum-with-essence/.

3.2   The Research Questions

The practices and tools used by the teams recorded a lot of data concerning the process enacted by the teams. We study how agile processes can be improved, thus we aimed to compare the teamwork performances, asking the following research questions:

RQ1: *How can we evaluate the teamwork performed during the project?*
RQ2: *How can we evaluate how Agile was the teamwork?*

We used a teamwork quality model in order to answer RQ1 and an Agile maturity model to answer RQ2. We also compared the two evaluations.

The teamwork quality model is inspired from [8], thus we name it the *Hoegl-Gemuenden model*. It is based on the assumption that any human behaviour in a team can be summarized in two major areas: activities and interactions. Inspired by the Hackman model [7], which sustained that interactions influence product, performance, and satisfaction, Hoegl and Gemuenden created a survey to analyze the aspects which followed the conceptual model shown in Fig. 2.

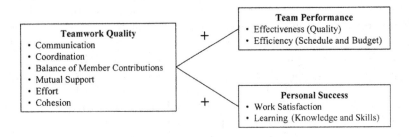

Fig. 2. Conceptual representation of Hoegl-Gemuenden's quality model [8].

The paper [15] reformulated the Hoegl-Gemuenden approach to apply it to Agile teams. Similarly, our analysis is also inspired by the Hoegl-Gemuenden model, but we applied some changes due to our educational context. Our evaluation constructs are the following:

- interaction analysis, with all the six constructs of Hoegl-Gemuenden's teamwork quality category;
- effectiveness analysis about software quality;
- work efficiency, which only considers schedule efficiency, because there was no budget;
- satisfaction analysis, which considers team satisfaction about learning, product, and process of Hoegl-Gemuenden's "personal success" category. Since our study was conducted in a short time period, questions about future personal success of team members were excluded.

Since the data collection involved different evaluation metrics (1 to 5 Likert scale for students' opinions from questionnaire about team interactions, decimal scale for instructors' evaluation of process and product, marks of SonarQube for the product internal quality ratings, and percentages of completing user stories and tasks), in the data processing they were all converted in percentages.

The Agile maturity model we used is inspired by the Yin model presented in [31]. It includes five maturity levels and explores seven inner categories of analyses. The conceptual model is shown in Fig. 3.

Level 1 - Initial. This maturity level represents the lack of achievement of level 2 goals. This level of Agile maturity does not have a clearly defined process for Agile development, and the possible project success depends solely on the competence of individuals.

Level 2 - Managed. This maturity level represents fulfillment of the two main goals: basic Scrum management and software requirements engineering. The first area of analysis ensures the minimum acceptable usage of the Scrum methodology and structure: Scrum roles, artifacts, and meetings are used by the team. The second area of analysis comprises product backlog management and successful sprint planning meetings.

Level 3 - Defined. This maturity level focuses on the relationship with clients and on timely delivery of software products (which includes best Agile practices associated with the technical programming aspects of engineering software). The first area of analysis requires the establishment of a *Definition of Done* (DoD), frequent meetings with PO, and systematic sprint review meetings. The second area of analysis requires sprint backlog management, continuous product deliveries, verifying software quality in each delivery, usage of pair or mob programming sessions.

Level 4 – Quantitatively Managed. This maturity level includes the achievement of a standardized - repeatable - software development process aided by the management of the process performance through measurement and analysis practices.

Level 5 – Optimizing. This level focuses on the achievement of continuous self-improvement and high levels of satisfaction of both the client and the development team. The main goal for this level is: performance management through daily Scrum meetings, successful sprint retrospective meetings, causal risk analysis and mitigation and resolution.

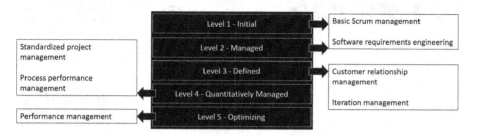

Fig. 3. Conceptual representation of Yin's Scrum maturity model.

Yin based his model on Patel's Agile Maturity Model [20]. The paper [24] using Yin's Model proposes a evaluation system based on Patel's Key Process

Area (KPA) formula. Following this approach, we set a GQM evaluation schema in which answers to questions are: "Yes", "No", "Partially", "Non applicable".

The Key Process Area (KPA) formula is:

$$\frac{\sum Y_n + \frac{1}{2}\sum P_m}{t - \sum NA_f} \times 100$$

where n is the number of "Yes" (Y) answers, m is the number of "Partially" (P) answers, t is the total number of questions in the GQM schema, f is the number of "Non applicable" (NA) answers.

To assess the maturity level in the software development process, all its internal categories have to be fully achieved so equal or above 86%.

3.3 Collecting the Data

As depicted in Fig. 4 data were collected by surveys and observing team projects and reports stored inside in two available services: gitlab and SonarQube.

"Survey 1" and "Survey 2" were addressed to Scrum Masters. Both surveys included questions about team efficiency in each sprint, which was analyzed by counting completed tasks and user stories done in each sprint backlog. Moreover "Survey 2" included questions about ratings of maintainability, reliability, and security as obtained in SonarQube. These ratings were confirmed by a direct observation of the values reported by each team inside their specific SonarQube data repository.

The "Final individual report" was a survey addressed to all the members of each team at the end of the last sprint. It included several questions, which mostly required an answer from 1 to 5 Likert scale. The questions investigated about interactions, productivity data (lines of code personally written and working hours personally spent, either individually or in teamwork) and open-ended questions about describing the personal IDE and logger tool usage, process and practices, personal satisfaction, strengths and weaknesses of the team.

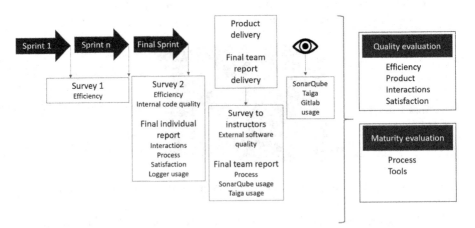

Fig. 4. Data collection process.

We performed a systematic analysis of data stored as Taiga artifacts (kanban, Wiki, tasks recorded by total power points), SonarQube reports (if each team used it in all sprints), Gitlab artifacts (if each team applied version control, updating the code throughout all work period observing contributors' graphs of commits).

4   Results

The radar graphs in Fig. 5 show the percentages obtained in each category of quality and maturity model, respectively.

Hackman's theory [7] about influence of internal interactions on satisfaction, effectiveness and efficiency is confirmed. Indeed teams which, on average, obtained the best evaluation in the teamwork quality model obtained high evaluations in these three aspects, while teams which, on average, obtained the worst evaluation resulted highly variable in these aspects.

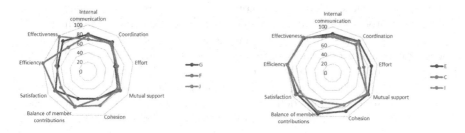

Fig. 5. Radar graphs of worst teams (G, F, J) and best teams (E, C, I) of areas analysis in team work quality

The teams which performed worst were characterized by:

- low quality of internal communication,
- low perception of effort spent in the project,
- unbalance of members' contribution to the project.

Moreover, these teams exposed often a conflict of opinions about team interactions, clearly indicating different perceptions and attitudes about teamwork.

We reported only internal communication because all teams said to not have consulted with experts or other teams. This is a behavior typical of our Computer Science students, who rarely ask for help outside their team.

Concerning the maturity model we can make two different observations about two aspects of the maturity model: one about each category of analysis, the other about levels reached by the teams.

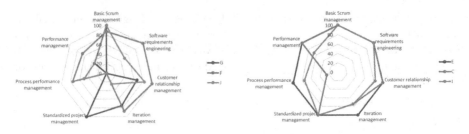

Fig. 6. Radar graphs of worst teams (G, F, J) and best teams (E, C, I) of areas analysis in Scrum maturity model

Considering the first aspect, let us consider the radar graphs in Fig. 6. Except for "basic Scrum management" category, the majority of worst teams obtained low evaluations in all categories. A common aspect of these teams is the absence of using Gitlab to apply a version control strategy, which corresponds to "Standardized project management" category.

Furthermore we observed some common difficulties in most teams in the categories of process performance management and iteration management.

Concerning process performance management, students were not constant in collecting personal productivity data neither using the logger tool which counted lines of code nor in updating burn down charts after each sprint.

Concerning iteration management, this included sprint backlog management in Taiga kanban, continuous delivery, use of SonarQube in each sprint to check and improve codebase quality, peer and mob programming sessions.

The only problematic aspect is the sprint backlog management in Taiga kanban: several teams forgot updating it most of the time, so many teams were evaluated with a "Partially" in this evaluation point. However, the majority of teams applied the other development techniques included in this category, in particular pair programming. Indeed several open-ended answers from students refer to pair programming as a valuable and useful technique. The answers underline it as a technique which encourages mutual improvement of knowledge, fast resolution of issues, a way to acquire more self-esteem about own code production, increased productivity, and creativity and fun.

Considering the second aspect of the maturity model, the majority of teams reached level two or higher, proving a basic Scrum management and good software requirements management.

In the leftmost image of Fig. 7 each point represents a team with its average KPA value in x-axis and average value of quality model evaluations in y-axis.

Data show a 0.8 Pearson correlation coefficient: this value suggests the possible presence of not perfect linear relationship among the two evaluations. Indeed the rightmost image in Fig. 7 shows a regression line not so far from the points. The average error of point distance from the line is 3.5.

We can assert that when there is a frequent use of Agile practices and control tools, there are also a good satisfaction, efficiency, product, and team work quality.

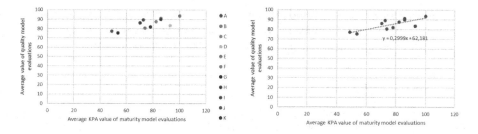

Fig. 7. Scatter graphs with average evaluations of the two models

Indeed in the analysis the worst and best teams were the same for both models. We remark that he students were not aware of any of the quality models we have used.

4.1 Students' Perceptions of Agile Practices

On the basis of students' answers to the open-ended question "List Agile practices used", as shown in Fig. 8 the top three practices used were sprint planning, pair programming, and daily scrum.

Sprint retrospective and sprint review, code refactoring, Essence and backlog usage were Agile practices quoted as useful and effective by at least 20% of students.

It is instead a strange result that kanban, burndown chart, versioning and continuous delivery were not quoted, because they were actually practices used by the majority of the teams. Our hypothesis is that since for all students this was the first experience with Agile and with Scrum, these practices were not perceived as crucial, but in some sense they were "part of the game" required by the project rules.

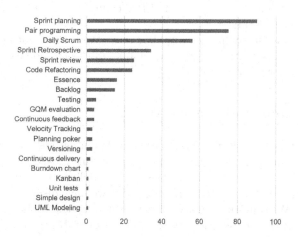

Fig. 8. Histogram of Agile practices

The uses of the kanban and versioning repository were actually widespread and effective. Instead, the idea of tracking the team's effort using the automatic burndown diagram capability of Taiga was neglected by some teams.

4.2 Threats to Validity

In this paragraph we discuss some threats to validity concerning this study. We focus first on issues connected with the pandemic, that impacted strongly the activities of this project.

First, we have chosen a specific set of open source tools, that not necessarily are the best ones for Agile developments and record data useful for quality evaluations. A different set of tools could result in different outcomes: an example is Jira, that however is not open source. Interestingly, although we insisted that the teams use the open source tools included in the environment we offered them, teams additionally used MS Teams and Discord, that are not open source but used daily for lectures and at no charge for the students. Some tools, e.g. the productivity logger, were used only partially because had some defects.

Second, the evaluation models we have used are taken and adapted from the literature of Agile developments in the industry, for teams working face to face. We found that most constructs and questions in questionnaires make sense in an academic context working remotely, however we had to delete or adapt a number of questions. We did not investigate for instance in this case study the impact of pandemic on non verbal interactions, that in Agile are quite relevant and we investigated in a recent work [3].

The students received a personal questionnaire and had to answer to questions concerning their teamwork and companions. We took measures to ensure the anonymity of the answers.

However, the same questionnaires may contain biased questions. For instance we avoided all questions connected to gender issues, but other bias could have remained unnoticed. In order to limit this aspect before sending the questionnaire to the students, we asked the opinion of two colleagues from another university expert in Agile development.

Finally, the case study has been applied once. We are replicating it in another academic context, with the same product but different students, to verify and possibly confirm or modify our findings.

5 Conclusions and Future Work

This research involved 107 students grouped in 21 teams, who worked for approximately three months at the end of 2020 and in the first weeks of 2021. All teams passed the final exam at the end of this period, delivering a product that was more or less usable and complete. In this paper we have discussed the quality of the teamwork. We remark that the data collected by the tools are available for further analyses. The experiment itself is also repeatable, as the CAS environment is all made of open source services and components.

Analyzing the results of the quality and maturity models we observed a linear relation. This relation is not perfect, indeed it has a medium error of 3.5, but it shows a possible relationship between teamwork quality and following closely a work methodology.

We argue that initiating the process with a team building game and exploiting Essence cards for guiding the teams during the retrospectives were activities very helpful for improving the quality of the teamwork observed during the project.

The main goal of this experiment was to exploit open source tools working remotely on a project developed with an Agile method and related practices, in order to collect data for quality evaluations. The teams were able to use some tools quite effectively, like Taiga, GitLab and SonarQube. Some teams decided also spontaneously to add Jenkins for automating their testing. In a future edition of our course we intend to suggest to use a tool for animating requirements [28].

Some other tools were less appreciated by our students, like Mattermost and the productivity logger. Mattermost, like Slack, is apparently superseded by MS Teams; moreover, teams based their communications on Telegram and Discord. These however are neither open source services, nor make available their data for inspections. We decided not to insist too much on using open source, trackable tools, in order to not increase the burden managed by the teams.

We believe that open source collaboration platforms, like Mattermost, need specific training when used for software development. We have also found that educating developers to self-tracking their own developing activity is quite difficult, and that the data recorded concerning productivity are not very reliable, as the developers tend to conceal or even to manipulate them. In the future we plan to improve the dashboard for self-tracking productivity data.

Acknowledgments. We wish to thank the students who participated to the project as developers.

References

1. Baham, C.: Teaching tip: implementing scrum wholesale in the classroom. J. Inf. Syst. Educ. (JISE) **30**, 141–159 (2019)
2. Blake, M.: Integrating large-scale group projects and software engineering approaches for early computer science courses. IEEE Trans. Educ. **48**(1), 63–72 (2005)
3. Ciancarini, P., Farina, M., Succi, G., Yermolaieva, S., Zagvozkina, N.: Non verbal communication in software engineering - an empirical study. IEEE Access (2021, to appear)
4. Ciancarini, P., Missiroli, M., Poggi, F., Russo, D.: An open source environment for an agile development model. In: Ivanov, V., Kruglov, A., Masyagin, S., Sillitti, A., Succi, G. (eds.) OSS 2020. IAICT, vol. 582, pp. 148–162. Springer, Cham (2020). https://doi.org/10.1007/978-3-030-47240-5_15
5. Ciancarini, P., Missiroli, M., Sillitti, A.: Preferred tools for agile development: a sociocultural perspective. In: Mazzara, M., Bruel, J.-M., Meyer, B., Petrenko, A. (eds.) TOOLS 2019. LNCS, vol. 11771, pp. 43–58. Springer, Cham (2019). https://doi.org/10.1007/978-3-030-29852-4_3

6. Dingsøyr, T., Dybå, T., Abrahamsson, P.: A preliminary roadmap for empirical research on agile software development. In: Agile Conference, pp. 83–94 (2008)
7. Hackman, J.: The design of work teams. In: Lorsch, W. (ed.) Handbook of Organizational Behavior, pp. 67–102. Prentice Hall (1987)
8. Hoegl, M., Gemuenden, H.G.: Teamwork quality and the success of innovative projects: a theoretical concept and empirical evidence. Organ. Sci. **12**(4), 435–449 (2001)
9. Jacobson, I., et al.: The Essentials of Modern Software Engineering: Free the Practices from the Method Prisons! Association for Computing Machinery and Morgan & Claypool (2019)
10. Ju, A., Fox, A.: TEAMSCOPE: measuring software engineering processes with teamwork telemetry. In: Proceedings of the 23rd ACM Conference on Innovation and Technology in Computer Science Education, pp. 123–128 (2018)
11. Kelter, U., Monecke, M., Schild, M.: Do we need 'Agile' software development tools? In: Aksit, M., Mezini, M., Unland, R. (eds.) NODe 2002. LNCS, vol. 2591, pp. 412–430. Springer, Heidelberg (2003). https://doi.org/10.1007/3-540-36557-5_29
12. Kropp, M., Meier, A.: Teaching agile software development at university level: values, management, and craftsmanship. In: Proceedings of the 26th International Conference on Software Engineering Education and Training (CSEE & T), pp. 179–188 (2013)
13. Lang, G.: Agile learning: sprinting through the semester. Inf. Syst. Educ. J. **15**, 14–21 (2017)
14. Lee, M., Barta, B.-Z., Juliff, P.: Software Quality and Productivity: Theory, Practice, Education and Training. Springer, Heidelberg (2013)
15. Lindsjørn, Y., et al.: Teamwork quality and project success in software development: a survey of agile development teams. J. Syst. Softw. **122**, 274–286 (2016)
16. Mahnic, V., Rožanc, I.: Students' perceptions of scrum practices. In: Proceedings of the 35th International Convention MIPRO, pp. 1178–1183 (2012)
17. Masood, Z., Hoda, R., Blincoe, K.: Adapting agile practices in university contexts. J. Syst. Softw. **144**, 501–510 (2018)
18. McEwan, D., et al.: The effectiveness of teamwork training on teamwork behaviors and team performance: a systematic review and meta-analysis of controlled interventions. PLoS One, **12**(1) (2017)
19. Paasivaara, M., et al.: Teaching students global software engineering skills using distributed Scrum. In: Proceedings of the 35th International Conference on Software Engineering (ICSE), pp. 1128–1137 (2013)
20. Patel, C., Ramachandran, M.: Agile maturity model (AMM): a software process improvement framework for agile software development practices. Int. J. Softw. Eng. (IJSE) **2**(1), 3–28 (2009)
21. Poth, A., Kottke, M., Riel, A.: Evaluation of agile team work quality. In: Paasivaara, M., Kruchten, P. (eds.) XP 2020. LNBIP, vol. 396, pp. 101–110. Springer, Cham (2020). https://doi.org/10.1007/978-3-030-58858-8_11
22. Poženel, M.: Assessing teamwork in a software engineering capstone course. World Trans. Eng. Technol. Educ. **11**(1), 6–12 (2013)
23. Raibulet, C., Fontana, F.A.: Collaborative and teamwork software development in an undergraduate software engineering course. J. Syst. Softw. **144**, 409–422 (2018)
24. Ridha, F., Hegarini, E.: Analysis of maturity level project management of software development in scrum framework: case research on tribe enterprise PT. XYZ. IT J. Res. Dev. **5**, 87–97 (2020)

25. Rodríguez, G., Soria, A., Campo, M.: Teaching scrum to software engineering students with virtual reality support. In: Cipolla-Ficarra, F., Veltman, K., Verber, D., Cipolla-Ficarra, M., Kammüller, F. (eds.) ADNTIIC 2011. LNCS, vol. 7547, pp. 140–150. Springer, Heidelberg (2012). https://doi.org/10.1007/978-3-642-34010-9_14
26. Scott, E., et al.: Are learning styles useful indicators to discover how students use Scrum for the first time? Comput. Hum. Behav. **36**, 56–64 (2014)
27. Steghöfer, J., Knauss, E., Alégroth, E., Hammouda, I., Burden, H., Ericsson, M.: Teaching agile - addressing the conflict between project delivery and application of agile methods. In: IEEE/ACM 38th International Conference on Software Engineering Companion (ICSE-C), pp. 303–312 (2016)
28. Sterling, L., Ciancarini, P., Turnidge, T.: On the animation of "not executable" specifications by prolog. Int. J. Softw. Eng. Knowl. Eng. **6**(01), 63–87 (1996)
29. Sussy, B.O., Calvo-Manzano, J.A., Gonzalo, C., et al.: Teaching team software process in graduate courses to increase productivity and improve software quality. In: Proceedings of the 32nd International Computer Software and Applications Conference, pp. 440–446. IEEE (2008)
30. Wedemann, G.: Scrum as a method of teaching software architecture. In: Proceedings of the 3rd European Conference on Software Engineering Education, pp. 108–112. ACM (2018)
31. Yin, A., et al.: Scrum maturity model: validation for IT organizations' roadmap to develop software centered on the client role. In: The Sixth International Conference on Software Engineering Advances, ICSEA 2011 (2011)
32. Young, P.E., Needham, D.M.: Using a class-wide, semester-long project to teach software engineering principles. GSTF J. Comput. (JoC) **3**(3) (2014)

STAMP 4 NLP – An Agile Framework for Rapid Quality-Driven NLP Applications Development

Philipp Kohl[1]([✉]), Oliver Schmidts[1], Lars Klöser[1], Henri Werth[1], Bodo Kraft[1], and Albert Zündorf[2]

[1] FH Aachen - University of Applied Sciences, 52428 Jülich, Germany
{p.kohl,schmidts,kloeser,werth,kraft}@fh-aachen.de
[2] University of Kassel, 34127 Kassel, Germany
zuendorf@uni-kassel.de

Abstract. The progress in natural language processing (NLP) research over the last years, offers novel business opportunities for companies, as automated user interaction or improved data analysis. Building sophisticated NLP applications requires dealing with modern machine learning (ML) technologies, which impedes enterprises from establishing successful NLP projects. Our experience in applied NLP research projects shows that the continuous integration of research prototypes in production-like environments with quality assurance builds trust in the software and shows convenience and usefulness regarding the business goal. We introduce STAMP 4 NLP as an iterative and incremental process model for developing NLP applications. With STAMP 4 NLP, we merge software engineering principles with best practices from data science. Instantiating our process model allows efficiently creating prototypes by utilizing templates, conventions, and implementations, enabling developers and data scientists to focus on the business goals. Due to our iterative-incremental approach, businesses can deploy an enhanced version of the prototype to their software environment after every iteration, maximizing potential business value and trust early and avoiding the cost of successful yet never deployed experiments.

Keywords: Natural language processing · Process model · Machine learning · Best practices · Avoiding pitfalls · Quality assurance

1 Introduction

The field of artificial intelligence in general and natural language processing as one of its sub-fields offers tremendous novel business opportunities in a steadily growing market [13]. Recent progress in NLP research shows the potential for business applications, leading to a demand for more advanced NLP applications [7].

The state-of-the-art in NLP differs from research to industrial domains. Besides the progress in research, the application of ML-based NLP in many

© Springer Nature Switzerland AG 2021
A. C. R. Paiva et al. (Eds.): QUATIC 2021, CCIS 1439, pp. 156–166, 2021.
https://doi.org/10.1007/978-3-030-85347-1_12

enterprises is severely limited [6]. The black-box behavior of ML models, missing know-how, complex technological landscape, and the decision on an appropriate tool stack discourage enterprises from implementing NLP approaches [1,10]. They discard promising projects due to the combination of high and uncertain effort estimation [23].

Many ML projects fail because of exceeding budgets, deadlines or they do not meet the business requirements [11]. The late integration of several projects can lead to a services shutdown [17,27]. We minimize the risk of these situations with agile methodology to handle the uncertainties and generate business value and feedback on the application as early as possible. This increases the quality and trust in the software for all involved stakeholders [5].

We propose a new process model adjusted for developing NLP applications: **S**tandardized **M**odeling **P**rocess for **N**atural **L**anguage **P**rocessing (STAMP 4 NLP).

With STAMP 4 NLP, we merge software engineering principles with best practices from data science to improve and accelerate the development cycle and integrate prototypes with every iteration into a test or production environment. STAMP 4 NLP provides a transparent development process, including roles, tasks, artifacts, and best practices.

Our main contributions[1] are:

- A novel process model for developing NLP applications, with formally specified roles, activities, and artifacts focusing on quality, and early business value.
- Usage of predefined environment and software templates based on prior experiences for accelerating the development start.

2 Related Work

Knowledge Discovery in Databases (KDD) [9] represents one of the first process models for data mining. It offers a generic guided process of the technical tasks to reveal patterns in data and building knowledge.

Cross Industry Standard Process for Data Mining (CRISP-DM) [4] also considers business requirements and models the application development process in an applied context in contrast to KDD. Modern ML process models originate from CRISP-DM. It consists of six stages: Business Understanding, Data Understanding, Data Preparation, Modeling, Evaluation, and Deployment. Depending on the stage's results, it allows transitions to previous stages.

CRISP-ML(Q) [24] extends CRISP-DM for machine learning and explicitly considers the differences between data mining (revealing patterns in data) and machine learning (training and inference). Studer et al. focus on quality assurance on every specific task. CRISP-ML(Q) merges Business Understanding and Data Understanding into a single stage and adds the Monitoring and Maintenance stage, addressing particular challenges of machine learning applications not considered by CRISP-DM.

---

[1] https://github.com/philipp-kohl/stamp4nlp.

While CRISP-DM and CRISP-ML(Q) mainly focus on application creation, Weber et al. [28] introduced an approach with defined transitions between model development and model operation. Thus, they cover the whole model lifecycle from planning over production until retirement. Their process does not explicitly consider business requirements.

Similar to KDD, Amershi et al. [2] focuses on the modern, mainly technical process for developing a machine learning model but also incorporates fundamental operational analytics with transitions to previous stages.

In contrast to the mentioned process models, we focus on NLP. We treat manual data annotations and annotation guidelines as central project artifacts. Our approach is especially suitable for supervised NLP tasks as information extraction. Further, our focus is on strong quality assurance with different levels of applied tests. We leverage approaches and best practices from software engineering, combining them with machine learning approaches, such as supporting versioning of code, data, models, and tracking experiment results [16].

Agile software development [5] uses iterations and increments instead of transitions between process stages. This leads to a stronger focus on running software during the development process. The incremental aspect allows isolated investigation of the experimental effects and the usage of continuous integration and delivery (CI/CD) [8]. Developers receive feedback, and stakeholders gain value and trust in the application with every deployed increment. In comparison to [24] with task-agnostic quality assurance, we measure technical and business-oriented metrics on a higher level after every iteration [18,19,22].

Inspired by Spring [14], maven archetypes [25] and NLPf [20], we deliver STAMP 4 NLP with a framework, which supports the developer with a predefined development environment, code for well-known standard tasks [12,26] for creating a rapid prototype as basline or proof of concept, which the developer enhances over iterations and increments. STAMP 4 NLP decreases the risk of not deployed valuable experiments and failing projects.

3   Process Model

STAMP 4 NLP is an instantiable, iterative, and incremental process model for developing natural language processing applications with a focus on quality, business value, and simplified prototyping.

STAMP 4 NLP uses agile methodology [5] by establishing software in increments developers enhance in various iterations (c.f. Fig. 1). The Evolution Loop works in sprints (e.g., 2–4 weeks) to create a new release candidate that the developers integrate into the customer's test or production environment to gain trust in the software and receive feedback for further improvements to fit the customer's needs [8]. The workflow is as follows: the developers start with the Evolution Loop to define or refine the requirements, followed by multiple iterations in the Development Loop (hours to days) to create a model that satisfies the specified requirements. Deployment and testing are also a part of the inner loop. Once the software fulfills them, the developers leave the inner loop and proceed to the outer loop to integrate and monitor the release candidate. Depending on the monitoring results, they trigger a new iteration.

The process model provides particular levels of transparency. At first, every stakeholder can follow the complex process, even if they are unfamiliar with NLP. They can also track the order of tasks by consulting the documentation. Thereby the responsibilities are clearly defined, and every involved party knows their tasks. Clearly defined responsibilities are helpful to prevent conflicts and create rational processes that the users can monitor and optimize. We use the *MEDIATION* [19] approach to provide the

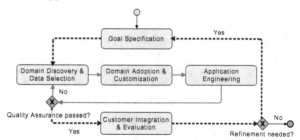

Fig. 1. STAMP 4 NLP consists of five subprocesses arraned in two nested loops: *Development Loop* (green + solid) for developing the NLP application and model. *Evolution Loop* (blue + dashed) surrounds the Development Loop and covers mainly the interaction with the customer: creation and refinement of the project goals with associated requirements and integration and monitoring of the application. Note: The solid and dashed connectors have the same meaning of sequence flow but help distinguish the loops in black and white print. (Color figure online)

application state transparent via a dashboard with project specific business metrics for all stakeholders.

The development environment equips the user with a standard set of tools for rapidly building a proof of concept while maintaining the flexibility to let the user choose other preferred libraries. Creating a project instance provides folder structure, development environment, documentation, and boilerplate code (e.g., REST-Service with predefined endpoints, etc.). The standard folder facilitates the automatic loading and storing of data, models, and results to their destination by convention. Furthermore, no settling-in period for already STAMP-involved members; they know where to find code, documentation, experiments, and data.

ML metrics serve as a common benchmark for different models. High or low metrics show the averaged performance but do not allow making conclusions which use-cases a model cannot handle appropriately. Model interpretability is a current research subject [1]. To minimize the interpretability gap in machine learning and to receive more feedback on a low application level, we incorporated CheckList [18] for creating behavioral tests aiming for specific capabilities the NLP application should cover. Besides CheckList, we use MEDIATION [19] for testing the NLP application on a business level: the developers and stakeholders define test cases strongly related to their intended use cases in the form of annotated documents. Thus, this additional test set serves as an indicator of the business readiness of the NLP application. In combination with the CI/CD approach, we receive this feedback for every iteration and increment. Involving testers or real user groups into the increment testing generates feedback for business and practical usage.

STAMP 4 NLP supports the user to keep the reproducibility of experiments and models as high as possible. We incorporated parts of Pineau's reproducibility list [16] into the process by documentation and tools supporting versioning of code, data, models, and tracking experiment's results.

In the following, we give a short description of each subprocess with its primary artifacts. We show exemplarily a detailed BPMN diagram of the Domain Adoption and Customization in Fig. 2. Our GitHub repository provides the other subprocess diagrams and the detailed description of each task and artifact.

3.1 Goal Specification

Description: The Goal Specification aims to establish a common business understanding. The stakeholders define and refine the business goals, and their associated technical, machine learning, business, and MEDIATION requirements and update the documentation accordingly. It includes an evaluation of all data sources and the data provision for the data scientists. This stage involves all currently relevant stakeholders to minimize the bias and possibly wrong model assumptions.

Artifacts: The primary artifacts are the refined and reviewed requirements, test cases, and access to all mandatory data sources.

3.2 Domain Discovery and Data Selection

Description: Data scientists and domain experts prepare the annotation process (c.f. Fig. 2). They identify NLP tasks and corresponding annotation schemas helpful to fulfill the business goals. Additionally, data scientists include domain knowledge from experts to steadily improve annotation guidelines and collect and evaluate data samples for the annotation process and necessary metadata.

Artifacts: The primary artifacts are the annotation guidelines, the new corpus versions prepared for annotation, and documentation about licenses, data protection, and data security.

3.3 Domain Adoption and Customization

Description: This subprocess (c.f. Fig. 2) includes data annotation and model training. The annotation process setup involves planning and, if necessary a domain training for annotators. The annotated texts build a new corpus version, which is used for training a new model. To minimize the annotation effort, we want to stop further annotating when noticing the resulting model's metrics

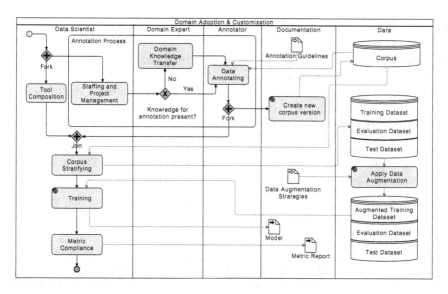

Fig. 2. Showing the task order of the subprocess *Domain Adoption and Customization* as BPMN Diagram with the involved roles displayed as swimlanes. Additional information is provided by *Documentation* and *Data* lane. *Create new corpus version, Training,* and *Apply Data Augmentation* are automatic tasks, which run without human interaction. *Training* requires the execution of one command as trigger.

stagnate. We incorporated the continuous integration and delivery approach of Schreiber et al. [21]. Thus, annotators receive feedback after each annotation session. The feedback can motivate to continue or stop annotating because the further annotations do not impact the model's performance remarkably.

Artifacts: The primary artifacts are the new corpus version, the new model, and metric reports about the model's performance.

3.4 Application Engineering

Description: Software developers package the model and all necessary dependencies. A CI/CD pipeline deploys the application in a test or production-like environment and runs evaluations to ensure the quality gates (software quality, machine learning metrics MEDIATION and behavioral tests via CheckList [18]) defined in the goal specification. The software package is versioned to provide transparency, whether the made modifications improved the previous version and for fallback solutions. Depending on the evaluation results, the application stays in the Development Loop or transitions into the Evolution Loop for integrating the software into the customer's application landscape (c.f. Fig. 1).

Artifacts: The primary artifacts are the software package and a quality assurance report.

3.5   Customer Integration and Evaluation

Description: Software developers integrate the packaged NLP application in the customer's application landscape. On the customer side, a monitoring service checks the model's performance. The resulting reports build the basis for a refinement of the quality gates comparable to [19,22] ensuring the fulfillment of the business requirements during the production phase.

Artifacts: An operation manual documents the deployment, and an integration plan explains the integration in the customer application. The performance reports support recommendations and business decisions.

4   Project Template

STAMP 4 NLP facilitates focusing on the project-specific challenges such as analyzing the data and the domain, annotating, experimenting with different concepts, and deep learning architectures. To decrease the overhead data scientists face while starting a new project, we offer a template with development environment, folder structure[2], tools, code and process documentation. Furthermore, the framework can generate customizable implementations for specific NLP tasks (e.g., named entity recognition (NER) [12], or text classification [26]) into the project, helping the developers implement a first baseline or proof of concept.

The template serves the paradigm *convention over configuration* [3]. Therefore the template comes with, but is not limited to a standard set of tools and libraries. If the user stays with the standard, no additional configuration is needed. But the user has the opportunity to use additional libraries or tools, resulting in extra configuration. The basic configuration provides, for example, the library spacy[3] to create prototypes quickly. Depending on the business goal, it is necessary to preserve more control over used architecture and training routines. Therefore the developer can exchange the conventional added spacy module with PyTorch[4] or similar frameworks. The same applies to the folder structure, environment, and infrastructure. We recommend to start with the standard configuration and specialize on demand.

5   Example

This section demonstrates a simplified STAMP 4 NLP usage over a few iterations to show the intuition behind the process model. We focus on a real-world project we performed with our business partners: The profile extraction from social media messages of an advertising group conversation. We use named

---

[2] Similar to https://drivendata.github.io/cookiecutter-data-science/.

[3] https://spacy.io/.

[4] https://pytorch.org/.

entity recognition (NER) as a standard NLP task, for which we can use existing approaches. NER describes the task of finding domain-relevant terms in documents: e.g., persons, brands, products, and their prices. On top of that, we implement a business layer to aggregate the named entities to a profile.

First Iteration – Requirements Analysis and Dry Run: The first iteration focuses on the requirements analysis and the infrastructure test run (also called *dry run*). Instantiating the process model provides a development environment including a prototypical web-service, a pre-configured CI/CD pipeline, and prepared documentation. We define and document the NER as the applied NLP task. Based on the documentation, we invoke the framework for generating a reference implementation for NER as a first baseline. Among others, we define the corresponding machine learning metrics we want to achieve with the NLP application. We skip the most tasks of all other subprocesses for this iteration since its the iteration's goal to ensure the infrastructure: training a model, embed the model into a software package, deploy into a test environment, model evaluation, publish results via a dashboard. The scores do not matter at this stage.

Second Iteration – Baseline: The second iteration focuses on creating a first baseline. This iteration covers the *Development Loop* exclusively. We prepare the annotation process by defining the annotation guidelines, deciding on a suitable corpus format, and transferring the data to the corpus format in Domain Discovery and Data Selection. Domain Adoption and Customization mainly focuses on annotating a subset of the data in this iteration to create the first baseline with the standard implementation. We embed the model into our software architecture and add a business layer to combine the named entities to a profile. Our CI/CD approach packages and deploys the software into the test environment, where the framework performs detailed quality assurance. The results are published on a dashboard (c.f. Fig. 3).

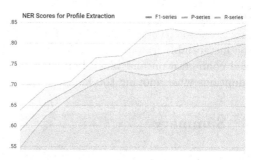

Fig. 3. An excerpt of a Grafana Dashboard visualizes the F1, precision, and recall score for the NER component over several iterations of annotating and architecture decision. Precision measures the correctness of positive classifications (here for a named entity) by penalizing false positives. Recall shows if our model has found all named entities by penalizing false negatives. F1 is the harmonic mean of precision and recall. It is commonly used for model evaluation and comparison.

Additional Iterations – Beat the Baseline: Further iterations focus isolated on specific aspects to enhance the baseline. We incorporate the aspects as isolated as possible to ensure the cause-effect relationships:

164   P. Kohl et al.

Annotations. Annotating new data points, improve existing annotations, decide to incorporate new labels, enhance annotation guideline based on gained experience.

Architectural Decisions. Use different common neural network components or pretrained contextualizes embedding layers [7,15].

If the application fulfills the requirements, we have a possible release candidate and exit the Development Loop and continue the Evolution Loop. If the results do not show the expected behavior or do not fulfill the business need, we begin a new iteration to investigate the cause and start new experiments improving the application's quality.

6   Limitations and Drawbacks

Our proposed process model has a strong focus on supervised NLP. We have many subprocesses with corresponding roles and artifacts for problems that include the manual annotation of corpora. They may be unbeneficial for unsupervised tasks. We further define clear responsibilities and processes but assume that a practical application involves loose compliance to those in some cases. The process needs to be adapted to each project individually. A significant benefit of the instantiable framework is a low application barrier. The resulting standardized configuration and black box code can lead to laborious error detection or adaptions when moving too far from these conventions.

7   Summary

We introduced STAMP 4 NLP a novel instantiable and iterative-incremental process model to develop NLP applications. It supports developers to create valuable and deployable increments rapidly, results in earlier feedback, and improves quality and trust in the application for all stakeholders.

Our approach equips the user with templates, development environment, and documentation to reduce the starting and integration overhead. That minimizes implementation barriers, avoids common pitfalls, and sets the focus on the business goal. Thus, STAMP 4 NLP reduces the risk of failing projects.

In the future, we plan to create a benchmark project for different groups to work on: some groups work with the STAMP 4 NLP and others work from scratch. Thus, we want to measure various project milestones, key performance indicators and observe the challenges the different teams face and pitfalls they could avoid. Furthermore, we want to use it for educational purposes to set the focus appropriately with incremental depth increase. We want to improve the development of generic NLP tasks, including unsupervised problem settings.

References

1. Adadi, A., Berrada, M.: Peeking inside the black-box: a survey on explainable artificial intelligence (XAI). IEEE Access **6**, 52138–52160 (2018). https://doi.org/10.1109/ACCESS.2018.2870052
2. Amershi, S., et al.: Software engineering for machine learning: a case study. In: Proceedings of the 41st International Conference on Software Engineering: Software Engineering in Practice, ICSE-SEIP 2019, pp. 291–300. IEEE Press (2019). https://doi.org/10.1109/ICSE-SEIP.2019.00042
3. Baechle, M., Kirchberg, P.: Ruby on rails. Softw. IEEE **24**, 105–108 (2007). https://doi.org/10.1109/MS.2007.176
4. Chapman, P., et al.: CRISP-DM 1.0 step-by-step data mining guide. In: SPSS (2000)
5. Cohn, M.: Succeeding with Agile: Software Development Using Scrum. Pearson Education Limited (2009). ISBN 978-0-32166-056-5
6. Costello, K.: Gartner survey shows 37 percent of organizations have implemented AI in some form (2019). https://www.gartner.com/en/newsroom/press-releases/2019-01-21-gartner-survey-shows-37-percent-of-organizations-have. Accessed 24 Apr 2021
7. Devlin, J., Chang, M.W., Lee, K., Toutanova, K.: BERT: pre-training of deep bidirectional transformers for language understanding. In: Proceedings of the 2019 Conference of the North American Chapter of the Association for Computational Linguistics: Human Language Technologies, vol. 1 (Long and Short Papers), pp. 4171–4186. Association for Computational Linguistics, Minneapolis (2019). https://doi.org/10.18653/v1/N19-1423. https://www.aclweb.org/anthology/N19-1423
8. Duvall, P., Matyas, S.M., Glover, A.: Continuous Integration: Improving Software Quality and Reducing Risk. Addison-Wesley Professional, Boston (2007).ISBN 0-32133-638-0
9. Fayyad, U., Piatetsky-Shapiro, G., Smyth, P.: From data mining to knowledge discovery in databases. AI Mag. **17**(3), 37 (1996)
10. Goasduff, L.: 3 barriers to AI adoption (2019). https://www.gartner.com/smarterwithgartner/3-barriers-to-ai-adoption/. Accessed 24 May 2021
11. Jyoti, R., Shirer, M.: Idc survey finds artificial intelligence adoption being driven by improved customer experience, greater employee efficiency, and accelerated innovation (2020). https://www.idc.com/getdoc.jsp?containerId=prUS46534820. Accessed 24 May 2021
12. Li, J., Sun, A., Han, J., Li, C.: A survey on deep learning for named entity recognition. IEEE Trans. Knowl. Data Eng, p. 1 (2020). https://doi.org/10.1109/TKDE.2020.2981314
13. Liu, S.: Global natural language processing market 2017–2025 (2020). https://www.statista.com/statistics/607891/worldwide-natural-language-processing-market-revenues/. Accessed 24 May 2021
14. Mane, D., Chitnis, K., Ojha, N.: The spring framework: an open source java platform for developing robust java applications. Int. J. Innov. Technol. Explor. Eng. (IJITEE) (2013)
15. Peters, M.E., et al.: Deep contextualized word representations. CoRR. abs/1802.05365 (2018). http://arxiv.org/abs/1802.05365
16. Pineau, J., et al.: Improving reproducibility in machine learning research (a report from the neurips 2019 reproducibility program) (2020). arXiv:2003.12206. Version 3

17. Reuters: Amazon ditched AI recruiting tool that favored men for technical jobs (2018). https://www.theguardian.com/technology/2018/oct/10/amazon-hiring-ai-gender-bias-recruiting-engine. Accessed 24 May 2021
18. Ribeiro, M.T., Wu, T., Guestrin, C., Singh, S.: Beyond accuracy: behavioral testing of NLP models with CheckList. In: Proceedings of the 58th Annual Meeting of the Association for Computational Linguistics, pp. 4902–4912. Association for Computational Linguistics, Online (2020). https://doi.org/10.18653/v1/2020.acl-main.442. https://www.aclweb.org/anthology/2020.acl-main.442
19. Schreiber, M., Kraft, B., Zündorf, A.: Metrics driven research collaboration: focusing on common project goals continuously. In: 2017 IEEE/ACM 4th International Workshop on Software Engineering Research and Industrial Practice (SER IP), pp. 41–47 (2017). https://doi.org/10.1109/SER-IP.2017.6
20. Schreiber, M.: Towards effective natural language application development. Dissertation, University of Kassel (2019). https://doi.org/10.17170/kobra-20190529539
21. Schreiber, M., Kraft, B., Zündorf, A.: Cost-efficient quality assurance of natural language processing tools through continuous monitoring with continuous integration. In: Proceedings of the 3rd International Workshop on Software Engineering Research and Industrial Practice, SER&IP 2016, pp. 46–52. Association for Computing Machinery, New York (2016). https://doi.org/10.1145/2897022.2897029
22. Sildatke, M., Karwanni, H., Kraft, B., Schmidts, O., Zündorf, A.: Automated software quality monitoring in research collaboration projects. In: Proceedings of the IEEE/ACM 42nd International Conference on Software Engineering Workshops, ICSEW'20, pp. 603–610. Association for Computing Machinery, New York (2020). https://doi.org/10.1145/3387940.3391478
23. Staff, V.: Why do 87% of data science projects never make it into production? (2019). https://venturebeat.com/2019/07/19/why-do-87-of-data-science-projects-never-make-it-into-production/. Accessed 24 May 2021
24. Studer, S., et al.: Towards CRISP-ML(Q): a machine learning process model with quality assurance methodology (2020). arXiv:2003.05155
25. Varanasi, B., Belida, S.: Maven archetypes. In: Introducing Maven. Apress, Berkeley (2014). https://doi.org/10.1007/978-1-4842-0841-0_6
26. Vijayan, V.K., Bindu, K.R., Parameswaran, L.: A comprehensive study of text classification algorithms. In: 2017 International Conference on Advances in Computing, Communications and Informatics (ICACCI), pp. 1109–1113 (2017). https://doi.org/10.1109/ICACCI.2017.8125990
27. Vincent, J.: Twitter taught microsoft's AI chatbot to be a racist asshole in less than a day (2016). https://www.theverge.com/2016/3/24/11297050/tay-microsoft-chatbot-racist. Accessed 24 May 2021
28. Weber, C., Hirmer, P., Reimann, P., Schwarz, H.: A new process model for the comprehensive management of machine learning models. In: Proceedings of the 21st International Conference on Enterprise Information Systems, vol. 1: ICEIS, pp. 415–422. INSTICC, SciTePress (2019). https://doi.org/10.5220/0007725304150422

Evaluating Predictive Business Process Monitoring Approaches on Small Event Logs

Martin Käppel[1]([✉]), Stefan Jablonski[1], and Stefan Schönig[2][ID]

[1] Institute for Computer Science, University of Bayreuth, Bayreuth, Germany
{martin.kaeppel,stefan.jablonski}@uni-bayreuth.de
[2] University of Regensburg, Regensburg, Germany
stefan.schoenig@ur.de

Abstract. Predictive business process monitoring is concerned with the prediction how a running process instance will unfold up to its completion at runtime. Most of the proposed approaches rely on a wide number of machine learning techniques. In the last years numerous studies revealed that these methods can be successfully applied for different prediction targets. However, these techniques require a qualitatively and quantitatively sufficient dataset. Unfortunately, there are many situations in business process management where only a quantitatively insufficient dataset is available. The problem of insufficient data in the context of BPM is still neglected. Hence, none of the comparative studies investigates the performance of predictive business process monitoring techniques in environments with small datasets. In this paper an evaluation framework for comparing existing approaches with regard to their suitability for small datasets is developed and exemplarily applied to state-of-the-art approaches in next activity prediction.

Keywords: Process mining · Predictive business process monitoring · Small sample learning · Process prediction

1 Introduction

Predictive business process monitoring aims at predicting how a running process instance will unfold up to its completion at runtime based on its current state of execution. This can help to identify problems before the process instance runs in and enables to take adequate preventive measures to avoid them. One can distinguish several prediction targets, e.g., performance predictions such as the remaining execution time [15], business rule violations [11,12], predictions regarding the outcome of a process instance [3,21], and predictions of the next event [6] including further information as when it / they will occur and which resource(s) is/are responsible for it [2,17]. The majority of the proposed approaches rely on a wide number of different machine learning (ML) techniques to perform these predictions.

© Springer Nature Switzerland AG 2021
A. C. R. Paiva et al. (Eds.): QUATIC 2021, CCIS 1439, pp. 167–182, 2021.
https://doi.org/10.1007/978-3-030-85347-1_13

In the last years numerous comparative studies, reviews, and benchmarks of predictive business monitoring approaches have been published [4,9,14,21,23]. These studies reveal that ML techniques can be successfully applied for all the mentioned prediction tasks. However, all ML techniques are faced with the fundamental requirement of a qualitatively and quantitatively sufficient dataset. In business process management (BPM) we can have an insufficient dataset since a process *(i)* is executed very seldom or has not been executed often yet, *(ii)* its instances are long running, *(iii)* legal regulations like the General Data Protection Regulation lead to significantly less data, or *(iv)* there are fundamental changes in the intended process execution so that some historic data are not usable anymore. Especially small and medium sized companies frequently cannot fulfill this fundamental requirements of ML since not enough data is recorded. On the other hand, small data can also be a desired objective because of limited computational power or real-time feedback. The latter is, for example, characteristic for Stream Process Mining or Concept Drift.

The problem of insufficient data in the context of BPM is still neglected [8]. Hence, none of the comparative studies or benchmarks investigates the performance of predictive business process monitoring techniques on small data, i.e., small event logs. Hence, the contribution of the paper is two-fold: *(i)* we introduce an evaluation framework for comparing existing approaches w.r.t. their suitability for small event logs, and *(ii)* analyse the suitability of existing state-of-the-art approaches in predictive business process monitoring on small event logs. This analysis is also a step towards answering the question of whether there is a lower bound for a minimum of required data for predictive business process monitoring and, if so, in which range this lower bound is located. Our results show that in many cases the algorithms allow a significant reduction of training data and, hence, training times and computational effort can be significantly reduced.

The remainder of the paper is structured as follows: In Sect. 2 we recall basic terminology and give a short introduction to the area of Small Sample Learning. Section 3 highlights the difference between this comparative study and other surveys. In Sect. 4 we describe our evaluation framework and how it can be tailored to the different areas of BPM. In Sect. 5 we use this framework for comparing selected state-of-the-art approaches for predicting the next activity w.r.t. their suitability for small event logs. Finally, Sect. 6 outlines future work.

2   Background

2.1   Process Mining

The input of process mining techniques is a *(process) event log*, i.e., a set of traces of a business process (model). A *trace* (also called *case*) is a temporaly ordered sequence of events that are related to the same process instance. An *event* is related to an activity (i.e., a step in a business process) and is characterized by various *event attributes* with at least a case id ($\mathcal{C}$), the name of the corresponding activity ($\mathcal{A}$), and the timestamp of occurrence ($\mathcal{T}$). Optionally, an event contains

Table 1. Sample process event log

Case ID	Event ID	Activity	Timestamp	Resource	Amount	Key
Case1	e_{11}	A	2020-10-09T14:50:17	MF		SD-1
Case1	e_{12}	T	2020-10-09T14:51:01	SL	100	HG-4
Case1	e_{13}	W	2020-11-09T12:54:39	KH		HZ-2
Case2	e_{21}	A	2019-04-03T08:55:38	MF		SD-2
Case2	e_{22}	T	2019-04-03T08:55:53	SL	340	HK-7
Case2	e_{23}	C	2019-05-19T09:00:28	KH		SGH-3
Case3	e_{31}	A	2019-11-06T10:47:35	MK		SD-3
Case3	e_{32}	T	2019-11-06T10:48:53	PE	235	UG-2
Case3	e_{33}	C	2019-11-25T08:18:07	SJ		KL-6
Case4	e_{41}	A	2019-04-05T08:59:38	MF		SD-5
Case4	e_{42}	T	2019-04-05T09:55:52	SL	140	HK-2

further event attributes, such as the resources or systems involved in executing the activity ($\mathcal{L}$) or further data payload ($\mathcal{D}_i$). Often additional event attributes (e.g., the role of a process participant) are derived by process mining approaches and added to the events.

Let us consider the sample event log shown in Table 1 that provides the following event attributes: a *case identifier*, the name of the executed *activity*, the *timestamp* of execution, the involved *resource*, and two further information (*amount, key*) in form of data payload.

Definition 1. *Let $\mathcal{E}$ be the universe of events, $\mathcal{P}$ the set of event attributes, and ε the empty element. For each event attribute $p \in \mathcal{P}$, we define a function $\pi_p : \mathcal{E} \rightarrow dom(\mathcal{P}) \cup \{\varepsilon\}$ that assigns a value of the domain of p to an event. However, ε can only be assigned to optional event attributes.*

For example, for event e_{13}, holds $\pi_{\mathcal{A}}(e_{13}) =$ "W", $\pi_{\mathcal{C}}(e_{13}) =$ "Case1", $\pi_{\mathcal{L}}(e_{13}) =$ "KH", $\pi_{\mathcal{T}}(e_{13}) =$ "2020-11-09T12:54:39", $\pi_{\mathcal{D}_{\text{Amount}}}(e_{13}) = \varepsilon$, and $\pi_{\mathcal{D}_{\text{Key}}}(e_{13}) =$ "HZ-2".

Definition 2. *Let S be the universe of traces. A **trace** $\sigma \in S$ is a finite non-empty sequence of events $\sigma = \langle e_1, ..., e_n \rangle$ such that for $1 \leq i < j \leq n : e_i, e_j \in \mathcal{E} \wedge \pi_{\mathcal{C}}(e_i) = \pi_{\mathcal{C}}(e_j) \wedge \pi_{\mathcal{T}}(e_i) \leq \pi_{\mathcal{T}}(e_j)$, where $|\sigma| = n$ denotes the length of σ and $\sigma(i)$ refers to the i-th element in σ.*

This definition states that each event is unique, time within a trace is increasing, and all events with the same case identifier refer to the same process instance.

If a process instance has finished, i.e., no additional events related to this instance are executed in the future, the trace is completed.

Definition 3. *A trace $\sigma \in S$ is called **completed** if there is no $e' \in \mathcal{E}$ such that $\pi_{\mathcal{C}}(e') = \pi_{\mathcal{C}}(e)$ with $e' \notin \sigma$ and $e \in \sigma$. An **event log** L is a set $L = \{\sigma_1, ..., \sigma_l\}$ of completed traces.*

As an example, the event log shown in Table 1 consists of four traces, related to the process instances Case1, Case2, Case3, and Case4. We consider traces to be equivalent with respect to one or more process perspectives (e.g., control flow) by introducing the concept of *trace variants*, which defines an equivalence relation on an event log:

Definition 4. *Let L be an event log, $\sigma_1, \sigma_2 \in L$ traces, and $\mathfrak{P} \subseteq \mathcal{P}$ a set of event attributes. We write $\sigma_1 \sim_\mathfrak{P} \sigma_2$, if σ_1 and σ_2 are equivalent with regard to $\mathfrak{P}$, i.e., for all $p \in \mathfrak{P}$ there is $\pi_p(\sigma_1(i)) = \pi_p(\sigma_2(i))$ for all $1 \leq i \leq max\{|\sigma_1|, |\sigma_2|\}$ with $\pi_p(\sigma(i)) = \varepsilon$ if $i > |\sigma|$. The set $[\sigma]_{\sim_\mathfrak{P}} := \{\sigma' \in L | \sigma' \sim_\mathfrak{P} \sigma\}$ is called a **trace variant**.*

It is obvious that $\sim_\mathfrak{P}$ is an equivalence relation. Applying this relation to an event log provides in dependency of $\mathfrak{P}$ a more abstract or a less fine-grained view on the event log, since we can disregard one or more process perspectives (to be exact event attributes). For example applying the relation with $\mathfrak{P} = \{\mathcal{A}\}$ on the event log in Table 1 results in three trace variants: the trace with id Case1 represents the trace variant $\langle A, T, W \rangle$; a second trace variant $\langle A, T, C \rangle$ is represented by the two remaining traces, since they are identical with regard to the controlflow; a third trace variant $\langle A, T \rangle$ is represented by trace with id Case4. If we additionally consider the organizational perspective, i.e., $\mathfrak{P} = \{\mathcal{A}, \mathcal{L}\}$ four trace variants evolve, since the traces with case id Case2, Case3, and Case4 differ with respect to the involved resources: $\langle (A, MF),(T, SL),(W, KH) \rangle$, $\langle (A, MF), (T, SL), (C, KH) \rangle$, $\langle (A, MK),(T, PE),(C, SJ) \rangle$, and $\langle (A, MF), (T, SL) \rangle$. On the other hand, if we only consider the organizational perspective, the traces with case id Case1 and Case2 represent the same trace variant ($\langle MF, SL, KH \rangle$). Usually the more event attributes are considered, the more trace variants occur since it is highly probable that they differ in one of the perspectives. We can consider the frequency distribution of the trace variants within the event log.

Definition 5. *Let L be an event log, Ω the set of trace variants with regard to $\sim_\mathfrak{P}$ on L, and $X : \Omega \to \mathbb{R}$ a discrete random variable that represents the trace variants. Then the probability for the occurence of a trace variant is given by:*

$$P(X = [\sigma]_{\sim_\mathfrak{P}}) = \frac{|[\sigma]_{\sim_\mathfrak{P}}|}{|L|}.$$

We call the frequency distribution of X the **distribution of the trace variants**.

For the example from Table 1, we obtain the following frequency distribution: If only the property $\mathcal{A}$ is considered, a frequency distribution of 0.33 to 0.67 follows. If additionally property $\mathcal{L}$ is regarded, three trace variants with equal probability of 0.33 result.

2.2 Small Sample Learning

In recent years a new and promising area in artificial intelligence research called *Small Sample Learning* (SSL) has emerged [18]. SSL deals with ML on quantitatively inadequate datasets. This also encompass partial insufficient datasets like imbalanced datasets, where for some classes are significantly more examples than for other classes. Although, SSL has its origins in the field of computer vision, meanwhile many SSL techniques are applied in various application areas. The current SSL research is divided into two main branches: *concept learning* and *experience learning* [18]. Experience learning attempts to solve a SSL problem by applying conventional ML techniques, by either transforming the problem into a classical ML problem through increasing the amount of data or reducing the preliminaries of the required ML algorithms. In contrast, concept learning aims to detect new concepts from only a small number of examples. Within the two branches numerous methods can be identified. Although there are numerous situations with qualitatively insufficient data in the context of BPM, the application of SSL methods is still neglected in this area. This might be caused by the fact that most common SSL techniques are strongly tailored to computer vision or NLP problems and must be adapted to BPM first in order to become applicable [8].

3 Related Work

This work relates to the stream of research in predictive business process monitoring and touches the area of SSL. Since, SSL methods are barely used in BPM so far, related work mainly focuses on comparative studies of existing business process monitoring approaches and the approaches themselves. The problem of quantitatively insufficient data in BPM was systematically addressed the first time in [8], where the authors propose the idea of leveraging SSL methods for this issue. They describe their concept by the example of predictive business process monitoring, suggests SSL methods that seems promising for BPM, and describe an idea of how the effectiveness of such methods can be proven. A survey of existing SSL methods outside of BPM is presented in [18].

The problem of insufficient training data in context of predictive business process monitoring in case of next event prediction was addressed in [20] where the authors proposed the use of Generative Adversarial Networks (GANs) for solving this issue. This network architecture outperforms other existing deep learning approaches w.r.t. accuracy and earliness of prediction. However, the authors use conventional, i.e., not small, event logs for training and evaluation. Hence, it is unclear whether it only improves results on conventional event logs or if it works for small event logs, too.

The necessity of evaluation frameworks for comparing the performance of different algorithms in BPM, respectively process mining, is not new, since the disparity of event logs, experimental setups, and different assumptions makes it often difficult to make fair comparisons [12,14]. In [16] the authors motivate the need of an evaluation framework for process mining approaches and propose a framework for comparing model discovery algorithms. In the subfield of predictive business process monitoring there is a plenty set of different comparative studies depending on the different prediction tasks [4,9,14,21,23]. However, all of them depend on large event logs and do not consider environments with a

Fig. 1. Conception of the evaluation framework

small amount of data. Outcome-oriented techniques are reviewed and compared in [21], in [9] with special focus on deep learning techniques. In [23] the authors give a survey and benchmark of remaining time predictions methods. In [14] the authors focus on deep learning techniques for next activity prediction, activity suffix prediction, next timestamp prediction, and remaining time prediction by evaluating approaches with publicly available source code on 12 real-life event logs from various domains.

The above discussed comparative studies observed that deep learning approaches for next activity prediction outperform classical predictions techniques, which use an explicit model representation such as Hidden Markov Models [10], probabilistic finite automata or state-transition [1,22]. These deep learning approaches are based on different types of neural networks. Most of them use Long-Short-Term-Memory (LSTM) Neural Networks [2,6,17,19], Gated Recurrent Units (GRUs) as a variant of LSTMs [7], or Convolutional Neural Networks (CNN) [5,13]. The approaches use different encoding techniques for sequences and events and consider different input data for making predictions. An overview about existing deep learning approaches including a detailed description of the underlying architectures is given in [14].

4   Evaluation Framework

In this section we describe the structure of our evaluation framework. We identify different challenges that must be considered by the evaluation framework.

4.1   The Issue of Small Event Logs

The evaluation framework (cf. Fig. 1) gets two inputs: the approaches to be compared and small event logs. However, providing small event logs is a crucial challenge. This is due to the missing definition of "small event log". This question is strongly related to the question what is "big data". Also, this is still an open question in research. Due to inconsistent and sometimes contradicting definitions, that often include time dependency (i.e., define as big data what is today the largest available amount of data), domain dependency or circular reasoning (e.g., big data is the opposite to small data) this question cannot be conclusively clarified. We bypass this technical and conceptual problem by reducing event logs with various reduction factors and thereby generate small event logs of different sizes. The use of different reduction factors enables us to fully cover the broad range of "smallness", which ranges from zero or a single case up to, for example, several 1000 cases. Hence, we are independent of concrete definitions. In a strict sense, the generated small event logs are rather "relatively small" event logs, than "small" event logs. The exact procedure of generating small event logs is described in detail in Sect. 4.3.

In addition to bypassing this definition problem, generating small event logs by reducing conventional event logs has another advantage: Since we can fall back to the non-reduced event log (so called *reference log*), it is possible to compare results of an analysis achieved on a small log with the results obtained on the reference log[1]. This comparison allows us to make quantitative statements about the impact of reducing an event log. Such a comparison is necessary to determine whether any potential loss of quality that goes in hand with the data reduction, can be better compensated by one method or by another. Hence, we measure how an approach performs depending on the reduction factor. It is likely that the achieved results also depend on the domain and structure of the considered event log (e.g., number of event per case).

4.2 Preserving Comparability

When we talk about comparability in our approach, we mean to compare the prediction quality of predictive business process monitoring approaches measured on the reference log and the generated small event logs. For preserving comparability, it is essential to evaluate all trained models with the same test data. Hence, we first divide the event log into training and test data and afterwards we reduce only the training data and not the whole reference log. The selection of the test data is discussed in Sect. 4.4. However, excluding the test data from reduction has a far-reaching consequence: Usually ML techniques, which require a split into training and test data, use training-test ratios like 80:20 or 70:30. Since we keep the test data and only reduce the training data the ratio between train and test data shifts more and more towards test data with increasing reduction factor. Hence, the less training data are used, the relatively more tests the model must pass afterwards. This seems to be unusual, however it ensures comparability and guarantees that the quality of the trained model and, as a result, the performance of the method used for training, are not overestimated but rather underestimated. In consequence, also the frequently used cross validation that enables the use of all available data for training as well as for testing are not applicable anymore, since through the reduction step reference log and small event logs differ. It should be noted that dispense on comparability would avoid this shift problem but would be accompanied with interpretation problems due to meaningless splits in training and test data. Suppose that a reduced event log would only contain 10 traces left and we would split this event log into training and test data using a ratio of 80:20. Then the metrics used for evaluation would hardly be meaningful. For example the accuracy metric could only attain three different values: 0%, 50%, or 100%.

---

[1] At this point we implicitly assume that the event logs currently used in research can be considered as quantitatively sufficient.

It is obvious that comparability and keeping the ratio between training and test data are diametrically opposed to each other. Since, the comparability between the reduced event logs is essential for our aims and cannot be neglected, we accept the shift of the training-test ratio in our evaluation framework.

4.3 Reducing Event Logs

The amount of training data is reduced by removing as many process instances from the training data such that a given reduction factor is reached. We select process instances for removal either randomly or along the time dimension. Removing instances randomly means selecting process instances randomly. When reducing along the time dimension, we order the process instances ascending by its first event timestamp and then remove the first process instances according to the reduction factor. Note that the way how the process instances to be removed are selected leads to different interpretations: In case of randomly removing process instances, we simulate that a process is executed very seldom or due to legal regulations there are only a few records available for analysis. Reason for this interpretation is that the underlying time window of the event log (spanned by the earliest and latest timestamp of an event) stays nearly unchanged. However, in case of removing process instances along the time dimension, the time window is shortened. Hence, this reduction method reflects a scenario where a process has not been executed often yet or due to fundamental changes in the intended process execution some historic data (up to a specific time) are not usable anymore. Hence, these two reduction methods are sufficient to simulate all in the introduction mentioned reasons for quantitatively insufficient event logs. Nevertheless, we implement some alternative selection methods, like removing the most recent data or removing only specific trace variants, as defined in Definition 4.

However, the reduction of the training data bears two further issues: *(i)* the possible loss of activities and resources, and *(ii)* statistical bias.

Loss of Activities and Resources. Since we generate small event logs out of large event logs, there is a risk that activities or resources get completely lost or are finally only represented in the test data. In case of getting completely lost, the trained model would not be able to handle these activities or resources, if they occur later in productive use, since they are not encoded and therefore are unknown to the model. Therefore, we extract and buffer all occurring activities and resources from the reference log before splitting into training and test data and before generating the small event logs. Hence, these activities and resources can be considered even if no training sample reflects them. However, this also implies that process instances in the test data that contain activities or resources that are not represented in the training data cannot be predicted well.

Statistical Bias. The reduction of the training data may be accompanied by statistical bias in the probability distribution of the trace variants (cf. Definition 5). Since most of the ML techniques are statistical methods, it affects the model quality and must therefore be considered adequately. Suppose that a trace variant is represented by exactly one representative in a training dataset, which consists of 100 traces. Then this trace variant has an empirical probability of 1%. If we reduce the training data by 50% and the representative of the considered trace variant is not removed, then the empirical probability of this trace variant increases to 2%. At the same time other trace variants are either completely eliminated or their empirical probability decreases. In case of an even stronger reduction and under the assumption that the considered trace variant is not removed, the increase of empirical probability could be much stronger. Hence, the probability distributions of the trace variants in the considered event logs can differ significantly or reflects no longer their occurrence frequency in reality.

However, the problem becomes less relevant the more process perspectives are considered, since process perspectives foster the singularity of traces and the number of trace variants represented in the event log tends to the number of traces in the event log. In the case that each trace variant occurs only once in the event log, removing a trace directly leads to a loss of a trace variant. This observation prohibits to reduce the event log along the distribution of its trace variants. However, considering this issue only from the perspective of trace variants is not sufficient. Because from the ML perspective there may be a significantly lower statistical bias since this perspective also takes the similarity between the trace variants into account (for example two trace variants only differ in a single event). Hence, often removing a trace variant is sufficiently compensated by another very similar trace variant that is still included in the event log. However, it is difficult to determine this compensatory effect, because it strongly depends on the considered ML technique and therefore cannot be adequately considered in the evaluation framework.

The effects discussed above are affected by the chosen reduction method. In case of a randomly reduction, the distribution of trace variants can be extremely distorted. The reduction along the time dimension alleviates this issue, since the distribution of the trace variants in a sufficiently large time window should be more similar to the distribution of the entire event log than the distribution in a randomly selected subset of the event log. This assumption also holds for the compensatory similarity effect. Hence, it is expected that via reduction along the time dimension the statistical bias can be reduced. However, it is clear, that it also depends on the particular event logs and in case of strong reduction the statistical bias cannot be longer compensated.

4.4 Splitting into Training and Test Data

Still, the question remains how the event log should be split into training and test data. We use the same procedure for selecting test data as for reducing the training data, i.e., the test data is either selected randomly or along the time dimension. In the latter case, the newest process instances are used for testing and the oldest for training. The chosen split procedure may affect the achieved results, since training and test data may overlap in time by splitting the event log randomly. This could be problematic if the underlying process evolves

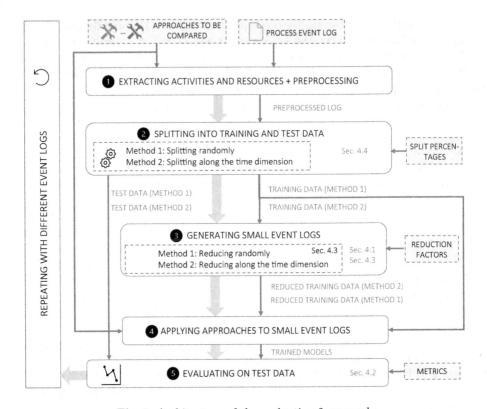

Fig. 2. Architecture of the evaluation framework

during time and, hence, different process variants are mixed up in the event log. However, splitting along the time dimension does not prevent this issue, since the splitting can lead to a separation of a specific process variant (i.e., the test data represents a process variant that does not occur in the training data). Nevertheless, splitting along the time dimension appears closer to reality, since knowledge of the past is used to predict the future. Furthermore, the splitting along the time dimension also provides a better reproducibility.

4.5   Architecture of the Evaluation Framework

In summary, the proposed evaluation framework depicted in Fig. 2 comprises five successive steps. In a first step, an event log is preprocessed depending on the selected approaches to be compared and all activities and resources of the event log are extracted and registered. Further preprocessing encompasses, for example, the removal of traces with events that have missing values. Afterwards (cf. Step 2) a preprocessed event log is split into training and test data according to one or more split ratios. The resulting training data is then reduced in the third step according to various reduction factors to generate a set of small event

Table 2. Statistic of the used event logs. Time related measures are shown in days.

Event Log	BPIC12	Helpdesk	BPIC13	BPIC15_2	BPIC15_5
Number of cases	9559	4580	1487	832	1156
Number of activities	36	14	7	410	389
Number of roles	8	4	4	11	10
Number of events	140863	21348	6660	44354	59083
Maximal case length	163	15	35	132	154
Minimal case length	3	2	1	1	5
Average case length	14.74	4.66	4.49	53.31	51.11
Maximal duration	76.90	59.99	2254.85	1325.96	1343.96

logs. The framework selects the traces to be removed with the same methods as used for selecting test and training data. The approaches to be compared are trained with the training data resulting from the splitting step as well as the reduced training data of the reduction step (cf. Step 4). In order to measure the performance of the considered approaches, the trained models are evaluated on the corresponding test data (cf. Step 5). For measuring the performance one or more suitable metrics are used. The selection of the metrics primarily depends on the types of approaches. After the completion of the evaluation step, all steps are repeated with further event logs to get representative results.

In general, the framework is extensible by adding alternative methods for splitting and reducing the processed data. In Fig. 2, all parts of the framework that can be adapted and configured are marked with dashed lines. Fields with a grey background represent input parameters that have to be set to configure the framework. The remaining dashed fields can be extended to add more functionality to the framework.

We conclude this section by a brief discussion whether the evaluation framework is tailored to specific process mining methods. Since the framework offers flexible preprocessing and the splitting into test and training data can be skipped it is also possible to evaluate unsupervised ML techniques. For ML techniques, which require a split into training, validation, and test data some smaller adaptions would be necessary. Since the evaluation framework does not implement any approach specific particularities, the framework can be considered as approach-agnostic.

5   Evaluation of Existing Approaches on Small Event Logs

5.1   Dataset Description and Experimental Setup

The first three steps of the framework that are responsible for generating small event logs are implemented as a Java application. Step 4 is covered by the modified implementations of the considered approaches. Modification becomes necessary, since approaches must deal with the generated small event logs and the test data generated in the previous steps. Hence, parts in the implementations of the considered approaches that are responsible for splitting into training and test data or extracting activities and resources must be modified. Also, the approach specific evaluation components must be replaced by the evaluation component of the framework (Step 5) to ensure a consistent evaluation procedure.

We evaluate our framework with a small comparative study of selected state-of-the-art approaches for next activity and role prediction. We select approaches [2] and [13] since they represent the most frequently used deep learning architectures (LSTM and CNN respectively) for next activity prediction, provides publicly available source code, and achieve good results in various comparative studies. We modified the approaches in the above described way and additional changed the implementations to run with Python 3.7 and to support training on GPU. The experiments are run on a system equipped with a Windows 10 operating system, an Intel Core i9-9900K CPU3.60GHz, 64GB RAM, and a NVIDIA Quadro RTX 4000 having 6GB of memory.

We perform our experiment using 5 real-life event logs from different domains with diverse characteristics (cf. Table 2) extracted from the *4TU Center for Research Data*[2]. For our experiment, we preprocess the event logs in the same way as it is done in the considered approaches. Due to the missing resource event attribute in some traces we removed 3528 of the 13087 traces in the BPIC12 log.

5.2   Tailoring the Evaluation Framework to Predictive Monitoring

We tailor the evaluation framework for evaluating predictive business process monitoring approaches in the following way. We use a training-test ratio of 70:30. The test data is selected by applying the two methods from Sec. 4.4: *(i)* splitting randomly, and *(ii)* splitting along the time dimension. Training data are reduced according to the following reduction factors: 0.2, 0.4, 0.6, 0.8, 0.9, 0.95, and 0.99. Hereby, the traces are either removed randomly or along the time dimension. For evaluation, we use the following common metrics that can be derived from the confusion matrix[3]: *(i) Recall* (also called sensitivity) defined as $R = TP/(TP + FN)$, *(ii) Precision* $P = TP/(TP + FP)$, *(iii) F-Measure* defined as harmonic mean $F = 2RP/(R + P)$ of precision and recall, and *(iv) Accuracy* defined as $A = (TP + TN)/(TP + FN + FP + FN)$. These metrics coincide with those from other comparative studies.

5.3   Results and Discussion

Due to the large number of trained models and measures and since the achieved results are comparable for all considered approaches we report in this paper only an exemplarily excerpt of the detailed measures (cf. Table 3 and 4) and

---

[2] https://data.4tu.nl.
[3] i.e., it can be calculated from true positives (TP), true negatives (TN), false positives (FP), and true positive (TP).

Table 3. Next activity prediction results (accuracy measures in %) for approach [2] (architecture "shared categorical")

| Event Log | Reduced along time dimension | | | | | | | | Reduced randomly | | | | | | | |
	Applied reduction factors								Applied reduction factors							
	0.0	0.2	0.4	0.6	0.8	0.9	0.95	0.99	0.0	0.2	0.4	0.6	0.8	0.9	0.95	0.99
BPIC_15_2	0.10	0.09	0.09	0.08	0.11	0.21	0.17	0.07	0.11	0.09	0.09	0.06	0.08	0.05	0.06	0.04
BPIC_15_5	0.16	0.20	0.24	0.28	0.28	0.26	0.22	0.22	0.16	0.14	0.13	0.14	0.09	0.09	0.08	0.03
BPIC_13	0.54	0.64	0.58	0.61	0.60	0.57	0.51	0.39	0.56	0.52	0.53	0.51	0.53	0.49	0.50	0.44
Helpdesk	0.74	0.74	0.79	0.79	0.78	0.79	0.78	0.70	0.74	0.74	0.73	0.74	0.73	0.73	0.72	0.72
BPIC_12	0.85	0.86	0.85	0.84	0.85	0.84	0.84	0.79	0.85	0.85	0.85	0.85	0.84	0.84	0.84	0.74

Table 4. Next role prediction results (accuracy measures in %) for approach [2] (architecture "shared categorical")

| Event Log | Reduced along time dimension | | | | | | | | Reduced randomly | | | | | | | |
	Applied reduction factors								Applied reduction factors							
	0.0	0.2	0.4	0.6	0.8	0.9	0.95	0.99	0.0	0.2	0.4	0.6	0.8	0.9	0.95	0.99
BPIC_15_2	0.85	0.87	0.86	0.86	0.86	0.82	0.84	0.55	0.87	0.78	0.75	0.85	0.85	0.82	0.68	0.55
BPIC_15_5	0.90	0.91	0.91	0.92	0.93	0.88	0.91	0.89	0.90	0.91	0.90	0.91	0.87	0.87	0.87	0.52
BPIC_13	0.96	0.96	0.92	0.96	0.95	0.93	0.83	0.63	0.97	0.97	0.97	0.97	0.97	0.93	0.91	0.95
Helpdesk	0.95	0.95	0.94	0.95	0.94	0.95	0.94	0.84	0.95	0.95	0.95	0.95	0.95	0.95	0.94	0.93
BPIC_12	0.97	0.97	0.97	0.97	0.97	0.97	0.97	0.94	0.97	0.97	0.97	0.97	0.97	0.96	0.96	0.93

limit ourselves to the discussion of the overall results. All further measures are provided in the repository of our implementation[4].

The most surprising observation is that only a very strong reduction factor of 95% or 99% significantly worsens the performance measured by different metrics. This applies for event logs where good results are achieved as well as for event logs that show poor results. A further surprising fact is that in case of a reduction along the time dimension the best results (highlighted in red) are not achieved by the reference values (reduction factor 0.0), i.e., often a reduced amount of training data achieves better results. However, this observation does not hold for a randomly performed reduction. This reduction method either achieves similar or slightly worse results. Hence, this observation supports the hypothesis of Sect. 4.3 that reduction along the time dimension leads to a more representative dataset. Since we remove those traces that have the earliest first timestamp this behaviour might also be an indicator that there is some process evolution within the logs. We also observe that the most complex event logs BPIC15_2 and BPIC15_5, which contain a relatively large number of activities for a comparatively small number of traces shows poor results. The reason for this behaviour seems to be the high number of activities per number of traces (cf. Table 2). This interpretation is supported by the fact that the prediction of

---

[4] https://github.com/mkaep/SSL-Evaluation-Framework.

the next roles performs significantly better. Hence, for learning such complex logs we would need significantly more training data.

In a deeper analysis of the results we analysed whether the prediction quality between the activities differ. This analysis reveals that all trained models (also the reference models) are good in predicting frequent activities but perform poor in predicting rare activities. As a result, frequent trace variants (i.e., standard cases) are predicted very well, while rare trace variants are barely predicted correct, since the prediction model treat them as standard cases. This is somehow natural, since ML methods try to generalize the data in a simple way by neglecting rare activities.

Hence, we can draw the following conclusions: for learning to predict frequent trace variants of less complex logs even a significantly reduced amount of data is sufficient. For learning rare trace variants, however, it is necessary to increase the amount of data, especially by better representing rare trace variants. For complex logs, like the BPIC15 logs, the currently available amount of data is not sufficient, to achieve acceptable results. Hence, our results reinforce the need for SSL methods in the area of predictive business process monitoring.

6   Future Work

In this paper, we propose a customizable evaluation framework for investigating predictive business process monitoring approaches w.r.t their suitability for small event logs. Our experiments reveal that training times and computational effort can be significantly reduced without any loss of quality with regard to the common metrics. For further improvement, however, it would be necessary to cope with the problem of rare trace variants. In future work the study should be extended to further approaches, event logs, and should investigate how different types of sequence and event encoding affect the performance. Furthermore, other prediction tasks, like the prediction of suffixes or the remaining time should be investigated. It is also necessary to adopt the framework for use in other subfields of process mining, like process model discovery or conformance checking.

References

1. Breuker, D., Matzner, M., Delfmann, P., Becker, J.: Comprehensible predictive models for business processes. MIS Q. **40**(4), 1009–1034 (2016)
2. Camargo, M., Dumas, M., González-Rojas, O.: Learning accurate LSTM models of business processes. In: Hildebrandt, T., van Dongen, B.F., Röglinger, M., Mendling, J. (eds.) BPM 2019. LNCS, vol. 11675, pp. 286–302. Springer, Cham (2019). https://doi.org/10.1007/978-3-030-26619-6_19
3. Conforti, R., de Leoni, M., La Rosa, M., van der Aalst, W.M.P.: Supporting risk-informed decisions during business process execution. In: Salinesi, C., Norrie, M.C., Pastor, Ó. (eds.) CAiSE 2013. LNCS, vol. 7908, pp. 116–132. Springer, Heidelberg (2013). https://doi.org/10.1007/978-3-642-38709-8_8

4. Di Francescomarino, C., Ghidini, C., Maggi, F.M., Milani, F.: Predictive process monitoring methods: which one suits me best? In: Weske, M., Montali, M., Weber, I., vom Brocke, J. (eds.) BPM 2018. LNCS, vol. 11080, pp. 462–479. Springer, Cham (2018). https://doi.org/10.1007/978-3-319-98648-7_27

5. Di Mauro, N., Appice, A., Basile, T.M.A.: Activity prediction of business process instances with inception CNN models. In: Alviano, M., Greco, G., Scarcello, F. (eds.) AI*IA 2019. LNCS (LNAI), vol. 11946, pp. 348–361. Springer, Cham (2019). https://doi.org/10.1007/978-3-030-35166-3_25

6. Evermann, J., Rehse, J.R., Fettke, P.: Predicting process behaviour using deep learning. Decis. Supp. Syst. **100**, 129–140 (2017)

7. Hinkka, M., Lehto, T., Heljanko, K.: Exploiting event log event attributes in RNN based prediction. In: Welzer, T., et al. (eds.) ADBIS 2019. CCIS, vol. 1064, pp. 405–416. Springer, Cham (2019). https://doi.org/10.1007/978-3-030-30278-8_40

8. Käppel, M., Schönig, S., Jablonski, S.: Leveraging small sample learning for business process management. Inf. Softw. Technol. **132**, 106472 (2020)

9. Kratsch, W., Manderscheid, J., Röglinger, M., Seyfried, J.: Machine learning in business process monitoring: a comparison of deep learning and classical approaches used for outcome prediction. BISE **63**, 261–271 (2020). https://doi.org/10.1007/s12599-020-00645-0

10. Lakshmanan, G.T., Shamsi, D., Doganata, Y.N., Unuvar, M., Khalaf, R.: A Markov prediction model for data-driven semi-structured business processes. Knowl. Inf. Syst. **42**(1), 97–126 (2013). https://doi.org/10.1007/s10115-013-0697-8

11. Maggi, F.M., Di Francescomarino, C., Dumas, M., Ghidini, C.: Predictive monitoring of business processes. In: Jarke, M., et al. (eds.) CAiSE 2014. LNCS, vol. 8484, pp. 457–472. Springer, Cham (2014). https://doi.org/10.1007/978-3-319-07881-6_31

12. Metzger, A., et al.: Comparing and combining predictive business process monitoring techniques. IEEE Trans. Syst. Man Cybern. **45**(2), 276–290 (2015)

13. Pasquadibisceglie, V., Appice, A., Castellano, G., Malerba, D.: Using convolutional neural networks for predictive process analytics. In: Proceedings of ICPM 2019 (2019)

14. Rama-Maneiro, E., Vidal, J., Lama, M.: Deep learning for predictive business process monitoring: review and benchmark. ArXiv arXiv:2009.13251 (2020)

15. Rogge-Solti, A., Weske, M.: Prediction of business process durations using non-Markovian stochastic petri nets. Inf. Syst. **54**, 1–14 (2015)

16. Rozinat, A., de Medeiros, A.K.A., Günther, C.W., Weijters, A.J.M.M., van der Aalst, W.M.P.: The need for a process mining evaluation framework in research and practice. In: ter Hofstede, A., Benatallah, B., Paik, H.-Y. (eds.) BPM 2007. LNCS, vol. 4928, pp. 84–89. Springer, Heidelberg (2008). https://doi.org/10.1007/978-3-540-78238-4_10

17. Schönig, S., Jasinski, R., Ackermann, L., Jablonski, S.: Deep learning process prediction with discrete and continuous data features. In: Proceedings of ENASE 2018 (2018)

18. Shu, J., Xu, Z., Meng, D.: Small sample learning in big data era. CoRR abs/1808.04572 (2018). arXiv:1808.04572

19. Tax, N., Verenich, I., La Rosa, M., Dumas, M.: Predictive business process monitoring with LSTM neural networks. In: Dubois, E., Pohl, K. (eds.) CAiSE 2017. LNCS, vol. 10253, pp. 477–492. Springer, Cham (2017). https://doi.org/10.1007/978-3-319-59536-8_30

20. Taymouri, F., Rosa, M.L., Erfani, S., Bozorgi, Z.D., Verenich, I.: Predictive business process monitoring via generative adversarial nets: the case of next event prediction. In: Fahland, D., Ghidini, C., Becker, J., Dumas, M. (eds.) BPM 2020. LNCS, vol. 12168, pp. 237–256. Springer, Cham (2020). https://doi.org/10.1007/978-3-030-58666-9_14
21. Teinemaa, I., Dumas, M., Rosa, M.L., Maggi, F.M.: Outcome-oriented predictive process monitoring: review and benchmark. TKDD **13**(2), 1–57 (2019)
22. Unuvar, M., Lakshmanan, G.T., Doganata, Y.N.: Leveraging path information to generate predictions for parallel business processes. Knowl. Inf. Syst. **47**(2), 433–461 (2015). https://doi.org/10.1007/s10115-015-0842-7
23. Verenich, I., Dumas, M., Rosa, M.L., Maggi, F.M., Teinemaa, I.: Survey and cross-benchmark comparison of remaining time prediction methods in business process monitoring. ACM TIST **10**(4), 1–34 (2019)

Analyzing a Process Core Ontology and Its Usefulness for Different Domains

Pablo Becker[✉], Fernanda Papa, Guido Tebes, and Luis Olsina

GIDIS_Web, Engineering School, UNLPam, General Pico, LP, Argentina
{beckerp,pmfer,guido_tebes,olsina1}@ing.unlpam.edu.ar

Abstract. A well-specified strategy should define and integrate consistently three capabilities: process, method, and common vocabulary specifications. The domain vocabularies of different strategies should be built on common reference terminologies. For example, a process ontology should be a common reference since it considers cross-cutting concerns for different domains. This work specifies and defines the main terms of ProcessCO (Process Core Ontology). This is an ontology placed at the core level in the context of a four-layered ontological architecture. A practical use of an upper-level ontology is to semantically enrich the lowest-level ontologies. For example, ThingFO (an ontology at the foundational level in that architecture) enriches ProcessCO. Since ProcessCO is at the core level, ontologies at the domain level benefit from reusing and extending its concepts. Therefore, ProcessCO can be seen as a reusable resource to semantically enrich domain ontologies. To illustrate its applicability, this work shows the semantic enrichment of two top-domain ontologies. By using ProcessCO (and other core ontologies) as a common terminological reference, the domain ontologies used in the different strategies are conceptually harmonized. Hence, strategies ensure terminological uniformity and consistency, thus facilitating the understanding of process and method specifications.

Keywords: Process · Vocabulary · Ontology · Core ontology · Ontological architecture · Semantic enrichment

1 Introduction

Engineering purposes can be classified into four main areas, such as evaluation, testing, development and maintenance [13]. For the development and/or maintenance categories, possible goal purposes are to create, add, delete or modify a specific feature and/or capability of a target entity and/or its context. On the other hand, examples of evaluation purposes may include to understand, monitor, control, improve, select an alternative, among others, while examples of testing purposes can embrace to find defects, review, verify, validate, find vulnerabilities, etc.

To achieve these goal purposes, strategies may be used. A strategy is a key resource of an organization that defines a specific course of action to follow. It specifies what to do and how to do it. As per [13], strategies should integrate process, method, and vocabulary specifications. These three capabilities promote, therefore, knowing what activities are

© Springer Nature Switzerland AG 2021
A. C. R. Paiva et al. (Eds.): QUATIC 2021, CCIS 1439, pp. 183–196, 2021.
https://doi.org/10.1007/978-3-030-85347-1_14

involved, and how to carry them out through methods and tools in the framework of a common vocabulary, which can be structured in an ontology [6, 10].

Summarizing each of these three capabilities, process specifications describe a set of domain activities, tasks, input and output artifacts, roles, and so forth to reach a specific goal purpose. Process specifications can consider process perspectives [7], such as functional, informational, behavioral and organizational. On the other hand, method specifications represent the particular ways to perform the activity descriptions. Finally, vocabularies explicitly establish the needed domain terms to specify processes and methods consistently. The use of a common vocabulary is very useful to avoid ambiguities, inconsistencies and incompleteness in the process and method specifications of a certain application domain. One example of an ontology is TestTDO (a *Top-Domain Ontology for Software Testing*) [19], and another is MEvalTDO (a *Top-Domain Ontology for Measurement and Evaluation*).

The authors of this paper are primarily interested in building strategies for different domains (e.g., testing, evaluation) that integrate the three abovementioned capabilities. Particularly, the domain vocabularies of the different strategies should be built on common reference terminologies. Heijst *et al.* [20] distinguish different types of ontologies regarding the subject of the conceptualization, e.g., *domain ontologies*, which express conceptualizations that are intended for particular domains (e.g. TestTDO and MEvalTDO); and *core* or *generic ontologies,* which include concepts that are considered to be general across many domains. Core ontologies can be used to enrich domain ontologies [17]. A process ontology should be a common reference since it considers cross-cutting concerns for different domains. Process terms such as activity, task, method, tool, agent and work product, among others, are used in different domains. For instance, the terms 'evaluation specification' (in MEvalTDO) and 'test case' (in TestTDO) have the semantics of 'artifact' (i.e. a kind of 'work product'), from the process terminology standpoint. Therefore, a core ontology for processes can be seen as a reusable resource, useful to enrich semantically diverse domain ontologies, for example, those used in the set of strategy families.

This paper analyzes ProcessCO, which is an ontology placed at the core level in the context of a four-layered ontological architecture called FCD-OntoArch (*Foundational, Core, and Domain Ontological Architecture for Sciences*) [14]. This architecture considers foundational, core, domain and instance levels. In FCD-OntoArch, ontologies at the same level can be related to each other. In addition, ontologies at lower levels can be semantically enriched by ontologies at upper levels. For instance, TestTDO at the domain level is enriched by concepts of the ProcessCO ontology placed at the core level. In turn, the latter is enriched by concepts of ThingFO [14] at the foundational level, as will be seen later. It is important to remark that ProcessCO is based on [3], but expanding it by including new process terms, properties and relationships, and harmonizing it in the framework of FCD-OntoArch.

In summary, as a contribution, this work documents and analyzes ProcessCO ontology and its terminological harmonization with the four-layered ontological architecture. To analyze the usefulness of ProcessCO to enrich domain ontologies, it also illustrates enriched terms of a couple of ontologies at the domain level such as TestTDO and MEvalTDO. To this end, the applicability of ProcessCO to enrich not only terms but also to reuse some of its properties and relationships is shown. Additionally, the reuse or mirroring of some ProcessCO conceptual blocks or patterns is also described. As a result, by using ProcessCO (and other core ontologies) as a common terminological reference, the domain ontologies used in the different strategies are conceptually harmonized. Hence, strategies ensure terminological uniformity and consistency, thus facilitating the understanding of their specifications.

The remaining sections are arranged as follows: Sect. 2 provides a summary of related work on process ontologies. Section 3 gives an overview of FCD-OntoArch. Section 4 documents and analyzes the main concepts included in ProcessCO. Section 5 illustrates the usefulness of ProcessCO for enriching the terms of a couple of domain ontologies. Finally, Sect. 6 summarizes conclusions and future work.

2 Related Work

When analyzing related work for ontologies or vocabularies of process, some syntactic disagreement is observed, as well as in the semantics of some terms, properties and relationships. It seems that so far there is no broad and unanimous consensus on many key terms and their meaning for work processes.

A work cited in the process area is ISO 12207 [12], which is structured as a glossary. Also, it depicts a diagram where the relations between process, activity and task terms are represented. According to this diagram, a process can group other processes, and can also contain at least one activity; in turn, an activity can group one or more related tasks. ProcessCO adopts to a great extent this process/activity/task hierarchy.

In an effort to standardize terms for the process domain, OMG (*Object Management Group*) developed SPEM (*Software & Systems Process Engineering Meta-Model Specification*), a meta-model for process engineering as well as a conceptual framework, which provides the concepts necessary to model, document and manage processes [15]. SPEM focuses on defining a generic framework for process modeling. Note that in SPEM a process is defined as a special type of activity, so that the hierarchy between activity and process differs from that in ISO 12207, where a process groups activities, and an activity groups tasks.

In [18], authors present Software Engineering Ontology Network (SEON), which is a collection of ontologies related together and organized in layers. Briefly, in the bottom layer, they put foundational ontologies. In the middle layer of SEON, they include core ontologies to represent the general domain knowledge. Finally, in the top layer, there are (sub) domain ontologies, which describe the more specific knowledge. Particularly, a core ontology is named Software Process Ontology (SPO) [4]. It is based on UFO (*Unified Foundational Ontology*) [11], which provides robustness to SPO -as indicated by authors. However, some semantic inconsistencies are observed, for example: in the SPO version documented in [11], the authors show that hardware resource, software resource and human resource inherit from resource, while in [4] a human resource is not a resource. On the other hand, SPO uses terminology that to some extent differs from recognized standards such as SPEM and ISO 12207. Thus, instead of using the work product term, they use the artifact term, not making the distinction between outcome and service terms. In addition, they do not use the task term but rather the atomic activity term.

A recent work is [9], which presents a Verification-Oriented Process Ontology that supports verification of behavioral properties of processes. The ontological representation of the processes is oriented both to the application of formal verification methods and to the extraction of information from technical documentation. However, this ontology is neither placed nor harmonized in an ontological architecture nor is it based on a foundational ontology. Additionally, it does not include very common terms of the quoted standards like work product, activity and task, among others.

In order to provide a shared and explicit vocabulary related to business process, in [16] the authors developed the Business Process Ontology (BPO). It focuses on business process definition, not addressing business process execution. BPO is based on UFO and business process literature. It is modular, being divided into three sub-ontologies: Business Process Goals and Types, which addresses organization's goals, business processes types and relations between them; Business Processes and Activities, dealing with the definition of business processes and their activities; and Business Process Supporting Enterprise Applications, dealing with applications, applications services and their support to business processes and activities. Since BPO is for business processes has fewer general (core) terms than ProcessCO.

Lastly, in [3] authors specify a process ontology, which considers SPEM and ISO 12207, among other process seminal works. ProcessCO builds on [3], but expanding it by adding more terms, such as Process Model, Allocation, among others. The ontology presented in [3] does not allow to know if its included terms were domain-dependent or not, since the ontology was not located in a layered architecture like FCD-OntoArch. Instead, ProcessCO is included in it and is enriched by the ThingFO foundational ontology. While UFO is made up of a set of ontologies: UFO-A (endurants), UFO-B (perdurants or events) and UFO-C (social entities, built on top of UFO-A and B), FCD-OntoArch includes just one foundational ontology, i.e., ThingFO. It has a small set of terms that makes it easy to specialize in lower-level ontologies, such as ProcessCO.

On the other hand, in [13], the authors use their process ontology to specify a family of strategies for evaluation. Although they model the processes of evaluation strategies from different perspectives, the ontology of [3] does not include terms such as Process Model and Process Perspective, which are terms included in ProcessCO.

3   ProcessCO in the Context of the Ontological Architecture

As commented in the Introduction Section, ProcessCO is placed at the core-domain level into FCD-OntoArch. It is a four-layered ontological architecture, which considers foundational, core, domain and instance levels. In turn, the domain level is split down into two sub-levels, namely: top-domain and low-domain. As depicted in Fig. 1, ontologies at the same level can be related to each other, except for the foundational level where only the ThingFO ontology is. Additionally, lower-level ontologies can be semantically enriched with higher-level ontologies. For example, TestTDO placed at the top-domain level is mainly enriched by terms, properties and relationships of the SituationCO and ProcessCO ontologies placed at the core level. In turn, both are enriched by the concepts of ThingFO.

At this point, what does it mean that ontologies at one level can be semantically enriched by other higher-level ontologies? This means that the terms, properties and/or relationships of an ontology at a certain level (e.g. top-domain or core) can reuse or 'inherit' the semantics of the corresponding more general terms/properties and/or relationships. For example, Artifact is a core term in ProcessCO, and Test Specification in TestTDO is semantically enriched by it. That is, Test Specification is an Artifact, or inherits the semantics, or is semantically enriched by the Artifact term. Moreover, Artifact has the semantics of particular Thing, which is a term in ThingFO. Therefore, the definition of the term Test Specification must be defined according to the test domain, but the designer already has the advantage of knowing the holistic meaning of the term Artifact, as it is explicitly defined in the ProcessCO ontology. In other words, these core terms provide a semantic basis that gives support to better define and understand more specific domain terms.

As commented above, ThingFO is at the foundational level. Therefore, its terms such as Thing, Thing Category and Assertion semantically enrich terms of components at lower levels. Thing represents a particular or concrete, tangible or intangible object of a given particular world, but not a universal category or class –which is modeled by the term Thing Category. Additionally, Assertion is defined as *"positive and explicit statement that somebody makes about something concerning Things, or their categories, based on thoughts, perceptions, facts, intuitions, intentions, and/or beliefs that is conceived with an attempt at furnishing current or subsequent evidence"* [14]. Assertions can be represented and modeled using informal, semiformal or formal specification languages. There are Assertion on Particulars for Thing, and Assertion on Universals for Thing Category.

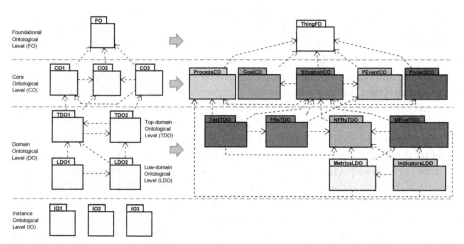

Fig. 1. Four-layered ontological architecture, which considers Foundational, Core, Domain and Instance levels. Some conceptual components are shown at the corresponding level. Note that NFRs stands for Non-Functional Requirements, FRs for Functional Requirements, MEval for Measurement and Evaluation, and PEvent for Particular Event. Also note that this figure is adapted from [14]

Dealing with a Thing through the use of Assertions, ThingFO allows specifying aspects of its action, substance, relations, structure, behavior, intentionality, quantity and quality, among other aspects. For example, the conceptualization of an ontology as an artifact (e.g., ProcessCO in Fig. 2) represents a mixture of substance-, relation-, structure-, intention-, and situation-related assertions. Axioms of an ontology are constraint-related assertions.

4   ProcessCO: A Process Core Ontology

Key terms in ProcessCO are Work Process, Activity and Task. Specifically, a Work Process -term thus labeled to differentiate it from a natural process- is composed of sub-processes and/or Activities, and in turn, an Activity is formed by sub-activities and/or Tasks. A Task is an atomic, fine-grained Work Entity that cannot be decomposed. The semantics given to these three terms comply with the meaning given in ISO 12207 [12]. As represented in Fig. 2, these three terms are kinds of Work Entities. While the Work Process, Activity and Task terms have slightly different semantics, they do share common properties such as name, objective, description, status and start/end dates. Also, they involve Roles, consume Product Entities, produce Work Products and have Conditions –both preconditions and postconditions. Note in Fig. 2 that the high-level Work Entity term has the semantics of Thing (from ThingFO). The Work Entity term is defined as "*a Thing (a particular) that describes the work by means of consumed and produced Work Products, Conditions, and involved Roles*".

It is important to note that ontologies in this work use stereotypes as a particular mechanism to semantically enrich and harmonize terms. Regarding the procedural way to enrich a given term from a higher-level term, in [3] authors argued that stereotypes are a more suitable mechanism than inheritance relationships, since it generates a loose coupling between a lower-level component and a higher-level component. Conversely, in some cases, defining a term as a specialization (inheritance relationship) of less specific terms can minimize the reuse of, for instance, a domain ontology, in addition to promoting tight coupling between components. Furthermore, stereotypes can reduce the complexity of the model, also promoting understandability and communicability.

As commented above, a Work Entity has a description (work description), which specifies the steps for achieving its objective. It represents "what" should be done instead of "how" should be performed. The "how" is represented by the Method term, i.e., the specific and particular way to perform the specified steps for instance in a Task. Note in Fig. 2 that the Method concept has the procedure and rules properties. A procedure is an arranged set of method instructions or operations, which specifies how the steps of a description of a Work Entity must be performed. On the other hand, a rule is a set of principles, conditions, heuristics, axioms, etc., associated with the procedure. The explicit relationship between Method (the "how") and work description (the "what") is not made as clear in other proposals as in this one.

It should be noted that to perform a Work Entity, i.e., a Task, an Activity or a Work Process, an Allocation of Work Resources should be done. Useful Work Resources in any project are Method, Tool and Agent (i.e. a performer playing a Role), among others.

Another key concept is Work Product, where Outcome, Artifact and Service are kinds of Work Products. Outcome is defined as "*a Work Product that is intangible,*

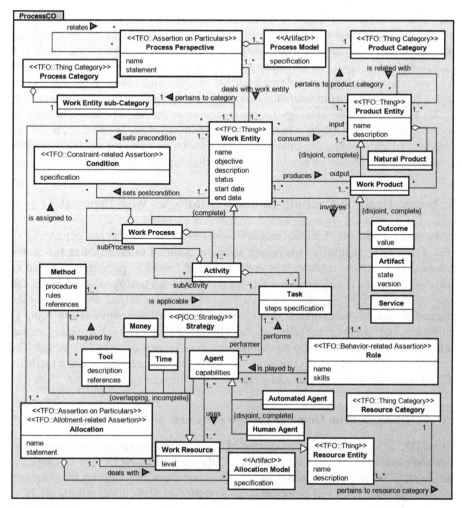

Fig. 2. Main terms, properties and relationships of the ProcessCO ontology. Note that TFO stands for ThingFO and PjCO for ProjectCO represented in Fig. 1

storable and processable", while Artifact "*is a tangible or intangible, versionable Work Product, which can be delivered*". Lastly, Service is defined as "*a Work Product that is intangible, non-storable and deliverable*". Note in Fig. 2 that a Work Product is a kind of Product Entity. Natural Product is another type of Product Entity. A key difference between Work Product and Natural Product is that the latter is not produced by a Work Entity, however it can be consumed by a Work Entity.

Finally, a Work Entity can be represented from different Process Perspectives [7], such as: i) *functional* that includes the Work Entities' structure, Work Products as inputs and outputs, etc.; ii) *informational* that includes the structure and interrelationships among Work Products produced or consumed by Work Entities; iii) *behavioral* that models the dynamic view of Work Entities, including Conditions; and, iv) *organizational* that deals with Agents and Roles. A Process Model specifies and models one or more related Process Perspectives using a given process specification language. Note in Fig. 2 that a Process Perspective has the semantics of Assertion on Particulars, which is a term reused from ThingFO. Depending on the particular situation at hand a Process Perspective may be a Behavior-related Assertion, or a Structure-related Assertion, among others. For example, the informational view shown in [2] is a Structure-related Assertion.

Ultimately, this core ontology for process contains the key concepts that are able to enrich semantically different domains as exemplified below. The reader can see the ProcessCO documentation, i.e., the definitions of the terms, properties and relationships as well as the verification of non-taxonomic relationships at http://bit.ly/P_CO.

5   Semantically Enriching Domain Ontologies with ProcessCO

In the sequel, Sub-sect. 5.1 describes how some ProcessCO terms are stereotyped in MEvalTDO to semantically enrich their terms, in addition to highlighting how some ProcessCO properties, relationships and conceptual blocks or patterns are reused or extended in MEvalTDO. Similarly, Sub-sect. 5.2 does an analogous description and analysis for TestTDO. Finally, Sub-sect. 5.3 includes an abridged discussion on the ProcessCO quality evaluation. It is important to note that this paper is not going to emphasize and discuss the content of the MEvalTDO and TestTDO ontologies, but rather the enrichment and reuse mechanism of terms, properties and relationships. The reader interested in MEvalTDO ontology can see its documentation at http://bit.ly/MEv alTDO, while for TestTDO can take a closer look at the reference [19].

5.1   Enriching Domain Ontologies for Measurement and Evaluation

MEvalTDO is a top-domain ontology that addresses measurement and evaluation activities and methods in general. While MetricsLDO and IndicatorsLDO are ontologies at the low-domain level as depicted in Fig. 1, which addresses, in particular, measurement and evaluation activities and methods based on metrics and indicators, respectively. Note that MEvalTDO can also be specialized by other low-domain ontologies such as QuestionsLDO, i.e., a Questionnaire-based Measurement Low-Domain Ontology (not shown in Fig. 1).

Figure 3 depicts an excerpt from the MEvalTDO ontology with some terms and relationships semantically enriched or reused from ProcessCO. Some terms (highlighted in orange in Fig. 3) are enriched semantically by Work Process and Activity terms, such as Evaluation, Design Measurement and Implement Measurement; some terms have the semantics of Work Product (highlighted in light blue), such as Measurement Specification (Artifact) and Measurement Value (Outcome); and other terms are enriched with Method (highlighted in green), such as Measurement Method and Evaluation Method.

Note that some terms enriched by Method (e.g. Measurement Design Method, which is defined as "*a Measurement and Evaluation Design Method for a task included in the Design Measurement activity*") and Artifact (e.g. Conclusion Report, which is defined as "*an Artifact that documents the analysis of all Measurement and Evaluation Values*") are not included in Fig. 3 so as not to overload the model with too many terms.

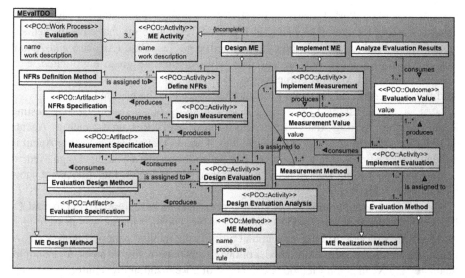

Fig. 3. Some terms, relationships and properties of MEvalTDO enriched semantically with ProcessCO (PCO) terms. Note that ME stands for Measurement and Evaluation

Additionally, MEvalTDO reuses and extends some conceptual blocks or patterns represented in ProcessCO. For example, the consumes/produces pattern, which indicates that all Work Entity consumes one or more Product Entities and produces one or more Work Products (Fig. 2), is mirrored in MEvalTDO.

As an example, in Fig. 3, Design Evaluation (which has the semantics of Activity and, in turn, of Work Entity) consumes one or more Measurement Specifications and one NFRs Specification (which are Artifacts and, in turn, have the semantics of Work Product and Product Entity). In the same way, Design Evaluation produces one or more Evaluation Specifications (which are Artifacts and, in turn, share the semantics of Work Product).

Another reused conceptual block is the work breakdown pattern, which indicates that a Work Process is composed of sub-Processes and Activities, and the latter by sub-Activities and Tasks (see in Fig. 2 the aggregation relationships between these terms). MEvalTDO considers this pattern since an Evaluation work process aggregates at least three Measurement and Evaluation Activities (at least one Design Measurement and Evaluation, one Implement Measurement and Evaluation, and one Analyze Evaluation Results- note that this restriction is supported by an axiom not shown here). Also, the Design ME aggregates sub-activities such as Define NFRs, Design Measurement, among others.

5.2 Enriching a Domain Ontology for Software Testing

TestTDO is a top-domain ontology for software testing activities and methods. Figure 4 depicts an excerpt from TestTDO ontology with some terms, properties and relationships semantically enriched or reused from ProcessCO. Like in MEvalTDO, terms enriched semantically with Work Process and Activity are orange highlighted in Fig. 4, e.g., Testing, Testing Design and Functional Dynamic Testing; terms that have the semantics of Work Product are light-blue highlighted, e.g., Test Case (Artifact) and Actual Result (Outcome); terms that are enriched with Method are green highlighted, e.g., Specification-based Method, Structure-based Method and Experience-based Method. Additionally, terms enriched with Role and Agent are blue highlighted.

It should be noted that to perform a Testing Activity, i.e., a Testing Design, Testing Realization and Testing Analysis, an Allocation of Work Resources, such as Agents and Methods should be done. Particularly, Fig. 4 shows that at least a Testing Agent is assigned to a Testing Activity. Moreover, Fig. 4 also shows that a Testing Design Method is assigned to a Testing Design activity. Note that, like in Fig. 3, Fig. 4 does not show all the TestTDO terms.

TestTDO also reuses and extends some conceptual blocks represented in ProcessCO. For example, the consumes/produces and work breakdown patterns, which were analyzed for MEvalTDO. Another conceptual block is the method pattern. Figure 2 shows that procedure is a property of Method. Following this pattern, Fig. 4 shows, for example, that a Testing Realization Method is composed of a Realization Procedure.

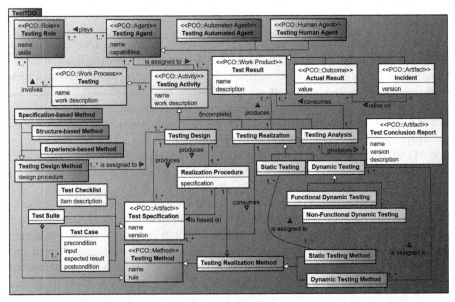

Fig. 4. Some terms, relationships and properties of TestTDO enriched semantically with ProcessCO (PCO) terms

5.3 Quality Evaluation of ProcessCO

In order to evaluate some aspects of the quality of ProcessCO, a non-functional requirements (NFRs) tree was built (see the first column of Table 1 and its defintions at http://

bit.ly/NFRdefs). For this, some dimensions or characteristics were considered for "beautiful ontologies" identified by D'Aquin *et al.* [8] from quality practices in the design of ontologies. Two (out of three) dimensions are formal structure and conceptual coverage, which are characterized by if the ontology is designed in a principled way; it is formally rigorous; it implements also non-taxonomic relations; it implements an international standard; and it reuses foundational ontologies, among others. Note that the considered NFRs tree in Table 1, even with limitations as to the number of characteristics and attributes included, is useful to evaluate any ontology at any level.

After building the NFRs tree, metrics and elementary indicators were designed for each attribute. Also, a linear additive scoring model was selected for derived indicators considering the characteristics and sub-characteristics. Table 1 conveys the obtained values for metrics and indicators for each quality attribute and characteristic.

For the sake of illustration only the indirect metric and the elementary indicator related to the "Balanced NTR/TR Availability" (1.1.3.2) attribute is considered in this paper. The indirect metric named "Percentage of Taxonomic Level" (%TxOntoLvl) has the formula (1). See the entire specification at http://bit.ly/metricSpec.

$$\%TxOntoLvl = (\#TR/(\#TR + \#NTR)) * 100 \qquad (1)$$

where #TR is the amount of taxonomic relationships; #NTR is the amount of non-taxonomic relationships; and $(\#TR + \#NTR) \neq 0$.

The measured value for 1.1.3.2 using the formula (1) is 59%. Then, by interpreting this percentage using the indicator "Performance Level of the Balanced NTR Availability", it is possible to know if an ontology is well balanced regarding the amount of taxonomic relationships (TR) and non-taxonomic relationships (NTR). To this end, the elementary indicator considers the formula (elementary model) and decision criteria shown in Fig. 5.

As shown in Table 1, the performance level for 1.1.3.2 attribute is 86.36% (●), which is satisfactory. This attribute is part of the Balanced Relationships Availability (1.1.3) sub-characteristic, which is defined as "Degree to which an ontology has a balance between the amount of NTR and TR in addition to the former are defined". Note that NTRs are those that are not 'kind of' (is_a) or 'whole-part' (part_of). Therefore, they should be defined.

As a result of the 1.1.3 sub-characteristic, ProcessCO met the satisfactory acceptability level (93.18% ●). For the Ontological Structural Quality (1.1), ProcessCO has met 97.72% (●) since all the terms and properties are explicitly defined but it is not perfectly balanced. Looking at the Compliance to other Vocabularies (1.2), ProcessCO adheres to some extent its terminology to the ISO 12207 glossary, as commented in Sect. 2. Also, ProcessCO was built considering the ThingFO foundational ontology. Finally, the Ontological Internal Quality achieved 98.86% (●).

It is important to mention that the data produced by metrics often allow interesting findings. For example, the ontologies described in [1] and [5] have fully taxonomic relations (%TxOntoLvl = 100). So these are taxonomies rather than ontologies, as the authors claim. In both cases, all represented relationships are 'kind of'.

194   P. Becker et al.

Elementary model:
Specification: the mapping is:

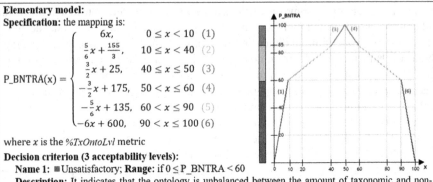

$$
P\_BNTRA(x) = \begin{cases}
6x, & 0 \le x < 10 \ (1) \\
\frac{5}{6}x + \frac{155}{3}, & 10 \le x < 40 \ (2) \\
\frac{3}{2}x + 25, & 40 \le x \le 50 \ (3) \\
-\frac{3}{2}x + 175, & 50 < x \le 60 \ (4) \\
-\frac{5}{6}x + 135, & 60 < x \le 90 \ (5) \\
-6x + 600, & 90 < x \le 100 \ (6)
\end{cases}
$$

where x is the *%TxOntoLvl* metric

Decision criterion (3 acceptability levels):
  Name 1: ■Unsatisfactory; **Range:** if $0 \le P\_BNTRA < 60$
  Description: It indicates that the ontology is unbalanced between the amount of taxonomic and non-taxonomic relationships. Therefore, change actions must be taken into account with high priority.
  Name 2: ◆Marginal;   **Range:** if $60 \le P\_BNTRA < 85$
  Description: It indicates that the ontology is moderately balanced between the amount of taxonomic and non-taxonomic relationships. Therefore, change actions should be taken into account.
  Name 3: ●Satisfactory;   **Range:** if $85 \le P\_BNTRA \le 100$
  Description: It indicates that the ontology is well balanced between the amount of taxonomic and non-taxonomic relationships. Therefore, no change actions are needed.

Fig. 5. Excerpt from the "Performance Level of the Balanced NTR Availability" elementary indicator specification. Note that the values of the Ranges are expressed in [%]

Table 1. Evaluation results of the Ontological Internal Quality characteristic for ProcessCO. The green icon (●) indicates a satisfactory acceptability level. Values for Measure, Elementary Indicators (EI) and Derived Indicators (DI) are expressed in [%]. NTR stands for Non-Taxonomic Relationships while TR for Taxonomic Relationships

Characteristic/*Attribute*	Measure	EI Value	DI Value
1. Ontological Internal Quality			98.86●
1.1 Ontological Structural Quality			97.72●
1.1.1 Defined Terms Availability	*100*	*100*●	
1.1.2 Defined Properties Availability	*100*	*100*●	
1.1.3 Balanced Relationships Availability			93.18●
1.1.3.1 Defined NTR Availability	*100*	*100*●	
1.1.3.2 Balanced NTR/TR Availability	*59.09*	*86.36*●	
1.2 Compliance to other Vocabularies			100●
1.2.1 Terminological use of International Standard Glossaries	*2*	*100*●	
1.2.2 Terminological Compliance to Foundational Ontologies	*yes*	*100*●	

6 Concluding Remarks and Future Work

This work has documented and analyzed ProcessCO, which is a domain-independent ontology for work processes placed at the core level in the context of a four-layered ontological architecture. This multilayer ontological architecture promotes a clear separation of concerns by considering the ontological levels that allow the allocation of conceptual components accordingly. This architecture thus encourages modularity, extensibility and reuse of ontological elements at all lower levels. Since ProcessCO is at the core level, ontologies at lower levels benefit from reusing and extending its key concepts. Therefore, ProcessCO can be seen as a reusable artifact and resource, which can be used to enrich semantically many domain ontologies, both top domain and low domain. In turn, ProcessCO extends the key three terms of ThingFO, namely Thing, Thing Category and Assertion. It also specializes its non-taxonomic relationships, which were verified for consistency as documented in the link provided in Sect. 4.

Furthermore, to analyze the applicability and usefulness of ProcessCO, this work has illustrated the semantically enriched terms of the MEvalTDO and TestTDO ontologies at the top-domain level. In particular, to show the applicability of ProcessCO alongside these two domain ontologies, it also addressed the mechanism to not only enrich terms, but also to reuse properties and specialize relationships. Moreover, this work has also presented how some conceptual blocks or patterns available in ProcessCO were clearly reflected in MEvalTDO and TestTDO.

The goals to build ontologies can be manifold, such as: to share a common understanding and then facilitating the communication among people and software agents; to reuse and integrate the disparate and heterogeneous representations; to formalize the representation of a domain problem or theory; and, as the basis to support semantic reasoning to full-fledged knowledge-based applications, among other aims. Particularly, considering that authors of this paper are primarily interested in building strategies for different domains, by using ProcessCO (and other core ontologies) as a common terminological base, the domain ontologies, which nourish different strategies, can be harmonized. So, strategies may ensure terminological uniformity and consistency, favoring thus the specifications of their processes and methods.

Authors in [13] developed a set of evaluation strategies but these were not well-founded considering domain ontologies in the framework of the ontological architecture depicted in Fig. 1. Therefore, a future work is to improve these strategies so that their terminologies harmonize with the FCD-OntoArch framework. In addition, strategies for testing are being developed, thus expanding the family of strategies proposed by [13].

Acknowledgments. This line of research is supported partially by the Engineering School at UNLPam, in the project named "Family of Strategies for Functional and Non-Functional Software Testing considering Different Test Goal Purposes".

References

1. Arnicans, G., Romans, D., Straujums, U.: Semi-automatic generation of a software testing lightweight ontology from a glossary based on the ONTO6 methodology. In: Frontiers in Artificial Intelligence and Applications, vol. 249, pp. 263–276 (2013)
2. Becker, P., Olsina, L., Peppino, D., Tebes, G.: Specifying the process model for systematic reviews: an augmented proposal. J. Softw. Eng. Res. Dev. (JSERD) 7, 1–23 (2019). https://doi.org/10.5753/jserd.2019.460
3. Becker, P., Papa, F., Olsina, L.: Process ontology specification for enhancing the process compliance of a measurement and evaluation strategy. CLEI Electron. J. 18(1), 1–26 (2015). https://doi.org/10.19153/cleiej.18.1.2

4. Bringuente, A.C., Falbo, R.A., Guizzardi, G.: Using a foundational ontology for reengineering a software process ontology. J. Inf. Data Manag. **2**(3), 511–526 (2011)
5. Cai, L., Tong, W., Liu, Z., Zhang, J.: Test case reuse based on ontology. In: 15th IEEE Pacific Rim International Symposium on Dependable Computing, pp. 103–108 (2009)
6. Corcho, O., Fernández-López, M., Gómez-Pérez, A.: Methodologies, tools and languages for building ontologies. Where is their meeting point? Data Knowl. Eng. **46**(1), 41–64 (2003)
7. Curtis, B., Kellner, M., Over, J.: Process modelling. Commun. ACM **35**(9), 75–90 (1992)
8. D'Aquin, M., Gangemi, A.: Is there beauty in ontologies? Appl. Ontol. **6**(3), 165–175 (2011)
9. Garanina, N.O., Anureev, I.S., Borovikova, O.I.: Verification-oriented process ontology. Autom. Control. Comput. Sci. **53**(7), 584–594 (2019). https://doi.org/10.3103/S01464116 19070058
10. Gruber, T.R.: A translation approach to portable ontologies. Knowl. Acquis. **5**(2), 199–220 (1993)
11. Guizzardi, G., Falbo, R., Guizzardi, R.: Grounding software domain ontologies in the unified foundational ontology (UFO): the case of the ODE software process ontology. In: 11th Conferencia Iberoamericana de Software Engineering (CIbSE 2008), pp. 127–140 (2008)
12. ISO/IEC 12207: Systems and software engineering - Software life cycle processes (2008)
13. Olsina, L., Becker, P.: Family of strategies for different evaluation purposes. In: 20th Conferencia Iberoamericana en Software Engineering (CIbSE 2017) held in the framework of ICSE, CABA, Argentina, pp. 221–234. Curran Associates (2017)
14. Olsina, L.: Analyzing the usefulness of ThingFO as a foundational ontology for sciences. In: Proceedings of ASSE 2020, Argentine Symposium on Software Engineering, 49 JAIIO, Held Virtually, CABA, Argentina, October 2020, pp. 172–191 (2020). ISSN 2451-7593
15. OMG-SPEM: Software & Systems Process Engineering Meta-Model Specification v2.0 (2008)
16. Renault, L., Barcellos, M., Falbo, R.: Using an ontology-based approach for integrating applications to support software processes. In: 17th Brazilian Symposium on Software Quality (SBQS), pp. 220–229. ACM, New York (2018)
17. Ruiz, F., Hilera, J.R.: Using ontologies in software engineering and technology. In: Calero, C., Ruiz, F., Piattini, M. (eds.) Ontologies in Software Engineering and Software Technology, pp. 49–102. Springer, Heidelberg (2006). https://doi.org/10.1007/3-540-34518-3_2
18. Ruy, F.B., Falbo, R.A., Barcellos, M.P., Costa, S.D., Guizzardi, G.: SEON: a software engineering ontology network. In: 20th International Conference on Knowledge Engineering and Knowledge Management, pp. 527–542 (2016)
19. Tebes, G., Olsina, L., Peppino, D., Becker, P.: TestTDO: a top-domain software testing ontology. In: 23rd CIbSE 2020, pp. 364–377. Curran Associates (2020)
20. van Heijst, G., Schreiber, A.Th., Wielinga, B.J.: Using explicit ontologies in KBS development. Int. J. Hum.-Comput. Stud. **46**, 183–292 (1997)

Towards Understanding Quality-Related Characteristics in Knowledge-Intensive Processes - A Systematic Literature Review

Rachel Vital Simões[1]([✉]) [iD], Glaucia Melo[2] [iD], Fernando Brito e Abreu[3] [iD], and Toacy Oliveira[1] [iD]

[1] Federal University of Rio de Janeiro, Rio de Janeiro, Brazil
{rachelvital,toacy}@cos.ufrj.br
[2] University of Waterloo, Waterloo, Canada
gmelo@uwaterloo.ca
[3] ISTAR-Iscte, University Institute of Lisbon, Lisbon, Portugal
fba@iscte-iul.pt

Abstract. *Context:* Contemporary process management systems have been supporting users during the execution of repetitive, predefined business processes. Many business processes are no longer limited to explicit business rules as processes can be unpredictable, knowledge-driven and emergent. In recent years, knowledge-intensive processes (KIPs) have become more important for many businesses. However, quality-related aspects of these processes are still scarce. Therefore, it is hard to evaluate these types of processes in terms of their quality. *Objective*: In this paper, we present a Systematic Literature Review aiming at investigating and reporting quality-related aspects of KIPs. *Results*: We identified in the selected studies the characteristics and methods related to KIPs. Although several papers present quality aspects of processes, literature still lacks directions on the quality-related approaches in KIPs.

Keywords: Knowledge-intensive processes · Knowledge intensive business process · Process flexibility · KIP quality

1 Introduction

In recent years, many changes have been observed in the approaches of business processes. In many cases, business processes are flexible, unpredictable, adaptable and knowledge-driven. The characteristics of these processes also vary in organizations. Hence, knowing these characteristics could potentially aid the understanding of the mechanisms for improving these types of processes.

Moreover, the quality aspects of Knowledge-Intensive Processes (KIPs) are an important source of competitive advantages for contemporary companies. The quality-related characteristics have been carried out in the literature in several

A. C. R. Paiva et al. (Eds.): QUATIC 2021, CCIS 1439, pp. 197–207, 2021.
https://doi.org/10.1007/978-3-030-85347-1_15

ways. Although several papers present some relation with quality aspects, there is a lack of studies that focus on quality-related characteristics in KIPs.

The importance and complexity of KIPs were exposed as hardly predefined, and compliance can be ensured only at run-time [7]. Therefore, the application of traditional Business Process Management (BPM) practices is difficult to implement in KIP environments and new ways to handle KIP processes need to be researched.

In this paper, we present a Systematic Literature Review on quality-related characteristics of KIPs to address the lack of literature on the topic. We contribute by exposing the lack of studies that present quality aspects for KIPs, and suggest avenues for defining quality metrics for KIPs.

The structure of this article is as follows. We start by laying an introduction to the topic. Then, in Sect. 2, we present the Related Work. Section 3 presents the protocol of the Systematic Literature Review, and the results of the study. Following, Sect. 4 discusses the threats of this research and Sect. 5 concludes the paper with our main considerations.

2   Related Work

Some quality metrics of business process models are used to evaluate a traditional process (prescriptive) model such as the number of elements, the complexity of the flow control, the immersion of the depth decision, the degree of clarity and the complexity of interconnections [25]. However, in the context of KIPs, these metrics are not fully applicable.

During our studies, we did not find specific treatments that address quality in knowledge-intensive processes. However, analyzing the state of the art we observed that many works address the related and repeated characteristics even in various contexts.

We highlight four papers that present critical studies in knowledge-intensive processes: Di Ciccio et al., 2015 [10]; Isik et al., 2012 [38]; Marjanovic and Freeze, 2012 [22]; Sarnikar and Deokar, 2010 [29]. KIPs are often associated with Adaptive Case Management (ACM). Pillaerds et al. (2017) [26] assesses the characteristics cited by Di Ciccio et al. (2015) in four different Business Process Support Systems (BPSS) as ACM and others.

Observing these characteristics is fundamental for the development of future works that evaluate the quality of the KIPS.

3   Systematic Literature Review

The Systematic Literature Review presented in this paper is based on the methodology proposed by Kitchenham et al. [19]. This methodology was conceived with a particular emphasis on Systematic Literature Review (SLR) conducted within the software engineering domain. Kitchenham's methodology is structured according to the following three steps, which have to be performed one after the other, as presented in Fig. 1.

Each of the three presented steps is described next.

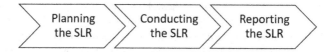

Fig. 1. SLR methodology steps [19].

- **Planning** - In the first step, we lay the objectives and needs for this review. We have defined the set of research questions and the review protocol.
- **Conduction** - In this second step, we have defined a search strategy to select a set of relevant research studies. The search was done according to the protocol established. This step has executed by two researchers, using a pair review strategy. This refinement step was quite critical since we had the opportunity to compare results. Finally the data extraction is performed and classified according to its relevant characteristics for each selected research work.
- **Reporting** - In this last step, we present the results and answers to the defined research questions.

Next, we present the details of each step of the systematic study.

3.1 Planning

In this section, we present the planning of this SLR. First, we introduce research questions. Then, we present the details of the applied protocol of the search.

Research Questions. We defined the following research questions to discover references in the state-of-the-art that could include relevant quality characteristics in KIPs. The questions resulted from sets of brainstorming sessions carried on by the authors and are listed next.

RQ1. What are the quality factors associated with Knowledge-Intensive Processes? This question aims to discover which quality characteristics are associated with KIPs.

RQ2. What methods, instruments or techniques are used to deal with KIPs? This question aims to understand the instruments, methods or techniques that handle KIPs and support these processes' quality aspects.

Developing the Protocol. The protocol has been defined according to Kitchenham's suggestions [19]. To retrieve relevant research papers, we performed an automatic search on Scopus Science, IEEE Xplore and ACM Digital Library in April 2021. The search string defined in Table 1.

We tested several combinations of keywords until we had achieved a suitable search string. To assess the quality of the search string, we first defined two control papers, depicted in Table 2. The control papers CP1 and CP2 were defined based on the results of pilot searches, before defining the final search string.

Table 1. Search string.

("Knowledge-intensive process" OR "flexible Process" OR "process flexibility" OR "Intentional Process" OR "Goal-oriented process") AND ("Quality" OR "Assessment" OR "Maturity") AND ("Business process" OR "BPM" OR "Process aware information system")

Table 2. Control papers.

ID	Title	Year	Reference
CP1	Assessing suitability of adaptive case management	2017	[26]
CP2	Improve Performance Management in Flexible Business Processes	2017	[11]

As part of the protocol implementation, a set of inclusion/exclusion criteria was specified and is reported in Table 3. These criteria secure that only relevant papers are included in the study.

Table 3. Selection criteria.

ID	Inclusion Criteria
I.1	Included studies must have been published in the last 6 years (included)
I.2	The work is a primary study
ID	Exclusion Criteria
E.1	Works outside the computing area
E.2	The work does not relate to the context of BPM and flexible processes
E.3	The paper is not written in English Language

3.2   Conduction

Identification and Selection of the Research Papers. The study selection process was performed by two researchers, as advised in the protocol, to mitigate possible biases.

For the selected articles, the two researchers independently filled out a spreadsheet with the basic information about the paper (e.g. title, authors, year of publication) and the option for including or not including the article in this study. The authors read the title and abstract of papers in this phase. The papers included were considered eligible when the researchers evaluated that the article should be included in our research. The data from the eligibility forms were stored in the spreadsheet, and the validation procedure was carried out. To measure the disagreements between the researchers on the eligibility of some papers, we used Cohen's kappa to assess the reliability of the diagnosis by measuring the agreement between the two judges.

Cohen's kappa is a measure of the agreement between two raters who determine which category a finite number of subjects belonging to whereby agreement due to chance is factored out. The two raters either agree or disagree. There are no degrees of disagreement (i.e., no weightings) [21].

To select the set of relevant studies, the following steps were performed. First, the search string was used in the selected databases returning an initial set of papers. Next, duplicates were identified and removed. After, we evaluated the papers according to the contents of their title and abstract using both the inclusion and exclusion criteria. This step was separately performed by two researchers.

In the face of results, we applied Cohen's kappa (k) agreement measure to determine the level of agreement between two judges, as shown in Table 4.

Table 4. Author's agreement results.

Judge B	Judge A			
	Read	Exclude	Include	Total
Read	27	3	0	30
Exclude	0	30	3	33
Include	2	1	0	3
Total	29	34	3	66

Considering the results shown in Table 4, we observed 57 papers with a perfect agreement between the judges, where 27 papers the researchers agreed that they should be read and 30 papers both agreed that they should be excluded from the study. Only six different papers are in total disagreement, where three papers have found by judge A and he rated them as valid articles for the study. Three others papers were found by judge B and they have rated these additional papers as valid as well.

The Cohen's k are calculated in Table 5. To interpret your Cohen's Kappa, the classification below was used [21]:

Table 5. Percentage of agreement among researchers.

	Read	Exclude	Include	Total
Agreement (pa)	27	30	0	57
By chance	14.54	15.5	0.14	30.18
(%) Perc. of Agreement	86.36%			
Cohen's k	74.87%			

- 1%–20%: slight agreement
- 21%–40%: fair agreement
- 41%–60%: moderate agreement
- 61%–80%: substantial agreement
- 81%–100%: almost perfect or perfect agreement

We verified a percentage of agreement of 86.36% in Table 5. Furthermore, the Cohen's k index was 74,87% following the adopted classification, representing a substantial agreement in the results.

Finally, of the 66 papers retrieved by the researchers, 33 were selected for the last step for data extraction and synthesis. These 33 papers were fully read and we extracted the information related to the defined RQs, which consists of quality-related characteristics and methods/approaches for deal with KIP processes. These studies constituted the new selection for the next step of the study.

Data Extraction and Synthesis. The data extraction and synthesis step aim to design a suitable form to record and collect the relevant information obtained from fully reading the selected research papers. The 33 relevant studies the two researchers selected were fully read, and the pertinent data to the research questions were extracted and recorded in a spreadsheet. Finally, we have analyzed the results, focusing on producing the desired answers for the RQs.

3.3 Reporting Results

In this section, we present the results of the SLR. At first, we reported some general information on the collected data in Sect. 3.2. Then considering the research questions listed in Sect. 3.1 we discuss (1) quality-related characteristics of Knowledge-Intensive Processes and (2) methods to deal with KIP.

- *RQ1. What are the quality factors associated with Knowledge-Intensive Processes?*

We observed a gap in studies about **quality** in knowledge-intensive processes, as literature lacks specific studies that aim at understanding and exploring this topic. Acknowledging this gap is essential to encourage increases in specific quality studies associated with KIPs.

Di Ciccio, Marrella and Russo [10] defined eight main key representative characteristics of KIPs: Knowledge-driven, Collaboration-oriented, Unpredictable, Emergent, Goal-oriented, Event-driven, Constraint- and rule-driven and Non-repeatable. Their work provides a precise characterization of KIPs and, starting from three real-world application scenarios. In our study, we extended this analysis to 33 more papers with different application scenarios. To classify the 33 papers, we build the following tables with synonyms, in Table 6. These synonyms were extracted from the selected papers and classified by the author.

Table 6. Synonyms for KIP characteristics based on DiCiccio et al. [10].

	Characteristics	Synonyms
C1	Knowledge-driven	Data-oriented, human, information exchange, people-centric, user decision, drive human
C2	Collaboration-oriented	Multi-user environment, participants with different roles, human-centred, transfer the data, interactive
C3	Unpredictable	Can be fully specified, iterative and incremental, unexpected conditions, flexibility, weak structured, may change during process execution
C4	Emergent	Ad-hoc changes, adaptability, uncertainty, complex
C5	Goal-oriented	Milestones to be achieved, objectives determined at run-time, intermediate goals
C6	Event-driven	Changes in the process, decisions, contextual changes
C7	Constraint- and rule-driven	Adapt to changes/change during process execution/Unpredictable situations
C8	Non-repeatable	Customizable, temporal changes, multi-variant

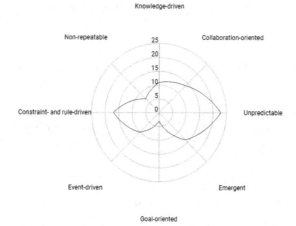

Fig. 2. Main characteristics of KIPs per occurrences.

In the selected studies, we found the following characteristics cited by Di Ciccio, demonstrated in Fig. 2. In addition to these characteristics defined in [10], we found characteristics such as traceability, control and transparency, as presented in Table 7.

– *RQ2. What methods, instruments or techniques are used to deal with KIPs?*

The studies found show several instruments and mechanisms to deal with KIPs. We have not found works that specifically focus on the quality of KIPs.

Table 7. Characteristics' summary.

Characteristics	Papers
C1 - Knowledge-driven	[2,6,12,14,17,26,27,31,33,35,36]
C2 - Collaboration-oriented	[2–4,6,11,12,17,18,23,23,26,28,32,35]
C3 - Unpredictable	[1,2,4,9,11,12,14,15,17,18,23,24,26–28,30,30,33–36,36,37]
C4 - Emergent	[3,5,9,14,16,17,20,24,26–28,34–36]
C5 - Goal-oriented	[12,18,26]
C6 - Event-driven	[3,12,18,23,24,26,30,33,34,36]
C7 - Constraint- and rule-driven	[2–4,8,11,12,14,18,23,26,27,30,33–37]
C8 - Non-repeatable	[11,12,14,23,26,30,35]
C9 - Control	[6,13]
C10 - Traceability	[16]
C10 - Transparent	[26]

However, all the proposals found seek, somehow, innovative ways to approach these types of processes.

4   Threats to Validity

We present the categorization (Sect. 3.3) based on the characteristics presented by [10]. This is a threat because the classification was defined based on Table 6 carried out by just one researcher. However, we believe that the result presented can be interesting because it reinforces the characteristics of KIPs in different environments.

5   Conclusions and Future Work

This SLR has identified a gap in qualitative aspects to measure or qualify knowledge-intensive processes. We did not find models, guidelines or good practices in the studies for dealing with quality aspects in these processes. Although [10] defines the characteristics of KIPs processes well, we did not find applicable quality models in this context. We also have not found basic concepts that can serve as an initial guideline for developing quality models for KIPs. In this work, we seek to encourage and discover new ways of research to deal with aspects of qualities in KIPs.

We provided an overview of the current works on quality-related characteristics in Knowledge-Intensive Processes. In this paper, we performed an SLR using Kitchenham's guidelines [19]. The results confirmed the importance of the topic as an important research area. We examined several groups of contributions: *i* we found the characteristics cited by [10] in 33 different domains and application scenarios; *ii* we identified mechanisms to deal with KIPs in recent works.

In terms of concepts or methods of quality assurance of KIP processes, we did not find a comprehensive picture of the topic in the literature. Despite the significant efforts of researchers and practitioners in the domain, more research is still required to enhance KIP's environments mainly when we need to think about quality aspects.

As future work, we propose to define coding protocols to better classified the papers found according to KIP characteristics presented by [10]. The authors could discuss the coded studies to identify discrepancies and shortcomings in the codes. We can use coding techniques to characterize the methods, instruments or mechanisms used to deal with KIP in these studies. We propose to use some of the quality aspects found in structured process analysis and use these as a start when analyzing KIPs. In this sense, we propose to include the evaluation in the most detailed study on the use of ISO/IEC 25000 (systems and software product quality) and ISO/IEC 3300X (Process assessment) in KIPs. Evaluating quality models that do not meet knowledge-intensive processes are also important contributions to the area.

References

1. Abbad Andaloussi, A., Davis, C.J., Burattin, A., López, H.A., Slaats, T., Weber, B.: Understanding quality in declarative process modeling through the mental models of experts. In: Fahland, D., Ghidini, C., Becker, J., Dumas, M. (eds.) BPM 2020. LNCS, vol. 12168, pp. 417–434. Springer, Cham (2020). https://doi.org/10.1007/978-3-030-58666-9_24
2. Andrews, K., Steinau, S., Reichert, M.: Enabling ad-hoc changes to object-aware processes, pp. 85–94. Institute of Electrical and Electronics Engineers Inc. (2018)
3. Andrews, K., Steinau, S., Reichert, M.: Enabling runtime flexibility in data-centric and data-driven process execution engines. Inf. Syst. (2019)
4. Benner-Wickner, M., Brückmann, T., Gruhn, V., Book, M.: Process mining for knowledge-intensive business processes, 21–22-October-2015, pp. 1–8. Association for Computing Machinery (2015)
5. Bernardi, M.L., Cimitile, M., Maggi, F.M.: Automated development of constraint-driven web applications, 04–08-April-2016, pp. 1196–1203. Association for Computing Machinery (2016)
6. Bider, I., Jalali, A.: Limiting variety by standardizing and controlling knowledge intensive processes, 2016-September, pp. 33–41. Institute of Electrical and Electronics Engineers Inc. (2016)
7. Boissier, F., Rychkova, I., Le Grand, B.: Challenges in knowledge intensive process management, 2019-October, pp. 65–74. Institute of Electrical and Electronics Engineers Inc. (2019)
8. Botangen, K.A., Yu, J., Sheng, M.: Towards measuring the adaptability of an ao4bpel process. Association for Computing Machinery (2017)
9. BădicĂ, A., BădicĂ, C., Leon, F., Buligiu, I.: Modeling and enactment of business agents using Jason. 18–20-May-2016, Association for Computing Machinery (2016)

10. Di Ciccio, C., Marrella, A., Russo, A.: Knowledge-intensive processes: characteristics, requirements and analysis of contemporary approaches. J. Data Semant. **4**, 29–57 (2015)
11. Estrada-Torres, B.: Improve performance management in flexible business processes, vol. 2, pp. 145–149. Association for Computing Machinery (2017)
12. Estrada-Torres, B., et al.: Measuring performance in knowledge-intensive processes. ACM Trans. Internet Technol. **19**, 1–26 (2019)
13. Fichtner, M., Schönig, S., Jablonski, S.: Process management enhancement by using image mining techniques: a position paper, vol. 1, pp. 249–255. SciTePress (2020)
14. Haarmann, S.: Fragment-based case management models: metamodel, consistency, and correctness, vol. 2839, pp. 1–8. CEUR-WS (2021)
15. Heinrich, B., Schiller, A., Schön, D., Szubartowicz, M.: Adapting process models via an automated planning approach. J. Decis. Syst. **29**, 223–259 (2020)
16. Hildebrandt, T.T., et al.: Ecoknow: engineering effective, co-created and compliant adaptive case management systems for knowledge workers, pp. 155–164. Association for Computing Machinery Inc. (2020)
17. Huber, S., Schott, P., Lederer, M.: Adaptive open innovation - solution approach and tool support, 23–24-April-2015. Association for Computing Machinery (2015)
18. Jaanus, J., Sihver, M., Ley, T.: Managing requirements knowledge in business networks: a case study, 21–22-October-2015. Association for Computing Machinery (2015)
19. Kitchenham, B., Charters, S.: Guidelines for performing systematic literature reviews in software engineering (2007)
20. Koehler, J., Woodtly, R., Hofstetter, J.: An impact-oriented maturity model for it-based case management. Inf. Syst. **47**, 278–291 (2015)
21. Landis, J.R., Koch, G.G.: The measurement of observer agreement for categorical data. JSTOR, Biometrics (1977)
22. Marjanovic, O., Freeze, R.: Knowledge-intensive business process: deriving a sustainable competitive advantage through business process management and knowledge management integration. Knowl. Process Manag. **19**, 180–188 (2012)
23. Marrella, A., Mecella, M., Sardina, S.: Intelligent process adaptation in the SmartPm system. ACM Trans. Intell. Syst. Technol. **8**, 11 (2017)
24. Moyon, F., Beckers, K., Klepper, S., Lachberger, P., Bruegge, B.: Towards continuous security compliance in agile software development at scale, pp. 31–34. IEEE Computer Society (2018)
25. Pavlicek, J., Hronza, R., Pavlickova, P., Jelinkova, K.: The business process model quality metrics. In: Pergl, R., Lock, R., Babkin, E., Molhanec, M. (eds.) EOMAS 2017. LNBIP, vol. 298, pp. 134–148. Springer, Heidelberg (2017). https://doi.org/10.1007/978-3-319-68185-6_10
26. Pillaerds, J., Eshuis, R.: Assessing suitability of adaptive case management, pp. 566–580. Association for Information Systems (2017)
27. Rapina, R., Martusa, R., Wijaya, I.N.A., Zelien, A.: The impact of a collection of tasks and activities on accounting information quality: survey in Indonesia, pp. 233–236. Association for Computing Machinery (2020)
28. Russo, D., Ciancarini, P., Falasconi, T., Tomasi, M.: A meta-model for information systems quality: a mixed study of the financial sector. ACM Trans. Manag. Inf. Syst. **9**, 9 (2018)
29. Sarnikar, S., Deokar, A.: Knowledge management systems for knowledge-intensive processes: design approach and an illustrative example (2010)

30. Sigmanek, C., Lantow, B.: The staps method: Process-Taylored introduction of knowledge management solutions, vol. 3, pp. 181–189. SciTePress (2016)
31. De Souza, E.F., et al.: Experience report on developing an ontology-based approach for knowledge management in software testing. Association for Computing Machinery (2020)
32. Vukšic, V.B., Vugec, D.S., Lovric, A.: Social business process management: Croatian IT company case study. Bus. Syst. Res. **8**, 60–70 (2017)
33. Wen, S.F.: Learning secure programming in open source software communities: a socio-technical view, pp. 25–32. Association for Computing Machinery (2018)
34. Wondoh, J., Grossmann, G., Stumptner, M.: Dynamic temporal constraints in business processes. Association for Computing Machinery (2017)
35. Wu, H., Lu, T., Wang, X., Zhang, P., Jiang, P., Xu, C.: KBCBP: a knowledge-based collaborative business process model supporting dynamic procuratorial activities and roles. In: Sun, Y., Lu, T., Yu, Z., Fan, H., Gao, L. (eds.) ChineseCSCW 2019. CCIS, vol. 1042, pp. 311–319. Springer, Singapore (2019). https://doi.org/10.1007/978-981-15-1377-0_24
36. Zhang, Y., Chen, J.L.: Knowledge-learning service construction based on events, pp. 681–688. Institute of Electrical and Electronics Engineers Inc. (2016)
37. Zhao, X., Liu, C., Yongchareon, S., Kowalkiewicz, M., Sadiq, W.: Role-based process view derivation and composition. ACM Trans. Manag. Inf. Syst. **6**, 5 (2015)
38. Işik, Ö., Van Den Bergh, J., Mertens, W.: Knowledge intensive business processes: an exploratory study, pp. 3817–3826. IEEE Computer Society (2012)

Quality Aspects in Quantum Computing

KDM to UML Model Transformation for Quantum Software Modernization

Luis Jiménez-Navajas⬛, Ricardo Pérez-Castillo(✉) ⬛, and Mario Piattini⬛

University of Castilla-La Mancha, 13071 Ciudad Real, Spain
{luis.jimeneznavajas,ricardo.pdelcastillo,
mario.piattini}@uclm.es

Abstract. Thanks to the last engineering advances, quantum computing is gaining an increasing importance in many sectors that will be benefited from its superior computational power. Before achieving all those promising benefits, companies must be able to combine their classical information systems and the new quantum software to operate with the so-called hybrid information systems. This implies, at some point of such a modernization process, that hybrid information systems will have to be (re)designed. UML can be used for defining abstract design models, not only for the classical part as done before, but also for the quantum software in an integrated manner. This paper proposes a model transformation for generating UML models that represents quantum circuits as activity diagrams. Thanks to the usage of UML, these designs are technological-independent which contributes to the modernization of hybrid information systems. The outgoing UML models are compliant with a vast amount of design tools and might be understood by a big community.

Keywords: Quantum software engineering · Modernization · Reengineering · KDM · UML · Model transformation

1 Introduction

In the last few years, the interest in quantum computing has been dramatically increased. More and more organizations have become aware of the benefits that this new computing paradigm can bring to the society [1]. This is due to researchers around the world are providing evidence, albeit still theoretical, of the benefits and challenges of quantum computing. This means that companies around the world must be prepared for this new technological leap, which may leverage a new "golden age" in the software engineering field [2].

Nevertheless, this technological leap cannot be made by discarding everything that has been built up to now and starting from scratch with the quantum paradigm [3]. There are several reasons for this, one of them being that, possibly, there are certain operations in the systems of the companies that are so simple that it does not make sense to implement them using quantum computing because of the cost versus the potential gain [4]. Another reason is that companies have based strategic decisions on the business

© Springer Nature Switzerland AG 2021
A. C. R. Paiva et al. (Eds.): QUATIC 2021, CCIS 1439, pp. 211–224, 2021.
https://doi.org/10.1007/978-3-030-85347-1_16

rules embedded in their classical information systems overtime (which is not available anywhere else) and its replacement becomes too risky.

The solution to this problem is simply not to replace the currently systems (henceforth called classical systems), but to modernize those systems that could benefit from the computational power of the quantum paradigm. So, create classical-quantum information systems, also known as hybrid information systems. The software modernization challenge is actually claimed by the Talavera Manifesto on Software Engineering and Programming [6].

ADM (Architecture Driven Modernization) [5] may be the right path to accomplish the evolution of classical systems toward hybrid ones, as it has been proved in the past to be effective in the evolution of legacy systems. ADM is the evolution of traditional reengineering by following a MDE (Model Driven Engineering) approach. The concept of Quantum Software Reengineering was introduced in [3], where it was depicted how the reverse engineering phase must be extended in order to work with the different quantum entities. In particular, this paper focuses on the restructuring phase, the next step in the modernization software approach. The main contribution is the transformation of extended KDM models to UML. This model transformation has been accomplished employing ATL [7]. The outgoing UML model uses the quantum UML profile proposed in [8] and allows to represent quantum circuits in UML activity diagrams. These models can be integrated into bigger UML models with other design concerns, both classical and quantum ones.

The main implication of this proposal is that, at some point of the hybrid systems modernization it will be necessary to (re)design the target system. We believe that adapting UML to be capable of analyzing and identifying quantum components is the right path forward for its development. Additionally, the usage of UML ensures the independence of quantum technology and software platforms, as well as its support in many design tools.

The remaining of this paper is structured as follows: Sect. 2 introduces the different reasons for believing that hybrid systems will be implemented in a future and then how the classical systems will be modernized toward them. Section 3 explains how KDM and UML have been extended for the purpose of working with the quantum components. In Sect. 4 is detailed the transformation of KDM models to UML. Finally, in Sect. 5 conclusions and future work are related.

2 Modernization Towards Hybrid Information Systems

This section first introduces the concept of hybrid information systems, i.e., classical-quantum software systems (cf. Sect. 2.1). Then, the software modernization process for this kind of systems is explained (cf. Sect. 2.2).

2.1 Hybrid Information Systems

Quantum computing brings us many benefits to the different fields of science, like in finances [9], chemistry [10] or machine learning [11]. Even those benefits are only theoretical, the expectation for implementing quantum computers is huge.

Once the commercial quantum computers arrive (with an acceptable number of qubits), companies will migrate part of those classical systems with complex and/or demanding algorithms to quantum computers. The implementation of quantum computing does not necessarily imply a full replacement of the classical information systems, but at some point both paradigms could work together, creating hybrid classical-quantum information. However, this evolution of the systems does not imply discarding the whole classical information systems given that they are still useful for their organizations. Those systems may embed a vast amount of critical-mission knowledge that probably is not located elsewhere, and their replacement is highly risky.

The hybrid information systems will consist of parts developed using quantum computing and the others according to the classical paradigm. The classical part will perform those processes and procedures that do not make sense to do using quantum computing due to the cost and complexity that it would entail compared to the gain acquired, e.g., simplistic functionalities.

This evolution of the actual systems can be accomplished through software modernization. This software modernization is the evolution traditional reengineering but following an MDE approach and it has been proved being successful in the last decades in industrial projects, as in the European projects MOMOCS [12] and MODELWARE [13].

However, the software modernization must be adapted in order to being capable to work with the quantum paradigm and so, to allow the evolution of the classical systems towards hybrid systems. Such adaptation of the modernization will be explained in Sect. 2.2.

2.2 Software Modernization of Hybrid Information Systems

Software engineering has evolved as new technologies and methodologies have emerged by adapting to the problems that have arisen in the development of new systems. Now, even though we are dealing the new quantum paradigm, we still face the same development problems as in classical systems.

A solution based on reengineering and, more specifically on ADM [14], was already proposed in [4] to achieve the evolution of classical information systems towards hybrid ones. That solution introduced "Quantum software reengineering" and ensured that it might be used in three complementary scenarios (see Fig. 1):

1. Migrate existing, isolated quantum algorithms and integrate them into the hybrid information systems.
2. Migrate classical legacy information systems toward hybrid architectures that support the integration of classical-quantum information systems.
3. Transform or add new business operations supported by quantum software that will be integrated into the target hybrid systems.

Figure 1 shows the complete quantum software reengineering process and as can be seen, the use of already existing KDM or UML standards is proposed. The first phase is reverse engineering, where the artifacts (either source code or database schemas) of the classical systems (scenario 1) and quantum if they exist (scenario 2) will be

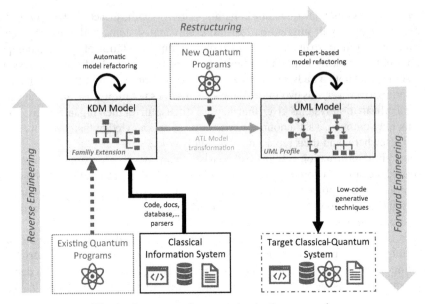

Fig. 1. Quantum software modernization approach.

analyzed, and a model will be generated that will represent, in a technology-agnostic way, the components and their interrelationships of the system. The restructuring phase (the second reengineering phase) is the scope of this paper. The restructuring phase consists of the transformation of the previously generated KDM models into a different high-abstraction level models that may be used later to generate the target code. The metamodel chosen has been UML as it is a well-proven modelling language that has been widely employed by industry for some time. UML also follows the philosophy of the previous step for representing models in a technological-agnostic manner. Finally, the last phase consists of forward engineering, where tools can be used to automatically generate code fragments of the hybrid system designed in UML. Although there are currently tools that generate code based on UML diagrams, they cannot automatically implement quantum algorithms.

Using UML for system design has several advantages, such as the possibility of being able to visualize the same system from different viewpoints thanks to the various diagrams that exist or the large number of tools that allow modelling UML designs, which are known by a broad community. Additionally, it should be noticed that UML represents a collection of best practices and its use in the design of complex systems has already been validated [15].

This paper defines a model transformation for automatically generate UML models from KDM models that were generated from existing quantum programs, i.e., scenario 1. Scenarios 2 and 3 are outside of this research.

3   Quantum Metamodel Extensions

For defining the model transformation between KDM and UML, KDM and UML metamodels have been extended to incorporate quantum semantics. These extensions have been proposed in two previous papers. Next sections summarize the metamodel extensions provided that are involved in the model transformation.

3.1   Quantum KDM Extension

The Knowledge Discovery Metamodel-ISO /IEC 19506 is a standard developed for the modernization of those systems that have suffered the passing of time and the technology with which they have been developed is obsolete or close to being obsolete. These systems are known as legacy information systems.

KDM was the first of the standards proposed within ADM and it provides a comprehensive view of the application structure and data [16]. KDM identifies the different components of the systems and its interrelationships and represents it in a technology-agnostic way at a higher abstraction level. However, KDM was not created with the aim to evolve classical information systems toward hybrid ones. Therefore, it was necessary to extend it through its built-in extension mechanism to support the representation of the different quantum entities. The full headway of the adaptation of KDM to quantum programs was proposed in [4], which is briefly summarized in the next lines.

The default extension mechanism provided by KDM is the extension family. In this extension family the different components that can be found in a quantum programming language are represented in this group, shown in Fig. 2. This mechanism collects a set of stereotypes that are then used in the ordinary elements provided by KDM.

Table 1 shows the KDM elements in which each stereotype is applied to represent all the different quantum entities (shown in Fig. 2). In KDM, the *CodeModel* are those elements which collect the facts of the same program, so as it will appears once in every program, it was assigned the stereotype *Quantum Program*. The *Quantum Operations* are the typical methods of any usual programming language that we already know, but these ones use quantum components. Nevertheless, because the different *Quantum Operations* can be called between them, were assigned the *CallableUnit* element. The *ActionElement* element is assigned to those elements whose describe a basic unit of behavior, just like the *Quantum Gate* and *Qubit measure* (this last stereotype is assigned to the Measure gate) do.

```
<extensionFamily>
    <stereotype name="quantum programming language" />
    <stereotype name="quantum program" />
    <stereotype name="quantum operation" />
    <stereotype name="quantum gate" />
    <stereotype name="qubit" />
    <stereotype name="qubit measure" />
    <stereotype name="control qubit" />
    <stereotype name="qubit array" />
</extensionFamily>
```

Fig. 2. Extension family of KDM for quantum components.

The *Qubit* and *Qubit Array* stereotype are mapped in KDM to *StorableUnit* since in the different quantum programming languages, a qubit is nothing more than a variable with a stored value (in this case a 0 or 1). Further details about the usage of the KDM extension are in previous work [4].

Table 1. Matching KDM elements with the defined one of the extension family.

KDM Element	Extension Family Element
CodeModel	Quantum program
CallableUnit	Quantum operation
ActionElement	Quantum gate
StorableUnit and ParameterUnit	Qubit
ActionElement	Qubit measure
ActionRelation	Control qubit
StorableUnit	Qubit array

3.2 Quantum UML Extension

In order to manage all the different quantum entities in UML, it is necessary to extend the UML metamodel. There are several ways to do this, but we proposed [8] an extension by creating an UML Profile. UML profiles are created as a set of stereotypes, tagged values and constraints defined for some of the existing UML elements. A key aspect of this extension mechanism is that the defined profile would remain fully compliant with UML. This advantage would allow us to use existing modelling tools.

In Fig. 3 can be seen the preliminary UML profile to graphically represent quantum programs by means of activity diagrams. On the right side of the image, the stereotypes that have been added to be able to work with the different quantum entities are grouped together: *quantum circuit, qubit, quantum gate, controlled qubit, measure and reset.* The left side of Fig. 3 shows the UML metamodel excerpt for representing UML Activity Diagrams. Leftwards arrows from stereotypes to metaclass elements in are extension elements that are used to indicate that the properties of a metaclass are extended through the respective stereotype.

The <<*QuantumCircuit*>> stereotype points directly to the *Activity* metaclass because, to represent a quantum algorithm, a single activity diagram with the <<*QuantumCircuit*>> stereotype will be used. Within this activity diagram, qubits will be represented as *ActivityPartition* with the <<*Qubit*>> stereotype. Graphically, the qubits can be seen as horizontal lines where the different quantum gates can be placed. This way of representing qubits is similar to the way IBM Quantum Experience [17] does it. All the quantum gates are *action* elements but depending on the way they act or behave on a qubit they will have one stereotype or another. The gates that affect the state of the qubit without any control qubit (such as the Hadamard gate or the Pauli's family) are represented as *call operation actions* plus the stereotype <<*QuantumGate*>>. However, those quantum gates employing a control qubit are represented by multiple *action* elements. The control qubit of the gate is represented as *send signal action* with the stereotype <<*controlled qubit*>> and the other part of the gate as *accept event action* with the <<*quantum gate*>> stereotype. In order to keep the relationship between both parts, *constraints* have been used between the involved elements. Additionally, special operations like qubit measuring and qubit resetting are represented with value specification action elements and the respective stereotypes <<*measure*>> and <<*reset*>>.

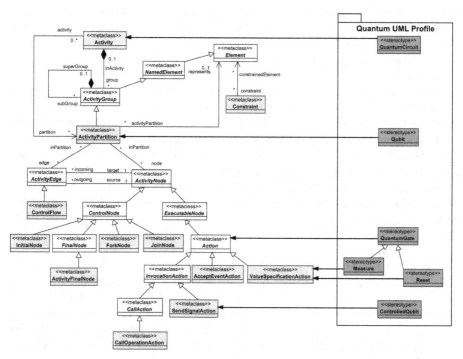

Fig. 3. Quantum UML profile extracted from [8]

4 KDM to UML Model Transformation

This section explains in detail the main contribution of this paper, the transformation from KDM to UML models for quantum information. This proposal is framed in the restructuring stage of the overall quantum software reengineering process [3] (cf. Sect. 2).

KDM models, represented according to the quantum extension family [4], are able to manage all the different quantum programs' components and their interrelationships (e.g., quantum circuits, qubits, quantum gates, etc.). Additionally, KDM represents such components independently on the quantum technology and programming languages. Such standardization of the quantum code allows to manage quantum elements without a specific concern on the quantum platform or framework where it was developed. The proposal of this paper follows the same technology-agnostic approach since it focuses on transforming KDM models into the well-known standard UML. The outgoing UML models are useful since these can be used for capturing further analysis and design details for hybrid information systems in restructuring and forward engineering stages.

The designed KDM-to-UML has been formally defined in ATL [7]. ATL is a model transformation language as a combination of declarative and imperative language that provides mechanisms to produce a set of target models compliant with the specified metamodel, from a set of source models. ATL additionally supports OCL [18] for defining additional constraints in transformation rules. An ATL transformation program is composed of rules that define what elements of the input metamodel are transformed in other elements regarding the output metamodel.

A key part for designing the model transformation is to define the input and output metamodels. The input metamodel is an extension of KDM which allows the identification of quantum elements proposed in [4] and explained in Sect. 2. The output metamodel is the ECORE metamodel for UML version 2.5.1, which defines the abstract syntax of UML. This ECORE metamodel can be seen in [19] and contains the UML model description compliant with EMOF metamodel [20]. The UML metamodel is used as is, although a quantum UML profile as depicted in [8] is used for modelling quantum circuits as UML activity diagrams (cf. Sect. 3).

Having defined the metamodels, the design of the ATL transformation attempts to identify which quantum entities could match with elements of the UML metamodel. In Sect. 3 is explained on detail the Quantum UML Profile and the reasoning of its equivalences. This identification of the elements with the metamodel is essential for the transformation.

The KDM-to-UML transformation followed a top-down order. Thus, the first KDM elements that were transformed to UML are those that group the remaining nested elements, i.e., the *Segment* element as the KDM model's root element (which may contains from different perspectives, the description of a whole system, including its components and interrelationships [21]). Whilst the last, and more atomic, KDM element is the *actionRelation*, which specifies on which qubit a quantum gate acted and its flow control.

The remainder of this section will be devoted to explaining the ATL rules employed on transformation of the main sets of KDM elements, which are the quantum program (referred to the whole quantum algorithm file), the qubit declaration, the quantum gate usage (as the different kinds of quantum gates) and the execution flow.

4.1 Quantum Program Rule

In KDM, the full quantum program is represented as a *CompilationUnit,* because it defines a container of all the program elements, so it was an essential element on the transformation. This *CompilationUnit* has been transformed into *Interaction* due to the similarities in its definitions, since this last one groups all the elements or actions that share a common objective.

As in the KDM model, all elements that are nested in the same *CompilationUnit* will be nested in *Interaction* but with corresponding transformations, such as the declaration of a qubit or the usage of a quantum gate.

A simplified and graphical example of this transformation can be seen in Fig. 4. On the left-hand side of the image is located the input model defined in KDM that contains a *CompilationUnit* and inside it is nested a qubit (with the attribute *"name"*) and a Hadamard gate (which has the attribute *"target"* that defines the qubit on which it acts). In the middle of the image is the transformation program with the *CompUnit2Interaction* rule, where it is defined that all qubits will be of type *edge* and the Hadamard gate of type *ownedNode*. Finally, on the right side of the image is the resulting model, with the *CompilationUnit* transformed to *Interaction* and with it, the nested elements together with their attributes.

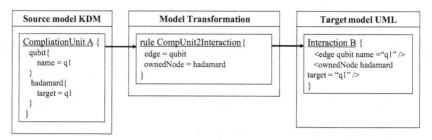

Fig. 4. Quantum program rule transformation

The *CompilationUnit* to *Interaction* transformation rule can be seen in Fig. 5, where the type of element to be identified is specified in line 3 and the type to which it has to be transformed in line 5. From line 6 to 7 it is specified by means of OCL that the *ownedBehavior* attribute of the output model will have as attributes the *CallableUnit* type elements of the input model.

4.2 Qubit Declaration Rules

In order to define the qubits in the KDM model, *StorableUnit* has been used, this is because qubits, when implementing algorithms, are nothing more than variables with a stored value (in this case 0 or 1). For the UML model, these *StorableUnit* have been transformed to *ActivityPartition* because the qubits in the final model will be represented as horizontal lines where the quantum gates can be placed, thus representing that such a quantum gate acts on a certain qubit. This way of representing qubits is the same way we can find in the different graphical editors of quantum algorithms, such as IBM Q Experience or Quirk. The rule used to transform the *StorableUnit* into *ActivityPartition* can be seen in Fig. 6, where the *ActivityPartition* simply has the same *"name"* attribute as the *StorableUnit*.

```
1 rule CompilationUnitToInteraction {
2  from
3      src: kdm!CompilationUnit
4  to
5     tgt: uml!Interaction (
6        ownedBehavior <- src.codeElement -> select(e | e.
7              oclIsTypeOf(kdm!CallableUnit))
8     )
9 }
```

Fig. 5. Compilation unit to interaction ATL rule.

```
1 rule StorableUnitToActivityPartition {
2  from
3      src : kdm!StorableUnit
4  to
5     tgt : uml!ActivityPartition(
6        name <- src.name
7     )
8 }
```

Fig. 6. StorableUnit to ActivityPartition rule.

4.3   Quantum Gates Rules and Execution Flow

In KDM, all quantum gates are identified as *ActionElement* because they have a behavior on another element (in this context, on a qubit). However, UML allows to define more precisely what kind of behavior it is. Therefore, depending on the type of quantum gate, they will be of one type or another or will have certain attributes or not.

The whole Hadamard's gate transformation to UML can be seen in Fig. 7. As it just affects to the state of a qubit, it has been defined as *CallOperationAction* in UML. This is because *CallOperationAction* transmits an operation call request to a target object. In the left side of the image is located the gate represented in KDM with two attributes ("*name*" and "*id*") and three children (one "*source*" and two "*actionRelation*"). The *actionRelation* element of type *Addresses* points with the *to* attribute to the qubit which the quantum gate is applied and with *from* to the gate that acts (itself). The *actionRelation* element of type *Flow* specifies the flow that the information follow, where the *to* attribute points to the quantum entity that precedes.

In the middle of Fig. 7 are located the two rules necessary for the transformation. At the upper part is located the rule for the transformation of *Address* to *CallOperationAction* (to make it simpler, the methods that check whether such quantum gate is Hadamard or not have been omitted), where the attributes of the output model defined in that rule are "*name*" and "*inPartition*". The "*name*" attribute specifies the name of the gate and is taken from the element pointed to by its "*from*" attribute and the "*inPartition*" attribute defines which qubit is the quantum gate acting on, that is why the "*to*" attribute is used as explained previously. In the lower middle part of the image, you can see the rule to transform the actionRelation from *Flow* to *ControlFlow* type. The standard mechanism of UML for specify the flow of the information is by means of *ControlFlow,* therefore this transformation is one of the most important. So, for defining the target and source of the flow of the information, were employed the *to* and *from* attributes of *Flow*.

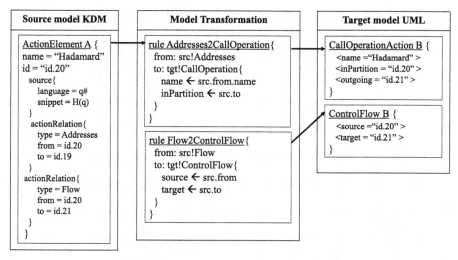

Fig. 7. Hadamard's gate transformation.

Finally, in the right side of Fig. 7 can be seen how the transformation ends, with *CallOperationAction* and *ControlFlow* each one with its corresponded attributes. Thanks to the bidirectionality of the transformation, the *outgoing* attribute is set automatically in *CallOperationAction* due to the *target* attribute in *ControlFlow*. The real UML representation of the Hadamard's gate can be seen in Fig. 8.

```
1   <ownedNode xsi:type="uml:CallOperationAction" name="Hadamard"
2       incoming="1/@packagedElement.0/@packagedElement.0/@ownedBehavior.0/@edge.5"
3       outgoing="1/@packagedElement.0/@packagedElement.0/@ownedBehavior.0/@edge.0"
4       inPartition= "1/@packagedElement.0/@packagedElement.0/@ownedBehavior.0/@ownedGroup.0"/>
5   <edge xsi:type="uml:ControlFlow"
6       target="1/@packagedElement.0/@packagedElement.0/@ownedBehavior.0/@ownedNode.2"
7       source="1/@packagedElement.0/@packagedElement.0/@ownedBehavior.0/@ownedNode.1"/>
```

Fig. 8. Hadamard's gate in UML.

4.4 Running Example

As an example of the transformation of KDM to UML, Fig. 9 briefly shows the result of transforming the quantum teleportation algorithm. The teleportation Q# code from which the KDM model was build is available in [22]. Due to the extension limitations, the input and output model are visualized hierarchically with the modelling tools of the Eclipse IDE [23]. The whole resources for this example can be found at [24] (i.e., metamodel, input and output models).

The generation of the KDM model by reverse engineering can be observed on the left-hand side of Fig. 9. The definition of the extension family (previously explained) is placed at the beginning of the model. The elements of the KDM model *Teleport, TeleportClassicalMessage* and *TeleportRandomMessage* belong to the *CallableUnit* type because, as explained in Sect. 3.1, they correspond to the methods working with qubits, being in the case of the *Callable Unit Teleport,* the qubit with the name *register.* In case the qubits are passed by reference, those qubits will be found as children of an element of type *Signature.*

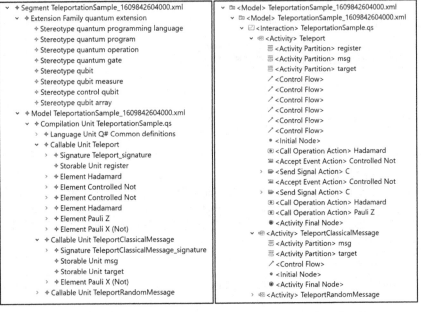

Fig. 9. Result of the model transformation for the teleportation algorithm.

The right-hand side of Fig. 9 is shown the outgoing UML model (available in [24]). Unlike the KDM model, the methods defined on the previous paragraph are now of *Activity* type. We can distinguish that, at the beginning of each *Activity,* an *Initial Node* is declared to denote where the action flow starts and a *Final Node* to indicate where it ends. In contrast with the KDM model, to denote the flow of action, in UML it is done through the *Control Flow* that can be observed at the beginning of each method, while in KDM it is done through attributes of the elements.

One major change with respect the KDM model, is that depending on the type of action a quantum gate does, in the UML model has on type or another, whereas on KDM model they are all just *Elements.* Furthermore, the Controlled Not gate in the UML model is divided into two elements, one for the lecture of the control qubit as a *Send Signal Action* and the other one for representing the qubit state transformation with a *Accept Event Action.*

5   Conclusions and Future Work

This paper presented a solution for addressing the challenge of the modernization of classical information systems towards hybrid ones. This research specially focuses on the designing of hybrid systems through UML. In order to perform the design of the new systems, paper proposes a model transformation between KDM and UML models, which has been implemented in ATL. The corresponding metamodels have been extended to work with the different quantum entities (qubits, quantum gates, etc.). In particular, the quantum circuits are modelled as activity diagrams by using a specific quantum UML profile.

The KDM-to-UML transformation has been accomplished and its usage with a real model has been demonstrated. Thus, quantum algorithms can be modelled as UML activity diagrams that can be combined with the other design models of the system. This integration contributes to define high-level designs within the modernization process of hybrid information systems. Additionally, this research makes it possible to visualize quantum algorithms in UML designs, enabling a graphical view of the flow of the action through activity diagrams.

When gathering quantum algorithms into KDM models, specific quantum information is already abstracted thanks to KDM. Then, the proposed model transformation is performed between KDM and UML that could be considered to be at the same abstraction level. However, the future research will study in-depth how affect the gap between the abstraction level of UML (originally intended to deal with object-oriented software) and circuits (set a very low abstraction level). Furthermore, as future work, we will define transformations to other types of UML diagrams, like classes, sequence, or state.

Acknowledgments. This work is part of the SMOQUIN project (PID2019-104791RBI00) funded by the Spanish Ministry of Science and Innovation (MICINN) and "QHealth: Quantum Pharmacogenomics Applied to Aging", 2020 CDTI Missions Programme (Center for the Development of Industrial Technology of the Ministry of Science and Innovation of Spain). We would like to thank all the aQuantum members, and particularly Guido Peterssen and Pepe Hevia, for their help and support.

References

1. Haroche, S., Raimond, J.-M.J.P.T.: Quantum computing: dream or nightmare? Phys. Today **49**(8), 51–54 (1996)
2. Piattini, M., Peterssen, G., Pérez-Castillo, R.: Quantum computing: a new software engineering golden age. ACM SIGSOFT Softw. Eng. Notes **45**(3), 12–14 (2020). https://doi.org/10.1145/3402127.3402131
3. Pérez-Castillo, R., Serrano, M.A., Piattini, M.: Software modernization to embrace quantum technology. Adv. Eng. Softw. **151**, 102933 (2021)
4. Jiménez-Navajas, L., Pérez-Castillo, R., Piattini, M.: Reverse engineering of quantum programs toward KDM models. In: Shepperd, M., Brito e Abreu, F., Rodrigues da Silva, A., Pérez-Castillo, R. (eds.) QUATIC 2020. CCIS, vol. 1266, pp. 249–262. Springer, Cham (2020). https://doi.org/10.1007/978-3-030-58793-2_20

5. OMG. ADM Task Force by OMG (2020). Accessed 25 May 2020. https://www.omg.org/adm/
6. Piattini, M., et al.: The talavera manifesto for quantum software engineering and programming. In: QANSWER (2020)
7. Foundation, E.: ATL - a model transformation technology. https://www.eclipse.org/atl/
8. Pérez-Castillo, R., Jiménez-Navajas, L., Piattini, M.: Modelling quantum circuits with UML. In: Second International Workshop on Quantum Software Engineering (Q-SE 2021). IEEE Computer Society, Madrid (2021). In Press
9. Egger, D.J., et al.: Quantum computing for finance: state of the art and future prospects (2020)
10. Cao, Y., et al.: Quantum chemistry in the age of quantum computing. Chem. Rev. **119**(19), 10856–10915 (2019)
11. Ristè, D., et al.: Demonstration of quantum advantage in machine learning. npj Quant. Inf. **3**(1), 1–5 (2017)
12. Bagnato, A., et al.: MOMOCS: MDE for the modernization of complex systems. Genie Log. **85**, 49–52 (2008)
13. Comission, E.: MODELWARE: a new approach to model-driven development (2005). https://cordis.europa.eu/article/id/97188-modelware-a-new-approach-to-modeldriven-development
14. Pérez-Castillo, R., de Guzmán, I.G.R., Piattini, M.: Architecture-driven modernization. In: Modern Software Engineering Concepts and Practices: Advanced Approaches, pp. 75–103. IGI Global (2011)
15. Selic, B.: Using UML for modeling complex real-time systems. In: Mueller, F., Bestavros, A. (eds.) LCTES 1998. LNCS, vol. 1474, pp. 250–260. Springer, Heidelberg (1998). https://doi.org/10.1007/BFb0057795
16. Pérez-Castillo, R., et al.: Knowledge discovery metamodel-ISO/IEC 19506: a standard to modernize legacy systems. Comput. Stand. Interfaces. **33**(6), 519–532 (2011)
17. IBM. IBM Quantum Experience Webpage. https://quantum-computing.ibm.com/
18. OMG. Object Constraint Language (2014). https://www.omg.org/spec/OCL/2.4. Accessed 18 Mar 2021
19. UML ECORE. https://github.com/ricpdc/qrev-api/blob/main/qrev-api/resources/metamodels/uml.ecore
20. Eclipse. EMF, ECore & Meta Model. https://www.eclipse.org/modeling/emft/search/concepts/subtopic.html. Accessed 27 March 2021
21. OMG. Architecture-Driven Modernization: Knowledge Discovery Meta-Model (KDM) (2016). https://www.omg.org/spec/KDM/1.4/PDF
22. Microsoft. Teleportation Algorithm in Q#. https://github.com/ricpdc/qrev-api/blob/main/qrev-api/test/casestudy/qsharp_programs/TeleportationSample.qs
23. Eclipse. Eclipse Modeling Project Website. https://www.eclipse.org/modeling/
24. Luis Jiménez-Navajas, R.P.-C.: Folder in a Github repository with the resources (2021). https://github.com/ricpdc/qrev-api/tree/main/qrev-api/test/es/alarcos/qrev/atl/models

Hybrid Classical-Quantum Software Services Systems: Exploration of the Rough Edges

David Valencia[ID], Jose Garcia-Alonso[(✉)][ID], Javier Rojo[ID], Enrique Moguel[ID],
Javier Berrocal[ID], and Juan Manuel Murillo[ID]

Social and Pervasive Innovation Lab (SPILab), University of Extremadura,
Avda. de la Universidad s/n, 10003 Cáceres, Spain
{davaleco,jgaralo,javirojo,enrique,jberolm,juanmamu}@unex.es
http://spilab.es/

Abstract. The development that quantum computing technologies are achieving is beginning to attract the interest of companies that could potentially be users of quantum software. Thus, it is perfectly feasible that during the next few years hybrid systems will start to appear integrating both the classical software systems of companies and new quantum ones providing solutions to problems that still remain unmanageable today. A natural way to support such integration is Service-Oriented Computing. While conceptually the invocation of a quantum software service is similar to that of a classical one, technically there are many differences. To highlight these differences and the difficulties to develop quality quantum services, this paper takes a well-known problem to which a quantum solution can be provided, integer factorization, and the Amazon Braket quantum service platform. The exercise of trying to provide the factorization as a quantum service is carried out. This case study is used to show the rough edges that arise in the integration of classical-quantum hybrid systems using Service-Oriented Computing. The conclusion of the study allows us to point out directions in which to focus research efforts in order to achieve effective Quantum Service-Oriented Computing.

Keywords: Quantum services · Classical services · Quality

1 Introduction

Quantum computing is starting to establish itself as a commercial reality [15]. Several major computing corporations have already built working quantum computers, there are tens of quantum programming languages and simulators, and real quantum computers can already be used by the general public through the cloud. All this is motivating software development companies to take the first steps by launching their own proposals for the integral development of quantum software [2,22,23,25,31]. All of these signals are an urgent call to software engineers to prepare and enroll to sail the quantum seas.

© Springer Nature Switzerland AG 2021
A. C. R. Paiva et al. (Eds.): QUATIC 2021, CCIS 1439, pp. 225–238, 2021.
https://doi.org/10.1007/978-3-030-85347-1_17

It is generally assumed that on the way to a new world in which software systems are mostly quantum there will be a transition time in which classical and quantum systems must not only coexist but collaborate by interacting with each other [27]. This is what has been called classical-quantum hybrid systems [16,17]. The advances provided by software engineering in the last two decades allow us to affirm that a natural way to approach such collaborative coexistence is by following the principles of service engineering and service computing.

Among the reasons for this, two can be highlighted. On the one hand, as hardware technology matures and achieves more affordable costs, it is reasonable to think that companies will be inclined to use quantum infrastructure and quantum software as a service, as they are used to do nowadays with classical computing resources. On the other hand, it is reasonable to think that, at least initially, quantum systems will be used to solve only those parts of problems that cannot be solved by classical architectures, while those parts of problems that are already efficiently solved by classical architectures will continue to be treated as before. A natural way to achieve these quantum solutions is by consuming quantum services.

Conceptually, the invocation of a quantum program is similar to that of a classical service. A piece of software needs a result to be produced by a quantum system and to do so it consumes a service. For the sake of service engineering principles, such an invocation should even be agnostic of whether the service that will return the result is quantum or not. Technically, however, the invocation of a quantum service is very different from that of a classical service and still poses a challenge today. This is due to the inherent nature of quantum computing, meaning that a quantum service differs from classical services in which it includes entanglement and superposition of solutions, and will collapse to a single solution when interacting with external world, leading to having a probability amplitude associated to the results obtained upon observations of the quantum system.

Servitizing a quantum piece of software, namely converting it in a service endpoint that can be invoked through a standard service request, is possible with the existing technology. However, in the current status of quantum software it means eliminating most of the advantages that made Service-Oriented Computing a commercial success. Specially, those related with software quality like composability, modularity, maintainability, reusability, etc.

The reasons for this are multiple. First and foremost, the specificity of each architecture makes quantum algorithms and their parameters dependent on the specific quantum hardware in which they will be executed. But also, the return of the result of a quantum process is subject to errors or does not support the intermediate verification of results (due to the system collapse). Thus, different quantum architectures require very different skillsets. For example, circuit based quantum programming require developers to know the details of quantum gates [31], while quantum annealing programming requires to adapt the problem to that specific metaheuristic [3]. Consequently, invoking a quantum program in an agnostic way is impossible today and violates all the principles of service engineering. All above highlights the need for the development of Quantum Service Engineering.

In this paper we explore the current state of quantum software engineering from a service-oriented point of view. The integer factorization problem [11,20] is used to illustrate the different problems that arise when a quantum piece of code is tried to be used as a service. Amazon Braket[1], the quantum computing service offered by Amazon as part of their AWS suite is used as the services platform. Amazon is globally recognized as the leader company in services technology and through Braket they offer access to quantum computers from three different hardware providers. Using this platform as the basis for quantum services development, we identify the problems and limitations of current technology using the lessons learned from service-oriented computing. The paper provides an exploration of the problems to be addressed pointing out different research directions for the development of a future Quantum Service Engineering.

In order to do that, the rest of the paper is organized as follows. Section 2 details this work background in both fields service-oriented computing and quantum software development. Section 3 addresses the servitization of quantum software using Amazon Braket. Section 4 lists the main limitations found in today technology that limits the benefits of quantum services. Section 5 details the most relevant related works. And finally, Sect. 6 presents the paper conclusion and future works.

2 Background

Service-oriented computing is a paradigm that utilizes services as the fundamental elements for developing software [21]. One of its pillars is Service Oriented Architecture (SOA) that proposes the implementation of complex software solutions through the use of a set of services that are composed and choreographed [7]. The basic composition mechanism is the service call that allows a service to be invoked from another piece of code (potentially another service) agnostically with respect to the place, technology or architecture of the invoked service. The services can thus be maintained, evolved, replaced and reused independently without affecting the software that invokes them. It is precisely these properties what makes them especially attractive to create quality software. Over the last two decades, service-oriented computing and SOA in general, and web services in particular, have been at the center of intense research [4] leading to monolithic software being gradually replaced by service-based software run in the cloud.

The success of Service-Oriented Computing has been possible, to a great extent, thanks to the development of Cloud Computing as a paradigm that aims to provide reliable and customized dynamic computing environments [29]. Some of the main reasons behind the success of the cloud includes: the ability for companies to better control their costs, since they do not have to buy, upgrade and maintain expensive hardware and only pay for their use; and the flexibility and scalability provided by cloud vendors that allow companies to instantly increase or decrease their hardware capabilities according to their needs. These have made the cloud one of the most successful business models of the last

---

[1] https://aws.amazon.com/braket/.

decades. Recent estimations calculate that, in the USA only, cloud computing contributed with approximately 214 billion dollars in value-added to the GDP and 2.15 million jobs in 2017 [9].

Given these numbers is not a surprise that current quantum computers, which are still a very expensive hardware to build and operate, are being offered following this model. In its current form, most quantum computers can be accessed through the cloud in a model called by some researchers Quantum Computing as a Service (QCaaS) [26]. This model can be compared to the classical Infrastructure as a Service (IaaS) model offered in cloud computing. QCaaS allows developers to access some of the world existing quantum computers, nevertheless, this access is very dependent of the specific hardware and developers must have great proficiency in Quantum Computing to benefit from its advantages.

To increase the abstraction level of QCaaS, there are multiple ongoing research efforts. From a commercial perspective, platforms like the above mentioned Amazon Braket provide a development environment for quantum software engineers or, like QPath[2], an ecosystem that covers a wide range of possible applications by integrating the software classical and quantum worlds in a quantum development and application life-cycle platform for high-quality quantum software.

From a more academic perspective, a significant number of works are starting to appear in the field of quantum software engineering [24,32]. These works focus on translating the lessons learnt in classical software engineering to improve the quality of quantum software. However, as far as the authors know, very few works focus on the perspective of service engineering for quantum and hybrid software.

However, some works are starting to appear in this domain, like [1] where Quantum application as a Service (QaaS) is proposed to narrow the gap between classical service engineering and quantum software. Works like this reveal the need to focus on a service oriented approach for the development of quantum services.

3 Quantum Servitization: The Amazon Braket Case

To address the current state of quantum services, in this paper we have decided to use Amazon Braket. Amazon defines Braket as a fully managed quantum computing service. Specifically, Braket provides a development environment to build quantum algorithms, test them on quantum circuit simulators, and run them on different quantum hardware technologies.

Given that Amazon is currently the global leader regarding cloud computing and services technologies through AWS, Braket seems a good alternative to develop quantum services. Nevertheless, since the state of quantum software development is roughly the same in the different existing platforms, we expect similar results to the ones presented in this paper if the quantum services were developed on a different platform.

---

[2] https://www.quantumpath.es/.

The basic building block of service-oriented computing is a service, defined as a self-describing, platform-agnostic computational element that support rapid, low-cost composition of distributed applications [21]. However, Braket is not directly prepared to offer the developed quantum algorithms as services that can be invoked through an endpoint to compose a more complex application.

This shortcoming can be addressed by wrapping the quantum algorithm in a classical service. This implies including a classical computer to run the classical service that, in turn, invokes the quantum computer. As far as the authors know, there is currently no way of directly invoking a quantum algorithm as a service. Figure 1 shows an example of this approach. One of the simplest and well-known quantum circuits, the one used to create Bell states between two qubits is wrapped by a Flask[3] service. This Flask service can be deployed in a classical computer and provides a simple way to include quantum algorithms in a complex service-oriented solution.

Next, we present a more complex quantum algorithm used as a case study to identify the problems and limitations of current technology from the perspective of Service-Oriented Computing.

3.1   Integer Factorization Case Study

In order to make the analysis as broad and interdisciplinary as possible, we have decided to select a problem well-known by the scientific community working in quantum computing. At the same time, the selected problem is simple enough to be comprehended by any newcomer. Between the several applications that satisfy both conditions, we have decided to tackle on Integer Factorization, more precisely with a particular application of the later denoted Prime Factorization. As we all know, although this fundamental problem in number theory is computationally hard, it is not believed to belong to the NP-hard class of problems [11]. Nonetheless, it is a problem that has been used as a basic hardness assumption for cryptographic algorithms, such as the famous RSA algorithm. Thus, integer factorization and identification of new methods to address this task acquire an important role in information security.

There are multiple proposals and algorithms for the solution of this problem, being the most famous Shor's algorithm [20]. This algorithm is normally described in terms of quantum gates and circuits, suitable for development and execution on machines such as IBM's Q computing chip [8], but when considering other approaches to quantum computing, such as Adiabatic Quantum Computing based on concepts such as quantum annealing, it is not possible to implement Shor's algorithm directly. Nonetheless, other algorithms have been proposed for prime factoring, such is the case of the algorithm proposed by Wang et al. in [28]. Thus, in the studies conducted on this paper these will be the algorithms proposed for integer factorization: Shor's algorithms for quantum machines programmed with quantum circuits and gates, such as Rigetti's [19] and IonQ's

---

[3] https://flask.palletsprojects.com/.

```
from flask import Flask, request, jsonify, send_file
from flask_cors import CORS
import matplotlib.pyplot as plt

from braket.circuits import Circuit          } Braket libraries for quantum computing
from braket.devices import LocalSimulator

app = Flask(__name__)
CORS(app)
                                              Classical wrapping service
@app.route('/execute', methods=["get"])
def execute_quantum_task():

    bell = Circuit().h(0).cnot(control=0, target=1)
    device = LocalSimulator()                       } Quantum algorithm
    result = device.run(bell, shots=1000).result()
    counts = result.measurement_counts

    plt.bar(counts.keys(), counts.values())
    plt.xlabel('bitstrings')
    plt.ylabel('counts')
    plt.savefig("result.png")

    return send_file("result.png", mimetype='image/png')

if __name__ == '__main__':
    app.run(host="localhost", port=33888)
```

Fig. 1. Quantum algorithm wrapped by a classical service

[12]; and integer factorization based on quantum annealing for adiabatic quantum machines such as D-Wave's [10].

These algorithms also serve as an illustration of a problem derived of the relative novelty of quantum computing and its different existing implementations. Namely, the nonexistence of algorithms with do-it-yourself characteristics. This is mainly due to the complex nature of the problems addressed by quantum computing and to the proximity of the algorithms with the underlying hardware used. This context is producing problems similar to those of the 60's software crisis [18], where each algorithm was designed for each particular computing hardware, many times having to recreate the algorithms for each new machine or even for each new increment of the problem. A reminiscent of this is found, for example, when having to generate a new circuit in Shor's algorithm for primes to be factorized. Although this is done relatively easy by using algorithms to generate these circuits automatically, for the great majority of possible users of quantum computing, the ability of being able to create these types of "meta-algorithms" is beyond their capabilities, complicating the expansion of quantum computing usage out of the specialized field. Thus, it is necessary to offer solutions to non-specialized users for the utilization of quantum computing, such as the case of deployment of quantum services which allow to hide the complexity to users, only providing with entry end-points and returning the results of the execution.

3.2   Integer Factorization in Amazon Braket

To illustrate the actual situation of quantum services that can be developed on Amazon Braket we have translated the above mentioned integer factorization algorithms to this platform.

At the moment of writing this paper Braket support three different quantum computer simulators and real quantum computers from three different hardware vendors. Specifically, the supported quantum computers include two vendors whose development is based on quantum circuits, Rigetti and IonQ, and one vendor based on quantum annealing, D-Wave. The integer factorization algorithms have been tested in all supported quantum machines and simulators.

Since the supported simulators are also based on quantum circuits, Shor's algorithm has been used in both, simulators and quantum circuits hardware. Figure 2 shows a fragment of the quantum period-finding subroutine of Shor's algorithm implemented using Amazon Braket. The complete circuit for Shor's algorithm can be executed without changes in the three simulators and the two circuit based computers supported by Braket. Nevertheless, is interesting to note that the measurement and reinitialization of qubits supported by many other existing simulators, and that can be therefore found in public implementations of Shor's algorithm, are not supported by Braket. In the figure, this part of the algorithm is left commented as an example. This difference with other existing solutions causes that the implementation presented here only works on certain occasions. Shor's algorithm can be adapted to avoid the use of these operations which means additional efforts to adapt one of the most well-known algorithms to the specifics of a given quantum platform.

Although, the quantum circuit would be the same regardless of the quantum hardware or simulator used, the way in which the algorithm is invoked changes depending on where it will be run. Figure 3 shows the Braket invocation code for the three simulators and the two quantum computers supported. As can be seen in the Figure, using the local simulator is the most straightforward invocation. To run the algorithms in the other simulators an s3 (Amazon simple storage system) destination has to be defined, where results will be stored, alongside a timeout for polling these results (if polling timeout is too short, results may not be returned within the polling time). Finally, for running the algorithm on real quantum computers a recovery task has to be defined. The quantum algorithm execution is an asynchronous operation and the developer is in charge of consulting the results when ready.

Finally, the code has to change significantly to run integer factorization in an adiabatic quantum machine, such as D-Wave's, since they are based on the adiabatic theorem closely related to quantum annealing. Thus, the mapping challenge differs from gate-based machines rendering quantum circuits inappropriate. Figure 4 shows the Braket code to factorize the number 21 using a D-Wave quantum machine.

```
def period(a,N, selected_device="LocalSimulator"):
    global Ran_Quantum_period_finding
    Ran_Quantum_period_finding = 1
    num_qubits = 5
    C_reg = [0,0,0]
    cr = C_reg
    qc = Circuit()
    Shor1 = qc
    Shor1.x(0)
    Shor1.h(4)
    Shor1.h(4)
#   Shor1.measure(4,C_reg[0]) #TODO operation not implemented
#   # Reinitialize to |0>
#   Shor1.reset(4) #TODO operation not implemented

    Shor1.h(4)
    for k in range(2):
        cmod(Shor1,a)
    if C_reg[0] == 1:
        Shor1.rz(4,pi/2.0)
    Shor1.h(4)

    Shor1.h(4)
    cmod(Shor1,a)
    if C_reg[1] == 1 :
        Shor1.rz(4,pi/2.0)
    if C_reg[0] == 1 :
        Shor1.rz(4,pi/2.0)
    Shor1.h(4)

    result = run_on_device(Shor1, selected_device)

    counts = result.measurement_counts
```

Fig. 2. Fragment of the quantum circuit needed to run Shor's algorithm in Amazon Braket

These examples, although small, are enough to remark the current limitations of quantum software from the point of view of service-oriented computing.

4   Current Limitation of Quantum Services

The analysis carried out during and after the experiments allows us to conclude that there is some roughness, limitations and problems that arise when a quantum piece of software is expected to be provided as a service. The mentioned limitations are not related to the fact that quantum services cannot be built but to the fact that, by implementing quantum services with current service technologies, the potential benefits of Service-Oriented Computing are lost. Such roughness can be classified into three different types depending on their nature.

```
if(selected_device=="LocalSimulator"):
    device = LocalSimulator()
    return device.run(circuit, shots=1000).result()
elif (selected_device=="SV1"):
    device = AwsDevice("arn:aws:braket:::device/quantum-simulator/amazon/sv1")
    return device.run(circuit, s3_folder, shots=1000, poll_timeout_seconds=24*60*60).result()
elif (selected_device=="TN1"):
    device = AwsDevice("arn:aws:braket:::device/quantum-simulator/amazon/tn1")
    return device.run(circuit, s3_folder, shots=1000, poll_timeout_seconds=24*60*60).result()

elif (selected_device=="Rigetti"):
    device = AwsDevice("arn:aws:braket:::device/qpu/rigetti/Aspen-8")
    task = device.run(circuit, s3_folder, shots=1000, poll_timeout_seconds=5*24*60*60)
    return recover_task_result(task)
elif (selected_device=="IonQ"):
    device = AwsDevice("arn:aws:braket:::device/qpu/ionq/ionQdevice")
    task = device.run(circuit, s3_folder, shots=1000, poll_timeout_seconds=5*24*60*60)
    return recover_task_result(task)
```

Fig. 3. Fragment of the Amazon Braket code to invoke the Shor's algorithm in different devices

```
sampler = BraketDWaveSampler(s3_folder,'arn:aws:braket:::device/qpu/d-wave/DW_2000Q_6')
sampler_embedding=EmbeddingComposite(sampler)
h={'s1': 580, 's2': 420, 's3': 144, 's4': 128}
J={('s1','s2'): 152, ('s1','s3'): -144, ('s1','s4'): -512, ('s2','s3'): 16,('s2','s4'): -512, ('s3','s4'): 128}
sampleset=sampler_embedding.sample_ising(h,J,num_reads=100)
```

Fig. 4. Fragment of the Amazon Braket code to run the integer factorization algorithm in a D-Wave device

First, those related to the impossibility of abstracting the service from the architecture in which they are executed. Second, those associated with shortcomings of the actual abstractions to express or conceive architectures of quantum services. Finally, a third category related to the lack of support infrastructure for quantum services execution. The rest of this section delves into each of these categories.

In the case of the first category, problems related with the impossibility of abstracting the service from the architecture in which they are executed, they can be directly connected to vendor locking. This creates many different complications when generating and deploying services, such as, different types of parameters depending on the underlying machine to execute the code, as can be seen in the previous examples (see Figs. 3 and 4). In particular, when considering quantum annealing, the architecture itself restricts the specification of the problems. In this particular machine, the specification must be formulated using a QUBO or Ising form (see Fig. 4), defining it by means of graphs with valued vertex and valued links between these vertex. Any high order interrelation such as those found on terms involving 3 or greater number of variables must be mathematically transformed to simpler 2 variables related terms, a task with great complexity due to the necessity of ample and profound comprehension of the problem and dexterity on mathematical knowledge and tools.

Another difficulty of this category lies in the results generated. This is linked to the underlying physical phenomena that serve as base for the quantum architecture, such as the case of ion traps or quantum chips. Thus, apart from the well-known situation where the algorithms must be run several times to ensure statistical certainty adding a probability term to the results, depending on the architecture one must work with a panoply of solutions ranging from energy levels of solutions to "simple" probabilities and cases. This is directly incompatible with the philosophy of services.

Thus, to tackle these particular problems, the science of quantum services has to determine ways to abstract the algorithms and their results of the particularities of the machines.

Continuing with the categories, in the case of problems associated with shortcomings of the actual abstractions to express or conceive architectures of quantum services, this could be related to the misconception of directly using classical software abstractions for quantum software development. Reality posses that these abstractions are, in the best case, limited or directly inappropriate to express quantum services architectures. For example, the transparency and feature hiding typical of services cannot be achieved, even when working with solutions thought to serve as a simplification such as Amazon Braket. In other words, taking as starting point code developed in a well-known quantum programming language, almost standard of fact, such as Qiskit [31], the migration of the code to Amazon bracket's platform forces a conversion of code to the particular solution, having to generate new code and not doing a simple change of gates or functions denomination, along with different forms of invocations depending on the architecture selected to execute the code. This is a subset of a bigger drawback of quantum computing algorithms such are defined nowadays, first, having to accommodate the problems to new formulations to be used on quantum computing, such as the case of changing from integer factorization to period finding in the case of Shor's algorithm. Second, in many cases it is necessary "almost" significant modifications of the algorithm for each significant step of the problem size, i.e. different circuits for Shor's algorithm for factoring 15, 143 and so on. In order to work on this and further develop quantum services, it is necessary to rethink actual software development for quantum computing, having to abandon easy-to-carry preconceptions and contemplate the possibility and necessity of new quantum software engineering strategies.

Lastly, the problems related to the lack of general infrastructure for quantum services execution induces some situations that make it difficult to further implement and deploy quantum services. Such is the case of not being able to deploy quantum code on a quantum machine and only being able to execute it through remote invocations, along with other aspects related on how to manage the business side of quantum services, such as uptime, usage, and so on. Thus, quantum service researchers will have to further explore the transformations needed to evolve from small number of quantum machines owned by few enterprises to quantum cloud ecosystems fully available to a more general public.

5   Related Works

Due to the young nature of the quantum software engineering discipline, there is still not a lot of works focusing on quantum servitization. Nevertheless, some researchers are staring to delve in this area.

Works like [13] start to explore the potential of quantum services in the cloud and the research opportunities of quantum as a service. Some of the research opportunities presented are similar to the problems detected in this work. Specifically, the different implementations of the same quantum algorithms between different vendors or the problems to deploy quantum services in quantum computers.

Further exploring the deployment of quantum services, in [30] authors propose the use of TOSCA for quantum services. TOSCA is a standard for automating the deployment and orchestration of cloud applications. In this work, the authors define an extension to allow TOSCA to deploy quantum software. This proposal is similar to the work presented here in the sense that, since quantum applications must be newly deployed for each invocation, a classical computer is needed to host and deploy them. In our case, our wrapping classical service, as shown in Fig. 1, meets both function, hosting and deploying the quantum algorithm when invoked, but also converting the quantum algorithm in a service that can be included in a service-oriented architecture.

From a commercial perspective, along with Amazon Braket, there are other proposals also related to the simplification and homogenization of quantum access to machines and services. Such is the case of Azure Quantum [6], the counterpart of Amazon Braket. Azure Quantum not only includes Microsoft and IonQ, but also other partners such as Honeywell, Quantum Circuits Inc., 1Qloud and Toshiba. Azure Quantum provides a quantum development kit that allows the unification of an heterogeneous set of hardware and software solutions.

Similarly, other companies and software developers are creating high level development environments, toolkits and APIs to increase the abstraction level of quantum software. For example, IBM proposes IBM Quantum [5], although it only allows developers to run quantum algorithms in IBM quantum hardware or simulators. While other focus on specific domains like quantum machine learning [10]. However, as far as the authors know they do not provide any advance on quantum services over Amazon Braket.

Moreover, to be able to offer quality quantum services is not enough to simplify the development and deployment of quantum algorithms. Other aspects of quality service engineering [14] cannot be overlooked. Specifically, works needs to be done in the areas of orchestration, testing, security... of quantum services.

6   Conclusion and Future Works

In this paper we have presented an analysis of current quantum software from the point of view of Service-Oriented Computing. We have used Amazon Braket to deploy quantum services by wrapping them on a classical service and used the integer factorization problem to show the differences of running the same service on different quantum hardware, even when doing it under the common umbrella of Braket.

This experiment has allowed us to clearly present the current limitations in building and using quantum services. We have organized these limitations under three different categories and argued that intensive research efforts are needed to bring the benefits of Service-Oriented Computing to the quantum world.

Due to the young nature of quantum software engineering most areas in this discipline, including Service-Oriented Computing, are still giving their first steps. Nevertheless, the paradigm change that underlies quantum computing implies that there cannot be a direct translation of proposals and techniques. Running quantum algorithms as traditional services is not enough to bring the benefit of Service-Oriented Computing to the quantum era. There needs to be an effort to generate new techniques, methodologies and tools that bring all these benefits, already shown by the cloud and service computing, to quantum software and services.

Acknowledgements. This work was supported by the projects 0499_4IE_PLUS_4_E (Interreg V-A España-Portugal 2014–2020) and RTI2018-094591-B-I00 (MCIU/AEI/ FEDER, UE), by the FPU19/03965 grant, by the Department of Economy and Infrastructure of the Government of Extremadura (GR18112, IB18030), and by the European Regional Development Fund.

References

1. Barzen, J., Leymann, F., Falkenthal, M., Vietz, D., Weder, B., Wild, K.: Relevance of near-term quantum computing in the cloud: a humanities perspective. In: Ferguson, D., Pahl, C., Helfert, M. (eds.) CLOSER 2020. CCIS, vol. 1399, pp. 25–58. Springer, Cham (2021). https://doi.org/10.1007/978-3-030-72369-9_2
2. Bergholm, V., et al.: Pennylane: automatic differentiation of hybrid quantum-classical computations. arXiv preprint arXiv:1811.04968 (2018)
3. Boixo, S., Albash, T., Spedalieri, F.M., Chancellor, N., Lidar, D.A.: Experimental signature of programmable quantum annealing. Nat. Commun. **4**(1), 1–8 (2013)
4. Bouguettaya, A., et al.: A service computing manifesto: the next 10 years. Commun. ACM **60**(4), 64–72 (2017)
5. Cross, A.: The IBM Q experience and QISKIT open-source quantum computing software. APS March Meet. Abs. **2018**, L58-003 (2018)
6. Cuomo, D., Caleffi, M., Cacciapuoti, A.S.: Towards a distributed quantum computing ecosystem. IET Quantum Commun. **1**(1), 3–8 (2020)
7. Endrei, M., et al.: Patterns: service-oriented architecture and web services. IBM Corporation, International Technical Support Organization, New York (2004)
8. Haring, R., et al.: The IBM blue GENE/Q compute chip. IEEE Micro **32**(2), 48–60 (2011)
9. Hooton, C.: Examining the economic contributions of the cloud to the United States economy. Report. Internet Association, Washington, DC (2019)
10. Hu, F., Wang, B.N., Wang, N., Wang, C.: Quantum machine learning with d-wave quantum computer. Quantum Eng. **1**(2), e12 (2019)

11. Jiang, S., Britt, K.A., McCaskey, A.J., Humble, T.S., Kais, S.: Quantum annealing for prime factorization. Sci. Rep. **8**(1), 1–9 (2018)
12. Kielpinski, D., Monroe, C., Wineland, D.J.: Architecture for a large-scale ion-trap quantum computer. Nature **417**(6890), 709–711 (2002)
13. Leymann, F., Barzen, J., Falkenthal, M., Vietz, D., Weder, B., Wild, K.: Quantum in the cloud: application potentials and research opportunities. In: Proceedings of the 10th International Conference on Cloud Computing and Service Science (CLOSER 2020), pp. 9–24. SciTePress (2020). https://doi.org/10.5220/0009819800090024
14. Li, S., et al.: Understanding and addressing quality attributes of microservices architecture: a systematic literature review. Inf. Softw. Technol. **131**, 106449 (2021)
15. MacQuarrie, E.R., Simon, C., Simmons, S., Maine, E.: The emerging commercial landscape of quantum computing. Nat. Rev. Phys. **2**(11), 596–598 (2020)
16. McCaskey, A., Dumitrescu, E., Liakh, D., Humble, T.: Hybrid programming for near-term quantum computing systems. In: 2018 IEEE International Conference on Rebooting Computing (ICRC), pp. 1–12. IEEE (2018)
17. McCaskey, A.J., Lyakh, D.I., Dumitrescu, E.F., Powers, S.S., Humble, T.S.: XACC: a system-level software infrastructure for heterogeneous quantum-classical computing. Quantum Sci. Technol. **5**(2), 024002 (2020)
18. Moguel, E., Berrocal, J., García-Alonso, J., Murillo, J.M.: A roadmap for quantum software engineering: applying the lessons learned from the classics. In: Pérez-Castillo, R., Piattini, M., Peterssen, G., Hevia, J.L. (eds.) Short Papers Proceedings of the 1st International Workshop on Software Engineering & Technology (Q-SET'20) co-located with IEEE International Conference on Quantum Computing and Engineering (IEEE Quantum Week 2020), (Online Conference) Broomfield, Colorado, USA, October 2020. CEUR Workshop Proceedings, vol. 2705, pp. 5–13. CEUR-WS.org (2020). http://ceur-ws.org/Vol-2705/short1.pdf
19. Motta, M., et al.: Determining eigenstates and thermal states on a quantum computer using quantum imaginary time evolution. Nat. Phys. **16**(2), 205–210 (2020)
20. Nielsen, M.A., Chuang, I.: Quantum computation and quantum information (2002)
21. Papazoglou, M.P.: Service-oriented computing: concepts, characteristics and directions. In: Proceedings of the Fourth International Conference on Web Information Systems Engineering, WISE 2003, pp. 3–12. IEEE (2003)
22. Pérez-Castillo, R., Piattini, M.: The quantum software engineering path. In: Pérez-Castillo, R., Piattini, M., Peterssen, G., Hevia, J.L. (eds.) Short Papers Proceedings of the 1st International Workshop on Software Engineering & Technology (Q-SET'20) co-located with IEEE International Conference on Quantum Computing and Engineering (IEEE Quantum Week 2020) Broomfield, Colorado, USA, October 2020. CEUR Workshop Proceedings, vol. 2705, pp. 1–4. CEUR-WS.org (2020). http://ceur-ws.org/Vol-2705/invited1.pdf
23. Pérez-Castillo, R., Serrano, M.A., Piattini, M.: Software modernization to embrace quantum technology. Adv. Eng. Softw. **151**, 102933 (2021)
24. Piattini, M., Peterssen, G., Pérez-Castillo, R.: Quantum computing: A new software engineering golden age. ACM SIGSOFT Softw. Eng. Notes **45**(3), 12–14 (2020)
25. Piattini, M., Serrano, M., Perez-Castillo, R., Petersen, G., Hevia, J.L.: Toward a quantum software engineering. IT Prof. **23**(1), 62–66 (2021)
26. Rahaman, M., Islam, M.M.: A review on progress and problems of quantum computing as a service (QCAAS) in the perspective of cloud computing. Glob. J. Comput. Sci. Technol. (2015)

27. Sodhi, B.: Quality attributes on quantum computing platforms. arXiv preprint arXiv:1803.07407 (2018)
28. Wang, B., Hu, F., Yao, H., Wang, C.: Prime factorization algorithm based on parameter optimization of Ising model. Sci. Rep. **10**(1), 1–10 (2020)
29. Wang, L., et al.: Cloud computing: a perspective study. New Gener. Comput. **28**(2), 137–146 (2010)
30. Wild, K., Breitenbücher, U., Harzenetter, L., Leymann, F., Vietz, D., Zimmermann, M.: TOSCA4QC: two modeling styles for TOSCA to automate the deployment and orchestration of quantum applications. In: 24th IEEE International Enterprise Distributed Object Computing Conference, EDOC 2020, Eindhoven, The Netherlands, 5–8 October 2020, pp. 125–134. IEEE (2020). https://doi.org/10.1109/EDOC49727.2020.00024
31. Wille, R., Van Meter, R., Naveh, Y.: IBM'S Qiskit tool chain: working with and developing for real quantum computers. In: 2019 Design, Automation & Test in Europe Conference & Exhibition (DATE), pp. 1234–1240. IEEE (2019)
32. Zhao, J.: Quantum software engineering: landscapes and horizons. CoRR abs/2007.07047 (2020). https://arxiv.org/abs/2007.07047

Towards a Set of Metrics for Quantum Circuits Understandability

José A. Cruz-Lemus[(✉)] ⓘ, Luis A. Marcelo ⓘ, and Mario Piattini ⓘ

Institute of Technologies and Information Systems and Escuela Superior de Informática, University of Castilla-La Mancha, 13071 Ciudad Real, Spain
{JoseAntonio.Cruz,Mario.Piattini}@uclm.es,
LuisAlberto.Marcelo@alu.uclm.es

Abstract. Quantum computing is the basis of a new revolution. Several quantum computers are already available and, with them, quantum programming languages, quantum software development kits and platforms, quantum error correction and optimization tools are proposed and presented continuously. In connection with this, disciplines such as the Quantum Software Engineering are appearing for applying the knowledge acquired through time in their corresponding classical relatives. Besides, measurement is well known as a key factor for assessing, and improving if needed, the quality of any model in terms of, for instance, its understandability. The easier to understand a model is, the easier to maintain, reuse, etc. In this work, we present the definition of a set of metrics for assessing the understandability of quantum circuits. Some examples of the calculation of the metrics are also presented. This is just the beginning of a more thorough process in which they will be empirically validated by the performance of empirical studies, especially experiments.

Keywords: Quantum circuits · Quantum metrics · Quantum circuits understandability · Quantum circuits complexity

1 Introduction

If the 19th century was the machine age and the 20th century was the information age, the 21st century will be the quantum age [18]. Several knowledge and business areas might be benefited by quantum computing: economics and finance services, chemistry, medicine and health, supply chain and logistics, energy and agriculture, cybersecurity, artificial intelligence, etc.

In fact, several quantum computers are already available: D-Wave, Google Quantum, IBM Q, IonQ, Microsoft Quantum, Rigetti, etc. Dozens of quantum programming languages (e.g., OpenQASM, Q Language, qGCL, Qiskit, QML, Quipper, Q#) [11, 22], quantum software development kits (e.g., Cirq, Forest, Orquestra, QDK, Qiskit) [19], platforms (e.g., Forge, LIQUi|>, IQ Experience, Quantum Inspire, Quantum Playground), and quantum error correction and optimization tools have been proposed in the recent years. Several quantum algorithms have been created since the seminal ones of Shor, Grover and Deutsch [1].

© Springer Nature Switzerland AG 2021
A. C. R. Paiva et al. (Eds.): QUATIC 2021, CCIS 1439, pp. 239–249, 2021.
https://doi.org/10.1007/978-3-030-85347-1_18

Besides, the Quantum Software Manifesto, promoted by several researchers and practitioners, states that *"Given the recent rapid advances in quantum hardware, it is urgent that we step up our efforts in quantum software"*. This Manifesto stresses the importance of quantum software. But quantum software is not enough on its own. It is necessary to go a step further and raise awareness on "Quantum Software Engineering" (QSE) to produce quantum software with the adequate quality and productivity [29].

The main approach for quantum computing is the *gate-based quantum computing,* consisting in dividing an algorithm into a sequence of a few very basic primitive operations or gates. So, one of the most used tools for creating quantum programs is the quantum circuit. There exist several quantum circuits simulators (e.g., Quirk[1]), while IBM uses the circuit as the main element for Qiskit[2] programming.

Quantum circuits could be taken as quantum software models and they must be understandable and flexible enough to easily incorporate modifications that reflect changes in the thing they model. It is well known that a model that is easy to understand will be easier to maintain, reuse, etc. In fact, understandability has traditionally been recognized as one of the main factors influencing software quality. Before any desired changed of any model -including quantum circuits- can be identified, designed or implemented, it must be well understood first. Understandability of conceptual models has been widely recognized in the literature as a relevant quality attribute [9, 12–14, 23, 31] but, as far as we are concerned, it has not been studied yet in the context of quantum circuits. So, we claim that it is very important that quantum programmers and designers understand the quantum circuits properly in order to design high quality circuits. Having this idea in mind, it would be important to have metrics at a conceptual level because, as stated in the *Talavera Manifesto*, Quantum Software Engineering must be agnostic [28].

That intends to be precisely the main contribution of this work: the initial proposal of a set of metrics for establishing the basis of the measurement of quantum circuits understandability.

In the remainder of this paper, Sect. 2 introduces an overview of quantum circuits; Sect. 3 summarized the related work, focusing on several metrics which have already been proposed related to different aspects of quantum software; Sect. 4 presents the set of proposed metrics; an example of calculation of these is explained in Sect. 5; and finally, Sect. 6 highlights the main conclusions of this work, together to the following steps to be taken as future work.

2   Quantum Circuits

A circuit model for quantum computation describes all computations in terms of a circuit composed of simple gates followed by a sequence of measurements [30].

Quantum circuits were originally described by Deutsch in 1989 [10] while the standard acyclic variant of the quantum circuit model was proposed and investigated a few years later by Yao [34].

---

[1] https://algassert.com/quirk.

[2] https://qiskit.org/.

A quantum circuit generalizes the idea of classical circuit families, replacing the AND, OR, and NOT gates by elementary quantum gates, which can also be represented as $2^n x 2^n$ matrices and will be applied to n qubits. But a significant distinction between classical (i.e., CMOS) and quantum circuits design is that all quantum mechanical operations are unitary or reversible. Every quantum circuit is composed of gates which represent quantum mechanical operations. Thus, all quantum circuits must have a one-to-one correspondence and be reversible. Because of this, quantum circuit designers must use reversible gates and, sometimes, additional resource costs, such as ancilla qubits [33].

3   Related Work

There is a lot of research about metrics for classical conceptual models [9, 12–14, 23, 31], but very few for quantum software.

For quantum circuits, there exist the 'quantum volume' metric which summarizes performance against some factors: number of physical qubits, number of gates, connectivity of the device, and number of operations that can be run in parallel [5]. But it is thought as a hardware performance metric (measuring the useful amount of quantum computing done by a device in space and time, as an alternative means for formalizing quantum algorithms complexity [30], for reduction in the physical layer and implementation costs [16], or for quantum circuit simulation [7].

Quantum volume is very useful for quantum researchers to systematically measure and understand how incremental technology, configuration, and design changes affect a quantum computer's overall power and performance. Also, it would benefit the CEO or investor who lacks the in-depth technical knowledge necessary to make confident investment decisions in the technology[3].

Maslov and Miller [20] proposed three different measures:

- The NCV-111 cost of a circuit composed of NCV gates as the number of gates (quantum NOT, CNOT, controlled-V and controlled-V +) in the circuit.
- The NCV-012 cost of an NCV circuit linear with weights 0, 1, and 2 associated with the gates NOT, CNOT, controlled-V and controlled-V +, respectively.
- The NCV-155 cost of an NCV circuit linear with weights 1, 5, and 5 associated with the gates NOT, CNOT, controlled-V and controlled-V +, respectively.

They used these metrics in their breadth-first search method for determining optimal 3-line circuits composed of quantum circuits.

Thapliyal and Muñoz-Coreas [33] point out different 'quantum circuit performance measures':

- Qubit cost: total number of qubits required to design the quantum circuit.
- Gate count: total number of gates used in quantum circuit.

---

[3] https://www.forbes.com/sites/moorinsights/2019/11/23/quantum-volume-a-yardstick-to-measure-the-power-of-quantum-computers/?sh=1b74bacd5bf4.

- Garbage outputs: any outputs which exist to preserve reversibility but are not primary inputs or useful outputs.
- *Ancillae*: all constant inputs to the quantum circuit.
- Depth: the number of gate layers in the circuit.

Oumarou *et al.* [26] propose QUANTIFY, an open-source framework for the quantitative analysis of quantum circuits. The metrics used are the number of physical qubits (determined by the width of the computation) and the amount of time for operating the physical qubits (determined by the depth of the computation). These metrics also influence on the total energy consumed to perform the computation.

Miller [20] propose to use T-count, the number of Toffoli and Fredkin (CSWAP) gates to produce accurate resource estimations of the implemented circuits.

Azad *et al.* [4] uses the circuit size and the circuit depth on the interaction and connection between different qubits circuit centric quantum architecture design.

Other authors focus the quantum metrics on the quantum algorithm complexity. For instance, Chaudhuri *et al.* [8] define some metrics as the Number of Gates required in a network, the Quantum Cost, the Number of Two-Qubit Gates required for generating the given network and the Complexity of the network. The Quantum Cost (QC) of a reversible function f(X) is defined as $\sum^n TOFx_i$; where $TOFx_i$ is the cost of the ith Toffoli Gate. And the Complexity 'C_f' of a given m-variable reversible function f(X) is given by $\sum_{i=0}^{m-1} \delta(A_i, B_i)$; where A_i and B_i are the corresponding 2^m input-output patterns of f(X).

Haug *et al.* [17] investigate the capacity and trainability of hardware efficient PQC (Parametrized Quantum Circuits) using the quantum geometric structure of the parameter space. They introduce the effective quantum dimension GC and the parameter dimension DC as a quantitative measure of the capacity of a PQC. The parameter dimension DC measures the total number of independent parameters a quantum state defined by the PQC can express. And the effective quantum dimension GC is a local measure to quantify the space of states that can be accessed by locally perturbing the parameters of the PQC.

Bu *et al.* [6] focus on quantum machine learning and measure the power of a learning model, which depends on its statistical complexity, proposing some measures as the Vapnik-Chervonenkis (VC) dimension, the metric entropy, the Rademacher complexity, and the Gaussian complexity.

Nevertheless, all these algorithms, learning model computational complexity, or resource (hardware oriented) cost metrics are not enough, and it is necessary to define metrics considering quantum software complexity.

In this sense, Sicilia *et al.* [32] propose a preliminary study on the structure of the source code of quantum software, using initially the same metrics typically used in classical software, and focused on the Q# language. But these metrics were defined at a logical level not at a conceptual one.

Zhao [36] recently proposed some software metrics to measure the inherent complexity for quantum software measuring:

- Code Size, by Lines-of-Code (LOC) and Halstead's Software Science
- Design Size, by considering Architectural Design Size and Detailed Design Size.

- Specification Size, based on an extension of UML, called Q-UML [26] by counting the number of quantum classes (objects), number of quantum elements (quantum variables or quantum operations), number of quantum interfaces, number of quantum attributes, and the number of all quantum methods.

The best-known artifact for designing quantum software is the quantum circuit. So, after the review stated in this section, we could conclude that there is still a need for quantum circuits metrics oriented to the designers' needs, understandability among others.

4 Metrics Proposal

In this section, the definition of the proposed metrics for assessing the understandability of quantum circuits is presented. They have been grouped by several categories.

- Circuit size. Intuitively, the bigger a circuit is the more complex to be understood should be too.

- **Width**: Number of qubits in the circuit.
- **Depth**: Maximum number of operations applied to a qubit in the circuit.

- Circuit density. As Fig. 1 shows, we can find several equivalent circuits in which the gates are deployed differently. Thus, the density of the circuit is referred to the quantity of gates applied to each qubit of the circuit at a certain step of it.

- **MaxDens**: Maximum number of operations applied to the circuit qubits in parallel.
- **AvgDens**: Average of the number of operations applied to the circuit qubits in parallel.

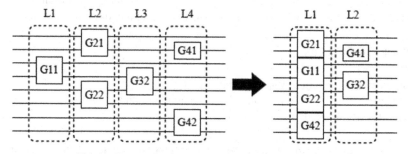

Fig. 1. Two equivalent circuits with different densities

- Single qubit gates. The most commonly used gates in quantum circuits.

- **NoP-X**: Number of Pauli-X (NOT) gates.
- **NoP-Y**: Number of Pauli-Y gates.
- **NoP-Z**: Number of Pauli-Z gates.
- **TNo-P**: Total number of Pauli gates in the circuit (calculated as the addition of the previous three).
- **NoH**: Number of Hadamard gates.
- **%SpposQ**: Ratio of qubits with a Hadamard gate as initial gate (qubits in superposition state).
- **NoOtherSG**: Number of other[4] single-qubit gates in the circuit.
- **TNoSQG**: Total number of single-qubit gates.
- **TNoCSQG**: Total number of controlled single-qubit gates.

- Multiple qubit gates. Gates involving several qubits as input and output.

- **NoCAnyG**: Number of controlled (any) gates.
- **NoSWAP:** Number of swap gates.
- **NoCNOT**; Number of Controlled NOT (CNOT) gates.
- **%QinCNOT**: Ratio of qubits affected by CNOT gates.

  - Both the controlled and the target qubit in a CNOT will be considered as affected for the calculation of this metric.

- **AvgCNOT**: Average number of CNOT gates targeting any qubit of a circuit.
- **MaxCNOT**: Maximum number of CNOT gates targeting any qubit of a circuit.
- **NoToff**: Number of Toffoli gates.
- **%QinToff**: Ratio of qubits affected by Toffoli gates.

  - The controlled qubit and the target qubits will be taken into account as affected for the calculation.

- **AvgToff**: Average number of Toffoli gates targeting any qubit of a circuit.
- **MaxToff**: Maximum number of Toffoli gates targeting any qubit of a circuit.

- All gates in the circuit.

- **NoGates**: Total number of gates in the circuit.
- **NoCGates**: Total number of controlled gates in the circuit.
- **%SGates**: Ratio single vs total gates.

- Oracles. We are aware that there are certain characteristics relatives to the use of oracles in quantum circuits which could affect their understandability but, while behaving as 'black boxes' are not possible to be calculated. Nevertheless, a thorough study of how oracles affect the understandability of quantum circuits is intended as a future work.

---

[4] Other is referred to any other single-qubit gate which is not any of the Pauli nor a Hadamard gate.

– **NoOr**: Number of oracles in the circuit.
– **NoCOr**: Number of controlled oracles in the circuit.
– **%QinOr**: Ratio of qubits affected by oracles.

  • Only the input qubits of the oracle will be considered as affected for the calculation of this metric.

– **%QinCOr**: Ratio of qubits affected by controlled oracles.

  • The controlled qubit and input qubits of the oracle will be considered as affected for the calculation of this metric.

– **AvgOrD**: Average depth of an oracle in the circuit.
– **MaxOrD**: Maximum depth of an oracle in the circuit.

• Measurement gates.

– **NoQM**: Number of qubits measured.
– **%QM:** Ratio of qubits measured.

• Other.

– **%Anc**: Ratio of ancilla (auxiliary) qubits in the circuit.

The definition of these metrics is just a first step mainly based in the experience of the authors dealing with other models understandability measurement [9]. The metrics validity, in terms of their relationship with the understandability of quantum circuits needs to be confirmed through the performance of empirical studies such as experiments.

5 Metric Calculation Examples

In this section, a couple of examples are used for illustrating the calculation of the metrics proposed in the previous section. Table 1 shows these calculations when applied to the examples in Fig. 2.

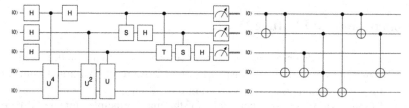

Fig. 2. Two examples of quantum circuits

Table 1. Calculation of the proposed metrics

Metric	Value (Fig. 2-left)	Value (Fig. 2-right)	Explanation
Width	5	5	
Depth	10	7	Measurement gates are not taken into account
MaxDens	3	1	
AvgDens	1.20	1	12/10 -- 7/7
NoP-X	0	0	NOT in CNOT are not taken into account
NoP-Y	0	0	
NoP-Z	0	0	
TNo-P	0	0	
NoH	6	0	
%SpposQ	0.60	0.00	
NoOtherSG	3	0	S, T
TNoSQG	9	0	
TNoCSQG	3	0	
NoCAnyG	6	7	
NoSWAP	0	0	
NoCNOT	0	6	
%QinCNOT	0	1.00	q0, q1, q2, q3, q4
AvgCNOT	0	1.20	0(q0) 2(q1) 0(q2) 3(q3) 1(q4)
MaxCNOT	0	3	q3
NoToff	0	1	q1, q3, q4
%QinToff	0	0.60	
AvgToff(q)	0	0.20	q4
MaxToff(q)	0	1	q4
NoGates	12	7	
NoCGates	6	7	
%SGates	0.75	1.00	
NoOr	3	0	
NoCOr	3	0	
%QinOr	0.40	0	
%QinCOr	1.00	0	
AvgOrD	2	0	3 oracles, 2 depth each
MaxOrD	2	0	
NoQM	3	0	
%QM	0.60	0.00	
%Anc	0.40	0.00	s_0, s_1

6 Conclusions and Future Work

We are involved in the dawning of a new era in software in which quantum computing will take down the limitations established by the hardware of traditional computers. Establishing strong foundations when creating new disciplines, such as the Quantum Software Engineering (QSE) is crucial. One of the main principles for the QSE is set the establishment of a QSE agnostic regarding quantum programming languages and technologies which assures the quality of quantum software [27]. Thus, we are aware that the easier to understand a quantum circuit (or any other kind of modeling artifact) is, the easier the tasks of quantum software debugging, testing and, in general, maintaining it will become.

It is necessary to develop several refactoring techniques for quantum circuits which allow us to improve their understandability in any new improved and equivalent version which keeps every original functionality [7]. This is why in this work, we have introduced a set of metrics for assessing the understandability of quantum circuits, as a first step.

After this first step there are several challenges in which we will put our efforts. The first one will, obviously, consists in the validation of this set of metrics through the performance of empirical studies, such as experiments and case studies. Our intention is also to develop a software tool able to automatize the calculation of the validated metrics, as well as the correct visualization and interpretation of their results. We also intend to explore the definition of a set of more complex metrics, derived from the initial set of metrics, proposed in this paper, which get empirically validated. Possible correlations and interactions among the metrics will also be estudied.

We are also interested in having a closer look at how the presence of oracles affects the understandability of quantum circuits. Moreover, being able to spot design patterns in quantum circuits is another topic we will be able to face in the future, and another promising topic of the QSE: to which extent this set of metrics can be used for easing the reuse of circuits [36] as it could allow the design-by-reuse of quantum circuits [2].

In a nearby concept, we are also interested in studying in depth the use of subcircuits in quantum circuits. A quantum algorithm comes normally down to a sequence of elementary gates and measurements, but many quantum algorithms are more naturally described in terms of manipulations at the level of entire sub-circuits, rather than individual gates [15]. In [3] a method is introduced that breaks a circuit into smaller subcircuits or fragments, and thus makes it possible to run circuits that are either too wide or too deep for a given quantum processor. We consider that this circuit 'fragmentation' could be very promising in order to increase a quantum circuit understandability.

Finally, an interesting aspect to study in the future is to which extent the complexity of a quantum circuit affects the complexity of the quantum programs generated from it in the different existing quantum platforms.

Acknowledgments. We would like to thank all the aQuantum members, especially Guido Peterssen and Pepe Hevia, for their help and support. This work was partially funded by the "QHealth: Quantum Pharmacogenomics Applied to Aging" project, part of the 2020 CDTI Missions Program (Center for the Development of Industrial Technology of the Ministry of Science and Innovation of Spain) and the GEMA and TESTIMO projects, funded by "Consejería de Educación, Cultura y Deportes de la Junta de Comunidades de Castilla La Mancha" and "Fondo Europeo de Desarrollo Regional FEDER" under Grants SBPLY/17/180501/000293 (GEMA) and SBPLY/17/180501/000503 (TESTIMO).

References

1. Abhijith, J., et al.: Quantum algorithm implementations for beginners. arXiv:1804.03719v2 (2020)

2. Allouche, C., Baboulin, M., Goubault de Brugière, T., Valiron, B.: Reuse Method for Quantum Circuit Synthesis. In: Kilgour, D.M., Kunze, H., Makarov, R., Melnik, R., Wang, Xu. (eds.) AMMCS 2017. SPMS, vol. 259, pp. 3–12. Springer, Cham (2018). https://doi.org/10.1007/978-3-319-99719-3_1

3. Ayral, T., Le Régent, F., Saleem, Z., Alexeev, Y., Suchara, M. Quantum divide and compute: hardware demonstrations and noisy simulations. arXiv:2005.12874v1 (2020)

4. Azad, U., Papneja, A., Saini, R., Behera, B., Panigrahi, P.: Circuit centric quantum architecture design. IET Quantum Commun. **2**, 14–25 (2021)

5. Bishop, L., Bravyi, S., Cross, A., Gambetta, J., Smolin, J. Quantum volume. https://storageconsortium.de/content/sites/default/files/quantum-volumehp08co1vbo0cc8fr.pdf. Accessed 14 May 2021

6. Bu, K., Koh, D., Li, L., Luo, Q., Zhang, Y.: Effects of quantum resources on the statistical complexity of quantum circuits. arXiv:2102.03282 (2021)

7. Burgholzer, L., Wille, R., Advanced equivalence checking for quantum circuits. IEEE Trans. Comput.-Aided Des. Integr. Circuits Syst. (2020). https://doi.org/10.1109/TCAD.2020.3032630

8. Chaudhuri, A., Sultana, M., Sengupta, D., Chaudhuri, A.: A novel reversible two's complement gate (TCG) and its quantum mapping. In: Devices for Integrated Circuit (DevIC), 252–256. Kalyani, India (2017)

9. Cruz-Lemus, J., Maes, A., Genero, M., Poels, G., Piattini, M.: The impact of structural complexity on the understandability of UML statechart diagrams. Inf. Sci. **180**(11), 2209–2220 (2010)

10. Deutsch, D.: Quantum computational networks. Proc. R. Soc. Lond. **A425**, 73–90 (1989)

11. Garhwal, S., Ghorani, M., Ahmad, A.: Quantum programming language: a systematic review of research topic and top cited languages. Arch. Comput. Methods Eng. **28**, 289–310 (2021)

12. Genero, M., Piattini, M., Calero, C.: A survey of metrics for UML class diagrams. J. Object Technol. **4**(9), 59–92 (2005)

13. Genero, M., Manso, M., Visaggio, C., Canfora, G., Piattini, M.: Building measure-based prediction models for UML class maintainability. Empir. Softw. Eng. **12**(5), 517–549 (2007)

14. Genero, M., Piattini, M., Chaudron, M.: Quality of UML models. Inf. Softw. Technol. **51**(12), 1629–1630 (2009)

15. Green, A., Lumsdaine, P., Ross, N., Selinger, P., Valiron, B.: Quipper: a scalable quantum programming language. ACM SIGPLAN Not. **48**(6), 333–342 (2013)

16. Gyongyosi, L., Imre, S. Optimizing high-efficiency quantum memory with quantum machine learning for near-term quantum devices. Sci. Rep. **10**, 135 (2020)

17. Haug, T., Bharti, K., Kim, M. Capacity and quantum geometry of parametrized quantum circuits. arXiv:2102.01659v1 (2021)

18. Humble, T., Thapiliyal, H., Muñoz-Correas, E., Mohiyaddin, F., Bennink, R.: Quantum computing circuits and devices. IEEE Des. Test **36**(3), 69–94 (2019)

19. LaRose, R. (2019). Overview and comparison of gate level quantum software platforms. Quantum 3, 130. arXiv:1807.02500v2 (2019)

20. Maslov, D., Miller, M.: Comparison of the cost metrics for reversible and quantum logic synthesis. IET Comput. Digital Tech. **1**(2), 98–104 (2007)

21. Miller, S.: Quantum resource counts for operations constructed from an addition circuit. In: 2020 IEEE Computer Society Annual Symposium on VLSI (ISVLSI), 141–146. Limassol, Cyprus (2020)

22. Mosca, M., Roetteler, M., Selinger, P.: Quantum programming languages (Dagstuhl Seminar 10381). Dagstuhl Rep. **8**, 112–132 (2018)

23. Nelson, H., Poels, G., Genero, M., Piattini, M.: Quality in conceptual modeling: five examples of the state of the art. Data Knowl. Eng. **55**(3), 237–242 (2005)

24. Nielsen, M., Chuang, L.: Quantum Computation and Quantum Information. Cambridge University Press, UK (2010)
25. Oumarou, O., Paler A., Basmadjian, R.: QUANTIFY: a framework for resource analysis and design verification of quantum circuits. In: 2020 IEEE Computer Society Annual Symposium on VLSI (ISVLSI), 126–131, Limassol, Cyprus. (2020)
26. Pérez-Delgado, C., Perez-Gonzalez, H.: Towards a quantum software modeling language. In: First International Workshop on Quantum Software Engineering (Q-SE 2020), 442–444 (2020)
27. Piattini, M., Peterssen, G., Pérez-Castillo, R.: Quantum Computing: a new Software Engineering Golden Age. ACM SIGSOFT Softw. Eng. Newsl. **45**(3), 12–14 (2020)
28. Piattini, M., et al.: The talavera manifesto for quantum software engineering and programming. In: 1st International Workshop on the Quantum Software Engineering and Programming (QANSWER 2020), 11–12. Talavera de la Reina, Spain (2020)
29. Piattini, M., Serrano, M., Pérez-Castillo, R., Peterssen, G., Hevia, J.: Toward a quantum software engineering. IT Prof. **23**(1), 62–66 (2021)
30. Rieffel, E., Polak, W.: Quantum computing: a gentle introduction. The MIT Press (2011)
31. Serrano, M., Trujillo, J., Calero, C., Piattini, M.: Metrics for data warehouse conceptual models understandability. Inf. Softw. Technol. **49**(8), 851–870 (2007)
32. Sicilia, M.-A., Sánchez-Alonso, S., Mora-Cantallops, M., García-Barriocanal, E.: On the source code structure of quantum code: insights from Q# and QDK. In: Shepperd, M., Brito e Abreu, F., Rodrigues da Silva, A., Pérez-Castillo, R. (eds.) QUATIC 2020. CCIS, vol. 1266, pp. 292–299. Springer, Cham (2020). https://doi.org/10.1007/978-3-030-58793-2_24
33. Thapliyal, H., Muñoz-Coreas, E.: Design of quantum computing circuits. IT Prof. **21**(6), 22–26 (2019)
34. Yao, A.: Quantum circuit complexity. In: Proceedings of the 34th Annual IEEE Symposium on Foundations of Computer Science, 352–361. Palo Alto, USA (1993)
35. Zhao, J.: Quantum software engineering. Landscapes and Horizons. arXiv:2007.07047v1 (2020)
36. Zhao, J.: Some size and structure metrics for quantum software. In: Second International Workshop on Quantum Software Engineering (Q-SE 2021) co-located with ICSE 2021. Madrid, Spain. arXiv:2103.08815v1 (2021)

Safety, Security and Privacy

A Critique on the Use of Machine Learning on Public Datasets for Intrusion Detection

Marta Catillo[(✉)], Andrea Del Vecchio, Antonio Pecchia, and Umberto Villano

Dipartimento di Ingegneria, Università degli Studi del Sannio, Benevento, Italy
{marta.catillo,andrea.delvecchio,antonio.pecchia,villano}@unisannio.it

Abstract. Intrusion detection has become an open challenge in any modern ICT system due to the ever-growing urge towards assuring security of present day networks. Various machine learning methods have been proposed for finding an effective solution to detect and prevent network intrusions. Many approaches, tuned and tested by means of public datasets, capitalize on well-known classifiers, which often reach detection accuracy close to 1. However, these results strongly depend on the training data, which may not be representative of real production environments and ever-evolving attacks. This paper is an initial exploration around this problem. After having learned a detector on the top of a public intrusion detection dataset, we test it against held-out data not used for learning and additional data gathered by attack emulation in a controlled network. The experiments presented are focused on Denial of Service attacks and based on the CICIDS2017 dataset. Overall, the figures gathered confirm that results obtained in the context of synthetic datasets may not generalize in practice.

Keywords: Denial of service · Machine learning · Public intrusion datasets

1 Introduction

The research community strongly relies on **public intrusion datasets**, such as UNSW-NB15 [17], NDSec-1 2016 [3] and CICIDS2017 [19], for designing, evaluating and comparing novel Intrusion Detection Systems (IDS). To this aim, a large number of public datasets have been proposed over the past years [18]. Public datasets provide ready-to-use network packets and labeled numeric records –known as *network flows*– collected under normative operations and attack conditions, which makes it straightforward to develop **machine** and **deep learning** models for intrusion detection. Not surprisingly, the intersection of intrusion detection and machine learning is an extremely hyped research topic. A plethora of attack detectors have spread in the literature [7,14]. Noteworthy, some of these detectors achieve astonishing results. For example, solutions proposed in [11] and [2] achieve an accuracy of 0.999 and 0.996, respectively. At the time being,

A. C. R. Paiva et al. (Eds.): QUATIC 2021, CCIS 1439, pp. 253–266, 2021.
https://doi.org/10.1007/978-3-030-85347-1_19

intrusion detection would seem a perfectly solved problem with no room for further improvements.

Most of the existing –and impressive– intrusion detection results hold just in the context of the datasets that were used to obtain the results themselves. We believe that the results obtained on the top of synthetic and "lab-made" attacks (such as those provided by many public datasets around) cannot be generalized to production networks. Synthetic intrusion datasets simply do not summarize *complexity* and *uncertainty* of **production networks**, which is intertwined with ever-evolving sophistication of the attacks, heterogeneous and non-stationary workloads, configurations and defense mechanisms of real-life servers. In consequence, an attempt to learn intrusion detectors on top of a public dataset may lead to partial –if not incorrect– patterns, which cannot be used to drive general and rigorous security claims on the effectiveness of a given IDS technique. In our opinion, the implications of using public datasets for advancing the state-of-the-practice in intrusion detection and cybersecurity remain quite opaque.

This paper proposes an initial exploration of the proposition above with a focus on the detection of Denial of Service (DoS) attacks. Detection is pursued by capitalizing on network flows, which summarize the conversation between pairs of endpoints, e.g., the attacker and the victim of an attack, through quantitative features, such as *duration, number* and *length of packets* and *flag counts*. We leverage benign and DoS network flows both (i) available in CICIDS2017 and (ii) obtained by direct emulation of DoS attacks against a victim server in a controlled testbed. It is worth noting that CICIDS2017 is a public dataset that is gaining increasing attention by the community.

Our critique is based on a twofold experiment. First, we **learn** an intrusion detector on the top of the flows of CICIDS2017, which encompasses benign traffic and various types of DoS attacks and related tools, such as hulk, slowloris and showhttptest. Second, we **test** the detector against held-out, i.e., not used for learning, benign and DoS flows of CICIDS2017 and those gathered in our testbed after the emulation of slowloris attacks (a specific type of DoS attack available also in CICIDS2017). The effectiveness of the detector is assessed with the consolidated metrics of *accuracy, precision, recall* and *F1 score*. The detector achieves 0.9991 accuracy when tested with CICIDS2017 data, which is extremely high and consistent with existing literature. Surprisingly, the same detector –instructed to detect a wider class of DoS attacks beside slowloris– performs quite poorly, i.e., 0.821 accuracy, against a slowloris attack conducted in our testbed; even much worse, it achieves only 0.257 detection accuracy for a mitigated variant of slowloris –obtained by hardening the configuration of the victim server through a defense module– being capable of significantly disrupt operations in spite of the activation of the defense. Overall, the experiment indicates that results obtained within the "ideal" world of a synthetic dataset may not generalize in practice.

The rest of the paper is organized as follows. Section 2 presents related work in the area. Section 3 describes the experimental testbed and how experiments have been conducted. Section 4 provides an overview of the datasets available in this study. Section 5 presents the results and lessons learned from our experiment. Section 6 concludes the paper and provides future perspectives of our work.

2 Related Work

Nowadays **intrusion detection datasets** have become increasingly pervasive among researchers and practitioners, due to their *usability* and *availability*. In general, data play a key role for the validation of any intrusion detection approach. However, datasets composed of network packets or flows from real-life environments are not easily available due to privacy issues. Therefore in recent years public intrusion detection datasets have been widely used by the security community with the aim of tuning and testing detection algorithms. The majority of these datasets are generated in synthetic environments under normative conditions and different intrusion scenarios. They emulate real network traffic –at least in theory– and they do not contain any confidential data. Most datasets are distributed as labeled network flows, organized in comma-separated values files specially crafted to apply modern machine learning techniques. In particular, each record is a flow and the label states if it is malicious or not. Customarily, data are also distributed as Packet Capture (pcap) files. These files are an ordered collection of network packets originating from one or more benign or malicious sources. The usability of any intrusion detection dataset reflects its power to provide information necessary for training intrusion detection models efficiently. This is confirmed by numerous solutions available in the literature, which capitalize around these datasets by achieving high levels of *accuracy* and *recall*, often close to 1.

The earliest effort to create a public intrusion detection dataset was made by DARPA (Defence Advanced Research Project Agency) in 1999 by providing a comprehensive and realistic intrusion detection benchmarking dataset, named KDD-CUP'99[1]. It includes two weeks of attacks-free instances and five weeks of attack instances that make it suitable for anomaly detection. Numerous intrusion detection solutions have been tested using the KDD-CUP'99 dataset over the last few decades, such as [22]. However, although this dataset was an essential contribution to the research on intrusion detection, its accuracy and capability to consider real-life conditions have been widely criticized [9,16]. This is also true for the more recent NSL-KDD[2] [21], a version of KDD-CUP'99 dataset with duplicates removed and reduced in size. A public intrusion detection dataset that has experienced strong popularity among the security world-wide researchers is certainly **CICIDS2017**[3] [19]. Released by the Canadian Institute for Cybersecurity (CIC) in 2017, it simulates real-world network data and uses the tool CICFlowMeter [12] to extract key statistics on network connections in order to produce labeled flows. Its Authors implemented a testbed framework with the aim to generate benign and attack data systematically using different profiles. Another recent public intrusion detection dataset is **UNSW-NB15**[4] [17], whose synthetic network data were collected by the Australian Center for Cyber

---

[1] http://kdd.ics.uci.edu/databases/kddcup99/kddcup99.html.
[2] https://www.unb.ca/cic/datasets/nsl.html.
[3] https://www.unb.ca/cic/datasets/ids-2017.html.
[4] https://www.unsw.adfa.edu.au/unsw-canberra-cyber/cybersecurity/ADFA-NB15-Datasets/.

Security (ACCS) by means of the IXIA Perfect-Storm tool[5], used as a normal and abnormal traffic generator. It leverages the CVE vulnerability database[6] to create a modern threat environment. The dataset is accessible in comma-separated values file and in pcap raw format. Since the aforementioned datasets are generated in a synthetic environment, they might fail to represent real-life network behaviors. An attempt to overcome this limitation is suggested by the Authors of the **UGR'16** dataset[7] [15], proposed by the University of Granada. In particular, this dataset is a collection of netflow traces representing four months of network traffic from an Internet Service Provider (ISP). UGR'16 includes unidirectional flows, which identify both benign traffic and attacks. Other known public intrusion datasets are **NDSec-2016**[8] [3], **MILCOM2016**[9] [4] and **TRAbID**[10] [23]. They are all accessible both as network flows and as raw pcap and contain different types of attacks. The interested reader is referred to [18] for a complete survey of existing literature on intrusion detection datasets.

It is worth noting that in the last few years works that look more critically at these datasets have spread. In particular, some of them, such as [20], consider the quality of the data by analyzing statistical flaws that might introduce bias in the model training phase. Other papers, such as [6] and [8], analyze instead the representativeness of the data contained in public intrusion detection datasets. In reference [10] it is reported a detailed analysis that considers the majority of public intrusion detection datasets issues. In particular, the Authors state that public datasets do not fit real-life conditions, and therefore the value of analysis performed against them may be of questionable value.

Over the years, the usability of public datasets has fostered the spread of machine-learning based intrusion detection systems tuned and tested on such data. Frequently, intrusion detectors are implemented with well-known classifiers, which are able to detect almost all the attacks contained in the dataset used for the training phase. For example, a comparative analysis between different classifiers is reported in [1]. All algorithms are evaluated by means of the CICIDS2017 dataset. In [11], instead, it is reported a feature reduction approach based on the combination of filter-based algorithms, namely Information Gain Ratio (IGR), Correlation (CR), and ReliefF (ReF). The proposed approach aims to reduce the number of features and exploits a rule-based classifier called Projective Adaptive Resonance Theory (PART) in order to detect DoS attacks. The Authors obtain 99.9593% accuracy with the CICIDS2017 dataset. The solution proposed in [24] is specifically focused on DoS detection; a neural-network based approach relying on the implementation of a simple Multi-Layer Perceptron is compared to the Random Forest technique. Again focused on DoS detection is the paper [13], where well-known machine learning approaches (e.g., Naïve Bayes and Logistic Regression) are used to distinguish normative conditions

---

[5] https://www.ixiacom.com/products/perfectstorm.

[6] https://cve.mitre.org.

[7] https://nesg.ugr.es/nesg-ugr16/.

[8] https://www2.hs-fulda.de/NDSec/NDSec-1/Files/.

[9] https://www.netresec.com/?page=ACS_MILCOM_2016.

[10] https://secplab.ppgia.pucpr.br/?q=trabid.

from malicious ones. In [2], instead, the Authors propose a method that exploits the Bayesian Regularization (BR) backpropagation and Scaled Conjugate Gradient (SCG) descent backpropagation algorithm. The results are promising for the detection of DoS attacks. In particular, the model achieves an accuracy of 99.6% using Bayesian Regularization and of 97.7% in Scaled Conjugate Gradient Descent. It is worth pointing out that all the aforementioned works achieve encouraging results in terms of performance metrics such as *accuracy* and *recall*. However, all of them *blindly* use data and none of them make a *speculative analysis* of the attacks considered during the experiments.

3 Experimental Testbed

Network flows that we consider during the experimentation come from both DoS attacks of the CICIDS2017 dataset, and from our testbed after the emulation of slowloris attacks against a victim web server. In order to evaluate the progression and the effect of the emulated attacks, we collect service metrics by monitoring the victim. In the following we present the experimental environment and the data collection procedure.

3.1 Experimental Testbed

Our experiments were conducted on a private network infrastructure at the University of Sannio. The experimental testbed consists of three Ubuntu 18.04 LTS nodes, equipped with Intel Xeon E5-2650V2 8 cores (with multithreading) 2.60 GHz CPU and 64 GB RAM, within a local area network (LAN). The structure of the testbed is sketched in Fig. 1.

The **"victim" node** hosts an installation of Apache web server 2.4.29. This server is a significant case study, due its wide use for hosting real-world sites and web apps. Furthermore, it can fit a wide range of attack targets available in public intrusion datasets. The Apache web server supports a variety of modules –including security-related ones– that can be enabled by adjusting the configuration of the baseline server installation. In particular, for our case study, we have selected `mod_reqtimeout`. This module can mitigate some DoS attacks, such as slowloris, and is typically enabled by default in the baseline server after installation from the standard Ubuntu repository, which means that its disablement requires explicit changes of the configuration by the user.

In particular, it allows to set –according to the environment and domain where the web server is deployed– minimum data rates and timeouts for receiving HTTP request headers and body from clients. These conditions need to be met in order to keep a connection open. If the conditions are violated, the connection is dropped and the server responds with a `408 REQUEST TIMEOUT` error. We configured the `mod_reqtimeout` according to the instructions from the Apache docs[11]. At any time, `mod_reqtimeout` can be seamlessly enabled or disabled by acting on the configuration and re-starting the web server.

---

[11] https://httpd.apache.org/docs/2.4/mod/mod_reqtimeout.html.

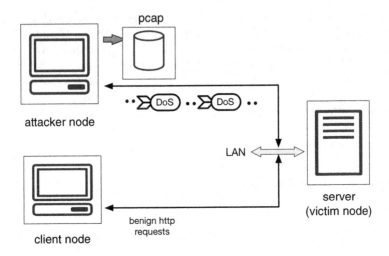

Fig. 1. Experimental testbed.

The **"attacker" node** generates potentially dangerous DoS traffic against the victim server. Attacks are performed by means of a dedicated slowloris tool (more on this later). The attacker node also runs an instance of `tcpdump`, which is used to capture the traffic between the attacker and the victim in a `pcap` packet data file. It is worth noting that the `pcap` file obtained after a given attack is successively processed to obtain the network flows.

The **"client" node** hosts `httperf`[12], which is a well-known load generator. This tool makes it possible to set a desired level of workload by setting several parameters. In our testbed, it is used to probe the web server by collecting several convenient metrics that summarize its operational status.

Our experiments are performed according to the following schedule:

1. *setup*: boot of `tcpdump` and the web server;
2. *metrics collection*: start of `httperf`, which continuously exercises the web server with *benign* HTTP requests –referred to as *load* (L) in the following– and collects service metrics during the whole progression of the experiment;
3. *attack*: execution of a DoS attack by means of a dedicated tool; the web server is under both benign load and DoS traffic;
4. *experiment completion*: shutdown of the attack tool, `httperf`, `tcpdump` and web server, storage of the `pcap` packet data file, service metrics and event logs for subsequent analysis. The `pcap` data file is processed to obtain network flows, as previously mentioned.

It is worth pointing out that, in order to ensure independent experimental conditions between pairs of subsequent experiments, we clear the logs of the web server (i.e., access and error log), stop the workload generator, attack scripts and the web server, and reboot the nodes. The web server is operated with the

---

[12] https://github.com/httperf/httperf.

default configuration –in terms of thread limits and maximum workers– available after a typical installation of the web server (e.g., by means of `apt-get install apache2`, pointing to the standard Ubuntu repository[13]).

4 Datasets

4.1 CICIDS2017

CICIDS2017 (See footnote 3) is a public dataset created in 2017 by the Canadian Institute for Cybersecurity (CIC) [19]. It consists of benign traffic synthesized by the abstract behavior of 25 users, mixed with malicious traffic from most common attacks. In order to create the dataset, a laboratory environment with attacker and victim networks has been set up. The dataset is delivered both as a set of packet capture (`pcap`) files and bidirectional labeled flow format (`csv`). In the latter format, each record is a labeled flow, obtained from the network traffic by means of the tool CICFlowMeter and identified by 84 features. These are mainly network traffic features (source IP, destination IP, source port, destination port, protocol, etc.) along with the label, stating if the flow belongs to normal traffic or to an attack. The data capture period started at 9 a.m., Monday, July 3, 2017 and ended at 5 p.m., Friday, July 7, 2017, for a total of 5 days. *Monday* is the "normal day" and contains only benign traffic; in the morning and afternoon of Tuesday, Wednesday, Thursday and Friday, in addition to normal traffic, attacks were performed belonging to the categories Brute Force FTP, Brute Force SSH, DoS, Heartbleed, Web Attack, Infiltration, Botnet and DDoS. DoS attacks, such as `hulk`, `slowloris` and `slowhttptest`, belong to the capture of *"Wednesday"*, i.e., the "DoS day". In particular, the attacker was a Kali Linux node and the victim an Ubuntu 16.04 system with an Apache web server.

4.2 Slowloris Data from USB-IDS-1

Slowloris data obtained by means of the testbed in Sect. 3 belong to a wider collection named USB-IDS-1[14], which is a recent public intrusion detection dataset developed at the University of Sannio [5]. In particular, slowloris attacks, were carried out by means of a publicly-available DoS tool: `slowloris`. It accomplishes a DoS attack by sending slow HTTP requests (*slow DoS attacks*) against a victim server. This category of attacks uses *low-bandwidth* approaches, which exploit a weakness in the management of TCP fragmentation of the HTTP protocol. We launched this attack by means of a well-known `Python` attack script[15]. In particular, this implements the slow DoS attack by sending incomplete HTTP requests. If the server closes a malicious connection, this is re-established by keeping constant the total number of open connections. We gathered regular network traffic and the attacks `pcap` files as described in Sect. 3. In order to

---

[13] http://it.archive.ubuntu.com/ubuntubionic-updates/main amd64 Packages.
[14] http://idsdata.ding.unisannio.it/.
[15] https://github.com/gkbrk/slowloris.

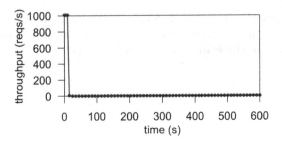

Fig. 2. Throughput of the web server during the progression of the slowloris attack (*no defense* experiment).

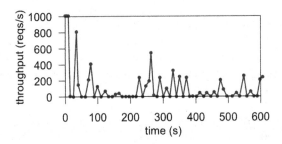

Fig. 3. Throughput of the web server during the progression of the slowloris attack in case of defense (mod_reqtimeout experiment).

obtain network labeled flows the `pcap` files obtained from the attack are successively processed by means of the CICFlowMeter[16] tool. The attacks collected from our testbed are obtained in two different operating conditions, which lead to the following datasets:

- **NoDefense-TEST**: flows obtained by running the `slowloris` DoS tool against the web server with no defense module in place;
- **Reqtimeout-TEST**: flows obtained by running the `slowloris` DoS tool after starting the web server with `mod_reqtimeout` defense enabled.

The duration of each experiment is 600 s; the web server is exercised with a client load L = 1000 reqs/s by `httperf` during the entire progression of the attack. It is worth pointing out that we also collect information on the effectiveness of the attack. In particular, Fig. 2 and Fig. 3 show the throughput (T), i.e., HTTP requests accomplished by the web server within the time unit measured in reqs/s, during the progression of the attacks. Figure 2 –*no defense* experiment– clearly shows the effectiveness of slowloris: the throughput is almost zero for entire duration of the attack. Figure 3 –`mod_reqtimeout` experiment– instead shows an interesting result. The slowloris attack still remains effective despite the `mod_reqtimeout` defense module. Except for few spikes, which indicate a

---

[16] https://github.com/ahlashkari/CICFlowMeter.

sporadic recovery of the server, very low values of the throughput are observed for the entire duration of the attack. Therefore, we can state that even the mitigated version of the attack is effective. It is worth pointing out that, for both cases, in attack-free conditions the throughput of the server is steady at 1000 reqs/s; on the contrary, it can be noted that the attack significantly impacts the throughput.

5 Results

5.1 Data Preprocessing and Analysis Framework

As for any machine learning experiment, we preprocess the CICIDS2017 "Wednesday" file and our slowloris data to make them suitable for the analysis. First, we remove non-relevant or biasing features, i.e., *timestamp* and *id* of the flows, *source address* and *port*, *destination address* and *port*, which leads to total 78 remaining features (label included). Moreover, it is worth noting that the presented experiment refers to a binary classification scenario. As such, flows referring to different types of attacks are considered as belonging to a unique general class named ATTACK – encoded with the *0* numeric label; on the other hand, BENIGN flows are assigned *1* as label.

Flows contained in the aforementioned CICIDS2017 "Wednesday" file are split into three **disjoint subsets** used for the *training*, *validation* and *test* of the IDS model. While splitting the file, we adopt a stratified sampling strategy with no replacement, which means that (i) the ratio between benign and attack classes of the original file is preserved in the output splits and (ii) each flow of the original file is assigned to a unique split. The original CICIDS2017 file contains 692,703 flows, where 1,297 were discarded due to the presence of malformed or unsuitable values (e.g., "Infinity" or "NaN"). The remaining 691,406 total flows are divided as follows:

– **CICIDS-TRAINING**: *70%* of the total (i.e., 483,982) divided into 307,778 BENIGN and 176,204 ATTACK flows;
– **CICIDS-VALIDATION**: *15%* of the total (i.e., 103,707), divided into 65,952 BENIGN and 37,755 ATTACK flows;
– **CICIDS-TEST**: *15%* of the total (i.e., 103,707), divided into 65,952 BENIGN and 37,755 ATTACK flows.

It should be noted that the three splits above sum up to 691,396, i.e., 10 flows less than the total. Occasionally, the chosen percentages did not return an integer number of flows to be assigned to a given split; in such cases, the number is rounded down to the highest preceding integer.

Figure 4 provides a representation of the learning and evaluation framework on the top of available datasets. CICIDS-TRAINING and CICIDS-VALIDATION are used to learn the IDS model; CICIDS-TEST jointly with NoDefense-TEST and Reqtimeout-TEST –our slowloris dataset– represent the test sets used for evaluating the IDS model. CICIDS-TEST, NoDefense-TEST

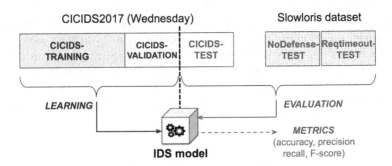

Fig. 4. IDS learning and evaluation framework.

and Reqtimeout-TEST provide held-out benign and attack flows, i.e., not seen at all by the IDS model during learning.

Evaluation is based on the typical metrics of *accuracy* (A), *precision* (P), *recall* (R) and *F-score* (F). They are computed from the total number of true negative (TN), true positive (TP), false negative (FN) and false positive (FP) obtained by running the test sets against the IDS model. For instance, a TN is a BENIGN flow of the test set that is classified BENIGN by the model; a FN is an ATTACK flow of the test set that is deemed BENIGN by the model. Metrics are computed as follows:

$$A = \frac{TP+TN}{TP+TN+FP+FN} \quad P = \frac{TP}{TP+FP} \quad R = \frac{TP}{TP+FN} \quad F = 2 \cdot \frac{P \cdot R}{P+R} \tag{1}$$

5.2   IDS Learning

Our experiment is based on a very popular machine learning technique, i.e., the **decision tree**. This technique is widely used in the literature to learn IDS models because of its capability to infer explicable rules for classifying network flows. The decision tree consists of predicates, i.e., *nodes* of the tree, which are tested on a given input flow to be classified: based on the outcomes of the tests, decision moves down through the tree until it is reached the class –either BENIGN or ATTACK in our study– of the flow, i.e., a *leaf* of the tree.

The tree is learned from both BENIGN and ATTACK flows. Most notably, decision tree is a supervised technique: in consequence, learning needs for the availability of the labels of the flows. We capitalize on the python implementation of the decision tree provided by the package scikit-learn[17]. According to Fig. 4, we learn the decision tree with the flows in CICIDS-TRAINING and CICIDS-VALIDATION. Learning is based on the hypopt[18] package. More detailed, hypopt performs an exhaustive search over desired ranges and combinations of the hyperparameters of the tree, such as the maximum depth of the

---

[17] https://scikit-learn.org/stable/.
[18] https://pypi.org/project/hypopt/.

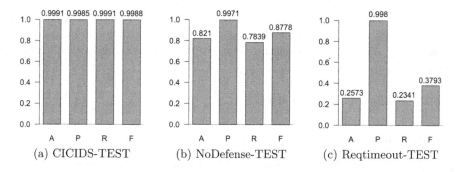

Fig. 5. Evaluation metrics of the IDS model across the test sets.

tree, which is the length of the path from the root to the furthest leaf of the tree, or the minimum number of samples per leaf, i.e. the minimum number of samples that needs to be collected by a leaf during the training phase, in order to be accepted in the final configuration. During the search, hypopt (i) trains the decision tree by means of CICIDS-TRAINING, and (ii) tests it with the flows in CICIDS-VALIDATION. The learning stops when hypopt finds the optimal combination of hyperparameters.

5.3   Evaluation of the Detection Metrics

Firstly we test the decision tree with **CICIDS-TEST**. The obtained metrics are shown in Fig. 5a. The most striking result is that all the metrics are above 0.99, i.e., almost *perfect detection*. In fact, this is the finding achieved by most of the papers on IDSs when machine learning techniques are applied to public intrusion datasets. The values of the metrics represent an "ideal" baseline. Our critique is that such impressive results will likely not hold outside the public dataset itself.

In order to explore this proposition, we test the model against the network flows of slowloris obtained in our testbed. Figure 5b shows the results for **NoDefense-TEST**. It can be noted that the IDS model, although trained to detect different types of DoS attacks –including slowloris– performs quite poorly. For example, A and R drop from 0.991 (Fig. 5a) to 0.8210 and 0.7839, respectively. This finding is quite surprising because the slowloris attack in NoDefense-TEST is so obvious and proven to be 100% disruptive through all the duration of the data collection, as clearly shown in Fig. 2 in Sect. 4. The IDS model was purposely trained on a variety of DoS attacks to achieve more flexibility and avoid that the model was "overfitted" only on slowloris data. However, according to the outcome, embedding such attack knowledge in the model did not help to achieve satisfactory results.

As for **Reqtimeout-TEST** in Fig. 5c, the evaluation metrics get even worse. In this case accuracy and recall drop to 0.2573 and 0.2341, respectively. As said, Reqtimeout-TEST hinges on a mitigated variant of slowloris obtained by enabling the `req_timeout` defense module. In principle, the reader may think that an attack done under defense is harmless and not worthy to be detected; however, Fig. 3 in Sect. 4 demonstrates that it is not the case for slowloris, which strongly disrupts operations in spite of the defense. Our experiment indicates that a model trained to detect a given attack might be ineffective to reveal a "weaker" variant of the same attack.

5.4   Lessons Learned

There are several interesting lessons learned from our experience. We notice that the "ideal" IDS model obtained in the context of its originating dataset –CICIDS2017 in this study– *does not* generalize to a much more simple proof-of-concept experiment. In consequence, it is hard to see if/how that IDS model would generalize to a real-life network affected by all the sources of complexity and uncertainty that do not exist in our small-scale, controlled, testbed.

More importantly, a minor difference with respect to the data gathering environment of the public dataset, such as the enablement of a defense module, can totally invalidate an IDS model inferred on the top of it. It must be noted that defense modules are just a marginal example out of the large number of uncontrollable factors (e.g., sophistication of the attacks, workloads and configuration) that characterize a production network. Public intrusion datasets provide only a limited and incomplete view: our initial experiment demonstrates that *one single variation of the factors changes it all*.

Overall, the implications of using public datasets for advancing the state-of-the-practice of real-life networks and to drive general and rigorous security claims on machine learning and IDS techniques remain quite opaque.

6   Conclusion

The recent spread of machine learning techniques has boosted significantly the performance of intrusion detection systems. Machine learning models can learn normal and anomalous patterns from training data and generate classifiers that are successively used to detect attacks. Most proposals in the literature leverage public intrusion detection datasets and achieve detection rates that often are very impressive. However, these classifiers are hardly ever employed in real-life networks as they could be ineffective under realistic traffic conditions.

This paper proposed an initial investigation of the inefficacy of machine learning on public datasets, with a focus on DoS attacks. In particular, we trained an intrusion detector based on the flows of CICIDS2017 dataset, by considering both benign and DoS attack traffic. In order to validate the effectiveness of this detector, we tested it with held-out data, i.e., not used for learning. We leveraged benign and DoS network test flows from the CICIDS2017 dataset and from a testbed emulating a `slowloris` attack. The detector exhibits 99% accuracy when tested with data from CICIDS2017. Notably, performance drops against the `slowloris` attack conducted in our testbed. This indicates that the "ideal" conditions that identify most intrusion detection datasets are not generalizable to real-life environments. The finding contributes to establishing new knowledge in this area and poses novel open challenges.

Our results are extremely relevant both for the release of new datasets and for the implementation of machine learning algorithms, for the purpose of designing increasingly robust and performing intrusion detection systems. In our future work, we will extend the analysis by emulating other different DoS attacks. More important, our long-term objective is to extend our study to other similar public datasets and machine learning approaches. Our aim is also to analyze *deep learning* techniques as far as their use on real-world data is concerned, since at least in theory they could not be affected by the issues pointed out in this paper.

Acknowledgment. Andrea Del Vecchio gratefully acknowledges support by the "Orio Carlini" 2020 GARR Consortium Fellowship.

References

1. Ahmim, A., Maglaras, L., Ferrag, M.A., Derdour, M., Janicke, H.: A novel hierarchical intrusion detection system based on decision tree and rules-based models. In: Proceedings of International Conference on Distributed Computing in Sensor Systems, pp. 228–233 (2019)
2. Ali, O., Cotae, P.: Towards DoS/DDoS attack detection using artificial neural networks. In: Proceedings of 9th IEEE Annual Ubiquitous Computing, Electronics Mobile Communication Conference, pp. 229–234 (2018)
3. Beer, F., Hofer, T., Karimi, D., Bühler, U.: A new attack composition for network security. In: DFN-Forum Kommunikationstechnologien, pp. 11–20. Gesellschaft für Informatik e.V. (2017)
4. Bowen, T., Poylisher, A., Serban, C., Chadha, R., Jason Chiang, C., Marvel, L.M.: Enabling reproducible cyber research - four labeled datasets. In: Proceedings of Military Communications Conference, pp. 539–544. IEEE (2016)
5. Catillo, M., Del Vecchio, A., Ocone, L., Pecchia, A., Villano, U.: USB-IDS-1: a public multilayer dataset of labeled network flows for IDS evaluation. In: Proceedings of International Conference on Dependable Systems and Networks - Supplemental Volume. IEEE (2021)
6. Catillo, M., Pecchia, A., Rak, M., Villano, U.: A case study on the representativeness of public DoS network traffic data for cybersecurity research. In: Proceedings of International Conference on Availability, Reliability and Security, pp. 1–10, Art. no. 6. ACM (2020)
7. Catillo, M., Rak, M., Villano, U.: 2L-ZED-IDS: a two-level anomaly detector for multiple attack classes. In: Barolli, L., Amato, F., Moscato, F., Enokido, T., Takizawa, M. (eds.) WAINA 2020. AISC, vol. 1150, pp. 687–696. Springer, Cham (2020). https://doi.org/10.1007/978-3-030-44038-1_63
8. Catillo, M., Pecchia, A., Rak, M., Villano, U.: Demystifying the role of public intrusion datasets: a replication study of DoS network traffic data. Comput. Secur. 102341 (2021)
9. Kayacık, H.G., Zincir-Heywood, N.: Analysis of three intrusion detection system benchmark datasets using machine learning algorithms. In: Kantor, P., et al. (eds.) ISI 2005. LNCS, vol. 3495, pp. 362–367. Springer, Heidelberg (2005). https://doi.org/10.1007/11427995_29

10. Kenyon, A., Deka, L., Elizondo, D.: Are public intrusion datasets fit for purpose characterising the state of the art in intrusion event datasets. Comput. Secur. **99**, 102022 (2020)
11. Kshirsagar, D., Kumar, S.: An efficient feature reduction method for the detection of DoS attack. ICT Express (2021)
12. Lashkari, A.H., Gil, G.D., Mamun, M.S.I., Ghorbani, A.A.: Characterization of Tor traffic using time based features. In: Proceedings of International Conference on Information Systems Security and Privacy, pp. 253–262 (2017)
13. Lee, J., Kim, J., Kim, I., Han, K.: Cyber threat detection based on artificial neural networks using event profiles. IEEE Access **7**, 165607–165626 (2019)
14. Liu, H., Lang, B.: Machine learning and deep learning methods for intrusion detection systems: a survey. Appl. Sci. **9**(20), 4396 (2019)
15. Maciá-Fernández, G., Camacho, J., Magán-Carrión, R., García-Teodoro, P., Therón, R.: UGR'16: a new dataset for the evaluation of cyclostationarity-based network IDSs. Comput. Secur. **73**, 411–424 (2017)
16. McHugh, J.: Testing Intrusion detection systems: a critique of the 1998 and 1999 DARPA intrusion detection system evaluations as performed by Lincoln Laboratory. ACM Trans. Inf. Syst. Secur. **3**(4), 262–294 (2000)
17. Moustafa, N., Slay, J.: UNSW-NB15: a comprehensive data set for network intrusion detection systems (UNSW-NB15 network data set). In: Proceedings of Military Communications and Information Systems Conference, pp. 1–6. IEEE (2015)
18. Ring, M., Wunderlich, S., Scheuring, D., Landes, D., Hotho, A.: A survey of network-based intrusion detection data sets. Comput. Secur. **86**, 147–167 (2019)
19. Sharafaldin, I., Lashkari, A.H., Ghorbani., A.A.: Toward generating a new intrusion detection dataset and intrusion traffic characterization. In: Proceedings of International Conference on Information Systems Security and Privacy, pp. 108–116. SciTePress (2018)
20. Silva, J.V.V., Lopez, M.A., Mattos, D.M.F.: Attackers are not stealthy: Statistical analysis of the well-known and infamous KDD network security dataset. In: Proceedings of Conference on Cloud and Internet of Things, pp. 1–8 (2020)
21. Tavallaee, M., Bagheri, E., Lu, W., Ghorbani, A.A.: A detailed analysis of the KDD CUP 99 data set. In: Proceedings of Symposium on Computational Intelligence for Security and Defense Applications, pp. 1–6. IEEE (2009)
22. Tavallaee, M., Stakhanova, N., Ghorbani, A.A.: Toward credible evaluation of anomaly-based intrusion-detection methods. IEEE Trans. Syst. Man Cybern. Part C (Appl. Rev.) **40**(5), 516–524 (2010)
23. Viegas, E.K., Santin, A.O., Oliveira, L.S.: Toward a reliable anomaly-based intrusion detection in real-world environments. Comput. Netw. **127**(C), 200–216 (2017)
24. Wankhede, S., Kshirsagar, D.: DoS attack detection using machine learning and neural network. In: Proceedings of 4th International Conference on Computing Communication Control and Automation, pp. 1–5 (2018)

A Comparison of Different Source Code Representation Methods for Vulnerability Prediction in Python

Amirreza Bagheri[1] and Péter Hegedűs[2,3(✉)]

[1] Software Engineering Department, University of Szeged, Szeged, Hungary
bagheri@inf.u-szeged.hu
[2] MTA-SZTE Research Group on Artificial Intelligence, ELKH, Szeged, Hungary
hpeter@inf.u-szeged.hu
[3] FrontEndART Ltd., Szeged, Hungary

Abstract. In the age of big data and machine learning, at a time when the techniques and methods of software development are evolving rapidly, a problem has arisen: programmers can no longer detect all the security flaws and vulnerabilities in their code manually. To overcome this problem, developers can now rely on automatic techniques, like machine learning based prediction models, to detect such issues. An inherent property of such approaches is that they work with numeric vectors (i.e., feature vectors) as inputs. Therefore, one needs to transform the source code into such feature vectors, often referred to as *code embedding*. A popular approach for code embedding is to adapt natural language processing techniques, like text representation, to automatically derive the necessary features from the source code. However, the suitability and comparison of different text representation techniques for solving Software Engineering (SE) problems is rarely studied systematically. In this paper, we present a comparative study on three popular text representation methods, word2vec, fastText, and BERT applied to the SE task of detecting vulnerabilities in Python code. Using a data mining approach, we collected a large volume of Python source code in both vulnerable and fixed forms that we embedded with word2vec, fastText, and BERT to vectors and used a Long Short-Term Memory network to train on them. Using the same LSTM architecture, we could compare the efficiency of the different embeddings in deriving meaningful feature vectors. Our findings show that all the text representation methods are suitable for code representation in this particular task, but the BERT model is the most promising as it is the least time consuming and the LSTM model based on it achieved the best overall accuracy (93.8%) in predicting Python source code vulnerabilities.

Keywords: Vulnerability prediction · Code embedding · Comparative study · Machine learning

ⓒ Springer Nature Switzerland AG 2021
A. C. R. Paiva et al. (Eds.): QUATIC 2021, CCIS 1439, pp. 267–281, 2021.
https://doi.org/10.1007/978-3-030-85347-1_20

1   Introduction

Security bugs (i.e., vulnerabilities) in software are becoming more and more difficult to identify in today's applications, allowing hackers and attackers to profit from their exploit. Every year, tens of thousands of such vulnerabilities are discovered and fixed. Manually auditing source code and finding vulnerabilities is costly at best, if not impossible at all. Therefore, researchers and practitioners have proposed various tools that can help in discovering vulnerabilities automatically. Classical vulnerability detection tools rely on static [3,10,17] or dynamic [20,22,24] code analysis, symbolic execution or taint analysis. However, with the advent of efficient machine learning techniques, new approaches appear that try to solve Software Engineering (SE) problems by training AI prediction models on large amount of annotated code samples. Vulnerability detection is one typical such SE task that has been addressed with these new ML approaches. As of today, using prediction models to decide if a source code fragment is vulnerable or has became a very common and effective approach. An inherent property of such approaches is that they can work with numeric vectors (i.e., feature vectors) as inputs. Therefore, one needs to transform the source code into such feature vectors, often referred to as *code embedding*. This process can be either manual (i.e., defining and extracting features from source code manually, like lines of code, number of branches, code complexity) or automatic (i.e., applying ML based techniques to automatically learn the vector representation of code). A popular approach for automatic code embedding is to adapt natural language processing techniques, like text representation [26], to automatically derive the necessary features from the source code. Despite their popularity, the suitability and comparison of different text representation techniques for solving SE problems has been rarely studied systematically. Given the fact that the accuracy of prediction models relies heavily on the appropriate representation of input data, we need empirical data about the effect of such representations on the underlying SE task to be solved.

In this paper, we present a comparative study of three popular text representation methods, word2vec [9], fastText [15], and BERT [11] applied to the SE task of detecting vulnerabilities in Python code. We applied a data mining approach to collect a suitable training data for training vulnerability prediction models. Using a heuristic approach (i.e., searching for simple terms indicating security fixes in commit logs) we collected a large volume of Python source code from GitHub in both vulnerable and fixed forms. We generated the vector representation of these code fragments using automatic code embedding based on the word2vec, fastText, and BERT text representation methods and used a Long Short-Term Memory [23] network to create a vulnerability prediction model based on them. Training the LSTM model with the same architecture on each of the different code representations, we could compare the efficiency of the various embeddings in deriving meaningful feature vectors for vulnerability prediction. We investigated the following two research questions using the above described methodology:

RQ1: Is there a significant difference in the performance of the vulnerability prediction models based on the different code embedding methods?
RQ2: Are some of the code embedding methods more suitable for predicting certain types of vulnerabilities than others?

Our findings show that all the text representation methods are suitable for code representation in this particular task, but the BERT model is the most promising, as it is the least time consuming, and the LSTM model based on it achieved the best overall accuracy (93.8%) in predicting Python source code vulnerabilities. Regarding the various vulnerability types, we observed slight variances in model performances based on the applied source code embeddings. Nonetheless, the prediction model based on the word2vec representation of code clearly outperformed models based on fastText and BERT for detecting SQL injection, while in case of Command Injection, Cross-Site Request Forgery (XSRF), Remote Code Execution (RCE), and Path Disclosure the BERT based models achieved better results than models based on the other two embeddings.

The rest of the paper is organized as follows. In Sect. 2 we introduce works that are similar to ours. Section 3 gives details about our dataset collection methodology, while in Sect. 4 we describe our overall approach for the systematic comparison of the different source code embedding methods. Section 5 contains the comparison results. We summarize the set of threats to the validity of our work in Sect. 6 and conclude our findings in Sect. 7.

2   Related Work

Solving a SE task with machine learning requires the input source code to be represented as a numeric vector. Therefore many approaches have been proposed for deriving meaningful code representations to feed into ML models.

Alon et al. [2] introduce code2vec, a neural model for representing snippets of code as continuous distributed vectors. The method first breaks down the code to a collection of paths in its abstract syntax tree. Then, the network learns the atomic representation of each path while simultaneously learning how to aggregate a set of them.

Lozoya et al. [16] introduce a new code embedding technique called commit2vec based on code2vec. This representation focuses on embedding code changes rather than code snapshots, which they used to successfully train models to detect vulnerability fixing commits.

Ben-Nun et al. [4] propose a code embedding technique called inst2vec that is based on an Intermediate Representation (IR) of the code that is independent of the source programming language. They provide a novel definition of *contextual flow* for this IR, leveraging both the underlying data- and control-flow of the program. The authors of the paper demonstrate the effectiveness of the approach on compute device mapping, optimal thread coarsening and algorithm classification.

Mou et al. [18] propose the "coding criterion" to build program vector representations, which are the premise of deep learning for program analysis. They evaluate the learned vector representations both qualitatively and quantitatively.

In our work, we do not propose new code embedding techniques, rather evaluate the impact of different text representation methods (i.e., word embeddings) used as code representations for vulnerability prediction. As these techniques are usually used under the hood of the more complex code representations, this is a natural first step towards better understanding the application of natural language processing techniques for solving SE tasks.

There are also many related works that focus on vulnerability prediction or similar SE tasks based on word embeddings in particular. Harer et al. [13] use word2vec to create word embeddings for C/C++ tokens. Based on this code representation they successfully train machine learning models to predict the results of static analyzers.

White et al. [27] apply word2vec in the scope of automatic program repair. In their approach, DeepRepair, they create Java token embeddings that they use to start a recursive encoder for abstract syntax trees. Chen and Monperrus [7] use word2vec to create Java token embeddings for automated program repair as well, in order to find the correct ingredients.

Unlike the works mentioned above, we are not focusing on creating a state-of-the-art prediction model for a particular SE task. Rather, we investigate the capabilities of various text vectorization techniques as source code representations in the context of identifying vulnerabilities in Python code with ML.

The work of Russel et al. [19] is the closest one to ours. They developed a fast and scalable vulnerability detection tool based on deep feature representation learning that directly interprets lexed source code. They compared the bag-of-words (BOW) based simple source code embedding with code representations learned by CNN and RNN models automatically (i.e., with an embedding layer). Although our approach is similar, we do not compare different ML models and automatic code representation learning, but explicitly compare the effect of applying word embeddings as features for an LSTM prediction model. To the best of our knowledge, ours is the first attempt to systematically evaluate the impact of word2vec, fastText, and BERT-based code embeddings on vulnerability prediction.

3   Dataset Extraction

In order to compare the various word embedding based code representations, we need a training dataset for the vulnerability prediction model relying on them. We applied a data mining approach to gather actual vulnerability fixes from various repositories and use them to train our model to recognize different patterns of security vulnerabilities in source code. We chose GitHub as our data source as it contains a wide range of open source applications, including Python source code, which we focus on in this work. We searched for commits in Python projects with some vulnerability related keywords included in their

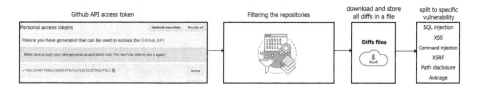

Fig. 1. GitHub data mining process to find vulnerability fixes

commit messages. There are numerous types of security vulnerabilities in programming languages, but most of them are spread across languages. We focus on some of the most popular vulnerability types, namely SQL and command injection, cross-site scripting, cross-site request forgery, remote code execution, and path disclosure. Our overall data mining process is displayed in Fig. 1.

3.1 Mining GitHub

We followed the guidance provided by Chaturvedi et al. [6], who demonstrated how to use tools and datasets to mine database repositories and assist us in gathering data in this time-consuming task. The first step is to collect a large number of commits that are candidate vulnerability fixes. We searched for vulnerability fixing commits by querying GitHub data through its public REST API. Because of GitHub constraints, we first had to extract a dataset containing commits coming from different language projects and then filter out data related to Python projects. We ended up collecting approximately 70k commits yielding to 140k Python code snippets (vulnerable and fixed together) from 14k different Python projects. To facilitate reproducibility, we published all the collected data and processing scripts in the form of an online appendix.[1]

3.2 Filtering the Data

After collecting the candidate commits, we filtered them based on some security relevant keywords. Some sample keywords we use in the heuristic data collection scripts are shown in Fig. 2. For the complete list of search terms, see the script source in the online appendix package.

We used the PyDriller tool [21] to download repositories and look for relevant commits and extract information from them. We also filtered out commits that did not contain changes in files with '.py' extension. Once we identified the commits that are related to vulnerability fixes, we downloaded the changed source code before and after the fixes. It turned out that downloading the source code in a reasonable amount of time was possible if all of the scanning was done ahead of time in a clever way to keep the number of downloaded repositories to a bare minimum. The diffs files we downloaded are essentially large text files that represent the changes in the source code introduced by a commit; however, they

---

[1] https://doi.org/10.5281/zenodo.4703996.

["buffer overflow","denial of service","XSS","cross site","directory traversal","remote
code execution","XSRF","cross site request forgery","click jack","clickjack","
session fixation","cross origin","brute force","buffer overflow","cache overflow","
command injection","cross frame scripting","csv injection","eval injection","
execution after redirect","format string","path disclosure","function injection","
replay attack","session hijacking","smurf","sql injection","flooding","tampering","
sanitize","sanitise", "unauthorized", "unauthorised"]

Fig. 2. Security related search terms used by our heuristic data collection script

contained some unnecessary details (file name, line number) that we eliminated
before assembling the final dataset using the previous and subsequent versions of
the code snippet. Both snippets contained the changed lines so we could extract
and label the functions in the previous version as vulnerable while after the fix,
they become not vulnerable.

3.3 Labels

After filtering the commits based on their messages and downloaded the relevant
code changes in form of diffs, we created the final labeled dataset as follows. We
removed the comments from the affected code blocks because they are unlikely to
impact a file's vulnerability. After that, we extracted the fragments of code (i.e.,
code blocks) from the diff files that were affected by the fix in the commit and
assigned the vulnerable label to its pre-fixed version while not vulnerable label
was assigned to its fixed form. However, it is not trivial to identify the exact
code blocks within the whole source file that were affected by a vulnerability
fixing change. For this, we analyzed the downloaded diff files and implemented
the algorithm presented by Hovsepyan et al. [14] and Wartschinski et al. [25] to
find the appropriate code block.

4 Approach

The primary goal of this work is to compare various embedding layers based
on text representations in order to determine their capabilities in detecting vulnerabilities in Python programs. To achieve an objective comparison, we need
to apply the different source code embedding methods selected with the same
ML algorithm trained on the same dataset. We evaluate the embedding methods
by training a Long Short-Term Memory (LSTM) model with the same hyper-
parameters on the dataset described in Sect. 3.

4.1 The Evaluated Embedding Layers

To encode the code tokens we need to transfer the code tokens into vectors
using one of our selected embedding methods (word2vec, fastText and BERT).

For word2vec and fastText we need to train a model that learns the embeddings based on a large corpus of Python source code. To collect this, we also mined GitHub for popular Python projects.

Word2vec: Word2vec is one of the most widely adopted word embedding methods to represent source code in vector form. To derive word2vec based source code embeddings, we needed to train a suitable word2vec model on Python source code to encode the code tokens into word2vec vectors. Training the word2vec model requires a large corpus of Python source code (for further reference, see the works of Bhoopchand et al. [5] and Allamanis et al. [1]).

To collect such a corpus, we searched for popular projects on GitHub. GitHub uses two metrics to measure a repository's popularity: stars (user-created highlights) and forks (number of copies of a repository). The list of selected repositories with a high number of stars and forks used as a code corpus is available in our online appendix. We used PyDriller [21] for querying the most popular projects and downloading their source files. The resulting source code, 11 million lines in total from 38 of the most popular projects, is simply concatenated to create a single massive Python code file. Another script is then used to fix any issues with the text, such as indentation errors. We transform the Python programs into Python tokens using the built-in Python tokenizer. We delete the comments from files and add new lines at the end of the file. Tabs and indentations have been normalized. The word2vec model is then trained on the corpus using the Gensim[2] Python package (see Fig. 3). All the word2vec training scripts are also part of our online appendix.

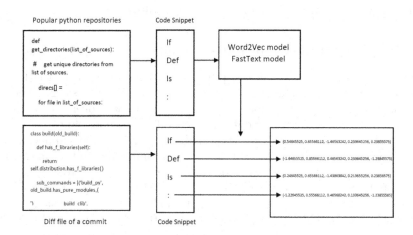

Fig. 3. Transforming code into vectors

---

[2] https://radimrehurek.com/gensim/.

FastText: We use the exact same process for calculating fastText [15] embeddings as for word2vec. This means, we apply the same data analysis and tokenizer scripts and train the embedding model with the same Python code corpus. We chose fastText as a study subject because word2vec only learns vectors for words that are complete in the training corpus. FastText, on the other hand, learns vectors for both the n-grams and the full words contained inside each word. FastText uses the mean of the target word vector and its component n-gram vectors for training at each step. The change derived from the error is then applied uniformly to all of the vectors that were combined to form the target. This adds a significant amount of extra computation to the training step. A word must sum and average its n-gram component parts at each point.

BERT: Bidirectional Encoder Representations from Transformers (BERT) is a Google-developed Transformer-based machine learning technique for natural language processing (NLP) pre-training [11]. Jacob Devlin and his Google colleagues developed and released BERT in 2018. We selected this embedding method for comparison due to its recent successes within the NLP field. As the BERT model is pre-trained on natural language texts, to adopt it to source code, we used its Microsoft's variant, called CodeBERT [12]. CodeBERT is a pre-trained BERT model for programming languages. In the context of this paper, we used BERT only as an embedding method and we feed all output tokens to an LSTM model. The biggest difference between BERT and the other two embedding methods is that the training part of the embedding model is done in advance using a huge corpus in case of BERT, while for word2vec and fastText, we need to do the training locally. This means that CodeBERT can be used out of the box, without having to train a model for token embeddings.

4.2   Preparing the Data for Classification

The collected vulnerability dataset (see Sect. 3) contains data in the form of vulnerable and not vulnerable code snippets. We need to transform these into a list of tokens (such as '+', 'for', 'init') and convert each token into its vector representation according to the different embedding methods. Each list of such vectors (representing the list of tokens of the underlying code snippet) will be labeled, where label '1' means that the code is vulnerable and '0' means it is not vulnerable. Since ML models require a fix-sized input, we took the overall length of the concatenated vectors for the longest code snippet in our dataset and padded all the shorter ones with zeros to make them have the same length.

We split the training dataset into three sets, train, validation and test. 80% of the data selected randomly is used for training, 10% for validating and 10% for testing. Note that the validation data is only used to evaluate the model performance but all the results are presented on the test data, which the model has never seen before, applying a 10-fold cross-validation.

4.3   Training the LSTM

After transforming each of our learning samples into a fix-sized numeric vector, we are ready for training the LSTM model on them. For the implementation of the model, we used the Keras library [8]. The first component of the model is the LSTM layer, which learns the features associated with the label of the code snippet (i.e., whether it is vulnerable or not). We can use a variety of hyper-parameters for the model, like dropout.

Then, there is an activation layer that creates a dense output layer with one neuron. We used the Sigmoid activation function as our aim is to predict between two classes: vulnerable and not vulnerable. We applied different hyper-parameters and tried out several different combinations of them as a set. Technically, the evaluation metric and loss functions are also hyper-parameters. We chose to compare the model performances based on the F1-score metric.

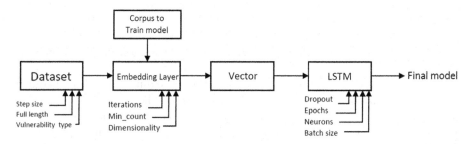

Fig. 4. The steps of creating and evaluating the vulnerability prediction models based on different code representations

Our model's base hyper-parameter is the number of neurons, which has a direct impact on its learning capacity; the more neurons we use, the more complex structures our model can recognize, but the training can also take longer. Finally, we have the number of epochs, or the number of times the learning algorithm can iterate over the entire training data set, which we set to 100 and 200. The high-level overview of our code representation evaluation/comparison process is shown in Fig. 4.

5   Results

With data mining, we created a large dataset of Python code snippets from GitHub and labeled them as being vulnerable or not vulnerable based on detected vulnerability fixing commits. The dataset covers six common types of vulnerabilities (SQL and command injection, cross-site scripting, cross-site request forgery, remote code execution, and path disclosure). We trained an LSTM classifier using different embedding layers (i.e., word2vec, fastText, and BERT) with different hyper-parameters to compare the impact of the three

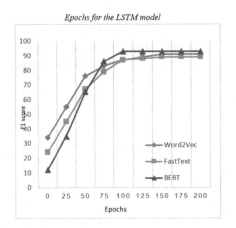
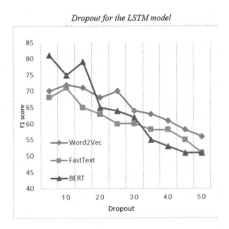

Fig. 5. LSTM model results using word2vec, fastText and BERT with various epochs and dropout ratio

different source code embeddings on vulnerability detection predicting performance.

The results of the LSTM models based on the three different code embedding layers are displayed in Figs. 5 and 6. Figure 5 shows the changes in F1 scores based on the number of epochs and ratio of dropout applied for the training. As can be seen, the results are very close for the three embedding approaches. Word2vec based results are slightly outperforming the others for small number of epochs and high dropout rate. However, for more than 75 epochs and a dropout rate lower than 20%, BERT based models perform the best.

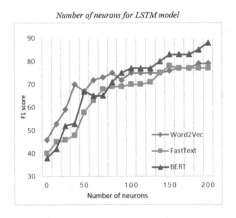
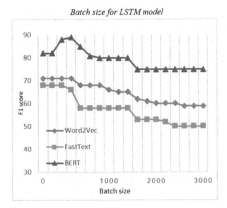

Fig. 6. LSTM model results using word2vec, fastText and BERT with various number of neurons and batch sizes

Figure 6 depicts F1 score changes based on the hyper-parameters of neuron counts and batch sizes. Again, the results achieved with the different embedding methods are very close. For smaller number of neurons, word2vec based models work better, while for large number of neurons, BERT becomes superior to others. BERT is also the best performing model when it comes to various batch sizes. It works best with batch sizes between 400 and 600. It is also true, that word2vec slightly outperforms fastText when applying larger batch sizes.

LSTM models using the BERT-based code representation achieve, on average, an accuracy of 93.8%, a recall of 83.2%, a precision of 91.4%, and an F1 score of 87.1%. The models based on the word2vec code representation achieve, on average, an accuracy of 91%, a recall of 86.1%, a precision of 88.2%, and an F1 score of 85.6%. While fastText code representation based models achieve, on average, an accuracy of 91.8%, a recall of 86.4%, a precision of 85.1%, and an F1 score of 84%, on average, an accuracy of 91%, a recall of 81%, a precision of 90% and an F1 score of 82%. Based on the results, we can answer RQ1 as follows.

> **RQ1.** We did not observe significant differences in the vulnerability prediction performances of the LSTM models trained on different code embeddings. All of them are suitable the represent code for this task (all the models achieve an accuracy above 90%). However, for BERT based models seems to perform slightly better, especially using larger batch sizes and smaller dropout rate.

To answer RQ2, we calculated the same performance measures grouped by the different vulnerability types. We categorized each code snippet according to the keywords found in the vulnerability fixing commit. As it can be seen from Figs. 7, 8, and 9, there is not much variance in model performance values within the categories.

Vulnerability	Accuracy	Precision	Recall	F1
SQL injection	92.5%	86.2%	86.0%	86.1%
XSS	91.2%	87.9%	80.8%	84.2%
Command injection	90.3%	88.0%	82.3%	84.0%
XSRF	90.1%	87.6%	84.4%	85.9%
Remote code execution.	90.0%	86.0%	85.1%	85.8%
Path disclosure	89.3%	89.0%	86.4%	86.1%
Average	*91 %*	*88.2%*	*86.1%*	*85.6%*

Fig. 7. LSTM+word2vec results for each vulnerability categories

The word2vec based models (see Fig. 7) show the least variance in model performances within vulnerability categories. The only minor exception is the recall for XSS, which is clearly lower than that of the others or the average, mostly because finding good vulnerable dataset of it is difficult and we think that we didn't train it with enough data. On the other hand, word2vec based models perform the best among all in detecting SQL injection vulnerabilities.

Vulnerability	Accuracy	Precision	Recall	F1
SQL injection	91.2%	82.2%	88.0%	85.0%
XSS	92.8%	83.8%	80.8%	82.2%
Command injection	91.2%	89.0%	87.3%	88.1%
XSRF	92.3%	82.7%	81.3%	81.9%
Remote code execution.	90.2%	86.0%	82.8%	83.7%
Path disclosure	89.8%	82.0%	81.1%	81.5%
Average	*91.8%*	*86.4%*	*85.1%*	*84%*

Fig. 8. LSTM+fastText results for each vulnerability categories

The fastText based models (see Fig. 8) show a higher variance within vulnerability categories. They have similar average performance values to the word2vec based models, but are less effective in finding XSS, XSRF, and Path disclosure types of vulnerabilities.

Vulnerability	Accuracy	Precision	Recall	F1
SQL injection	92.5%	82.2%	78.0%	80.1%
XSS	93.8%	91.9%	80.8%	86.0%
Command injection	95.8%	94.0%	87.2%	90.5%
XSRF	92.2%	92.9%	85.4%	89.0%
Remote code execution.	91.1%	96.0%	82.6%	88.8%
Path disclosure	91.3%	92.0%	84.4%	88.1%
Average	*93.8%*	*91.4%*	*83.2%*	*87.1%*

Fig. 9. LSTM+BERT results for each vulnerability categories

The BERT based models (see Fig. 9) have the highest average performance measures and the variance in the values is small within the categories. The only exception is SQL injection, where BERT based models are less efficient than the other models (recall of 78%, F1 score of 80.1%). However, in case of Command Injection, Cross-Site Request Forgery (XSRF), Remote Code Execution (RCE), and Path Disclosure the BERT based models achieved better results than models based on other embeddings. We can sum up the above observations to answer RQ2 as follows.

> **RQ2.** The prediction models based on the different code representations show balanced performance measures within vulnerability categories. However, we found that vulnerability fix detection on top of word2vec-based embedded code outperform others in detecting SQL injection, while all the remaining vulnerability types are detected most effectively when BERT based models were used for code embedding.

6   Threats to Validity

The heuristic data collection is a major threat to the validity of the results. With a keyword based commit search we might include irrelevant commits (that do not fix vulnerabilities) and we might miss out those that fix vulnerabilities but do not contain the searched keywords. To mitigate this threat, we manually investigated a small sample of the collected data, which we found to be accurate in the majority of cases. Since we collected a very large amount of such training data, the impact of several mis-classified commits should be negligible.

Many scenarios exist where a weakness arises from the interaction of lines of code that are distributed over a large file (or multiple files). However, since the examples for vulnerabilities used to train the model only concentrate on the immediate vicinity of fixed lines, the model might be unable to learn the consequences of far-reaching dependencies. Even though our results might not generalize to all of the different types of vulnerabilities, we believe these preliminary empirical results are already valuable.

Limitations in the chosen approach may also be a threat to the internal validity. We selected one specific prediction model to compare three different code embedding algorithms. Different ML models might yield to different results. In the future, we plan to extend our scope and add multiple ML models and code embeddings to the comparison.

7   Conclusion

In this paper, we presented an empirical study where we performed the comparison of three word embedding based code representation methods in the context of vulnerability prediction in Python code. These methods – word2vec, fastText, and BERT – adopted from the field of natural language processing, are widely used in practice to represent source code as numeric vectors and solve SE tasks (e.g., code summarization, bug detection, or finding copy-pasted code parts) with ML models trained on these representations. Despite their popularity, very few works evaluate and compare their impact on the prediction performances of the ML models relying on them.

With a data mining approach, we collected vulnerability fixing commits from which we could extract vulnerable (before the fix) and not vulnerable (after the fix) code snippets that formed our training dataset (140k Python code snippets in total). We applied the three investigated code embeddings to these code snippets and fed the resulting vectors into the same LSTM architecture to train a prediction model. Our findings show that all the text representation methods are suitable for code representation in this particular task, but the BERT model is the most promising as it is the least time consuming and the LSTM model based on it achieved the best overall accuracy (93.8%) in predicting source code vulnerabilities. Regarding the various vulnerability types, we observed slight variances in model performances based on the applied source code embeddings. Nonetheless, the prediction model based on the word2vec representation of code clearly outperformed models based on fastText and BERT for detecting SQL injection, while in case of Command Injection, Cross-Site Request Forgery (XSRF), Remote Code Execution (RCE), and Path Disclosure the BERT based models achieved better results than models based on other embeddings.

Our future work will focus on using different classifiers and improving the approach for labelling the data, collecting a dataset of higher quality, and leveraging the commit context to create actionable fix recommendations. The work could also be extended to other programming languages or types of vulnerabilities.

Acknowledgment. The presented work was carried out within the SETIT Project (2018-1.2.1-NKP-2018-00004)[3] and supported by the Ministry of Innovation and Technology NRDI Office within the framework of the Artificial Intelligence National Laboratory Program (MILAB). The research was partly supported by the EU-funded project AssureMOSS (Grant no. 952647).

Furthermore, Péter Hegedűs was supported by the Bolyai János Scholarship of the Hungarian Academy of Sciences and the ÚNKP-20-5-SZTE-650 New National Excellence Program of the Ministry for Innovation and Technology.

References

1. Allamanis, M., Sutton, C.: Mining source code repositories at massive scale using language modeling. In: 2013 10th Working Conference on Mining Software Repositories (MSR), pp. 207–216. IEEE (2013)
2. Alon, U., Zilberstein, M., Levy, O., Yahav, E.: code2vec: learning distributed representations of code. In: Proceedings of the ACM on Programming Languages, vol. 3(POPL), pp. 1–29 (2019)
3. Arroyo, M., Chiotta, F., Bavera, F.: An user configurable clang static analyzer taint checker. In: 2016 35th International Conference of the Chilean Computer Science Society (SCCC), pp. 1–12. IEEE (2016)
4. Ben-Nun, T., Jakobovits, A.S., Hoefler, T.: Neural code comprehension: a learnable representation of code semantics. In: Proceedings of the 32nd International Conference on Neural Information Processing Systems, NIPS 2018, Red Hook, NY, USA, pp. 3589–3601. Curran Associates Inc. (2018)
5. Bhoopchand, A., Rocktäschel, T., Barr, E., Riedel, S.: Learning python code suggestion with a sparse pointer network. arXiv preprint arXiv:1611.08307 (2016)
6. Chaturvedi, K.K., Sing, V., Singh, P.: Tools in mining software repositories. In: 2013 13th International Conference on Computational Science and Its Applications, pp. 89–98. IEEE (2013)
7. Chen, Z., Monperrus, M.: The remarkable role of similarity in redundancy-based program repair. arXiv preprint arXiv:1811.05703 (2018)
8. Chollet, F., et al.: Keras: the python deep learning library. Astrophysics Source Code Library, p. ascl-1806 (2018)
9. Church, K.W.: Word2vec. Nat. Lang. Eng. **23**(1), 155–162 (2017)

---

[3] Project no. 2018-1.2.1-NKP-2018-00004 has been implemented with the support provided from the National Research, Development and Innovation Fund of Hungary, financed under the 2018-1.2.1-NKP funding scheme.

10. Cousot, P., et al.: The ASTREÉ analyzer. In: Sagiv, M. (ed.) ESOP 2005. LNCS, vol. 3444, pp. 21–30. Springer, Heidelberg (2005). https://doi.org/10.1007/978-3-540-31987-0_3

11. Devlin, J., Chang, M.W., Lee, K., Toutanova, K.: BERT: pre-training of deep bidirectional transformers for language understanding. arXiv:1810.04805 (2018)

12. Feng, Z., et al.: CodeBERT: a pre-trained model for programming and natural languages. arXiv preprint arXiv:2002.08155 (2020)

13. Harer, J.A., et al.: Automated software vulnerability detection with machine learning (2018)

14. Hovsepyan, A., Scandariato, R., Joosen, W., Walden, J.: Software vulnerability prediction using text analysis techniques. In: Proceedings of the 4th International Workshop on Security Measurements and Metrics, pp. 7–10 (2012)

15. Joulin, A., Grave, E., Bojanowski, P., Douze, M., Jégou, H., Mikolov, T.: Fast-Text.zip: Compressing text classification models. arXiv:1612.03651 (2016)

16. Lozoya, R.C., Baumann, A., Sabetta, A., Bezzi, M.: Commit2vec: learning distributed representations of code changes. SN Comput. Sci. **2**(3), 1–16 (2021)

17. Olesen, M.C., Hansen, R.R., Lawall, J.L., Palix, N.: Coccinelle: tool support for automated CERT C secure coding standard certification. Sci. Comput. Program. **91**, 141–160 (2014)

18. Peng, H., Mou, L., Li, G., Liu, Y., Zhang, L., Jin, Z.: Building program vector representations for deep learning. In: Zhang, S., Wirsing, M., Zhang, Z. (eds.) KSEM 2015. LNCS (LNAI), vol. 9403, pp. 547–553. Springer, Cham (2015). https://doi.org/10.1007/978-3-319-25159-2_49

19. Russell, R., et al.: Automated vulnerability detection in source code using deep representation learning. In: 2018 17th IEEE International Conference on Machine Learning and Applications (ICMLA), pp. 757–762. IEEE (2018)

20. Skaletsky, A., et al.: Dynamic program analysis of Microsoft windows applications. In: 2010 IEEE International Symposium on Performance Analysis of Systems & Software (ISPASS), pp. 2–12. IEEE (2010)

21. Spadini, D., Aniche, M., Bacchelli, A.: Pydriller: Python framework for mining software repositories. In: Proceedings of the 2018 26th ACM Joint Meeting on European Software Engineering Conference and Symposium on the Foundations of Software Engineering, pp. 908–911 (2018)

22. Srivastava, A., Eustace, A.: ATOM: a system for building customized program analysis tools. ACM SIGPLAN Not. **39**(4), 528–539 (2004)

23. Sundermeyer, M., Schlüter, R., Ney, H.: LSTM neural networks for language modeling. In: 13th Annual Conference of the International Speech Communication Association (2012)

24. Waddington, D.G., Roy, N., Schmidt, D.C.: Dynamic analysis and profiling of multithreaded systems. In: Advanced Operating Systems and Kernel Applications: Techniques and Technologies, pp. 156–199. IGI Global (2010)

25. Wartschinski, L.: Detecting software vulnerabilities with deep learning. Master's thesis, Humboldt University, Berlin (2014)

26. Wen, Y., Zhang, W., Luo, R., Wang, J.: Learning text representation using recurrent convolutional neural network with highway layers. arXiv preprint arXiv:1606.06905 (2016)

27. White, M., Tufano, M., Martinez, M., Monperrus, M., Poshyvanyk, D.: Sorting and transforming program repair ingredients via deep learning code similarities. In: 2019 IEEE 26th International Conference on Software Analysis, Evolution and Reengineering (SANER), February 2019

Threat Modeling of Edge-Based IoT Applications

Massimo Ficco[ID], Daniele Granata[(✉)][ID], Massimiliano Rak[ID],
and Giovanni Salzillo[ID]

Department of Engineering, University of Campania Luigi Vanvitelli,
via Roma 29, 81031 Aversa, CE, Italy
{massimo.ficco,daniele.granata,massimiliano.rak,
giovanni.salzillo}@unicampania.it

Abstract. The Multi-access Edge Computing (MEC) computing model
provides on-demand cloud resources and services to the edge of the network, to offer storage and computing capacity, mobility, and context
awareness support for emerging Internet of Things (IoT) applications.
On the other hand, its complex hierarchical model introduces new vulnerabilities, which can influence the security of IoT applications. The
use of different enabling technologies at the edge of the network, such
as various wireless access and virtualization technologies, implies several
threats and challenges that make the security analysis and the deployment of security mechanisms a technically challenging problem. This
paper proposes a technique to model Edge-based systems and automatically extract security threats and plan possible security tests. The proposed approach is tested against a simple, but significant case study. The
main contribution consists of a threat catalog that can be used to derive
a threat model and perform a risk analysis process of specific MEC-based
IoT scenarios.

Keywords: IoT · Edge · Internet of Things · Threat model · Security

1 Introduction

The Multi-access Edge Computing (MEC) extends the cloud computing capabilities to the edge of the network, in order to fulfil more stringent end to end
latency-sensitive, high-computing and -bandwidth-demanding, location awareness, and mobility of the typical Internet of Things (IoT) applications [8,26].
Edge computing enables orchestrating and coordinate optimization actions over
local resources, with minimal interaction with remote resources, taking into
account the behaviour of local users. On the other hand, this emerging paradigm
introduces new security challenges because of the multiple interactions with
different access technologies, including WiFi, Bluetooth, Long Term Evolution
(LTE)/5G, etc., making the edge infrastructure more prone to attacks, such
as Denial-of-Service (DoS), wireless jamming, and man-in-the-middle attacks

© Springer Nature Switzerland AG 2021
A. C. R. Paiva et al. (Eds.): QUATIC 2021, CCIS 1439, pp. 282–296, 2021.
https://doi.org/10.1007/978-3-030-85347-1_21

for traffic injection or eavesdropping [25]. Moreover, the provisioning of virtual resources beyond the cloud to the edge nodes has negative effects: nodes could be compromised by malicious users to orchestrate geographically coordinated attacks, as well as used to collect fine-grained information, such as sensitive users' data [17]. The security assessment for IoT and Edge infrastructures is a complex task, due to its highly distributed and heterogeneous nature: each located nodes may suffer different security weakness, needing different countermeasures.

In recent works, we proposed a set of techniques that aims at identifying security issues and suggests correct countermeasures in an almost automated way [6,20,23], in the context of IoT and cloud environments. The methodology relies on a threat-based approach: starting from the architectural model of the system under analysis, we automatically construct a threats model, i.e. the set of threats the system is subject to. From the resulting threat list, supported by automated risk analysis, we identify a set of possible attack patterns that can be easily tested to verify possible security problems. The technique can be applied to perform a systematic security assessment and risk analysis, and/or to drive penetration tests.

In this paper, we propose an extension of the proposed approach in order to take into account MEC architectures. As a summary, the main contribution of this work is: (i) an extension of our model to support Edge architectures, (ii) a threat catalogue that can be used to derive a threat model and perform a risk analysis process of specific edge scenarios, and (iii) a demonstration of our threat-based penetration testing approach over a simple case study.

The remainder of the paper is organized as follows: Sect. 2 analyzes the state of the art of edge systems in terms of security, Sect. 3 summarizes the threat-based security assessment approach and the case-study application. Section 4 describes the proposed modelling technique, together with the new Edge extension and a model of the case study. Section 5 illustrates our threat catalogue for MEC servers, applying it to the case study. In Sect. 6, the conclusions and the future works are described.

2   State of the Art

On the one hand, the Edge systems aim at improving performance and ensure customers' privacy, on the other hand, they could expose them to multiple classes of security threats, if security is not taken properly into account. Abbas et al. [2] evaluates the security problems deriving from the new emerging architectures that impact on the confidentiality of the data exchanged with the cloud servers. The authors also highlight how the MEC ecosystems involve various actors (end-users, service providers and infrastructure providers). This could cause cloud identification problems and man-in-the-middle attack scenarios. Cloud computing systems, but also grid computing have a lot of security problems, as stated by the authors [4] who underline how the integration between cloud paradigm and grid paradigm can lead to security issues. Unlike cloud systems, MEC-based

IoT applications introduce new security threats also due to several interactions with various wireless access technologies, multi-tenant infrastructures, virtualization, and different MEC based IoT applications [24]. One of the major security threat is related to the lack of a well-defined global perimeter of the Edge-IoT ecosystem. In particular, the whole ecosystem will not be controlled by one single mobile network operator. Moreover, small companies, like stores, can also deploy their own micro-edge data-centres, and allow their users to become active participants in the provisioning of services. This makes a such ecosystem more heterogeneous and vulnerable. The lack of a well-defined perimeter exposes this paradigm to the external attackers (which do not control any infrastructure element), as well as to malicious internal or external users that control elements of the infrastructure (such as device users, servers, virtual machine, edge data-centres, and entire network sections) with which they can influence the provided services. The geographical distribution of the MEC gateways/servers to provide services in the close proximity of local sources of data (e.g., mobile devices, entities inside a building), involves that each component of the infrastructure can be indirectly targeted by malicious users. If an attacker compromises an edge data-centre, he could control the services provided in neighbouring geographical locations. Moreover, the MEC paradigm can provide micro-servers (e.g., deployed on a SBC[1], such as a Raspberry Pi) and user devices (mobile phones) to provide their services. On these devices, the security policies might not be properly implemented or maintained. In fact, the MEC paradigm allows the creation of clusters of devices at the very edge of the network for providing services, for example to exploit parallel mechanisms, which can be used to inject malware and perform DoS attacks against legit participants. Roman et al. [21] presented an overview of the threats that affect a generic MEC architecture. In particular, at infrastructure level, the edge network is part of the last-mile network. Therefore, different technologies are typically employed to build a network, making the MEC infrastructure exposed to different attacks. For example, the Denial-of-Service (DoS) and the wireless jamming are two of the most common attacks used to consume the bandwidth and computing resources of the edge nodes. Man-in-the-middle attacks could be used to take control of a portion of the network, or inject and eavesdrop on traffic from the nodes. It could be also used to gain access to the gateway network interfaces that connects 3G and other wireless networks. Similarly, a malicious gateway can be added to a cluster of nearby user devices to eavesdrop on and/or inject traffic. Also, the virtualisation environments adopted to share resources among ME applications could be exploited to deploy malicious virtual machines/malware for depleting the computing/networking resources shared between different VMs. Moreover, although the MEC core infrastructure is typically managed by the same network operator that deploys the edge data-centres, the interactions with a cloud provider could be un-trusted and be the target of cloud-oriented attacks [10]. There are some solutions in the literature for the security problems described above. Yahuka et al. [27] have classified the security requirements related to Edge

---

[1] Single-Board-Computer.

systems by providing a taxonomy of techniques to be used to guarantee them. The available solutions require an assessment of the risks associated with these systems. These techniques are described in a generic way and are valid only in particular circumstances. A research conducted by Jiang et al. [15], analyzed the security risks for a grid Edge computing system and proposed an analysis model aimed at solving the security problems of grid Edge computing. Another study was conducted by Karim [13], describing the security challenges for Fog Computing. The author produced a list of potential threats describing possible attacks, cataloged according to the CIAA process (Confidentiality, Integrity, Availability, Authentication) and the STRIDE classification [3]. Another study was conducted by The European Union Agency for Cybersecurity (ENISA), which reported a threat landscape in 5G context, also considering Edge solutions. Some specific threats for MEC Server are used in next sections to build a threat catalog. In [18], authors carried out a comparative analysis on systems composed by MEC Servers and other Edge/Cloud components. In particular, they focused on the security challenges in the Cloud and in the Edge, producing a list of threats applicable in both the contexts.

3   Security Assessment Methodology

Hereafter are described the steps required by the security assessment methodology adopted within this work. The methodology was previously introduced in [20,23] and enables less-skilled penetration testers to perform a threat-modeling-driven penetration testing security evaluation, guiding them to look for system vulnerabilities on a per threats-basis. As highlighted in Fig. 1, the approach relies on four phases: (*i*) the *System Modeling*, during which a (semi-)formal description of the system under test is produced, (*ii*) the *Threat Modeling*, a phase devoted to the threat enumeration and identification, (*iii*) the *Planning phase*, for the security test selection and attack planning, and (*iv*) the final *Penetration Testing* phase, for the actual attack execution.

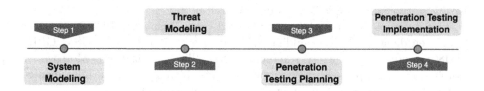

Fig. 1. The steps of the adopted methodology.

According to our approach, the *System-under-Test* (SuT) is described in the Multi-cloud Application Composition Model (MACM) formalism [6], a graph-based system modelling formalism, described in Sect. 4, that aims at offering a simplified description of the system devoted to automate threat modelling and security assessment and annotate security-concerning information [9]. Thanks to the techniques described in [6,11], it is possible to generate a full list of threats for the SuT, starting from a pre-organized and general-purpose catalog.

In the planning phase, penetration testers analyze the identified threats and select the most promising one, on the basis of his experience and his own competencies in terms of possible attacks. Currently, we are working on techniques that aim at automating this step (in [20] and in [23] are presented two alternative approaches). Once selected the targeted component and the security objectives to be tested, a penetration tester looks for available vulnerabilities and, eventually, set up the appropriate tools and frameworks to exploit and put into effect the chosen threats.

3.1   A Walk-Through Case Study

The considered Edge-IoT experimental scenario consists of a Smart Building Control system deployed to produce significant savings through its ability to react quickly even to small changes that occur in the building (such as the air temperature, the levels of occupation, and brightness of the environments).

The IoT infrastructure consists of smart sensors (meters, thermostats, advanced lighting systems, etc.), deployed in different places of the building, for monitoring and controlling the environment, e.g. temperature, gas presence, etc. Transferring such a considerable amount of (personal) data to the centralized cloud servers could be impractical. Moreover, each apartment in the building may have a different configuration and could involve different IoT devices.

Therefore, the MEC can leverage specialized local services for processing and storage capabilities for the large IoT data produced within the building, extending the gateway functionalities to the edge of the network and reducing the communication latency. As an example, the MEC would collect temperature from different apartments and activate the cooling system just in some interleaved apartments, thus reducing the overall energy consumption and continuing to regulate the building temperature in a smarter way.

At the device level, these smart devices are able to collect and transmit environmental parameters, whereas the local IoT Gateway collects such data locally (a typical example is a system adopted in [6]).

Our proof-of-concept edge server, based on a Raspberry Pi 3 Model B+, have been deployed in the building. The node is equipped with a GSM/GPRS SIM808 module (with a GPS antenna for satellite localization). Moreover, a simple Android App has been developed to remotely monitoring the implemented scenario (e.g., monitor the temperature, the vital signs, etc.).

A custom Python script deployed on the MEC server collects data from the IoT systems (they could be sent by IoT gateways and/or directly by smart devices), react to an abnormal situation, and send data to a private cloud data centre. All the communication with the local IoT systems relies on the MQTT protocol, which is tailored for communication in resource-constrained environments such as IoT. At cloud level, an application, running a low-consumption control workload, formats and displays the alerts and the data collected in user-friendly interfaces (with basics search & filtering capabilities).

Our proof-of-concept simply matches a pretty common configuration, which is able to outline a typical Edge scenario, that includes an intermediary among IoT systems and the remote cloud services, managed by a third party.

4   MACM Model for Edge Systems

The first step of our methodology is the system modelling that, as anticipated, relies on the MACM (Multi-Application Cloud Composition Model) formalism [19]. MACM is a graph-based model in which each graph node represents a component of the system, and each link characterizes the existing connection between two different components. The MACM offers a modelling technique to catch the main features of a reference architecture and to (automatically) identify security threats. In order to extend the proposed model to Edge systems, we need to analyze the target architecture and their features, so that we can: (i) extend the model and (ii) enrich our catalogue of threats for the new assets.

A general Edge-IoT architecture is represented in Fig. 2. Different types of mobile devices and smart sensors are connected to the Internet through the MEC nodes, whereas the cloud network can be reached through the core network. The MEC consists of geo-distributed virtual servers/gateways deployed at the user's premises, for example, in a fixed outdoor or indoor location (e.g., a shopping center, a bus terminal, a smart building, a park, etc.) and on devices located in moving object (e.g., buses and cars). Each MEC gateway supports a set of built-in services specific for the target environment, and exploits wireless network elements for the communication, including WiFi access points, the cellular base stations, including low power femtocells.

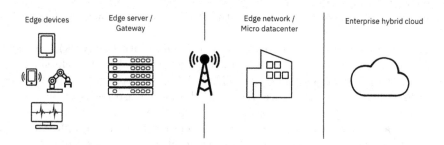

Fig. 2. MEC-IoT architectural model.

As there is no widely accepted standard for edge computing, the reference architecture (RA) [1] provided by the Edge Computing Consortium describes the paradigm from a conceptual, technological, and deployment point of view. The RA outlines that edge systems are built in such a way that IoT devices produce data that is processed and stored not in the cloud, but through intermediate processing systems (ECNs). Data processing on intermediate nodes gives the system reduced response times. Possible Edge Nodes (ECNs) are classified as: smart asset, smart gateway, and smart system. Smart assets (i.e., smart street lamp, smart elevator) can be connected to smart service through a three-layer model, in which there is a gateway that processes information near the device. However, alternative reference architectures are proposed in other papers, like [16,26]. At state of art, there is no affirmed standard that states the components of edge architectures. Something similar happened in IoT systems, as outlined in [7], even if nowadays standards like ISO ISO30141 [14] are being commonly accepted. It is worth noticing the core difference among pure IoT systems and Edge concepts: IoT commonly relies on devices and gateways installed and configured by the end-user, and may use (cloud) service. Instead, Edge solutions, assume that an intermediary (ECNs and/or MEC server) acts between the IoT devices/gateways and the (cloud) services. Such components behave similarly to the IoT gateways but: (i) they are provided by an external provider, (ii) they could be able to manage multiple independent IoT systems (i.e., IoT devices that refers to different customers), and (iii) they are (differently from cloud services) physically located nearby to the managed systems. As summary, Edge architecture introduces a new type of asset with respect to cloud and IoT: the ECN (Edge Compute Network) or MEC (Multi-access Edge Compute), which is provided by CSP. It is physically located near to IoT systems and is able to offer services that partially overlap the cloud services, but, at the same time, have lower latency and are able to manage temporary data without the need to remotely store them in the cloud. ECN/MEC may use remote cloud services in order to perform the more complex evaluation or store historical data. Last, but not least, an ECN/MEC system may coordinate with others physically near ECN/MEC. A different technological solution may implement all or only a few of such choices, depending on the vendor evaluations, but our modelling technique is able to support each of them, outlining the possible interaction (when they exist): in fact, each additional feature introduces, even, additional possible threats.

As anticipated, MACM models IoT, cloud, and (with this work) Edge systems through a graph-based model. Each node has a label that classifies the component in the system deployment. These labels describe typical party roles, like *CSP*, Cloud Service Provider, *CSC*, Cloud Service Customer, or assets types, e.g., *IaaS* (infrastructure-as-a-service) for infrastructure services or *IoTDevice* for physical devices, etc. Labels affect the relationships (the graph edges) in which the nodes can be involved. Moreover, each node has a set of properties that specifies the character of the node. A mandatory property, for the service components, is the *type*, a field that specifies the *Asset Type* according to the concepts expressed in the previous section. The Asset Type specifies the details needed during the threat modelling phase to identify the threats to which an asset is subject. As an example, *IaaS* nodes can be of type *VM* or *container*, whereas a *SaaS* service can be a *Web Application*, a *Database* or a *IDS* (Identity Management System). MACM supports many different types of assets, in particular, [6] summarizes the asset types introduced for IoT systems, based on the ISO 30141 standard [14]. Table 1 summarizes some of the MACM nodes, labels,

Table 1. MACM node labels and assets.

Labels	Asset type (s)	Example of asset
CSC	CSC.Human	A customer that uses services
CSP	CSP	A service Provider like Amazon, Google, or a telecom provider
IaaS	VM, Container	Virtual Machine or Containers
SaaS	Service.Web, Service.DB	Services offering Web applications or Databases
Network	Network.WAN, Network.WiFi, Network.LAN, Network.BLE, Network.ZigBee	Network, the assets differs depending on the involved technologies
HW	HW.server, HW.PC, HW.micro	A physical hosting hardware
IoTDevice	Device.IoT, Device.UE	IoT Devices, or user equipments like Mobile phones or tablets
IoTGW	Device.IoTGW	An IoT gateway
ECN	**Device.MEC**	**A MEC Server acting as an Edge Compute Node**

asset types, and the relationships for the supported cloud and IoT systems. Note that, the labels depend on the reference architectures of the supported systems, while the asset types are more specific and include technologies and vendor-specific solutions. The MACM was extended by introducing a new label node (*ECN*), outlined in the table in bold, modelling a generic Edge node, together with an additional asset type (*EDGE.MEC*) to represent a generic Multi-access Edge compute. In future, we aim at adding additional asset types to differentiate the different MEC servers available in the literature. The (directed) edges of the graph represent the relationship between the nodes. The model adopts different kinds of relationships, such as: *provides*, *hosts* and *uses*. The relationship outlines how components interact, as, for example, the *uses* relationship between two services outlines that a service uses the capabilities offered by the other service. The model allows to associate properties to relationships, e.g., it is possible to specify a *protocol* attribute to an *uses* relationship, with a value indicating the protocol involved in the interaction. Table 2 summarizes the MACM relationships for the supported Cloud and IoT systems. It is worth to note that, the model supports different relationship labels, indicating different kinds of interaction. Edge extension to MACM are outlined by the new label *ECN* in the table. Note that, a CSP directly provides the ECN (while CSP does not provides IoT gateways) and the node is able to offer services of various kind, which can be connected through network (differently from services, which are simply provided to anyone that is connected on Internet). Moreover, ECNs may use other ECNs,

Table 2. Relationship in MACM models.

Relationship	Start node(s)	End node(s)
uses	CSC, IaaS, SaaS, PaaS, IOTDevice, IoTGW **ECN**	IaaS, SaaS, PaaS, IOTDevice, IoTGW, HW **ECN**
provides	CSP	IaaS, SaaS, PaaS, Network, **ECN**
hosts	IaaS, HW, PaaS, **ECN**	SaaS, PaaS
connects	Network	IaaS, IOTDevice, IoTGW, HW, **ECN**

other cloud services (SaaS) and IoT gateways. IoT gateways and devices may use the ECNs [5,6,19,20].

4.1   Smart Building MACM Model

Figure 3 shows the MACM model of our simple case study. Each node contains a label that reports its asset type, whereas the relationships are reported near the connecting edges. The proposed model outlines that the solution relies on two different CSPs, one providing the cloud services and the second one devoted to Edge components (it provides the ECN node). Although from a functional point of view this choice could be non-relevant, from the security perspective this heavily affects the system, due to both the different security grants that each CSP may offer and the needed interaction between them. The proof-of-concept MEC server relies on a simple node hosting two key assets: the MQTT broker devoted to the collection of data packets from the IoT systems and the optimization service (the Python code implementing the Edge logic), which performs some local reductions and stores historical data in the cloud. CSPs, ECN, and IoT gateways are able to communicate through Internet (connected through the WAN network), while the IoTGW and the ECN are even connected through a LAN network: we assume that the Smart Building Edge provider simply installs an ECN node in each building and every apartment is able to connect its own IoT system to the ECN through a dedicated connection. It is worth noticing that, the MACM modelling process helps to define the key features of the proposed architecture, driving the analyst in the identification of some key features that could affect the security aspect of the system, even if they can be easily neglected by developers, for which such features are completely transparent. Moreover, the model mutates when new assets are added to the system and/or some of the components of the connection changes. Adding a BLE component and/or a smartphone that can control the system affects the model: in fact, each of such actions affects the global security of the infrastructure. It is worth noticing that, it is very easy to maintain our models and keep them updated, thanks to the adoption of graph databases, where we maintain the MACM model of the systems under analysis. The description of such tools is out of the scope of this paper.

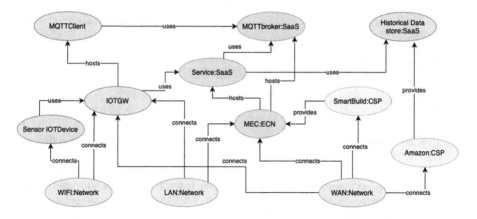

Fig. 3. A simple MACM model for the Smart Building example.

5   EDGE Security and ECN/MEC Threat Catalog

In this chapter we highlight some edge security issues and how we built a catalogue of threats applicable to the ECN/MEC asset. The construction of the catalogue is based on the study of the state of the art described in Sect. 2. Secondly, we report an attack planning phase in which we show how we plan attacks based on the selected threats.

5.1   The Extended Threat Catalogue

In our methodology, a threat is modelled as the triple {Threat Agent, Asset, Behavior}, representing the possibility of a *Threat Agent*, i.e., a malicious actor, to cause damage to an *Asset*, i.e., something that has a value in the system, through a specific *Behavior*, i.e., a set of actions that implies human and/or automated interactions with the target systems [11]. All the threats in the catalogue are linked to the assets of the system under analysis, through the *asset type* field and are obtained in an automated way through ad-hoc queries on threat catalogue. While in previous works, we already collected the typical threats for IoT-related assets, in this work we concentrate on the ECN/MEC introduced with the edge extension for MACM. The following threat catalogue lists all the threats applicable to the MEC server and was built through a detailed analysis of the state of art, and by reformulating all the security issues and the threats according to our format and concepts. The catalogue, which is independent of our tools, will be used to automatically collect the threat model for the full system architecture.

Threat catalog list

1. *False or rogue MEC Gateway* - The open nature of edge gateways allows a malicious user to deploy their own gateway devices, this threat can produce the same result as a Man-in-the-Middle attack.
2. *Edge node overload* - This threat refers to attacks on edge nodes by flooding the node with requests from mobile Apps or IoT devices.
3. *Abuse of edge open application programming interfaces (APIs)* - The need for open APIs in MEC is mainly to provide support for federated services and interactions with different providers and content creators. This threat can be associated with DoS, man-in-the-middle, malicious mode problems, privacy leakages.
4. *Compromised supply chain, vendor and service providers* - Threat from third parties' personnel accessing Mobile Network Operator's facilities.
5. *Erroneous use or administration of the network, systems and devices* - The errors resulting from a poorly maintained and administrated network may compromise the confidentially, integrity and availability of the network.
6. *Misconfigured or poorly configured systems/networks* - The exploitation of a misconfigured system creates the opportunity for a threat actor to reach critical assets in the network or stage an attack.
7. *Inadequate designs and planning or lack of adaption* - Outdated system or network from the lack of update or patch management.
8. *Snooping on Buffered Information* - One of the core objectives of Edge node is to act as an intermediate buffer between the end devices and the cloud. A malicious user can look into buffer systems such as hard disk.
9. *System Profiling* - A malicious user can use the unprotected ports of the nodes.
10. *Sniffing Network Traffic* - MEC-based system rely on network communication. An attacker can sniff network channel for exposed data.
11. *Memory Acquisition* - An attacker can steal information from this de-allocated memory by using any kind of memory acquisition tools.
12. *Network Communication Jamming* - An attacker can launch jamming attack in these mediums to damage the integrity of the packets. She can flood the wired network or broadcast in same wireless frequency.
13. *Modifying Metadata* - Since the Edge system is heavily virtualized, it has to keep track of many logs. An attacker can manipulate log files and corrupt parts of the system.
14. *Memory Tampering* - An attacker can acquire memory and read information from it using any kind of memory accusation tool. With proper security privilege they can access storage memory blocks and tamper the stored data.
15. *Exhausting Log Space* - Log files must be maintained on Edge systems in order to ensure traceability of actions. An attacker can attempt to write garbage values on these files and consume the log space.
16. *Exhausting Buffer Space* - An attacker can create a large number of unnecessary files and request them continuously fill the available space. Also, attacker can request buffer space with unresponsive connection similar to syn-flood attack in TCP/IP communication.
17. *Network Communication Distruptor* - Adversaries can jam or disrupt the network communication medium using different congestion techniques.

18. *User Impersonation* - An attacker can impersonate an user by retrieving her credentials.
19. *Power Disruption* - Fog/Edge node can often be located at public space where security is minimum. Adversaries can disrupt the power supply which will make the Fog/Edge node unavailable for service.
20. *Communication Disruption* - An attacker can cut off the network line or break the communication antenna.
21. *Device Theft* - An attacker can open the MEC server and detach the storage unit.
22. *Physical Destruction* - A MEC node can be physically damaged by the adversaries. One can simply damaged a Fog node by hitting it with heavy object or putting it in fire or pouring liquid like water.
23. *Hardware Based Attack* - An attacker can easily attach an USB stick and install malicious software. Also, an attacker can connect to MEC node directly connecting it via its own terminal at the location.
24. *Privacy Leakage* - The possibilities of adversaries accessing the information stored at the upper layer of the edge infrastructure could warrant substantial concerns for privacy leakage.
25. *Man in the Middle* - A Third malicious party interposed between two or more communicating parties or entities and secretly relaying or altering the communication between such parties.

Due to space limitation we avoided to report a more detailed description of the proposed threats. For what regards the threat agents, we identified them using the methodology proposed in [11]. The technique provides a list of possible threat agent categories based on some assumptions made by the system owner. In this work, we only considered hostile attackers, and classified the "damage", "destroy" or "copy" data exchanged with the IoT devices as the most threatening actions exploitable to have a technological and business advantage. Under these assumptions, we have identified 5 possible threat agent categories: Competitor, Data Miner, Government Spy, Irrational Individual, Cyber Vandal. The characterization of these categories enabled us to define the concept of threat applicable to the scenario described in Sect. 3.1.

5.2   Attack Planning

The Smart Building threat model lists the threats in the form {*Threat Agent, Asset, Behaviour*} and it can be automatically generated through our techniques. It relies on the threat catalogues collected in other works for each of the assets supported in MACM. The threat model offers the basis to set up the penetration test plans, as described in [23] and constructs accordingly specific attacks. The test plans include possible tests at different levels of the proposed Edge architecture. Most of them, like the one that focuses on the lowest level, i.e., the sensor and the local network level, includes attacks specific for different IoT pairing protocols and networks or communication technologies that were already analyzed in previous works [12,20,22,23]. This collection is continuously updated. Among the others, we illustrate a particular attack concerning the MQTT protocol that implements the MITM threat on the MQTT session established between the IoT Gateway and the MQTT broker hosted by the MEC server. It is worth noticing that, as described in [23]. This threat requires the control of a personal WiFi network in order to be implemented in an IoT context (this is possible through the attacks described in [12,22]), whereas if applied to an Edge context, the attacker can leverage the network segment shared among different systems, subject to different control policies. Even though the MQTT protocol is a standard and broadly adopted protocols, it is subjected to multiple classes of threats and attacks and, as a consequence, it could expose the customers or the management networks to severe risks if its security parameters are not configured correctly. Starting from the MITM threats of our threat model, we selected the MITM attack plans specifically for the MQTT protocol [23]. The attack on which we focused requires the attacker to perform an L2 ARP-poisoning on the LAN network segment, enabling it to put itself in the middle between the gateway and the MQTT broker. By relaying MQTT traffic back and forth in a completely transparent way, the attacker can steal all the sensible data collected by the sensor network. Additionally, he can manipulate the sensor measurements to alter, for example, the building temperature control systems. As an example, in a very warm day, the attacker could overwrite the measured temperature $-1\,°C$, thus triggering the heating system to the max power in every apartment of the building. This is possible because the considered MQTT implementation (in our proof-of-concept) did not implement the TLS and the HMAC security measures (disable by default in multiple frameworks). As a matter of fact, the proposed test plans outline the possible misconfigurations and, if applied before the system deployment, can help to prevent many security issues.

6   Conclusion

Although the use of the Edge paradigm offers important advantages in terms of information processing performance and latency reduction, it introduces new security vulnerabilities, which affects the security of a typical IoT application. Therefore, this paper provides a basis for the security assessment of Edge architectures, which is used to extend the presented MACM model to the Edge Compute Network, adding new labels (the ECN) and introducing new asset types (such as the EDGE-MEC). The extended MACM can be used to drive the analysis of the tested scenario in order to outline some key features affecting the security of the involved systems. In the future work, a framework to analyze how the derived threat model and the related attacks affect the different layers of a specific MEC-IoT scenario.

References

1. Edge Computing Reference Architecture 2.0. Technical report, Edge Computing Consortium, November 2017
2. Abbas, N., Zhang, Y.: Mobile edge computing: a survey. IEEE Internet Things J. 5(1), 16 (2018)

3. Ansari, M.T., Pandey, D., Alenezi, M.: STORE: security threat oriented requirements engineering methodology, January 2019
4. Casola, V., Rak, M., Villano, U.: Identity federation in cloud computing, pp. 253–259 (2010). https://doi.org/10.1109/ISIAS.2010.5604074, cited by 13
5. Casola, V., De Benedictis, A., Rak, M., Salzillo, G.: A cloud SecDevOps methodology: from design to testing. In: Shepperd, M., Brito e Abreu, F., Rodrigues da Silva, A., Pérez-Castillo, R. (eds.) QUATIC 2020. CCIS, vol. 1266, pp. 317–331. Springer, Cham (2020). https://doi.org/10.1007/978-3-030-58793-2_26
6. Casola, V., De Benedictis, A., Rak, M., Villano, U.: Toward the automation of threat modeling and risk assessment in IoT systems. Internet Things **7**, 100056 (2019)
7. Di Martino, B., Rak, M., Ficco, M., Esposito, A., Maisto, S.A., Nacchia, S.: Internet of things reference architectures, security and interoperability: a survey. Internet Things **1**, 99–112 (2018)
8. Ficco, M., Esposito, C., Xiang, Y., Palmieri, F.: Pseudo-dynamic testing of realistic edge-fog cloud ecosystems. IEEE Commun. Mag. **55**, 98–104 (2017)
9. Ficco, M., Palmieri, F., Castiglione, A.: Modeling security requirements for cloud-based system development. Concurr. Comput. **27**, 2107–2124 (2015)
10. Ficco, M., Rak, M.: Intrusion tolerance as a service: a SLA-based solution. In: Proceedings of the 2nd International Conference on Cloud Computing and Services Science, pp. 375–384 (2012)
11. Granata, D., Rak, M.: Design and development of a technique for the automation of the risk analysis process in IT security, p. 14 (2021)
12. Granata, D., Rak, M., Salzillo, G., Barbato, U.: Security in IoT pairing & authentication protocols, a threat model and a case study analysis, p. 10 (2021)
13. Hoque, M.A., Hasan, R.: Towards a threat model for vehicular fog computing, pp. 1051–1057 (2019)
14. ISO: Internet of Things Reference Architecture (IoT RA) ISO/IEC CD 30141
15. Jiang, Y., et al.: Security risk analysis of grid edge computing. IOP Conf. Ser. Earth Environ. Sci. **693**(1), 12–34 (2021)
16. Khan, W.Z., Ahmed, E., Hakak, S., Yaqoob, I., Ahmed, A.: Edge computing: a survey. Futur. Gener. Comput. Syst. **97**, 219–235 (2019)
17. Kounev, S., et al.: Providing dependability and resilience in the cloud: challenges and opportunities. In: Wolter, K., Avritzer, A., Vieira, M., van Moorsel, A. (eds.) Resilience Assessment and Evaluation of Computing Systems, pp. 65–81. Springer, Heidelberg (2012). https://doi.org/10.1007/978-3-642-29032-9_4
18. Okwuibe, J., Liyanage, M., Ahmad, I., Ylianttila, M.: Cloud and MEC security, pp. 373–397, January 2018
19. Rak, M.: Security assurance of (multi-)cloud application with security SLA composition. In: Au, M.H.A., Castiglione, A., Choo, K.-K.R., Palmieri, F., Li, K.-C. (eds.) GPC 2017. LNCS, vol. 10232, pp. 786–799. Springer, Cham (2017). https://doi.org/10.1007/978-3-319-57186-7_57
20. Rak, M., Salzillo, G., Romeo, C.: Systematic IoT penetration testing: Alexa case study **2597**, 190–200 (2020)
21. Roman, R., Lopez, J., Mambo, M.: Mobile edge computing, Fog et al.: a survey and analysis of security threats and challenges. Future Gener. Comput. Syst. **78**, 680–698 (2018)
22. Salzillo, G., Rak, M.: A (in)secure-by-design IoT protocol: the ESP touch protocol and a case study analysis from the real market. In: Proceedings of the 2020 Joint Workshop on CPS&IoT Security and Privacy, CPSIOTSEC 2020, New York, NY, USA, pp. 37–48. Association for Computing Machinery (2020)

23. Salzillo, G., Rak, M., Moretta, F.: Threat modeling based penetration testing: the open energy monitor case study. In: 13th International Conference on Security of Information and Networks, SIN 2020, New York, NY, USA. Association for Computing Machinery (2020)
24. Shirazi, S.N., et al.: The extended cloud: review and analysis of mobile edge computing and fog from a security and resilience perspective. IEEE J. Sel. Areas Commun. **35**(11), 2586–2595 (2017)
25. Shropshire, J.: Extending the cloud with fog: security challenges & opportunities. In: 20th Americas Conference on Information Systems, AMCIS 2014, January 2014
26. Weyrich, M., Ebert, C.: Reference architectures for the Internet of Things. IEEE Softw. **33**, 112–116 (2015)
27. Yahuza, M., et al.: Systematic review on security and privacy requirements in edge computing: state of the art and future research opportunities. IEEE Access **8**, 76541–76567 (2020)

Enforcing Mutual Authentication and Confidentiality in Wireless Sensor Networks Using Physically Unclonable Functions: A Case Study

Mario Barbareschi⬤, Salvatore Barone$^{(\boxtimes)}$⬤, Alfonso Fezza, and Erasmo La Montagna⬤

Department of Electrical Engineering and Information Technologies, University of Naples Federico II, Via Claudio, 21, 80125 Naples, Italy
{mario.barbareschi,salvatore.barone,erasmo.lamontagna}@unina.it, al.fezza@studenti.unina.it

Abstract. The technological progress we witnessed in recent years has led to a pervasive usage of smart and embedded devices in many application domains. The monitoring of Power Delivery Networks (PDNs) is an example: the use of interconnected sensors makes it possible to detect faults and to dynamically adapt the network topology to isolate and compensate for them. In this paper we discuss how Fault-Detection, Isolation and Service Recovery (FDISR) for PDNs can be modeled according to the fog-computing paradigm, which distributes part of the computation among edge nodes and the cloud. In particular, we consider an FDISR application on Medium-Voltage PDNs (MV-PDNs) based on a Wireless Sensor Network (WSN) whose nodes make use of the Long Range (LoRa) technology to communicate with each other. Security concerns and the attack model of such application are discussed, then the use of a communication protocol based on the Physically Unclonable Functions (PUFs) mechanism is proposed to achieve both mutual authentication and confidentiality. Finally, an implementation of the proposal is presented and evaluated w.r.t. security concerns and communication overhead.

Keywords: Wireless Sensor Networks · Power Delivery Networks · Smart grid · PUF · Mutual authentication · Fault detection and isolation

1 Introduction

One of the most immediate advantages of the technological progress in the information technology field is the general reduction in costs, size and energy consumption of devices, which leads to a number of applications that would otherwise be precluded. One of these applications is the continuous monitoring of complex systems that extend over large geographical areas, such as medium-voltage

© Springer Nature Switzerland AG 2021
A. C. R. Paiva et al. (Eds.): QUATIC 2021, CCIS 1439, pp. 297–310, 2021.
https://doi.org/10.1007/978-3-030-85347-1_22

power distribution networks. These systems typically feed industrial facilities that, in case of interruption of the energy supply service, can suffer considerable damages and loss of quality of service. In order to minimize damages, electricity distributors adopt protection systems aimed at detecting and isolating faults that occur on the network and, consequently, minimizing the portion of the line and the number of users affected by the fault [39].

Many of these monitoring systems make use of a Wireless Sensor Network (WSN), i.e. a network of sensor nodes – distributed throughout the entire Power Distribution Network (PDN) – that cooperate with each other to detect and isolate faults while communicating using wireless communication [17]. Sensor nodes consist of low power micro-controllers, equipped with sensors, and low energy communication devices are employed. They cooperate by processing and exchanging large amounts of data, including sensible information, which is sent to central nodes to be further analyzed, according to a scheme known as fog-computing [35].

Nevertheless, most of these devices are deployed in unattended environment and may be subject to a wide-range of attacks aiming at disclosing the secrets stored in devices [4]. Although apparently insignificant, in PDNs for instance, a successful attack may prevent nodes from detecting a fault, causing damage to the network, or mislead sensors causing them to detect a bogus fault, causing service disruption to customers. Therefore, the most critical challenges in such applications are security and safety: device identification and authentication are fundamental requirements in order to protect data and prevent attacks [4]. Traditional encryption often require substantial computational resources [9] as well as a key management and distribution system.

In this paper, a lightweight mutual-authentication approach is proposed. The protocol allows sensor nodes to authenticate each other while exchanging encrypted messages without constantly relying upon the authentication server intervention.

In particular, a wireless sensor network for Fault-Detection, Isolation and Service Recovery (FDISR) on a Medium-Voltage Power Distribution Network is used as a case study to discuss and evaluate the adoption of the Extended Physical Hardware-Enabled Mutual Authentication Protocol (ExPHEMAP), compared to well known strategies based on symmetric key encryption.

In addition, the overhead due to the protocol and the attacks that can be prevented by adopting it will be evaluated with respect to classical encryption schemes and plain-text solutions.

The remainder of this paper is organized as follows: Sect. 2 reports the state-of-the-art for authentication protocols and the FDISR in PDN, Sect. 3 provides preliminaries on Physical Unclonable Functions (PUFs) and Physical Hardware-Enabled Mutual Authentication Protocol (PHEMAP), in order to present issues and challenges faced by these protocols. The implementation of our approach, the experiments we carried out for evaluation and the result we obtained are discussed in Sect. 4 and Sect. 5 respectively. Finally, Sect. 6 draws the conclusion.

2   Related Works

A Wireless Sensor Network, capable of monitoring a Power Distribution Network, can be modeled according to the fog-computing paradigm: resource-constrained devices (e.g., sensors, actuators, etc.) at the edge of the network extract information from the environment or execute commands received from an upper layer, exchanging data by means of low-power communication technologies [36]. In fog-computing, edge nodes communicate directly with closer devices, without cloud server intercession, providing location awareness, low latency and improving quality of service for real-time applications. As discussed in [19,22,26,31], since they are distributed in unattended and potentially hostile environments, WSN nodes are exposed to several attacks, whatever the medium being chosen to interconnect them. A comprehensive analysis of such attacks is available in [7]. These attacks include physical tampering, man-in-the-middle attacks, jamming on the communication channel, identity forgery, denial of service attacks to deplete resources of the nodes, etc. The distributed nature of the WSN ecosystem makes the devices easily exploitable, threats like tampering and authentication failure are very typical in this scenario. In addition, nodes must be identified and be able to mutually authenticate with one another, without relying upon any centralized authentication service or user intervention [5]. As usual, WSN nodes have low energy, memory, computational capabilities, furthermore they rely on constrained communication channels. Thus, lightweight encryption is preferable over traditional cryptography primitives.

Authors in [18] identified four classes of security challenges in Internet of Things (IoT) environments: identity management, data provenance and integrity, trust management and privacy. Many of the proposed mechanisms that guarantee integrity and confidentiality are based on classical encryption schemes: the parties, each provided with a pair of public and private keys, exchange a session key using the key-exchange protocols, such as the Deffie-Helmann method [16]. As proposed in [14,24], sensor nodes exchange a symmetric encryption key, namely a session key, using asymmetric encryption; then, the parties use the session key to exchange authenticated messages, providing both integrity and confidentiality. An elliptic curve cryptography based authentication mechanism was proposed in [23] while a lightweight Merkle hash-tree based message authentication mechanism was proposed in [21], in order to address replay and message forgery attacks. Nevertheless, all these protocols require significant computational resources, which may not be available in typical low-cost sensor nodes for WSN. In addition, many of these protocols are only able to authenticate messages but not network nodes, so they are not effective against node theft.

Taking into account all the existing constraints, hardware security approaches can be leveraged to build a secure Internet of Things (IoT) system. Several approaches based on the symbiosis between the Radio-Frequency IDentification (RFID) technology and both lightweight and traditional cryptography are presented in [10]. Traditional encryption has larger computational and storage overhead, while lightweight encryption relies on random number generators, checksums and bit-wise operations, thus introduces negligible overhead and it is best suited for our purposes. Authors in [38] proved the feasibility of an ultra-lightweight mutual authentication protocol, based on RFID and bit-wise operations, that is able to ensure resiliency against man-in-the-middle, replay and disclosure attacks as well as confidentiality and integrity of data. However, as pointed out by authors in [20], RFID tags are subject to several security threats due to their physical nature. In particular, tags may be cloned by first capturing identification data from a legitimate tag and then copying them to a new unauthorized chip. Furthermore, RFID tags do not provide mutual authentication, as a reader can properly authenticate the transponder embedded on a chip, but not vice-versa. The approach proposed in [3] leverages the concept of PUFs, which are hardware primitives that, when stimulated by a bit string, return an output that is guaranteed to be unique, unclonable and tamper-evident [27]. Unfortunately, the protocol proposed in [3] is subject to man-in-the-middle attack and does not provide mutual-authentication; thus, the PHEMAP [4,5] was proposed. It allows nodes to mutually authenticate each other and provide confidentiality without using cryptographic primitives. Both PUF and the PHEMAP will be detailed in Sect. 3, since our proposal is based on these two fundamental concepts.

3   Preliminaries

3.1   Physical Unclonable Functions (PUFs)

PUFs, firstly introduced in [27], offer the possibility to harden device security by providing a unique and unclonable physical fingerprints. Basically, PUFs map a set of input bit-strings, namely *challenges*, into a set of output bit-strings, called *responses*. Nevertheless, PUFs can be also used without any input, in order to generate an unique code which may be useful for device identification.

Properties of PUFs are directly inherited from unpredictability of the manufacturing process, thus the mapping mechanism between challenges and responses is unique for a particular device; moreover, it can be computed in polynomial time but it is hard to predict, so PUFs can also be employed to provide cryptographic keys. However, PUF responses are subject to working conditions of the circuits built into the devices, thus they are a non-negligible source of instabilities and are not suitable for getting involved as secret keys in cryptography schemes as they are. To deal with this issue, a recovering technique known as Fuzzy Extractor (FE) has been proposed in [12]. Briefly, FE operate in two different phases. During the *enrollment* phase (top part of Fig. 1), performed once and within a secure perimeter, the key is computed from a PUF response and an hash function (Privacy Amplification). The helper data is computed by making use of a randomly-chosen secret symbol and an Error Correcting Code (ECC). Contrary to the key, which must be kept secret and undisclosed, the helper data do not require secrecy. Once the device has been deployed, it executes the *information reconciliation* phase of the FE (bottom part of Fig. 1), where the device is able to recover the key from the helper data and a noisy PUF response (different from the one of the enrollment phase).

There are many possibilities to realize PUFs: an overview can be found in [30]. The approach proposed by us makes use of a memory-based Static Random Access Memory (SRAM)-PUF [8,11,33,40], that exploits the random pattern generated by memory circuits when being powered-up, since, by design, they are not initialized on a given initial state.

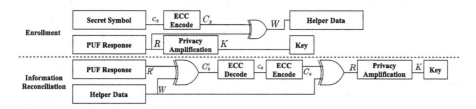

Fig. 1. Fuzzy extractor algorithm phases

3.2 Mutual Authentication Using PUFs

Embedding PUFs within devices can solve problems such as maliciously modified sensors, provide a unique device identification to cope with fake identity attacks, and act as lightweight encryption functions to protect against confidentiality attacks such as eavesdropping [15,32,37].

In order to enable authentication, both the node to be authenticated –from now on, simply the node – and the authenticator node – i.e. the *verifier*, or the Authentication Service (AS) – must share some knowledge about the PUF embedded into the device, i.e. the verifier must collect a significant amount of Challenge-Response Pairs (CRPs) during the enrollment phase. So, in a basic authentication protocol, the verifier issues a challenge to the node and then compares its response with the expected one [3]. However, this simple protocol may be subject to man-in-the-middle attacks because an attacker may intercept and collect CRP, in order to use them later. Moreover, it does not provide any mechanism to the node to authenticate the verifier, so mutual authentication is still not provided.

To cope with this issue, PHEMAP has been proposed in [4,5]. The protocol relies on a set of distinct *chains*, extracted from the PUF embedded into the device; a chain is generated from the device by recursively applying responses as challenges, starting from a randomly chosen initial challenge. The enrollment phase could benefit from using PUF-chains because the verifier follows the chain, rather that issuing random challenges. During the enrollment phase, the verifier generates a set of PUF chains for each device by picking different random initial challenges, in order to generate different chains. The latter are then stored in a secure database and will be used in a revised version of the challenge-response protocol introduced in [3]. On the device side, the protocol only requires devices to embed a register Q to store the last consumed link on the current chain. This register is the only hardware status information maintained by the device and it must be included in a tamper-proof secure perimeter, such that it cannot be altered by a malicious user during the protocol execution.

PHEMAP leverages the concept of *sentinel* nodes, which are defined a-priori and are known to both the verifier and the device. Sentinels protect against tampering with the protocol by ensuring that no more than a given amount of chain links are exposed during any of the phases of the protocol.

The basic PHEMAP protocol consists in two distinct phases: initialization and verification. The initialization procedure is always started by the verifier and consists in the exchange of messages made up of *nonces* and chain links. After the initialization, both device and verifier are synchronized on a certain link of the chain selected by the verifier. The next link on the chain, right after the initialization phase, is called the *root sentinel*, and it will not be exchanged during any of the following operations. The verification phase can be initiated by both verifier or the device. It consists in a simple link exchange involving two consecutive links on the chain. Basically, being l_k the link sent by the initiator, the other party must prove that it knows l_{k+1}. Obviously, in order to prevent reply attacks, each CRP must be used only once.

In [5] an accurate analysis of the protocol has been performed. This analysis proved that the protocol is immune to man-in-the-middle attacks, since the un-clonability property of PUFs inherently ensures that malicious devices cannot be authenticated by the verifier. The basic PHEMAP protocol is not suitable for Cloud-Edge (CE) applications, since the centralized verifier would easily become a bottleneck and since it allows mutual authentication only between terminal nodes and verifier, therefore no communication between terminal nodes is possible without the verifier acting as an intermediary. The ExPHEMAP [4] protocol overcomes the aforementioned difficulties of the basic protocol in CE scenarios. It consists in two sub-protocols: Salted-PHEMAP, that enables a node (equipped with a PUF circuit) and its reference gateway (an Edge node without a PUF circuit) to mutually prove their identity while communicating, and Babelchain PHEMAP (BC-PHEMAP), that enables mutual authentication between two nodes both embedding a PUF circuit. In [4,5] a full description of the protocol is provided.

3.3   Mutual Authentication Between Sensor Nodes

BC-PHEMAP allows two heterogeneous devices to mutually authenticate each other, without the constant participation of the AS, leveraging the concept of *carnet* to let devices accomplish only a limited number of authentication operations. Consider two nodes, namely A and B, and suppose A wants to communicate with B for the first time. The BC-PHEMAP setup procedure requires the exchange of two authentication messages between A and AS:

1. A sends a request to communicate with B to the AS; this request message contains the next non-sentinel link on the chain and it also specifies the expected number of interactions;

2. if the AS is able to authenticate the A node, it generates a *carnet* by extracting a given amount of links from the current chain of the A and B, and XOR-ing homologous links so that only A and B can make use of the carnet to communicate to each other respectively; then it sends such carnet to A;

Since the carnet does not disclose any sensitive information about chains, it can be exchanged in plain text and stored in local memory without causing harm. All subsequent communications between A and B are carried out in the following way:

1. A sends a message to B, by extracting a link from the carnet;
2. if B is able to authenticate A – i.e. the message B received contains the next non-sentinel link on the chain – then it replies to A with the immediate next link on the chain;
3. A compares the content of the received message with the next link in the carnet; if they match, then A is able to successfully authenticate B.

4 Fault-Detection and Isolation on Medium-Voltage PDN (MV-PDN)

As reported in [34], Zone Selectivity (ZS) can be effectively applied to isolate faults and to restore the power supply in MV-PDN. The typical structure of a Fault-Detection, Isolation and Service Recovery (FDISR) system for MV-PDNs is depicted in Fig. 2 [6,13]. The structure can be seen as a sort of ring, with high-voltage to medium-voltage transformers connecting the MV-PDN to the high voltage backbone. Sensors capable of detecting over-voltage and/or over-current are deployed along the network in order to implement ZS; these sensors impose the opening of a normally-closed circuit-breaker, also known as *protection-relay*, in the event a fault is detected on the section downstream of the sensor. HV/MV transformer nodes are often equipped with the same sensors. The ring is split in the middle by a normally-open circuit-breaker, known as the *tie-recloser*, that could be closed to restore the service after a failure has been correctly isolated.

Suppose a fault is detected between nodes B and C in the network depicted in Fig. 2. Since, wherever the failure happens, the fault is detected by all upstream nodes (on the right side of Fig. 2), A and B open their *protection-relay* and,

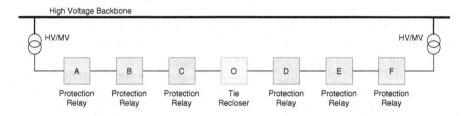

Fig. 2. Structure of an MV-PDN.

at the same time, send an *ignore* message to the upstream node. Once a node receives such kind of message, it knows that the downstream node detected the fault, thus, it can close its circuit breaker to restore the power supply to the downstream section. Conversely, if no *ignore* message is received after detecting a fault, it means that the node is immediately upstream of the fault (in this case B); as a consequence, in order to perform isolation and service restoration, the node sends an *isolate* message to the downstream node – the *C* node in Fig. 2, in the considered example – which cannot detect the fault, in order to inform it that a fault has been detected on the network immediately ahead of its location. Once a node receives the *isolate* message, it opens its circuit breaker, isolating the failure. Moreover, a *connect* message to the *tie-recloser* is sent, so that the faulty section is totally disconnected from the network and the supply on the section downstream of the fault is restored. The *connect* message can be sent either from the node immediately upstream the failure – i.e. the one that does not receive the *ignore* message – or from the node downstream the failure –i.e. the one that receives the *isolate* message. These two solutions are theoretically equivalent, although the second allows to be confident that the supply is restored only after isolating the faulty section.

Timing factor is of major importance in MV-PDN protection: if too much time elapses between the occurrence of a fault and the reaction of the FDISR system, the failure could propagate and cause severe damage to the entire network. On the other hand, customers may witness severe economic damage in case the portion of the network they belong to provides no energy supply for a long period of time. Figure 3 shows the structure of the WSN for the protection of MV-PDN in the fog-computing context: all protection-relays belonging to the same ring form a sub-network, whose gateway node is the *tie-recloser*. In the following, we will focus on the communication within a sub-network, while omitting aspects related to communication between gateways and AS. As in [2], we make use of the Long Range (LoRa) technology to interconnect nodes belonging to the same sub-network. In this case study, rather than using plain text, the BC-PHEMAP, which guarantees confidentiality and mutual authentication, is employed.

4.1   Achieving Mutual Authentication and Confidentiality

In order to embed a PUF into nodes, we referred to [1]; consequently, in order to generate 128 bits long device fingerprints intended to be used as cryptographic keys, 2816 SRAM bits are fed to SHA-256 while considering only the 128 less significant bits of the hashsum. We implemented the fuzzy extractor scheme by making use of first order, seventh grade Reed-Muller ECC [25,29] while AES-128 provides the privacy-amplification primitive. Therefore, challenges, responses as well as chain links are 128 bits, i.e. 16 bytes, long.

The initialization of the devices follows the protocol specification reported in [4]; nevertheless, a slight adaptation of the BC-PHEMAP protocol is required to accomplish the FDISR application. Since each of the protection-relays, besides the gateway of the sub-network to which it belongs, needs to be able to communicate with the protection-relay upstream and downstream of its position, three

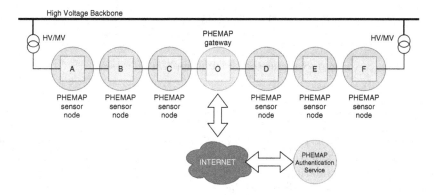

Fig. 3. View of the MV-PDN in the fog-computing context.

different Q-registers and suitable mechanisms are needed to communicate with different devices at the same time, allowing to manage chain links consumption separately and keeping the chains up to date at each node. During the start-up phase of the FDISR system, thus the initialization phase of the PHEMAP, the procedure that the node performs to obtain a carnet to be able to communicate with the upstream node is fully compliant with that specified by the BC-PHEMAP protocol. However, as an additional step, the AS must notify B in order to let it aware that A wants to communicate using a certain number of messages. Thus, B must update the Q register, in order to keep talking to the AS, and it will store the first link it eventually receives from A in a different Q register, to be able to talk with A. The purpose of the notification message the AS sends is to align the Q register the node uses to talk to the AS to the correct link, to allow communication with different devices at the same time.

The structure of a FDISR application message is reported in Fig. 4: it embeds the source node identifier (SRC ID), the message type (MSG – ignore, connect, isolate) and a Cyclic Redundancy Check (CRC). Since the set of messages is fixed and predetermined, it is possible to pre-construct all of them, CRC included, without any harm. Please note that part of the message is unused, but reserved for future evolution.

The message construction process is invariant w.r.t. the particular FDISR message: the node must merge the appropriate pre-computed FDISR message – *ignore*, for instance – together with the first unused link from the current carnet, using a bitwise XOR. Once a device receives a FDISR message, all it has to do is compute the bitwise XOR between the message and the appropriate Q register; then, by computing the CRC on the whole decoded message, it is able to determine both the integrity of the message and the identity of the sender.

SRC ID	MSG	Reserved	CRC
1 Byte	1 Byte	10 Bytes	4 Bytes

Fig. 4. Structure of a FDISR application message

5   Evaluation

In this Section we will discuss the advantages and drawbacks of adopting the BC-PHEMAP protocol for nodes belonging to the same sub-network. In order to get a truthful evaluation, close to that of a real world case, we built a scale prototype of the network shown in Fig. 3.

The AS is designed to manage multiple connections at the same time and it has been implemented on an ordinary personal computer running GNU/Linux. Each one of the protection-relays (sensor nodes) consists of two ST-Microelectronics STM32L152RE development board, equipped with a 32-bit ARM Cortex M3 CPU, 512 Kbytes of Flash memory and 80 Kbytes of RAM. Each board is equipped with an SX1272MB2xAS extension boards, that integrate a LoRa SX1272 half-duplex transceiver. The tie-recloser (the gateway node) consists in a STM32H745I board and a STM32L152RE development boards, both equipped with a SX1272MB2xAS LoRa extension board. The former provides the gateway node with the capability to connect to the Internet via a Gigabit Ethernet interface, while the latter is used only as a transmitter. The need to use two development boards for the gateway node is related to the fact that the available transceiver only allows half-duplex communications. Since each node must always be ready to receive and transmit, and since there is no possibility to assemble two extension boards on the same development board, it was considered appropriate to separate the transmitter and the receiver. The receiver board, which is the one on that runs the protocol, is configured to listen on a fixed frequency, which is different for each node in the sub-net, while the frequency on which the transmitter operates is changed according to the destination.

The base frequency for LoRa has been set at 868 MHz and the transmission power at 14 dBm to comply with European standards. The on-air time for a generic message can be expressed as the sum of the time needed to transmit the LoRa preamble and the time needed to transmit the actual message payload, both computed as a function of the $T_s = \frac{2^{SF}}{BW}$, i.e. the symbol-time, where SF is the LoRa spreading factor and BW is the bandwidth. Taking into account the recommendations in [28], we set the SF to 7 and the bandwidth to 500 KHz. Consequently, approximately 13 ms are needed to transmit each of the 16 bytes long messages, LoRa preamble and CRC included.

5.1   Protocol Overhead Evaluation

As mentioned above, the most time-critical aspect of an FDISR application is the reaction to a fault being detected, which could be affected by the overhead introduced by the protocol. However, since after the initialization phase of the protocol the Q register already holds the link to be used to compose an *ignore* message, and since nothing forbids to construct such a message beforehand, the overhead due to the protocol depends only on the authentication message that the upstream node must send in order to accomplish the mutual-authentication. Therefore, we can express the protocol overhead as $T_{L_0} + T_{xor}$, where T_{L_0} is the time to transmit the link while T_{xor} is the time to make the bitwise XOR operation.

In order to measure the average time needed to resolve a fault both in plain-text and using the PHEMAP we firstly measured the average time needed to complete the transmission of a 16 bytes long message, which is about 19 ms. This measure takes into account the time required by the transceiver to synchronize on the desired transmitting frequency, which is approximately 7 ms. The average time required to resolve a fault in plain-text and with PHEMAP is 35, 867 ms and 51, 571 ms, respectively, with a variance of 9,677 in the former case and 13,416 in the latter. The difference between the mean values gives us the overhead that is equal to 15, 704 ms in accordance with the result we expected. To ensure that we have statistical significance, a T-test was performed on the samples and the null hypothesis was rejected with $\alpha = 0.01$.

5.2   Threats Analysis

Among the various attacks that can be carried out, the replay attacks are potentially the most dangerous. In particular, there are two messages that can cause the most problems. The first attack scenario, foresees that an attacker sends an *isolate* message to a node, causing the opening of its relay and leaving a portion, or even the entire network, without power. The second scenario, instead, foresees that a malicious attacker creates a fault on the network, let's say between node A and node B, and sends an *ignore* message to node A pretending to be B. Node B does not notice the fault and therefore node A should not receive any *ignore* message and leave its relay open. Receiving this message causes A to close its protection relay and the FDISR system to fail, resulting in damage to network equipment. Obviously, when PHEMAP is used, these two attacks are not possible, since nodes A and B are mutually authenticated. Moreover, since the chain links are only used once and since we make use of a CRC, we are guaranteed by PHEMAP both confidentiality and data integrity, as discussed extensively in [4]. This ensures that man-in-the-middle attacks cannot be carried out. Additionally, given the use of PUF for link generation, and assuming it has strong PUF characteristics, forgery attacks, as well as all other attacks that aim to take control of a node, are not feasible. Moreover, when compared to a classic protocol, PHEMAP does not expose any kind of sensitive information and it does not store the key at any time, making it the ideal protocol for nodes deployed in unattended and hostile environment in which it is easy for an attacker to try to get hold of one of the nodes. Finally, it does not require high computational resources, which makes it suitable for use with low-performance and inexpensive sensor nodes.

6   Conclusion

In this paper it has been shown that a state-of-the-art mutual authentication and confidentiality protocol – i.e. that is not based on the classic key-exchange and encryption schema – can be adopted in resource limited WSN, considering a fault detection, isolation and service recovery system for PDN as a case study. In particular, considering the ZS application for MV-PDNs, it has been discussed how to implement the BC-PHEMAP protocol, to allow mutual authentication of sensor nodes within the network while ensuring confidentiality for application messages.

The advantages of using such protocol have been highlighted, both w.r.t. a plain-text system and a system that adopts a classical encryption scheme. Although the proposed solution increases overhead and variance, these value remain acceptable as demonstrated by the experimental evaluation. Attacks that the adoption of the protocol would help to prevent have been also discussed. In addition, the overhead due to the adoption of the protocol versus the plain text solution has been analytically expressed and measured by referring to a scaled prototype of the proposed solution. The analysis, which was reflected in the measurements made, allows to establish the actual suitability of the solution when the time constraints of the particular MV-PDN considered come into play, showing that the transmission medium is the most significant factor to take into account.

References

1. Barbareschi, M., Bagnasco, P., Amelino, D., Mazzeo, A.: Designing an SRAM PUF-based secret extractor for resource-constrained devices. Int. J. Embedded Syst. **9**, 353–364 (2017)
2. Angrisani, L., Bonavolontà, F., Liccardo, A., Schiano Lo Moriello, R.: On the use of LoRa technology for logic selectivity in MV distribution networks. Energies **11**(11), 3079 (2018)
3. Barbareschi, M., Bagnasco, P., Mazzeo, A.: Authenticating IoT devices with physically unclonable functions models. In: 2015 10th International Conference on P2P, Parallel, Grid, Cloud and Internet Computing (3PGCIC), pp. 563–567. IEEE (2015)
4. Barbareschi, M., De Benedictis, A., La Montagna, E., Mazzeo, A., Mazzocca, N.: A PUF-based mutual authentication scheme for cloud-edges IoT systems. Futur. Gener. Comput. Syst. **101**, 246–261 (2019)
5. Barbareschi, M., De Benedictis, A., Mazzocca, N.: A PUF-based hardware mutual authentication protocol. J. Parallel Distrib. Comput. **119**, 107–120 (2018)
6. Botton, S., Cavalletto, L., Marmeggi, F.: Schema project-innovative criteria for management and operation of a closed ring mv network. In: 22th International Conference and Exhibition on Electricity Distribution (CIRED 2013). IET (2013)
7. Bou-Harb, E., Fachkha, C., Pourzandi, M., Debbabi, M., Assi, C.: Communication security for smart grid distribution networks. IEEE Commun. Mag. **51**(1), 42–49 (2013)
8. Böhm, C., Hofer, M., Pribyl, W.: A microcontroller SRAM-PUF. In: 2011 5th International Conference on Network and System Security, pp. 269–273 (2011)

9. Casola, V., Benedictis, A.D., Drago, A., Mazzocca, N.: Analysis and comparison of security protocols in wireless sensor networks. In: 30th IEEE Symposium on Reliable Distributed Systems Workshops, SRDS Workshops 2011, Madrid, Spain, 4–7 October 2011, pp. 52–56. IEEE Computer Society (2011)
10. Chien, H.: SASI: a new ultralightweight RFID authentication protocol providing strong authentication and strong integrity. IEEE Trans. Dependable Sec. Comput. **4**, 337–340 (2007)
11. Cortez, M., Dargar, A., Hamdioui, S., Schrijen, G.J.: Modeling SRAM start-up behavior for physical unclonable functions. In: 2012 IEEE International Symposium on Defect and Fault Tolerance in VLSI and Nanotechnology Systems (DFT), pp. 1–6. IEEE (2012)
12. Dodis, Y., Reyzin, L., Smith, A.: Fuzzy extractors: how to generate strong keys from biometrics and other noisy data. In: Cachin, C., Camenisch, J.L. (eds.) EUROCRYPT 2004. LNCS, vol. 3027, pp. 523–540. Springer, Heidelberg (2004). https://doi.org/10.1007/978-3-540-24676-3_31
13. D'Orazio, L., Calone, R.: Innovative protection system on distribution network. In: 22th International Conference and Exhibition on Electricity Distribution (CIRED 2013). IET (2013)
14. Fouda, M.M., Fadlullah, Z.M., Kato, N., Lu, R., Shen, X.S.: A lightweight message authentication scheme for smart grid communications. IEEE Trans. Smart Grid **2**(4), 675–685 (2011)
15. Frikken, K.B., Blanton, M., Atallah, M.J.: Robust authentication using physically unclonable functions. In: Samarati, P., Yung, M., Martinelli, F., Ardagna, C.A. (eds.) ISC 2009. LNCS, vol. 5735, pp. 262–277. Springer, Heidelberg (2009). https://doi.org/10.1007/978-3-642-04474-8_22
16. Hellman, M.E.: An overview of public key cryptography. IEEE Commun. Mag. **40**(5), 42–49 (2002)
17. Hung, K., et al.: On wireless sensors communication for overhead transmission line monitoring in power delivery systems. In: 2010 First IEEE International Conference on Smart Grid Communications, pp. 309–314. IEEE (2010)
18. Kanuparthi, A., Karri, R., Addepalli, S.: Hardware and embedded security in the context of Internet of Things. In: Proceedings of the 2013 ACM Workshop on Security, Privacy & Dependability for Cyber Vehicles, pp. 61–64 (2013)
19. Khan, M.A., Salah, K.: IoT security: review, blockchain solutions, and open challenges. Futur. Gener. Comput. Syst. **82**, 395–411 (2018)
20. Kulkarni, G., Shelke, R., Sutar, R., Mohite, S.: RFID security issues & challenges. In: 2014 International Conference on Electronics and Communication Systems (ICECS), pp. 1–4, February 2014
21. Li, H., Lu, R., Zhou, L., Yang, B., Shen, X.: An efficient Merkle-tree-based authentication scheme for smart grid. IEEE Syst. J. **8**(2), 655–663 (2013)
22. Lin, J., Yu, W., Zhang, N., Yang, X., Zhang, H., Zhao, W.: A survey on internet of things: architecture, enabling technologies, security and privacy, and applications. IEEE Internet Things J. **4**(5), 1125–1142 (2017)
23. Mahmood, K., Chaudhry, S.A., Naqvi, H., Kumari, S., Li, X., Sangaiah, A.K.: An elliptic curve cryptography based lightweight authentication scheme for smart grid communication. Futur. Gener. Comput. Syst. **81**, 557–565 (2018)
24. Mahmood, K., Chaudhry, S.A., Naqvi, H., Shon, T., Ahmad, H.F.: A lightweight message authentication scheme for smart grid communications in power sector. Comput. Electr. Eng. **52**, 114–124 (2016)
25. Muller, D.E.: Application of Boolean algebra to switching circuit design and to error detection. Trans. IRE Prof. Group Electron. Comput. **3**, 6–12 (1954)

26. Ni, J., Zhang, K., Lin, X., Shen, X.S.: Securing fog computing for internet of things applications: challenges and solutions. IEEE Commun. Surv. Tutor. **20**(1), 601–628 (2018)

27. Pappu, R., Recht, B., Taylor, J., Gershenfeld, N.: Physical one-way functions. Science **297**(5589), 2026–2030 (2002)

28. Raychowdhury, A., Pramanik, A.: Survey on LoRa technology: solution for Internet of Things. In: Thampi, S.M., et al. (eds.) Intelligent Systems, Technologies and Applications. AISC, vol. 1148, pp. 259–271. Springer, Singapore (2020). https://doi.org/10.1007/978-981-15-3914-5_20

29. Reed, I.S.: A class of multiple-error-correcting codes and the decoding scheme. Technical report, Massachusetts Institute of Technology, Lincoln Laboratory, Lexington (1953)

30. Roel, M.: Physically unclonable functions: constructions, properties and applications. Katholieke Universiteit Leuven, Belgium (2012)

31. Roman, R., Lopez, J., Mambo, M.: Mobile edge computing, Fog et al.: a survey and analysis of security threats and challenges. Futur. Gener. Comput. Syst. **78**, 680–698 (2018)

32. Rostami, M., Majzoobi, M., Koushanfar, F., Wallach, D.S., Devadas, S.: Robust and reverse-engineering resilient PUF authentication and key-exchange by substring matching. IEEE Trans. Emerg. Top. Comput. **2**(1), 37–49 (2014)

33. Schrijen, G., van der Leest, V.: Comparative analysis of SRAM memories used as PUF primitives. In: 2012 Design, Automation Test in Europe Conference Exhibition (DATE), pp. 1319–1324 (2012)

34. Spalding, R.A., et al.: Fault location, isolation and service restoration (FLISR) functionalities tests in a smart grids laboratory for evaluation of the quality of service. In: 2016 17th International Conference on Harmonics and Quality of Power (ICHQP), pp. 879–884. IEEE (2016)

35. Stojmenovic, I., Wen, S.: The Fog computing paradigm: scenarios and security issues. In: 2014 Federated Conference on Computer Science and Information Systems, pp. 1–8, September 2014

36. Stojmenovic, I., Wen, S., Huang, X., Luan, H.: An overview of fog computing and its security issues. Concurr. Comput. Practice Exp. **28**(10), 2991–3005 (2016)

37. Suh, G.E., Devadas, S.: Physical unclonable functions for device authentication and secret key generation. In: 2007 44th ACM/IEEE Design Automation Conference, pp. 9–14. IEEE (2007)

38. Tewari, A., Gupta, B.B.: Cryptanalysis of a novel ultra-lightweight mutual authentication protocol for IoT devices using RFID tags. J. Supercomput. **73**(3), 1085–1102 (2017)

39. Valdes, M.E., Dougherty, J.J.: Advances in protective device interlocking for improved protection and selectivity. IEEE Trans. Ind. Appl. **50**(3), 1639–1648 (2013)

40. Xiao, K., Rahman, M.T., Forte, D., Huang, Y., Su, M., Tehranipoor, M.: Bit selection algorithm suitable for high-volume production of SRAM-PUF. In: 2014 IEEE International Symposium on Hardware-Oriented Security and Trust (HOST), pp. 101–106 (2014)

GRADUATION: A GDPR-Based Mutation Methodology

Said Daoudagh[1,2]($\boxtimes$) (iD) and Eda Marchetti[1] (iD)

[1] ISTI-CNR, Pisa, Italy
{said.daoudagh,eda.marchetti}@isti.cnr.it
[2] University of Pisa, Pisa, Italy

Abstract. The adoption of the General Data Protection Regulation (GDPR) is enhancing different business and research opportunities that evidence the necessity of appropriate solutions supporting specification, processing, testing, and assessing the overall (personal) data management. This paper proposes GRADUATION (GdpR-bAseD mUtATION) methodology, for mutation analysis of data protection policies test cases. The new methodology provides generic mutation operators in reference to the currently applicable EU Data Protection Regulation. The preliminary implementation of the steps involved in the GDPR-based mutants derivation is also described.

Keywords: Data protection · GDPR · Mutation Operators · Privacy Policies · Security policies

1 Introduction

The widespread adoption of the General Data Protection Regulation (GDPR), i.e., the EU Data Protection Regulation [12], if on the one hand is enhancing different business and research opportunities within the Information and Communication Technology (ICT) environment, on the other hand is struggling in the definition of appropriate procedures and technical solutions for specifying the privacy requirements, processing personal data, and testing the overall data management. Indeed, privacy legislation's requires to deploy adequate fine-grained mechanisms that are able to continuously enforce and verify legal requirements, such as the data usage purpose, the user consent and the data retention period. To this purpose, different proposals are currently available for automatic defining, implementing and testing privacy knowledge and rules [1,3,7,23,24], but few attention is still devoted to the assessment of the testing suites or strategies adopted for validating the different GDPR implementation aspects. Indeed, the fault detection effectiveness is a fundamental parameter for ensuring the quality properties of the final products and for prioritizing and/or selecting test cases for regression testing activities [15]. To this purpose, one of the most adopted approaches is the Mutation testing, i.e., a technique in which syntactic faults, simulating typical programmer's mistakes, are seeded in the original program in

© Springer Nature Switzerland AG 2021
A. C. R. Paiva et al. (Eds.): QUATIC 2021, CCIS 1439, pp. 311–324, 2021.
https://doi.org/10.1007/978-3-030-85347-1_23

order to produce a set of faulty programs, called mutants, each containing one fault. Therefore, a predefined set of test cases is executed both on the original program and its mutants, and outputs collected: if the mutant's output is different from the original program's one, the fault is detected and the mutant is said to be killed. The mutation score is the ratio of the number of detected faults over the total number of seeded faults and indicates the effectiveness of the test suite.

In the context of the GDPR, and data privacy management in general, only few proposals are targeting the definition of mutation operators able to deal with the specific privacy characteristics and requirements of the privacy standards [2]. In these cases, the proposed mutation operators do not exhaustively cover all the important criticalities of the GDPR. For instance, they do not consider mutation operators concerning the erroneous use of the purpose defined by the controller and the consent given by the data subject.

In this paper, we move a step ahead in this research direction by presenting the new GdpR-bAseD mUtATION (GRADUATION) methodology, partially supported by a prototype tool, for: 1. analysing and managing model-based specifications of legal text (such as the GDPR), so as to extract main concepts and useful data; 2. selecting and applying a set of mutation operators to a specific GDPR-based model instance, so as to derive its mutated versions.

To better clarify the methodology application, we present the specialization of the GRADUATION in the context of GDPR-based authorization systems. Indeed, privacy legislation requires organizations to deploy adequate fine-grained Access Control (AC) mechanisms [14] that take into account additional legal requirements, such as the data usage purpose, the user consent and the data retention period. Consequently, this rises up the problem of developing effective and efficient test strategies able to guarantee the lack of unauthorized access to personal data (*security perspective*) and unlawful processing (*legal perspective*).

It is important to notice that even if the specialization of the GRADUA-TION tool refers to the AC mechanisms based on the Attribute-Based Access Control (ABAC) model [14], the GRADUATION methodology, and in particular its mutation operators set, is agnostic with respect to the AC mechanisms specification language, and can be applicable to any system that dealing with the GDPR.

In this paper, with the aim of providing a comprehensive assessment environment, the specialization of the GRADUATION presented includes: 1) all the currently available AC-based mutation operators [8], i.e., the traditional ABAC mutation operators [8]; and 2) the new conceived operators based on the GDPR's peculiarities.

Summarizing, the main contributions of this paper are:

- a generic methodology, called GRADUATION for automatically generating GDPR-based mutants;
- a set of GDPR-based mutation operators focusing on the GDPR's peculiarities;

– a preliminary implementation of the steps involved in application of mutation operators and mutants generation in the ABAC context; and
– an example of application GRADUATION methodology in the ABAC context.

The objective therefore is to define an abstract process for the automatic generation of GDPR-based mutants, useful for assessing generic GDPR-based testing strategies through mutation analysis. Indeed, the derived test suites can be used by:

1. The Controller to assess the GDPR's readiness of the Processor, i.e., the responsible of the Personal Data processing.
2. The Supervisor Authority for verifying the GDPR compliance of the processes defined by the Controller; and
3. The Data Protection Officer (DPO) for ensuring that the organisation processes Personal Data in compliance with the data protection rules.

Outline. Section 2 presents the background knowledge about the GDPR, ABAC and mutation analysis; whereas, Sect. 3 illustrates related work. We present GRADUATION methodology in Sect. 4, and the specific GDPR-based mutation operators in Sect. 5. In Sect. 6, the implementation of the steps involved in mutants generation are presented, while an example of the application of GRADUATION methodology is provided in Sect. 7. Finally, Sect. 8 concludes the paper by also hinting at future work.

2   Background

In this section, we briefly provide an overview of the GDPR and ABAC model. Other basic concepts, useful for understanding the proposal are provided in line within the text in Sect. 4.

GDPR Concepts. The GDPR [12] defines Personal Data as any information relating to an identified or identifiable natural person called Data Subject. In this view the, a Data Subject is a Natural Person and her/his data are managed by a *Controller.* The GDPR rules the processing of personal data, whether it is automated (even partially) or not. The GDPR relies on the following principles and demands: *Purposes,* i.e., data should only be collected for determined, explicit and legitimate purposes, and should not be processed later for other purposes; *Accuracy,* i.e., the processed data must be accurate and up-to-date regularly; *Retention,* i.e., data must be deleted after a limited period; *Subject explicit consent,* i.e., data may be collected and processed only if the data subject has given her or his explicit consent. The most adopted model-based representation of the GDPR relies on ontologies [4,16,20,21,25].

ABAC and Mutation. ABAC [14] is currently one of the mostly adopted AC model in industrial environment [13] and "supplements and subsumes" the other models [14]. The National Institute of Standards and Technology (NIST) defines ABAC as "[a]n access control method where subject requests to perform operations on objects are granted or denied based on assigned attributes of the subject, assigned attributes of the object, environment conditions, and a set of policies that are specified in terms of those attributes and conditions" [13]. In the recent years, several proposals used ABAC model to represent GDPR's concepts [5,6,10,11], by casting the conceived representation into the eXtensible Access Control Markup Language (XACML) standard [19]. Indeed, XACML is the only available standard implementation of ABAC model, and it is a platform-independent XML-based language for the specification of Access Control Policies (ACPs). The main purpose of an XACML policy is to define the constraints that a subject (e.g., Data Subject or Controller) needs to comply with for accessing a resource (e.g., Personal Data) and doing an action (e.g., a processing activity) in a given environment (e.g., purpose and consent). However, as stated in the previous section, developing XACML-based ACPs rises up the problem of developing effective and efficient test strategies able to guarantee the lack of unauthorized access to personal data (*security perspective*) and unlawful processing (*legal perspective*). Therefore, mutation analysis [22] can be applied on ACPs for measuring the adequacy of the generated test suites. The general process of mutation analysis consists of two steps: first, change the original program (e.g., ACP) with predefined mutation operators and generates a set of mutated program, called mutants; then, the mutants are executed against a test suite, and information is collected during the execution for various purpose of analysis.

3   Related Work

In the context of the GDPR, and data privacy management in general, only few proposals are targeting the definition of mutation operators able to deal with the specific privacy characteristics and requirements of the privacy standards [2]. And in these cases, the proposed mutation operators do not exhaustively cover all the important criticalities of the GDPR. For instance, they do not consider mutation operators concerning the erroneous use of the purpose defined by the controller and the consent given by the data subject.

Focusing in particular on mutation testing in the context of access control, the most noteworthy proposals are: the fault models and relative set of mutation operators simulating syntactic faults of XACML access control policies proposed by [17]; the generic metamodel for the specification rule-based security policy and the relative set of mutation operators provided by [18]; the XACMUT tool [8], which includes and enhances the mutation operators of [17] and [18] addressing specific faults of the XACML 2.0 language; and the proposal of [9] which implements mutation analysis at the level of the policy evaluation engine instead of applying it at the level of access control policy.

On the contrary, considering the mutation testing in the context of the GDPR, to the best of our knowledge the only proposal currently available is represented by [2]. Indeed, this paper is the first attempts of extending mutation operators for validating ontologies expressing the GDPR's provisions. However, even if generic, the mutation operators proposed in the paper do not cover all the specific aspects of the privacy standard.

Therefore, our proposal on the one hand extends the set of mutation operators, so as to validating the test suites or strategies against the GDPR peculiarities, on the other provides an implementation able to integrating into a unique environment all the existing approaches for mutation testing in the area of access control system.

4   Methodology for GDPR-Based Mutants Derivation

GRADUATION methodology is composed of four main steps (see Fig. 1): (1) Model Derivation; (2) Model Parsing; (3) Implementation Parsing; and (4) Mutation Application.

Although grounded in a domain-related implementation (i.e., the GDPR), GRADUATION yields a more general spectrum, since it can be applied to different data protection regulations and more in general to any legal text that implicitly contains, or suggests, data protection requirements. In the following, details about the methodology steps are provided.

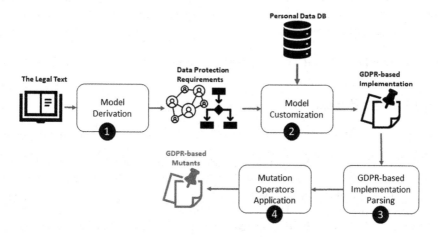

Fig. 1. GDPR-based mutation methodology.

Model Derivation (Step ①). Starting from a legal text, in our case the GDPR, the model representing the main concepts and the relations between them is obtained. To this purpose, in literature different proposals focused on the derivation of a formal representation of legal text are available [4,16,20,21,25]. It is out of the scope of this work investigating the most suitable approaches for this purpose. The hypothesis of our work is that a GDPR-based model is available in terms of a specification language, for instance an ontological representation, a UML model or an access control model.

Model Customization (Step ②). This step takes as input both the legal text model and concrete inputs stored in *Personal Data DB*. In this step the legal-based model (in our case the GDPR-based model) is analyzed to identify main legal concepts and associate to each of them the proper input domain (i.e., the data contained in *Personal Data DB*). Examples of legal data could be: personal data, data subject, controller, processor, consent and purpose. The legal-based model and the identified input are then used for deriving a specialized GDPR-based implementation of the considered model.

GDPR-Based Implementation Parsing (Step ③). According to the mutation testing approach, the derived GDPR-based implementation is classified as *gold* implementation, and it is used for: i) identifying the set of data entities, such as for instance the current ID of the Processor, the name of a Data Subject and so on; ii) instrumenting the *gold* implementation so as to let the automatic derivation of its mutated versions (i.e., mutants set).

Mutation Operators Application (Step ④). The set of GDPR-based mutation operators is applied to the gold implementation so as to derive the mutants set. In this step, two kinds of mutations are considered: *intra-implementation* and *inter-implementation mutations*. The former set refers to the application of mutation operators managing only the information and data extracted from the *gold* implementation (i.e., during Step ③). The latter set refers to mutation operator managing the information relative to the GDPR-based model (i.e., the model derived during the Step ②).

The conceived GDPR-based mutation operators are reported in Sect. 5.

5   GDPR-Based Mutation Operators

The GDPR-based mutation operators can be classified in three main categories:

1. operators targeting the purpose of processing and the consent given by data subject;
2. mutation operators targeting the roles defined in the GDPR such as Data Subject, Controller and Processor; and finally,
3. operators focusing on Personal Data, i.e., the object of the EU legal framework, and their categories.

These operators have the ability to be applied to different domains, because voluntarily conceived as generic. Therefore, depending on the specific language or formalism used for defining the GDPR's requirements, they can be implemented and applied accordingly.

The new generic GDPR-based mutation operators are as in the following:

Giving Consent (GC) this operator changes the value of the Consent given by the data subject.

Withdraw Consent (WC) this operator is dual to GC, and it changes the value of the consent element in the targeted implementation.

Change Purpose (CP) this operator replaces a purpose with other defined in the considered implementation. In case there is only one purpose, CP operator changes the purpose with a random one defined in the GDPR model or in other available supporting sources.

Change Controller (CC) this operator replaces a Controller with another one. In case missing candidates, CC changes the current Controller with a randomly generated Controller. This operator is applied also when Joint Controllers exit and involved in the processing of Personal Data, i.e., in defining the Purpose of processing, obtaining the consent and using Personal Data accordingly.

Replace Data Subject (RDS) this operator is able to replace a Data Subject with another one. Similar to CC and CP operators, i.e., in case of missing candidates, RDS chooses random Data Subject that replaces the current one.

Replace Controller with Processor (RCP) this operator changes a Controller with a Processor presented in the current implementation;

Replace Processor (RP) this operator replaces a Processor with another Processor.

Change Personal Data (CPD) this operator is able to change a personal data with another one.

Change Personal Data Category (CPDC) this operator changes the category of given personal data with another one.

6   GDPR-Based Mutation Operators Implementation

In this section, we describe the contextualization of GRADUATION methodology in the context of ABAC-based systems. For this purpose, steps of the GRADUATION methodology (see Sect. 4) have been divided into three modules: Module (A) refers to the activities for modeling the GDPR and deriving the ABAC policies (Steps (1) and (2) of Fig. 1); Module (B) refers to the ABAC policy parsing (Step (3) of Fig. 1); and Module (C) contains specific activities for the mutation testing application (Step (3) of Fig. 1).

In this section, however, we only provide the implementation of Modules (B) and (C), which are the most specific for the ABAC context[1].

As reported in Fig. 2, Module (B) is implemented as parser of the ABAC policy. Its role is to extract the data for deriving the mutated versions of the ABAC policy. An example of the information collected by this parser is provided in Table 1 of the following section.

Module (C) is composed of the following components:

– *Mutation Operators Selector (Component (a))*: this component implements two set of mutation operators: (i) the GDPR-based Mutation Operators

---

[1] GRADUATION has been implemented in Java, and it is currently available at: http://security.isti.cnr.it/tools/graduation.

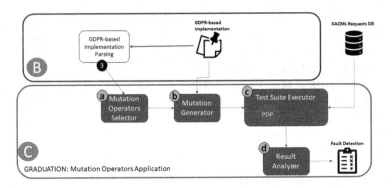

Fig. 2. Overview of GRADUATION.

defined in the previous section; and (ii) Standard ABAC Mutation Operators. This last set of operators can be categorized based on the ABAC policy
elements. There are operators emulating fault at: (1) Policy Set element level
such as Policy Set Target True (PSTT), Policy Set Target False (PSTF) and
Change Policy Combining Algorithm (CPC); (2) Policy element level, e.g.,
Change Rule Combining Algorithm (CRC) and Policy Target False (PTF);
(3) Rule element level, such as Rule Target True (RTT), Rule Condition
False (RCF) and Change Rule Effect (CRE); and finally, (4) Policy Functions level, for instance RemoveUniquenessFunction (RUF), ChangeLogical-
Function (CLF) and AddNotFunction (ANF). For a more detailed description
and comprehensive overview of the standard AC mutation operators, we refer
the reader to [8].

- *Mutants Generator (Component ⓑ)*: this component has the responsibility
of generating mutated versions of the Gold (GDPR-based) policy by applying
the selected mutation operators (both standard and GDPR-based) by end-
user.
- *Test Suite Executor (Component ⓒ)*: this component executes the AC
requests provided by the user on the original GDPR-based ABAC policy
(Gold Policy) and on the generated set of mutated policies. For requests evaluation this component integrates an ABAC PDP engine, which is able to
provide the corresponding result (Permit, Deny, NotApplicable or Indetermi-
nate) for a given policy P and a request *Req*.
- *Results Analyzer (Component ⓓ)*: this component takes as input the results
obtained by the execution of the test suites on the original GDPR-based policy
and on its set of mutants, and computes the fault detection effectiveness. It
works as follows: for each request the result obtained by its execution on the
original policy is compared with that obtained on its mutants set. If the results
are different, the mutant is classified as killed. The component provides as
output the list of killed mutants, survived mutants, and the percentage of fault
detection effectiveness obtained by the requests execution. It also provides
functionalities allowing to filter by mutation operators, by test cases, and

by the expected authorization decision. This is useful for providing different perspective of the data and for analyzing deeply the different aspects of these mutation data views.

For the aim of completeness, even if out of the scope of this paper, components ©️ and ⓓ have been described in this section because part of the implementation of Module ©️. However, they will be not further detailed in the reminder of this paper.

7   Using GRADUATION Methodology

In this section, we briefly detail the application GRADUATION methodology (see Sect. 4) by considering a use case scenario concerning a fitness environment taken from the literature [10]. Specifically, we consider the situation in which Alice, a Data Subject, wants to use a smart fitness application to monitor her daily activities to achieve a predefined training objective. In this case, we suppose that a customized (mobile) application is provided by a generic myFitness company (the Controller). To meet Alice's needs, myFitness has so far defined two purposes (MyCholesterol and Untargeted Marketing), each related to a specific data set of Personal Data and achieved by allowing access to perform a specific set of Actions. More precisely, the MyCholesterol purpose is achieved by performing AGGREGATE, DERIVE and QUERY actions; whereas the Untargeted Marketing purpose is achieved by performing COLLECT, QUERY and SEND actions.

At the time of subscribing to the myFitness application, Alice provided her personal data (i.e., e-mail, Age, Gender, and Blood Cholesterol) and gave her consent to process her e-mail and Age for Untargeted Marketing purpose, and her Blood Cholesterol for MyCholesterol purpose. Additionally, Alice withhold her consent to share her personal data with a third-party company named xxx-HealthOrg company. In turn, myFitness gave to Alice controller's contacts that include: piiController, orgName, address, e-mail, and phone number.

According to GRADUATION methodology, the application of the first two activities (see Fig. 1) involves:

- **Model Derivation (Step ①):** starting from the GDPR text, among the different proposals, the Privacy Ontology (PrOnto) [20,21] ontology representation of the GDPR is used for deriving the GDPR's entities useful for modeling GDPR-based ABAC policy. In particular we considered:
  1. *Data* that is the object of the GDPR and it is target of its protection. Data can be: Personal Data, non-personal data, anonymized data and pseudonymised data;
  2. *Agents and Roles* such as data subject, controller, processor, supervisory authority and the new introduced figure the Data Protection Officer(DPO), as well as third-party;
  3. *Processing activities* expressed as a set of actions such as delete, transmit and store;

4. *Purposes and legal bases* such as the consent; and finally,

5. *Legal rules* such as right, obligation, permission and prohibition.

According to the methodology presented in [6], an example of an abstract representation of a GDPR-based ABAC policy model is reported below:

((Subject = Controller OR DataSubject) ∧ (Resource = PersonalData) ∧ (Action = processing) ∧ (Action.purpose = PersonalData.purpose) ∧ (PersonalData.purpose.consent = YES)) ⟹ (Authorization = Permit)

– **Model Customization (Step ②):** the GDPR-based ABAC policy model is then analyzed to identify main legal concepts and associate to each of them the proper input domain. In particular, based on the above scenario, a possible access control policy can be derived as reported here below. The policy allows a lawfulness of processing of personal data related to Alice in case of subscription to the myFitness specific service for two different purposes.

LawfulnessOfProcessingPolicy:

R1: permission(Controller=myFitness, DataSubject=Alice PersonalData=Blood Cholesterol, purpose=MyCholesterol, Action=DERIVE Consent=TRUE)

R2: permission(Controller=myFitness, DataSubject=Alice, PersonalData=EmailDS, purpose=UntargetedMarketing, Action=SEND Consent=TRUE)

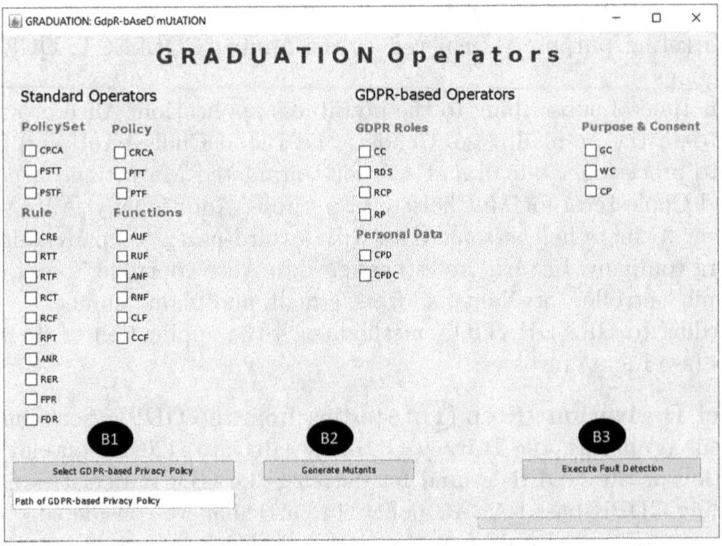

Fig. 3. GRADUATION main GUI. (Color figure online)

The **GDPR-based Implementation Parsing (Step ③)** is being performed through the application of the implementation of Module Ⓑ (see Fig. 2). The end-user interaction is managed through an User Interface (UI) as depicted in Fig. 3. Through this interface, the end-user can select the GDPR-based policy (button **B1** in Fig. 3) and starts its parsing. This access control policy, representing the gold implementation, is then analyzed for identifying the data useful for deriving its mutated versions. In Table 1, the result of this activity is represented. In particular, the table reports the set of GDPR-based entities (column *GDPR Entity*), their classification (column *Category*), their names (column *Name*) and related values (column *Value*). In the following, we describe the application of the GDPR-based mutation operators by considering the above policy named *LawfulnessOfProcessingPolicy*.

Table 1. The GDPR entities extracted from the model.

GDPR entity	Category	Name	Value
Controller	Agent	orgName	myFitness
Controller	Biodata	piiController	myFitnessID
Controller	Biodata	address	-
Controller	Biodata	e-mailC	-
Controller	Biodata	phone number	-
Third-party	Agent	orgName	xxx-HealthOrg
Data Subject	Agent	DSName	Alice
Personal Data	Biodata	Age	-
Personal Data	Biodata	Gender	-
Personal Data	Biodata	Blood Cholesterol	-
Personal Data	Biodata	e-mailDS	-
Purpose	-	Purpose	MyCholesterol
Purpose	-	Purpose	Untargeted Marketing
Processing	-	Action	AGGREGATE
Processing	-	Action	DERIVE
Processing	-	Action	QUERY
Processing	-	Action	COLLECT
Processing	-	Action	SEND

The **Mutation Operators Application (Step ④)** is performed through Module ⓒ. In particular, by means of the User Interface (UI) (see Fig. 3) the end-user can select the GDPR-based mutation operators and the standard ones, and apply them to the selected policy (button **B2**).

In the following, some examples of mutants related to *LawfulnessOfProcessingPolicy* are reported. In particular, in bold-italics text we report the name of the applied Mutation Operator, whereas in bold-blue we highlight the applied mutation operators within **R1** and **R2** rules.

Finally, the end-user can execute the policy mutants against a given test suite (button **B3** of the User Interface (UI) of Fig. 3).

WC MUTANT
LawfulnessOfProcessingPolicy-WC1:

R1: permission(Controller=myFitness, DataSubject=Alice PersonalData=Blood Cholesterol, purpose=MyCholesterol, Action=DERIVE **Consent=FALSE**)
R2: permission(Controller=myFitness, DataSubject=Alice, PersonalData=e-mailDS, pur-
pose=UntargetedMarketing, Action=SEND Consent=YES)

CP MUTANT
LawfulnessOfProcessingPolicy-CP2:

R1: permission(Controller=myFitness, DataSubject=Alice PersonalData=Blood Cholesterol, **purpose=UntargetedMarketing**, Action=DERIVE Consent=TRUE)
R2: permission(Controller=myFitness, DataSubject=Alice, PersonalData=e-mailDS, pur-
pose=UntargetedMarketing, Action=SEND Consent=TRUE)

CPD MUTANT
LawfulnessOfProcessingPolicy-CPD:

R1: permission(Controller=myFitness, DataSubject=Alice **PersonalData=AGE**, pur-
pose=MyCholesterol, Action=DERIVE Consent=TRUE)
R2: permission(Controller=myFitness, DataSubject=Alice, PersonalData=e-mailDS, pur-
pose=UntargetedMarketing, Action=SEND Consent=YES)

In particular, this step involves the selection of the set of AC requests to be evaluated; the execution of the policy and the derived mutants against test suite; and the evaluation of which mutants (both standard and GDPR-based) have been killed by the application of the selected test suite. It is out of the scope of this work discussing the results of this step because it strictly depends on the test generation strategy or the test suite to be evaluated. The aim of this work is therefore to present a mutation strategy targeting the GDPR's peculiarities, and provides specific mutation operators based on the GDPR.

8 Conclusions

In this paper, we introduced GRADUATION, a comprehensive methodology for defining and applying mutation operators specifically conceived in the context of the GDPR. The methodology and the proposed mutation operators have been voluntarily conceived independent from any modeling language, used for formally represent the GDPR. Although grounded in a domain-related implementation (i.e., the GDPR), GRADUATION yields a more general spectrum, since it can be applied to different data protection regulations, and more in general to any legal text that implicitly contains, or suggests, data protection requirements. The applicability of GRADUATION has been exemplified in the context of ABAC domain. Thus, the ABAC-based GRADUATION implementation has been used to generate mutated versions of GDPR-based ABAC Privacy policies. Currently, we are working to extend the GDPR-based mutation operators set so as to cover other GDPR's demands as well as to improve its validation with real case studies. Ongoing work includes also the specialization of GRADUATION methodology considering other formalisms and languages such as UML and Semantic Web Technologies.

Acknowledgment. This work is partially supported by the project BIECO H2020 Grant Agreement No. 952702, and by CyberSec4Europe H2020 Grant Agreement No. 830929.

References

1. Barsocchi, P., et al.: A privacy-by-design architecture for indoor localization systems. In: Shepperd, M., Brito e Abreu, F., Rodrigues da Silva, A., Pérez-Castillo, R. (eds.) QUATIC 2020. CCIS, vol. 1266, pp. 358–366. Springer, Cham (2020). https://doi.org/10.1007/978-3-030-58793-2_29
2. Bartolini, C.: Software testing techniques revisited for OWL ontologies. In: Hammoudi, S., Pires, L.F., Selic, B., Desfray, P. (eds.) MODELSWARD 2016. CCIS, vol. 692, pp. 132–153. Springer, Cham (2017). https://doi.org/10.1007/978-3-319-66302-9_7
3. Bartolini, C., Calabrò, A., Marchetti, E.: Enhancing business process modelling with data protection compliance: an ontology-based proposal. In: Proceedings of the 5th International Conference on Information Systems Security and Privacy, ICISSP 2019, Prague, Czech Republic, 23–25 February 2019, pp. 421–428 (2019)
4. Bartolini, C., Calabrò, A., Marchetti, E.: GDPR and business processes: an effective solution. In: Proceedings of the 2nd International Conference on Applications of Intelligent Systems, APPIS 2019, Las Palmas de Gran Canaria, Spain, 07–09 January 2019, pp. 7:1–7:5 (2019)
5. Bartolini, C., Daoudagh, S., Lenzini, G., Marchetti, E.: GDPR-based user stories in the access control perspective. In: Piattini, M., Rupino da Cunha, P., García Rodríguez de Guzmán, I., Pérez-Castillo, R. (eds.) QUATIC 2019. CCIS, vol. 1010, pp. 3–17. Springer, Cham (2019). https://doi.org/10.1007/978-3-030-29238-6_1
6. Bartolini., C., Daoudagh, S., Lenzini., G., Marchetti., E.: Towards a lawful authorized access: a preliminary GDPR-based authorized access. In: Proceedings of the 14th International Conference on Software Technologies: ICSOFT, vol. 1, pp. 331–338. INSTICC, SciTePress (2019)
7. Basin, D., Debois, S., Hildebrandt, T.: On purpose and by necessity: compliance under the GDPR. In: Meiklejohn, S., Sako, K. (eds.) FC 2018. LNCS, vol. 10957, pp. 20–37. Springer, Heidelberg (2018). https://doi.org/10.1007/978-3-662-58387-6_2
8. Bertolino, A., Daoudagh, S., Lonetti, F., Marchetti., E.: XACMUT: XACML 2.0 mutants generator. In: Proceedings of 8th International Workshop on Mutation Analysis, pp. 28–33 (2013)
9. Daoudagh, S., Lonetti, F., Marchetti, E.: Assessment of access control systems using mutation testing. In: Proceedings of the First International Workshop on TEchnical and LEgal Aspects of Data pRIvacy, pp. 8–13. IEEE Press (2015)
10. Daoudagh, S., Marchetti, E., Savarino, V., Bernardo, R.D., Alessi, M.: How to improve the GDPR compliance through consent management and access control. In: Proceedings of the 7th International Conference on Information Systems Security and Privacy, ICISSP 2021, Online Streaming, 11–13 February 2021, pp. 534–541. SCITEPRESS (2021)
11. Davari, M., Bertino, E.: Access control model extensions to support data privacy protection based on GDPR. In: 2019 IEEE International Conference on Big Data (Big Data), pp. 4017–4024 (2019)

12. Regulation (EU) 2016/679 of the European Parliament and of the Council of 27 April 2016 on the protection of natural persons with regard to the processing of personal data and on the free movement of such data, and repealing Directive 95/46/EC (General Data Protection Regulation). Official Journal of the European Union L119, pp. 1–88, May 2016. http://eur-lex.europa.eu/legal-content/EN/TXT/?uri=OJ:L:2016:119:TOC

13. Hu, C.T., et al.: Guide to attribute based access control (ABAC) definition and considerations [includes updates as of 02-25-2019]. Technical report (2019)

14. Jin, X., Krishnan, R., Sandhu, R.: A unified attribute-based access control model covering DAC, MAC and RBAC. In: Cuppens-Boulahia, N., Cuppens, F., Garcia-Alfaro, J. (eds.) DBSec 2012. LNCS, vol. 7371, pp. 41–55. Springer, Heidelberg (2012). https://doi.org/10.1007/978-3-642-31540-4_4

15. Khatibsyarbini, M., Isa, M.A., Jawawi, D.N., Tumeng, R.: Test case prioritization approaches in regression testing: a systematic literature review. Inf. Softw. Technol. **93**, 74–93 (2018)

16. Libal, T., Steen, A.: Towards an executable methodology for the formalization of legal texts. In: Dastani, M., Dong, H., van der Torre, L. (eds.) CLAR 2020. LNCS (LNAI), vol. 12061, pp. 151–165. Springer, Cham (2020). https://doi.org/10.1007/978-3-030-44638-3_10

17. Martin, E., Xie, T.: A fault model and mutation testing of access control policies. In: Proceedings of WWW, pp. 667–676 (2007)

18. Mouelhi, T., Fleurey, F., Baudry, B.: A generic metamodel for security policies mutation. In: Proceedings of ICSTW, pp. 278–286 (2008)

19. OASIS: eXtensible Access Control Markup Language (XACML) Version 3.0 (2013). http://docs.oasis-open.org/xacml/3.0/xacml-3.0-core-spec-os-en.html

20. Palmirani, M., Martoni, M., Rossi, A., Bartolini, C., Robaldo, L.: Legal ontology for modelling GDPR concepts and norms. In: Legal Knowledge and Information Systems - JURIX 2018: The Thirty-first Annual Conference, Groningen, The Netherlands, 12–14 December 2018, pp. 91–100 (2018)

21. Palmirani, M., Martoni, M., Rossi, A., Bartolini, C., Robaldo, L.: PrOnto: privacy ontology for legal reasoning. In: Kő, A., Francesconi, E. (eds.) EGOVIS 2018. LNCS, vol. 11032, pp. 139–152. Springer, Cham (2018). https://doi.org/10.1007/978-3-319-98349-3_11

22. Papadakis, M., Kintis, M., Zhang, J., Jia, Y., Le Traon, Y., Harman, M.: Mutation testing advances: an analysis and survey. In: Advances in Computers, vol. 112, pp. 275–378. Elsevier (2019)

23. Ramadan, Q., Salnitriy, M., Strüber, D., Jürjens, J., Giorgini, P.: From secure business process modeling to design-level security verification. In: Proceedings of MODELS 2017, pp. 123–133. IEEE, September 2017

24. Ranise, S., Siswantoro, H.: Automated legal compliance checking by security policy analysis. In: Tonetta, S., Schoitsch, E., Bitsch, F. (eds.) SAFECOMP 2017. LNCS, vol. 10489, pp. 361–372. Springer, Cham (2017). https://doi.org/10.1007/978-3-319-66284-8_30

25. Robaldo, L., Bartolini, C., Palmirani, M., Rossi, A., Martoni, M., Lenzini, G.: Formalizing GDPR provisions in reified I/O logic: the DAPRECO knowledge base. J. Logic Lang. Inform. **29**(4), 401–449 (2020)

A Proposal for the Classification of Methods for Verification and Validation of Safety, Cybersecurity, and Privacy of Automated Systems

Jose Luis de la Vara[1]([✉]), Thomas Bauer[2], Bernhard Fischer[3], Mustafa Karaca[4],
Henrique Madeira[5], Martin Matschnig[3], Silvia Mazzini[6], Giann Spilere Nandi[7],
Fabio Patrone[8], David Pereira[7], José Proença[7], Rupert Schlick[9], Stefano Tonetta[10],
Ugur Yayan[4], and Behrooz Sangchoolie[11]

[1] Universidad de Castilla-La Mancha, Albacete, Spain
joseluis.delavara@uclm.es
[2] Fraunhofer IESE, Kaiserslautern, Germany
thomas.bauer@iese.fraunhofer.de
[3] Siemens, Vienna, Austria
{bernhard.bf.fischer,martin.matschnig}@siemens.com
[4] Inovasyon Muhendislik, Odunpazari, Turkey
{mustafa.karaca,ugur.yayan}@inovasyonmuhendislik.com
[5] Universidade de Coimbra, Coimbra, Portugal
henrique@dei.uc.pt
[6] Intecs, Pisa, Italy
silvia.mazzini@intecs.it
[7] ISEP, Porto, Portugal
{giann,drp,pro}@isep.ipp.pt
[8] University of Genoa, Genova, Italy
f.patrone@edu.unige.it
[9] AIT, Vienna, Austria
rupert.schlick@ait.ac.at
[10] FBK, Povo, Italy
tonettas@fbk.eu
[11] RISE, Borås, Sweden
behrooz.sangchoolie@ri.se

Abstract. As our dependence on automated systems grows, so does the need for guaranteeing their safety, cybersecurity, and privacy (SCP). Dedicated methods for verification and validation (V&V) must be used to this end and it is necessary that the methods and their characteristics can be clearly differentiated. This can be achieved via method classifications. However, we have experienced that existing classifications are not suitable to categorise V&V methods for SCP of automated systems. They do not pay enough attention to the distinguishing characteristics of this system type and of these quality concerns. As a solution, we present a new classification developed in the scope of a large-scale industry-academia project. The classification considers both the method type, e.g., testing, and the concern addressed, e.g., safety. Over 70 people have successfully used the classification on

A. C. R. Paiva et al. (Eds.): QUATIC 2021, CCIS 1439, pp. 325–340, 2021.
https://doi.org/10.1007/978-3-030-85347-1_24

53 methods. We argue that the classification is a more suitable means to categorise V&V methods for SCP of automated systems and that it can help other researchers and practitioners.

Keywords: Verification and validation · V&V · Method · Classification · Safety · Cybersecurity · Privacy · Automated system

1 Introduction

Automated systems such as industrial robots and advanced driving systems play an increasingly important role in society. They support many daily-life activities and we strongly depend on them. On the other hand, as the use and complexity of these systems are growing, system manufacturers and component suppliers require methods that help them to confirm that safety, cybersecurity, and privacy (SCP) requirements are satisfied [4]. This is necessary so that the systems can be deemed dependable. From a general perspective, a method corresponds to a particular procedure for accomplishing or approaching something, especially a systematic or established one [31]. In this paper we focus on methods for verification and validation (V&V) of automated systems. Examples of these methods are fault injection [30] and model-based testing [26].

The features of the new generation of automated systems require that dedicated V&V methods (usually a combination of methods) are applied to them [4, 12]. The methods must consider how to cope with the scale and complexity of the systems, the aspects that make them cyber-physical, and their specific quality needs, among other issues. For example, the use of software-focused V&V methods alone is often not sufficient. This also implies that manufacturers and suppliers need to clearly distinguish among different V&V methods and their characteristics to be able to select the most adequate ones during a system's lifecycle. Method classifications can aid in this task.

However, when involved in the analysis and characterisation of V&V methods for SCP of automated systems, we have experienced that existing classifications are not suitable. Among the issues identified, the classifications do not pay enough attention to specific aspects such as the need for analysing possible faults and attacks at early development stages or for ascertaining what SCP aspect a given V&V method deals with. The descriptions of existing classification are also usually not clear enough to help users decide upon how to best classify a V&V method and to select the most suitable method for a given V&V need. If these problems arise, then the selection and use of V&V methods for SCP of automated systems can be less effective, ultimately impacting the cost and dependability of a system.

We aim to address these issues by proposing a new classification of V&V methods. We have created it in the scope of VALU3S [4], a large-scale industry-academia project in which 41 partners from ten countries are cooperating towards improving how automated systems are verified and validated with respect to SCP requirements. Among the activities of the project, we identify, analyse, and classify methods that could improve V&V of specific industrial use cases from the automotive, agriculture, railway, healthcare, aerospace, and industrial automation domains.

The classification distinguishes between two main facets of a V&V method: *the general method type* and *the concern addressed*. For example, penetration testing [44] is a testing method for cybersecurity. Thanks to the classification, we have managed to classify tens of V&V methods and differentiate among them more precisely. Our initial aim in VALU3S was to reuse some existing classification, but we found issues such as insufficient consideration of automated system SCP needs and insufficient clarity to know how to best classify a method. Nonetheless, relationships can be established between our classification and others.

We consider that the classification can be useful for both researchers and practitioners. A more precise classification of V&V methods for SCP of automated systems can help others to better determine the circumstances under which a given method should be used, possible improvements and extensions on the methods, methods that can be combined to jointly cover a wider V&V scope, and areas in which new methods could be needed.

The rest of the paper is organised as follows. Section 2 reviews related work. Sections 3 and 4 present the classification and its application, respectively. Finally, Sect. 5 summarises our main conclusions.

2 Related Work

As part of the work done in VALU3S, we searched for and analysed existing V&V method classifications to assess their adoption in the project.

Nair et al. [29] identified evidence types for certification of safety-critical systems and created a taxonomy. Results of V&V methods is one of the types. It is refined into tool-supported V&V and manual V&V. The former is divided into testing (13 basic types for objective-based, environment-based, or target-based testing), simulation, and formal verification (three basic types). Similar V&V method types are referred to in engineering standards, e.g., EN 50128 [9] for railway software. The main issues with the classification by Nair et al. are its focus on safety, thus cybersecurity and privacy aspects are not sufficiently covered, and that it pays a much larger attention to testing than to other method types. This results in an unbalanced classification for our purpose.

The Amalthea4public project [1] reviewed V&V methods for embedded multi- and many-core software systems. The methods were divided into informal methods, static methods, dynamic methods, formal methods, testing, simulation, and product line analysis. The main issue that we found in this classification was that it was not clear how some methods should be classified, e.g., dynamic methods vs. formal methods or testing, as defined by the project. SCP requirements are also not explicitly addressed.

We identified the same issues with several other classifications, e.g., one proposed by the US Department of Defense [42]. This classification distinguishes four main method types: informal V&V methods, static V&V methods, dynamic V&V methods, and formal V&V methods. These method types are commonly used. However, we consider that it is necessary to distinguish among informal, semi-formal, and formal methods, as well as explicitly among different types of dynamic methods such as testing and simulation. This distinction is typical in engineering standards such as IEC 61508 [20], thus it is a relevant aspect for systems in regulated application domains.

There also exist classifications that specify the V&V methods that could be used in the different system lifecycle activities [22]. We regard these classifications in isolation as less useful because they do not represent well the reasons to use a method, how formal it is, or the type of requirements addressed.

In summary, our classification fills gaps in prior work by considering a broader range of general V&V method types, explicitly focusing on SCP, and providing a detailed description of its elements, how they can be distinguished, and how to use them.

3   Classification for V&V Methods for SCP of Automated Systems

This section presents the classification that we propose for V&V methods. It is the result of an effort in the VALU3S project to decide upon how to best categorise V&V methods that we identified as relevant for evaluation of SCP of automated systems. We also analysed the methods [43]. The current structure of the classification is the result of several iterations and has been discussed among VALU3S partners.

The classification is based on two main facets of the V&V methods: the general method type and the concern addressed. When categorising a method, a user of the classification must choose (1) one or several general method types and (2) one or several concerns. This is justified in the following paragraphs.

The general method types considered are:

- **Injection**, when some phenomenon is introduced in a system to analyse its response.
- **Simulation**, when the behaviour of a model of a system is studied.
- **Testing**, when system execution under certain conditions is checked before operation.
- **Runtime verification**, when system execution is evaluated during operation.
- **Formal analysis**, for V&V methods with a mathematical basis.
- **Semi-formal analysis**, for V&V methods that exploit some structured means but without a full mathematical basis.
- **Informal analysis**, for V&V methods that do not follow any predefined structure or do not have a mathematical basis.

We have identified five main concerns that SCP V&V methods for automated systems might have to address:

- **Safety**, as the ability of a system to avoid injury, serious injury, or death.
- **Cybersecurity**, as the ability of a system to avoid unauthorised access, use, or modification.
- **Privacy**, as the ability of a system to avoid disclosure of sensitive data.
- **General**, when a V&V method analyses a general characteristic of a system that does not directly contribute to SCP, but indirectly, e.g., traceability.
- **System-type-focused**, when a V&V method focuses on specific and distinguishing characteristics of a system type, e.g., a method for CPUs.

The selection of general method types is based on categories in related classifications and on the decision upon how to fill the gaps that we found in the classifications.

Regarding the concerns, we started focusing on SCP and realised that they needed to be extended to also consider general V&V needs and system-type-focused ones.

Among the characteristics that differentiate the classification and its use, we believe that considering injection as a separate independent general method type is very important for automated systems. Injection-based V&V methods focus on SCP evaluation, are essential for early system V&V, and can cope well with V&V of specific characteristics of cyber-physical systems, addressing injection from the software, hardware, network, mechanical, and real-world environment perspectives.

We also treat methods in a way that allows a user of the classification to consider very specific methods or broader ones. This is inspired by how engineering standards for critical systems [9, 20] present methods and it is also in line with how VALU3S industrial partners distinguish V&V methods. For example, the standards can refer both to general methods and categories such as performance testing and to specialisations such as stress testing and response time analysis. Therefore, the classification needs to be flexible regarding the abstraction level of the methods. This also implies that the classification of broader methods, for which specialised ones or sub-methods could be distinguished, might not be mapped to a single general method type or concern, but to several. For example, failure detection and diagnosis in robotic systems can be mapped to simulation and runtime monitoring as general method type and to safety and cybersecurity as concerns. This is shown in more detail in Sect. 4.

The following sub-sections present each general method type and how specific methods can be mapped to them, also considering the different concerns.

3.1 Injection

Injection-based V&V methods focus on introducing certain characteristics in a system, providing a certain type of input, or triggering certain events, to confirm that the system behaves suitably under the corresponding conditions. Two specific types of injection are discussed: fault injection and attack injection.

Fault injection refers to deliberate insertion of artificial (yet realistic) faults in a computer system or component. This way, it is possible to assess the behaviour of a system in the presence of faults and allow the characterization of specific dependability measures or fault tolerant mechanisms available in the system. According to the well-known concepts and terminology proposed by Avizienis et al. [3], a fault is the "adjudged or hypothesized cause of an error", and an "error is the part of the total state of the system that may lead to its subsequent service failure". In other words, the faults injected may lead to errors that, subsequently, may cause erroneous behaviour of the target component. These errors may propagate in the system and may cause failures in other components or even system failures. Fault injection can be seen as an approach to accelerate the occurrence of faults in order to help in V&V of the fault handling mechanisms available in the system under evaluation.

Avizienis et al. [3] define an attack as a special type of fault which is human made, deliberate and malicious, affecting (or breaching) hardware or software from external system boundaries and occurring during the operational phase. The system breach exploits the vulnerabilities in a system and could result into a compromised system. The compromised system could result in a system failure such as software or hardware complete failure or degraded performance. Thus, attack injection in a system is analogous to fault injection. However, the aim is to evaluate the impact of cybersecurity attacks on the overall security or safety of a system.

Fault and attack injection can be used in different phases of system development to evaluate (or even predict) how systems and specific components behave in the presence of faults, or to assess dependability properties such as safety, security, privacy, availability, or reliability. Typically, faults injected in models (structural or behaviour-based models) are useful in the early stages of system development, while faults injected in prototypes or in real systems in controlled experiments allow V&V of actual properties of deployed systems.

Examples of injection-based V&V methods for the different concerns include:

- **Safety:** *Model-implemented fault injection* [37], to evaluate the safety aspects of a system's design by injecting fault models directly into simulated system models (such as Simulink ones) at early product development phases.
- **Cybersecurity:** *Vulnerability and attack injection in real systems or prototypes* [15], to evaluate globally how a system copes with attacks and to assess specific security mechanisms in the target system.
- **Privacy:** *SQL injection* [17], to assess the possibility of unrestricted access to databases.
- **General:** *Noise injection* [27], to add irrelevant data to the inputs during neural network training and assess the impact for V&V.
- **System-type-focused:** *Failure detection and diagnosis in robotic systems* [24], to analyse failures and possible failures in robotic system components via fault injection.

3.2 Simulation

Simulation enables early V&V of systems and components. It is based on the development or use of digital models that behave or operate like real-world systems or components, and on the provision of real-world-like inputs. Simulation-based V&V methods provide virtual validation in software-intensive systems. Possible issues in automated systems can be experimented and analysed through simulation.

This type of V&V methods provides solutions for different challenges for efficient early V&V. For example, simulation methods enable integration tests and behaviour tests without dealing with expensive hardware or test equipment. Test scenarios can be created easily for most of real-world scenarios. Simulation-based test approaches do not introduce direct safety risks in cases where human-machine interaction exists. However, the effort and cost of the development of simulation and its test processes can be high. The trade-off between simulation accuracy on the one hand, and simulation speed, resource consumption, and effort for constructing simulation models on the other hand, has to be considered.

Simulation supports different approaches for tackling challenges in V&V processes. An approach is the virtual validation of complex systems and system architectures by coupling simulation models and simulators, existing code, and virtual hardware plat-forms [25]. Another is the study of the safety and efficiency of human-robot collabora-tion [40]. There exist also approaches that provide solutions for machine learning-based systems through the provision of simulation environments for perception, planning, and decision-making systems [19].

Simulation is closely related to other V&V method types. Injection-based methods can be used in simulated environment. When aiming to highlight these characteristics, they can be referred to, e.g., as simulation-based attack injection for cybersecurity and simulation-based fault injection for safety. Simulation methods also usually exploit semi-formal methods, e.g., models, and testing aspects, e.g., test case management.

A major advantage of simulation is that V&V can be conducted without producing any physical item and adding risk to the environment. On the other hand, simulation-based applications mostly run on hierarchical models. This narrows the availability of both academic and industrial resources in development. Simulation tools can require significant computational power and limit real-time applications.

Examples of simulation methods for the different concerns include:

- **Safety:** *Simulation-based robot verification* [40], to assure a robot's trajectory safety and in turn to increase flexibility and robustness by maintaining the level of productivity.
- **Cybersecurity:** *V&V of machine learning-based systems using simulators* [19], which aims to provide efficient and effective V&V of SCP requirements of machine learning in simulated environments without endangering human safety.
- **Privacy:** *Simulation of obfuscation and negotiation* [14], to safeguard location information.
- **General:** *Virtual and augmented reality-based user interaction V&V* [6], for human factor analysis and technology acceptance by end users before a system is built or deployed.
- **System-type-focused:** *CPU verification* [18], to ensure that a CPU delivers its functionality correctly and as intended, and which can exploit simulation.

3.3 Testing

This type of V&V methods focuses on validating a system by executing it in the frame of so-called test cases. A test case contains at least two fundamental sets of information: input data to be provided to the System Under Test (SUT) and a description of the expected output or behaviour. To run a test case, an environment is used. It allows the tester to feed the SUT with the input data in a controlled manner, as well as to monitor SUT reactions. This environment is sometimes called test harness. Furthermore, usually a means is needed to judge whether SUT reactions conform to expectations. Such means is sometimes referred to as test oracle. For testing, the SUT can be the final system as well as any artefact used during its development, such as models or specific hardware or software components. The methods that focus on testing of models are especially useful for early detection of conceptual flaws.

Among the different ways to distinguish them, testing approaches can be divided into black-box testing and white-box testing. In black-box testing, only the interfaces of the SUT are considered and its interior is considered as a black box. White-box testing monitors the SUT's interior, e.g., inner states. A combination of both, i.e., grey box testing, is also possible. The scope of testing can be functional, when assessing whether the SUT behaves as expected (i.e., it fulfils its functions), and non-functional, when characteristics such as performance, robustness, and security are assessed. Therefore, testing can contribute significantly to establishing SCP. However, it must be considered that testing is usually incomplete. Even successfully passing a large set of test cases (a test suite) is no guarantee for the SUT's correctness. A test suite's quality is correlated with two aspects: how good it covers the addressed issues (functionality, robustness, etc.) and how efficiently it achieves this.

A way to get high quality test cases is (automated) test case generation, which is used by many testing methods. Furthermore, various coverage criteria can be addressed, such as scenarios, potential implementation faults, or potential impact of cybersecurity attacks on safety. Many V&V methods for critical systems address testing of non-functional issues such as safety, robustness, and cybersecurity, and also novel properties of automated systems, e.g., machine learning.

Examples of V&V methods of this type for the different concerns include:

- **Safety:** *Model-Based Robustness Testing* [38], to derive unexpected or slightly out of specification stimuli in order to check the robustness of the system or component under test.
- **Cybersecurity:** *Assessment of cybersecurity-informed safety* [39], to black-box test security-informed safety of automated driving systems and in turn produce an understanding of the interplay between safety and security.
- **Privacy:** *System testing for GDPR (General Data Protection Regulation) compliance* [33], to confirm adherence to its requirements before deployment.
- **General:** *Model-based testing* [26], to derive tests from (semi-)formal behaviour models or to test models.
- **System-type-focused:** *Penetration testing of industrial systems* [44], to analyse sensor data and server-PLC communication for evaluation (1) of system robustness in the case of sensor data manipulation and (2) of effects of data manipulation in communication.

3.4 Runtime Verification

Runtime verification is a method that allows checking whether a run of a target system satisfies or violates a set of correctness properties. It trades the computationally costly approach adopted by exhaustive offline verification techniques by a lightweight and limited, but still rigorous and precise, verification mechanism during execution time.

This V&V method type uses monitors to verify that a system's behaviour complies with its specification. In this context, behaviour expresses how the system evolves concerning the passage of time and its states' changes. To issue such verdicts, monitors collect and analyse execution traces, using them to verify if the current system state, or a set of recorded system actions, complies with a given specification. Such a specification is in general encoded in some formal language typically belonging to the family of temporal logics, state machines, rule systems, or regular expressions.

The process of collecting data from the system and feeding them to monitors, called instrumentation, is an essential part of this method type. Ideally, the instrumentation process should be considered at design time, as overheads can be minimized and performance can be optimized. However, legacy systems could also benefit from runtime verification solutions. The way monitors can be implemented is classified in various ways [8], covering aspects such as temporal and logical isolation from the monitored system, how much a monitor synchronizes with the system's execution flow, and whether a monitor is hardware- or software-based.

Although runtime verification solutions have a broad spectrum of applicability, V&V of embedded safety-critical systems seems to be the area where it shines the most. Considering their demanding safety and security levels, runtime verification is becoming widespread given its ability to identify faulty behaviour accurately and in a timely way, given its formal reasoning and lightweight resource usage.

Runtime verification methods are also especially suitable to verify properties that static formal verification techniques fail to confirm in a timely and resource-constrained way. On top of that, runtime verification tools need fewer model assumptions to work, which is also a notorious downside of static tools. Testing is another area that lately has been benefiting from runtime verification solutions as it can complement traditional testing techniques, speeding up the validation of complex system parts.

Examples of runtime verification methods for the different concerns include:

- **Safety:** *Dynamic analysis of concurrent programs* [13], to find errors in synchronisation of concurrently executing threads, processes, or any other tasks executed concurrently.
- **Cybersecurity:** *Test oracle observation at runtime* [5], to dynamically assess system behaviour by measuring how far the system is from satisfying or violating a property specified formally, e.g., a cybersecurity property.
- **Privacy:** *Monitoring of GDPR compliance* [2], to confirm adherence to GDPR requirements after a system is deployed, and to identify violations.
- **General:** *Runtime verification based on formal specification* [10], to formally specify properties of runtime observations and verify them with monitors.
- **System-type-focused:** *Model-based formal specification and verification of robotic systems* [28], to formally verify these systems with models that cope with the intractable state space of complex systems, improving V&V coverage and assurance by combining formal methods and runtime verification.

3.5 Formal Analysis

Formal analysis denotes a set of methods to prove properties of a system with formal methods based on mathematical system models. Formal analysis is typically not focused on single executions of a system, but on proving properties exhaustively on all executions. Formal analysis comprises both V&V: for verification, the properties formalize the system requirements specification, while for validation, the properties are used to check if the model is the right representation of the system, e.g., consistency checking, reachability of states, and vacuous satisfaction of requirements.

Model checking [11] is a prominent class of formal analysis methods. It uses a variety of languages to represent systems, from finite-state to infinite-state machines, from discrete-time to timed or hybrid systems, from non-deterministic automata to stochastic models, and from synchronous to asynchronous communicating programs. Given a formal semantics of the input language, model checking can also be applied to models defined for other purposes, e.g., architectural description or simulation, or directly to source code. There is a wide range of options for property specification, ranging from simple reachability or invariant properties to temporal properties, and from safety to liveness properties. Depending on the modelling language, temporal properties can be specified in different logics, e.g., either propositional or first-order. The model checking problem is solved algorithmically by a procedure that decides if the model satisfies the property or finds a counterexample. When the problem is undecidable, e.g., for software, the model checking procedure may be incomplete.

Another major class of formal analysis methods corresponds to those based on deductive verification [11]. Properties and systems are usually represented in first-order logic, higher-order logics, or specific theories (arithmetic, sets, continuous functions). Deductive verification methods are based on the generation of proof obligations that encode the correctness of the system. Depending on the underlying logic, these proof obligations are discharged by interactive theorem provers, automatic theorem provers where the proof is extracted from the specification and additional annotations, or Satisfiability Modulo Theories (SMT) solvers.

In general, formal analysis methods are independent of specific concerns and can be applied to SCP concerns as long as the requirements can be formalised in the property language. There exist however more specific formal analysis methods for SCP taking into account faults or attacker models.

Examples of formal analysis methods for the different concerns include:

- **Safety:** *Model-based safety analysis* [7], to formally analyse the fault configurations leading to a system failure, given a behavioural model.
- **Cybersecurity:** *Source code static analysis* [36], to derive various runtime properties and find various kinds of errors in programs without executing them, and which can address cybersecurity considerations.
- **Privacy:** *GDPR compliance formal verification* [23], to formally ensure that a system satisfies GDPR requirements.
- **General:** *Deductive verification* [21], to ensure that source code conforms to its formal specification.
- **System-type-focused:** *Reachability analysis-based verification for safety-critical hybrid systems* [41], to exhaustively explore a system's evolution over time, given an initial input range.

3.6 Semi-formal Analysis

This type of V&V methods deals with the evaluation of systems and components by using structured means whose application does not result in a mathematical proof. The methods enable that confidence in system dependability is developed in relation to characteristics of an automated system such as risks, faults, vulnerabilities, and threats. The methods also contribute to the avoidance and identification of these issues, and to the recovery from them.

As a mathematically rigorous approach to SCP V&V of complex systems is unfeasible in many cases, semi-formal techniques are used to complement formal V&V. System decomposition, abstraction, and specific models reduce SCP V&V to sub-problems of limited scope that may be addressed using semi-formal methods and tools. These methods and tools can rely on models, architectural principles, mathematical or probabilistic calculus, qualitative and quantitative analysis, and simulation, among other means, while also addressing compliance with engineering and assurance standards.

Semi-formal analysis also enables the evaluation of general characteristics of a system that contribute to SCP, e.g., about the traceability between system artefacts. These characteristics indirectly address automated system SCP by confirming the fulfilment of conditions needed for SCP. For instance, requirements traceability contributes to assuring that the correct and expected functionality has been implemented in a system. This in turn contributes to developing confidence in system reliability and consequently in SCP. In other words, if someone cannot confirm that the correct and expected functionality has been implemented in a system, it might not be possible to develop sufficient confidence in system SCP.

Examples of V&V methods of this type for the different concerns include:

- **Safety:** *Model-based dependability assessment* [16], with which system and safety engineers share a common system model created using a model-based development process and extend the system model with a fault model as well as relevant portions of the physical system to be controlled, also enabling safety analysis automation.
- **Cybersecurity:** *Wireless interface network security assessment* [32], to analyse a system's robustness against network security attacks carried out through wireless interfaces by evaluating (1) CANBUS-based control network security and teleoperation and (2) supervision network security.
- **Privacy:** *Model-based assurance and certification* [12], to justify system dependability in compliance with standards, e.g., privacy ones, by taking advantage of structured information specifications about a system, about the standards, and about their relation.
- **General:** *Knowledge-centric system artefact quality analysis* [34], to quantitatively determine the suitability of system artefacts by exploiting ontologies and semantic information, and according to selected criteria such as correctness, consistency, and completeness.
- **System-type-focused:** *Model-based avionics software specification and verification* [35], which is based on the modelling of the DO-178C standard and can contribute to requirements V&V, among other tasks.

3.7 Informal Analysis

Although in VALU3S we have not reviewed informal analysis methods, we include them in our classification for completeness. These methods are based on human reasoning and subjectivity, without a predefined underlying formalism or structure.

Walkthrough [20] is among the most common informal analysis methods. It corresponds to the situation in which the producer of some system artefact presents it to others for defect identification. A programmer performing a source code peer review is another example. In both cases, the application of the method could aim to detect SCP issues, as well as to analyse some general or system-type-focused characteristic.

4   Application of the Classification

The proposed classification scheme has been used for the review of V&V methods [43] in VALU3S. Such usage shows how the classification has helped in a real method classification effort. The outcome also allows us to claim that the scheme can be a feasible means for the classification of V&V methods for SCP of automated system.

Seventy-three people from 31 organisations contributed to the review of 53 V&V methods for automated systems. The people cover different roles for automated system V&V, such as researchers, systems engineers, and tool vendors, and the organisations include large enterprises, small and medium-sized enterprises, and research institutions from the automotive, agriculture, railway, healthcare, aerospace, and industrial automation domains. The complete list of methods is presented in Table 1, considering their different method types and concerns (Safety – Sa, Cybersecurity – C, Privacy – P, General – G, System-type-focused – Sy). Some V&V methods map to several types. For

Table 1. Classification of V&V methods with the proposed scheme.

Injection: Fault injection in FPGAs (Sa, Sy), Interface fault inj. (G), Model-based fault inj. for safety analysis (Sa), Model-implemented attack inj. (C), Model-implemented fault inj. (Sa), Simulation-based attack inj. at system-level (C), Simulation-based fault inj. at system-level (Sa), Software-implemented fault inj. (Sa, G), Vulnerability and attack inj. (C)

Simulation: Assessment of cybersecurity-informed safety (Sa, C), CPU verification (Sa, C, G, Sy), Failure detection and diagnosis in robotic systems (Sa, C, G, Sy), Fault injection in FPGAs (Sa, Sy), Kalman filter-based fault detector (C), Model-implemented attack inj. (C), Model-implemented fault inj. (Sa), Simulation-based fault inj. at system-level (Sa), Simulation-based fault inj. at system-level (Sa), Simulation-based testing for human-robot collaboration (Sa, Sy), Test optimization for simulation-based testing of automated systems (Sa, G), V&V of machine learning-based systems using simulators (Sa, C), Virtual & augmented reality-based user interaction V&V and technology acceptance (Sa, G), Simulation-based robot verif. (Sa, G, Sy), Virtual architecture development and simulated evaluation of software concepts (Sa, G)

Testing: Assessment of cybersecurity-informed safety (Sa, C), Behaviour-driven formal model dev. (Sa, G), Behaviour-driven model dev. and test-driven model review (G), CPU verification (Sa, C, G, Sy), Fault inj. in FPGAs (Sa, Sy), Interface fault inj. (G), Intrusion detection for wireless sensor networks based on Weak Model Processes state estimation (C), Machine learning model validation (Sa, G, Sy), Model-based mutation testing (G), Model-based robustness testing (G), Model-based testing (G), Penetration testing of industrial systems (C, Sy), Risk-based testing (G), Signal analysis and probing (G, Sy), Simulation-based testing for human-robot collab. (Sa, Sy), Software component testing (Sa, G), Software-implemented fault inj. (Sa, G), Test parallelization and automation (G), Vulnerability and attack inj. (C), Wireless interface network security assessment (C)

(continued)

Table 1. (*continued*)

Runtime verification: Behaviour-driven model dev. and test-driven model review (G), Dynamic analysis of concurrent programs (Sa, G, Sy), Failure detection and diagnosis in robotic systems (Sa, C, G, Sy), Fault inj. in FPGAs (Sa, Sy), Model-based formal specification and verif. of robotic systems (Sa, G, Sy), Runtime verif. based on formal specification (Sa, G), Simulation-based robot verif. (Sa, G, Sy), Test oracle observation at runtime (Sa, G)

Formal Analysis: Behaviour-driven formal model dev. (Sa, G), CPU verification (Sa, C, G, Sy), Deductive verif. (Sa, G), Formal requirements validation (Sa, G), Model checking (Sa, G), Model-based design verif. (Sa, G), Model-based fault inj. for safety analysis (Sa), Model-based formal specification and verif. of robotic systems (Sa, G, Sy), Model-based safety analysis (Sa, C), Reachability-analysis-based verif. for safety-critical hybrid systems (Sa, G, Sy), Source code static analysis (Sa, C, P, G), Theorem proving and satisfiability modulo theories solving (Sa, G), V&V of machine learning-based systems using simulators (Sa, C)

Semi-formal Analysis: Behaviour-driven model dev. and test-driven model review (G), Code design and coding standard compliance checking (Sa), Failure detection and diagnosis in robotic systems (Sa, C, G, Sy), Human interaction safety analysis (Sa), Intrusion detection for wireless sensor networks based on Weak Model Processes state estimation (C), Kalman filter-based fault detector (C), Knowledge-centric system artefact quality analysis (Sa, C, P, G), Knowledge-centric traceability mngmt. (Sa, C, P, G), Model-based assurance and certification (Sa, C, P, G), Model-based design verif. (Sa, G), Model-based safety analysis (Sa, C), Model-based threat analysis (C), Risk analysis (Sa, C), Source code static analysis (Sa, C, P, G), Traceability mngmt. of safety software (Sa), Vulnerability analysis of cryptographic modules against hardware-based attacks (C), Wireless interface network security assessment (C)

---

instance, simulation-based robot verification uses both simulation and runtime verification. Further information about the review of the methods can be found in [43], including a description of the methods, an analysis of the relationships between them, information about tool support, and an assessment of strengths and limitations.

5 Conclusion

It is essential that the manufacturers and component suppliers of automated systems use adequate verification and validation (V&V) methods to confirm that the systems' safety, cybersecurity, and privacy (SCP) requirements are satisfied. This requires that the manufacturers and suppliers clearly understand the characteristics of the methods, when the methods should be used, and for what purposes.

We have presented a new classification scheme to categorise V&V methods used to evaluate automated systems with respect to SCP requirements. The scheme provides practitioners and researchers with a clear and easy-to-understand set of categories where V&V methods could be selected from. For example, the scheme can aid in identifying V&V methods to evaluate safety of a system based on its response to some phenomenon introduced. The method types considered are injection, simulation, testing, runtime verification, formal analysis, semi-formal analysis, and informal analysis. The methods can deal with different concerns: SCP, general concerns that indirectly contribute to SCP, or system-type-focused concerns.

The scheme has been successfully used by 73 researchers and practitioners to classify 53 V&V methods, covering six different application domains. This makes us confident in the validity of the classification scheme.

As future work, we will continue classifying V&V methods with the proposed scheme, e.g., methods combined or developed in VALU3S. This will allow us to further validate the classification. It will also be useful to extend the guidance on how to use the classification and how to select methods from the classified ones.

Acknowledgments. The research leading to this paper has received funding from the VALU3S (H2020-ECSEL grant agreement no 876852; Spain's MICINN ref. PCI2020-112001), iRel4.0 (H2020-ECSEL grant agreement no 876659; MICINN ref. PCI2020-112240), and Treasure (JCCM SBPLY/19/180501/000270; European Regional Development Fund) projects, and from the Ramon y Cajal Program (MICINN RYC-2017-22836; European Social Fund). We are also grateful to all the VALU3S partners that have provided input and feedback for the development of the classification.

References

1. Amalthea4public project: D3.1 - Analysis of state of the art V&V techniques (2015)
2. Arfelt, E., Basin, D., Debois, S.: Monitoring the GDPR. In: Sako, K., Schneider, S., Ryan, P.Y.A. (eds.) ESORICS 2019. LNCS, vol. 11735, pp. 681–699. Springer, Cham (2019). https://doi.org/10.1007/978-3-030-29959-0_33
3. Avizienis, A., et al.: Fundamental concepts of dependability. University of Newcastle (2001)
4. Barbosa, R., et al.: The VALU3S ECSEL project: verification and validation of automated systems safety and security. In: DSD 2020 (2020)
5. Bartocci, E., Manjunath, N., Mariani, L., Mateis, C., Ničković, D.: Automatic failure explanation in CPS models. In: Ölveczky, P.C., Salaün, G. (eds.) SEFM 2019. LNCS, vol. 11724, pp. 69–86. Springer, Cham (2019). https://doi.org/10.1007/978-3-030-30446-1_4
6. Belmonte, L., et al.: Feeling of safety and comfort towards a socially assistive unmanned aerial vehicle that monitors people in a virtual home. Sensors 21(3), 908 (2021)
7. Bozzano, M., Cimatti, A., Griggio, A., Mattarei, C.: Efficient anytime techniques for model-based safety analysis. In: Kroening, D., Păsăreanu, C.S. (eds.) CAV 2015. LNCS, vol. 9206, pp. 603–621. Springer, Cham (2015). https://doi.org/10.1007/978-3-319-21690-4_41
8. Cassar, I., et al: A survey of runtime monitoring instrumentation techniques. PrePost@iFM (2017)
9. CENELEC: EN 50128 - Railway applications - Communication, signalling and processing systems - Software for railway control and protection systems (2020)
10. Cimatti, A., Tian, C., Tonetta, S.: Assumption-based runtime verification with partial observability and resets. In: Finkbeiner, B., Mariani, L. (eds.) RV 2019. LNCS, vol. 11757, pp. 165–184. Springer, Cham (2019). https://doi.org/10.1007/978-3-030-32079-9_10
11. Clarke, E.M., et al.: Handbook of Model Checking. Springer, Heidelberg (2018). https://doi.org/10.1007/978-3-319-10575-8
12. de la Vara, J.L., et al.: Assurance and certification of cyber-physical systems: the AMASS open source ecosystem. J. Syst. Softw. 171, 110812 (2021)
13. Dias, R., et al.: Verifying concurrent programs using contracts. In: ICST 2017 (2017)
14. Duckham, M., Kulik, L.: Simulation of obfuscation and negotiation for location privacy. In: Cohn, A.G., Mark, D.M. (eds.) COSIT 2005. LNCS, vol. 3693, pp. 31–48. Springer, Heidelberg (2005). https://doi.org/10.1007/11556114_3

15. Fonseca, J., et al.: Analysis of field data on web security vulnerabilities. IEEE Trans. Dependable Secure Comput. **11**(2), 89–100 (2014)
16. Gallina, B., et al.: Multi-concern dependability-centered assurance for space systems via ConcertoFLA. Ada-Europe (2018)
17. Halfind, W.G.J., et al.: A classification of SQL injection attacks and countermeasures. In: ISSSE 2006 (2006)
18. Herdt, V., et al.: Efficient cross-level testing for processor verification: a RISC-V case-study. In: FDL 2020 (2020)
19. Humbatova, N., et al.: Taxonomy of real faults in deep learning systems. In: ICSE 2020 (2020)
20. IEC: IEC 61508 - Functional safety of electrical/electronic/programmable electronic safety-related systems (2011)
21. Hähnle, R., Huisman, M.: Deductive software verification: from pen-and-paper proofs to industrial tools. In: Steffen, B., Woeginger, G. (eds.) Computing and Software Science. LNCS, vol. 10000, pp. 345–373. Springer, Cham (2019). https://doi.org/10.1007/978-3-319-91908-9_18
22. IEEE: IEEE Std 1012 - IEEE Standard for System, Software, and Hardware V&V (2016)
23. Kammueller, F.: Formal modeling and analysis of data protection for GDPR compliance of IoT healthcare systems. In: SMC 2018 (2018)
24. Khalastchi, E., Kalech, M.: On fault detection and diagnosis in robotic systems. ACM Comput. Surv. **51**(1), 9 (2018)
25. Kuhn, T., Antonino, P.O., Bachorek, A.: A simulator coupling architecture for the creation of digital twins. In: Muccini, H., et al. (eds.) ECSA 2020. CCIS, vol. 1269, pp. 326–339. Springer, Cham (2020). https://doi.org/10.1007/978-3-030-59155-7_25
26. Kramer, A., Legeard, B.: Model-Based Testing Essentials. Wiley, Hoboken (2016)
27. Laskey, M., et al.: DART: noise injection for robust imitation learning. In: CoRL 2017 (2017)
28. Luckcuck, M., et al.: Formal specification and verification of autonomous robotic systems: a survey. ACM Comput. Surv. **52**(5), 100 (2019)
29. Nair, S., et al.: An extended systematic literature review on provision of evidence for safety certification. Inf. Softw. Technol. **56**(7), 689–717 (2014)
30. Natella, R., et al.: Assessing dependability with software fault injection: a survey. ACM Comput. Surv. **48**(3), 44 (2016)
31. Oxford UK Dictionary: method (2021). https://www.lexico.com/definition/method
32. Pan, L., et al.: Cyber security attacks to modern vehicular systems. J. Inf. Secur. Appl. **36**, 30–100 (2017)
33. Pandit, H.J., O'Sullivan, D., Lewis, D.: Test-driven approach towards GDPR compliance. In: Acosta, M., Cudré-Mauroux, P., Maleshkova, M., Pellegrini, T., Sack, H., Sure-Vetter, Y. (eds.) SEMANTiCS 2019. LNCS, vol. 11702, pp. 19–33. Springer, Cham (2019). https://doi.org/10.1007/978-3-030-33220-4_2
34. Parra, E., et al.: Advances in artefact quality analysis for safety-critical systems. In: ISSRE 2019 (2019)
35. Paz, A., El Boussaidi, G.: A requirements modelling language to facilitate avionics software verification and certification. In: RET 2019 (2019)
36. Rival, X., Yi, K.: Introduction to Static Analysis. An Abstract Interpretation Perspective. MIT Press (2020)
37. Sangchoolie, B., et al.: A study of the interplay between safety and security using model-implemented fault injection. In: EDCC 2018 (2018)
38. Savary, A., Frappier, M., Leuschel, M., Lanet, J.-L.: Model-based robustness testing in event-B using mutation. In: Calinescu, R., Rumpe, B. (eds.) SEFM 2015. LNCS, vol. 9276, pp. 132–147. Springer, Cham (2015). https://doi.org/10.1007/978-3-319-22969-0_10
39. Skoglund, M., et al.: Black-box testing for security-informed safety of automated driving systems. In: VTC 2021-Spring (2021)

40. Timperley, C.S., et al.: Crashing simulated planes is cheap: Can simulation detect robotics bugs early? In: ICST 2018 (2018)
41. Tsachouridis, V.A., et al.: Formal analysis of the Schulz matrix inversion algorithm: a paradigm towards computer aided verification of general matrix flow solvers. Numer. Algebra Control Optim. **10**(2), 177–206 (2020)
42. US DoD: Defense Modeling & Simulation Coordination Office, V&V Technique Taxonomy (2001). https://vva.msco.mil/default.htm?Ref_Docs/VVTechniques/
43. VALU3S project: D3.1 - V&V methods for SCP evaluation of automated systems (2021)
44. Yang, Y., et al.: Man-in-the-middle attack test-bed investigating cyber-security vulnerabilities in smart grid SCADA systems. In: SUPERGEN 2012 (2012)

Risk Identification Based on Architectural Patterns

Maritta Heisel[1]([✉]) and Aida Omerovic[2]

[1] University of Duisburg-Essen, Duisburg, Germany
maritta.heisel@uni-due.de
[2] Norwegian Computing Center, Oslo, Norway
aida@nr.no

Abstract. We present a novel approach for the identification of risks for IT-based systems, where we base risk identification on the system architecture, in particular, the architectural principles a system is built on. Such principles can be expressed as architectural patterns, which are amenable to specific risks. We represent those risks – concerning e.g. safety, security or fault tolerance – as *Risk Issue Questionnaires* (RIQs). A RIQ enumerates the typical risks associated with a given architectural pattern. Risk identification proceeds by identifying the architectural patterns contained in a system architecture and processing the associated RIQs, i.e., for each issue in the RIQ it has to be assessed whether it is relevant for the system under analysis or not. We present an example of a RIQ, a RIQ-driven risk identification method, an application example, and the results of an initial experiment evaluating the RIQ method.

1 Introduction

For critical IT-based systems, it is crucial to establish a proper risk management process. Such a process consists of five steps (see e.g. [1]): 1) Establish the context; 2) Identify risks; 3) Estimate risks; 4) Evaluate risks; 5) Treat risks. The identification of relevant risks plays a crucial role, because risks that are overlooked in the risk identification step will not be taken into account in the subsequent steps of the risk management process. Note, however, that risk identification is not concerned with identifying possible risk mitigation measures.

This work aims at making the risk identification process systematic, repeatable, and as complete as possible, building on previously acquired risk knowledge for similar systems. For this purpose, the architecture of the system to be analyzed is taken into account. Critical systems are often structured according to general architectural principles, such as redundancy, or control loops. These provide valuable information about the possible risks involved with the system and hence are a good basis to identify risks.

Each architectural principle can be represented by a pattern, and is associated with typical risks. For example, an interactive system where operators are involved has the risk of a misbehavior or misconception of the operator. Every communication channel between system components can be subject to attacks,

© Springer Nature Switzerland AG 2021
A. C. R. Paiva et al. (Eds.): QUATIC 2021, CCIS 1439, pp. 341–355, 2021.
https://doi.org/10.1007/978-3-030-85347-1_25

etc. We propose *risk issue questionnaires* (RIQs) as a means to document the risks that are relevant for an architectural pattern. Such risks can be related to safety, security, or reliability in general. RIQs make up a knowledge base that can be updated over time, when new risks become known for some class of system.

We start out from the architecture of the system to be analyzed for risks. Either, that architecture is already implemented, or it has been chosen in the design phase of the system development process. Then, our method can be used to validate the architectural decisions before realizing them. The first step in the risk identification process is to identify all architectural patterns that are present in the system architecture, and to determine the instantiations of these patterns. Then, the RIQs for the relevant patterns are processed, i.e., for each risk enumerated in a RIQ, it is decided whether that risk is relevant for the given system or not. In this way, all known risks (i.e., all risks documented in a RIQ) that are associated with architectural patterns underlying the system are collected and can be used as the basis for subsequent risk management steps.

This procedure helps to identify all relevant risks in a structured manner, and serves as a documentation of the risk identification process, which may be relevant for certification and assurance purposes.

We discuss RIQs in general and give an example of a RIQ in Sect. 2. Section 3 describes a risk identification method based on RIQs. Section 4 gives an example of a risk identification for a patient monitoring system. That system was also used for an experiment, where two groups of students were given the task to identify risks, one using RIQs and one without (Sect. 5). Related work is discussed in Sect. 6, before concluding and giving an outlook on future work in Sect. 7.

2   Risk Issue Questionnaires

Risk Issue Questionnaires refer to architectural patterns[1] that can be given as informal drawings, see Fig. 1. Here, we number the components and connections and refer to these numbers in the corresponding RIQ. Different kinds of system architectures are vulnerable to specific kinds of risks. For example, the process monitoring architecture given in Fig. 1 has risks related to the functioning of sensors and display, but also related to the communication channels between those and the control software.

Each risk is associated with unwanted incidents that harm an asset, and a risk level, often expressed by the likelihood of that incident to happen. The issues in the RIQs describe conditions or scenarios that might lead to harm of an asset. We use the term "issue" because we do not want to distinguish between threats, vulnerabilities, attacks, etc. Everything that can lead to harm of an asset can be listed in a RIQ. Thus, RIQs are independent of concrete threat models.

Issues deemed relevant must be investigated further, in later steps of the risk management process. The unwanted incidents are not part of the RIQ, because they depend on the concrete system and the assets related to it.

---

[1] See e.g. [2] for software architectural patterns. System architectures are more general than software architectures, because they can contain hardware components, as well.

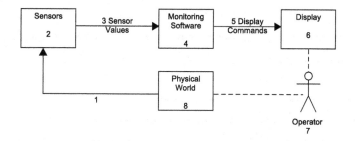

Fig. 1. Architectural pattern: process monitoring

We have set up RIQs for a number of different architectural patterns, instances of which often occur as parts of critical IT-based systems. In the following, we present the RIQ for process monitoring systems in Sect. 2.1. Further RIQs are sketched in Sect. 2.2.

The architectural patterns for which we have set up RIQs occur in many existing critical systems, but, of course, other kinds of architectures (e.g., peer-to-peer systems) are relevant, too, and should also be equipped with RIQs in the future. The RIQs existing so far were set up by the authors of this paper, who have long-lasting experience in risk management, as well as safety and security of IT-based systems. However, we do not claim that those RIQs are indeed complete. The contribution of this work is not only the content of the specific RIQs, but – more importantly – the idea to exploit architectural properties of critical systems for risk identification. We aim for evolving RIQ repositories, where many contributors can add new knowledge and experience.

2.1   RIQ for Process Monitoring

Figure 1 shows the architectural pattern for process monitoring systems. Such systems use sensors to monitor a part of the physical world to inform operators about its state, using a display. Based on the displayed information, the operator may take actions that are outside the scope of the system to be analyzed.

In the following, we present the RIQ for process monitoring systems, using a different font. The numbers of the RIQ items refer to the numbers used in Fig. 1. Each entry describes a possible risk, and the question to be answered is whether the described risk issue is relevant for the system under analysis or not. Each high-level issue (numbered 1–8) may contain sub-issues that further detail the high-level issue. If a high-level issue is assessed not to be relevant, its sub-issues are irrelevant, too.

RIQ 1 Process Monitoring (PM)

1 Sensors cannot read entities from physical world properly (even though they function as intended)
  1.1 Sensors not correctly installed
  1.2 Inappropriate Sensors
    1.2.1 Sensors not fast enough
    1.2.2 Sensors do not measure what is needed
2 Sensor delivers wrong (HAZOP[2]) values
  2.1 Sensor is single point of failure (insufficient redundancy)
  2.2 Sensor not sufficiently physically protected against environmental influences
  2.3 Sensor not sufficiently physically protected against attacks
  2.4 Sensor needs maintenance / repair
  2.5 Sensor is hacked
  2.6 Sensor values do not reflect reality
3 Monitoring Software receives wrong (HAZOP) values from sensors
  3.1 Because of wrong sensor values, see issue 2
  3.2 Wrong value received from fake sensor (man-in-the-middle)
  3.3 Issues with communication channel. Process RIQ for communication channels
4 Monitoring Software affected
  4.1 Monitoring Software has inaccurate/wrong internal state
    4.1.1 Because of wrong sensor values, see issues 1 - 3
    4.1.2 Internal state not properly initialized
    4.1.3 Wrong computation of internal state
    4.1.4 Integrity of internal state destroyed by attack
  4.2 Monitoring Software is broken down
    4.2.1 Due to hardware problems
    4.2.2 Due to attack on availability
    4.2.3 Due to problems with system software
  4.3 Monitoring Software computes wrong / incoherent (HAZOP) display commands due to attack
  4.4 Monitoring Software computes wrong / incoherent (HAZOP) display commands due to programming errors
5 Display receives wrong (HAZOP) commands
  5.1 Due to problems with Control Software (see issue 4)
  5.2 Wrong command received from fake component (man-in-the-middle)
  5.3 Issues with communication channel. Process RIQ_CC
6 Display does not function correctly (HAZOP)
  6.1 Display is single point of failure (insufficient redundancy)
  6.2 Display not sufficiently physically protected against environmental influences
  6.3 Display not sufficiently physically protected against attacks
  6.4 Display needs maintenance / repair
  6.5 Display is hacked
7 Operator does not react as intended
  7.1 Operator cannot correctly interpret displayed information
    7.1.1 Too much information given
    7.1.2 Not enough information given
    7.1.3 Irrelevant information given
    7.1.4 Information incomprehensible
  7.2 Problems with Operator
    7.2.1 Operator is malicious
    7.2.2 Operator is naive / careless / not concentrated

---

[2] When we mention the term "HAZOP", we mean that the HAZOP guide-words should be considered to determine what "wrong" values may be: NO OR NOT, MORE, LESS, AS WELL AS, PART OF, REVERSE, OTHER THAN / INSTEAD, EARLY, LATE, BEFORE, AFTER.

7.2.3 Operator is mistaken about the situation / has wrong information
7.2.4 Operator is not authentic
  7.3 Operator cannot act as intended
 8 Unexpected condition in physical world

Note that this RIQ covers issues related to security (e.g., Issue 4.2.2) as
well as to safety (e.g., Issue 2.2) and fault tolerance (e.g., Issue 2.1). Also non-
technical risks are taken into account (e.g., Issue 7.2.2). In general, there is no
limitation to what kind of risk can be addressed in a RIQ.

2.2 Further RIQs

In addition to the RIQ for process monitoring systems, we have set up RIQs for
the following architectural patterns:

Process control systems. Such systems are similar to process monitoring
systems, but are equipped with actuators instead of a display, in order to
control the surrounding physical world. The corresponding RIQ has large
parts in common with RIQ 1.
Communication channels. The corresponding RIQ considers risks concerning
the connection between two components. Risks concerning the connected
components are not considered. The issues mainly concern confidentiality
and integrity of the data transmitted via the channel, as well as bandwidth
problems and hardware failures.
Interactive systems. The corresponding architecture consists of a system that
is connected to a user via input and output devices. The RIQ issues concern
malicious or non-authentic users (similarly to issue 7 of RIQ 1), as well as
failing or attacked input/output devices.
Persistent Storage Systems. Here, the architecture consists of a storage component and its clients. Risk issues concern confidentiality, integrity and availability of the storage component.

3 Risk Identification Method

RIQs can be used to systematically identify risks for a given IT-based system,
based on its system architecture. Apart from the system architecture, the assets
that shall be protected are input to the method. The steps of the method are:

1. Identify the architectural patterns that are used in the system. This is done
   based on a static architectural description of the system.
2. For each such pattern, instantiate it and the corresponding RIQs.
3. For each instantiated RIQ, cross out the issues that are not relevant; annotate
   the reason why they are not relevant. For those issues that are relevant,
   describe the corresponding risk.

In the first step of the method, the architectural patterns that are contained
in the system architecture must be identified, in order to determine the RIQs
that need to be processed. Then, in step 2, the identified architectural patterns

as well as the corresponding RIQs have to be instantiated. Thus, patterns and the questions of the RIQ become specialized for the system to be analyzed. For example, if the operator in the process monitoring part of a system is instantiated with a nurse, then Issue 7.2.2 of the RIQ becomes: "Nurse is naive/careless/not concentrated".

The so instantiated RIQ can then be processed (step 3). For each instantiated issue, it is determined whether it is relevant or not. If a top-level issue is deemed to be not relevant, its sub-issues do not need to be considered. The reasons for assessing an issue to be irrelevant need to be documented. Often, systems are subject to change, which makes it necessary to re-consider the identified risks. When the reasons for disregarding an issue are documented, this helps to determine whether the given reasons are still valid or not. For each issue assessed to be relevant, the affected asset must be documented. There only is a risk for the system, if one of its associated assets could be harmed. Furthermore, it is of importance to document the unwanted incident that is made possible by the condition or scenario described in the RIQ.

4   Example

We have applied the risk identification method on the example of a patient monitoring system in an intensive care unit (ICU) of a hospital, taken from [3]. The informal description is as follows:

> A patient monitoring program is required for the intensive-care unit of a hospital. Each patient is monitored by an analog device which measures factors such as pulse, temperature, blood pressure, and skin resistance. The program reads these factors on a periodic basis (specified for each patient) and stores the factors in a database. For each patient, safe ranges for each factor are also specified by medical staff. If a factor falls outside a patient's safe range, or if an analog device fails, then the nurses' station is notified.

The system architecture is given in Fig. 2. As relevant assets we identify the health of the patient, which is safety-related, and the confidentiality of the patients' data, which is security-related. This constitutes the input for the risk identification method described in Sect. 3.

We identify four architectural patterns contained in the system architecture (step 1):

- *Process Monitoring*. The instance of that pattern (as part of step 2 of the method) is given in Fig. 3.
- *Interactive System*, where the instance consists of the Medical Staff as a user, the Keyboard/ Mouse as an input device, and the Screen as an output device.

- Two instances of *Persistent Storage*, one with Periods & Ranges, one with Factors Database as the persistent storage, both connected to the Monitor Machine.
- Two instances of *Communication Channel*, one for the channel *Register Value* between the Analog Devices and the Monitor Machine, the other for the channel *Notify* between the Monitor Machine and the Nurses' Station.

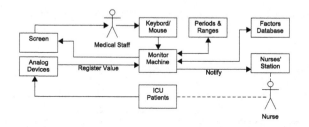

Fig. 2. System architecture for patient monitoring system

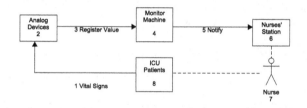

Fig. 3. Process monitoring part of patient monitoring system

After instantiating the architectural patterns, the RIQs have to be instantiated, too (step 2), and subsequently, all issues contained in the instantiated RIQs have to be processed (step 3).

We present the results of processing the RIQ for process monitoring in RIQ 2, using the instantiated RIQ 1. Issues that are assessed to be irrelevant are grayed out. For irrelevant issues, the sub-issues are not shown. Comments are given below.

RIQ 2 Instantiated RIQ_PM for Patient Monitoring System

1 Analog Devices cannot read entities from physical world properly (even though they function as intended)
  1.1 Analog Devices not correctly installed
  1.2 Inappropriate Analog Devices
2 Analog Devices delivers wrong (HAZOP) values
  2.1 Analog Devices are single point of failure (insufficient redundancy)
  2.2 Analog Devices not sufficiently physically protected against environmental influences
  2.3 Analog Devices not sufficiently physically protected against attacks
  2.4 Analog Devices need maintenance / repair
  2.5 Analog Devices are hacked
  2.6 Analog Devices values do not reflect reality
3 Monitor Machine receives wrong (HAZOP) values from sensors
  3.1 Because of wrong sensor values, see Issue 2
  3.2 Wrong value received from fake sensor (man-in-the-middle)
  3.3 Issues with communication channel. Process RIQ_CC
4 Monitor Machine affected
  4.1 Monitor Machine has inaccurate/wrong internal state
    4.1.1 Because of wrong sensor values, see Issues 1 - 3
    4.1.2 Internal state not properly initialized
    4.1.3 Wrong computation of internal state
    4.1.4 Integrity of internal state destroyed by attack
  4.2 Monitor Machine is broken down
    4.2.1 Due to hardware problems
    4.2.2 Due to attack on availability
    4.2.3 Due to problems with system software
  4.3 Monitor Machine computes wrong / incoherent (HAZOP) display commands due to attack
  4.4 Monitor Machine computes wrong / incoherent (HAZOP) display commands due to programming errors
5 Nurses' Station receives wrong (HAZOP) commands
  5.1 Due to problems with Control Software (see Issue 4)
  5.2 Wrong command received from fake component
  5.3 Issues with communication channel. Process RIQ_CC
6 Nurses' Station does not function correctly (HAZOP)
  6.1 Nurses' Station is single point of failure (insufficient redundancy)
  6.2 Nurses' Station not sufficiently physically protected against environmental influences
  6.3 Nurses' Station not sufficiently physically protected against attacks
  6.4 Nurses' Station needs maintenance / repair
  6.5 Nurses' Station is hacked
7 Nurse does not react as intended
  7.1 Nurse cannot correctly interpret displayed information
  7.2 Problems with Nurse
    7.2.1 Nurse is malicious
    7.2.2 Nurse is naive / careless / not concentrated
    7.2.3 Nurse is mistaken about the situation / has wrong information
    7.2.4 Nurse is not authentic
  7.3 Nurse cannot act as intended
8 Unexpected condition in ICU Patients

By default, all issues should be considered relevant. Issues should be excluded from further analysis only if there are good reasons to do so. That assessment very much depends on the specific situation. For example, if the system is already in use for some time, some issues can be eliminated because of past experience with the system.

For our example, we assume that the system is already in operation. Then, we can exclude for example Issues 1.2, 2.1, 2.6, 4.1.2, 4.1.3, 4.2.3. Regular maintenance leads to an exclusion of Issue 2.4. If we assume that the loudspeaker in the Nurses' Station is robust, installed in a room with no extreme environmental conditions, and is protected against physical manipulation, we can exclude Issues 6.2 and 6.3.

As for the issues under 7, the intended reaction of the nurse is to go and look after the patient whose vital signs lead to raising the alarm, or check the failed Analog Device. Because of past experience, one can exclude the issues under 7.1. In contrast, the issues under 7.2 cannot be excluded, except 7.2.3, because the nurses know what their task is. Issue 7.3 only needs to be considered if the situation that a nurse falls ill in the Nurses' Station and cannot go and see a patient or inspect an Analog Device should be taken into account. An unexpected situation among the ICU patients (Issue 8) might be that a patient disconnects himself or herself from the Analog Devices.

For the Process Monitoring part of the patient monitoring system, all issues concern the asset "health of the patient". The unwanted incident is that exceeded limits of vital signs are not noticed and not treated. Issues concerning the confidentiality of patients' data become apparent when processing the RIQs for Persistent Storage and Communication Channels.

The RIQs corresponding to the other identified architectural patterns are processed in a similar way.

5   Evaluation

To evaluate our method, we conducted an experiment with students of Computer Science at the Master level, who took a course on the development of safe and secure software, but had no experience in risk identification. The experiment should serve to investigate whether a larger number of relevant risks could be identified for a system when using RIQs than without. Two groups of about equal size (about 8 persons each) were formed: the treatment group that received the RIQs, and the corresponding method, and the control group that only received information on the architectural patterns contained in the system to be considered, namely the patient monitoring system discussed in Sect. 4. The two assets ("health of the patient" and "confidentiality of patients' data") were given to both groups.

Both groups received a 10-minute introduction to the patient monitoring system, the contained architectural styles, and the risk identification task to be performed. Afterwords, both groups were given an informal example of a simple risk identification for a party plan (taken from [3]), lasting 5 min and not using

RIQs. No further input was provided to the control group. Both groups had about 60 min to complete their risk identification. The control group did not use the entire 60 min.

The treatment group was given a third presentation of about 10 min, introducing the concept of RIQs and the risk identification method presented in Sect. 3, which was exemplified with the same party plan example that both groups had seen before. For the treatment group, it has to be noted that the participants mostly processed the top-level issues only and ignored the sub-issues. This lead to identified risks that are quite high-level.

Considering the RIQ for Process Monitoring, the control group identified only 3 risks out of 8 (considering only the top-level issues), which amounts to 5 false negatives. The treatment group correctly assessed that there are risks associated with Issues 1–7. Issue 8 was mis-interpreted by the treatment group, which can be counted as a false positive.

Considering the RIQ for Communication Channels, the participants of the treatment group unfortunately did not distinguish between the two channels, for which different risks are relevant. They did not see that the bandwidth of the *Notify* channel is not an issue, because that channel only needs a very low bandwidth. Hence, one can count a false positive here. The control group identified 4 risks that can be related to communication channels, one of which was very general and could not be mapped to a RIQ issue, and one was incomprehensible.

Considering the RIQ for Persistent Storage, the treatment group correctly identified each of the 4 RIQ issues as relevant, but did not consider sub-Issues. The control group, on the other hand, identified 2 risks that can be related to sub-issues of the RIQ, but had 2 false negatives.

Considering the RIQ for Interactive Systems, the treatment group correctly identified 7 high-level risks, in comparison to 3 in the control group.

Furthermore, the control group identified 3 risks that were relevant but out of scope, because they were not related to the system under consideration but to general technical or organizational issues (e.g., blackout).

An in all, we can summarize the results of the experiment as follows:

- The control group missed a number of relevant risks, i.e., there were quite a number of false negatives. This is more severe than false positives, which would be detected in later phases of the risk management process.
- The control group identified risks not related to RIQs. However, these risks are not specific to the patient monitoring system but apply to every socio-technical system. Hence, there is no indication that the RIQs narrow the scope of the analyzes too much.
- The treatment group did not produce false negatives, but rather false positives. This means, they just instantiated the RIQs and did not reflect whether the identified risks were indeed relevant. However, this is less severe than overlooking relevant risks.
- The treatment group disregarded the sub-issues of the RIQs and referred only to the top-level issues. Hence, the identified risks are more general than necessary. This means that the work to be done is postponed to the subsequent

phases of the risk management life-cycle, which also is the case for the false positives.

All in all, the experiment indicates that the RIQs help to not overlook relevant risks, which is the most important goal associated with their use.

We also tried out our method on the real-life example of a self-healing smart power grid. An outline of the self-healing concepts as well as a part of its security risk model are presented in [4]. The system architecture given in the paper contains, among others, client-server and peer-to-peer parts, but also a process control part and an interactive part. Those risks reported in [4] that are related to the latter two architectural patterns would have been found using our RIQs. For the distributed parts, we have set up preliminary RIQs that still need refinement, but that are suitable to identify the risks enumerated in the paper.

6   Related Work

There are a number of collections of risk issues such as vulnerabilities, weaknesses or best practices that are published by different organizations on the Internet. They are exclusively concerned with cyber-security risks and do not consider other kinds of risks. We mention just a few of them:

- Common Vulnerability Scoring System (CVSS)[2] "is an open framework for communicating the characteristics and severity of software vulnerabilities."
- Common Weakness enumeration (CWE)[3]: "is a list of software and hardware weaknesses types."
- Common Weakness Risk Analysis Framework (CWRAF)[4] "provides a framework for scoring software weaknesses in a consistent, flexible, open manner, while accommodating context for the various business domains."
- Common Vulnerabilities and Exposures (CVE)[5] "is a dictionary of publicly disclosed cyber-security vulnerabilities and exposures"
- ENISA IoT security checklist[6]: "ENISA's online tool for IoT and Smart Infrastructures Security"
- ATT&CK for Industrial Control Systems[7] "is a knowledge base useful for describing the actions an adversary may take while operating within an ICS network."

All of these lists have in common that they are quite specific for cyber-security or specific kinds of systems such as IoT (Internet of Things) systems, or industrial

---

[2] https://www.first.org/cvss/, accessed April 19, 2020.

[3] https://cwe.mitre.org/data/index.html, accessed April 19, 2021.

[4] https://cwe.mitre.org/cwraf/, accessed April 19, 2021.

[5] https://cve.mitre.org/cve/, accessed April 19, 2021.

[6] https://www.enisa.europa.eu/news/enisa-news/your-must-have-iot-security-checkl ist-enisas-online-tool-for-iot-and-smart-infrastructures-security, accessed April 19, 2021.

[7] https://collaborate.mitre.org/attackics/index.php, accessed April 19, 2021.

control systems. Some of them focus on vulnerabilities of specific technologies, some enumerate best practices (i.e., they are concerned with risk mitigation, not risk identification). CWRAF mentions different kinds of systems, such as Control Systems and Network Communications, which are associated with so-called vignettes[8]: "A vignette provides a shareable, formalized way to define a particular environment, the role that software plays within that environment, and an organization's priorities with respect to software security." Thus, vignettes can be regarded as a kind of pattern.

Apart from being specialized for security, none of the above-mentioned lists takes architectural patterns as the basis for risk identification.

STRIDE [5] stands for Spoofing, Tampering, Repudiation, Information disclosure, Denial of service, Elevation of privilege. It is a method for identifying security threats, which is based on a dataflow diagram of the system, rather than its architecture.

The method for identification and modeling of cyber-security risks in the context of smart power grids elaborated by Omerovic et al. [4] relies on brainstorming sessions between risk and domain experts to identify relevant risks. Risk identification is not reported to rely on the properties of the system architecture.

Pattern-based approaches to security analysis are abuse frames [6] and attack patterns [7], which do not take the system architecture into account, as well as misuse patterns [8], which are specialized to cloud computing.

The method proposed by Halikidis et al. [9] considers software architectures that already contain security patterns. Their method assesses security risks for such systems by using fuzzy-set theory and fuzzy fault trees. Thus, the method does not address risk identification but supports later steps of the risk management process.

Wirtz and Heisel have proposed patterns to represent threats [10]. Using such patterns, they have defined a method for security risk identification [11], which is based on problem-frame models of the functional requirements for the system in question. System architectures are not taken into account. Casola et al. [12] propose a format for a threat catalog that can be used in a risk analysis process.

All of the above-mentioned approaches to risk identification have in common that none of them takes the system architecture as the basis for risk identification, and they all focus on security risks. RIQs, in contrast, can also be used to identify safety and other kinds of risk.

In safety, risks are often analyzed starting from unwanted incidents, mostly accidents, which are possible because of hazards. Fault tree analysis (FTA) (see e.g., [13]), Failure Modes and Effects Analysis (FMEA) [14], and Hazard and Operability Study (HAZOP) [15] are well-known hazard analysis methods. The more recent approach System-Theoretic Process Analysis (STPA) [16] also uses guide-words, and is thus similar to HAZOP. Furthermore, safety standards such as ISO 26262 [17] require a Hazard Analysis and Risk Assessment (HARA) without specifying in detail how this has to be performed.

---

[8] https://cwe.mitre.org/cwraf/data/vignettes.html, accessed April 19, 2021.

Beckers et al. [18] have proposed a model-based method for HARA in the automotive sector, also using guide-words and taking ASILs (automotive safety integrity levels) into account.

However, to the best of our knowledge, no risk identification method has been proposed so far that is based on principles of system architectures (i.e., architectural patterns) and that is not specialized to identifying specific kinds of risk, but supports the identification of all relevant kinds of risk.

Slyngstad et al. [19] use questionnaires to identify risks in the context of software evolution. However, the identified risks are different from the ones that we consider: they are not related to the operation of an IT-based system, but rather its development process. The risks are problems that occur when the architecture of some software needs to be changed.

7   Conclusion and Outlook

In this paper, we have presented a novel method for risk identification that is based on the system architecture of the system to be analyzed. Risks are identified by determining the architectural patterns used in the system architecture, and processing risk issue questionnaires associated with such patterns. Considering the risk management process mentioned in Sect. 1, our method provides a traceable link between step 1 (context establishment) and step 2 (risk identification), where the system architecture is a necessary part of the context.

Our method is neither confined to specific kinds of systems (such industrial control systems), nor to specific kinds of risks (such as security risks). Hence, it can be applied for any system for which risk management is deemed necessary, provided that the system architecture contains patterns. Such patterns represent best practices in system design; hence, instantiations of such patterns can expected to be found in a great number of existing and future IT-based systems.

Since a system architecture can be expected to contain more than one architectural pattern, one and the same component can play different roles when the instantiations of architectural patterns overlap. Then, they are assessed according to all of the roles they can play, which contributes to the completeness of the analysis. In our example, this holds for the Monitor Machine (see Fig. 2). On the one hand, it plays the role of monitoring software. On the other hand, it also plays the role of an interactive system that has to communicate with its users. Both of these roles are covered by processing the associated RIQs.

As a limitation of the method one can consider that – in its present form – it cannot detect risks that emerge from the composition of different sub-systems. Connecting sub-systems in the wrong way can lead to new risks that cannot be identified by analyzing the subsystems in isolation. If the subsystems share instantiations of architectural patterns, as discussed in the previous paragraph, then the RIQ method may find emergent risks. However, there may be cases where the composition is more intricate.

In the future, we will investigate possibilities to connect RIQs with the risk issue collections discussed in Sect. 6. Furthermore, we will look for possibilities to collectively work on completing existing RIQs and setting up new ones, in order to cover a broad range of systems. Also the documentation of the RIQs can be enhanced by giving more detailed descriptions of the different issues.

To also address further steps of risk management, we will connect our risk identification method using RIQs with risk modeling, e.g., using the CORAS language [1]. For this purpose, we will annotate the RIQs with modeling rules. First investigations of this topic have yielded promising results.

References

1. Lund, M.S., Solhaug, B., Stølen, K.: Model-Driven Risk Analysis. The CORAS Approach. Springer, Heidelberg (2010). https://doi.org/10.1007/978-3-642-12323-8
2. Buschmann, F., Meunier, R., Rohnert, H., Sommerlad, P., Stal, M.: Pattern-Oriented Software Architecture: A System of Patterns. Wiley, Hoboken (1996)
3. Jackson, M.: Problem Frames: Analyzing and Structuring Software Development Problems. Addison-Wesley Longman Publishing Co., Inc., Boston (2001)
4. Omerovic, A., Vefsnmo, H., Erdogan, G., Gjerde, O., Gramme, E., Simonsen, S.: A feasibility study of a method for identification and modelling of cybersecurity risks in the context of smart power grids. In: Muñoz, V.M., Firouzi, F., Estrada, E., Chang, V., (eds.) Proceedings of the 4th International Conference on Complexity, Future Information Systems and Risk, pp. 39–51. COMPLEXIS, SciTePress (2019)
5. Shostack, A.: Threat Modeling: Designing for Security. Wiley, Hoboken (2014)
6. Lin, L., Nuseibeh, B., Ince, D.C., Jackson, M., Moffett, J.D.: Introducing abuse frames for analysing security requirements. In: 11th IEEE International Conference on Requirements Engineering, RE, pp. 371–372. IEEE Computer Society (2003)
7. Li, T., Paja, E., Mylopoulos, J., Horkoff, J., Beckers, K.: Security attack analysis using attack patterns. In: Tenth IEEE International Conference on Research Challenges in Information Science, RCIS, pp. 1–13. IEEE (2016)
8. Hashizume, K., Fernández, E.B., Yoshioka, N.: Misuse patterns for cloud computing. In: Proceedings of the 23rd International Conference on Software Engineering & Knowledge Engineering (SEKE'2011), Eden Roc Renaissance, Miami Beach, USA, 7–9 July 2011, pp. 683–686. Knowledge Systems Institute Graduate School (2011)
9. Halkidis, S.T., Tsantalis, N., Member, S., Chatzigeorgiou, E., Stephanides, G.: Architectural risk analysis of software systems based on security patterns. IEEE Trans. Dependable Secure Comput. 5, 129–142 (2008)
10. Wirtz, R., Heisel, M.: A systematic method to describe and identify security threats based on functional requirements. In: Zemmari, A., Mosbah, M., Cuppens-Boulahia, N., Cuppens, F. (eds.) CRiSIS 2018. LNCS, vol. 11391, pp. 205–221. Springer, Cham (2019). https://doi.org/10.1007/978-3-030-12143-3_17
11. Wirtz., R., Heisel., M.: Risk identification: from requirements to threat models. In: Proceedings of the 6th International Conference on Information Systems Security and Privacy, vol. 1: ICISSP, pp. 385–396. INSTICC, SciTePress (2020)
12. Casola, V., Benedictis, A.D., Rak, M., Villano, U.: A novel security-by-design methodology: modeling and assessing security by SLAs with a quantitative approach. J. Syst. Softw. 163, 110537 (2020)
13. Leveson, N.: Safeware: System Safety and Computers. Addison-Wesley, Boston (1995)

14. Safety Management System and Safety Culture Working Group (SMS WG): Guidance on hazard identification. Technical report (2009)
15. IEC: Hazard and Operability Studies (HAZOP studies). IEC 61882, International Electrotechnical Commission (IEC) (2001)
16. Leveson, N.: Engineering a Safer World?: Systems Thinking Applied to Safety. MIT Press, Cambridge (2011)
17. International Organization for Standardization: ISO 26262 road vehicles - functional safety (2011)
18. Beckers, K., Frese, T., Hatebur, D., Heisel, M.: A structured and model-based hazard analysis and risk assessment method for automotive systems. In: Proceedings of the 24th IEEE International Symposium on Software Reliability Engineering, pp. 238–247. IEEE Computer Society (2013)
19. Slyngstad, O.P.N., Li, J., Conradi, R., Babar, M.A.: Identifying and understanding architectural risks in software evolution: an empirical study. In: Jedlitschka, A., Salo, O. (eds.) PROFES 2008. LNCS, vol. 5089, pp. 400–414. Springer, Heidelberg (2008). https://doi.org/10.1007/978-3-540-69566-0_32

Expressing Structural Temporal Properties of Safety Critical Hierarchical Systems

Massimo Benerecetti⬤, Fabio Mogavero⬤, Adriano Peron⬤,
and Luigi Libero Lucio Starace$^{(\boxtimes)}$⬤

University of Naples Federico II, Naples, Italy
{massimo.benecetti,fabio.mogavero,adrperon,
luigiliberolucio.starace}@unina.it

Abstract. Software-intensive safety critical systems are becoming more and more widespread and are involved in many aspects of our daily lives. Since a failure of these systems could lead to unacceptable consequences, it is imperative to guarantee high safety standards. In practice, as a way to handle their increasing complexity, these systems are often modelled as hierarchical systems.

To date, a good deal of work has focused on the definition and analysis of hierarchical modelling languages and on their integration within model-driven development frameworks. Less work, however, has been directed towards formalisms to effectively express, in a precise and rigorous way, relevant behavioural properties of such systems (e.g.: safety requirements).

In this work, we propose a novel extension of classic Linear Temporal Logic (LTL) called Hierarchical Linear Temporal Logic (HLTL), designed to express, in a natural yet rigorous way, behavioural properties of hierarhical systems. The formalism we propose does not commit to any specific modelling language, and can be used to predicate over a large variety of hierarchical systems.

Keywords: Formal specification · Safety-critical software systems · Formal verification · Temporal logics

1 Introduction and Related Works

In today's world, computer and software systems are ubiquitous and involved in almost every aspect of daily life. From railway-traffic control systems to smartphones, from medical appliances to the stock exchange market, from power plants to communication networks, society relies on such systems to an ever-growing extent, making their reliability an issue of great social importance. Furthermore, it is increasingly rarer to find isolated computer systems, as they are typically embedded in larger contexts, interacting with several other concurrently-executing systems over wired and wireless networks. Due to this interconnection

© Springer Nature Switzerland AG 2021
A. C. R. Paiva et al. (Eds.): QUATIC 2021, CCIS 1439, pp. 356–369, 2021.
https://doi.org/10.1007/978-3-030-85347-1_26

trend and to the increasing variety and complexity of the performed tasks, the complexity of computer systems is growing apace, along with the difficulty in their design, specification, implementation and verification.

Of greatest concern, in particular, are the so-called *safety-critical systems*, i.e., those systems whose failure could lead to consequences that are determined to be unacceptable. Typical examples of safety-critical systems include medical care devices, aircraft and railway traffic controllers, nuclear power plants, and so on. However, a way broader class of systems has the potential for very high consequences of failure, and these systems should be considered to be safety-critical as well. For example, it is obvious and sadly known [10] that a malfunctioning in commercial aircraft could lead to loss of lives. It is not obvious, on the other hand, that also a malfunction in a telephone exchange system could kill people. Indeed, a protracted loss of 911 service has very high potential of resulting in serious consequences [12].

When dealing with the specification and design of large and complex software-intensive reactive systems, the notion of hierarchy arises quite naturally as witnessed by the establishment of hierarchical specification languages such as Statechart [9] as a standard in the Software Engineering community. Such systems can be indeed described as collections of nested components, or modules, organized in a tree-like structures, evolving concurrently and interacting with each other in some meaningful way.

Quite a lot of work has been directed towards the definition of hierarchical models [3,7,13,15], towards the study of the complexity of basic decision problems, such as reachability and model checking of classic temporal logic properties [2], and towards their integration within model-driven development frameworks [5,6,14]. Less work, however, has been devoted to languages to express relevant behavioural properties of such models, taking into account also their intrinsic hierarchical structure.

A notable exception is [8], which proposes a formal model for recursive concurrent programs, namely Communicating Recursive State Machines (CRMS). In that work, the authors also propose a logic called ConCaRet, extending with parallel operators the linear logic for Call and Return CaRet [1]. ConCaRet is designed to specify behavioural properties of recursive sequential systems such as CRMS, in which a computation can be seen as a sequence of (possibly unbounded) ranked trees to model recursive calls. ConCaRet introduces operators to reason about tree paths corresponding to computation treads. Temporal operators moves along a thread, intertwining temporal displacements and moves within the recursive structure.

In this paper we propose a different extension of classic Linear Temporal Logic (LTL [17]) called Hierarchical Linear Temporal Logic (HLTL). Among temporal logics, Linear-time Temporal Logic (LTL) has been widely used as a specification language to formalize behavioural properties of systems [16,18]. LTL allows for reasoning about behaviours represented as sequences of unstructured (flat) system states. When dealing with hierarchical models, however, the ability of naturally contextualizing behavioural properties with respect to the horizontal and vertical modular structure of the specification could prove to be very useful. To this end, HLTL combines the analysis of the standard temporal dimension of LTL with two additional orthogonal dimensions that account for the hierarchical and concurrent nature that characterizes the computations of hierarchical systems. This allows HLTL to naturally express behavioural local properties of modules instead of being limited to reasoning about global system states. Unlike ConCaRet, HLTL syntactically separates temporal moves along a computation from the moves along its vertical and horizontal dimensions. The clear separation between the temporal and the structural operators in HLTL gives a clear way to precisely contextualize properties in a module of the system, as opposed to ConCaRet which lacks this specification ability.

This paper is structured as follows. In Sect. 2 we provide some basic preliminary notions on Dynamic State Machines (DSTM), a recently-proposed hierarchical modelling language explicitly devised to meet industrial requirements in design, verification and validation of complex, multi-process, control systems. In Sect. 3 we introduce the logical formalism we propose, and show how it can be applied to express properties of hierarchical systems, and in particular of DSTMs. In Sect. 4, we hint at possible direct applications of HLTL in different phases of the system development lifecycle. At last, in Sect. 5, we draw some closing remarks and discuss future research directions.

2   Dynamic State Machines and Hierarchical Computations

In this section, we provide some preliminary notions on hierarchical modelling languages and on the formalization of their behaviours by giving an overview of one of such formalisms, namely Dynamic State Machines (DSTM). For a complete account of the formal syntax and semantics of DSTM we refer to [5].

2.1   Dynamic State Machines

The Dynamic STate Machine (DSTM) formalism is a recently-developed modelling language originally proposed in [15] and explicitly devised to meet industrial requirements in design, verification and validation of complex control systems. DSTM features both complex control flow constructs such as asynchronous forks, preemptive termination, recursive execution and complex data flow constructs such as custom complex type definition, parametric machines, and inter-process communication through global channels and variables.

DSTM takes many syntactic elements from UML Statecharts, and extends them with the notion of re-usable module and with the possibility of recursion and dynamic instantiation. A machine is capable of dynamically instantiating one of its modules when the number of concurrently-executing instances of said module is decided at run-time.

In more detail, a Dynamic STate Machine (DSTM) model is a sequence of machines $\langle M_1, M_2, \ldots, M_n \rangle$ communicating over a set X of global variables and a set C of global communication channels. The first of such machines M_1 is the so-called *initial machine*, i.e., the highest level of the hierarchical system. A machine M_i represents a module in the hierarchical specification and is defined as a state-transition diagram composed by vertices connected by transitions. The following kinds of vertices are defined:

node basic stable control state of a machine;

entering node initial pseudo-node of a machine. A machine may have multiple entering nodes, corresponding to different initial conditions;

initial node default entering pseudo-node of a machine, to be used when no entering node is explicitly specified. There must be exactly one for each machine;

exit node final (or exiting) node of a machine. A machine may specify multiple exiting nodes, corresponding to different termination conditions;

box node modelling the parallel activation of machines associated with the box itself. A transition entering a box represents the parallel activation of the corresponding machines, while a transition exiting a box corresponds to a return from said activation.

fork control pseudo-node modelling the activation of new processes. Such activation may be either *synchronous* (the forking process is suspended and waits for the activated processes to terminate) or *asynchronous* (the forking process continues its activity along the newly-activated processes).

join control pseudo-node used to synchronize the termination of concurrently executing processes or to force their termination when necessary (*preemptive join*).

In the description above the vertices corresponding to stable, meaningful control points are called *nodes*. On the other hand, *pseudo-nodes* represent transient points.

Transitions represent changes in the control state of a machine. A transition is labelled with a name and decorated with a *trigger* (an input event originating from the external environment or from other concurrent machines), a *guard* (a Boolean condition on the current contents of variables and channels) and an *action* (one or more statements on variables and channels). For a transition to be fired it is necessary that its trigger is fulfilled and that its guard is satisfied. When a transition fires, its action is executed with possible side-effects.

Example 1 (The Counting *DSTM).* As an example, consider the *Counting* DSTM, consisting of the machines *Main, Counter* and *Incrementer* represented in Fig. 1. In the proposed graphical formalism, default entering pseudo-nodes are depicted as black circles, entering pseudo-nodes as white circles, final nodes as crossed-out white circles. Boxes are represented by rectangles and decorated with a comma-separated list of associated machines enclosed in square brackets. Nodes are drawn as rounded rectangles and fork and join pseudo-nodes are represented by black bars. Each node and pseudo-node is decorated with its name. Transitions are, as usual, drawn as directed edges between the source and the target vertices. The transitions for these machines are detailed in Table 1,

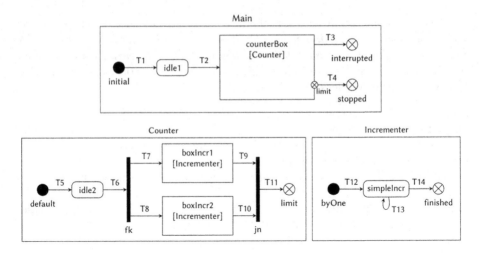

Fig. 1. The *Counting* DSTM specification

in which we denote the trivial trigger and the trivial guard, which are always satisfied, respectively with τ and *True*. The empty list of actions, which produces no side-effects, is represented with ε. As for the semantics of the *Counting* DSTM, we describe it informally as follows. The initial machine, and highest module in the hierarchy, is the *Main* DSTM, and its initial stable state is idle1. Subsequently, by executing transition T2 (which has trivial trigger, guard, and actions, and thus is always executable and has no side effects), *Main* performs a call operation instantiating a *Counter* module by entering the *counterBox* box. After instantiation, the *Counter* machine will be in its local stable state idle2. After performing the fork operation consisting in transitions T6,T7,T8, the counter *Counter* module can instantiate two instances of the *Incrementer* module, which will run in parallel at the same level of the hierarchy. Back to the *Main* module, notice that transition T3 can be executed at anytime when the signal? trigger, which requires that a message is present on the communication channel named signal, is fulfilled. If T3 is executed, the *Counter* module (and eventually the modules the latter instantiated) will be pre-emptively terminated and deallocated. Transition T4, on the other hand, can be executed only if the *counter* module has reached its limit termination state, which can happen only once both the *Incrementer* modules have terminated and the join operation represented by transitions T9,T10,T11 is executed. As for the *Incrementer* module, its initial stable state is simpleIncr. Then, until the global variable x is incremented to 10 and transition T14 becomes executable, only transition T13 can be executed. This transition does not lead to a different local state, but is associated with an action having the side-effect of incrementing x by 1. Summarizing, the two *Incrementer* modules instantiated in parallel by Counter will, at each computation step, increment each the global variable x by 1. After 5 computation steps, x will be incremented up to 10, and the *Incrementer* modules will execute transition T4, reaching their exiting finished states. Subsequently, the *Counter* module will perform the join operation we previously mentioned, reaching its final limit state, and the *Main* module will be able to terminate, reaching its stopped final state.

Table 1. Transition structure for the DSTM model *Counting*

T_1	Source	Target	Trigger	Guard	Action
T1	initial	idle1	τ	*True*	ε
T2	idle1	counterBox	τ	*True*	ε
T3	counterBox	interrupted	signal?	*True*	ε
T4	(counterBox, limit)	stopped	τ	*True*	ε
T5	default	idle2	τ	*True*	ε
T6	idle2	fk	τ	*True*	ε
T7	fk	boxIncr1	τ	*True*	ε
T8	fk	boxIncr2	τ	*True*	ε
T9	boxIncr1	jn	τ	*True*	ε
T10	boxIncr2	jn	τ	*True*	ε
T11	jn	limit	τ	*True*	ε
T12	byOne	simpleIncr	τ	*True*	ε
T13	simpleIncr	simpleIncr	τ	x<10	x++
T14	simpleIncr	finished	τ	x$\geq$10	ε

2.2 Hierarchical Computations

The evolution of a dynamic system can, in general, be seen as a sequence of stable system states. When dealing with hierarchical systems such as DSTM, each state has an intrinsic hierarchical structure, and thus can be represented using a tree-like structure reflecting the internal organization of modules. In such a tree-like representation, which we call *configuration tree*, each node represents a currently active module, and a module is a child of another if the latter instantiated the former. Hence, sibling modules execute concurrently at the same level of the hierarchy and are instantiated by the same parent module. A behaviour of a hierarchical system, i.e., a *hierarchical computation*, is thus a sequence of configuration trees, each representing a state of the entire system. Adjacent configuration trees in a hierarchical computation are the source and the target of a single computation step of the system.

Along a hierarchical computation, adjacent configuration trees are not structurally unrelated, but must reflect possible structural changes induced by computational steps of the underlying system. To capture this intuition, the concept of *frontier* is introduced. A frontier is a possibly empty subset of nodes of a configuration tree marking the modules that take part in the current computation step. All the points that are not descendant of the frontier remain unchanged during the step, since they are not performing any action. In more detail, if a point belongs to the frontier, we assume that the module instantiated in that point is performing an action. Otherwise, if an ancestor of a point belongs to the frontier, then the module instantiated in that point is deallocated. Finally, if a module is an ancestor of a point belonging to the frontier, then the current computation step affects a module internally invoked by the considered module.

As an example of hierarchical computation, consider the partial behaviour of the *Counting* DSTM depicted in Fig. 2.

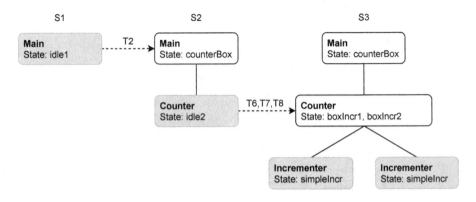

Fig. 2. A partial computation of the *Counting* DSTM

In the initial state $S1$, only the *Main* module is active, and is in its local *idle1* state. Then, after performing transition $T2$, the system reaches state $S2$, in which, in addition to the *Main* module, also a *Counter* module is active. In particular, the *Counter* module is instantiated by the *Main* one via the box *counterBox*, and hence is its child in the hierarchy. The *Counter* module will be in its *idle2* local state. Subsequently, in our example, the *Counter* module performs a fork operation instantiating two *Incrementer* modules. As a result of this operation (which corresponds to transitions T6, T7 and T8 in the DSTM model), the overall state of the systems is $S3$, in which the two *Incrementer* modules are added as children of *Counter*. In our representation, modules belonging to the frontier of each state are highlighted with a yellow background.

3   Hierarchical Linear-Time Temporal Logic

Temporal logic is a widely-used formalism for describing behaviours of dynamic systems, which can be seen as a sequence of system states representing the system evolution over time. Temporal logic extends propositional or predicate logic with modalities that permit to refer to the the temporal dimension of behaviours. They provide a very intuitive but mathematically precise notation for expressing properties about the relations between states in a behaviour [4].

Among temporal logics, Linear-time Temporal Logic (LTL), originally proposed in [17], has been widely used as a specification language to formalize behavioural properties of systems [16,18]. LTL allows for reasoning about sequences of unstructured (flat) states. However, as discussed in the previous section, hierarhical models such as DSTM represent systems whose global state in a given instant can be described by tree-like structures. As a consequence, a behaviour of such system can be represented as sequence of tree-structured states. As a consequence, LTL cannot be used to express, in a natural way, system properties that take into account the intrinsic structure of hierarchical systems.

To address this issue, we propose an extension of LTL, which we name Hierarchical Linear-time Temporal Logic (HLTL), which is designed to express properties of hierarchical computations, i.e., of sequences of tree-structured states. HLTL is able to explicitly reference the tree-like structure of each state. The main intuition behind HLTL is to use classic LTL operators to reason about the evolution of a given module, while additional operators are used to contextualize formulae in the hierarchy of activated modules. A HLTL formula is locally evaluated with regard to a context (i.e. a given module, corresponding to a vertex in the tree-like hierarchical structure of the current state), and the context can change during the evaluation of a formula by moving along both the vertical and the horizontal dimension. The vertical dimension is related to the hierarchy (caller/called relations), while the horizontal one is related to concurrency (left/right sibling in the tree).

Suppose that the current context is fixed in a given point of a configuration tree, corresponding to a module committed to a call, which is to say that that point has children (the modules it invoked) in the current state. It is possible to express the fact that the formula ϕ is required to hold in the i-th child of that module by means of the formula $\downarrow_i(\phi)$. Notice that in HLTL it is possible to navigate the vertical dimension only downwards. If the context has siblings in the current state (i.e. is executing concurrently with other modules as a result of a call operation performed by its parent), then it is possible to express the fact that the formula ϕ is required to hold in its left (resp. right) sibling with the formula $\leftarrow(\phi)$ (resp. $\rightarrow(\phi)$).

These vertical and horizontal displacement operators can be freely combined with linear temporal operators that allow for expressing behavioural properties of a module with regard to the temporal dimension.

Before going into details about the syntax and semantics of HLTL, we firstly formalize the notion of hierarchical computation, which was informally introduced in Sect. 2.

Definition 1 (Hierarchical computation). *A hierarchical computation over a set of atomic propositions* $\mathcal{P}$ *is a sequence of the form*

$$\langle (T_0, v_0), Fr_0 \rangle, \langle (T_1, v_1), Fr_1 \rangle, \ldots, \langle (T_i, v_i), Fr_i \rangle, \ldots$$

such that, for all $i \geq 0$:

1. (T_i, v_i) *is a labelled tree representing, with* $v_i : T_i \rightarrow 2^{\mathcal{P}}$;
2. *the frontier* Fr_i *is a subset of the* T_i;
3. *all the nodes in* T_i *that are not descendant of the nodes in the frontier* Fr_i *cannot be deallocated, i.e., they belong to* T_{i+1};
4. *for all the nodes* $t \in T_i \setminus Fr_i$ *it holds that* $v_i(t) = v_{i+1}(t)$.

In the above definition, Item 1 captures the idea that each state in a hierarchical computation has a tree structure in which each node is a currently active module. The labelling function $v_i : T_i \rightarrow 2^{\mathcal{P}}$ is used to assign, to each module in the configuration tree, a set of atomic propositions that are satisfied in that module. Item 2 requires that the set of nodes belonging to the frontier is well-formed, i.e., it is a subset of the modules that are currently active. Of course, since the frontier represents nodes that are involved in the current computation step, only currently active modules can belong to it. Items 3 and 4 capture the fact that adjacent configuration trees in a hierarchical computation are not structurally unrelated, but must reflect changes induced by the computation step the system performs. In particular, Item 3 guarantees that only nodes that are descendant of the frontier can be deallocated (i.e., can be removed in the subsequent configuration tree) as a result of a preemptive termination performed by their ancestor in the frontier. Item 4, on the other hand, requires that the labelling remains unchanged for all the modules that do not belong to the frontier, capturing the intuition that modules that do not take part in the current computation step must remain unchanged, and thus must satisfy the same atomic propositions.

When dealing with sequences of states, the standard interpretation of LTL has a *global* character, i.e. the concept of *next* state is relative to the overall system state. With flat, unstructured states, this classic interpretation is perfectly adequate, but it falls short when dealing with sequences of structured states of concurrent hierarchical modular systems, as it is not able to fully capture the concurrent nature of computations. To better capture the concurrent and hierarchical nature of these computations, HLTL considers a *local* interpretation of next, capturing a local notion of successor, which requires that the context is directly interested by a local change. As follows, we formalize the notion of local next we considered.

Definition 2 (Local interpretation of next). *Given an interrupting hierarchical word*

$$\xi = \xi_0, \xi_1, \ldots, \xi_k, \ldots,$$

with $\xi_i = \langle (T_i, v_i), Fr_i \rangle$, *for all* $i \geq 0$ *and* $t \in T_i$ *(t is a node in the tree* T_i*) the local* next *of a given module* t *in* ξ_i, *in symbols* $Next(\xi_i, t)$, *is the hierarchical computation symbol* ξ_j *(if any) such that* $j > i$ *is the least index such that* $t \in Fr_{j-1}$ *and, for each* $i < \ell < j$ *there is no prefix* t' *of* t *with* $t' \in Fr_\ell$.

As usual, $Next^*(\xi_i, t)$, denotes the reflexive and transitive closure of $Next^*(\xi_i, t)$ and is defined inductively as the set of hierarchical symbols such that:

1. $\xi_i \in Next^*(\xi_i, t)$;
2. $\xi_j \in Next^*(\xi_i, t)$ iff $\xi_j \in Next(\xi_k, t)$ and $\xi_k \in Next^*(\xi_i, t)$.

As an example, consider the hierarchical computation $\xi = \xi_0, \xi_1, \xi_2, \xi_3, \xi_4$ in Fig. 3, in which each node is represented by a circle and decorated with the atomic proposition it satisfies, and nodes belonging to the frontier are depicted with a double circle. In the figure, the local successor relation is depicted as a dashed arrow connecting a module with its local next. Consider the only module in the first state ξ_0 of ξ. Its local next is the root in the subsequent state ξ_1, since 1 is the least index greater than 0 such that the root module belongs to the frontier Fr_0. When considering the root module in the state ξ_1, on the other hand, the local next is the corresponding module in state ξ_4.

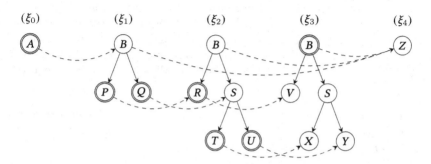

Fig. 3. An hierarchical computation decorated with the *local* next relation

With the definitions of hierarchical computation and local next in place, we can introduce the syntax and semantics of HLTL.

Definition 3 (HLTL syntax). *HLTL formulae are inductively defined as follows:*

$$\phi ::= \top \mid p \in \mathcal{P} \mid \neg\phi \mid \phi \vee \phi \mid \phi \wedge \phi \mid \downarrow_n(\phi) \mid \leftarrow(\phi) \mid \rightarrow(\phi) \mid \mathbf{X}\phi \mid \phi\mathbf{U}\phi \mid \phi\mathbf{R}\phi,$$

where $\mathcal{P}$ is a set of atomic propositions.

A HLTL formula is interpreted over interrupting hierarchical computations according to the following semantics.

Definition 4 (HLTL semantics). *The satisfaction of an HLTL formula ϕ in node $t \in T_i$ at the i-th symbol of a hierarchical computation $\xi = \xi_0, \xi_1, \ldots, \xi_k, \ldots$, with $\xi_i = \langle(T_i, v_i), Fr_i\rangle$, is defined recursively as follows:*

- $\langle\xi_i, t\rangle \vDash p$ *iff* $p \in v_i(t)$, *with* $p \in \mathcal{P}$;

- *Boolean connectives are defined as usual;*
- $\langle \xi_i, t \rangle \vDash \downarrow_j \phi$ *iff there exists a node* $t' \in T_i$ *being the j-th child of t and* $\langle \xi_i, t' \rangle \vDash \phi$;
- $\langle \xi_i, t \rangle \vDash \leftarrow(\phi)$ *iff there exists a node* $t' \in T_i$ *that is the left sibling of t and* $\langle \xi_i, t' \rangle \vDash \phi$;
- $\langle \xi_i, t \rangle \vDash \rightarrow(\phi)$ *iff there exists a node* $t' \in T_i$ *that is the right sibling of t and and* $\langle \xi_i, t' \rangle \vDash \phi$;
- $\langle \xi_i, t \rangle \vDash X(\phi)$, *iff there exists* ξ_j *such that* $\xi_j = \text{Next}(\xi_i, t)$ *and* $\langle \xi_j, t \rangle \vDash \phi$.
- $\langle \xi_i, t \rangle \vDash \phi U \psi$ *iff there exists* $\xi_j \in \text{Next}^*$ *such that* $\langle \xi_j, t \rangle \vDash \psi$ *and, for all* $\xi_k \in \text{Next}^*$, *with* $i \leq k < j$, $\langle \xi_k, t \rangle \vDash \phi$.
- $\langle \xi_i, t \rangle \vDash \phi R \psi$ *iff, for all* $\xi_j \in \text{Next}^*(\xi_i, t)$, *if* $\langle \xi_j, t \rangle \nvDash \psi$, *then there exists* $\xi_k \in \text{Next}^*$, *with* $i \leq k < j$, *such that* $\langle \xi_k, t \rangle \vDash \phi$.

A hierarchical computation ξ *satisfies a HLTL$^{\xi}$ formula* ϕ, *in symbols* $\xi \vDash \phi$, *if* ϕ *holds in the root of the first configuration tree.*

The following abbreviations will be used hereafter: $\bot$ for $\neg \top$; $\phi \Rightarrow \psi$ for $\neg \phi \vee \psi$; $Stop_x$ for $\neg X \top$, expressing the fact that the current context has no local future. Derived temporal operators *eventually* F and *globally* G can be defined as follows. F ϕ, requiring that, in some future point in $Next^*$, ϕ holds, is equivalent to $\top U \phi$. Similarly, G ϕ, requiring for ϕ to hold in all points in $Next^*$, is equivalent to $\bot R \phi$.

Example 2 (HLTL formulae). In this example, we hint at the expressive power of HLTL through some examples which are then evaluated against the hierarchical computation ξ depicted in Fig. 3.

1. Let ε denote the root node of each configuration tree in xi. It holds that $\langle \xi_{i \in \{1,2,3\}}, \varepsilon \rangle \vDash X Z$, since in each of these contexts, the local next $\langle \xi_4, \varepsilon \rangle \vDash Z$. The HLTL formula $X Z$, on the other hand, is not satisfied in the root of ξ_0, since its local next is the root of ξ_1, and $\langle \xi_1, \varepsilon \rangle \nvDash Z$.
2. The formula $\phi = (A \vee B) U(X Z)$ is satisfied by ξ, i.e., $\langle \xi_0, \varepsilon \rangle \vDash \phi$, since there exists the symbol ξ_1 in $Next^*(\xi_0, \varepsilon)$ such that $\langle \xi_1, \varepsilon \rangle \vDash X Z$ and $\langle \xi_0, \varepsilon \rangle \vDash (A \vee B)$.
3. The formula $\psi = G((\downarrow_1(R)) \Rightarrow (\downarrow_2(Stop)))$ requires that, in each state of the computation, if the first child of the primary module satisfies R, then the second child has no local next. It is easy to see that it holds that $\xi \vDash \psi$.
4. The formula $\mu = X(\downarrow_1(P \Rightarrow \rightarrow(X(S))))$ requires that, in the local next relative to its context, if the first child satisfies P, then its right sibling has a local next satisfying S. This formula is satisfied in ξ.
5. The formula $\lambda = G(\downarrow_2(S \Rightarrow \downarrow_1(T \vee \rightarrow(Y))))$ requires that, at each step of the computation, if the second module instantiated by the primary module satisfies S, then its first child must either satisfy T, or have a right sibling satisfying Y. It is easy to see that $\xi \vDash \lambda$, as well.

4 Towards Automatic Verification of HLTL Properties for Hierarchical Systems

We envision that HLTL could prove to be a valuable tool in the specification of behavioural properties of hierarchical systems, supporting different phases of the system development lifecycle. For instance, HLTL could be used to formalize system requirements in a more natural yet rigorous way, assisting requirement engineers in the initial phases of system development. Moreover, by integrating HLTL within existing verification frameworks, it is also possible to allow for the fully-automatic verification (*model checking*) of HLTL properties against hierarchical models.

As an example of this, let us consider again the existing work on DSTM presented in [5,6]. These works define a toolchain to '*translate*' a DSTM model into a semantically equivalent Promela specification for the well-known SPIN model checker [11], enabling simulation and test case generation for DSTM models. This translation was designed in such a way that the concurrent and hierarchical nature of DSTM modules is preserved in the Promela encoding. That toolchain could be extended to support automatic verification of HLTL properties by including an additional module that translates a HLTL specification into a semantically-equivalent, although possibly way more complex and less natural, LTL one. With the LTL equivalent in place, the SPIN Model Checker, which natively supports LTL specifications, could then be used to perform automatic verification. An overview of the resulting DSTM verification framework is shown in Fig. 4.

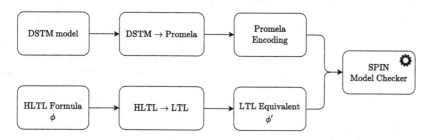

Fig. 4. Automatic HLTL verification framework for DSTM models

5 Conclusions and Future Works

Driven by the increasing need of methodologies to support the design and verification of safety critical systems, quite a lot of work has been directed towards the definition of hierarchical models such as StateChart, Simulink, or Dynamic State Machines. Less work, however, has been devoted to formal languages to express in a precise, non-ambiguous and practical way properties of the computations of such systems.

In this work, we present a novel formalism named Hierarchical Linear-time Temporal Logic (HLTL), an extension of the well-known Linear-time Temporal Logic (LTL) designed to express linear properties of hierarchical systems. Thanks to the introduction of specific operators, our approach allows practitioners to concisely express linear-time properties of hierarchical system that take into account the intrinsic hierarchical structure of the states of such systems.

In future works, as discussed in Sect. 4, we plan to integrate HLTL within the modelling framework for Dynamic State Machines (DSTM) proposed in [5, 6], allowing for fully-automated verification of properties, expressed as HLTL formulae, of DSTM systems.

References

1. Alur, R., Etessami, K., Madhusudan, P.: A temporal logic of nested calls and returns. In: Jensen, K., Podelski, A. (eds.) TACAS 2004. LNCS, vol. 2988, pp. 467–481. Springer, Heidelberg (2004). https://doi.org/10.1007/978-3-540-24730-2_35

2. Alur, R., Henzinger, T.A., Mang, F.Y.C., Qadeer, S., Rajamani, S.K., Tasiran, S.: MOCHA: modularity in model checking. In: Hu, A.J., Vardi, M.Y. (eds.) CAV 1998. LNCS, vol. 1427, pp. 521–525. Springer, Heidelberg (1998). https://doi.org/10.1007/BFb0028774

3. Alur, R., Kannan, S., Yannakakis, M.: Communicating hierarchical state machines. In: Wiedermann, J., van Emde Boas, P., Nielsen, M. (eds.) ICALP 1999. LNCS, vol. 1644, pp. 169–178. Springer, Heidelberg (1999). https://doi.org/10.1007/3-540-48523-6_14

4. Baier, C., Katoen, J.P.: Principles of Model Checking. MIT press, Cambridge (2008)

5. Benerecetti, M., et al.: Dynamic state machines for modelling railway control systems. Sci. Comput. Program. **133**, 116–153 (2017). https://doi.org/10.1016/j.scico.2016.09.002, https://www.sciencedirect.com/science/article/pii/S0167642316301332. formal Techniques for Safety-Critical Systems (FTSCS 2014)

6. Benerecetti, M., et al.: From dynamic state machines to promela. In: Biondi, F., Given-Wilson, T., Legay, A. (eds.) Model Checking Software. SPIN 2019. Lecture Notes in Computer Science, vol. 11636. Springer, Cham (2019). https://doi.org/10.1007/978-3-030-30923-7_4

7. Benerecetti, M., Peron, A.: Timed recursive state machines: expressiveness and complexity. Theor. Comput. Sci. **625**, 85–124 (2016). https://doi.org/10.1016/j.tcs.2016.02.021

8. Bozzelli, L., Torre, S.L., Peron, A.: Verification of well-formed communicating recursive state machines. Theor. Comput. Sci. **403**(2–3), 382–405 (2008)

9. Harel, D.: Statecharts: a visual formalism for complex systems. Sci. Comput. Program. **8**(3), 231–274 (1987)

10. Herkert, J., Borenstein, J., Miller, K.: The boeing 737 max: lessons for engineering ethics. Sci. Eng. Ethics **26**(6), 2957–2974 (2020)

11. Holzmann, G.J.: The model checker spin. IEEE Trans. Softw. Eng. **23**(5), 279–295 (1997)
12. Knight, J.C.: Safety critical systems: challenges and directions. In: Proceedings of the 24th International Conference on Software Engineering, pp. 547–550 (2002)
13. Lanotte, R., Maggiolo-Schettini, A., Peron, A., Tini, S.: Dynamic hierarchical machines. Fund. Inform. **54**(2–3), 237–252 (2003)
14. Matinnejad, R., Nejati, S., Briand, L.C., Bruckmann, T.: Test generation and test prioritization for simulink models with dynamic behavior. IEEE Trans. Softw. Eng. **45**(9), 919–944 (2018)
15. Nardone, R., et al.: Dynamic state machines for formalizing railway control system specifications. In: Artho, C., Ölveczky, P.C. (eds.) FTSCS 2014. CCIS, vol. 476, pp. 93–109. Springer, Cham (2015). https://doi.org/10.1007/978-3-319-17581-2_7
16. Oyeleke, R.O., Chang, C.K., Margrett, J.: Situation-driven context-aware safety model for risk mitigation using ltl in a smart home environment. In: 2020 IEEE World Congress on Services (SERVICES), pp. 22–24. IEEE (2020)
17. Pnueli, A.: The temporal logic of programs. In: 18th Annual Symposium on Foundations of Computer Science (sfcs 1977), pp. 46–57 (Oct 1977). https://doi.org/10.1109/SFCS.1977.32
18. Zhang, S., Zhai, J., Bu, L., Chen, M., Wang, L., Li, X.: Automated generation of ltl specifications for smart home iot using natural language. In: 2020 Design, Automation & Test in Europe Conference & Exhibition (DATE), pp. 622–625. IEEE (2020)

Quality Aspects in Machine Learning, AI and Data Analytics

Facing Many Objectives for Fairness in Machine Learning

David Villar and Jorge Casillas[(✉)] [iD]

Department of Computer Science and Artificial Intelligence,
Data Science and Computational Intelligence Institute (DaSCI),
University of Granada, Granada 18071, Spain
daalma7@ugr.es, casillas@decsai.ugr.es
http://ccia.ugr.es/~casillas

Abstract. Fairness is an increasingly important topic in the world of Artificial Intelligence. Machine learning techniques are widely used nowadays to solve huge amounts of problems, but those techniques may be biased against certain social groups due to different reasons. Using fair classification methods we can attenuate this discrimination source. Nevertheless, there are lots of valid fairness definitions which may be mutually incompatible.

The aim of this paper is to propose a method which generates fair solutions for machine learning binary classification problems with one sensitive attribute. As we want accurate, fair and interpretable solutions, our method is based on Many Objective Evolutionary Algorithms (MaOEAs). The decision space will represent hyperparameters for training our classifiers, which will be decision trees, while the objective space will be a four-dimensional space representing the quality of the classifier in terms of an accuracy measure, two contradictory fairness criteria and an interpretability indicator.

Experimentation have been done using four well known fairness datasets. As we will see, our algorithm generates good solutions compared to previous work, and a presumably well populated pareto-optimal population is found so that different classifiers could be used depending on our needs.

Keywords: Fairness in machine learning · Many objective evolutionary algorithm · Decision trees

1 Introduction

In the last few years, fairness has become one of the main research topics in the field of Machine Learning (ML). The problem of bias in ML has always been there, as it comes from statistics. Dataset labeling and other kinds of data

---

Supported by FEDER and the Spanish Ministry of Science and Innovation, Institute of Health Carlos III, grant no. PI20/01435.

A. C. R. Paiva et al. (Eds.): QUATIC 2021, CCIS 1439, pp. 373–386, 2021.
https://doi.org/10.1007/978-3-030-85347-1_27

collection or even selecting a representative sample of the whole population, as it is done by human experts, because of their inherent human nature, it is a biased process, so algorithms have great bias tendencies.

Even though this inherent problem has been well known for several decades, it has not got the relevance and attention it deserves until these days [5,17] due to a variety of factors, including more social awareness and criticism in terms of inequalities and discrimination or famous cases which stimulated that feeling in ML community [2,16]. Bias is a serious problem, as it goes against some subsets of the population, whose individuals share a certain or multiple features, being even totally unrelated within the context of that task. This fact has been observed in an extensive range of fields, such as human rights, privacy, health or economics [2,6,16,23].

When an algorithm is biased against a social group, it can be worse than only being harmful, as it can even lead to an increase of that biasing tendency for that group as time goes by [8,15]. For this reason, trying to figure out how can we reduce bias impact in our data driven decision models is a crucial task [20,24]. Having understood this context, we want to develop a method which not only tries to optimise accuracy as further as possible, but that takes fairness into account trying to minimise this negative impact.

But another problem arises when trying to come up with a mathematical definition of fairness such that can be considered in ML systems. A wide range of them have been proposed, which are closely related to legal and social science legal concepts [13]. They can belong to three different classes: group, individual and counterfactual fairness measures. Group fairness measures have a clear advantage over the others, as they only depend on probabilities which can be directly calculated independently of the context, while individual and counterfactual measures require additional definitions of distances or causal graphs respectively. Nonetheless, some group fairness metrics are incompatible [4].

We can divide algorithms which incorporate fairness into three non mutually exclusive classes: preprocessing, inprocessing and postprocessing algorithms [9]. The method we have developed belongs to the inprocessing class. Group fairness definitions are considered as objectives to optimise, as well as other criteria, in this case, accuracy and interpretability. This last criterion is interesting as a decision tree interpretability may greatly vary depending on its structure, thus reducing their usefulness. There are intrinsical tradeoffs between accuracy and fairness criteria [14] too, but we are still able to push the further as we can in an optimization process, trying to get the best possible models, and expecting them to be better than some current existing models [18].

Our algorithm interprets problems as a many objectives optimization ones, using model hyperparameters as our decision space, and the objective space will be built in terms of the criteria we want to optimise. It is based on Many Objectives Evolutionary Algorithms (MaOEAs) which have been proven to be really useful in this context. Furthermore, lots of different non Pareto dominated decision trees will be generated and will describe the limits of our optimization process.

2 Background

In this section we will expose a general background about simultaneous optimization of accuracy and fairness in ML, as well as MaOEAs.

2.1 Accuracy and Fairness Optimization Background

With respect to simultaneous optimization of fairness and accuracy, efforts have tended to introduce fairness constraints and optimizing for both criteria [22]. In terms of Decision Trees, work incorporating fairness criteria in the own learning process by modifying the information gain function has been done, exploring some variants [11]. It has also been proposed to reinterpret the problem of fair classification in order to incorporate cost functions which lead the learning process [1]. In Zafar et al. [21] a problem which could be formulated as a convex constrained optimization problem was considered. That formulation incorporated fairness in terms of a measure of the decision boundary. Thanks to that, several statistical based fairness metrics are considered at the same time. In [10], using Support Vector Machines regularization techniques showed that applying strict fairness criteria may lead to worse welfare for the considered groups.

The recent work of Valdivia et al. [18] incorporated NSGA-II multiobjective optimization based techniques to Decision Trees hyperparameters, optimising for both accuracy and fairness. That work showed how are we able to optimise our methods up to much further limits than some of historically applied ML algorithms, such as COMPAS. In terms of the current work, we will generalise the concept introduced in this paper, applying more sophisticated algorithms and a more elaborated method to find Pareto optimal solutions using a Many Objectives perspective, rather than use a 2-objective minimisation one.

2.2 MaOEAs Background

Let Ω and Θ be 2 sets such that $\Omega \subset \mathbb{R}^n, \Theta \subset \mathbb{R}^m : m > 1$. Let be $f : \Omega \to \Theta$, with $f(\omega) = (f_1(\omega), f_2(\omega), ..., f_m(\omega)), \forall \omega \in \Omega$, being each $f_i : \Omega \to \mathbb{R}, \forall i \in \{1, 2, ...m\}$. A multiobjective minimization optimization problem consists of:

$$\min_{\omega \in \Omega} \text{ or } \max_{\omega \in \Omega}(f_1(\omega), f_2(\omega), ..., f_m(\omega))$$

Where n is the dimension of the space Ω, which is also named as decision space, whereas m is the dimension of the space Θ, also named objective space. Each of the functions f_i are named single objective functions, while f is our multiobjective function.

We will try to minimise all functions at the same time, and it is clear that, apart from extreme cases which have no interest of linear correlated single objective functions, we will reach a point where we will not be able to keep minimising a single objective without having a tradeoff with at least 1 other objective.

A solution $x \in \Omega$ Pareto dominates or simply dominates another solution, $y \in \Omega$ which will be written as $x \prec y \Leftrightarrow f_i(x) \leq f_i(y) \forall i \in \{1, ..., m\} \wedge \exists j \in$

$\{1, ..., m\} : f_j(x) < f_j(y)$. Solve a multiobjective problem consists of finding as much non dominated solutions as we can for this problem, while also having good distribution properties. This solutions are named Pareto optimal solutions, and their image under f is named Pareto front (PF). For solving these problems, Multiobjective Evolutionary Algorithms (MOEAs) are widely used and generate high quality solutions.

A Many Objectives Optimization Problem is a multiobjective optimization problem where $m > 3$. High dimensionality greatly hinders the task of finding pareto optimal solutions, as it is more difficult that one solution dominates another and the objective space grows in orders of magnitude in terms of dimension, so the size of the Pareto front tends to grow in size analogously. During last years, MaOEAs have been widely utilised since they report good quality Pareto fronts.

3   MaOEA to Achive Accurate, Fair, and Interpretable Solutions

In this section we will discuss the design of our method. We will start showing how both the objective and decision spaces are built. Then, a brief explanation of the three base algorithms employed is exposed.

3.1   Objective Space

We want our solutions to be accurate, fair and interpretable. For that reason, an accuracy metric, two group fairness metrics belonging to contradictory subfamilies and an interpretability measure will be employed. Notating $\hat{y}$ as our binary classifier output, y as the true class and a being the protected attribute, those metrics deffinitions are the following:

- Accuracy criterion: gmean_inv. This criteron is calculated as $1 - \text{G-mean}(\hat{y}, y)$, where $\text{G-mean}((\hat{y}, y) = \sqrt{\text{TPR} \cdot \text{TNR}} = \sqrt{P[\hat{y} = 1 | y = 1] \cdot P[\hat{y} = 0 | y = 0]}$. Minimizing this measure, we ensure that both TPR and TNR are low, so the accuracy of the prediction is high.
- 1st fairness criterion: FPR_{diff} or difference between False Positive Rates. This measure is calculated as: $\text{FPR}_{\text{diff}} = |P[\hat{y} = 1 | y = 0, a = 0] - P[\hat{y} = 1 | y = 0, a = 1]|$. This is an objective to minimise. It will be minimum, when there is no difference on the FPR value for both demographic groups. This fairness criterion belongs to the subfamily of Equalised Odds, defined as $P[\hat{y} | y, a = 0] = P[\hat{y} | y, a = 1]$.
- 2nd fairness criterion : PPV_{diff}, or difference between Positive Predictive Values. This measure is calculated as: $\text{PPV}_{\text{diff}} = |P[y = 1 | \hat{y} = 1, a = 0] - P[y = 1 | \hat{y} = 1, a = 1]|$. This is a measure to minimise, and will be minimum when there is no difference between PPVs for both demographic groups. This fairness criterion belongs to the subfamily of Predictive Rate Parity, defined as $P[y | \hat{y}, a = 0] = P[y | \hat{y}, a = 1]$. No classifier can fulfill measures from both Equalised Odds and Predictive Rate Parity at the same time [4].

– Interpretability criterion: Number of leaves. This measure is a direct estimator about interpretability of the model, as those leaves represent decision paths that our model can make. The least paths there are, the easier the whole process will be to interpret.

3.2 Decision Space: Hyperparameters

Our base binary classifiers to apply learning processes will be Decision Trees. We have used the implementation of scikit-learn, therefore our hyperparameters and their range will be a subset of those available. These hyperparameters will be:

– criterion: Represents the function which will measure the quality of a split. Possible values we will use are Gini and Entropy.
– max_depth: The maximum depth the tree could have. Possible values we will use are $\{n \in \mathbb{N} : n \geq 3\}$ plus a value which represents unrestriction, ∞.
– min_samples_split: The minimum number of samples required to divide an internal node. Possible values we will use are $\{n \in \mathbb{N} : 2 \leq n \leq 40\}$.
– max_leaf_nodes: Maximum number of nodes the tree could have. Possible values we will use are $\{n \in \mathbb{N} : n \geq 2\}$, plus a value which represents unrestriction (∞).
– class_weight: This parameter gives a weight to each class, which is really useful for unbalanced datasets. It takes values in the range $[0, 1]$, and a value of $\frac{1}{2}$ means that both classes are evenly considered. Possible values we will use are $\{\frac{n}{10} : n \in \mathbb{N}, 1 \leq n \leq 9\}$.

3.3 Initial Population

The initial population will contain at least 2 individuals represented with the following hyperparameters: (Gini, ∞, 2, ∞, $\frac{1}{2}$), (Entropy, ∞, 2, ∞, $\frac{1}{2}$). This will generate the biggest possible trees, and we will use them to upper bound all unbounded hyperparemeters. The rest of the initial population will be generated using random values randomly distributed with uniform probability in the range of each hyperparameter using the just calculated upper bounds when necessary.

3.4 MaOEAs Based Methods

As we know, MaOEAs suffer optimization problems due to the high dimensionality of the objective function. The number of non Pareto dominated solutions increase exponentially, as well as the number of solutions we need to describe and have a better understanding of the shape of the Pareto front [12]. Consequently, we decided to program and adjust three different algortihms,with them being NSGA-II, SMS-EMOA, and GrEA. Each of them has different properties, which may initially lead to some different Pareto front approximations.

NSGA-II Based Method. We will start with NSGA-II (Non-dominated Sorting Genetic Algorithm). We chose this algorithm because it is a staple in the context of Multiobjective Evolutionary Algorithms. It was the algorithm employed in Valdivia et al. [18], giving really good results, and we want to assess the behaviour of this algorithm in a Many Objectives Optimization context. The same structure and parameters as in that paper were used.

NSGA-II performance quickly decreases as the number of objectives start to grow, as it is particularly sensitive to the dominance resistance phenomenon and active diversity promotion [12]. In order to overcome these problems, many MaOEAs were specifically designed. We have selected two of them, both with different features and based on different concepts, to have a decent variety of methodologies. This is important as some of them could be better suited for certain problems than others.

SMS-EMOA Based Method. The second algorithm considered is SMS-EMOA (S metric Selection-EMOA) [7]. This algorithm uses S metric (better known as hypervolume) contribution as an elitist selection criterion. For that reason it belongs to the class of MaEOAs named indicator based measures, and to the subclass of hypervolume driven algorithms [12].

This algorithm generates a single new individual on each generation, and after adding it to the population, it removes the least contributing individual. SBX crossover and polynomial mutation are operator used, as proposed by the authors. Only for tournament purposes, crowding distance is calculated considering individuals on each Pareto Dominance rank, just as in NSGA-II. For maximizing hypervolume in a minimisation optimization problem, we have to compute the worst objective point in the objective space. To not be biased against any objective, every objective whose maximum value is greater than 1 is normalised to the range $[0, 1]$ in terms of the worse individual for that objective in the considered population.

GrEA Based Method. Finally, we have considered as our third algorithm GrEA (Grid based Evolutionary Algorithm) [19]. This algorithm belongs to the class of Relaxed dominance based MaOEAs, and in particular to Value-Based Dominance MaOEAs [12].

GrEA's main idea is to introduce a grid setting in the objective space, in which individuals are placed, which changes dynamically depending on the individuals forming the population. Thanks to that grid structure, we can change tournament and environmental selection criteria. For tournament, criteria used are standard domination, grid domination and grid crowding distance. For selection, grid rating, grid crowding distance and grid coordinate point distance are used.

4   Experimental Design

We have designed an experimentation process using four different ML problems which have been deeply studied in the context of fairness in ML, varying in scale and domain. All of these datasets are public and free to download from GitHub: https://github.com/algofairness/fairness-comparison/tree/master/fairness/data (last date accessed 24 March 2020). The data sets are as follows:

- Adult: U.S. citizens information in 1994. There are 32561 instances and 14 attributes. The prediction task is to asses wether an individual earns more than $50k per year or not. The sensitive attribute is race.
- German: Individuals' financial information. There are 1000 instances and 20 attributes. The prediction task is to asses the credit risk of individuals. The protected attribute considered is age.
- ProPublica Recidivism: Individuals' information from the Broward County (Florida) in 2013 and 2014. There are 72144 individuals containing 52 attributes. We want to predict if a person will reoffend in two years or not. From these attributes, we have used the following 12 in the experiments of this paper: sex, age, age_cat, race, juv_fel_count, juv_misd_count, juv_other_count, priors_count, c_charge_degree, c_charge_desc, decile_score, score_text. The protected attribute is race.
- ProPublica Violent Recidivism: This data set describes the same scenario as the previous one, but in this case the outcome is whether the rearrest happened within 2 years was because of a violent crime. It contains 4743 individuals and the same 12 attributes. The protected attribute is race.

We have executed each algorithm 10 times with different random seeds. Each execution was made with a population size of 150 individuals and 300 generations. The probability of mutation is 0.3, probability of crossover 0.9, and $\gamma = 2$ as stated in Valdivia et al. [18], for all methods which require those parameters.

To have a real Pareto front approximation to which evaluate convergence, we will join Pareto fronts found by each run of each given algorithm for a given problem, and then we filter those solutions sets, extracting only the non Pareto dominated individuals among them.

We will use a good range of quality measures which evaluate different aspects from the solution sets obtained. This measures help us to evaluate performance regarding convergence, uniformity and spread of solutions. With the purpose of defining those metrics, we will notate A as a set of solutions, and PF will represent our best Pareto front approximation after all the processes previously discussed:

- Hypervolume: It is defined as $\int_{(0,1)^m} \mathbb{1}_{D_A}(z)dz$ being $D_A = \{z = (z_1, ..., z_m) \in (0,1)^m : \exists a \in A : a \prec z\}$ and $\mathbb{1}_{D_A}$ being the indicator function of D_A. The bigger it is, the better is the set in a general way, as it may have better convergence, be more spread or have better uniformity on the distribution of the solutions.

- Generational Distance (GD): It is defined as $\frac{(\sum_{i=0}^{|A|} d_i^2)^{1/2}}{|A|}$, where d_i is calculated for a solution $x_i \in A$ as $\min\{||f(x_i) - f(y)||_2 : y \in PF\}$. The lower it is, the more converged is A with respect to PF on average.
- Inverted Generational Distance: It is defined as $\frac{(\sum_{i=0}^{|PF|} d_i^2)^{1/2}}{|PF|}$, where d_i is calculated for a solution $x_i \in PF$ as $\min\{||f(x_i) - f(y)||_2 : y \in A\}$. It is similar to GD, but from a different perspective, which is better suited to analyse convergence to PF analysing real Pareto front representation.
- Proportion: Proportion of PF solutions that also appear in A, i.e., $\frac{|B|}{|PF|}$, where $B = \{x \in A \cap PF\}$
- Error Ratio: $\frac{|B|}{|A|}$ where $B = \{x \in A \wedge x \notin PF\}$
- Spacing: It is defined as $\sqrt{\frac{1}{|A|-1} \sum_{i=1}^{|A|} (\overline{d} - d_i)^2}$, where $d_i = \min_{x_j \in A, x_j \neq x_i} \{||f(x_i) - f(x_j)||_1\}$, and $\overline{d} = \frac{\sum_{i=0}^{|A|} d_i}{|A|}$. The bigger it is, the more separated is each solution to each nearest neighbour, on average.
- Maximum spread: It is defined as $||z||_2$ where $z_\alpha = \max_{x_i, x_j \in A} |f_\alpha(x_i) - f_\alpha(x_j)|$. The bigger it is, the more extreme values on each coordinate of the objective space are found.
- Overall Pareto front spread: It is defined as $\prod_{i=1}^{m} \frac{|\max_{x \in A} f_i(x) - \min_{x \in A} f_i(x)|}{|P_{N_i} - P_{I_i}|}$, where P_N is an approximation of the nadir point, and P_I is an approximation of the ideal point [3], which are calculated as follows: $P_{I_\alpha} = \min_{x \in PF} f_\alpha(x)$, and $P_{N_\alpha} = \max_{x \in PF} f_\alpha(x)$. The bigger it is, the exploration of extreme points considering only 1 coordinate at a time better approaches the behaviour of PF, leading to a better representation of it.

5   Experimental Results

We will first compare our results to a similar process as that done in Valdivia et al. [18] and thus we will also execute our program using NSGA-II optimising for both gmean_inv and FPR$_{\text{diff}}$. In order to perform a fairer comparison, we used the same execution parameters as for the rest of executions. Both PPV$_{\text{diff}}$ and number of leaves were calculated for each individual generated. We will refer to it as NSGA-II$_2$, whereas our four objective optimisation NSGA-II will be referred as NSGA-II$_4$.

We will analyse how the value of each objective changed when we go up from optimising two to four objectives. We will take the mean of the median solutions in terms of validation error from the Pareto fronts of all NSGA-II$_2$ runs as a reference. Then, for each other algorithm, we will select the two individuals with the nearest value above in validation error with respect to the reference value, and the two nearest individuals below in each run. Once found, we will calculate a weighted average of those individuals, depending on how far in validation error are them from that reference median value, being less significant the further they are. Doing this, we can observe how algorithms behave at the same level of error, for the rest of objectives, and thus we can compare their multiobjective performance. Results can be seen on Table 1.

As we can see, solutions found by our four objectives algorithms tend to behave better on the objectives which NSGA-II$_2$ was not prepared to optimise, but worse on FPR$_{\text{diff, v}}$. This was expected as the two objective algorithm tries to minimise both error and FPR$_{\text{diff}}$ without taking into account the other two objectives, leading for worse results on the other objectives as they are contradictory, while in our four objective algorithms, as all objectives are taken into account, it generates more balanced solutions.

Table 1. Objective values of weighted average of individuals near the mean of the medians in NSGA-II$_2$ on validation error

| | | 4 Objectives | | | | | |
| | | 2 Objectives | | PPV$_{\text{diff,v}}$ | N.Leaves | Error$_t$ | FPR$_{\text{diff,t}}$ | PPV$_{\text{diff,t}}$ |
		Error$_v$	FPR$_{\text{diff,v}}$					
Adult	NSGA-II$_2$	0.2362	0.0169	0.1163	256.8000	0.2390	0.0346	0.0715
	NSGA-II$_4$	0.2362	0.0413	0.0741	278.5704	0.2366	0.0410	0.0770
	SMSEMOA	0.2362	0.0329	0.0604	210.8909	0.2374	0.0333	0.0722
	GrEA	0.2362	0.0330	0.0391	137.9508	0.2364	0.0303	0.0605
German	NSGA-II$_2$	0.3155	0.0202	0.1631	38.3000	0.3498	0.1041	0.0972
	NSGA-II$_4$	0.3177	0.0891	0.1240	30.7936	0.3387	0.1215	0.0854
	SMSEMOA	0.3172	0.0933	0.0941	34.3890	0.3436	0.1101	0.1035
	GrEA	0.3190	0.0967	0.1021	20.4307	0.3516	0.0872	0.1312
ProPub	NSGA-II$_2$	0.3708	0.0290	0.0922	258.8000	0.3822	0.0533	0.0820
	NSGA-II$_4$	0.3708	0.0869	0.0520	158.9334	0.3722	0.0894	0.0602
	SMSEMOA	0.3708	0.0504	0.0704	113.0509	0.3758	0.0742	0.0709
	GrEA	0.3708	0.0612	0.0577	107.6457	0.3765	0.0777	0.0676
ProP. V.	NSGA-II$_2$	0.3645	0.0235	0.1223	102.2000	0.3798	0.0474	0.0991
	NSGA-II$_4$	0.3645	0.0781	0.0779	92.8691	0.3816	0.0716	0.0957
	SMSEMOA	0.3645	0.0603	0.0703	99.5176	0.3763	0.0642	0.0898
	GrEA	0.3645	0.0686	0.0700	57.5332	0.3770	0.0696	0.0915

All of them behave better on PPV$_{\text{val}}$. It happens the same with the number of leaves except for NSGA-II$_4$ in Adult dataset. GrEA halves NSGA-II$_2$ number of leaves results. FPR$_{\text{val}}$ results are worse, as it is contradictory with respect to the other objectives. Our Many Objective algorithms tend to behave, in general, better than NSGA-II$_4$, although that is not the case in German dataset.

We will now join all solutions from all runs for each algorithm and calculate the coverage of these solution sets to each other. Results can be seen on Fig. 1. Coverage done by a set A to a set B is calculated as $C(A, B) = \frac{\{b \in B : \exists a \in A : a \prec b\}}{|B|}$. The bigger it is, the better solutions are in A with respect to those in B.

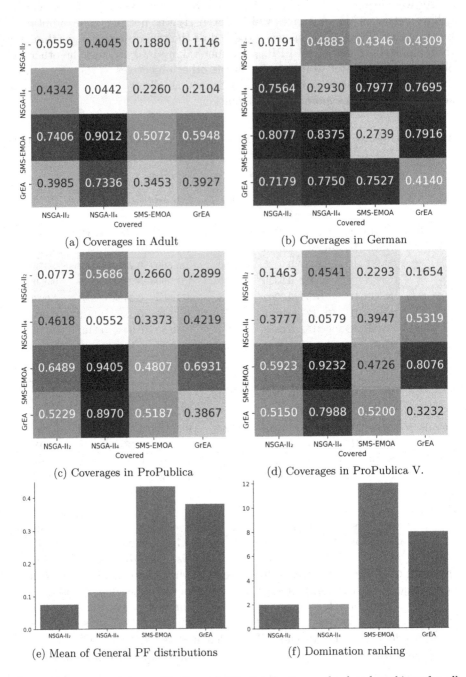

Fig. 1. Coverage matrices with General PF distribution and related rankings for all datasets and algorithms

We have also calculated all non Pareto dominated individuals from all runs and algorithms and join them together, giving the most accurate representation of the real Pareto front, which will be named General Pareto front (General PF). We then measure the proportion of those solutions that come from each algorithm. These values are shown at the diagonals of matrixes in Fig. 1. It is useful to understand which algorithm generated more solutions non dominated by those generated by any other algorithm, which is preferable. Also mean distribution proportions of General PF and a ranking of domination which shows how many times $C(A, B) > C(B, A)$ for solutions of an algorithm A compared to any other set of solutions B on the same dataset are shown in subfig. e and f.

We can now clearly see how SMS-EMOA and GrEA performed better in general than both variants of NSGA-II. They win in both rankings by a huge margin. SMS-EMOA solutions always cover more than others do with respect to them. They are, in general terms, the most represented solutions among all non dominated solutions found, with the exception of German dataset, where even NSGA-II$_4$ results are more represented. Both Many Objective algorithms tend to cover a great proportion of solutions from both NSGA-II, mostly NSGA-II$_4$ ones. NSGA-II$_2$ solutions are less covered as some of them have more opsimised results in error or FPR, while NSGA-II$_4$ are more balanced ones, and in this case they tend to be dominated with ease by solutions found by Many Objective algorithms. This supports our theory that Many Objectives algorithms are better suited for optimising fairness ML than NSGA-II in a 4 objective context.

In Table 2 we can see the quality measures previously discussed calculated using our the Pareto fronts of the 4 objectives algorithms. The General PF to which compare is now only calculated with respect to these algorithms. Measures than can be calculated over General PF are also shown. SMS-EMOA solutions are generally more converged than those from the rest of the algorithms, followed by GrEA, as their GD and Inverted GD for SMS-EMOA is the lowest considering every dataset except for German, meaning that they approximate well to the real Pareto front and they are quite representative. German dataset has much less instances, reason why their results consistently vary with respect to the rest of datasets. Proportion values follow the same distribution as before. Error ratio is consistent with results on proportion, as when one increases, the other one should decrease, meaning in this case that the size of Pareto fronts obtained by each run of all algorithms should be similar. In terms of spread measures we can not see a clear and direct relationship between them and the rest of measures or the quality of the solutions found by that algorithm. Both of them seem correlated as higher values on one of them mean higher values on the other, except for German dataset.

Table 2. Many-objective quality measures obtained in each problem

Data	Quality Measure	NSGA-II	SMS-EMOA	GrEA	General PF
Adult	Hypervolume	0.8190	0.8249	0.8164	0.8249
	GD	0.0068	0.0017	0.0023	–
	Inverted GD	0.0040	0.0035	0.0032	–
	Proportion	0.1114	0.4764	0.4122	1.0000
	Error ratio	0.6432	0.1159	0.2507	–
	Spacing	0.0229	0.0212	0.0162	0.0179
	Maximum spread	1.4379	1.1036	1.2532	1.4840
	Overall PF spread	0.9302	0.1386	0.5340	–
German	Hypervolume	0.7162	0.7189	0.7133	0.7190
	GD	0.0067	0.0086	0.0107	–
	Inverted GD	0.0082	0.0052	0.0099	–
	Proportion	0.3256	0.3101	0.3643	1.0000
	Error ratio	0.0968	0.1563	0.3493	–
	Spacing	0.0505	0.0443	0.0457	0.0404
	Maximum spread	0.8996	1.1768	0.9737	1.2161
	Overall PF spread	0.5217	0.7261	0.4982	–
ProPublica	Hypervolume	0.6683	0.6766	0.6708	0.6765
	GD	0.0076	0.0034	0.0034	–
	Inverted GD	0.0057	0.0037	0.0052	–
	Proportion	0.1689	0.4374	0.3937	1.0000
	Error ratio	0.5643	0.1843	0.2791	–
	Spacing	0.0257	0.0285	0.0194	0.0218
	Maximum spread	1.0338	1.2271	0.8307	1.2578
	Overall PF spread	0.6219	0.8109	0.2359	–
ProPublica V.	Hypervolume	0.6850	0.6903	0.6833	0.6903
	GD	0.0103	0.0041	0.0051	–
	Inverted GD	0.0074	0.0063	0.0074	–
	Proportion	0.1703	0.4444	0.3853	1.0000
	Error ratio	0.6678	0.1276	0.4061	–
	Spacing	0.0927	0.0288	0.0487	0.0542
	Maximum spread	1.8360	1.0903	1.2151	1.8374
	Overall PF spread	0.9974	0.0503	0.0590	–

6   Conclusions

In this paper we introduced an innovative method that generates a great variety
of models for ML problems considering several contradictory objectives, including fairness definitions. The method uses hyperparameters of learning algorithm

as decision space, employing decision trees as base classifier. Therefore, the method looks for optima settings of the learner to drive it to generate many models with different balances of accuracy, two fairness measures and interpretability. Since dealing with four contradictory criteria is a challenge, we opted by using the state-of-the-art many-objective optimization techniques SMS-EMOA and GrEA. The methodology shows that it is possible to obtain good results in terms of both equalized odds and predictive rate parity fairness while keeping a good accuracy and interpretability. This makes us reflect on the room for improvement in fairness that can be obtained without degrading accuracy.

Further studies using this method could involve employing other kinds of classifiers, or utilising other accuracy, fairness, or interpretability contradictory criteria. Adding more criteria could increase the gap in terms of quality of the solutions generated by NSGA-II and other MaOEAs. An interesting development path could involve incorporating fairness criteria in the own learning process of the decision tree, depending on a hyperparameter which controls how important fairness is. These models intrinsically consider fairness and add a relevant hyperparameter to the decision space, so they would be worth studying.

References

1. Agarwal, A., Beygelzimer, A., Dudík, M., Langford, J., Wallach, H.: A reductions approach to fair classification. arXiv preprint arXiv:1803.02453 (2018)
2. Angwin, J., Larson, J., Mattu, S., Kirchner, L.: Machine bias. ProPublica, 23 May 2016
3. Audet, C., Bigeon, J., Cartier, D., Le Digabel, S., Salomon, L.: Performance indicators in multiobjective optimization. Eur. J. Op. Res. (2020)
4. del Barrio, E., Gordaliza, P., Loubes, J.M.: Review of mathematical frameworks for fairness in machine learning (2020)
5. Binns, R., Van Kleek, M., Veale, M., Lyngs, U., Zhao, J., Shadbolt, N.: 'It's reducing a human being to a percentage' perceptions of justice in algorithmic decisions. In: Proceedings of the 2018 Chi conference on human factors in computing systems, pp. 1–14 (2018)
6. Bolukbasi, T., Chang, K.W., Zou, J.Y., Saligrama, V., Kalai, A.T.: Man is to computer programmer as woman is to homemaker? Debiasing word embeddings. Adv. Neural Inf. Process. Syst. **29**, 4349–4357 (2016)
7. Emmerich, M., Beume, N., Naujoks, B.: An EMO algorithm using the hypervolume measure as selection criterion. In: Coello Coello, C.A., Hernández Aguirre, A., Zitzler, E. (eds.) EMO 2005. LNCS, vol. 3410, pp. 62–76. Springer, Heidelberg (2005). https://doi.org/10.1007/978-3-540-31880-4_5
8. Eubanks, V.: Automating Inequality: How High-Tech Tools Profile, Police, and Punish the Poor. St. Martin's Press, New York (2018)
9. Friedler, S.A., Scheidegger, C., Venkatasubramanian, S., Choudhary, S., Hamilton, E.P., Roth, D.: A comparative study of fairness-enhancing interventions in machine learning. In: Proceedings of the Conference on Fairness, Accountability, and Transparency, pp. 329–338 (2019)
10. Hu, L., Chen, Y.: Fair classification and social welfare. In: Proceedings of the 2020 Conference on Fairness, Accountability, and Transparency, pp. 535–545 (2020)

11. Kamiran, F., Calders, T., Pechenizkiy, M.: Discrimination aware decision tree learning. In: 2010 IEEE International Conference on Data Mining, pp. 869–874. IEEE (2010)
12. Li, B., Li, J., Tang, K., Yao, X.: Many-objective evolutionary algorithms: a survey. ACM Comput. Surv. (CSUR) 48(1), 1–35 (2015)
13. Mehrabi, N., Morstatter, F., Saxena, N., Lerman, K., Galstyan, A.: A survey on bias and fairness in machine learning (2019)
14. Menon, A.K., Williamson, R.C.: The cost of fairness in binary classification. In: Conference on Fairness, Accountability and Transparency, pp. 107–118 (2018)
15. O'neil, C.: Weapons of Math Destruction: How Big Data Increases Inequality and Threatens Democracy. Broadway Books, Portland (2016)
16. S.C. of the United States: Ricci v. DeStefano. Technical report. U.S. 557 (2009)
17. Selbst, A.D., Boyd, D., Friedler, S.A., Venkatasubramanian, S., Vertesi, J.: Fairness and abstraction in sociotechnical systems. In: Proceedings of the Conference on Fairness, Accountability, and Transparency, pp. 59–68 (2019)
18. Valdivia, A., Sánchez-Monedero, J., Casillas, J.: How fair can we go in machine learning? Assessing the boundaries of accuracy and fairness. Int. J. Intell. Syst. 36(4), 1619–1643 (2021)
19. Yang, S., Li, M., Liu, X., Zheng, J.: A grid-based evolutionary algorithm for many-objective optimization. IEEE Trans. Evolut. Comput. 17(5), 721–736 (2013)
20. Zafar, M.B., Valera, I., Gomez Rodriguez, M., Gummadi, K.P.: Fairness beyond disparate treatment & disparate impact: learning classification without disparate mistreatment. In: Proceedings of the 26th International Conference on World Wide Web, pp. 1171–1180 (2017)
21. Zafar, M.B., Valera, I., Gomez-Rodriguez, M., Gummadi, K.P.: Fairness constraints: a flexible approach for fair classification. J. Mach. Learn. Res. 20(75), 1–42 (2019)
22. Zafar, M.B., Valera, I., Rogriguez, M.G., Gummadi, K.P.: Fairness constraints: mechanisms for fair classification. In: Artificial Intelligence and Statistics, pp. 962–970. PMLR (2017)
23. Zehlike, M., Bonchi, F., Castillo, C., Hajian, S., Megahed, M., Baeza-Yates, R.: Fa*ir: a fair top-k ranking algorithm. In: Proceedings of the 2017 ACM on Conference on Information and Knowledge Management, pp. 1569–1578 (2017)
24. Zehlike, M., Castillo, C.: Reducing disparate exposure in ranking: a learning to rank approach. In: Proceedings of The Web Conference 2020, pp. 2849–2855 (2020)

A Streaming Approach for Association Rule Analysis of Spanish Politics on Twitter

Pedro J. López, Elena Ruiz, and Jorge Casillas[(✉)] [ID]

Department of Computer Science and Artificial Intelligence,
Data Science and Computational Intelligence Institute (DaSCI),
University of Granada, Granada, Spain
casillas@decsai.ugr.es
http://ccia.ugr.es/ casillas

Abstract. The technological era in which we live has supposed an exponential rise in the quantity of data daily-generated in the Internet. Social networks and particularly Twitter has been one of the most disruptive factors in this era, allowing people to share easily opinions and ideas. Data generated in this social network is an example of streams, which are outlined by the challenges that arise from their particular features: continue, unlimited, high-speed arrivals, demand of fast reaction and with changes over time (known as concept drifts). The dynamism that characterizes this type of problem requires from a streaming analysis in order to perform an adequate treatment. In this situation, data stream mining appears as an emergent field of data science with specialized machine learning techniques according to the nature of streams. One of the most prominent tasks in this field is association stream mining, which focuses on the problem of dynamical extraction of interesting association rules from data features in a situation where it is not possible to assume an priori data structure and there is an evolution of these data features over the time. This paper aims to carry out a proof of concept focused on politics by studying a real collection of tweets related to the 2019 Spanish Investiture process. Thereby, Fuzzy-CSar-AFP algorithm has been applied in order to carry out an online analysis of association rules among a collection of terms of interest from our Twitter database.

Keywords: Data stream analysis · Association rules · Twitter analytics · Real-time systems

1 Introduction

Nowadays we live a technological era in which everything is automatized and everyone is connected. Therefore, an exponential increase in the production of

Supported by MINECO/FEDER under the Spanish National Research Project TIN2017-89517-P.

new information and content in the Internet has implied a rise in the amount of data that are generated. In this context, data sources that generate massive amounts of information in chronological order are becoming increasingly common (social networks, energy consumption, internet of things, network traffic, etc.). This has resulted in a growing interest in analyzing and understanding information as soon as it is produced. Many of these data sources are usually associated to some specific challenges, such as: high arrival rates, the requirement of immediate response or non-stationary distributions with the presence of concept drifts [9] (i.e., data distribution may suffer changes along time).

These aforementioned scenarios can be addressed by means of data streams, which are infinite sequences of structured records that arrive continuously. However, traditional data mining techniques cannot deal properly with them, since they assume that all data are available by the time of the analysis while this is not the case in data streams. Although one may be tempted to wait until all data are collected in order to perform an analysis, a real-time analysis is needed in some cases since the value of a data shrinks critically over time. Hence, an online adaptive approach is required in order to successfully analyze streams. An additional concern about streams is related to the management of computational resources, since data streams are loaded in memory and could eventually surpass the available resources depending on the amount and speed of upcoming data. Bearing this in mind, data structures are used in order to optimize memory space while keeping the information from data.

Data stream mining [8] arises as a field of data mining which gathers those techniques for streams analysis. These techniques apply particular methodologies and have mechanisms for adapting to changes in data. Data from stream are not stored in a permanent way but they are processed on-the-fly: each data is analyzed, processed and finally forgotten, making possible managing huge amounts of data in real-time. An interesting branch in the field of data stream mining is association stream mining, which addresses the conceptual ideas from association rules while keeping the online approach in order to deal with streams.

Twitter presents an ideal scenario in order to illustrate the aforementioned digitalization and has risen as a huge source of information in the last years. It is a microblogging social network in which millions of users post their opinions about any topic, share multimedia content and read hot news. In the Twitter domain, messages are called tweets. Tweets posted by users are an incessant source of data. Tweets are sequentially created in time and could eventually appear in a massive and unlimited quantity as a reaction to a trigger event. In addition, their content changes over time as new topics arise, old topics disappear and even for persistent topics changes might occur. Therefore, they are an example of textual stream, in which content is continuously created with no limit in amount or speed and their patterns are sensitive to evolve. Since a tweet consists on a collection of words, it could be considered as a transaction whose items are the words that compound it. Consequently, it is possible to mine association rules from a collection of tweets.

We have applied this idea in order to analyze the evolution of the association rules extracted from a stream of tweets about a specific topic. Concretely, we focused our efforts in those rules that present a link between terms and tweet sentiment, obtained by means of a pre-trained sentiment analysis model. Politics is undoubtedly one of the hot topics in social networks, which are used by political parties in order to foster their campaigns and attract voters. It has motivated us for carrying out our study for the Spanish politics and specifically for the process of Spanish Government investiture in 2019, which was quite controversial. To do so, we deal with tweets collected by ourselves between July 2019 and August 2019.

The originality of our proposal lies in the application of association stream mining to continuously create, update and delete association rules as new data are received. These rules allow us to connect different concepts of the tweet in a real-time manner, from the hashtags and keywords used to the sentiment with which the text was written. Therefore, the methodology we propose goes far beyond simple term frequency accounting, but rather uncovers reliable relationships between concepts that evolve over time as a result of modifications in the users opinions. These variations may be triggered by some landmark such as the release of new information, a statement from a political party or even a movement from some social groups. We present an elegant and visual approach for analyzing electoral periods, which could be used by political parties in order to prepare upcoming political campaigns as well as to enhance its comprehension of the electorate based in a (progressively more) representative population sample defined by Twitter community.

2   Related Work

Social networks are acquiring a key role in the current society, conforming an unexploited and powerful source of information in which data mining techniques could discover patterns on the users and their opinions. Streaming analysis appears as a promising tool for analyzing complex information that formerly was hardly accessible and have applications in business in order to attract customers or even set marketing strategies [3]. These applications could be potentially transferred to politics, since it is a topic progressively more bounded to Twitter. Bearing this in mind, it is not surprising that during last decades several researches prediction and analysis of political elections have been carried out using Twitter as a source of data.

Tasks like semantic association rule mining for a political context have been addressed in several researches by using variate sources of information. The research in Afolabi et al. [10] considers a semi-automatic creation of domain ontology in order to mine association rules from a collection of Nigerian politics-related news. They use the GARW (Generating Association Rules based on Weighting scheme) algorithm but just focus their approach in basic quality metrics such as support and confidence for a global study, without addressing any online analysis. Moreover, an interesting approach is presented in [1], where a time-window association rule mining is used in order to create an automated, streaming event detection in sports and politics for Twitter data. However, unlike our proposal, this approach is not purely online, but employs an offline algorithm (Apriori) for batches of data, which requires from defining an appropriate batch size and means losing adaptability when data arrival rates vary.

The main researches in politics and Twitter focus on predicting electoral results and monitoring political campaigns by heeding to patterns and sentiments. Wang *et al.* [19] applies a real-time analysis for USA elections based on a real-time data processing infrastructure and statistical sentiment model in order to evaluate public sentiment. In the same manner, elections in Europe have been also a subject to studies on the relation between Twitter and political results. 2013 Italian general elections motivated a Twitter-based study of several aspects, such as association between topics and political parties and correlations between volume of tweets and the election results [2]. Twitter sentiment analysis has also been tackled in several researches. Tumasjan *et al.* [17] studied Twitter importance in political discourse and analyzed if political sentiment on Twitter reflects real-life results in 2009 German federal election. While these works address interesting aspects such as an analysis at different timestamp and a topic relevance for candidates, they do not present neither a machine learning nor a real-time approach. Instead, they only take advantage of statistical calculations.. A forecasting of Singapore election was tackled by means of sentiment analysis in Choy *et al.* [4], who combine reweighting techniques and online sentiment divisions in order to avoid sampling bias. Although it is a compelling approach, they just focus their efforts in accomplishing an overall sentiment for each candidate within their respective party line. Meduru *et al.* [12] perform a sentiment analysis of mining tweets opinions about government issues and political reforms. In spite of an interesting tweet collection and processing, this approach does not investigate about the topics that raise a certain sentiment but just analyze the overall reaction of predefined country regions.

Regarding Spanish politics, Twitter has been recently used as a tool for mining voters opinions. Criado *et al.* [5] analyzed tweets about 2011 general elections, studying the correlation between the presence of political parties and the election results. On other hand, Solé *et al.* [16] perform a study of Twitter data in order to forecast Spanish political trends by means of a sentiment analysis and a political party affinity classification. As we can see, both works apply straightforward Machine Learning approaches without distinguishing from temporal aspects. However, as far as we know, association rule mining in a truly online fashion has never been used for this type of data.

Within our research, we have been addressed the application of Fuzzy-CSar-AFP [14] algorithm in a political context. Fuzzy-CSar-AFP is an evolution of Fuzzy-CSar [13], which follows a Michigan-style learning classifier system architecture with the aim of mining online fuzzy association rules from data streams. Fuzzy-CSar-AFP is a sophisticated version which includes two main improvements: new knowledge representations as well as new evolutionary operators in order to allow the use of fuzzy partitions with different granularities (i.e., number of linguistic terms), and an online mechanism for updating attributes ranges. This enhancements have meant fostering the capacity of the algorithm in order to ensure a set of rules with more robust descriptiveness and wider diversity. Both Fuzzy-CSar and Fuzzy-CSar-AFP performance as well as the quality of the generated rules have been widely analyzed for both real and synthetic data streams in Orriols *et al.* [13] and Ruiz and Casillas [15].

3   Proposed Methodology for Online Analysis of Tweets

3.1   Association Stream Mining

Association rules are an unsupervised technique used in order to mine patterns and relations between elements. This task is particularly interesting in streaming environments due to: (1) the demand of interpretability of the patterns discovered in data, (2) the need for discovering patterns while they are happening, and (3) the high and continuous volumes of data to be processed, which demand scalable learners. Some basic concepts in association rules terminology are as follow:

- **Itemset**: Given a database composed by a set of transactions, $\mathcal{T} = \{t_1, \ldots, t_K\}$, we could define a set of items, $\mathcal{I} = \{i_1, \ldots, i_N\}$, which define a collection of elements that appears together in a certain transaction t_i. Such a set is called itemset. If it contains k elements, it is called k-itemset.
- **Support**: Frequency count of a certain itemset in a database. It is a key aspect in order to extract interesting rules.
- **Frequent itemset**: Those itemsets whose support count in a database is greater than or equal to threshold support count specified by user.
- **Association rule**: Suppose two disjoint itemsets, X, Y such that $X \cap Y = \emptyset$, we define a rule $X \to Y$, where X is the antecedent and Y is the consequent.

Quality of rules is assessed by specific measurements of the representative of a rule within a database. For a rule $X \to Y$, we consider three main metrics:

- **Confidence**: Measures the strength of an association rule by calculating the ratio of the observed support of the rule and the support of its antecedent.
- **Lift**: Measures the ratio of the observed support of the rule and the expected if X and Y were independent. Originally, it was called Interest.

Considering the aforementioned features and challenges presented by streams, we required from an association rule mining technique which should be capable of extracting rules from a time-evolving data stream which makes no assumption about data structure.

In our study, we have applied **Fuzzy-CSar-AFP** [15], whose properties fit into the requirements of our task. Fuzzy-CSar-AFP is an online genetic fuzzy system designed to mine interesting association rules from streams of data in a single step, i.e., it does not build any list of frequent itemsets. Instead, Fuzzy-CSar-AFP directly evolves the set of fuzzy association rules. As it is presented in Ruiz and Casillas [15], it assumes that all the input variables can equally be part of the antecedent or the consequent part of the rules. Nonetheless, we have added to Fuzzy-CSar-AFP the capability of distinguishing between attributes to form the antecedent and attributes to form the consequent of the rules. To that aim, both the covering and genetic operators (crossover and mutation) [15] of the algorithm have been modified. The lists of attributes that can be used in each part of the rules are provided as input parameters of the algorithm. Using this new capability of the algorithm, sentiment variable was set to appear only in the consequent part. This allows the search space to be reduced and to focus on generating rules of interest, thus improving the efficacy of the algorithm.

3.2   Natural Language Processing and Sentiment Analysis

Raw Twitter data requires from a preprocessing step in order to improve the effectiveness of Machine Learning systems [7]. Since tweets are textual data, Natural Language Processing (NLP) emerges as a key task in order to enhance the quality in our analysis. NLP pursuits the understanding of unstructured, textual data. It comprehends a collection of techniques capable of preprocessing from raw messages in order to transform text into valuable information.

Special tweet features entail a need of a special preprocessing capable of extracting the best possible information from them. Tweet preprocessing requires from special considerations in order to deal with the special type of redaction from Twitter users [20]. For our purpose, NLP techniques such as lemmatization, stopwords suppression and part-of-speech have been applied in order to clean, standardize and structure messages. We also considered the need of shorting those words which are stretched out in order to emphasize a message as well as removing URLs that may be contained in tweets. Another technique in our NLP workflow is the detection of N-grams, which consist on a group of words which together present a special meaning and should be considered as a global concept. It is important for our work, since ignoring them will lead to the rise of rules with the N-grams words, which could cover up the rules that are actually interesting.

Sentiment analysis is applied in order to get the polarity of tweets. Sentiment analysis is the Machine Learning field focused on determining the opinion orientation expressed within textual data, identified as a sentiment, attitude or emotion. The popularity of this task has notably increased in last years due to the increase of available textual data, thanks to social networks. However, tweets are featured by their shortness, which hinder its performance. The effects of pre-processing techniques in the ability of tweet polarity classification systems has been addressed in several researches [11]. Sentiment analysis was a needed step in our analysis, since we were interested in those association rules that present a relation between key terms and sentiments from messages. Since our database of tweets was not labeled, we applied a pre-trained model for sentiment analysis, SentiStrength, which has been tested in several works [18]. It has been optimized for general short social web texts and is capable of dealing with several languages. For our purpose, we have considered three possible tweet sentiments: positive, neutral and negative.

4 Problem Statement and Data

4.1 Problem Statement

The aim of this work is to perform streaming association rule mining from Twitter data. The selected topic for this proof of concept was the Spanish investiture process from 2019, which was quite controversial since the fragmentation in the Parliament lead to a necessity of covenants between political parties in order to reach the Government. In this scenario, Twitter was an interesting tool for listening the opinion of the population. It is an interdisciplinar task which requires from several fields of Data Science previously introduced.

Tweets are preprocessed by means of a NLP analysis and tagged by a sentiment classifier. Although sentiment classification can be processed in streaming, our NLP task requires from a prior, offline analysis in order to be successfully addressed: we perform a preliminar analysis in Twitter to define a bag of words composed by the most representative political terms. These words will act as the items that form the transactions in our association rule mining analysis. In the same manner, the previously introduced analysis of N-grams should be based on a previous analysis due to the need of counting the words. Therefore, in this proof of concept we feed our streaming model with this information as a result of an external, previous analysis.

4.2 Data

Our database is composed by 261,080 tweets posted in a 45-day range, from 15th July to 29th August, 2019. The database was accomplished by using the official Twitter API, which allows us to retrieve those tweets which present specific targets that are related to the main Spanish political parties and the investiture process. We define the next set of hashtags as our targets: #PSOE, #PP, #UnidasPodemos, #CiudadanosCs, #VOX, #InvestiduraCongreso19, #InvestiDudaARV. Figure 1(a) shows the longitudinal distribution of tweets over time, with a maximum of 30k tweets in 25, July. In addition, data also have been labeled by using a pre-trained model for sentiment analysis: Fig. 1(b) displays a stream graph with the sentiments distribution in time.

As aforementioned, data has been preprocessed by means of NLP techniques which requires from a prior study in order to define standardize tweets. After that, we perform an analysis of our bag-of-words in order to define the terms of interest, which are those that were representative meaning in the political context as well as have a notably frequency. We have selected 40 terms that are shown in Fig. 2 as frequencies of appearance and word cloud. This set of terms are used as the items that will represent the tweets from our database.

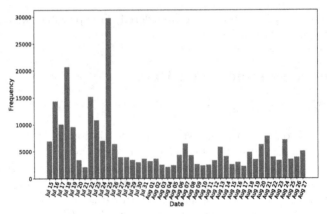

(a) Tweet distribution over time

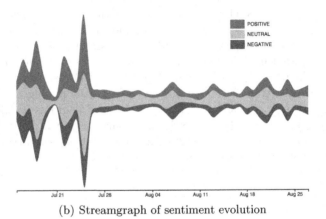

(b) Streamgraph of sentiment evolution

Fig. 1. Longitudinal distribution of the retrieved tweets though the time

5   Results

5.1   Association Rule Mining in Twitter Politics

Firstly, we analyzed the performance of our algorithms regarding the quality of the obtained rules so that we could verify whether these rules have enough quality when it comes to diversity and representativity. We have performed a quantitative analysis by means of Lift as our main metric for measuring the quality of the mined rules.

Figure 3(a) shows the evolution of the amount of rules which beat a lift threshold while the number of tweets increases in time. Total amount of rules is determined by the lift metric, which allows us to assess those rules that are more representative. We can observe that the higher the lift threshold the lower the quantity of extracted rules. A lift threshold of 1.0 retrieves an average of 70 rules while lift 1.2 and 1.4 lead to 20 and 10 rules, respectively. Regarding

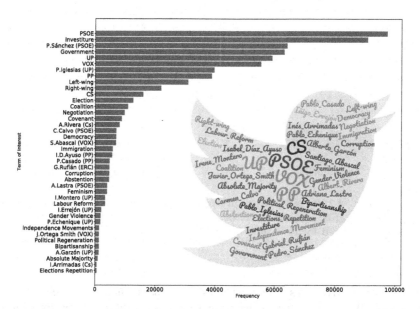

Fig. 2. Terms of interest (frequency distribution and word cloud) used in our study. For the shake of a better comprehension, terms has been translated into English and political personalities has been completed with tag indicating the party they belong to.

Fig. 3(b), it shows the amount of rules for a specific timestamp with regards to a minimum support threshold. We can observe how these quantities coincide with red line values in Fig. 3(a) when there is no support limitation.

Figure 4 displays the amount of rules over time that cite the main political parties in Spain. The rules considered for this analysis are those which include within its antecedent either political parties or the politicians that belong to them. We can observe that PSOE maintains its influence through time, while the other parties exhibit booms and busts. This behavior coincides with their influence during the investiture process, in which PSOE acted as the candidate to form Government, while the rest of them gain prominence in specific moments.

5.2 Concept Drift in Twitter Politics

Given the changing nature of the stream of tweets, a key aspect is the ability of the association stream mining method to react to changes in the patterns which may appear in the data by evolving the mined set of rules accordingly. We use a hybrid-chord diagrams as the visualization tool for rule representation. We have analyzed the presence of concept drift phenomenon from the retrieved patterns, which can be represented by a change in the type of rules for a specific concept in near timestamps. Concretely, we have focused our efforts in analyzing Fuzzy-CSar-AFP rules considering a 1.2 lift threshold.

A comparison between Fig. 5(a) and 5(b) allows us to illustrate the concept drift phenomenon: UP term suffers a sudden change in the found rules, going

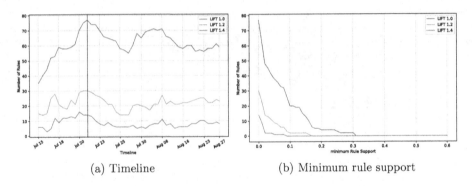

(a) Timeline   (b) Minimum rule support

Fig. 3. Amount of rules as data are processed and for minimum support thresholds in a specific time. Red-vertical line in (a) denotes the timestamp for support analysis. Results are compared for three lift thresholds (lift ≥ 1.0, lift≥ 1.2, lift ≥ 1.4) (Color figure online)

from a set of positive rules to neutral rules. In the same manner, Sánchez (PSOE) exhibits a drift from negative rules to neutral rules. In addition, it shows also a notably decrease of its importance, as it is shown by the reduction of the chord weight with respect to the whole diagram. PP term evolves from a set of just neutral rules to a set of neutral and positive rules in which positive has a bigger importance. On the contrary, Government shows an opposite behavior, running from a mix of three opinions to just neutral and positive rules. These cases are concept drift examples, in which retrieved rules evolve into different relations because of a variation in the pattern within the new published tweets. More examples of this behavior are available in terms like Iglesias(UP), Investiture, PSOE and CS. Furthermore, rules related to other terms arise in time as a results of new pattern in the posted messages. It is the case of terms such as VOX, Left-wing and Right-wing.

Similarly, Fig. 5(c) and 5(d) let us observe how some rules arise, such as CS with neutral sentiment and UP with positive sentiment, while other disappear (Investiture). We can observe that VOX loses some importance in the panorama despite the raise of neutral sentiment. Although it has gained rule diversity, its weight in the set of rules has decreased. On the contrary, PP and PSOE increase their weight in the panorama by new sentiments arising. Figure 5(a) shows a diverse scenario with several actors. An interesting behavior is performed by the main politicians in charge of the covenant (Sánchez and Iglesias), whose sentiment is opposed to the parties they lead. Figure 5(d) shows how at advanced stages parties have gathered prominence in Twitter debates, that agrees on a polarization phenomena where users have identified themselves with a posture.

In order to visualize how concept drift phenomenon appears for some key terms, we have studied the amount of rules through time for each sentiment by means of a streamgraph representation. For instance, in Fig. 6(a) we can observe how PP presents a change in the amount of rules for each sentiment: it starts with positive and neutral assessments among Twitter community. However, as

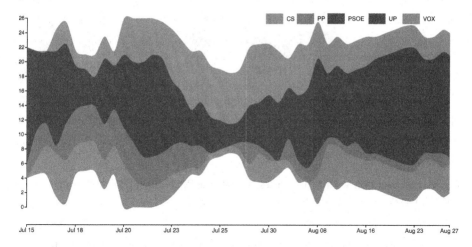

Fig. 4. Streamgraph of the amount of rules with lift ≥ 1.2 related to the main political parties by considering both political parties and the politicians that belong to them

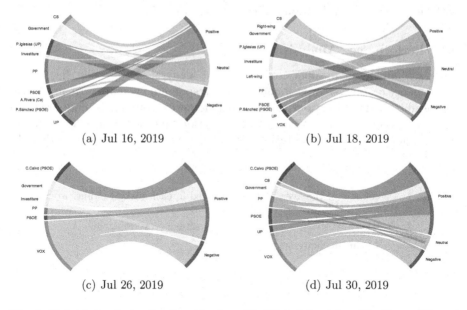

(a) Jul 16, 2019

(b) Jul 18, 2019

(c) Jul 26, 2019

(d) Jul 30, 2019

Fig. 5. Hybrid-chord visualization of rules with lift ≥ 1.2 retrieved by Fuzzy-CSar at several timestamps of the stream processing.

time passes it causes mix of sentiments, while towards the end of the stream it generates a negative opinion with a total agreement among the users of Twitter. Similarly, the analysis of PSOE (Fig. 6(b)) also shows a clear evolution in user opinions. It displays an interesting pattern, causing a mix of feelings in the early stages of the analyzed period, but finally leading to a clear predominance of

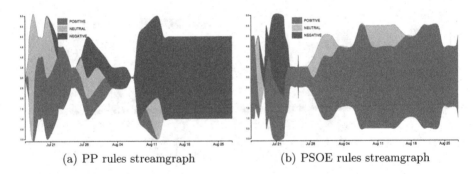

      (a) PP rules streamgraph   (b) PSOE rules streamgraph

Fig. 6. Streamgraph with evolution of rules for each sentiment for the terms (a) PP and (b) PSOE

positive sentiment among the community. Moreover, it is a term with sufficient relevance in the set of tweets as to be part of different rules during the entire duration of the stream. We can check that in both cases this behavior agrees with the hybrid-chord diagram representation in Fig. 5.

5.3 Performance Analysis

Since we pursue an unsupervised streaming analysis, a key point lies in the performance of the system: it should rapidly respond to upcoming streams which may lead to critical situations because of its features (continuous, unlimited and high speed arrivals). We have analyzed the performance for each task in order to identify those that are computationally expensive and could lead to bottlenecks (Table 1).

Table 1. Percentage of the average time invested in each task of online processing

Task	Percentage of average time
Sentiment analysis	64%
NLP	35.9%
Association rules extraction	0.09%

The study shows an average time of processing per message of 0.5 secs. Notice that the most of the time is invested in sentiment analysis task. Therefore, using a more sophisticated tool could lead to better results in performance.

6   Conclusions

By means of association stream mining techniques, we perform an analysis of users' opinion from Twitter in order to extract relations between a set of terms of interest and sentiments. The presented work is a novel application of streaming association rule analysis that, as far as we are aware, has not been used in order to analyze this type of data. The proposal continuously evolve association rules that allow us to relate in real time different concepts of the tweet, from the hashtags and keywords used to the sentiment with which the text was written.

Particularly, we conducted this research by working with a dataset of tweets related to Spanish government investiture process in 2019. We selected a hot-topic in social networks such as politics in which the online analysis of associations between terms and sentiments is quite interesting. This type of research is highly attractive since it allows to easily mine interesting conclusions about what is happening at every instant in an open, non-limited source such as Twitter. Our study of rule dynamics shows how user opinions go through different phases, leading to intriguing pattern variations. Its potential is prominent, since it could allow political parties to monitor political campaigns and gain leverage from Twitter in order to comprehend voters preferences by analyzing users reactions to events within the political scene.

As future lines of improvement, it could be interesting to incorporate a spam removal step in order to filter those messages which have a clear advertising intention. In addition, regarding the high amount of time invested in the sentiment analysis, the application of BERT architectures [6] in this task would be notably beneficial in order to speed processing up. Another feasible research line is to use this streaming approach for online detection and identification of events for a certain topic.

References

1. Adedoyin-Olowe, M., Gaber, M.M., Dancausa, C.M., Stahl, F., Gomes, J.A.B.: A rule dynamics approach to event detection in Twitter with its application to sports and politics. Expert Syst. Appl. **55**(C), 351–360 (2016). https://doi.org/10.1016/j.eswa.2016.02.028
2. Caldarelli, G., et al.: A multi-level geographical study of Italian political elections from Twitter data. PLoS ONE **9**, e95809 (2014). https://doi.org/10.1371/journal.pone.0095809
3. Chamlertwat, W., Bhattarakosol, P., Rungkasiri, T., Haruechaiyasak, C.: Discovering consumer insight from Twitter via sentiment analysis. J. Univ. Comput. Sci. **18**, 973–992 (2012)
4. Choy, M., Cheong, M., Laik, M.N., Shung, K.: A sentiment analysis of singapore presidential election 2011 using Twitter data with census correction. arXiv preprint:1108.5520 (2011)
5. Criado, J.I., Martínez-Fuentes, G., Silván, A.: Twitter en campaña: las elecciones municipales españolas de 2011. In: Revista de Investigaciones Políticas y Sociológicas (RIPS), vol. 12 (2013)
6. Devlin, J., Chang, M.W., Lee, K., Toutanova, K.: BERT: pre-training of deep bidirectional transformers for language understanding. In: Proceedings of the 2019 Conference of the North American Chapter of the Association for Computational Linguistics: Human Language Technologies, vol. 1 (Long and Short Papers), pp. 4171–4186. Association for Computational Linguistics, Minneapolis, Minnesota (June 2019). https://doi.org/10.18653/v1/N19-1423

7. Effrosynidis, D., Symeonidis, S., Arampatzis, A.: A comparison of pre-processing techniques for Twitter sentiment analysis. In: 21st International Conference on Theory and Practice of Digital Libraries (TPDL 2017) (2017). https://doi.org/10.1007/978-3-319-67008-9_31
8. Gama, J.: Knowledge Discovery from Data Streams. Chapman & Hall/CRC, Boca Raton (2010)
9. Gama, J., Žliobaitė, I., Bifet, A., Pechenizkiy, M., Bouchachia, A.: A survey on concept drift adaptation. ACM Comput. Surv. (CSUR) 46(4), 1–37 (2014). https://doi.org/10.1145/2523813
10. Ibukun, A., Okuboyejo, O., Daramola, O.: Semantic association rule mining in text using domain ontology. Int. J. Metadata Semant. Ontol. 12(1), 28–34 (2017). https://doi.org/10.1504/IJMSO.2017.087646
11. Krouska, A., Troussas, C., Virvou, M.: The effect of preprocessing techniques on Twitter sentiment analysis. In: 2016 7th International Conference on Information, Intelligence, Systems Applications (IISA), pp. 1–5 (2016). https://doi.org/10.1109/IISA.2016.7785373
12. Meduru, M., Mahimkar, A., Subramanian, K., Padiya, P.Y., Gunjgur, P.N.: Opinion mining using Twitter feeds for political analysis. Int. J. Comput. (IJC) 25(1), 116–123 (2017)
13. Orriols-Puig, A., Casillas, J., Martínez-López, F.J.: Automatic discovery of potential causal structures in marketing databases based on fuzzy association rules. In: Casillas, J., Martínez-López, F.J. (eds.) Marketing Intelligent Systems Using Soft Computing. Studies in Fuzziness and Soft Computing, vol. 258, pp. 181–206. Springer, Berlin, Heidelberg (2010). https://doi.org/10.1007/978-3-642-15606-9_14
14. Ruiz, E., Casillas, J.: Adaptive fuzzy partitions for evolving association rules in big data stream. Int. J. Approx. Reason. 93, 463–486 (2018). https://doi.org/10.1016/j.ijar.2017.11.014
15. Sancho-Asensio, A., Orriols-Puig, A., Casillas, J.: Evolving association streams. Inf. Sci. 334–335, 250–272 (2016). https://doi.org/10.1016/j.ins.2015.11.043
16. Solé Farré, M., Giné, F., Valls, M., Bijedic, N.: Real time classification of political tendency of Twitter Spanish users based on sentiment analysis. Int. J. Comput. Inf. Eng. 12(9), 697–706 (2018). https://doi.org/10.5281/zenodo.1474549
17. Tumasjan, A., Sprenger, T., Sandner, P., Welpe, I.: Predicting elections with Twitter: what 140 characters reveal about political sentiment. In: Fourth International AAAI Conference on Weblogs and Social Media, pp. 178–185 (2010)
18. Vilares, D., Thelwall, M., Alonso, M.A.: The megaphone of the people? Spanish SentiStrength for real-time analysis of political tweets. J. Inf. Sci. 41(6), 799–813 (2015). https://doi.org/10.1177/0165551515598926
19. Wang, H., Can, D., Kazemzadeh, A., Bar, F., Narayanan, S.: A system for real-time Twitter sentiment analysis of 2012 U.S. presidential election cycle. In: Proceedings of the ACL 2012 System Demonstrations, pp. 115–120. ACL (2012)
20. Zhao, J., Gui, X.: Comparison research on text pre-processing methods on Twitter sentiment analysis. IEEE Access 5, 2870–2879 (2017). https://doi.org/10.1109/ACCESS.2017.2672677

On the Trade-off Between Robustness and Complexity in Data Pipelines

Aiswarya Raj Munappy[1], Jan Bosch[1(✉)], and Helena Homström Olsson[2]

[1] Department of Computer Science and Engineering, Chalmers University of Technology, Hörselgången 11, 412 96 Gothenburg, Sweden
{aiswarya,jan.bosch}@chalmers.se
[2] Department of Computer Science and Media Technology, Malmö University, Nordenskiöldsgatan, 211 19 Malmö, Sweden
helena.holmstrom.olsson@mau.se

Abstract. Data pipelines play an important role throughout the data management process whether these are used for data analytics or machine learning. Data-driven organizations can make use of data pipelines for producing good quality data applications. Moreover, data pipelines ensure end-to-end velocity by automating the processes involved in extracting, transforming, combining, validating, and loading data for further analysis and visualization. However, the robustness of data pipelines is equally important since unhealthy data pipelines can add more noise to the input data. This paper identifies the essential elements for a robust data pipeline and analyses the trade-off between data pipeline robustness and complexity.

Keywords: Data pipelines · Trade-off · Robustness · Complexity · Composite nodes · Data quality

1 Introduction

The era of Artificial Intelligence and Big Data is bringing the urgent need of advanced mechanisms for the acquisition, management, and analysis of data [6]. Data analysis techniques like neural networks, data mining, machine learning, signal processing, and visualization methods demand high-quality data [2]. Recently, many organizations have begun implementing advanced, data-driven, and real-time analytics for both operational and strategic decision making [3,9]. Machine learning algorithms are the foundation for such initiatives [4]. However, poor data quality is the major factor challenging advanced analytics implementations as well as the performance of machine learning models [1]. To achieve good data quality, it is mandatory to control and co-ordinate end-to-end data process. Data pipelines play an important role throughout the data process whether it is data analytics, machine learning, or deep learning [8]. The activities in a data pipeline can be manual, semi-automated, or completely automated (without any human intervention) and can be triggered periodically by scripts that

A. C. R. Paiva et al. (Eds.): QUATIC 2021, CCIS 1439, pp. 401–415, 2021.
https://doi.org/10.1007/978-3-030-85347-1_29

run all the time. The activities in the pipeline are interchangeable enough such that the order of their execution does not matter. Alternatively, the order may be extremely important because the activities depend on where in the pipeline they run. In practice, data pipelines often encounter failures at different stages and the impact of the failure is carried to the successive steps causing accumulation of errors thereby negatively affecting the quality of data application. A failure or bug in a single step of a data pipeline has cascading effects that can require hours of manual intervention and cleanup. These kinds of issues consume time and effort of data engineers, data scientists, and data analysts which make teams wary of pushing out even the most innocuous changes to a data pipeline. Moreover, data quality is negatively affected causing eroded end-user confidence.

Although data pipelines facilitate automated data flow from the data source to the data sink, they can encounter failures at any stage of the data life cycle. Robust data pipelines are strong and healthy data pipelines that are capable of surviving failures. Robustness of data pipelines is critical as data pipelines are built to ensure reliability, transparency, reproducibility, and traceability in the data management process. Therefore, data pipelines should be monitored to detect the failure at every stage. The detection of failures wouldn't be enough to provide sufficient strength to the pipeline. Further, defining mitigation strategies is required to reduce the impact of failure. In this study, we model data pipelines with components called nodes and connectors with different capabilities. These components help to avoid data leakages through the links of the data pipeline and provide better traceability, monitoring, and failure notification. However, complexity is induced through the inclusion of components added to ensure robustness.

The contribution of this paper is two-fold. First, it identifies the essential components of a robust data pipeline. Second, it details the trade-off between robustness and complexity in a data pipeline. The design of a conceptual model for a robust data pipeline and its components are validated through a case study with three leading companies in telecommunication and automobile domains. The remainder of this paper is organized as follows. Section 2 discusses the research methodology adopted for conducting the study. Section 3 introduces the use cases and Sect. 4 describes the data pipeline model, its components, and capabilities. Section 5 details the conceptual model for robust data pipelines and Sect. 6 explains the trade-off between data pipeline robustness and complexity. Section 7 summarizes our study and the conclusions.

2   Research Methodology

The objective of this study is to explore the existing data pipelines at three case companies, identify the components of a pipeline, and to develop a conceptual model of a robust data pipeline with the least complexity. Based on the study objectives, we formulated the following research questions:

- **RQ1:** What are the essential components of a robust data pipeline?
- **RQ2:** How is the data pipeline complexity impacted when we apply our conceptual model of robust data pipeline?

2.1   Multiple Case Study

This study uses a multi-case study with an interpretive approach [11] as it allows the researchers to explore, study, and understand real-world cases in its context in more depth [11,13]. Multi-case study can facilitate a deep understanding of a topic through different lenses. Second, the multiple case study approach can investigate contemporary real-life situations and can provide a foundation for the application of ideas and extension of methods. Each case in the study pertains to a use case that makes use of data. Table 1 details the selected five use cases and roles of interviewed experts from three case companies.

Company A: Company A is a telecommunications equipment manufacturer that also provides solutions and services for managing network operations. Within Company A, we studied three data pipelines A1, A2, and A3.

Company B: Company B is a leading multinational automobile manufacturer. Within Company B, we have studied a data pipeline B1 that they use to create data quality reports based on the data collected from their manufacturing units, repair centers, and delivery centers.

Company C: Company C is an innovation center of an automotive company. Data pipeline C1 collects data from the data lake located at the development center, analyses it, and creates data quality reports out of it. According to the reports, actions are taken to fix the data quality issues and the good quality data thus generated is stored in refined storage for training their machine learning models.

2.2   Data Collection

Semi-structured interviews and weekly meetings [12] were the two research methods adopted for data collection. An interview guide with 30 questions categorized into six sections was formulated for conducting semi-structured interviews. The questions in the interview guide was formulated based on the objectives of the research which was to explore and study the applications consuming data in the companies. The first two sections intended on the background of the interviewee. Next two sections focused on the data life cycle activities in various use-cases. The remaining questions focused on the data pipelines failures and the final section had questions about data testing and monitoring practices. All interviews were conducted virtually via videoconferencing due to the COVID-19 pandemic. The duration of the interviews were between 60 and 80 min and

Table 1. Use cases and roles of interviewed Experts

Company	Use cases	Interviewed Experts	
		ID	Role
A	Pipeline for Data Collection	R1	Senior Data Scientist
A	Pipeline for Data Governance	R2	Data Scientist
		R3	Analytics System Architect
		R4	Software Developer
A	Data Pipeline for Machine learning model	R5	Data Scientist
		R6	Senior Data Scientist
		R7	Software Developer
		R8	Senior Data Scientist
B	Pipeline for Data Collection	R9	Senior Data Engineer
		R10	Data Engineer
		R11	Data Engineer
		R12	Data Analyst and Superuser
C	Pipeline for Data Quality monitoring	R13	Director of data analytics team
		R14	Data pipeline developer
		R15	Software Developer
		R16	Product Owner for data analytics team

were recorded with the permission of respondents and were transcribed later for analysis. Besides, the data was collected through by the first author who attends weekly meetings and discussions with data scientists and data analysts at companies A, B as part of action research.

2.3 Data Analysis

A summary of the interview was prepared by the first author to create an overall idea about the use cases, data pipeline stages, and associated challenges. The interview transcripts were investigated for identifying the stages of the data pipeline, the main purpose of the data pipeline, similarities, and dissimilarities between the use cases. The transcripts were open coded [5] to build themes from the transcripts. The first author prepared notes during the meetings with the team and analyzed it further. These notes together with the codes from transcripts were further analyzed to obtain an end-to-end view of data pipelines at the case companies. The themes developed from the transcripts helped to understand the parts common to all use cases. The first author developed the findings of the study after careful analysis of the empirical data and modified it based on the inputs from the other two authors which were then validated with the interviewees from the companies by conducting a follow-up meeting. For further validation, the findings were also presented before another panel including super users, managers, software developers, data engineers, and data scientists at all three companies. The reflections were about the increase in complexity that is induced with the introduction of fault detection, mitigation components.

3   Use Cases

Data was collected from three embedded system companies anonymized as companies A, B, and C owing to a confidentiality agreement. This section presents five data pipelines from these three case companies A, B, and C. For confidentiality reasons, we can only describe each data pipeline at a very high level of abstraction. Significant details have been studied by the authors, but cannot be presented in the paper.

3.1   Case A1: Data Collection Pipeline

The Company A has to collect data from various globally distributed devices which is a demanding task. The data collected from devices located in another country or customer network requires compliance with the legal agreement. Moreover, sensitive information like user details will be there in the network data which demands responsible attention. Data generated by sources can be of different formats and frequencies. For instance, data generation can be continuous, intermittent, or batches. Consequently, the data collection pipeline should be adaptable with different intensities of data flow. Figure 1 illustrates the automatic data collection pipeline that does data collection from multiple distributed devices. In this scenario, the data collection device is placed inside a piece of equipment owned by customers. However, the device data is extracted by filtering the customer's sensitive information. Base stations have data generation devices called nodes as well as a device for monitoring and managing the nodes. Data collection agents at the customer premise can interact either with nodes directly. However, access service is used for authentication. The data thus collected is transmitted through a secure tunnel to the data collection toolkit located at the company premise which also has access service for authentication. Data collection toolkit received the data and store it in the central data storage from where the teams can access the data using their data user credentials.

3.2   Case A2: Data Governance Pipeline

Figure 2 shows the data pipeline that serves the teams in the company who are working with data according to their requirement (The term 'data', here

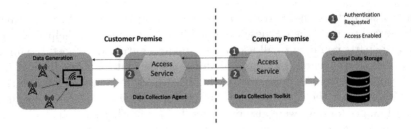

Fig. 1. Data collection pipeline - A1

indicate the link for downloading original data). The data pipeline A2 receives two types of data dumps: internal and external. The internal data dump is the data that is ingested by the teams inside the company and external data dump is the data collected directly from the devices in the fields. The data pipeline in case A2 gathers both types of data dumps from various sources and stores it in a data warehouse. The data ingestion method for internal data and external data are different. i.e. the data ingestion method varies according to the data source. The ingested data from multiple assorted sources are stored in the refined data storage for future use. The data can be encrypted and requires decryption before storing it for further uses. Therefore, data archiver module sends encrypted data dump to the third-party services for decryption. Decrypted links from the third party are sent to the archiver module which then stores it in the data storage. Thus, data from several distributed sources are made available in a central location. Teams can access data from any stage of the pipeline. The monitoring mechanism in the pipeline is manually carried out by the 'flow guardian' or data pipeline owner who manages the issues in the pipeline by arranging fix.

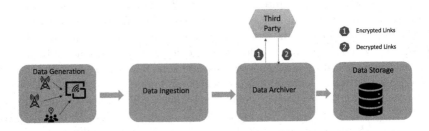

Fig. 2. Data governance pipeline - A2

3.3   Case A3: Data Pipeline for Machine Learning Applications

Figure 3 shows the data pipeline for machine learning applications. Ingest, store, transform, and aggregate are the four main steps in the data pipeline of case A3. The data generated by the source is collected from the devices that are deployed in the dedicated zone in the field. These dedicated zones in the field which collects the data and ingest into pipeline are connected to the data ingestion module. A periodic check is performed to find out the compressed files. If a compressed file is encountered, a transaction is logged and the file is downloaded. These files are loaded into the archive directory of the data cluster. Machine learning models cannot use the data directly from the cluster because either the data is in compressed form or data logs collected from different devices are of different formats. Data transformation step in the data pipeline checks for the new files in the archive directory and when found it is fetched, uncompressed, and processed to convert it to an appropriate format. Data aggregation module receives this uncompressed data, aggregate and summarize to form structured data which the machine learning models can use.

Fig. 3. Data pipeline for machine learning applications - A3

3.4   Case B1: Data Collection Pipeline

Three types of data plant data, delivery data, warranty data and repair data are collected and stored by Company B and is distributed to all the teams and co-working organization spread across the world. Manufacturing plants, service centers, delivery centers and warranty offices are the sources from which these data are collected. Every 24 h, from distributed manufacturing plants, company B collects product data. For each product built there, data is generated by these manufacturing units. The data collection agent at company B do not collect all the data generated by the plants. The data which is to be collected from the plants is demanded by the Group Quality IT platform in the company. In the company's warehouse, the data requested by the delivery centers are also collected and stored. The data collection pipeline working in company B is illustrated in Fig. 4. The data collected from different sources are in different formats and volumes and as a result data transfer mechanism and data storage are also different. The data is transformed into a uniform format and stored in data warehouse after ingesting it from the primary storage. For teams as well as other organizations that demands data, it then act as a supplier. For instance, data about the products that are manufactured in the plants are a requisite for the delivery centers.

3.5   Case C1: Data Quality Analysis Pipeline

Company B collects and stores data from manufacturing plants, delivery centers. Company C collects data from the data pipeline of company B and creates data

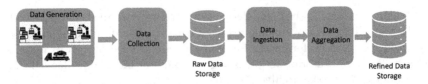

Fig. 4. Data collection pipeline - B1

quality reports which are used by the data scientists team at company C for analyzing the product quality. For example, the report can be used to identify the product model that is sent to repair centers frequently. The investigation is initiated if the data quality is not satisfactory, and actions are taken to fix the data quality issues. Company B sends data through a private network to company C and store it in their data storage. Data scientists from company C access the data for creating reports and training machine learning models. Figure 5 illustrates the data pipeline for data quality analysis at company C.

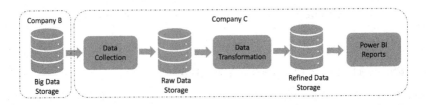

Fig. 5. Data quality analysis pipeline - C1

4   Components of a Robust Data Pipeline

This section gives an overview of components in a conceptual model of the data pipeline. Data Pipelines are a collection of data processing components connected such that the output of one component becomes the input to one or more others. Data-flow through the data pipelines starts from a data source and ends in a data sink. Use cases in Sect. 4 shows that data undergoes aggregation, cleaning, transformation, and processing before reaching the destination or data sink. Each of these steps can induce data error and data loss. Practitioners R2, R5, R6, R8, and R12 indicated that data loss happens during the process of aggregation, transformation, and cleaning. Therefore, we can infer that each component in the data pipeline is a potential threat to data quality.

Organizations depending on data for decision-making have to ensure the robustness of their data pipelines. A data pipeline is said to be robust when it is strong and healthy which means that the data pipeline should be capable of recovering from failures and produce the intended output with minimum errors.

To design such a robust data pipeline functionalities such as monitoring, fault detection and fault recovery are essential. To enable fault recovery, mitigation strategies are required. To prevent data breaches, authentication mechanisms should be included in the data pipeline. These functionalities are formulated based on the MECE principle. The Mutually Exclusive, Completely Exhaustive (MECE) is a methodology propounded by McKinsey and Company which means no omission and no duplication [10]. Therefore, to implement strong and healthy data pipelines, we need the components that perform data-flow monitoring, fault detection, mitigation strategies and authentication mechanism.

We have modelled data pipelines with basic elements called nodes and connectors as shown in Fig. 6. All data pipeline starts with a source node that produces data and ends with a sink node that is the ultimate destination of the data flowing through that pipeline. All the nodes in between the source and the sink are intermediate nodes as illustrated in Fig. 6(c). The ability of a component to perform an activity or task is called its capability. Therefore, the functionalities such as fault detection, fault recovery, authentication are incorporated as capabilities. Capabilities in a data pipeline can be classified as node level capabilities and connector level capabilities.

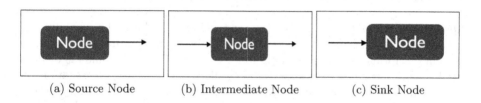

(a) Source Node   (b) Intermediate Node   (c) Sink Node

Fig. 6. Types of nodes

4.1   Node Level Capabilities

Node level Capability is the ability of a node to perform a certain activity. Data generation, data collection, data ingestion, data storage, data processing, and data reception are node level capabilities.

Data Generation: Data generation is typically the capability associated with the source node. However, there is no strict requirement that the source node of the data pipeline should have data generation capability. For instance, the source node in case C1 can't generate data. Instead, it can store data. Smart homes, grids, sensors in airplanes, networks, wearable devices, mobile phones, cars, etc. can be called data generation nodes.

Data Collection: Data collection nodes gather data from the source nodes. Most often, source nodes will be multiple and distributed. In those cases, data collection nodes will be also multiple and distributed as in cases A1, A2, A3, and B1. The data collection node performs the activity according to the legal agreement. Data generated/stored at the source can be in huge volumes. However, not all data are collected by the data collection agent due to the following reasons.

- Data collection agent doesn't have access to entire data (Case A1, A2, A3)
- Data pipeline requires only part of the data from the source (Case C1)
- Data collection agent can't handle huge volume of data (Case B1)

Therefore, either data collection node filters the data that is required for the data pipeline or the data source sends filtered data to the data collection agent.

Data Ingestion: Data ingestion is the process of collecting data from multiple assorted sources. Data ingestion can be real-time, as batches, or as a combination of real-time and batches. Kafka, Hive, or Spark are the tools used in the use cases described in the previous section. Cases A1, A2, and A3 use Kafka whereas case B1 and C1 use Hive, Spark, and Kafka as data ingestion tools. According to the type of data, the data ingestion method also varies within a single data pipeline. For instance, case A2 at company A has Continuous Integration data as well as Continuous Deployment data ingested using different methods.

Data Storage: Data Storage is often repeated in a pipeline. There are different types of storage such as data lakes, data warehouses, file systems, etc. Storage of data in raw format is critical as data processing, transformation, and aggregation mechanisms may cause data loss. Data granularity is lost during aggregation and transformation and consequently the data will come less suitable for applications that demands fine-grained data [7]. Moreover, machine learning models trained with processed data might not perform well while encountering real-time raw data. Therefore, data stored for the future is better in its original form.

Data Processing: Data processing is an umbrella term that includes several operations like data aggregation, data transformation, data extraction, data selection, etc. Real-world data is often incomplete, inconsistent, and/or missing certain behaviors, and is likely to contain several errors. Data pre-processing is an important capability implemented for resolving such issues.

Data Reception: Data reception is the capability of all nodes in a data pipeline as all except data sources are receiving data from the previous node.

4.2   Connector Level Capabilities

Connector level Capability is the ability of the connector to perform a certain activity. Capabilities like authentication, monitoring, fault detection, and mitigation are connector level capabilities.

Authentication: To ensure the security of the data flowing through the pipeline, authentication is essential. Authentication validates the right to access data and information, and protect against identity theft and fraud. Moreover, it ensures security tasks such as confidentiality, integrity, and availability. Confidentiality restricts data access to authorized persons whereas integrity ensures that data is modified only by authorized persons. Availability guarantees data availability to authorized users. Thus authentication is a central component that guards the data pipeline against external attacks.

Fault Detection: Continuous monitoring and fault detection is required in the pipeline to prevent data leakage and thereby maintaining data quality. With the increase in the number of nodes in the data pipeline, the chance for data leakage also increases. Therefore, it is necessary to anticipate failures throughout the data pipeline. For instance, in data pipeline A3, not all encrypted data links sent to the third party for decryption are sent back, leading to missing files and as a result, the quality of the final data product decreases. Similarly, each of the stages may encounter failures resulting in the degradation of data quality. Identifying a complete and exhaustive list of faults at each stage of the data pipeline is not a practical task. However, it is possible to define typical faults and thus try to minimize data loss or data quality degradation. Data Validation is a special type of fault detection method consisting of automated checks, performed to guarantee that the data input is rational and acceptable.

Data Validation: Data errors are a common challenge that cause significant performance degradation in data-intensive software systems. To ensure early detection of erroneous data and avoid the accumulation of bad data, research and industrial practice suggest incorporation of automated data validation into data pipelines. Thus, data validation is a critical component in the data pipeline that can ensure data quality. Implementing the data validation component at all steps of the data pipeline allows better traceability. On the other hand, it demands considerable time and effort. Also, it increases the data pipeline complexity.

Mitigation Strategies: Mitigation strategies are adopted to make the extent of an impact less severe. Detection of faults will not be sufficient in building robust data pipelines. Mitigation strategies also should be defined wherever possible so that the data-flow can continue by ameliorating the effect of faults. Mitigation strategies involve mitigation goals, mitigation actions, and an action plan for implementation. Mitigation strategies can be manual, automated, or semi-automated. For instance, a change in data format can be easily detected and as a mitigation strategy, the data can be transformed such that it becomes compatible with the data storage of the data pipeline. Sending alarms is another mitigation strategy that requires manual intervention. Although sending alarms is one of the mitigation strategies, it is added separately here since all practitioners mentioned that sending alarms is the first action taken while detecting a fault. Case A1, A2, A3, and B1 adopt this as their default and manual mitigation strategy even though it is not added as a component in their pipeline. Case C1 receives an alarm from the manufacturing units, repair units, and delivery units when their data sending job fails. According to experts R3, R9, R10, R11, and R14 sending alarms should be done even with the defined mitigation strategies as mitigation strategies does not resolve the fault completely.

Sending Alarms: Sending alarm is a mechanism through which the teams working with the data pipeline and consumers of the data pipeline can be notified whenever something unexpected happens. This strategy can be adopted in case of faults that cannot be fixed automatically or when the fault is encountered for the first time. Sending alarms to the responsible person is the most simple mitigation strategy. However, sending alarms continuously to the same person for the same fault should be prevented.

5 Conceptual Model of Robust Data Pipeline

The data pipelines described in Sect. 3 are operational. However, practitioners mentioned that they are not robust. Data pipelines in case A3 and case C1 are manually monitored which ensures that the flow of data is not broken in between while the remaining cases do not have monitoring or fault detection. Data pipeline connectors are prone to breakage at any time due to unexpected load, change in data format or malfunctioning of nodes. Consequently, data-flow will be interrupted which in turn leads to poor quality data product. Therefore, our model has connector level capabilities that can guard the data flow through the data pipeline. Failures in the data pipeline can be detected and mitigated using fault detection and mitigation components.

The Fig. 7 illustrates the conceptual model of a robust data pipeline that can be implemented for case A3. This data pipeline utilizes data generated by devices employed at base stations that act as data sources. Data collection is performed by a data collection agent that authenticates itself and gets access to data generated at the source. The data thus collected is stored in the raw data storage. Data ingestion is the process through which raw data stored in multiple repositories are ingested and made available to the data pipeline. Through data extraction, required data from the raw data dumps are obtained. The company uses supervised algorithms for training the machine learning model. Therefore, the data labeling step in the data pipeline annotates unlabeled data and stores it in the refined data storage from where it is validated and fed to the machine learning models for training. The trained model is evaluated using a test data set and when sufficient performance is achieved, the model is deployed. The deployed model also produces data while in operation. This data is again collected by the data collection agent and the cycle repeats. Each connector in the data pipeline has got six capabilities. Data transmission is the default activity performed by the connectors. Authentication, fault detection, data validation, mitigation, and sending alarms are the other five functionalities performed by the connectors among which fault detection, mitigation, and sending alarms are the capabilities that should be implemented at all the connectors whereas data validation and authentication are not mandatory for all connectors.

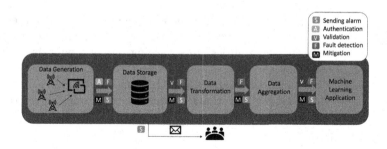

Fig. 7. Robust data pipeline model for case A3

6   Trade-off Between Data Pipeline Robustness and Complexity

Robustness is a critical factor for the data pipelines presented in Sect. 3 as they are serving various data applications. To ensure robustness, we have to continuously monitor the data pipeline and detect the faults at each stage. Further, we have to define mitigation strategies for reducing the impact of the faults. However, adding more details to the data pipeline increases complexity.

Robustness is critical for data pipelines to produce good quality software products. Section 5 clearly details how to model a robust data pipeline and what components need to be included to maintain data pipeline health. Traceability is also a factor contributing to robustness that can be ensured through the separation of capabilities at the node level. Although a node can have more than one capability, for better traceability we assign mutually exclusive capabilities to each node in the data pipeline. For instance, if the data processing node has the capabilities to aggregate and transform the data, it is difficult to identify whether aggregation or transformation induced error. It would become even worse if the fault is with the link between data generation and data storage as fault at the initial stage is carried until the last step. Furthermore, it takes time to identify the person who is responsible to fix the data pipeline breakage. However, modeling such a data pipeline increases the complexity of it from the developer's point of view. Practitioners R4 and R15 who are software developers and R14 who is a data pipeline developer raised the concern of difficulty in implementation. R4 and R14 also pointed out the difficulty in identifying all possible faults in the data pipeline stages.

None of the pipelines explained in Sect. 3 has implemented connector level capabilities. Thus, identifying the exact point that induced error is difficult with them. Moreover, significant human effort is required to fix the data pipeline in case of failure. Because data errors are identified at the final stage and once identified they have to manually search for the broken link in the data pipeline. Nevertheless, all those pipelines are comparatively easy to implement. Here "complexity" of a given data pipeline model is measured in terms of the number of components present in it. Therefore, the increased number of capabilities going from left to right is a warning sign of unnecessary complexity. On the other hand, very few connector capabilities are a warning sign of a poor data pipeline with few quality securing capabilities. Thus, robustness and complexity are two quality factors which are not attainable at the same time. The only possible option is to prioritize one factor without completely compromising the other.

7   Conclusions

In this paper, we have shown that robustness-complexity trade-off play an important role while modelling data pipelines and we have to prioritize either robustness or reducing complexity. Using five case studies we have demonstrated that it can be worthwhile to introduce connector level capabilities and node-level capabilities to maximize the quality of the data product. Further, we identified that robust data pipelines need capabilities such as fault detection, and mitigation strategies. However, an increased number of capabilities going from left to right of a data pipeline is a warning sign of unnecessary complexity. On the other hand, if there are very few connector capabilities, it is a warning sign of a poor data pipeline with quality securing capabilities. From the study, we learned that increased level of detail during data pipeline implementation saves effort and increases quality while increased complexity might still be acceptable. Our empirical study results show that it is essential to find the right balance between data pipeline complexity and robustness. Nevertheless, practitioners feel that robustness needs to be prioritized due to two reasons. First, data quality is critical for data-driven companies. Second, increased complexity can be compromised since data pipelines can be used for a long duration once implemented. However, we have not conducted a complexity-robustness analysis to find out when and how robustness needs to be compromised in a specific context to achieve simplicity in data pipelines. As future work, we plan to extend this study and frame guidelines for using composite nodes for reducing the complexity.

Acknowledgment. This work is in part supported by the Software Center. The authors would also like to express their gratitude for all the support provided by three Software Center companies involved in the study.

References

1. Cai, L., Zhu, Y.: The challenges of data quality and data quality assessment in the big data era. Data Sci. J. 14 (2015)
2. Chen, C.P., Zhang, C.Y.: Data-intensive applications, challenges, techniques and technologies: a survey on big data. Inf. Sci. **275**, 314–347 (2014)

3. Goodhope, K., et al.: Building linkedin's real-time activity data pipeline. IEEE Data Eng. Bull. **35**(2), 33–45 (2012)
4. Gudivada, V.N.: Data analytics: fundamentals. In: Data Analytics for Intelligent Transportation Systems, pp. 31–67. Elsevier (2017)
5. Holton, J.A.: The coding process and its challenges. Sage Handb. Grounded Theory **3**, 265–289 (2007)
6. Hu, H., Wen, Y., Chua, T.S., Li, X.: Toward scalable systems for big data analytics: a technology tutorial. IEEE Access **2**, 652–687 (2014)
7. Munappy, A., Bosch, J., Olsson, H.H., Arpteg, A., Brinne, B.: Data management challenges for deep learning. In: 2019 45th Euromicro Conference on Software Engineering and Advanced Applications (SEAA), pp. 140–147. IEEE (2019)
8. O'Donovan, P., Leahy, K., Bruton, K., O'Sullivan, D.T.J.: An industrial big data pipeline for data-driven analytics maintenance applications in large-scale smart manufacturing facilities. J. Big Data **2**(1), 1–26 (2015). https://doi.org/10.1186/s40537-015-0034-z
9. Provost, F., Fawcett, T.: Data science and its relationship to big data and data-driven decision making. Big Data **1**(1), 51–59 (2013)
10. Rasiel, E.M.: The McKinsey Way. McGraw Hill, New York (2019)
11. Runeson, P., Höst, M.: Guidelines for conducting and reporting case study research in software engineering. Empir. Softw. Eng. **14**(2), 131 (2009)
12. Singer, J., Sim, S.E., Lethbridge, T.C.: Software engineering data collection for field studies. In: Shull, F., Singer, J., Sjøberg, D.I.K. (eds.) Guide to Advanced Empirical Software Engineering, pp. 9–34. Springer, London (2008). https://doi.org/10.1007/978-1-84800-044-5_1
13. Verner, J.M., Sampson, J., Tosic, V., Bakar, N.A., Kitchenham, B.A.: Guidelines for industrially-based multiple case studies in software engineering. In: 2009 Third International Conference on Research Challenges in Information Science, pp. 313–324. IEEE (2009)

Big Data Quality Models: A Systematic Mapping Study

Osbel Montero[1]([✉]) [ID], Yania Crespo[1], and Mario Piatini[2]

[1] School of Computer Engineering, University of Valladolid, Valladolid, Spain
[2] Information Technologies and Systems Institute (ITSI), University of Castilla-La Mancha, 13071 Ciudad Real, Spain

Abstract. In the last decade, we have been witnesses of the considerable increment of projects based on big data applications and the evident growing interest in implementing these kind of systems. It has become a great challenge to assure the expected quality in Big Data contexts. In this paper, a Systematic Mapping Study (SMS) is conducted to reveal what quality models have been analyzed and proposed in the context of Big Data in the last decade, and which quality dimensions support those quality models. The results are exposed and analyzed for further research.

Keywords: Big data · Quality dimensions · Data quality models

1 Introduction

Big Data involves the management of large datasets that due to its size and structure exceed the capabilities of traditional programming tools for collecting, storing, and processing data in a reasonable time. In data generation the main big data sources are users, applications, services, systems, sensors, and technological devices, among others [18]. Them all contribute to Big Data in the form of documents, images, videos, software, files with a multi-diverse format style. The huge volume and heterogeneity present in Big Data applications contribute to the complexity of any engineering process involved.

Currently, different kinds of Big Data applications can be identified such as Recommendations, Feature Prediction and Pattern Recognition [72]. The real-life domains of big data applications include smart cities, smart carts, healthcare systems, financial, business intelligence, environmental control and so on.

The importance and relevance that Big Data is acquiring these days and the promising future we can expect on this knowledge area has been discussed widely. The lack of research on the adequate test modelling and coverage analysis for big data application systems, and the clear practitioners' demand for having stablished a well-defined test coverage criterion is an important issue [62]. In addition, how to effectively ensure the quality of big data applications is still a hot research issue [72].

© Springer Nature Switzerland AG 2021
A. C. R. Paiva et al. (Eds.): QUATIC 2021, CCIS 1439, pp. 416–430, 2021.
https://doi.org/10.1007/978-3-030-85347-1_30

For defining a Big Data quality evaluation system, is necessary to know what quality models have been investigated and proposed. The reminder of this study is organized as follows: Sect. 2 exposes related papers where similar topics were investigated; Sect. 3 presents the research methodology used to conduct this study. In Sect. 4 we reveals answers to our research questions, and finally in Sect. 5, we discuss considerations based on our analysis and threats to validity our mapping study.

2 Related Work

In [52] a review on key non-functional requirements in the domain of Big Data systems is presented, finding more than 40 different quality attributes related to these systems and concluding that non-functional requirements play a vital role at software architecture in Big Data systems.

[71] presents another review that evaluates the state of the art of proposed Quality of Services (QoS) approaches on the Internet of Things (IoT) where one of the research questions mentions the quality factors that quality approaches consider when measuring performance.

The research that comes closest to the actual work is [53]. In this paper a SMS is presented involving concepts like "quality models", "quality dimensions" and "machine learning". A selection of 10 papers is done where some quality models are reviewed and a total of 16 quality attributes are presented that have some effects on machine learning systems. Finally, the review is evaluated by conducting a set of Interviews with other experts.

3 Methodology

By applying a SMS, we attempts to identify the quality models that have been proposed to evaluate Big Data applications in the last decade by making a distinction between the different types of quality models applied in the context of Big Data applications.

3.1 Definition of the Research Questions

- RQ1: What quality models related to Big Data have been proposed in the last 10 years?
- RQ2: For which Big Data context have these quality models been proposed?
- RQ3: What Big Data quality characteristics are proposed as part of these quality models?
- RQ4: Have Big Data quality models been proposed to be applied to any type of Big Data application?

3.2 Inclusion/Exclusion Criteria

In Table 1, pre-defined criteria for inclusion/exclusion of the literature are presented. Papers included are published between 1st January 2010 and 31st December 2020 whose main contribution is the presentation of new or adapted quality models for Big Data applications or even the discussion of existing ones. A small database was prepared which contained all documents and a special column was defined to determine the expected level of correlation that the document might have with the topic being investigated.

Papers excluded where those duplicated in different databases or published in Journals and Conferences with the same topic. Papers which could not answer any of the research questions proposed were equally excluded. In addition, those that could not be accessed, or an additional payment was requested for access the full content, or with non-English redaction were similarly excluded.

Table 1. Inclusion and exclusion criteria

Inclusion criteria
Papers published between 2010 and 2020
Papers whose main topic is the presentation or discussion of a quality model for Big Data applications
Desirable: Papers published in a trustworthy and indexed source
Desirable: Papers with a peer-review
Exclusion criteria
Duplicate papers in different databases or under the same topic in different Conference papers and Journal articles
Papers that do not answer any of the research questions
Papers that require an additional payment to provide access
Papers with a low quality in the defined methodology
Papers with non-English redaction

3.3 Search and Selection Process

The following search string: "Big Data" AND "Quality Model" was defined to obtain papers which correlate these two concepts. After processing the results of these searches, other papers could be analyzed by the applying "snowballing".

Because the amount of information we are trying to collect, analyze and classify, we will focus on this paper the search on scientific databases like SCOPUS and ACM. Figure 1 resumes the steps conducted at this SMS following the review protocol and finally a filtered excel sheet has been obtained with the primary studies selected. SCOPUS database indexes also publications indexed in other databases such as IEEE and Springer. In such cases, a depuration was executed to eliminate duplicates.

After searching in Scopus and ACM databases additional papers were included using snowballing. From the total of 958 papers obtained, the inclusion/exclusion criteria were applied and finally a resumed of 67 papers were selected as the primary studies.

Reviewing the number of citations in the primary studies, it has been found that five papers stand out from the rest. The most cited with 121 citations, is related to measuring the quality of Open Government Data using data quality dimensions [65]. With 76 citations, [42] proposes a Quality-in-use-model through their "3As model" which involves Contextual Adequacy, Operational Adequacy and Temporal Adequacy. The third most cited paper has 66 citations and explores the Quality-of-Service (QoS) approaches in the context of Internet of Things (IoT) [71]. In [29] is reviewed the quality of social media data in big data architecture and has 48 citations. Finally, [39] with 40 citations, proposes a framework to evaluate the quality of open data portals on a national level.

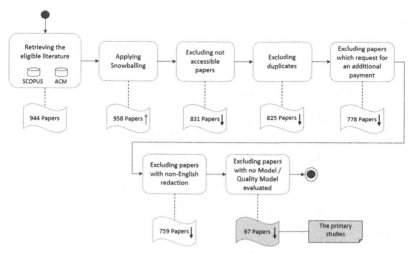

Fig. 1. Facets inside the search and filtering process.

3.4 Quality Assessment

To assess the quality of the chosen literature some parameters were defined as Quality Assessments (QA) such as:

- QA-1: Are the objectives and the scope clearly defined?
- QA-2: Do they proposes/discusses a quality model or related approaches? (if yes, the quality model is applied to a specific Big Data application?)
- QA-3: Do they discuss and present quality dimensions/characteristics for specific purpose?
- QA-4: Do they provide assessment metrics?
- QA-5: Where the results compared to other studies?
- QA-6: Where the results evaluated?
- QA-7: Do they present open themes for further searches?

At this point, the next step was assessing the quality to the selected primary studies which overall results are presented in Table 2. This is a process which complements the inclusion/exclusion is assigned to answer on each paper the quality assessments described above. These primary studies were scored to determine how well the seven quality items defined were satisfied. The punctuation system used was basically a predefined scale with Y-P-N (Y: Yes, P: Partially, N: No), which was weighted as Y: 1 point, P: 0.5 points, N: 0 points.

Table 2. Quality assessment overall results

Quality assessment	Total score	Compliance ratio
QA-1	66	98,51%
QA-2	67	100,00%
QA-3	56	83,58%
QA4-	22,5	33,58%
QA-5	8,5	12,69%
QA-6	31,5	47,01%
QA-7	52,5	78,36%

4   Results

The overall results of this SMS are presented in the current section. A distribution per document type exposed that the largest number of documents obtained (95,52%) are distributed as conference papers and journal articles.

Regarding the year of publication inside the initial range of 2010 – 2020, a gradual increase can be seen starting from 2014 in the number of studies published on the related topics. The 67% of all selected studies were published in the last three years (2018–2020), the 88% of all selected studies were published in the last five years (2016–2020) which is indicating that the issue of quality models in the context of Big Data is receiving more attention among the researchers, and if this trend continues the theme could become in one of the hottest research topics.

Regarding the publisher, Fig. 2 shows that most papers were published between Springer (26,87%), IEEE (25,37%), ACM (11,94%), and Elsevier (8,96%), most of them were indexed in SCOPUS.

Following, the research questions could be answered thanks to the review conducted, the findings are presented as follows.

RQ1: What quality models related to Big Data have been proposed in the last 10 years?

The study has revealed that 12 different quality model types has been published in the last 10 years, the most commons are those related with measuring Data Quality, Service Quality, Big Data Quality and Quality-In-Use. A complete distribution of these quality

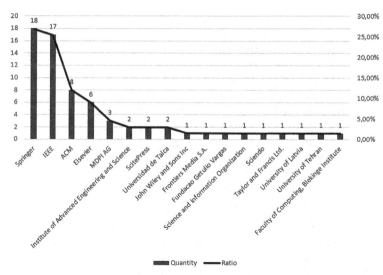

Fig. 2. Paper distribution per publisher

models can be viewed in Fig. 3. It is not a surprise that the largest number of quality models proposed are those related to measuring the quality of the data, representing almost half of all models found.

RQ2: In what Big Data context have these quality models been proposed?

The majority of quality models proposed can be applied to any Big Data project without distinguishing between the different types of Big Data applications. A number of 8 approaches have been identified as possible field of application which can be regarded in Table 3.

There is a differentiation between general Big Data projects and Open Data projects mainly because the dimensions presented for those Open Data are related such as free access, always available, data conciseness, data and source reputation, and objectivity among others, are specially required in Open Data projects. For Big Data Analytics, Decision Making and Machine Learning projects there is no such great differentiation with other Big Data projects, only in the case where non-functional requirements must be measured that are specific to the required purpose.

RQ3: What Big Data quality characteristics are proposed as part of these quality models?

In this case, is necessary to make a differentiation among the quality model types, because the authors have identified different quality dimensions depending upon the focus of the quality model inside Big Data context.

Data Quality Models: Are defined as a set of relevant attributes and relationships between them, which provides a framework for specifying data quality requirements

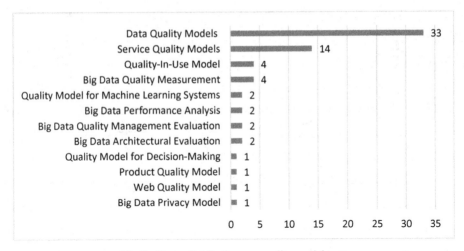

Fig. 3. Paper distribution per quality model type

Table 3. Quality model distribution per Big Data context

Context	Quantity	Ratio
Any Big Data Project	50	74,63%
Cloud Projects	6	8,96%
Social Information Services (Facebook, Twitter, etc.)	2	2,99%
Big Data Analytics	2	2,99%
Open Data Projects	2	2,99%
Decision Making process	2	2,99%
Machine Learning Projects	2	2,99%
Smart Cities Ecosystem Project	1	1,49%

and evaluating data quality. Represents data quality dimensions and the association of such dimensions to data. Good examples of those models are presented in [21, 29, 31, 48, 61, 65]. Figure 4 shows the categories that can be used to group the different data quality dimensions presented in the quality models.

Quality dimensions are presented in 28 from 33 papers related with data quality models. The most common dimensions for general data quality are:

- Completeness: characterizes the degree to which data have values for all attributes and instances required in a specific context of use. Also, data completeness is independent of other attributes (data may be complete but inaccurate).
- Accuracy: characterizes the degree to which data attributes represent the true value of the intended attributes in the real world, like a concept or event in a specific context of use.

- Consistency: characterizes the degree to which data attributes are not contradicted and are consistent with other data in a context of use.
- Timeliness: characterizes the latest state of a data attribute and its period of use.

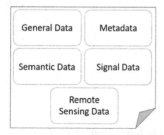

Fig. 4. Categories founded in the SMS that groups the data quality dimensions presented in the quality models.

In addition, for those quality models where the attention was focused on measuring the quality of metadata, in [29] the quality dimensions identified are believability, corroboration, coverage, validity, popularity, relevance, and verifiability. Other four dimensions are included apart from existing ones to Semantic Data [31] which are objectivity, reputation, value added and appropriate amount of data. For Signal Data [35], other dimensions were identified such as availability, noise, relevance, traceability, variance, and uniqueness. Finally, other two dimensions were included for Remote Sensing Data [7] which are resolution and readability.

It should be noted that quality dimensions proposed in each of these quality models refer to quality aspects that need to be verified by them in the specific context of use.

Service Quality Models: Are used to describe the way on how to achieve desired quality in services. This model measures the extent to which the service delivered meets the customer's expectations. Good examples of these models are presented in [8, 30, 32, 36, 41, 64]. The most common quality dimensions collected from those papers are: Reliability, Efficiency, Availability, Portability, Responsiveness, Real-time, Robustness, Scalability, Throughput.

Quality-In-Use Models: Defines the quality characteristics that the datasets that are used for a specific use must present to adapt to that use. In this research two papers were found that present such type of models [11] and [42], other papers discuss about them. These models are focused mainly in two dimensions: Consistency and Adequacy represented in Fig. 5.

It should be noted that, depending upon the quality characteristics that wants to be evaluated and the context of use, a different model should be applied. In those models, the two dimensions analyzed are presented as:

- Consistency: The capability of data and systems of keeping the uniformity of specific characteristics when datasets are transferred across the networks and shared by the various types of consistencies.

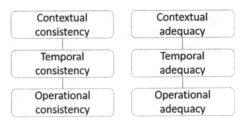

Fig. 5. Quality dimensions presented in Quality-In-Use Models

- Adequacy: The state or ability of being good enough or satisfactory for some requirement, purpose or need.

Big Data Systems Quality Models: There isn't a general definition for this types of models because the enormous number of different kinds. In this research will be defined as quality models applied to the context of Big Data viewed at a high level. Good examples of these models are presented in [28, 37, 50, 56]. The quality dimensions presented in these quality models are specified in Table 4, and can be separated in three groups:

- Dimensions for Big Data value chain
- Dimensions for Non-Functional requirements in Big Data Systems
- Dimensions for measuring Big Data characteristics.

Table 4. Quality dimensions for big data systems quality models

Big data value chain	Big data non-functional requirements (NFRs)	Big data characteristics
Timeliness	Scalability	Volume
Accuracy	High performance computing	Velocity
Completeness	Modularity	Variety
Consistency	Consistency	Veracity
	Security	Valence
	Real-time operations	Value
	Inter-operability	Volatility
	Availability	Vitality
		Vincularity

RQ4: Have Big Data quality models been proposed to be applied to any type of Big Data application or by considering the quality characteristics required in specific types of Big Data applications?

A Big Data application (BDA) processes a large amount of data by means of integrating platforms, tools, and mechanisms for parallel and distributed processing. As was presented in Table 3, the majority of quality models proposed (74,63%) can be applied to any Big Data project and only a few studies were developed specifically for Big Data Analytics such as [66], Decision Making process in [2] and Machine Learning presents in [54] and [55].

This could be means that researchers are not interested on develop a quality model for a specific Big Data application, instead a general quality model is proposed focusing on such topics like assuring the quality of data, the Quality-in-use, the quality of services involved, etc.

5   Threats to Validity of Our Mapping Study

The main threats to validity of our mapping study are:

- Selection of search terms and digital libraries. We search in two digital libraries and to complete our study other libraries should be included such as: IEEE, Springer, and Google scholar. In addition, because Big Data is an industrial issue it is recommended to include gray literature search [24] and achieve a Multivocal Literature Review (MLR).
- Selection of studies. Could be a better solution to apply other exclusion criteria such as the quality of papers. For example, if the results have been validated and compared to other studies.
- Quality model categorization. As a result of the small sample of papers in which quality models are not related to data quality, it is an arduous task to obtain sample quality metrics and quality dimensions for those Big Data quality models. With the amplification of the current study more samples could be obtained to support this task.
- Data categorization. We included all the categories identified in the primary papers, the extraction and categorization process was carried out by the first author, a MSc student with over five years of work experience in software and data engineering. The other two coauthors provided input to resolve ambiguities during the process. In this respect, the extraction and categorization process is partially validated.

6   Conclusions and Future Work

A SMS have been conducted to analyze and visualize the different quality models that have been proposed in the context of Big Data and the quality dimensions presented on each type of quality model. It has been found that different from what would have been thought, there is a considerable number of papers which do not present or partially discuss the quality metrics to evaluate the quality dimensions proposed in the model. Also, in the majority of studies the results of their research was not analyzed and compared with other similar studies.

This research have revealed that proposing, discussing, and evaluating new quality models in the context of Big Data is a topic that is currently receiving more attention from researchers and with the actual tendency we should expect an increase of papers related with quality models in Big Data context in the coming years.

As first topic for future work we will consider an in-depth review of the analyzed papers where common metrics, quality dimensions and quality models evaluations could be obtained for further analysis on each Big Data quality model type.

In the context of Big Data, most of the proposed quality models are designed for any Big Data application and they are not explicit in evaluating a specific type of Big Data application such as Feature Prediction Systems or Recommenders. Considering their different specificities to assess the expected quality in the final result when using these Big Data applications, we consider this as an open research topic.

References

1. Ali, K., Hamilton, M., Thevathayan, C., Zhang, X.: Big social data as a service: a service composition framework for social information service analysis. In: Jin, H., Wang, Q., Zhang, L.-J. (eds.) ICWS 2018. LNCS, vol. 10966, pp. 487–503. Springer, Cham (2018). https://doi.org/10.1007/978-3-319-94289-6_31
2. Alkatheeri, Y., Ameen, A., Isaac, O., Nusari, M., Duraisamy, B., Khalifa, G.S.A.: The effect of big data on the quality of decision-making in Abu Dhabi government organisations. In: Sharma, N., Chakrabarti, A., Balas, V.E. (eds.) Data Management, Analytics and Innovation. AISC, vol. 1016, pp. 231–248. Springer, Singapore (2020). https://doi.org/10.1007/978-981-13-9364-8_18
3. Asif, M.: Are QM models aligned with Industry 4.0? A perspective on current practices. J. Clean. Prod. **256**, 1–11 (2020)
4. Baillie, C., Edwards, P., Pignotti, E.: Qual: A provenance-aware quality model. J. Data Inf. Qual. **5**, 1–22 (2015)
5. Baldassarre, M.T., Caballero, I., Caivano, D., Garcia, B.R., Piattini, M.: From big data to smart data: a data quality perspective. In: ACM SIGSOFT International Workshop on Ensemble-Based Software Engineering, pp. 19–24 (2018)
6. Barbara Kitchenham, S.C.: Guidelines for performing systematic reviews in software engineering. Durham, UK: EBSE Technical report. EBSE-2007-01 Version 2.3 (2007)
7. Barsi, Á., et al.: Remote sensing data quality model: from data sources to lifecycle phases. Int. J. Image Data Fusion **10**, 280–299 (2019)
8. Basso, T., Silva, H., Moraes, R.: On the use of quality models to characterize trustworthiness properties. In: Calinescu, R., Di Giandomenico, F. (eds.) SERENE 2019. LNCS, vol. 11732, pp. 147–155. Springer, Cham (2019). https://doi.org/10.1007/978-3-030-30856-8_11
9. Behkamal, B., Kahani, M., Bagheri, E., Jeremic, Z.: A metrics-driven approach for quality assessment of linked open data. J. Theoret. Appl. Electron. Commer. Res. **9**, 64–79 (2014)
10. Bhutani, P., Saha, A., Gosain, A.: WSEMQT: a novel approach for quality-based evaluation of web data sources for a data warehouse. IET Softw. **14**, 806–815 (2020)
11. Caballero, I., Serrano, M., Piattini, M.: A data quality in use model for big data. In: Indulska, M., Purao, S. (eds.) ER 2014. LNCS, vol. 8823, pp. 65–74. Springer, Cham (2014). https://doi.org/10.1007/978-3-319-12256-4_7
12. Cappiello, C., et al.: Improving health monitoring with adaptive data movement in fog computing. Front. Robot. AI **7**, 1–17 (2020)
13. Cappiello, C., Samá, W., Vitali, M.: Quality awareness for a successful big data exploitation. In: International Database Engineering & Applications Symposium, pp. 37–44 (2018)
14. Castillo, R.P., et al.: DAQUA-MASS: an ISO 8000-61 based data quality management methodology for sensor data. Sensors (Switzerland) **18**, 1–24 (2018)

15. Cedillo, P., Valdez, W., Cárdenas-Delgado, P., Prado-Cabrera, D.: A data as a service metamodel for managing information of healthcare and internet of things applications. In: Rodriguez Morales, G., Fonseca C., E.R., Salgado, J.P., Pérez-Gosende, P., Orellana Cordero, M., Berrezueta, S. (eds.) TICEC 2020. CCIS, vol. 1307, pp. 272–286. Springer, Cham (2020). https://doi.org/10.1007/978-3-030-62833-8_21
16. Ciancarini, P., Poggi, F., Russo, D.: Big data quality: a roadmap for open data. In: International Conference on Big Data Computing Service and Applications, BigDataService, pp. 210–215 (2016)
17. Cichy, C., Rass, S.: An overview of data quality frameworks. IEEE Access **7**, 24634–24648 (2019)
18. Davoudian, A., Liu, M.: Big data systems: a software engineering perspective. ACM Comput. Surv. **53**, 1–39 (2020)
19. Demchenko, Y., Grosso, P., Laat, C.D., Membrey, P.: Addressing big data issues in Scientific data infrastructure. In: International Conference on Collaboration Technologies and Systems, CTS, pp. 48–55 (2013)
20. Fagúndez, S., Fleitas, J., Marotta, A.: Data streams quality evaluation for the generation of alarms in health domain. In: International Workshops on Web Information Systems Engineering, IWCSN, pp. 204–210 (2015)
21. Fernández, S.M., Jedlitschka, A., Guzmán, L., Vollmer, A.M.: A quality model for actionable analytics in rapid software development. In: Euromicro Conference on Software Engineering and Advanced Applications, SEAA, pp. 370–377 (2018)
22. Gao, T., Li, T., Jiang, R., Duan, R., Zhu, R., Yang, M.: A research about trustworthiness metric method of SaaS services based on AHP. In: Sun, X., Pan, Z., Bertino, E. (eds.) ICCCS 2018. LNCS, vol. 11063, pp. 207–218. Springer, Cham (2018). https://doi.org/10.1007/978-3-030-00006-6_18
23. Garises, V., Quenum, J.G.: An evaluation of big data architectures. In: 8th International Conference on Data Science, Technology and Applications, DATA, pp. 152–159 (2019)
24. Garousi, V., Felderer, M., Mäntylä, M.V.: Guidelines for including grey literature and conducting multivocal literature reviews in software engineering. Inf. Softw. Technol. **106**, 101–121 (2019). https://doi.org/10.1016/j.infsof.2018.09.006. ISSN 0950-5849
25. Ge, M., Lewoniewski, W.: Developing the quality model for collaborative open data. In: International Conference on Knowledge-Based and Intelligent Information and Engineering Systems, KES, pp. 1883–1892 (2020)
26. Gong, X., Yin, C., Li, X.: A grey correlation based supply–demand matching of machine tools with multiple quality factors in cloud manufacturing environment. J. Ambient. Intell. Humaniz. Comput. **10**(3), 1025–1038 (2018). https://doi.org/10.1007/s12652-018-0945-6
27. Gyulgyulyan, E., Aligon, J., Ravat, F., Astsatryan, H.: Data quality alerting model for big data analytics. In: Welzer, T., et al. (eds.) ADBIS 2019. CCIS, vol. 1064, pp. 489–500. Springer, Cham (2019). https://doi.org/10.1007/978-3-030-30278-8_47
28. Helfert, M., Ge, M.: Perspectives of big data quality in smart service ecosystems (quality of design and quality of conformance). J. Inf. Technol. Manag. **10**, 72–83 (2018)
29. Immonen, A., Paakkonen, P., Ovaska, E.: Evaluating the quality of social media data in big data architecture. IEEE Access **3**, 2028–2043 (2015)
30. Jagli, D., Seema Purohit, N., Chandra, S.: Saasqual: a quality model for evaluating SAAS on the cloud computing environment. In: Aggarwal, V.B., Bhatnagar, V., Mishra, D.K. (eds.) Big Data Analytics. AISC, vol. 654, pp. 429–437. Springer, Singapore (2018). https://doi.org/10.1007/978-981-10-6620-7_41
31. Jarwar, M.A., Chong, I.: Web objects based contextual data quality assessment model for semantic data application. Appl. Sci. (Switzerland) **10**, 1–33 (2020)

32. Jich-Yan, T., Wen, Y.X., Chien-Hua, W.: A framework for big data analytics on service quality evaluation of online bookstore. In: Deng, D.-J., Pang, A.-C., Lin, C.-C. (eds.) WiCON 2019. LNICSSITE, vol. 317, pp. 294–301. Springer, Cham (2019). https://doi.org/10.1007/978-3-030-52988-8_26

33. Jung, Y., Hur, C., Kim, M.: Sustainable situation-aware recommendation services with collective intelligence. Sustainability (Switzerland) **10**, 1–11 (2018)

34. Khurana, R., Bawa, R.K.: QoS based cloud service selection paradigms. In: International Conference on Cloud System and Big Data Engineering, Confluence, pp. 174–179 (2016)

35. Kirchen, I., Schutz, D., Folmer, J., Vogel-Heuser, B.: Metrics for the evaluation of data quality of signal data in industrial processes. In: International Conference on Industrial Informatics, INDIN, pp. 819–826 (2017)

36. Kiruthika, J., Khaddaj, S.: Software quality issues and challenges of internet of things. In: International Symposium on Distributed Computing and Applications for Business, Engineering and Science, DCABES, pp. 176–179 (2015)

37. Kläs, M., Putz, W., Lutz, T.: Quality evaluation for big data: a scalable assessment approach and first evaluation results. In: Joint Conference of the Int'l Workshop on and International Conference on Software Process and Product Measurement Software Measurement, pp. 115–124 (2017)

38. Liu, Z., Chen, Q., Cai, L.: Application of requirement-oriented data quality evaluation method. In: International Conference on Software Engineering, Artificial Intelligence, Networking and Parallel/Distributed Computing, SNPD, pp. 407–412 (2018)

39. Máchová, R., Lněnička, M.: Evaluating the quality of open data portals on the national level. J. Theor. Appl. Electron. Commer. Res. **12**, 21–41 (2017)

40. Manikam, S., Sahibudin, S., Kasinathan, V.: Business intelligence addressing service quality for big data analytics in public sector. Indonesian J. Electr. Eng. Comput. Sci. **16**, 491–499 (2019)

41. Mbonye, V., Price, C.S.: A model to evaluate the quality of Wi-Fi performance: case study at UKZN Westville campus. In: International Conference on Advances in Big Data, Computing and Data Communication Systems, icABCD, pp. 1–8 (2019)

42. Merino, J., Caballero, I., Rivas, B., Serrano, M., Piattini, M.: A data quality in use model for Big Data. Futur. Gener. Comput. Syst. **63**(1), 123–130 (2016)

43. Micic, N., Neagu, D., Campean, F., Zadeh, E.H.: Towards a data quality framework for heterogeneous data. In: Cyber, Physical and Social Computing, IEEE Smart Data, iThings-GreenCom-CPSCom-SmartDat, pp. 155–162 (2018)

44. Musto, J., Dahanayake, A.: Integrating data quality requirements to citizen science application design. In: International Conference on Management of Digital EcoSystems, MEDES, pp. 166–173 (2019)

45. Nadal, S., et al.: A software reference architecture for semantic-aware big data systems. Inf. Softw. Technol. **90**, 75–92 (2017)

46. Nakamichi, K., Ohashi, K., Aoyama, M., Joeckel, L., Siebert, J., Heidrich, J.: Requirements-driven method to determine quality characteristics and measurements for machine learning software and its evaluation. In: International Requirements Engineering Conference, RE, pp. 260–270 (2020)

47. Nikiforova, A.: Definition and evaluation of data quality: User-oriented data object-driven approach to data quality assessment. Baltic J. Mod. Comput. **8**, 391–432 (2020)

48. Oliveira, M.I., Oliveira, L.E., Batista, M.G., Lóscio, B.F.: Towards a meta-model for data ecosystems. In: Annual International Conference on Digital Government Research: Governance in the Data Age, pp. 1–10 (2018)

49. Olsina, L., Lew, P.: Specifying mobileapp quality characteristics that may influence trust. In: Central & Eastern European Software Engineering Conference in Russia, CEE-SECR, pp. 1–9 (2017)

50. Omidbakhsh, M., Ormandjieva, O.: Toward a new quality measurement model for big data. In: 9th International Conference on Data Science, Technology and Applications, pp. 193–199 (2020)
51. Valencia-Parra, Á., Parody, L., Varela-Vaca, Á.J., Caballero, I., Gómez-López, M.T.: DMN for data quality measurement and assessment. In: Di Francescomarino, C., Dijkman, R., Zdun, U. (eds.) BPM 2019. LNBIP, vol. 362, pp. 362–374. Springer, Cham (2019). https://doi.org/10.1007/978-3-030-37453-2_30
52. Pereira, J.D., et al.: A platform to enable self-adaptive cloud applications using trustworthiness properties. In: International Symposium on Software Engineering for Adaptive and Self-Managing Systems, SEAMS, pp. 71–77 (2020)
53. Rahman, M.S., Reza, H.: Systematic mapping study of non-functional requirements in big data system. In: IEEE International Conference on Electro Information Technology, pp. 25–31 (2020)
54. Rudraraju, N.V., Boyanapally, V.: Data quality model for machine learning. Faculty of Computing, Blekinge Institute of Technology, pp. 1–107 (2019)
55. Santhanam, P.: Quality management of machine learning systems. In: Shehory, O., Farchi, E., Barash, G. (eds.) EDSMLS 2020. CCIS, vol. 1272, pp. 1–13. Springer, Cham (2020). https://doi.org/10.1007/978-3-030-62144-5_1
56. Serhani, M.A., Kassabi, H.T., Taleb, I., Nujum, A.: An hybrid approach to quality evaluation across big data value chain. In: IEEE International Congress on Big Data, pp. 418–425 (2016)
57. Surendro, O.K.: Academic cloud ERP quality assessment model. Int. J. Electr. Comput. Eng. **6**, 1038–1047 (2016)
58. Taleb, I., Serhani, M.A., Dssouli, R.: Big data quality assessment model for unstructured data. In: International Conference on Innovations in Information Technology (IIT), pp. 69–74 (2018)
59. Taleb, I., Serhani, M.A., Dssouli, R.: Big data quality: a survey. In: 7th IEEE International Congress on Big Data, pp. 166–173 (2018)
60. Taleb, I., Serhani, M.A., Dssouli, R.: Big data quality: a data quality profiling model. In: Xia, Y., Zhang, L.-J. (eds.) SERVICES 2019. LNCS, vol. 11517, pp. 61–77. Springer, Cham (2019). https://doi.org/10.1007/978-3-030-23381-5_5
61. Talha, M., Elmarzouqi, N., Kalam, A.A.: Towards a powerful solution for data accuracy assessment in the big data context. Int. J. Adv. Comput. Sci. Appl. **11**, 419–429 (2020)
62. Tao, C., Gao, J.: Quality assurance for big data application - issues, challenges, and needs. In: International Conference on Software Engineering and Knowledge Engineering, SEKE, pp. 375–381 (2016)
63. Tepandi, J., et al.: The data quality framework for the Estonian public sector and its evaluation: Establishing a systematic process-oriented viewpoint on cross-organizational data quality. In: Hameurlain, A., Küng, J., Wagner, R., Sakr, S., Razzak, I., Riyad, A. (eds.) Transactions on Large-Scale Data- and Knowledge-Centered Systems XXXV. LNCS, pp. 1–26. Springer, Heidelberg (2017). https://doi.org/10.1007/978-3-662-56121-8_1
64. Vale, L.R., Sincorá, L.A., Milhomem, L.D.: The moderate effect of analytics capabilities on the service quality. J. Oper. Supp. Chain Manag. **11**, 101–113 (2018)
65. Vetrò, A., Canova, L., Torchiano, M., Minotas, C.O.: Open data quality measurement framework: definition and application to open government data. Gov. Inf. Q. **33**, 325–337 (2016)
66. Bautista Villalpando, L.E., April, A., Abran, A.: Performance analysis model for big data applications in cloud computing. J. Cloud Comput. **3**(1), 1–20 (2014). https://doi.org/10.1186/s13677-014-0019-z
67. Vostrovsky, V., Tyrychtr, J.: Consistency of Open data as prerequisite for usability in agriculture. Sci. Agric. Bohem. **49**, 333–339 (2018)

68. Wan, Y., Shi, W., Gao, L., Chen, P., Hua, Y.: A general framework for spatial data inspection and assessment. Earth Sci. Inf. **8**(4), 919–935 (2015). https://doi.org/10.1007/s12145-014-0196-9

69. Wang, B., Wen, J., Zheng, J.: Research on assessment and comparison of the forestry open government data quality between China and the United States. In: He, J., et al. (eds.) ICDS 2019. CCIS, vol. 1179, pp. 370–385. Springer, Singapore (2020). https://doi.org/10.1007/978-981-15-2810-1_36

70. Wang, C., Lu, Z., Wu, Z., Wu, J., Huang, S.: Optimizing multi-cloud CDN deployment and scheduling strategies using big data analysis. In: International Conference on Services Computing, SCC, pp. 273–280 (2017)

71. White, G., Nallur, V., Clarke, S.: Quality of service approaches in IoT: a systematic mapping. J. Syst. Softw. **132**, 186–203 (2017)

72. Zhang, P., Zhou, X., Li, W., Gao, J.: A survey on quality assurance techniques for big data applications. In: IEEE Third International Conference on Big Data Computing Service and Applications, pp. 313–319 (2017)

Business Process and Organizational Data Quality Model (BPODQM) for Integrated Process and Data Mining

Francisco Betancor, Federico Pérez, Adriana Marotta, and Andrea Delgado(✉)

Instituto de Computación, Facultad de Ingeniería, Universidad de la República,
J. Herrera y Reissig 565, Montevideo, Uruguay
{francisco.betancor.pallas,federico.andres.perez,
amarotta,adelgado}@fing.edu.uy

Abstract. Data Quality (DQ) is a key element in any Data Science project to guarantee that its results provide consistent and reliable information. Both process mining and data mining, as part of Data Science, operate over large sets of data from the organization, carrying out the analysis effort. In the first case, data represent the daily execution of business processes (BPs) in the organization, such as sales process or health process, and in the second case, they correspond to organizational data regarding the organization's domain such as clients, sales, patients, among others. This separate view on the data prevents organizations from having a complete view of their daily operation and corresponding evaluation, probably hiding useful information to improve their processes. Although there are several DQ approaches and models for organizational data, and a few DQ proposals for business process data, none of them takes an integrated view over process and organizational data. In this paper we present a quality model named Business Process and Organizational Data Quality Model (BPODQM) defining specific dimensions, factors and metrics for quality evaluation of integrated process and organizational data, in order to detect key issues in datasets used for process and data mining efforts.

Keywords: Data quality model · Process mining and Data mining · Data science · Integrated process and organizational data

1 Introduction

In last years the need to exploit available data in organizations has increased considerably, due to the continuous generation of data from different and interconnected sources. The complexity of socio-technical systems connecting people, things, data and business processes (BPs), integrating heterogeneous technologies and elements, also increases the complexity of integrating and generating useful datasets, as well as their management. Both Process mining [2] and Data mining [15], as part of Data Science [12], operate over large datasets from the

© Springer Nature Switzerland AG 2021
A. C. R. Paiva et al. (Eds.): QUATIC 2021, CCIS 1439, pp. 431–445, 2021.
https://doi.org/10.1007/978-3-030-85347-1_31

organization carrying out the analysis effort. In the first case, data represent the daily execution of BPs in the organization, such as sales process, health process, and in the second case, they correspond to organizational data regarding the organization's domain such as clients, sales, patients, among others. Most organizations manage their process and organizational data separately. This separate view on the data prevents organizations from having a complete view of their daily operation and corresponding evaluation, hindering the recovery of useful information to improve their processes.

On the one hand, Data Mining [15] aims at analyzing large datasets in search for general rules, providing predictions and behavior patterns based on the input data. Data Mining techniques are often classified as descriptive or predictive. Descriptive techniques include clustering and association rules to characterize data sets, while Predictive techniques are classification and regression, in the first case mainly decision trees and neural networks, and in the second regression functions, among others. On the other hand, Process Mining [2] focus on large datasets that are specific from process execution, in order to provide insight on process execution. Process mining provides three main perspectives: i) discovering BP models from event logs i.e. generating process models from execution data; ii) process conformance by checking BP models against the real execution in event logs; and iii) enhancing BP models with extra information such as participating roles and resources. Also, performance execution analysis can be performed such as bottlenecks, duration of process cases, average, etc.

Data Quality (DQ) [5,18] is a key element in any Data Science project to guarantee that its results provide consistent and reliable information. A DQ model defines dimensions conceptualizing different aspects of quality, which are composed of factors defining a specific quality aspect within a dimension, and metrics to specify the way that a factor is measured. Very well-known dimensions of data quality include *Accuracy, Consistency, Completeness, Uniqueness*, but several others can be taken into account depending on the context and domain at hand. Although there are several DQ approaches and models for organizational data, and a few DQ proposals for BPs data, none of them takes an integrated view over process and organizational data.

Business Process Management (BPM) [3,11,19] provides organizations with the basis for managing their BPs, which can be supported by traditional Information Systems or with process platforms such as BPM Systems [6]. In most BPMS settings, the process engine is in charge of BP execution i.e. the control flow defined within the process model registering all events in a database (schema) of its own, and the organizational data that is managed within the BP cases (i.e. instances) are registered in another (or several) database/s (schema) where other systems also register and query common organizational data i.e. clients, patients, etc. A key step towards BPs continuous improvement [10] is to be able to proactively assess their real execution to provide business people with Business Intelligence support for evidence-based decision making. To provide a complete view on data, process and organizational data must be integrated and analyzed in an integrated manner. To generate such integrated datasets, for each activity (human or automated) executed within a BP case, the organizational data that was involved in the execution of the activity must be related back to the corresponding activity.

In previous works we have addressed this problem by defining an integrated framework [9] and working with integrated process and organizational data [8], as well as identifying the need for a DQ model to be applied over the data before the mining effort can be carried out. In this paper we present such DQ model that we named Business Process and Organizational Data Quality Model (BPODQM), which defines specific dimensions, factors and metrics for quality evaluation of integrated process and organizational data, in order to detect key issues in integrated data sets used for process and data mining efforts.

The rest of this document is organized as follows: in Sect. 2 we present concepts and definitions and in Sect. 3 we introduced an example and preliminaries. In Sect. 4 we present our proposal of a BPO Data Quality Model (BPODQM), and in Sect. 5 we show an application of our proposal as proof of concept. In Sect. 6 we discuss other approaches to DQ for process and organizational data, and finally in Sect. 7 we present some conclusions.

2   Background

The model we present in this work is supported by some basic concepts of the Data Quality (DQ) area, which are introduced in this section. We also present concepts and definitions regarding BP event logs that contain process data for process mining, and the extension we have made to integrate organizational data.

2.1   Data Quality

DQ is managed with a multi-faceted approach, where the notion of quality is represented through dimensions that conceptualize different aspects of quality [5, 18]. Therefore, DQ dimensions address potential data problems, for example, a mistyping error is a data problem that is addressed by the DQ dimension *accuracy*. Additionally, as DQ dimensions are very general aspects, a second level of detail is considered, so that a DQ dimension is decomposed in DQ factors, i.e. a DQ factor is a specific quality aspect of a DQ dimension. Continuing with the example above, a mistyping error would be addressed by the DQ factor *syntactic accuracy*, which corresponds to the DQ dimension *accuracy*.

An essential part of DQ management is DQ measurement and evaluation. In order to measure DQ of a dataset, it is necessary to define metrics, which specify the way a DQ factor is measured, as well as the range of the numerical result that is obtained and the data granularity over which it is applied. For example, *syntactic accuracy* may be measured through a *string-distance* metric that is applied between a value of the dataset and the values of a referential dictionary of terms. The granularity of this metric is *data value* and the result range is $[0..1]$. Alternatively, if the metric obtained the percentage of correct values of a column of a data table, the granularity would be *column*. In addition, for each metric, different aggregations may be defined. An aggregation states the way that a set of measures, obtained through the metric application, are aggregated for obtaining a summarized measure that corresponds to a coarser data granularity. Continuing with the example, after applying the string-distance metric, whose granularity is data value, to all the values of a column, we can calculate an aggregation for obtaining one DQ value for the entire column.

The DQ literature shows a huge amount of DQ dimensions, factors and properties, as well as many different approaches for modeling quality characteristics. However, there is consensus in some main DQ concepts, such as dimensions and metrics, and in a basic set of dimensions, which address typical DQ problems and are present in most cases. These dimensions, which are usually represented with the same terms and have the same general semantics, are: *accuracy, completeness, consistency, timeliness/currency, uniqueness*. In recent times, where big data characteristics are present in most data scenarios, DQ dimensions related to credibility, trustworthiness and reputation, have gained much attention and relevance [14].

2.2 Process Mining and Event Logs

Process Mining [2] is a discipline within Data Science that uses and extends data mining techniques to discover information from process execution data, instead of organizational data i.e. clients, sales, etc. as data mining does. Data from process execution also come from organization's systems, where events that happen within each process instance (case) are registered as traces in a so-called event log. As mentioned before, process mining provides three main perspectives to: discover process models, check process models conformance and enhance process models with execution data.

Within BPM process mining can be used in the late phase of Evaluation in the BPs lifecycle in order to evaluate process execution and discover information based on process data to improve BPs and the operative of the organization, as described above, or can also be used in the first phase of Analysis as another input for the requirements elicitation and BP modeling. Whether there is a BP model in place for the process or not, real process data execution will help to get insights into the organization's operation. The BP model corresponds to the template of the process, where for structure process all execution possibilities should be included i.e. in domains such as banks, management, etc., while this is extremely challenging for unstructured BPs i.e. in domains such as health, knowledge management, etc. Each execution of the process is a BP case (instance) in which values of the specific execution are handled.

The input for process mining efforts is an Event log [2], which corresponds to only one process, and contains BP cases (instances) which in turn contains events that happened within the execution of the case. An event correspond to only one case and refers to work that is carried out in the organization i.e. activity, including when it is carried out (time stamps) and by whom (role, people, system). Events in a trace are ordered by execution time i.e. time stamp and a transaction type indicating the lifecycle event that is being registered e.g.

start or complete of an activity. Events can also have attributes such as cost, etc. The most common format for event logs data is the XES (eXtensible Event Stream) format [1], which is an XML format supported by process mining tools such as ProM[1]. In next Sect. 3.2 we show an example of the XES format within our extension for data integration.

3 Preliminaries

We present preliminary work over a real BP from our university that we have been working with throughout the application of our complete approach [9]. The aim of this section is to present the context of our work and the settings we are considering, as well as the extended Event log we generate from process and organizational data execution to which apply our BPODQM proposal. Although the BP has a simple control flow, the execution data i.e. event log contains process and organizational data that present cases and elements that are commonly included, so the quality example we present based on this process is both specific enough to this context and general enough to be applied to other processes.

3.1 BP Model and Organizational Data Model

The BP is named "Students Mobility" [8] and deals with granting scholarships for students who apply to exchange programs to attend courses in others country's universities which participate in the mobility programs. In Fig. 1a the BP model for the Students Mobility process is shown specified in BPMN 2.0, and in Fig. 1b the data model supporting the BP, extended from [8].

The BP Students Mobility depicted in Fig. 1a shows a simple path through the complete BP, which starts when the Register office receives applications to open Mobility programs from Students, and registers them in the task "Register application". After the period for applications is closed, registered applications are checked to be compliant with the requirements from the mobility program, in the task "Requirements assessment". After that, the confirmed applications i.e. the ones that comply with the requirements of the mobility call goes through an evaluation process in the "Evaluate applicants" task, where applicants are ordered and holders are selected, as well as substitutes. Then, with the list of ordered applications the task "Approve scholarships results" approve the results, then applicants are notified in task "Notify applicants" and in task "Sign contract and payment" holders sign and get the money granted by the scholarship.

It can be seen that the organizational data (from the data model in Fig. 1b) that is managed within the process is shown as a text comment associated to the corresponding task, e.g. in the "Register application" task the table Application is accessed in order to insert a new application for the Student with identification idStudent in the State "initiated". Other values are not shown, as the validation of courses or the corresponding Program to which the application

---

[1] https://www.promtools.org/.

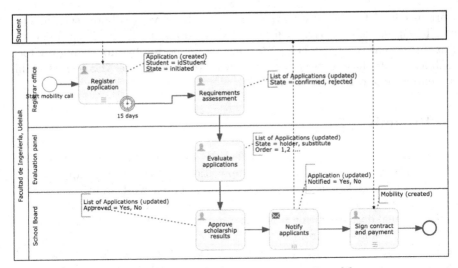

(a) Students Mobility business process from [8]

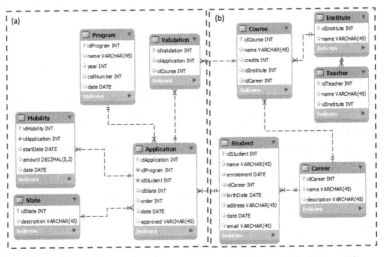

(b) Data model for the Students Mobility BP extended from [8]

Fig. 1. Students Mobility proof of concept

is being submitted. In the "Requirements assessment" task the list of applications is recovered from the organizational database, and it is updated with the confirmed or rejected result. In the subsequent tasks the list of applications is manipulated with corresponding updates and each application when the applicant is notified of the results. Finally, the last task creates a new record in the Mobility table including the start date of the mobility and the amount granted.

```xml
<?xml version="1.0" encoding="UTF-8"?>
<log xmlns="http://your_namespace"
     xmlns:xsi="http://www.w3.org/2001/XMLSchema-instance"
     xsi:schemaLocation="http://your_namespace"
     xes.version="1.0" xes.features="nested-attributes" >
     <extension name="Organizational" prefix="org" uri="http://www.xes-standard.org/org.xesext"/>
     <extension name="Time" prefix="time" uri="http://www.xes-standard.org/time.xesext"/>
     <extension name="Concept" prefix="concept" uri="http://www.xes-standard.org/concept.xesext"/>
     <extension name="OrganizationalData" prefix="orgdata" uri="http://www.xes-standard.org/orgdata.xesext"/>
     <string key="concept:name" value="Mobility"/>
     <trace>
               <string key="id" value="773783"/>
     <string key="concept:name" value="773783"/>
     <event>
               <string key="concept:name" value="Register application"/>
               <string key="lifecycle:transition" value="Start"/>
               <date key="time:timestamp" value="2020-11-16T09:36:33.784-0300"/>
               <string key="org:role" value="Jorge"/>
               <string key="org:resource" value="5394935"/>
               <string key="orgdata:elemType" value="UserTask"/>
               <list key="orgdata:varlist">
                         <variables>
                                   <string key="concept:varname" value="studentid">
                                             <string key="orgdata:varValue" value="89964588"/>
                                             <string key="orgdata:valueType" value="string"/>
                                             <date key="time:timestamp" value="2020-11-16T09:36:50.554-0300"/>
                                   </string>
                         </variables>
               </list>
               <list key="orgdata:entlist">
                    <entities>
                         <string key="concept:entname" value="application">
                              <list key="orgdata:attlist">
                                   <attributes>
                                        <string key="concept:attname" value="idapplication">
                                             <string key="orgdata:attValue" value="1592"/>
                                             <string key="orgdata:valueType" value="int4"/>
                                             <date key="time:timestamp" value="2020-11-16T09:36:50.863-0300"/>
                                        </string>
                                        <string key="concept:attname" value="idstate">
                                             <string key="orgdata:attValue" value="1"/>
                                             <string key="orgdata:valueType" value="int4"/>
                                             <date key="time:timestamp" value="2020-11-16T09:36:50.863-0300"/>
                                        </string>
                                        <string key="concept:attname" value="idprogram">
                                             <string key="orgdata:attValue" value="263"/>
                                             <string key="orgdata:valueType" value="int4"/>
                                             <date key="time:timestamp" value="2020-11-16T09:36:50.863-0300"/>
                                        </string>
                                        <string key="concept:attname" value="idstudent">
                                             <string key="orgdata:attValue" value="89964588"/>
                                             <string key="orgdata:valueType" value="int4"/>
                                             <date key="time:timestamp" value="2020-11-16T09:36:50.863-0300"/>
                                             <string key="orgdata:refVariable" value="studentid"/>
                                        </string>
                                        <string key="concept:attname" value="notified">
                                             <string key="orgdata:attValue" value="NULL"/>
                                             <string key="orgdata:valueType" value="int4"/>
                                             <date key="time:timestamp" value="2020-11-16T09:36:50.863-0300"/>
                                        </string>
                                   </attributes>
                              </list>
                         </string>
                         .....
                    </entities>
               </list>
     </event>
     ....
     </trace>
     .....
</log>
```

Fig. 2. Excerpt of the extended event log in XES format

3.2 Extended Event Log

Within our framework proposal we defined a XES extension for the Event logs to include integrated data from process and organizational data execution. Although the XES format allows to add attributes to events, they are added as tags without a logical order or correspondence to the event, as we provide in ours. As mentioned before, we integrate process execution data with corresponding organizational data [8] handled by the process, by means of several steps of data ETL from BPM systems and organizational databases, prior to the generation of the Event log. In Fig. 2 we present an excerpt of the extended Event log for the Students Mobility BP.

The extension adds two lists of attributes to the Event element: i) a variables list and ii) an entities list, which in turn contains a list of attributes. This extension reflects the integration of process and organizational data, in the following way. First, variables correspond to process variables that are handled by that event i.e. activity within the BPMS execution of the process, thus adding information from the process execution side. Secondly, entities and attributes correspond to organizational data that are handled by that event i.e. activity, within an organizational database different from the process one, thus adding information from the organizational data execution.

In the example, the activity that is shown corresponds to the "Register application" task, the process variable handled by the process execution is the "studentid" variable, which matches with the organizational database attribute "idstudent" of the entity (table) application. It can be noticed that the value for both elements is "89964588". This corresponds to the fact presented above that the "Register application" task inserted a new record in the application table of the organizational database, for each student application received, for the mobility program call. Thus, the application table, as shown in Fig. 1b has several references to other existing tables such as the Students and Program tables. As this is an excerpt of the extended event log, other variables, entities and attributes related to the "Register application" task are omitted for simplicity.

4   BPO Data Quality Model (BPODQM)

In this section we present the DQ model we developed for managing the quality of the integrated event log and organizational data (extended event log). For this, we first must present the format in which data is obtained as well as the granularities that are considered for its manipulation.

4.1   Data Format and Granularities

The extended event log shown in Fig. 2 is represented through the standard data format XES [1], as mentioned. In order to define a DQ model for the log, it is necessary to define the different granularities for identifying portions of data. These granularities are the following:

- **attribute value.** This is a particular value of an attribute. For example, in Fig. 2, the value "Register application".
- **attribute.** It refers to the set of values corresponding to the same key. For example, in Fig. 2, all the values that appear for key "concept:name".
- **event.** It involves all data included in an event data. For example, in Fig. 2, all data included in the event named "Register application"
- **log.** This granularity is used for properties that refer to the whole log.

4.2   BPODQM

This section presents the general DQ model BPODQM (Business Process and Organizational Data Quality Model) we have defined, in which specific dimensions, factors, and metrics for integrated process and organizational data are provided. It is based on previous quality models we have defined for other contexts [7,16], and on [17] which we have adapted and extended. This model is intended to serve as a general data quality model for the domain of integrated process and organizational data, which may be instantiated for any extended event log. Table 1 presents DQ dimensions, factors and metrics defined.

Accuracy dimension is composed by the following factors: (i) *syntactic accuracy*, which focuses on how the data is written, and whose metric measures if the data fits with the required format for the attribute, (ii) *semantic accuracy*, which refers to the existence of the attributes of an event with respect to reality, and may be measured through two different metrics, where the first one verifies the attributes that are not event identifiers, and the second one verifies the event identifiers, and finally, (iii) *precision*, which captures the detail level of a data item, and its metric is applied to an attribute value, which is a timestamp.

Consistency dimension is composed by the following factors: (i) *domain consistency*, which has two metrics, such that the first one compares an attribute value to a set of values and the second one verifies if an attribute value satisfy a values set definition, (ii) *inter-element consistency*, whose metric verifies if two attribute values of different events satisfy a consistency rule, and (iii) *intra-element consistency*, whose metric verifies if two attribute values of an event satisfy a consistency rule.

Completeness dimension has two factors: (i) *coverage*, which measures the proportion of the quantity of events contained in a trace wrt the quantity of events that the trace should contain, and (ii) *density*, for which there are three metrics, the first one verifies if an attribute value is Null, the second if certain attribute does not appear in an event, and the third one measures the density of an event considering weights over the different attributes.

Uniqueness dimension is composed by two factors: (i) *duplication-free*, which verifies if an attribute has duplicated values and if a trace has duplicated events, through two different metrics, and (ii) *contradiction-free*, whose metric evaluate if a trace has two different events that correspond to the same event in reality and have contradictory information.

For *Freshness* dimension we define only the factor *timeliness*. This factor has three different metrics, each one measuring attribute, event and trace timeliness, respectively. They verify if the timestamp of the object (attribute, event or trace) belongs to the time range of the parent object (event, trace or log, respectively).

Credibility dimension is composed of two factors: (i) *provenance*, which may be measured by three metrics; *responsibility*, which gives a score to the credibility of the person who is responsible of the log data, *origin*, which measures the credibility of the event origin, and *reproducibility*, which verifies if a log is reproducible following workflow rules, and (ii) *trustworthiness*, which may be measured through three different metrics that are applied over attribute values;

Table 1. BPODQM dimensions, factors and metrics

Dimension	Factor	Metric	Granularity
Accuracy	Syntactic Accuracy	Format	Attribute value
	Semantic Accuracy	Weak Semantic Accuracy	Event
		Strong Semantic Accuracy	Event
	Precision	Timestamp precision	Attribute value
Consistency	Domain Consistency	Extensional Values	Attribute value
		Intensional Values	Attribute value
	Inter-element Consistency	Inter-event Rule	Activity
	Intra-element Consistency	Intra-event Rule	Event
Completenes	Coverage	Coverage Ratio	Trace
	Density	Not Null	Attribute value
		Inexistent Value	Event
		Weighted Density	Event
Uniqueness	Duplication-free	Duplicate Attribute	Attribute value
		Duplicate Event	Event
	Contradiction-free	Contradictory Event	Event
Freshness	Timeliness	Attribute Timeliness	Attribute value
		Event Timeliness	Event
		Trace Timeliness	Trace
Credibility	Provenance	Responsibility	Log
		Origin	Event
		Reproducibility	Log
	Trustworthiness	Believability	Attribute value
		Reputation	Attribute value
		Verifiability	Attribute value
Security	User Permissions	Authorized User	Event
	Encrypted Data	Encrypted Attribute	Attribute value
		Ratio Encrypted Att	Event
	Anonymity	Anonymous Attribute	Attribute value
		Ratio Anonymous Att	Event

believability, which measures the degree of believability of the veracity of the data value, *reputation*, which refers to the reputation of the data source, and *verifiability*, which indicates if a data value es verifiable or not.

Finally, *security* dimension is composed by three factors: (i) *user permissions*, which verifies for an event, if the users that participated in it have the necessary rights, (ii) *encrypted data*, which has two metrics, one that verifies if all the values of an attribute are encrypted and another one that calculates the ratio of encrypted attributes of an event, and (iii) *anonymity*, which may be measured through a metric that verifies if an attribute is anonymized or a metric that calculates the ratio of anonymized attributes of an event.

All the results of a metric can be aggregated to the following granularity, calculating the percentage of results "1" over the total. For example, the metric *format* can be aggregated from *attribute value* to *attribute* granularity, obtaining the percentage of values that satisfy the required format for a given attribute.

5 Example of Application

In this section we present an example of BPODQM application on the extended event log we generated for the "Students Mobility" BP introduced in Sect. 3. In the first place, we have to select the quality characteristics from the BPODQM model, to be checked over the data in the extended event log. We have selected some basic ones in order to show its evaluation and to provide a discussion on the integrated process and organizational data to which we applied the model:

- Dimension: *Accuracy*, Factor: *Syntactic correctness*, Metric: *Format*
- Dimension: *Consistency*, Factor: *Domain consistency*, Metric: *Extensional values*
- Dimension: *Completeness*, Factor: *Density*, Metric: *Not null*
- Dimension: *Freshness*, Factor: *Timeliness*, Metrics: *Attribute Opportunity*

Each one is applied over a specific element of the extended event log which is also defined when selecting the characteristics to be evaluated, and specific metrics are defined for it to be calculated over the element. In what follows we present the definitions for each of the selected Metrics.

5.1 Metric Format

For this example, the Metric Format is applied to the existing timestamps in all levels i.e. event, variables and attributes. We defined a specific Metric that takes as correct format for the timestamp the one specified by the event log: *yyyy-MM-dd'T'HH:mm:ss*. We then defined a specific function in order to calculate the specific metric, with signature *timestampFormat(date, format): bool*, which returns true if the timestamp of an element of the log is in the defined format, false if not.

In this example, we had 1980 timestamp tags corresponding to event timestamps and the integrated data in variables timestamps and attributes timestamps, as shown in Fig. 2. As we automatically generated the extended event log from the integrated data formatting the timestamps as required, they all returned true in the correct format by construction. This is a basic example of the format metric that tools as ProM or Disco already check when importing event logs, but it can be checked for other attribute values including organizational data attributes that are domain specific for which specific formats are defined.

5.2   Extensional Values

We defined to check this factor in the extended event log for the values corresponding to the attribute *idstate* of the entity *application* as shown in Fig. 2. As introduced before, in the Students Mobility a new application is registered in the state "Initiated" whenever a student submits one for a mobility program. As the process progresses the application status values are updated, following domain predefined values, which are referenced from the application table i.e. "Initiated" = 1, "Approved" = 2, an so on. So we defined the domain values by extension as idstate = {1, 2, 3, 4} and we checked them within the extended event log, and the specific function *extensionalValueAttribute(attribute, dom): bool*, which returns true if the attribute value lies between the defined domain, false if not. In this case we did not find values off range.

5.3   Metric Not Null

We checked this factor at two levels: the process data and the organizational data, to ensure key elements for the mining analysis will not be null. At the process level we defined to check the *resource* attribute of the event, and at the organizational level the *notified* attribute of the application entity. Due to the specificity of the process implementation and supporting data model, the notified attributed will be (correctly) null when associated with the first four tasks of the model, until the process reaches the "Notify applicants" task where applicants are notified and the attribute is updated with values {Yes, No}. We defined the specific function *NotNullAttribute(attribute): bool*, which returns true if the attribute value is not null, false if not.

Checking for the resource attribute is useful if you are going to use the resource values for analysis, since tools such as ProM allows event logs without resources for process model discovering purposes. In our case, all resources where included either people or system values. Regarding the notified attribute, an interesting discussion arises, since most values of the attribute returned as null. It would be interesting to be able to select not only the attribute to be checked but the event to which the attribute should be attached and not be null, which in this case will be only the "Notify applicants" task.

5.4   Metric Attribute Timeliness

This metric was checked for all organizational data attributes of each entity within the corresponding event i.e. task to which they are related. We define the function *attributeTimelinessTimestamp(attribute):bool* which returns true if the timestamp of the organizational data attribute is within the timestamp of the corresponding event, and false if not. We detected several timestamps of attributes which had values that do not correspond to the timestamps of the event, i.e. were prior to the event timestamp. Although the log was correctly imported in ProM, since the extended log attributes are not taken into account in the checks, when importing it in Disco we got a warning on this fact, and several registers were not imported correctly. This fact helped us to dig into the generation of the log, the integration of data, and the process and organizational data from the sources, in order to find the problem.

6   Related Work

Data quality dimensions have been defined in the last decades generating a wide set of dimensions with focus on organizational data from which to choose. This is both and advantage and a disadvantage since it can be overwhelming to define, integrate and organize dimensions, factors and metrics in a model for an organization. However, there is a sub-set agreed and used by most authors [13,14] that could help in this task. [5] propose an organization of quality dimensions providing six clusters with which to cover key dimensions such as accuracy, completeness, consistency, among others. Data quality evaluation and cleaning is a key step in data mining and other analysis approaches e.g. data warehouses.

Regarding process data quality evaluation for process mining, there are some recent proposals which defined specific dimensions with focus on the process data at the event log level such as [17], without dealing with organizational data. It takes into account the guidelines for process data quality in [2], but it is not clearly structured in dimensions, factors and metrics as ours, only defining dimensions and less than ours. Also, metrics are defined in a fixed way and with a predefined score. [4] presents an approach and application for the health area, defining some dimensions and metrics.

Differently to these works, our proposal defines a quality model for integrated process and organizational data, that are put together in an extended event log where both quality and analysis take into account the complete data set of each process. The model is instantiated for the extended event log of each process.

7   Conclusions

This paper presents a DQ model, called BPODQM, for evaluating DQ in the extended event log, which is a log that contains data from process execution and the related organizational data. The proposed DQ model is a general model that can be instantiated for any extended event log, by selecting the most important DQ dimensions, factors, metrics and data to evaluate, according to the characteristics and requirements of the particular case. BPODQM contains a set of dimensions, factors and metrics that were selected, adapted and extended from the literature, considering the particularities of the BP domain, the goals of process mining activities and the characteristics of the extended event log we manage. On the other hand, this model was refined from its successive application to particular cases of BP. We illustrated the model application through a small part of an experience of DQ evaluation over a BP that deals with students applications and granting for mobility programs.

We believe that this DQ model is rich enough, and at the same time concise and practical, to address the most important issues that can appear when working with event logs and associated organizational data in order to perform process and data mining.

Acknowledgments. This work was supported by project "Minería de procesos y datos para la mejora de procesos en las organizaciones" funded by Comisión Sectorial de Investigación Científica (CSIC), Universidad de la República (UdelaR), Uruguay.

References

1. IEEE: standard for extensible event stream (xes) for achieving interoperability in event logs and event streams. IEEE Std. 1849–2016, pp. 1–50 (2016)
2. van der Aalst, W.M.P.: Process Mining - Data Science in Action, 2nd edn. Springer, Heidelberg (2016)
3. van der Aalst, W.M.P., ter Hofstede, A.H.M., Weske, M.: Business process management: a survey. In: van der Aalst, W.M.P., Weske, M. (eds.) BPM 2003. LNCS, vol. 2678, pp. 1–12. Springer, Heidelberg (2003). https://doi.org/10.1007/3-540-44895-0_1
4. Andrews, R., et al.: Leveraging data quality to better prepare for process mining: an approach illustrated through analysing road trauma pre-hospital retrieval and transport processes in Queensland. Int. J. Environ. Res. Pub. Health 16(7), 1138 (2019)
5. Batini, C., Scannapieco, M.: Data and Information Quality - Dimensions, Principles and Techniques. Data-Centric Systems and Applications, Springer, Heidelberg (2016)
6. Chang, J.: BPM Systems: Strategy and Implementation. CRC Press, Boca Raton (2016)
7. Cristalli, E., Serra, F., Marotta, A.: Data quality evaluation in document oriented data stores. In: Woo, C., Lu, J., Li, Z., Ling, T.W., Li, G., Lee, M.L. (eds.) ER 2018. LNCS, vol. 11158, pp. 309–318. Springer, Cham (2018). https://doi.org/10.1007/978-3-030-01391-2_35
8. Delgado, A., Calegari, D.: Towards a unified vision of business process and organizational data. In: XLVI Latin American Computing Conference, CLEI 2020. p. To appear. IEEE (2020)
9. Delgado, A., Marotta, A., González, L., Tansini, L., Calegari, D.: Towards a data science framework integrating process and data mining for organizational improvement. In: 15th International Conference on Software Technologies, ICSOFT 2020, pp. 492–500. ScitePress (2020)
10. Delgado, A., Weber, B., Ruiz, F., de Guzmán, I.G.R., Piattini, M.: An integrated approach based on execution measures for the continuous improvement of business processes realized by services. Inf. SW Technol. 56(2), 134–162 (2014)
11. Dumas, M., Rosa, M.L., Mendling, J., Reijers, H.A.: Fundamentals of BPM, 2nd edn. Springer, Heidelberg (2018)
12. IEEE: Task Force on Data Science & Adv. Analytics (2020). http://www.dsaa.co/
13. Scannapieco, M., Catarci, T.: Data quality under a computer science perspective. Arch. Comput. 2, 1–15 (2002)
14. Shankaranarayanan, G., Blake, R.: From content to context: the evolution and growth of data quality research. J. Data Inf. Qual. 8(2), 1–28 (2017)
15. Sumathi, S., Sivanandam, S.N.: Introduction to Data Mining and its Applications, Studies in Computational Intelligence, vol. 29. Springer, Heidelberg (2006)

16. Valverde, M.C., Vallespir, D., Marotta, A., Panach, J.I.: Applying a data quality model to experiments in software engineering. In: Indulska, M., Purao, S. (eds.) ER 2014. LNCS, vol. 8823, pp. 168–177. Springer, Cham (2014). https://doi.org/10.1007/978-3-319-12256-4_18

17. Verhulst, R.: Evaluating quality of event data within event logs: an extensible framework (2016)

18. Wang, R.Y., Strong, D.M.: Beyond accuracy: what data quality means to data consumers. J. Manag. Inf. Syst. **12**(4), 5–33 (1996)

19. Weske, M.: BPM - Concepts, Languages, Architectures, 3rd edn. Springer, Heidelberg (2019)

A Checklist for Explainable AI in the Insurance Domain

Olivier Koster[1]([✉]) [iD], Ruud Kosman[2,3] [iD], and Joost Visser[1] [iD]

[1] LIACS, Leiden University, Leiden, The Netherlands
j.visser@liacs.leidenuniv.nl
[2] SIVI, Utrecht, The Netherlands
[3] InnoValor, Enschede, The Netherlands

Abstract. Artificial intelligence (AI) is a powerful tool to accomplish a great many tasks. This exciting branch of technology is being adopted increasingly across varying sectors, including the insurance domain. With that power arise several complications. One of which is a lack of transparency and explainability of an algorithm for experts and non-experts alike. This brings into question both the usefulness as well as the accuracy of the algorithm, coupled with an added difficulty to assess potential biases within the data or the model. In this paper, we investigate the current usage of AI algorithms in the Dutch insurance industry and the adoption of explainable artificial intelligence (XAI) techniques. Armed with this knowledge we design a checklist for insurance companies that should help assure quality standards regarding XAI and a solid foundation for cooperation between organisations. This checklist extends an existing checklist that SIVI, the standardisation institute for digital cooperation and innovation in Dutch insurance.

Keywords: Artificial intelligence · Explainability · Insurance · Finance

1 Introduction

Artificial intelligence (AI) is one of the leading technologies paving the way for more efficient solutions and powerful automation. This exciting technology is being deployed increasingly across various industries. For instance, AI is aiding healthcare in its search for accurate diagnostic procedures in order to detect cancer early, assisting radiology by discovering patterns and accelerating medicine development [5]. Similarly, in the insurance industry, the use of AI is starting to gain traction, being used in assessing risks, handling claims and detecting fraud. Aside from all this added ability, AI too comes with its own downsides. Much like human cognition, technology has its flaws. The same goes for AI algorithms. While early AI systems were relatively easy to comprehend, we have seen a recent rise in opaque decision systems such as Deep Neural Networks. Although these types of algorithms increase accuracy, they come with a higher level of

A. C. R. Paiva et al. (Eds.): QUATIC 2021, CCIS 1439, pp. 446–456, 2021.
https://doi.org/10.1007/978-3-030-85347-1_32

algorithmic complexity, often consisting of hundreds of layers and millions of parameters [4]. In these instances, interpretability vastly decreases. This results in a black-box algorithm that is difficult to understand for experts and non-experts alike. This can create some unfavourable situations. In particular, when decisions made by an algorithm affect human lives. For example, when black-box algorithms make incorrect diagnoses, doctors may be subject to intense scrutiny for taking the wrong course of action, being unable to explain the proper reasoning behind a diagnosis. This phenomenon can have an even more severe impact on a larger scale. In 2020, The Dutch government deployed SyRi, an algorithmic fraud risk scoring system. It used a non-disclosed algorithmic risk model to profile citizens, allegedly targeting mostly low-income neighbourhoods and minority residents. Dutch court deemed SyRi illegal for lacking transparent data usage and violating privacy. Similarly, Apple revealed its AI driven credit risk system showed a striking bias, as it deemed men far more creditworthy than women. Consequently, individuals could be given different credit limits despite having the same accounts, cards or assets [7]. In precision medicine, decisions cannot be based on mere binary prediction, creating a need for extensive explanations supporting a model's output. The same holds true for other domains such as autonomous vehicles, transportation, security, and finance [10].

Evidently, using AI to make impactful decisions can be a dangerous practice when the legitimacy of the model is not justified. From this perspective, the responsibility of the algorithms' creator does not only concern its accuracy but also its interpretability and transparency. This reasoning has spawned a new field of research named Explainable Artificial Intelligence (XAI). Research on this topic has spiked in recent years, reflecting a growing need for XAI. Even so, to our knowledge, no prior research captures the state of AI adoption, and more specifically of XAI techniques, in the (Dutch) insurance industry.

In this paper, we examine the current adoption and future prospects of AI and XAI within the Dutch insurance industry. This is done through literature research coupled with conducting exploratory interviews of industry experts. All of this will lay the groundwork for the design of a checklist for insurance companies that should help assure quality standards regarding XAI and a solid foundation for cooperation between organisations. The checklist is evaluated and tested by conducting confirmatory interviews, creating a feedback loop for further refinement. The aforementioned checklist extends an existing checklist regarding AI that SIVI, the standardisation institute for digital cooperation and innovation in Dutch insurance.

2   Method

Our research methodology is based on the design science research paradigm for information systems [6]. Contrary to behavioural science, design science is focused on designing an artefact. In our case, this artefact is a checklist for explainable and transparent AI applications. Similar to the methodology discussed in [6], research is done in three iterative cycles.

448 O. Koster et al.

We conduct two types of interviews during our research. Firstly, we perform semi-structured exploratory interviews to assess the current state of the art with respect to AI techniques used within the insurance industry. This is helpful because, while current literature tells us a lot about the possibilities and practices of AI, it gives little insight into the actual adoption of AI techniques. Additionally, practical context is usually missing in most available literature. We interview four industry experts at companies that operate within the insurance industry, ranging from software suppliers to insurance companies. The findings can be found in Sect. 4. Secondly, we conduct confirmatory interviews with similar companies to evaluate our findings and checklist design. This will give us a strong indication of both the correctness, robustness as well as practicality of our design. Similarly to the exploratory interviews, evaluation is done by conducting four confirmatory interviews with industry experts from insurance companies, and their software suppliers. The evaluation findings can be found in Sect. 6. For privacy reasons we will not disclose the actual company names, nor will we disclose employee names and information that could be used to identify organisations and personnel. Instead, we will call the seven companies 'company A' through 'company G', respectively. Note, that with company B we have conducted both an exploratory interview as well as a confirmatory interview.

3 Literature Background

Taxonomy of XAI. According to Vilone and Longo [12], there is little agreement among scholars on what explanations are and what properties they might have, as well as the correct terminology that should be used. Fortunately, Fortunately, Barredo Arrieta et al. [2] have comprised a clear report on the most common terms used in XAI research and their respective meaning. Notably, they propose three distinct *levels of transparency*. Barredo Arrieta et al. [2] explain how these levels of transparency apply to different AI algorithms, enabling them to categorise the algorithms as either of type *transparent* or type *opaque* (or *non-transparent*). Of course, a system itself is never opaque but rather opaque with respect to some particular agent. Tomsett et al. [11] break down all different agent groups within a system in fine detail. Depending on what a particular agent is tasked with doing, they are likely to require a different kind of knowledge to do it and, thus, seek a different kind of explanation. Barredo Arrieta et al. [2] have comprised a list of the research goals that particular agents can achieve through model explainability. To get a better grip on the concept of explaining AI models, we must acknowledge that explanations come in many different proverbial shapes. Vilone and Longo [12] describe attributes and characteristics of explanations as well as define several types of explanations. In recent years, several XAI methods have been developed to increase model transparency and explainability. Vilone and Longo [12] have also compiled a list of all current *ante-hoc* and *post-hoc* XAI methods.

Responsible AI. AI bias is a phenomenon that occurs when an algorithm produces results that are systemically prejudiced due to either erroneous (or correct but undesired) assumptions in the machine learning process. This can happen with learning algorithms when they are trained on their dataset. In this case, we call the phenomenon *algorithmic bias*. Even so, other forms of bias exist. It can also result from human errors (e.g. faulty collection or representation of input data). Barocas and Selbst [1] break down all possible cause for bias. Sometimes biases can be functionally correct, but immoral to base results upon. These undesired biases stem from a black-box model's tendency to unintentionally create unfair decisions by including sensitive factors such as the individual's race or gender. This phenomenon gives rise to certain discriminatory issues, either explicitly (considering sensitive attributes) or implicitly (considering factors that correlate with sensitive attributes). Barredo Arrieta et al. [2] gives several degrees of fairness that should be considered to design responsible AI solutions.

Several guidelines for trustworthy AI have been proposed [3,8]. Similar to the checklist we propose, these frameworks aim to give general guidance for responsible use of AI. However, these frameworks, while being very high level in nature, are not actionable for working developers. Serban et al. [9] provide 14 engineering practices for trustworthy ML applications, of which several are related to explainability. These practices are not formulated in terms of checks.

4   Exploration

As mentioned, we carried out four exploratory interviews with industry experts from financial institutes, insurance companies, and their software suppliers. A summary of the interviewees is shown in Table 1. The priority of these interviews lies in achieving three primary goals. Firstly, we seek a more in-depth understanding of the insurance industry and its related processes, stakeholders, demands and concerns. Secondly, we want to know which AI techniques said companies deployed and which they plan to deploy in the future. Thirdly, we want to know how the industry values transparency and explainability.

Findings. The insurance industry is still in a preliminary phase when it comes to the deployment of AI technologies. All of the four companies interviewed have deployed some form of Rule-Based System (RBS), but some are hesitant to adopt more complex AI techniques, like Machine Learning (ML) and Deep Learning (DL). This is because most companies are focused on improving these Rule-Based Systems and ironing out any inefficiencies. Additionally, the interviewees from company B expressed a growing concern that people lack trust in ML algorithms. It takes time and effort to convince people that ML algorithms work better than Rule-Based Systems, even though oftentimes they are statistically proven to do so. Thus, at the moment, all of them prefer Rule-Based Systems because they are more explainable, even when the results that are explained are sometimes less accurate. Two out of four companies interviewed have already deployed ML algorithms in their processes. Notably, both company B and D

Table 1. Summary of exploratory interview company information *Also takes part in confirmatory interview

	Company A	Company B*	Company C	Company D
Core business	Insurance software supplier	Insurance intermediary (software)	Financial services	Financial services
# employees	100+	100+	1.000+	10.000+
Job-title interviewee(s)	Product owner	ML engineer & software engineer	Manager client contact financial services	Product Owner & Innovation Manager Business Automation
Uses RBS for	Various processes	Various processes	Various processes	Various processes
Uses ML for	–	Fraud detection	–	Fraud detection
Uses DL for	–	–	–	–

have deployed the technology for insurance claim handling, specifically to detect possible fraudulent activity. It is interesting to note, however, that both companies do so with different kinds of algorithms. Company B uses a decision tree classifier (supervised learning), whereas company D uses a k-means clustering algorithm for anomaly detection (unsupervised learning). Company B also uses ML algorithms for calculating car insurance premiums. They are also experimenting with ML algorithms to calculate a customer's risk coverage ratio, but this system has yet to be deployed. Importantly, neither use non-transparent algorithms (including DL) for these tasks. Company B and D are already experimenting with DL. However, none of the interviewed companies have deployed any DL systems thus far. There are four main reasons for this:

1. **DL is less explainable:** Even though DL algorithms are usually more accurate than ML algorithms (and Rule-bases Systems), they are even less explainable. A balance between accuracy and explainability has to be found. Insurance companies mostly choose explainability in favour of a marginal increase in accuracy. They need increased explainability to understand and convey why the system gives a certain output, otherwise, the results are not actionable.
2. **Understanding DL requires technical/mathematical expertise:** Because DL algorithms (and some ML algorithms for that matter) have such high complexity, they are less explainable. Thus, they require more expertise to be understood and used (this is the case for all system agent roles, but especially operators and executors). For most current employees this creates a knowledge gap that is hard to overcome. Furthermore, if they were to overcome this obstacle, their job description would change significantly. Claims handlers would turn into model experts.
3. **DL is less transferable:** DL algorithms are sometimes less transferable than other AI techniques. The input data that insurance companies use at

the moment is less suitable for these types of algorithms. Additionally, some of the data that could be used to extract the most out of DL algorithms are not present in the dataset or are off-limits due to privacy concerns.

4. **Streamlining RBS has more value in the short term:** More quality gain can be found in streamlining current RBSs and ML processes, instead of looking for accuracy gain with DL algorithms. Gains can especially be made in the refinement of input data (e.g. feature selection), as this is where most resource and thought is going at the moment.

Future prospects for all companies range from the initial deployment of ML to the deployment of complex DL algorithms when the aforementioned issues start to be resolved. Most expect to start incorporating (more of) these complex AI technologies near the end of the 2025.

5   Design

Purpose. The checklist should be a list of 'checks' that, if answered properly, should test the explainability and transparency of AI model applications, as well as highlight potential weaknesses and areas for improvement. We define a *check* as a component that features one or more questions, hence the collective is called a checklist. Every check comes with an elucidation to clear any confusion for the reader and to make sure the question is answered as intended. Checks either have open answers or multiple choice answers. The complete checklist can be found in the appendix. The checklist is designed with two main purposes in mind: Firstly, it should be used to confirm the quality and completeness of an AI application with regards to its explainability and transparency. In that way, the checklist can essentially be used as a guide to evaluate if all facets, that make a well designed explainable and transparent AI application, are accounted for. If, based on this checklist, one would conclude their application is not complete or lacks quality in certain key areas, it serves as an indication where further progress should be made. Secondly, the checklist, if properly filled in, could be shared with third parties (clients or companies) to show the quality and completeness of an AI applications with regards to explainability and transparency. This is especially helpful for collaboration between companies to give confidence that certain information or assets can be shared. Moreover, this could be interesting from a marketing standpoint, giving clients assurance that your application is well designed and responsible.

Constraints. To fulfil these purposes we formulate several constraints for the checklist design. The checklist is based on an existing checklist[1] named 'Checklist-KOAT' or 'Checklist Kwaliteit Onbemenste Advies- en Transactie-etoepassingen' by SIVI, the standardisation institute for digital cooperation and innovation in Dutch insurance. This existing checklist covers several topics with

---

[1] The Checklist-KOAT can be found at https://www.sivi.org/checklist-koat/.

regards to computer applications for financial advice and financial transactions. We can deduce several helpful constraints that are implied in this pre-existing checklist. We will use these implied constraints as well as our design guidelines to set constraints to design our checklist. The following constraints are used:

1. **Practical relevance:** We want our checklist to be applicable for practical use. That means that all covered topics should be relevant from a practical standpoint. Furthermore, the checklist cannot be overly long or be too technically in-depth, as this would disincline people from using it.
2. **Non-expert terminology:** The checks and elucidation should refrain from using expert terminology as much as possible. If used in a practical environment by actual employees of financial companies, expert terminology may be unclear and would not induce a full understanding of the covered topic.
3. **Broadness-precision balance:** Topics should be covered broadly enough to be appropriate for most, if not all, AI model applications. Yet, checks should be precise enough to get the most informative answer. A proper balance should be found between these two ends.

6   Validation

As mentioned in Sect. 2, similarly to the exploratory interviews, evaluation is done by conducting four confirmatory interviews with industry experts from insurance companies, and their software suppliers. A summary of the interviewees is shown in Table 2. Other than to evaluate our design, these interviews essentially helped us confirm whether our original findings are correct and if they still hold within new contexts. The structure of the interview is as follows: For every check and its elucidation, we ask three things: 1. "Is the phrasing and meaning clear?" 2. "How relevant is the check and its encompassing topic (with regards to the purposes mentioned in Sect. 5)?" and 3. "What would your answer be to the question for your specific application?" After all, topics are covered, we ask two general questions about the entire set of topics: 1. "Do you deem the sequence/order of topics logical and favourable?" 2. "Is the set of topics (and checks) complete or do you think a topic is missing?"

Conforming to our used design science research methodology, evaluation is done during the design phase. Therefore, the design process has an iterative nature. Consequently, a new checklist draft is designed after each confirmatory interview. This way the design is improved in a step by step manner. Most initial constructive criticism, in the interview with company E, was aimed at phrasing and meaning (of checks and their elucidation) being unclear. This resulted in the inclusion of additional elucidations were needed, or rephrasing of said unclear pieces of information. This was the case throughout the design. In most cases, an illustrative example was also added in an attempt to clear up any remaining confusion. The next iteration was found to be much more clear and comprehensible, although slight improvements kept being made from version to version. Until, in the last interview, no confusion was remarked explicitly.

Table 2. Summary of confirmatory interview company information *Also takes part in exploratory interview

	Company E	Company F	Company G	Company B*
Core business	Software supplier	Insurance & pensions	Software supplier (insurance & pensions)	Insurance intermediary (software)
# employees	10+	1.000+	10+	100+
Job-title interviewee(s)	CCO\CMO	sr. IT Architect	User interaction designer	ML engineer & software engineer
Use RBS for	Various processes	Various processes	Various processes	Various processes
Use ML for	–	–	Policy recommendation	Fraud detection
Use DL for	–	–	–	–

7 Discussion

In the final iteration of the design, all checks and elucidations seemed to be phrased clearly, to be fully understood by the interviewees, based on our assessment of their answers. Also, based on the results, all checks and topics present in the final iteration seemed to be relevant enough to be included in the design. Interviewees specifically expressed relevance for the topics spanning bias. Given this fact, more checks could be added towards this topic. Such questions could dive deeper into why they include and exclude certain biases in their model (thus, revealing which biases they would label as undesired biases). Eventually, we landed on a design that puts a heavy emphasis on questions formulated with open-ended answer in mind. This has two main advantages, whilst also running the risk of some potential drawbacks. The first advantage is that phrasing the questions in such a way, tends to squeeze as much interesting information out of a single check as possible, as long as the checklist user is motivated to explore the answer to the intended extent (interviewees have at least expressed the intention to do so). The second advantage is that this open-ended phrasing creates room for a certain broadness in the scope of a check's applicability. By restricting the answers too much, you run the risk of excluding some AI applications, rendering the check useless for their specific model.

At the end of the day, the checklist needs to be relevant for companies that only use RBSs, but must also be a guide to ML and DL technology, in order to aid with applications in the future. Based on the results of our confirmatory interviews, we feel our design fulfils this ambition.

8   Conclusion

Contributions. Several contributions stand out when compared to other literature that we could find on the topics of XAI and AI in general. Firstly, we propose a checklist that can be used to assess and help assure transparency and explainability for AI application in a practical environment. It can also be used to verify if enough thought has gone into the application and to share quality standards across parties. As such, our checklist is more actionable for the working developer than the frameworks mentioned in Sect. 3. Secondly, we give insight into AI and XAI adoption in the insurance industry. Few other papers talk about AI and XAI in the financial sector. Presumably, this comes down to the fact that most financial companies are only now starting to adopt AI algorithms effectively, as knowledge on the subject has only started to grow in recent years. After all, once a technology has been discovered, it takes some time for it to develop into a commercially viable product. Thirdly, we have, to some extent, validated existing theories and concepts about XAI in a practical environment.

Future Work. As with any study, some things could be done to further improve the design research carried out. For example, while interviews were conducted to learn about the adoption and prospects of AI and XAI techniques in the Dutch insurance industry as a whole, more interviews would give a more complete view of the industry. Additionally, since industry experts employed at insurance companies and software suppliers were targeted for the interviews, end-customers, consumers and lawmakers were not consulted. Moreover, only a small number of companies in the industry are now starting to gain traction with ML and DL concepts. This means that knowledge of the technologies among industry experts is still relatively scarce. Considering, that in the future this knowledge will grow, more detailed analyses could be done on the topic.

Finally, as initially mentioned, the checklist is meant to extend an existing checklist, named 'Checklist-KOAT', which is made by SIVI. Specifically, the design mentioned in this paper serves as a base for the eventual integration into the 'Checklist-KOAT'. This integration will be done by SIVI itself. SIVI will keep improving the integrated design through field testing with associated member companies. We presume the design will remain relevant for the foreseeable future, although, as time progresses and new techniques become prevalent, eventual updates will inevitably be advisable.

While developed and validated in the context of the insurance domain, our checklist can likely be generalized to other domains.

Appendix: Checklist for AI in Insurance Applications

Transparency & explainability

Transparency refers to how understandable the inner workings of the application are and how well its individual components and their interrelationships can be viewed. By explainability, we mean the way an application conveys to the user (from customer to expert) in a human-understandable way, how the input leads to the results (i.e. output), which in turn can lead to novel or confirming insights about the model and its dataset. Both aspects ensure that the application as a whole becomes more robust. It can help increase the accuracy of your model, justify its functionality, prevent unwanted biases, uncover new knowledge and help prevent and correct errors.

#	Subject	Check	Answer type	Elucidation
1	Transparency	Elaborate whether the application itself is already transparent to the user or whether external techniques are needed to increase transparency and explainability?	Open answer	We can divide AI algorithms into two categories. Namely, *transparent algorithms* and *non-transparent algorithms*. Transparent algorithms include *rule-based systems*, *linear/logistic regression*, *decision trees*, *k-nearest neighbours*, *rule-based learners*, *general additive models*, *bayesian models*. Non-transparent algorithms include *tree ensembles*, *support vector machines* and *neural networks*. It is also possible that your application falls somewhere between the two extremes.
2	Purpose	Which of these reasons is most important with regard to the application's explainability. You can choose more than one option.	Multiple choice	The need to explain a model mainly stems from one of four reasons: 1) increasing the model's accuracy. 2) discovering or confirming causality. 3) verifying and justifying the model's fairness & robustness. 4) Checking the model for errors and removing bugs.
3	Development	Explain how the right balance has been found between accuracy and explainability in the development process and where priority has been placed.	Open answer	AI applications are often developed with the highest possible accuracy as the main priority. In such a case, a compromise is usually made between accuracy on the one hand and transparency on the other. In practice, explainability and transparency are often just as important and sometimes even more important for the use of an application.
4	Impact	1) Explain what the results of the application are used for (i.e. what role do the results fulfil). Are the results advisory to the user or does the application make autonomous decisions based on these results, or something in	Open answer	The application's impact on the organization is influenced by the role that the application's result must fulfil. If the application plays an advisory role, the result's impact on the end customer is relatively less than if the results play a decisive role (meaning the application makes autonomous decisions based on the results). If the application makes autonomous choices and implements incorrect logic, incorrect decisions can go unnoticed. After which they can only be corrected
5	Ante-hoc methods	1) What external ante-hoc techniques have been used to improve explainability? 2) Explain how these techniques increase the explainability of the application.	Open answers	There are external techniques that can increase the transparency and explainability of AI applications. Some of these techniques involve baking in explainability from the beginning. This has to do, for example, with paying extra attention to input processing or training on the dataset. These techniques are called *ante-hoc techniques*. Think of techniques such as *Reversed Time Attention Model (RETAIN)*, *Bayesian deep learning (BDL)*, etc.
6	Post-hoc methods	1) What external post-hoc techniques have been used to improve explainability? 2) Explain how these techniques increase the application's explainability.	Open answer	There are external techniques that increase an application's explainability after or during the model run-time. These techniques are called *post-hoc techniques*. There are post-hoc techniques that are universal for all algorithm types, but also for specific algorithms types. Think of techniques such as *Local Interpretable Model-Agnostic Explanations (LIME)*, SHapley Additive exPlanations (SHAP), Layer-wise Relevance Propagation (LRP)), etc.
7	Explanation output type	Explain what type of explanation is outputted?	Open answer	The outputted explanation of the application can be given in several types. The possible options are *textual, numeric, categorical, pictorial, time series or rule-based.*
8	Stakeholders	For each relevant stakeholder, explain... 1) what demands they have concerning the application's explainability and 2) how these interests are fulfilled by the application's explanations:	Open answer	Different people in and outside the organization have different demands concerning the application's explainability. The organisation must take these different demands into account, so that an application is as robust and usable as possible, while also considering ethical concerns and legislation. (stakeholders: *creator, examiner, operator, executor, decision-subject, data-subject*) (demands: *informativeness, causality, trustworthiness, confidence, accessibility, interactivity, transferability, privacy-awareness*)
9	Redress (Question and complaint handling)	Explain how the consumer receives more information when he or she has an in-depth question or complaint regarding	Open answer	If the application affects consumers, they may sometimes need further explanation about their situation. In such a case, the application's results may have to be explained to this person. This can happen, for instance, if the application makes a mistake, or the consumer has a
10	Bias	Explain... 1) which end-customer groups may be unfairly disadvantaged by the application and how this is prevented. 2) whether the explanations provided reveal (unwanted) biases (in the data or the algorithm)?	Open answer	Undesired biases can arise in applications that are trained on data. These unwanted biases must be actively prevented. Explainability and transparency can be a means to that end. Example of bias: Statistically, red cars take more damage. However, does this mean that red car owners have to pay a higher premium?
11	Expertise	Explain whether new expertise concerning explainability and ethics were needed in the company, since the implementation of the application?	Open answer	Some companies hire 'explanation experts' and 'ethics experts' to support their AI projects.

References

1. Barocas, S., Selbst, A.D.: Big data's disparate impact. Calif. Law Rev. **104**, 671 (2016)
2. Barredo Arrieta, A., et al.: Explainable artificial intelligence (XAI): concepts, taxonomies, opportunities and challenges toward responsible AI. Inf. Fusion **58**, 82–115 (2020). ISSN 1566-2535. https://doi.org/10.1016/j.inffus.2019.12.012. http://www.sciencedirect.com/science/article/pii/S1566253519308103
3. Van der Burgt, J.: General principles for the use of artificial intelligence in the financial sector (2019). https://www.dnb.nl/media/voffsric/general-principles-for-the-use-of-artificial-intelligence-in-the-financial-sector.pdf. Guidance Document from De Nederlandsche Bank. Accessed 25 May 2021
4. Castelvecchi, D.: Can we open the black box of AI? Nature **538**(7623), 20–23 (2016). https://doi.org/10.1038/538020a
5. Daley, S.: 32 examples of AI in healthcare that will make you feel better about the future (2019). https://builtin.com/artificial-intelligence/artificial-intelligence-healthcare. Accessed 25 May 2021
6. Hevner, A.R., March, S.T., Park, J., Ram, S.: Design science in information systems research. MIS Q. **28**(1), 75–105 (2004). ISSN 02767783. http://www.jstor.org/stable/25148625
7. Kroes, M.: Fact-AI: a framework towards responsible AI (2020). https://www.viqtordavis.com/en-us/media/whitepaper-fact-ai. Whitepaper from Viqtor Davies. Accessed 25 May 2021
8. Reisman, D., Schultz, J., Crawfordand, K., Whittaker, M.: Algorithmic impact assessments: a practical framework for public agency accountability (2018). https://ainowinstitute.org/aiareport2018.pdf. Report from AI Now Institute. Accessed 25 May 2021
9. Serban, A., van der Blom, K., Hoos, H., Visser, J.: Practices for engineering trustworthy machine learning applications. In: 1st Workshop on AI Engineering, WAIN 2021 (2021). https://arxiv.org/abs/2103.00964
10. Tjoa, E., Guan, C.: A survey on explainable artificial intelligence (XAI): toward medical XAI. IEEE Trans. Neural Netw. Learn. Syst. 1–21 (2020). ISSN 2162-2388. https://doi.org/10.1109/tnnls.2020.3027314
11. Tomsett, R., Braines, D., Harborne, D., Preece, A., Chakraborty, S.: Interpretable to whom? A role-based model for analyzing interpretable machine learning systems. arXiv preprint arXiv:1810.00184 (2018)
12. Vilone, G., Longo, L.: Explainable Artificial Intelligence: A Systematic Review (2020)

Evidence-Based Software Quality Engineering

Where the Bugs are: A Quasi-replication Study of the Effect of Inheritance Depth and Width in Java Systems

Steve Counsell[1]([✉]), Stephen Swift[1], and Amjed Tahir[2]

[1] Department of Computer Science, Brunel University, London, UK
steve.counsell@brunel.ac.uk
[2] School of Fundamental Sciences, Massey University,
Palmerston North, New Zealand

Abstract. The role of inheritance in the OO paradigm and its inherent complexity has caused conflicting results in the software engineering community. In a seminal empirical study, Basili et al., suggest that, based on a critique of the Chidamber and Kemerer OO metrics suite, a class located deeper in an inheritance hierarchy will introduce more bugs because it inherits a large number of definitions from its ancestors. Equally, classes with a large number of *children* (i.e., descendants) are difficult to modify and usually require more testing because the class potentially affects all of its children. In this paper, we use a large data set containing bug and inheritance data from eleven Java systems (seven open-source and four commercial) to explore these two research questions. We explore whether it is the case that a class deeper in the hierarchy is more buggy because of its deep position. Equally, we explore whether there is a positive relationship between the number of children and bugs, if classes with large numbers of children are indeed more difficult to modify. Results showed no specific trend for classes deeper in the hierarchy to be more buggy *vis-a-vis* shallower classes; the four commercial systems actually showed a negative relationship. The majority of classes across the hierarchy were also found to have no children and those classes included the most buggy.

1 Introduction

The concept of inheritance is a cornerstone of the OO paradigm and plays a key role in the functioning of any reasonably-sized OO system [12]. Inheritance promotes reuse, encourages specialisation and is meant to reflect the way that humans naturally structure information [4]. Controversy still surrounds inheritance, not least because the deep levels that were typically envisaged in systems have not materialised; systems still tend to be relatively flat with shallow inheritance structures [5]. Past studies have also argued about the optimum level of inheritance, some suggesting that three levels of inheritance is the most efficient depth for developers to or that *flat* systems without any significant depth to the

© Springer Nature Switzerland AG 2021
A. C. R. Paiva et al. (Eds.): QUATIC 2021, CCIS 1439, pp. 459–472, 2021.
https://doi.org/10.1007/978-3-030-85347-1_33

hierarchy is less likely to cause maintenance problems [7]. Very few empirical studies have looked at inheritance particularly with respect to "buggyness" in the past five to ten years and because of the different application type, nature, artefacts, subjects used and research questions of studies that have looked at inheritance in the past and our desire to cast light on those results, the most we can hope to achieve is a "quasi-replication". So we see our work as supporting or refuting prior results, but with the many caveats of aforementioned factors.

In an early paper of Basili et al. [2] the six metrics of Chidamber and Kemerer (C&K) [6] were validated using eight C++ systems as a basis. The analysis included the Depth in the Inheritance Tree of a class (DIT) and Number of Children (NOC) C&K metrics. The DIT is a measure of the distance from the root (in Java, the root is class Object from which all classes inherit). So, a class at DIT level 1 is a class with only Object as its superclass; a class at DIT has 2 classes which it inherits from (in a line) between it and root etc. The NOC metric is the number of immediate descendants below a class. So, if two classes X and Y inherit from class Z, then Z has an NOC value of 2. The basis of their analysis and validation of the DIT metric was the assumption that "....a class located deeper in a class inheritance lattice is supposed to be more fault-prone because the class inherits a large number of definitions from its ancestors." Equally, the study of NOC in the same paper was made on the basis that "a class with numerous children has to provide services in a larger number of contexts and must be more flexible. We expect this to introduce more complexity into the class design." The assumptions of Basili et al., were heavily informed by the claims of the two metrics by C&K in their original paper.

In this paper, we use a large data set of seven open-source systems and four commercial systems containing thousands of classes to explore the relationship between DIT, NOC and bugs. Since we have no developer maintenance information for the systems analysed, we use bugs as a surrogate for maintenance complexity. We justify this on the basis that a class with higher numbers of bugs reflects a class which is likely to be complex and has, over its lifetime, been more difficult to maintain. We investigate two research questions. Firstly, we explore whether there is a correspondence between the level of inheritance and the incidence of bugs. Put another way, are classes at deep levels of inheritance more buggy than shallower classes? Secondly, is there a relationship between NOC and bugs? In other words, does a larger number of children belonging to a class (given by a higher NOC) indicate that the class will be more bug-prone? Results showed no specific trend for classes deeper in the hierarchy vis-a-vis shallow classes; the majority of the open-source systems showed no relationship between DIT and bugs. The four commercial systems showed a strong negative relationship for our first question. In terms of the other research question related to NOC, the vast bulk of classes across the hierarchy were found to have zero children, including the one hundred most bug-prone classes in every system. The message seems from our work is quite stark: empirical studies provide useful results and others may support and refute those results. Ultimately however, a "one size fits all" approach to the use of inheritance and advocating a specific depth or width of inheritance may simply be unattainable.

The remainder of the paper is structured as follows. In the next section, we describe preliminary information. We then analyse our two research questions by examining bug data in the eleven systems (Sects. 3 and 4). In Sect. 5, we look at related work and threats to our study before concluding and pointing to future work (Sect. 6).

2 Preliminaries

The data used in this study was originally produced by Madeyski et al. [11] and comprises a range of metrics from 43 releases of eleven Java open source and 27 releases of 6 industrial Java projects. The four industrial projects belonged to the insurance domain and all projects were developed by the same software development company. We note that the data used in this study is freely available to download from a repository link in the original paper by Madeyski et al. [11]. In contrast to our work, the analysis described in their paper was not related specifically to inheritance; the study empirically evaluated process metrics for those which most significantly improved defect prediction models based on product metrics. In their work, the cjkm tool [16] was used to collect the DIT and NOC metrics and the BugInfo tool, developed by one of the authors of [11], was used to collect bug information.

Table 1 shows the number of classes, the mean DIT and NOC and corresponding median (med.) values for all classes where there was **at least one bug** across the eleven systems we studied[1]. We note that class `Object` is considered to be at DIT level 0. The four commercial systems are named Prop-1 to Prop-4 in the table. We can see, for example, that the Ant system has 350 buggy classes and the mean DIT of those classes is 2.55, with median 3. The mean NOC for this system is 0.67, with median 0. The DIT data seems to suggest that for the open-source systems, it is between DIT level 1 (below root) and DIT level 2 that the bulk of the bugs seem to lie; for the four commercial systems, there is a clear pattern for classes at DIT level 3 to be the source of problems - all four DIT mean and median values for the commercial systems are approximately 3. This is an interesting characteristic of the data since at least one study in the past has suggested that DIT level 3 may be the point beyond which code comprehension starts to become excessively complex for developers [7] and that is when problems start arising in the maintenance process. The four commercial systems stand out from the rest of the table in that sense.

A further striking feature of the table are the low values for NOC across all systems. For the set of bug-prone classes shown in the table, only one system (Camel) has an NOC value exceeding 1. The lowest NOC value was for the jEdit system (with an NOC value of just 0.20); all median NOC values were 0. The low values for NOC in our systems reflect the similar conclusion by Basili et al.

---

[1] ant.apache.org, camel.apache.org, ant.apache.org/ivy, jedit.org, logging.apache.org/log4j, lucene.apache.org, poi.apache.org.

Table 1. Summary of DIT and NOC (all systems)

System	#Classes	DIT mean	med.	NOC mean	med.
Ant	350	2.55	3.00	0.67	0.00
Camel	562	1.98	2.00	1.23	0.00
Ivy	119	1.73	1.00	0.52	0.00
jEdit	303	3.23	2.00	0.20	0.00
Log4j	260	1.71	1.00	0.32	0.00
Lucene	438	1.78	2.00	0.71	0.00
Poi	707	1.84	2.00	0.89	0.00
Prop-1	2436	3.02	3.00	0.79	0.00
Prop-2	1514	3.09	3.00	0.72	0.00
Prop-3	840	3.10	3.00	0.35	0.00
Prop-4	1299	3.45	3.00	0.80	0.00

[2] that most classes do not tend have more than one child and that flat systems (with low levels of DIT) are frequent [5].

3   DIT Metric Analysis

3.1   Summary of DIT Data

For our analysis, we first explore the relationship between DIT and bugs and we then consider NOC. Henceforward, for expressiveness and clarity, we now refer to classes at inheritance level 1, 2 as simply DIT1, DIT2, respectively. Table 2 summarises the number of classes at each inheritance level (given by the DIT) for the eleven systems. Here, we report DIT6 and greater as a single total in the final column of the table for the purposes of brevity (this is chiefly because relatively few classes were found at levels greater than 6). For example, for the Ant system, there were 997 classes at DIT1, 498 classes at DIT2 and 521 classes at DIT3 etc.

The most noticeable feature of the table is the relatively stable numbers of classes evenly distributed across the four proprietary systems, when compared with the seven open-source systems. To put this into perspective, only 13943 classes from a total of 53649 (25.99%) for the four commercial systems were found at DIT1; for the open-source systems, the corresponding figure was 6917 from 13942 classes; this represents 49.61% of the total number of classes across the seven systems. For the four proprietary systems, DIT3 contained more classes than its corresponding DIT1 value in every case, reflecting the relatively even spread of classes in those systems. It is also interesting to note that the number of classes in the DIT $\geq$ 6 category for the seven open-source systems was far lower compared to the four commercial systems. Only jEdit shows significant numbers of classes at DIT6 and greater. jEdit is an editor tool and that type of

Table 2. Summary of DIT levels (per system)

System/Depth	DIT1	DIT2	DIT3	DIT4	DIT5	DIT ≥ 6
Ant	997	498	521	265	130	31
Camel	1827	683	584	182	127	25
Ivy	617	149	64	63	22	18
jEdit	1971	919	151	63	167	424
Log4j	349	130	43	18	6	11
Lucene	590	426	144	40	5	0
Poi	566	966	111	26	12	2
Prop-1	4343	1682	6364	4744	2087	3838
Prop-2	3100	1312	3939	2125	2150	527
Prop-3	2162	621	2724	1014	940	1406
Prop-4	1395	386	2129	2073	1969	619

system (based on panels, frames, boxes and labels) is acknowledged to contain a richer inheritance structure because of their very structured nature. We note that the maximum depths across all eleven systems was 9 (Prop-3) followed by DIT8 for jEdit, Prop-1 and Prop-4. Ant, Log4j and Prop-2 all had maximum DIT7, so the systems were broadly comparable in that sense.

Table 3 shows the eleven systems studied, the number of classes in each system, the number of bug-prone classes (i.e., classes containing at least one bug) and the number of bug-free classes of that total. It also provides the percentages that these values represent. For example, Ant comprised 2442 classes, of which 350 were bug-prone and 2092 bug-free. This represents 14.33% and 85.67% of the total, respectively. The table shows that the most buggy of the eleven systems was Log4j, where 46.68% of classes contained at least one bug. The least buggy

Table 3. System summary by bugs

System	#Classes	Buggy	Bug-free	%Buggy	#Bugs
Ant	2442	350	2092	14.33	637
Camel	3428	562	2866	16.39	1371
Ivy	933	119	814	12.75	307
jEdit	3695	303	3392	8.20	943
Log4j	557	260	297	46.68	645
Lucene	1205	438	767	36.35	1314
Poi	1683	707	976	42.00	1377
Prop-1	23058	2436	20622	10.56	4102
Prop-2	13153	1514	11642	11.49	2167
Prop-3	8867	840	8027	9.47	1362
Prop-4	8571	1299	7272	15.52	1930

system was jEdit, where only 8.2% of classes contained at least one bug. Generally speaking, the four proprietary systems were less bug-prone than the seven open-source systems; however Prop-4 stood out from the other three commercial systems, with a relatively high bug level (15.52%).

3.2 Correlation of DIT vs Bugs

One way of determining the relationship between DIT and bugs is through correlation of the variables studied. Table 4 shows the results of correlation between DIT and bugs for the eleven systems and for completeness we provide three correlation coefficients: Pearson's r, Spearman's and Kendall's rank. Pearson's is a parametric measure and Spearman's and Kendall's coefficients are non-parametric, making no assumption about the data distribution [8]. Here, single asterisked values ("*") in the table represent significance at the 1% level and double asterisked values ("**") represent significance at the 5% level.

Table 4. Correlation of DIT and bugs

System	Pearson's	Spearman's	Kendall's
Ant	0.04	0.10	0.08
Camel	−0.04	−0.01	0.00
Ivy	−0.01	0.10	0.09
jEdit	−0.01	−0.02	−0.02
Log4j	0.10	0.20*	0.17*
Lucene	−0.04	0.00	0.00
Poi	−0.20*	−0.11*	−0.10*
Prop-1	−0.14*	−0.08*	−007*
Prop-2	−0.09*	−0.09*	−0.07*
Prop-3	−0.07**	0.04	0.03
Prop-4	−0.19*	−0.11*	−0.10*

The table shows a clear trend for the set of open-source systems; only two of the seven sets of correlation values show any significance and they are in opposing direction to each other (one is positive and one negative); for five of the open-source systems, there is clearly no notable relationship between DIT and bugs, with all values around the zero mark (i.e., just below or just above). This supports the view that there is no observable pattern to the distribution of bugs across the systems in terms of a DIT "landscape". So, it does *not* seem to be the case that classes at deep levels of the inheritance hierarchy are more buggy than at lower levels and, if we associate bugs with classes that are difficult to maintain, which is a reasonable assumption, then buggy classes do not seem to discriminate between one level or another.

The POI system stands out from Table 4, since the correlation values for this system are all negative and significant at the 1% level. In these cases, a higher DIT therefore suggests a lower incidence of bugs. In terms of OO theory, this is what we might expect to occur, since classes at deeper levels of the inheritance hierarchy would be smaller (because of specialisation), be more maintainable as a result and therefore be the source of fewer bugs. But that is not how in practice it seems to work out. For the set of four proprietary systems, a different, yet equally distinct pattern can be seen; for three of the four systems there is a negative, significant association between DIT and bugs which was only present in one of the open-source systems (we saw the same for the POI system). The data for the four industry systems suggests that the deeper in the inheritance hierarchy a class resides, the lower its propensity for bugs. Prop-4 has the highest correlation coefficients overall.

From Table 4, we also see that the Log4j system is positively and significantly correlated at the 1% level. It is worth remarking that this system had the highest percentage of bugs (46.68%), as can be seen from Table 3. For this system, it appears that a higher DIT value does indicate a higher propensity for bugs, but this is probably because there are so many bugs in this system that this result was inevitable anyway. Table 5 shows the distribution of bugs across the DIT levels for this system. For example, at DIT1 there were 345 bugs, representing 52.83% of the total number of bugs (i.e., 636). The table also shows "bug-density" values which we define as the number of bugs at a particular DIT level, divided by the number of classes at that level containing at least one bug; this reflects the average number of bugs per class. If we now inspect these values, we see an interesting trend. The lowest bug-density of 2.25 was found at DIT1 and the highest at DIT4 (value 3.6). In other words, the highest propensity for bugs was found at DIT4 and the lowest bug density at DIT1.

Table 5. Bugs and bug-density (Log4j)

Depth	DIT1	DIT2	DIT3	DIT4	DIT5	DIT $\geq$ 6
# Bugs	345	201	51	18	11	19
% Bugs	52.83	31.60	8.02	2.83	1.73	2.99
# Classes	153	71	18	5	4	8
Bug-density	2.25	2.83	2.83	3.6	2.75	2.38

Figure 1 shows the bug-densities for the seven open-source systems and Fig. 2 the corresponding values for the four commercial systems. The most striking feature is for the jEdit system which stands out for the peak at DIT4 (bug density 9.43). The most notable feature across the two figures more generally is that the bug density varies, but for the four commercial systems that variance is relatively small. The bug density ranges between 1.14 and 2.44 for those systems, indicating that bugs do not seem to dominate any particular level. While the

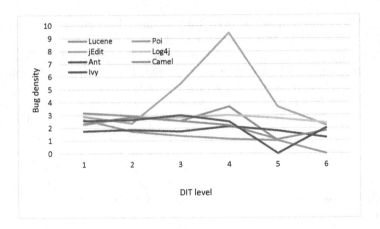

Fig. 1. DIT vs. Bug density (seven open-source systems)

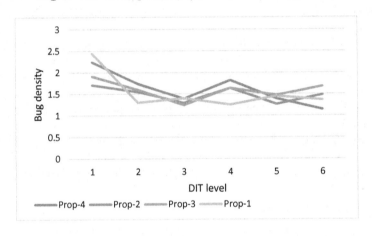

Fig. 2. DIT vs. Bug density (four commercial systems)

variance is wider for the open-source systems (values range between 0 and 3.67 in most cases) there seems to be no standout DIT. The two figures support thus the view that there is no harmful, useful or remarkable level of inheritance - a view stated unequivocally by Prechelt et al. [14].

3.3   The Role of Class Size

One relevant question that arises from the preceding analysis is why there are such differences between the open-source systems and the proprietary systems in terms of results from Table 4 and from Figs. 1 and 2? One possible explanation is that commercial systems are arguably better maintained and have cleaner code structures than open-source systems (although we cannot generalise in this sense). They may also be subjected more to practices such as refactoring

[9] throughout their lifetime, which has the effect of stemming code decay and stopping code smells emerging. Smaller class sizes would be the norm and smaller classes we know are generally easier to maintain than larger classes, as well as generating fewer bugs on average. Table 6 shows the median and mean class sizes for each of the eleven systems. We again measure class size using the C&K WMC metric.

Table 6. WMC data per system

System	Median	Mean	Max.
Ant	8.74	5	120
Camel	6.93	4	166
Ivy	9.43	5	205
jEdit	7.59	3	413
Log4j	6.64	5	105
Lucene	7.68	5	166
Poi	12.23	9	134
Prop-1	4.84	4	347
Prop-2	4.42	3	140
Prop-3	4.30	3	136
Prop-4	3.96	2	212

The table shows that for only one open-source system (jEdit) is the median lower than the commercial systems and no mean WMC is lower in across the set of open-source systems. The most striking aspect of the table is the low class sizes for the four commercial systems. This evidence, together with the results from Table 4 and Fig. 2 suggests that keeping classes relatively small may be one way of preserving a system's structure and, although our analysis is based on just eleven systems, potentially minimising the number of bugs in the system. To verify that smaller classes arise across the hierarchy, Table 7 shows the correlation values of DIT versus WMC for all eleven systems.

As we might expect, for the four commercial systems Prop-1 to Prop-4, Spearman's and Kendall's values are positive and significant at the 1% level. The same cannot necessarily be said of the seven open-source systems (where only Ivy shows the same type of relationship). Our belief that the commercial systems (Prop-1 to Prop-4) may be better maintained and looked after seems to have some traction. That said, whichever way this is looked at, bugs still do not seem to discriminate at any particular DIT level. It also suggests that there is no pattern in terms of the size of a class at any level.

Table 7. Correlation of DIT vs. WMC per system

System	Pearson's	Spearman's	Kendall's
Ant	0.04	0.09	0.07
Camel	−0.13*	−0.12*	−0.09*
Ivy	0.04	0.32*	0.26*
jEdit	−0.06	−0.08	−0.07
Log4j	−0.10	0.07	0.06
Lucene	−0.15*	−0.15*	−0.12*
Poi	−0.08**	0.06	0.05
Prop-1	−0.16*	0.26*	0.23*
Prop-2	0.01	0.24*	0.20*
Prop-3	−0.13*	0.29*	0.25*
Prop-4	−0.14*	0.34*	0.29*

Summary: No clear pattern to the relationship between the depth of a class (given by DIT) and the incidence of bugs was found for the eleven systems studied.

4 NOC Metric Analysis

The study of Basili et al., suggests from C&K's suite of metrics that classes with a high NOC value would be more complex and difficult to maintain. In their words: "*Classes with large number of children are difficult to modify and usually require more testing because the class potentially affects all of its children. Thus, a class with numerous children has to provide services in a larger number of contexts and must be more flexible.* We also believe that classes with a high NOC value will contain more bugs than classes with a low or zero NOC because of the extra complexity in classes with that high NOC. As per DIT, and for brevity, we now refer to a class with zero children as NOC0.

4.1 Correlation of NOC vs. Bugs

To explore the relationship between NOC and bugs, we correlated their values across the eleven systems. Table 8 shows these correlation values for all classes containing at least one bug.

As we found for the DIT analysis, there is no clear trend in the data. For the open-source systems, there is only one system with a positive, significant relationship (Log4j). Interestingly, the same system showed the same result for DIT. This system had the highest percentage of bugs and it may simply be that is the only reason why the correlations were so significant. Most of the values in the table are close to zero, suggesting no obvious or standout relationship

Table 8. Correlation of NOC and bugs

System	Pearson's	Spearman's	Kendall's
Ant	−0.03	0.04	0.03
Camel	0.09**	0.06	0.06
Ivy	0.00	0.07	0.07
jEdit	−0.02	−0.14*	−0.13*
Log4j	0.13**	0.13**	0.11**
Lucene	0.00	0.05	0.04
Poi	0.00	−0.05	−0.05
Prop-1	0.04	0.10*	0.10*
Prop-2	−0.01	0.06**	0.06**
Prop-3	−0.01	0.02	0.02
Prop-4	0.00	0.02	0.02

between NOC and bugs. For the four commercial systems, there is some evidence of positive, significant relationships, but it only applies to two systems (Prop-1 and Prop-2).

One explanation for the lack of any trend in the NOC data and a feature of the eight systems studied by Basili et al. [2] is that most classes in the eleven systems had few or mostly zero children. Inspection of the NOC data revealed that for example, in the Ant system, 2163 of the 2442 classes (88.57%) had zero children; for the Camel system, the corresponding value was 90.15%. For Prop-1, the figure was 95.75% and for Prop-2, 94.45% of classes had zero children. We then listed the hundred most buggy classes in each of the eleven systems and found that for the Ant system, 77 of those 100 classes were at NOC0. For the Camel system, we found the corresponding value of 71 classes. For Prop-1, the number of classes with NOC0 in the top 100 buggy classes was 90 and for Prop-2, the figure was 88. Our original research question regarding whether classes with large numbers of children were more bug-prone seems to be largely overshadowed by the fact that so few classes in all the systems have children at all and that the most buggy classes are contained in that group.

Summary: No clear pattern to the relationship between NOC belonging to a class and the incidence of bugs was found for the eleven systems studied. The vast majority of classes had zero children.

5   Related Work

There have been many (often conflicting) empirical results on the role of inheritance and as a community we are still no nearer establishing an optimal level of inheritance depth. Perhaps, as our study suggests, it will always elude us.

Twenty-four years ago, Daly et al. [7] published the results of a controlled experiment into inheritance and its relationship with class maintainability using the C++ language. The study evaluated subjects in their task of maintaining code written with different levels of inheritance (3 and 5); these were then compared with the effectiveness of similar tasks on systems containing no inheritance (flat systems). Results showed that subjects maintaining code with three levels of inheritance completed the tasks more quickly than those working on tasks on the flat system. The interesting observation however, was that subjects working on code with five levels of inheritance struggled with the inherent complexity at that depth and took longer to complete than tasks for the corresponding flat system. This suggests that beyond a level of inheritance, maintenance becomes problematic. One study that did "semi-replicate" the work of Daly et al., was by Prechelt et al. [14]. In their empirical study, they used a longer and more complex program and added a different type of maintenance task also. They cast doubt on the results of Daly et el., and concluded that: *"....previous results plus ours suggest that there is no such thing as usefulness or harmfulness of a certain inheritance depth as such"*. Results from the paper herein seem to back up this claim.

In our paper, we also note that a big impediment to analysis of NOC was the high number of NOC0 values (i.e.. most classes having zero children). Interestingly, previous work on inheritance by Nasseri et al. [13] showed that, over time and as they evolved, inheritance hierarchies in open-source systems tended to collapse to bring classes up to shallower levels. Perhaps it is the case that as systems evolve, structures start to fragment through maintenance and it is simply easier to amalgamate classes and move them to shallower levels closer to the root than to try to maintain them at the deeper levels. This feature of systems ties with work by Bieman et al. [3] who describe a study of nineteen C++ systems (with 2744 classes in total); only 37% of these systems had a median class DIT >1. Other studies have shown that flat systems (with low inheritance depths) are more easily maintained. Perhaps flat systems leads to fewer "mistakes" by developers and by implication, fewer bugs. Alternatively, moving classes to shallower levels is what the developers hope will happen. Finally, the danger of using inheritance were pointed out by Wood et al. [17]: inheritance should only be used with care and only when it is felt absolutely necessary.

5.1   Threats to Validity

For any empirical study, need to consider the threats to its validity [1, 15]. Firstly, we only used eleven systems in our study. In this paper, our intention was to highlight key features of inheritance through the prism of DIT and NOC and while there is no such thing as the *right* number of systems to use in any empirical study, we feel that the work gives a fairly representative insight in the more broader issues typical of all systems. The four industrial systems were all developed in the same company and so we accept that this represents a "sub-threat" in this category. Secondly, we have made the assumption throughout the paper that bugs are a surrogate for complex classes and that a complex class will harbour and generate more bugs than a simple, less complex class. While we accept that this may not always be true, we feel that in the absence of developer maintenance data to work with, this is a reasonable assumption to make. Thirdly, class size *per se* would influence the propensity for bugs (larger classes, more bugs) and we have looked at depth versus bugs as one indicator; however, this factor was not a key motivator of our work - rather that a class had experienced at least one bug. Fourthly, many of the previous empirical studies of inheritance used C++ systems, whereas we use Java. We defend this stance on the basis that while there are significant differences between the two languages, the OO paradigm is common to both and developer behaviour when maintaining systems does not seem to differ that greatly in the OO paradigm; one could argue that the different constructs used by OO languages may however have made a difference (this is a topic for future work). Fifthly, we have focused on classes where at least one bug was found and also of the twenty-five systems at their latest version point; this is because we wanted to understand the distribution of those bugs across inheritance as it stands presently. The study could be criticised because it failed to compare those results to classes without any bugs or indeed to look at version data. In our defence however, we were trying to quasi-replicate earlier work of studies where bugs were the dependent variable (and versions/version history were not explored). Sixthly, we have used a data set with different projects (open source and commercial), built by different developers, facing different development issues. This presents a risk to the generalisability of the results. Finally, the reader will have noted that the literature on empirical studies of inheritance has been fairly static over the past ten years. (The references in this paper are mostly from the mid-90's to around latest 2010.) We feel however, that this in no way undermines the need for studies like ours. In fact, it begs the question "why have there been no contemporary studies of inheritance on an empirical basis?" And also "what has changed in the past ten years?" such that no researchers are exploring this facet of systems any more.

6 Conclusions and Further Work

In this paper, we explored two research questions related to inheritance. The first explored the relationship between the depth of a class in the inheritance hierarchy and bugs and the second that a high number of children belonging to a class would render that class as more buggy. We found no evidence that classes at a specific depth of inheritance were more bug-prone than at any other depth. We did note some interesting differences between commercial and open-source systems, however, suggesting that the former are better maintained and looked after more generally. We also found no evidence to support the view that classes with a high NOC were any more buggy than other classes. The overwhelming number of classes had no children. Inheritance hierarchies, either through design or evolution do not tend to follow that pattern. One conclusion is that how a system evolves depends on factors such as the type of system, whether open-source or commercial and possibly system age. Work by Harrison et al. [10] suggested that large systems were equally difficult to maintain regardless of use of inheritance. Perhaps it is the case that as systems grow and evolve, inheritance is just one more problem amongst an array of other problems that a developer faces. It thus becomes relatively less of a problem.

Future work will focus on extending the study to more commercial and open-source systems. We would also like to investigate the role that refactoring and code smells [9] play in the removal and possible introduction of bugs into code at different levels and the difference that such practices make to the shape of a system.

References

1. Ampatzoglou, A., Bibi, S., Avgeriou, P., Chatzigeorgiou, A.: Guidelines for managing threats to validity of secondary studies in software engineering. In: Felderer, M., Travassos, G. (eds.) Contemporary Empirical Methods in Software Engineering, pp. 415–441. Springer, Cham (2020). https://doi.org/10.1007/978-3-030-32489-6_15
2. Basili, V.R., Briand, L.C., Melo, W.L.: A validation of object-oriented design metrics as quality indicators. IEEE Trans. Softw. Eng. 22(10), 751–761 (1996)
3. Bieman, J.M., Zhao, J.: Reuse through inheritance: a quantitative study of C++ software. In: ACM SIGSOFT Symposium on Software Reusability, Seattle, USA, pp. 47–52 (1995)
4. Booch, G.: Object-oriented development. IEEE Trans. Softw. Eng. 12(2), 211–221 (1986)
5. Cartwright, M., Shepperd, M.: An empirical investigation of an object-oriented software system. IEEE Trans. Soft. Eng. 26(8), 786–796 (2000)
6. Chidamber, S., Kemerer, C.: A metrics suite for object oriented design. IEEE Trans. Softw. Eng. 20(6), 476–493 (1994)
7. Daly, J., Brooks, A., Miller, J., Roper, M., Wood, M.: Evaluating inheritance depth on the maintainability of object-oriented software. Empir. Softw. Eng. 1(2), 109–132 (1996)
8. Field, A.: Discovering Statistics Using IBM SPSS Statistics, 4th edn. Sage Publications Ltd. (2013)
9. Fowler, M.: Refactoring: Improving the Design of Existing Code. Addison-Wesley, Boston (1999)
10. Harrison, R., Counsell, S., Nithi, R.: Experimental assessment of the effect of inheritance on the maintainability of object-oriented systems. J. Syst. Softw. 52(2–3), 173–179 (2000)
11. Madeyski, L., Jureczko, M.: Which process metrics can significantly improve defect prediction models? An empirical study. Softw. Qual. J. 23(3), 393–422 (2015)
12. Meyer, B.: Object-Oriented Software Construction. Prentice-Hall, Hoboken (1997)
13. Nasseri, E., Shepperd, M.J.: Class movement and re-location: an empirical study of java inheritance evolution. J. Syst. Softw. 83(2), 303–315 (2010)
14. Prechelt, L., Unger, B., Philippsen, M., Tichy, W.: A controlled experiment on inheritance depth as a cost factor for code maintenance. J. Syst. Softw. 65(2), 115–126 (2003)
15. Runeson, P., Host, M., Rainer, A., Regnell, B.: Case Study Research in Software Engineering: Guidelines and Examples, 1st edn. Wiley, Hoboken (2012)
16. Spinellis, D.: Tool writing: a forgotten art? IEEE Softw. 22(4), 9–11 (2005)
17. Wood, M., Daly, J., Miller, J., Roper, M.: Multi-method research: an empirical investigation of object-oriented technology. J. Syst. Softw. 48(1), 13–26 (1999)

30 Years of Automated GUI Testing: A Bibliometric Analysis

Olivia Rodríguez-Valdés[1]([✉]), Tanja E. J. Vos[1,2][iD], Pekka Aho[1], and Beatriz Marín[2][iD]

[1] Open Universiteit, Heerlen, The Netherlands
orv@ou.nl
[2] Universitat Politècnica de València, Valencia, Spain

Abstract. *Context:* Over the last 30 years, GUIs have changed considerably, becoming everyday part of our lives through smart phones and other devices. More complex GUIs and multitude of platforms have increased the challenges when testing software through the GUI. *Objective:* To visualise how the field of automated GUI testing has evolved by studying the growth of the field; types of publications; influential events, papers and authors; collaboration among authors; and trends on GUI testing. *Method:* To conduct a bibliometric analysis of automated GUI testing by performing a systematic search of primary studies in Scopus from 1990 to 2020. *Results:* 744 publications were selected as primary studies. The majority of them were conference papers, the most cited paper was published on 2013, and the most published author has 53 papers. *Conclusions:* Automated GUI testing has continuously grown. Keywords show that testing applied to mobile interfaces will be the trend in next years, along with the integration of Artificial Intelligence and automated exploration techniques.

Keywords: Automated testing · Graphical user interface · Bibliometric analysis · Secondary study

1 Introduction

A Graphical User Interface (GUI) is a human-computer interface that includes graphical elements commonly called widgets, for example buttons, menus, textboxes, scrollbars, and icons. The first GUIs were developed in early 70s to improve the usability of operating software systems. Before GUIs, the only way to interact with the systems was through CLIs (Command Line Interfaces). GUIs allow end-users to interact with the system functionality more easily, and provide output and feedback in a graphical form based on the actions of end-users.

In GUI testing, the system is tested through the elements of the GUI and their properties. To do that, test sequences are comprised of actions (such as click, type, drag and drop) and the corresponding test oracles to check the state of the system after the execution of the actions. GUI testing is of paramount importance since it allows testing systems from the end-user's point of view.

© Springer Nature Switzerland AG 2021
A. C. R. Paiva et al. (Eds.): QUATIC 2021, CCIS 1439, pp. 473–488, 2021.
https://doi.org/10.1007/978-3-030-85347-1_34

Automated GUI testing has been researched for over three decades. The first papers on this topic are from the late 80s [8]. Automating GUI testing faces several challenges. GUIs change frequently during the life cycle of a system (e.g., controls are removed or re-positioned, new controls are added, etc.). This has severe implications for the practice of automated testing: instead of creating new test cases to find new faults, testers struggle with repairing the old ones in order to maintain the test suite and adapt it to the changed GUI layout.

Over the last 30 years, in accordance to the evolution of programming languages from 3rd generation to the 5th, GUIs have evolved with better graphics, becoming more realistic and their graphical components more skeuomorphic. A lot of desktop applications have been replaced by web applications, representing challenges to testing in form of distributed services and systems of systems. With the rise of smartphones and other portable devices, new testing challenges arose due to a much smaller screen and more complex interactions. Mobile GUIs have to be more simple (with less elements), but at the same time, the complexity on the functionality of applications is growing.

To cover the state of the art of GUI testing, Bao et al. [1] conducted a mapping study from 1991 to 2011 that included 136 publications. The field has been growing considerably since then.

To understand the community, publication patterns and trends in automated GUI testing, this paper presents a bibliometric study [17]. As far as we know, this paper presents the first bibliometric analysis on this field over the last 30 years. The main contributions are to:

1. Provide facts about the size and growth of the field.
2. Indicate the type of publications and their rankings, including most cited papers, most prolific authors, and most influential journals and conferences.
3. Show the distribution of the publications among the available sources and over the years using a spectroscopy.
4. Present and discuss the productivity and the level of collaboration among researchers in the literature.
5. Use the bibliometric laws of Bradford [3] to know the most influencing journals, and of Lotka [11] to evaluate scientific productivity of authors.
6. Show the evolution of the major research topics in the field by analysing the keywords used by the authors.
7. Make a public repository for Automated GUI testing.

The rest of the paper is organized as follows. Section 2 defines the scope of the study. Section 3 presents the methodology for the bibliometric analysis, and the results are presented in Sect. 4. Section 5 presents the main conclusions.

2   Scope: Automated GUI Testing

To make the scope of the study clear, this section explains the definition of *automated GUI testing* that was used to decide which papers should be included in this bibliometric study. Executing sequences of events on the GUI widgets of a system under test (SUT) and checking test oracles is called *GUI testing*.

Table 1. Family of words for the search string

Term	Family
Automated	Automated OR automatic OR automatically OR automation OR automating OR automate OR generation OR generate OR generating OR generator
GUI	GUI OR UI OR "graphical user interface"
Testing	Testing OR test OR tested

The goal of executing these tests – like in any other type of testing – is finding failures, reducing risks, and analysing and increasing the quality of the SUT.

Evidently, it is possible to **automate the execution** of these test sequences and call it *automated GUI testing*. However, more activities related to GUI testing can be automated. To be able to define clear inclusion/exclusion criteria for the papers of this bibliometric analysis, the definition of automated GUI testing was refined to include also other activities of GUI testing, as follows:

Automating the creation of test sequences: Test sequences in GUI testing consist of sequences of GUI actions/events on widgets together with input values. Test sequences are made to cover some test goal of the SUT (e.g., checking some specific functionality or finding a failure). Test sequence defines which path through the SUT should be taken (which *states* should be visited), i.e., *what* actions will be executed, and in which *order*.

Automating the definition or checking of the oracles: Oracles [2] are procedures that distinguish between the correct and incorrect behavior of the SUT. Since test cases in GUI testing are sequences, we can check the oracles after each action (test step) during the execution (online oracle), just one time at the end of each sequence, or analyse the results after the execution (offline oracle). Test oracle automation is important for removing the current bottleneck that inhibits greater overall test automation [2]. Without test oracle automation, a human has to determine whether observed behaviour is correct.

Automating the analysis of test results: This consists of analysing, for example, the failures that were found in a specific SUT, or evaluating the quality of the test cases that were executed, using a set of defined metrics.

When at least one of these activities is automated, it will be considered *automated GUI testing* (even when the test execution is done manually), and therefore, the corresponding papers will be included in this study.

3   Methodology

In this study, we follow the workflow for bibliometric analysis defined in [6].

3.1   Data Retrieval

We used Scopus for the search process since it is the largest database of peer-reviewed literature with the largest coverage in comparison to other scientific

1: (TITLE-ABS-KEY((*Automated* W/5 *Testing*) AND *GUI*)
2:    OR TITLE-ABS-KEY ((*Automated* W/5 *GUI*) AND *Testing*)
3:    OR TITLE-ABS-KEY((*GUI* W/5 *Testing*) AND *Automated*))
4: **AND**   LIMIT-TO(LANGUAGE , "English")
5: **AND**   PUBYEAR > 1989 AND PUBYEAR < 2021
6: **AND**
7: (LIMIT-TO(DOCTYPE , "cp") OR LIMIT-TO(DOCTYPE , "ar") OR
8:    LIMIT-TO(DOCTYPE , "ch") OR LIMIT-TO(DOCTYPE , "Undefined"))
9: **AND**
10: (LIMIT-TO(SUBJAREA , "COMP") OR LIMIT-TO(SUBJAREA , "ENGI")
11:    OR LIMIT-TO(SUBJAREA , "MATH"))

Fig. 1. The used search query

repositories, such as WoS [20]. The search string evolved from the initial terms "Automated GUI testing" – to reduce the probability of missing relevant papers, a family of words was derived from every term (see Table 1).

The complete search query is shown in Fig. 1. As can be seen in lines 1–3, the terms must appear in the article's title, abstract or keywords since the Scopus operator TITLE-ABS-KEY is used. To fine-tune the results, a minimum distance of terms was established, using the "W/" operator. The distance was set to 5 after several tests observing the results. In Fig. 1, each family of words is represented by its main term. Each term was replaced by the derived family of terms, using the OR operator to accept the appearance of at least one of the terms within its family. Using the Scopus facilities, papers were also excluded according to their type, language and publication date, excluding works that:

exC1: are not written in English (in line 4, using the Scopus Document field code: LANGUAGE and limiting it to "English")
exC2: are published before year 1990 and after 2020 (in line 5 using the Scopus Publication field code: PUBYEAR)
exC3: are not conference, workshop, journal publications or book chapters (in lines 7 and 8) using the Scopus Document field code: DOCTYPE and limiting it to types Conference Paper-"cp", Article-"ar", Book Chapter-"ch" and "Undefined"). The last one was included because some documents that have been accepted for publication, but have not yet been assigned to a journal or conference, so that they are temporarily indexed as "Undefined".
exC4: do not belong computer science area (in lines 10 and 11) using the Scopus subject areas: COMP, ENGI and MATH.

The search was performed on January 2021. The total amount of papers retrieved was 2240.

3.2   Pre-processing

First of all, we manually excluded in Scopus the papers belonging to other fields, reducing the total amount of papers to 1233. This was needed because, for instance, a document can be classified as Computer Science and Social Science because it describes a social science study using some computational system. Since these papers are also categorized as COMP, ENG or MATH, they were retrieved by the search query, even if they also belonged to other fields. The papers that were clearly off-topic were manually rejected.

Driven by our additional goal to create a GUI testing research repository, we searched for a simple and flexible environment that, besides assisting our work, would allow future interactions with the extracted papers. Thus, we decided to use BUHOS [4], an open source web-based paper management system. We uploaded the 1233 papers in BUHOS, we defined additional exclusion criteria (exC5 and exC6 below), and manually applied these exclusion criteria by screening the title and abstract of each paper.

exC5: clearly off topic, i.e. not at all related to the scope (Sect. 2)
exC6: not a primary study

The 1233 papers were divided among the authors, who, after reading the title and abstract, marked them as included, excluded or undecided. Next, a collective analysis was carried out to make a final decision on the undecided papers, resulting 720 papers. Then, a backward snowballing [21] on the 720 papers resulted 50 new papers that were screened based on the title and abstract. This added 24 papers, resulting in the total of 744 included publications.

3.3 Analysis and Visualization

CRExplorer [19] and Biblioshiny[1] were used to analyse and visualize the data. These tools were selected because they have specific functionalities to visualize bibliometric maps. In addition, Scopus was used in conjunction with Excel to generate the charts. Before the analysis, normalization was required on the keywords using a thesaurus of synonyms[2], and the author's names by taking accents and different formatting into account. Related to the conferences, it was necessary to split the description in order to properly obtain the name of the conference separately from the publisher and the year of publication.

4 Results

4.1 Size of the Area and Growth

The number of publications in a field over time is a central piece of information to investigate its growth and development. In Fig. 2 the evolution of the growth per year along with the trend is depicted. The first decade covered by our study only has 18 papers related to field. There are even two years (1992 and 1993) with no papers at all. In the second decade of our study this increased to 170 works. And, in the third decade we found 556 works. Since a 41.4% of all documents have

---

[1] https://www.bibliometrix.org/Biblioshiny.html.
[2] https://gui-testing-repository.testar.org/keywords.

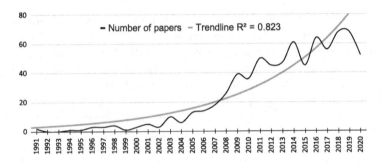

Fig. 2. Evolution of the number of publications

Table 2. Papers in journals (J), conferences (C), workshops (W) and chapters (B).

Total 1991–2020	J	C	W	B
744	122	528	87	7

been published in the last 5 years, we expect that the automated GUI testing field continues to grow like it did in the last decade.

Between 2009 and 2013 we see an increase in the amount of papers that deviates from the trend. Reasons for this could be various. In 2008 the first edition of the ICST conference was held, being the first international conference entirely dedicated to software testing. Moreover, in 2009 the first edition of the TESTBEDS workshop was celebrated at ICST. There was also an increase in papers related to web testing, this can be related to the fact that in 2009, it was decided to merge Selenium RC and Webdriver and called the new project Selenium WebDriver, or Selenium 2.0. A third reason might be that Sikuli started in 2009 [15]. Sikuli is a visual approach to search GUIs using screenshots, allowing users to take a screenshot of a GUI element (such as a toolbar button, icon, or dialog box) and query a help system using the screenshot instead of the element's name. Finally, in 2009 there is an increase on papers related to mobile testing. This is probably related to the fact that in July 2008 the Apple's App Store went live and in August, the Android Market.

During 2020, we observe that the number of publications decreases, this could be explained by the pandemic since several conferences were canceled, mobility was reduced and therefore the research outcomes could be affected.

4.2   Types of Publications and Their Ranking

We found papers published in journals, conferences, workshops and as book chapters. Table 2 and Fig. 3 show the amount of papers of each kind.

We can observe that the majority of papers have been published in conference proceedings. This make sense since conferences provide feedback to researchers more quickly than journals. Moreover, in many cases papers describing part of a larger solution are presented in conferences in order to obtain feedback and

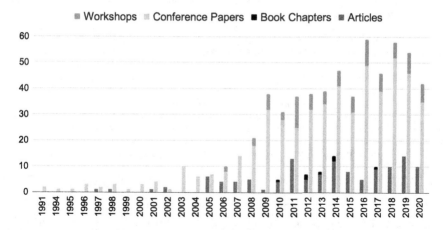

Fig. 3. Number of papers published in (journals + books) vs (conferences + workshops)

Table 3. Top 11 of most contributing journals

Journal name	# papers	%	SJR
Transactions on Software Engineering (TSE)	12	9,83%	1.19
Information and Software Technology (IST)	8	6,55%	0.78
Software Quality Journal (SQJ)	7	5,73%	0.36
IEEE Software	6	4,92%	0.81
Transactions on Software Engineering and Methodology (TOSEM)	5	4,10%	0.76
Software Testing Verification and Reliability (STVR)	5	4,10%	0.31
Empirical Software Engineering (ESE)	4	3,28%	1.08
Information Technology Journal	4	3,28%	0.11
ACM SIGPLAN Notices	3	2,46%	4.90
IEEE Access	3	2,46%	3.90
Innovations in Systems and Software Engineering	3	2,46%	1.90
Remaining 54 from the total of 65 journals	62	50,82%	
Total number of papers	**122**	**100%**	

validate each piece of work and later the entire proposal is presented in a journal. This is also the behavior in the entire Computer Science field [7].

Table 3 shows that IEEE Transactions on Software Engineering (TSE) has been the top one journal with 12 published articles on the field. Even though the automated GUI testing field has been steadily growing during the last 3 decades, STVR is the first journal that launched a special issue entirely dedicated to this field in only 2020. Papers included in that special issue have not been counted for our study because they were not yet published in 2020. By examining the data in Table 3, Bradford's Law [3] can be applied. This law establishes that the total set of journals in a research field can be divided into 3 categories or zones, each containing approximately one third of the total papers in the field. The

Table 4. Bradford's Law zones applying Leimkuhler model [9]

Zones	# journals	# papers
Zone 1	6	43
Zone 2	16	37
Zone 3	43	42
Total	65	122

Table 5. Top 10 of most influential Conferences

Conference name	# papers	%
International Conference on Software Engineering (ICSE)	37	7,01%
International Conference on Software Testing, Verification and Validation (ICST)	36	6,81%
International Conference on Automated Software Engineering (ASE)	27	5,11%
International Symposium on Software Testing and Analysis (ISSTA)	26	4,92%
Joint Meeting European Software Engineering Conference and Symposium on the Foundations of Software Engineering (ESEC/FSE)	22	4,17%
IEEE International Symposium on Software Reliability Engineering (ISSRE)	15	2,84%
International Conference on Software Maintenance (ICSM)	14	2,65%
International Computer Software and Applications Conference (COMPSAC)	11	2,08%
International Conference on Software Engineering and Knowledge Engineering (SEKE)	9	1,70%
International Conference on Software Quality, Reliability and Security (QRS)	9	1,70%
Remaining 45 conferences from the total of 56 conferences	322	60,98%
Total number of papers	**528**	**100%**

first category is related to articles which are published in an small number of journals, called core journals. The second category corresponds to the journals with an average of papers. And the last category corresponds to several journals that publish few papers.

From Table 3 we can derive that the top 6 journals are the core journals, since they correspond to 43 articles, which is 35.2% of all 122 journal papers. The next group is found in the next 16 journals (37 articles or 30.3%). In order to represent the last articles, the 42 remaining journal are necessary. The Bradford relation for journals is 6:16:43 and the details per zone can be found in Table 4.

The 528 papers were presented at 386 conferences of which 4.15% has CORE ranking A*, 16.32% CORE A, 16.84% CORE B, 10.36% CORE C and 37.31% has no CORE ranking. The remaining 14.51% conferences were in years when no CORE ranking was given (yet). The 87 workshop papers were presented at 56 workshops of which 37.50% was co-located at a CORE A* conference, 28.57% at a CORE A conference, 3.57% at CORE B conference and 12.50% at CORE C conference, 5.36% at conferences with no CORE ranking, and 5.36% at workshops not co-located with any conference. The remaining 7.15% workshops were in years when no CORE ranking was given (yet). Table 5 shows the most contributing conferences. ICSE and ICST are almost even at the top while in 2020 ICSE had celebrated 42 editions and ICST only 13.

4.3 Citations and Reference Publication Year Spectroscopy

In Table 6 we list the top 10 papers that have the most cites in Scopus, together with the year of publication, the complete reference, the number of cites retrieved by Scopus (Sc), and the number of cites retrieved by Google Scholar (GS). The cites from Scopus and Scholar differ in that Scholar has a much higher count. From [12], we learn that Scholar citation data is essentially a superset of Scopus, but with substantial extra coverage. We can see that 7 out of the top 10 most cited papers are concerned with Android testing. The remaining 3 papers are related to models (event-flow or state models) and widget detection (Sikuli).

The technique of Reference Publication Year Spectroscopy (RPYS) [13] is a quantitative method to identify the historical origins or turning points of research fields. This method analyzes the publication years of the references cited by all the papers in a specific field. A Reference Publication Year (RPY) is reflected in the spectrogram as a pronounced peak, usually corresponding to a publication that has been referenced very frequently. These publications are of significant importance, as they may represent the origins of the research field in question.

An RPYS chart was obtained using CRExplorer and is shown in Fig. 4, from 1960, although there are references up to 1901. The most influential year seems to be 2001, this is the year when Atif M. Memon finished his PhD entitled *A comprehensive framework for testing graphical user interfaces* [14]. In that year he published two final papers for his thesis. The first paper [MPS01] presents a new test case generation technique based on Artificial Intelligence Planning and using a model based on a GUI structure. Both Artificial Intelligence and Model-based Testing are trends that will guide the research field in the posterior years to this publication, as we explain later on in Sect. 4.7. In the second paper, Memon et al. [MSP01] introduce different coverage criteria for GUI testing and evaluate them through a case study, for the first time.

In addition, years 2012 and 2013 appear as peaks in the Spectroscopy chart. Five publications [AFT+12a,MTN13,CNS13,YPX13,AN13] appear among the most cited within the field. All of them have one common topic: Android testing.

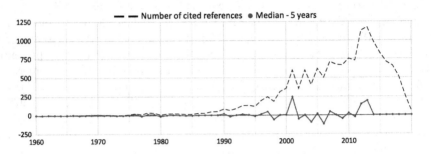

Fig. 4. Reference publication year spectroscopy

Table 6. Top 10 papers with most cites in Scopus (includes cites in Google Scholar) (https://gui-testing-repository.testar.org/bibliography)

Ref	Title	Author	Year	Sc	GS
[MTN13]	*Dynodroid: An input generation system for android apps*	Machiry, A., Tahiliani, R., Naik, M	2013	397	672
[AFT+12b]	*Using GUI ripping for automated testing of android applications*	Amalfitano, D., Fasolino, A., Tramontana, P., De Carmine, S., Memon, A	2012	343	563
[CGO16]	*Automated test input generation for android: Are we there yet?*	Choudhary S.R., Gorla A., Orso A	2016	245	401
[ANHY12]	*Automated concolic testing of smartphone apps*	Anand, S., Naik, M., Harrold, M., Yang, H	2012	231	428
[AOA05]	*Testing Web applications by modeling with FSMs*	Andrews A.A., Offutt J., Alexander R.T	2005	227	477
[YCM09a]	*Sikuli: Using GUI screenshots for search and automation*	Yeh T., Chang T.-H., Miller R.C	2009	217	400
[MHJ16]	*Sapienz: Multi-objective automated testing for android applications*	Mao K., Harman M., Jia Y	2016	207	336
[GNAM13]	*RERAN: Timing- and touch-sensitive record and replay for Android*	Gomez L., Neamtiu I., Azim T., Millstein T. Total	2013	202	341
[Mem07]	*An event-flow model of GUI-based applications for testing*	Memon A.M	2007	193	364
[HLN+14]	*PUMA: Programmable UI-automation for large-scale dynamic analysis of mobile apps*	Hao S., Liu B., Nath S., Halfond W.G.J., Govindan R	2014	192	321

Table 7. Ranking of author by number of publications in journals (J), conferences (C), workshops (W) and book chapters (B)

Name	Total	J	C	W	B	Year of first publication
Memon, A.M.	53	18	29	5	1	1999
Paiva, A.C.R.	31	6	20	5	0	2005
Alégroth, E.	17	3	8	5	1	2013
Vos, T.E.J.	16	2	11	3	0	2012
Xie, Q.	15	4	10	1	0	2004
Fasolino, A.R.	13	4	5	4	0	2010
Zeller, A.	13	1	10	2	0	2012
Aho, P.	12	0	7	4	1	2011
Amalfitano, D.	11	3	4	4	0	2010
Coppola, R.	11	4	3	4	0	2016
Ramler, R	11	1	8	2	0	2008

Table 8. Distributions of number of author per number of publications

Papers	1	2	3	4	5	6	7	8	9	10	11	12	13	15	16	17	31	53
Authors	1128	198	60	36	21	14	8	3	3	6	3	1	2	1	1	1	1	1

4.4 Most Influential Authors

The 744 documents that integrate this study have been written by a total of 1,488 authors. Table 7 shows the 11 most prolific authors, among them contributing 203 publications (27.28 %). For this ranking we count all authors of each paper, not only the first one. One notable fact is that 7 of the 11 authors published their first paper in the field since 2010, and only one published before 2000.

The distribution of the number of publications among authors is presented in Table 8. The largest group consists on authors who published a single paper, representing 75.81%. As show in the table, as the number of publications increases, the number of authors tends to decrease. The Lotka's law describes this behavior and states that the number of authors y publishing a certain amount of papers x is in inversely proportional to x, as $y = \frac{c}{x^n}$, where n and c are two constants to be estimated for every data set. We used the software Lotka [16], to apply the Maximal Likelihood method and estimate the parameters for this study, resulting in $n \approx 2.59$ and $c \approx 0.77$ i.e., our data set follows Lotka's general law as $y = \frac{0.77}{x^{2.59}}$. To assess the fitness between this hypothesized Lotka model and the actual distribution of the data, the Kolmogorov-Smirnov statistical test was applied. Even for a level of significance of 0.2, the results support the hypothesis.

4.5 Productivity and Funding

As shown in Fig. 5, there is a large gap between the most contributing country, United States, and the rest. China published its first papers in 2006 and since

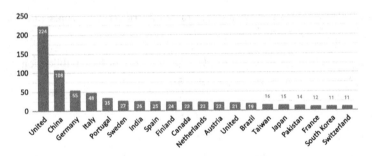

Fig. 5. Most contributing countries

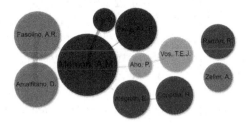

Fig. 6. Collaboration network of authors

then has contributed 108 publications, keeping a rate of 7.2 publications per year, similar to that of United States, with 7.5 annual papers since 1991.

Although China and the US are the main contributing countries to the field, the European region has had a boost in the last decade, and since 2015 occupies the first place with 308 publications. The Asian continent has contributed 242 publications, closely following North America with 245 publications so far.

A 21% of the papers included funding information. From all the mentions, 9,7% came from private funding by big companies such as Google, Microsoft, Amazon Web Services, and Boeing, amongst others. Asia is the continent that provides most funding resources for the majority of sponsored works (33,7%), followed by Europe (28,6%) and North America (27,1%). The leading funding agency in Asia is the National Natural Science Foundation of China. Likewise, the leading funding agencies in Europe and North America are the European Commission and the National Science Foundation, respectively. It is worth to mention that the only South American country that has funding is Brazil.

4.6   Collaboration

In Fig. 6 we depict the collaboration between the most prolific authors in the field from Table 7. Six authors have been co-authors with Atif M. Memon, who can also been related with another two authors through those six. Only 2 of the 11 authors do not have co-authorship with any of the most contributing authors.

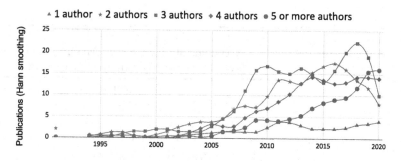

Fig. 7. Authorship evolution

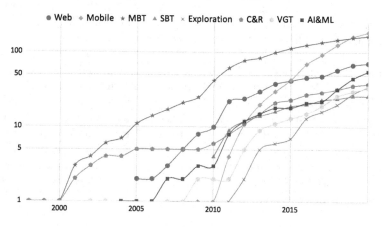

Fig. 8. Cumulative frequency of keywords

Figure 7 shows the evolution of author's collaboration over the 30 years. Single author publications have historically remained low, while publications of more than 4 authors have been increasing. However, only 18.95% of the papers have been the result of collaboration among affiliations from different countries.

4.7   Trends in Keywords

By analysing the keywords provided by the authors, we aim to reveal the details of a domain's major research topics and their introduction into the field. This is not as easy as just counting the most used keywords [5,18]. Many keywords do not give specific information on the details of the field because they are inherent to it, e.g. software testing, GUI testing, tools, regression testing, etc. In addition, different words can be used for describing the same concept, and thus we had to group them. We started standardizing plural forms into their singular form, by means of NLTK [10]. In order to group the keywords, the authors of this paper studied all the available keywords, and each made their individual classification. We set-up two brain-storming sessions to come to the following classification as a representation of relevant research themes in the domain that we want to study:

> web, mobile, model-based testing (MBT), search-based testing (SBT), visual-based testing (VBT), Artificial Intelligence and Machine Learning (AI&ML), Capture and Replay (C&R) and Automated Exploration

The objective is to study: *Web* and *mobile*: to distill the trend in the types of SUTs that are tested ; *MBT, SBT, VBT, AI&ML*: to visualize the timeline of the pick-up of different technologies into automated GUI testing; *C&R*: to investigate the evolution of the trend where the focus was on these tools; and *Automated Exploration*: for the shift from scripted to scriptless testing using random testing, traversal techniques and crawling. Figure 8 shows the cumulative frequency values per each group of keywords, annually. We see that both MBT and C&R have their first appearance in 1998. Since then MBT has been the main topic of the field, until Mobile reached a greater number of papers in 2019. As of 2010, two topics were introduced: SBT and Automated Exploration.

Publications mentioning Web-based SUT have remained constant. It is remarkable that 50% of MBT papers have been published as of 2014, being MBT one of the first topics in the field. C&R has seen a decrease in its frequency, coinciding with the considerable increase in VBT. This might indicate that C&R is being replaced by Image Recognition or Image Comparison techniques.

AI&ML has appeared in 56 papers: by 2013, it had appeared in 48 papers (26.79%) and it took 5 years to reach 50% of its total frequency. However, just one year was needed for AI&ML to reach 75%. In the last two years AI&ML appeared in as many papers as in the entire previous history of the field.

4.8 Discussion

To avoid internal validity threats, we use Scopus, the largest database of peer-reviewed scientific literature; we define a search string and we validate the results with a small set of relevant works. Since computer science works are mainly published in English, we advocate that we found the majority of works even though we aware that some works are not retrieved due to they are published in a different language.

Regarding the replicability of the study, we clearly define a protocol and documented all the process to mitigate this threat. We use the metadata of the works to perform the analysis to mitigate the threat that results may be biased by researchers' judgement. In order to deeper understand the techniques used for automated GUI testing, we propose to follow this work with a mapping review in order to establish the trends in the area.

5 Conclusions

This paper provides facts about automated GUI testing field. Publications have increased continuously, with exponential growth in the last decade. Lotka's Law and Bradford's Law were found applicable to the field. Analysis of author's collaboration, keywords and the geographic dispersion of the field was provided. The most common type of publication is the conference papers. The 6 core journals were identified, as well as the most prolific authors. A repository[3] was developed, with all the 744 referenced papers and further bibliometric results.

We conclude that this study offers relevant information for the field, its evolution over 30 years and trending topics for future research.

Acknowledgements. We thank Fernando Pastor for his valuable contribution. This research has been funded by DECODER (decoder-project.eu), iv4XR (iv4xr-project.eu), and IVVES (ivves.weebly.com) projects.

References

1. Banerjee, I., Nguyen, B., Garousi, V., Memon, A.: Graphical user interface testing: systematic mapping and repository. IST **55**(10), 1679–1694 (2013)
2. Barr, E.T., Harman, M., McMinn, P., Shahbaz, M., Yoo, S.: The oracle problem in software testing: a survey. TSE **41**(5), 507–525 (2015)
3. Bradford, S.C.: Sources of information on specific subjects. Engineering **137**, 85–86 (1934)
4. Navarrete, C.B., Malverde, M.G., Lagos, P.S., Mujica, A.D.: Buhos: a web-based systematic literature review management software. SoftwareX **7**, 360–372 (2018)
5. Chen, G., Xiao, L.: Selecting publication keywords for domain analysis in bibliometrics: a comparison of three methods. J. Informetr. **10**, 212–223 (2016)
6. Cobo, M., López-Herrera, A., Herrera-Viedma, E., Herrera, F.: Science mapping software tools: review, analysis, and cooperative study among tools. J. Am. Soc. Inform. Sci. Technol. **62**(7), 1382–1402 (2011)
7. Franceschet, M.: The role of conference publications in CS. Commun. ACM **53**(12), 129–132 (2010)
8. Johnson, M.: Automated testing of user interfaces. In: Pacific North West Software Quality Conference, pp. 285–293 (1987)
9. Leimkuhler, F.: An exact formulation of Bradford's law. J. Doc. (1980)
10. Loper, E., Bird, S.: NLTK: the natural language toolkit. arXiv:0205028 (2002)
11. Lotka, A.J.: The frequency distribution of scientific productivity. J. Wash. Acad. Sci. **16**(12), 317–323 (1926)
12. Martín-Martín, A., Orduna-Malea, E., Thelwall, M., Delgado López-Cózar, E.: Google scholar, web of science, and scopus: a systematic comparison of citations in 252 subject categories. J. Informetr. **12**(4), 1160–1177 (2018)
13. Marx, W., Bornmann, L., Barth, A., Leydesdorff, L.: Detecting the historical roots of research fields by reference publication year spectroscopy (RPYS). J. Am. Soc. Inf. Sci. **65**(4), 751–764 (2014)
14. Memon, A.M.: A comprehensive framework for testing graphical user interfaces. Ph.D. (2001). Advisors: Mary Lou Soffa and Martha Pollack; Committee members: Prof. Rajiv Gupta (University of Arizona), Prof. Adele E. Howe (Colorado State University), Prof. Lori Pollock (University of Delaware)

---

[3] https://gui-testing-repository.testar.org.

15. Paulos, E.: The rise of the expert amateur: DIY culture and citizen science. In: Proceedings of the 22nd Annual ACM Symposium on User Interface Software and Technology, pp. 181–182 (2009)

16. Rousseau, B., Rousseau, R.: LOTKA: a program to fit a power law distribution to observed frequency data. Cybern. Int. J. Scientometr. Informetr. Bibliometr. (4), 4 (2000)

17. Small, H.: Visualizing science by citation mapping. J. Am. Soc. Inf. Sci. **50**(9), 799–813 (1999)

18. Su, H.N., Lee, P.C.: Mapping knowledge structure by keyword co-occurrence: a first look at journal papers in Technology Foresight. Scientometrics **85**(1), 65–79 (2010). https://doi.org/10.1007/s11192-010-0259-8

19. Thor, A., Marx, W., Leydesdorff, L., Bornmann, L.: Introducing CitedReferencesExplorer (CRExplorer): a program for reference publication year spectroscopy with cited references standardization. J. Informet. **10**(2), 503–515 (2016)

20. Vieira, E.S., Gomes, J.A.N.F.: A comparison of scopus and web of science for a typical university. Scientometrics **81**(2), 587–600 (2009)

21. Wohlin, C.: Guidelines for snowballing in systematic literature studies and a replication in software engineering. In: Proceedings of the 18th International Conference on Evaluation and Assessment in Software Engineering, pp. 1–10 (2014)

A Large-Scale Investigation of Local Variable Names in Java Programs: Is Longer Name Better for Broader Scope Variable?

Hirohisa Aman[1]([✉]) [iD], Sousuke Amasaki[2] [iD], Tomoyuki Yokogawa[2] [iD],
and Minoru Kawahara[1] [iD]

[1] Ehime University, Matsuyama, Ehime 790-8577, Japan
{aman,kawahara}@ehime-u.ac.jp
[2] Okayama Prefectural University, Soja, Okayama 719-1197, Japan
{amasaki,t-yokoga}@cse.oka-pu.ac.jp

Abstract. Variables are fundamental elements of software, and their names hold vital clues to comprehending the source code. It is ideal that a variable's name should be informative that anyone quickly understands its role. When a variable's scope gets broader, the demand for such an informative name becomes higher. Although the standard naming conventions provide valuable guidelines for naming variables, there is a lack of concrete and quantitative criteria regarding a better name. That challenge in naming variables is the motivation of the quantitative investigation conducted in this paper. The investigation collects 637,077 local variables from 1,000 open-source Java projects to get a detailed view of the variable naming trend. The data analysis reveals frequently-used terms for variable names, the naming styles, and the length of names when the variable scopes are broad. The results showed that developers prefer to use fully spelled English words or compounded names for broad-scope variables, but they tend to avoid long names; Developers often use simple words or abbreviations shorter than seven or eight characters.

Keywords: Variable name · Variable scope · Quantitative investigation

1 Introduction

Variable names play essential roles in program comprehension [8,11]. Meaningful and easy-to-understand names enhance the readability of the source code [10]. By naming variables appropriately, both the author programmers themselves and other developers can easily understand and review the source code [16]. On the other hand, making a variable's name hard-to-understand is a fundamental way of code obfuscation. We can easily obfuscate a source code by replacing all variable names with single meaningless characters [9]. Hence, a variable name

© Springer Nature Switzerland AG 2021
A. C. R. Paiva et al. (Eds.): QUATIC 2021, CCIS 1439, pp. 489–500, 2021.
https://doi.org/10.1007/978-3-030-85347-1_35

can be a double-edged sword in terms of code quality because of its power of influence on the code readers.

The proper naming of variables has been attracting attention in the programming world. Many coding standards and practices mention the variable naming issue [2,13,16]. The standard rules and practices say that it is better to give a meaningful name to a variable. That is, it looks good to name a variable using a well-chosen English word or phrase (compounded words) describing the variable's role. On the other hand, developers sometimes prefer shorter names than fully-spelled English-word names or compounded ones. For example, many developers would favor "i" as the name of a loop counter rather than "loop_counter" if there is no chance of being misunderstood [2,16]. Indeed, we often see many variables whose names are "i" in various source programs for such a use case.

Here, we focus on the opposite case, such that a short variable name like "i" is undesirable. A representative example is a case that the variable's scope is broad. We are questionable whether "i" is suitable for the name of a loop counter even when its scope is broader than several dozen or more lines of code. In such a case, programmers may prefer a longer and more descriptive name for the variable to make it more informative. However, to the best of our knowledge, there are no clear and concrete criteria to decide whether a variable name is proper or not when the scope is broad. If such criteria become available, we can build them into a static analysis tool or an advanced editor to evaluate the variable names and recommend better names in an automated way. That is a challenge in naming variables, and it motivated us to conduct a large-scale quantitative investigation of variables. In this paper, we report our investigation and discuss the results.

2   Related Work

Caprile and Tonella [8] prepared a standard dictionary of terms used for identifiers and a pre-defined naming grammar (a set of naming patterns), then proposed a method for detecting meaningless names and renaming them. Allamanis et al. [3] proposed a more enhanced framework that infers the coding convention adopted in a development project by mining the code repository. Their framework works to detect the undesired variable names (identifiers) violating the project's coding convention and to suggest better names for renaming such undesired ones by utilizing natural language processing techniques. Although the studies in [3,8] provided helpful ways of improving variable names, the variables' scopes might also significantly impact their naming. Therefore, in this paper, we will conduct our investigation while considering the variable scope as well.

There have been large-scale investigations of variable names in the past. Beniamini et al. [6] focused on single-letter names such as "i" and investigated how programmers use those variables in their programs. They collected variable names from 1000 open-source projects whose languages include C, Java, JavaScript, PHP, and Perl. Although the single-letter name is the shortest name for a variable, their investigation revealed that some names could be meaningful in particular contexts, e.g., "i," and "j" as loop counters. Swidan et al. [17] conducted another investigation on Scratch programs and reported Scratch-specific variable naming trends: Scratch programmers tend to avoid single-letter names for variables and prefer longer names with 4–10 characters. The investigation reported in [6] motivated us to analyze the variable naming trends further. Moreover, the data reported in [17] shows the possibility that the naming trends vary from language to language. Thus, we focus only on one programming language (Java) and conduct a further investigation of variable names while considering other aspects of variables, including the variable types and scopes.

There have been studies focusing on the length of the variable name. Although a longer name is easier to describe its role, developers get harder to memorize the name as it becomes longer in their programming and code review. Binkley et al. [7] conducted an experiment involving 158 programmers to examine the relationship between the variable name's length and the programmer's short-term memory and proved that too long names adversely affect program comprehension. Moreover, they pointed out that a longer name may raise the risk of choosing a wrong name when programmers use a program editor's auto-completion function. Hofmeister et al. [15] and Aman et al. [4,5] reported empirical results showing that long names may have harmful impacts on program comprehension and fault-proneness. Thus, we have considered that a long and descriptive variable name is not always the best, even if its scope is broad. That thought is also one of our motivations for conducting a large-scale investigation.

3   Quantitative Investigation

We conducted a large-scale quantitative investigation regarding variable names in Java programs. In this section, we report and discuss the results.

3.1   Aim and Surveyed Software

This study aims to capture the features of broad-scope variable names through a data collection. Moreover, we can get a corpus of terms used in variable names by organizing the collected data. Such a corpus would help an automatic evaluation of variable names and a recommendation toward better namings. We discuss the following two research questions by analyzing the collected data.

RQ1: What are the features of the variable names when their scopes are broad?
RQ2: What kind of terms do developers use for broad-scope variable names?

As we mentioned in Sect. 2, we collect variable data from only Java software to avoid the impact caused by the difference in the programming language. Moreover, we focus only on the local variables[1] in this study because the names of the global variables, i.e., *fields* in Java, tend to depend on the class design, and the programmers may have no power to decide their names. Since local variables are available only within a method, the naming would usually be the programmer's discretion. We believe a large-scale data collection of variable names would be

---

[1] The local variables include the formal arguments (parameters) of methods.

worthwhile to understand the naming trend and the programmers' preference regarding broad-scope variables' names. In this study, we survey (collect data from) 1,000 Java open-source projects having high "stars" ranks at GitHub.

3.2 Results of Data Collection

As a result, we successfully got 472,665 Java source files from 971 projects. We could not analyze source files from 29 out of 1,000 projects due to one of the following three reasons: (a) the project had no Java source file (5 projects), (b) all source files were the ones to be excluded (e.g., test programs) (22 projects), and (c) our source file analysis failed because the source file path included a multi-byte character (2 projects). We could extract 637,077 local variables, i.e., the local variable declarations or formal argument declarations in methods.

Table 1 presents the distribution of variables' scope length. The scopes of the most variables were shorter than about 40 lines; the 90 percentile was 42 lines. The method length would cause this result because the local variables are available only within the method. On the other hand, we found variables whose scope lengths are broader than 3,000 lines. We manually checked the details of the variables with the broadest top 10 scopes. Then, we revealed that such ones appeared in a simple but huge method which only performs many assignments to an array. Such methods seem to be automatically generated code. Thus, we decided to exclude local variables with too-broad scopes from our analysis as outliers. Consequently, we use the variables whose scope ranges are between 90 and 99 percentiles (42 and 157 lines) as our sample set of broad-scope variables.

3.3 Results of Variable Name Categorization

Next, we report the results of our heuristic categorization of variable names. We began with four categories of variable names: i) single letter names, ii) dictionary-word ones, iii) compounded ones, and iv) other names. Then, we found 62,236 other names (9.8%), and we manually checked their names to explore a better categorization. Then, we detected the following six exceptions.

(a) **Technical terms:** We observed 131 technical terms that we usually see in programs, but Aspell's dictionary does not include them: for example, "default," "git," and "setter." We prepared a user dictionary that complements the default dictionary for capturing the above technical terms.

Table 1. Summary statistics of scope length.

min	Percentile (unit: source lines)									max
	10	20	30	40	50	60	70	80	90	
1	2	3	4	6	8	11	16	24	42	3,680

(b) Type-derived names: We encountered the variable name "`fos`." That name seems to be derived from its type, i.e., the class name, "`FileOutput-Stream`." Through our additional exploration, we also found the variable names that contain the type name as a substring (e.g., "`tLabel`" whose type is "`Label`"). Moreover, we noticed that there might be the plural form of a type-derived name such as "`mqs`" whose type is "`Set<MessageQueue>`"; It may mean that the variable contains two or more "`MessageQueue`" objects. Hence, we also check the above string matching for the name by dropping the trailing "`s`."

(c) Abbreviated words: Before our data collection, we expected to encounter local variables whose names are abbreviated words. However, we did not initially provide the name category of abbreviated words because it is challenging to prepare the complete list of abbreviations. Instead, we continued updating our abbreviation dictionary by checking the names included in the "other names" category to build the additional name category, "abbreviated words." When we update the dictionary, we checked if the abbreviated word is common or not by referencing https://www.abbreviations.com/. Our abbreviation dictionary consists of 201 terms, and it is available from our data website. We accept the plural form of abbreviations (e.g., `args`) as the ones being in this category.

(d) Numbered names: We saw many "numbered" names like "`x2`." Developers would add numbers to the end of variable names to declare two or more variables whose roles are similar. Any name in any category can become the base name of a numbered variable name, including single letter names, dictionary word ones, abbreviated word ones, compounded ones, and type-derived ones.

(e) Variants produced by adding an extra character: We also saw variants of dictionary names, which are produced by adding an extra character to the head or the end of the words (e.g., `fname`, `cellx`). We consider an additional category for such variants and denote it by "dict word name +1." We also introduce similar "+1" categories to the remaining categories to cover any variants.

(f) Concatenated names: There were exceptional names made by merely concatenating two words, such as "`filename`." Because there is no character-case change nor delimiter in such concatenated names, we implemented the following simple algorithm to fix the name category: if a name can be split into two substrings and both are in the English dictionary, our technical term dictionary, or our abbreviation dictionary, then we regard the original name as a compounded name. Although the above algorithm cannot work for a potential compounded name made by concatenating three or more words, there are almost no such names in our dataset, so we did not adopt a more sophisticated algorithm [12].

We have updated our variable name categories through heuristics, considering the above exceptions. Consequently, we made 17 categories of variable names shown in Table 2. Notice that we did not prepare the "+1" category (variant

Table 2. Local variable name category and frequency of names by category.

No.	Category	Frequency (%)		Example
		All variables	Broad scope only	
1	single letter	109,471 (17.2%)	2,884 (5.1%)	i
2	single letter + num	7,092 (1.1%)	1,074 (1.9%)	t1
3	dict word	251,723 (39.5%)	17,982 (32.1%)	result
4	dict word + 1	3,328 (0.5%)	464 (0.8%)	stepx (step + x)
5	dict word + num	5,422 (0.8%)	742 (1.3%)	count5
6	dict word + num + 1	109 (0.0%)	28 (0.0%)	inputp1 (input+p+1)
7	type derived	19,942 (3.1%)	1,578 (2.8%)	fos (FileOutputStream)
8	type derived + 1	1,097 (0.2%)	66 (0.1%)	jconf (j+Configuration)
9	type derived + num	433 (0.1%)	37 (0.1%)	str2
10	type derived + num + 1	26 (0.0%)	1 (0.0%)	tvecs2 (t+Vec[ ] +2)
11	abbrev word	10,625 (1.7%)	778 (1.4%)	buf
12	abbrev word + 1	433 (0.1%)	37 (0.1%)	imgw (img + w)
13	abbrev word + num	486 (0.1%)	29 (0.1%)	tmp2
14	abbrev word + num + 1	16 (0.0%)	0 (0.0%)	ctrly1 (ctrl+y+1)
15	compounded	218,138 (34.2%)	28,758 (51.3%)	commaIndex
16	compounded + num	2,910 (0.5%)	875 (1.6%)	upperString2
17	other	5,826 (0.9%)	727 (1.3%)	xy
	Total	637,077	56,060	

name category) for the single letter names (No. 1–2) and the compounded names (No. 15–16). In the case of a single letter name, it is hard to decide which character is the base name. For compounded names, we can split them into sub names. Then, the split sub names can also be classified into the remaining name categories. Although we could have divided the compounded name category by applying the remaining ones recursively, we avoided making the category organization too complex.

As a result, we classified the collected 637,077 local variables into the above 17 name categories, as shown in Table 2 (see "all variables" column). The most major categories are No. 3: dictionary word names (39.5%), No. 15: compounded names (34.2%), and No. 1: single letter names (17.2%). In the table, we also show the frequencies of names when we focus only on the broad-scope variables whose scope lengths are between 42 and 157 lines (see "broad scope only" column). For the broad-scope 56,060 variables, the most major category was the compound names, and about half of the variables belong to this category. The second and the third most major categories were the dictionary word names (32%) and the single-letter names (5%), respectively. Although we also observed type-derived names, abbreviated-word names, numbered names, and variants ("+1" names), all of their rates are about or less than 3%, so they seem to be the minorities in the Java local variable names regardless of their scope lengths.

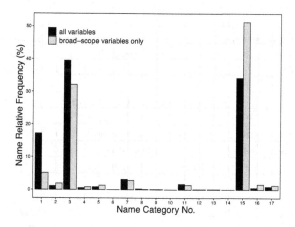

Fig. 1. A comparison of name category shares: all variables vs. broad-scope variables.

3.4   Discussion

We discuss the results from the perspective of our RQs.

RQ1 (What Are the Features of the Variable Names When Their Scopes Are Broad?). We regarded the variables whose scopes are between the 90 and 99 percentiles as the broad-scope variable samples. About half of the variables' names are compounded names, and about one-third of the ones are single dictionary (fully spelled) words, as we saw in Table 2. Developers seem to prefer such names when the variables' scopes get wider. Figure 1 presents the comparison of the name category shares between "all variables" and "broad-scope variables." Table 2 and Fig. 1 show that the following three name categories' shares are relatively specific to the broad-scope variables' names: No. 1 (single letter), No. 3 (dictionary word), and No. 15 (compounded names).

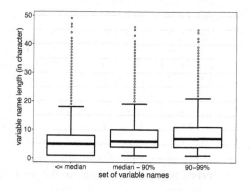

Fig. 2. A comparison of variable names' length.

While the shares of the single letter names and the dictionary ones decrease, the share of compounded names increases when the scope is broad. The remaining 14 categories' shares did not show large differences between "all variables" and "broad-scope variables." Thus, the broader scope would lead developers to adopt more descriptive compounded names rather than single-letter names and single-word names. Although developers also use single-letter names, its share is only about 5%. We additionally checked broad-scope variable samples with single-letter names and revealed that the symbolic names are "i" and "v." A variable "i" tends to play a control variable of a loop or an index of an array, and a variable "v" seems to be used for meaning a "value" of an object or a "vector" of objects.

Because developers tend to use compounded names for broad-scope variables, their variable name lengths may become longer than the others. We additionally examined the distribution of variable name length by counting the number of characters comprising the variable names. Figure 2 shows a comparison of the variable name lengths. In the figure, we considered three sets of variable names: (1) The variables whose scope lengths are equal to or narrower than the median; (2) The variables whose scope lengths are between the median and the 90 percentile; (3) Our broad-scope sample set, i.e., the variables whose scope lengths are between the 90 and 99 percentiles.

Although there is a gradually increasing trend as the variable scope gets broad, their differences are minor; the medians of variable name lengths are 5, 6, and 7, respectively. We cannot say the broad-scope variable has a notable long name. When a variable's scope gets broader, developers are likely to make the variable name more informative by successfully combining simple words or abbreviated words while controlling variable name length.

Therefore, we answer RQ1 as follows: Developers seem to name the broad-scope variables using compounded terms or fully spelled words, but they tend to avoid long names. The median name length is seven characters. Although single-letter names are not well-used, "i" and "v" are exceptions.

RQ2 (What Kind of Terms Do Developers Use for Broad-Scope Variable Names?). To comprehend the trend of words used for broad-scope variables' names, we tallied up the terms appearing in those variable names. Table 3 presents the most frequently-appearing terms (top 50), where the portions of a compounded name are also included; For example, when we have a compounded name "toString," we split it into "to" and "string" and tally up each of them.

The top 50 terms consist of 42 dictionary words, six abbreviations (id, max, num, pos, info, url), and two single letters (i and v). Here, we see that the length of the most terms (46 out of 50) is shorter than seven characters. Because well-used abbreviations "id" and "info" may be from "identifier" or "identification" (10 or 14 characters) and "information" (11 characters), developers might use shorter names instead. Interestingly, both "pos" and "position" ranked in the top 50 list. Some developers might consider the word "position" (8 characters) to be a bit longer for a variable name and preferred "pos." That is, such a length

Table 3. Most frequent terms used in single names or portions of compounded names of broad-scope variables (Top 50).

name	type	id	index	count	start	i	size	width	list
file	result	data	view	height	is	v	max	time	end
offset	value	path	to		current	num	key	field	line	new
length	text	item	last	in	pos	map	info	child	position
class	action	first	builder	left	request	url	color	string	layout

Table 4. Top 10 abbreviations.

num	idx	params	buf	src	args	tmp	param	arg	ret

may be a threshold to decide whether the name looks long or not, and this result corresponds to the trend of broad-scope variable's name length (the median is 7; see Fig. 2). Notice that our main focus of the above discussion is on the name length and not on the semantics. Because different programmers might use the same term to represent different concepts, the results might mix up such terms.

We further checked the details of 28,758 compounded names used for broad-scope variables. Then, we found that about 87% of compounded names consist of only dictionary words, and about 6% of them are mixups of dictionary words and abbreviations. That is, developers prefer to use dictionary words even in a compounded name. Table 4 presents the top 10 abbreviations, which appeared in broad-scope variable names. The abbreviations "param" and "params" would be valuable examples showing the above trend of avoiding longer names. Although we can consider a similar reason for "args," they may also have another reason: "args" often appears as the default parameter of "main" method in Java.

Therefore, we answer RQ2 as follows: For broad-scope variables, developers prefer fully spelled words to make their names informative even in a compounded name. However, they also tend to avoid making the name longer. The threshold of character counts would be seven or eight. When the name gets longer, developers will likely to replace the fully spelled words with their abbreviations. They often use short and meaningful terms shown in Tables 3 and 4.

Although our investigation is preliminary work on variable names, we could prove the trend that many programmers avoid long names even if their variables' scopes are broad. Such a trend seems to correspond to the harmfulness of too long names pointed out by Binkley et al. [7]. Moreover, we successfully found a quantitative baseline of name length to judge if a name is long or not. We plan to design an automated system for evaluating and recommending variable names using our findings and our dataset[2] of variable names in the future.

---

[2] Our dataset is available from https://bit.ly/3xLuaLK.

3.5 Threats to Validity

We describe threats to validity in our study below.

Construct Validity: We measured the length of a local variable's scope by focusing on the starting line number and the ending line number of the variable's scope in the source file. For example, when a variable is declared at the 15th line and is valid until the 26th line in the source file, we regard the length of the variable's scope as 12 lines (= 26 − 15 + 1). Because it might also count the comment lines and blank lines, the truth scope lengths might be slightly shorter than the values we reported in this paper. In addition to the camelCase names (e.g., `fileName`) and snake_case names (e.g., `file_name`), we classified the two-term concatenation names (e.g., `filename`) into the compounded name category as well. However, our classification cannot treat the exceptions made by concatenating three or more terms. We further checked the "other names" category and found 25 exceptional variable names like "`linestartpos`" which may be "`line`" + "`start`" + "`pos`" (position). We might successfully classify such exceptions if we utilized more sophisticated variable (identifier) splitting studies [14]. However, those exceptional names are less than 0.1% of the studied names, so we consider they have almost no impact on our findings.

Internal Validity: To automatically collect local variable data in this study, we developed a program analysis tool using the Eclipse Java development tools (JDT) [1]. Due to the version of the JDT parser we used, our tool does not support the Java lambda expressions using the arrow operator "->." That is, the tool misses the data on local variables appearing in the functional programming context. Although our dataset includes most of the local variables used in Java programs, such a lack of data is a threat to our study's internal validity.

External Validity: We conducted a large-scale investigation of local variable names by collecting the data from many open-source software projects. Because we chose popular projects without any bias in the project domain and scale (numbers of source files and developers), we believe our dataset is a sample set of the general trend regarding local variable names. However, our data collection is limited to Java open-source software. That is, our findings might not be generalized to commercial software or other programming language software.

4 Conclusion and Future Work

In this paper, we have focused on local variables' names in Java programs. Although programmers often use single-letter names for local variables, the naming trend might change to make a variable's name more informative when the variable's scope gets broader. To understand the naming trend for broad-scope variables, we conducted a large-scale quantitative investigation of local variable names with the following two research questions.

RQ1: What are the features of the variable names when their scopes are broad?
RQ2: What kind of terms do developers use for broad-scope variable names?

For RQ1, we found that developers tend to use compounded names or fully-spelled ones for broad-scope variables. Meanwhile, they are likely to avoid making long names; The median name length is seven characters. Although single-letter names are not well-used, "i" and "v" are exceptions. For RQ2, we affirmed that developers prefer short and meaningful dictionary words to make their names informative even in a compounded name. Nonetheless, they also tend to avoid long names, and the threshold of character counts would be seven or eight. When a variable's name gets longer, developers seem to shorten it by replacing the fully-spelled words with their abbreviated words or shorter other terms.

Although longer variable names would be more informative or descriptive, our investigation results proved that longer names are not always the better names for broad-scope variables. Choosing simple but meaningful terms would become the core of beneficial variable naming. Our data would be useful in an automated evaluation of variable names and a recommendation of proper names for enhancing the code readability; Our dataset is available from https://bit.ly/3xLuaLK.

Our future work includes applications of the investigation results into automatic aid for enhancing code readability. The naming trend and the variable name corpus would help enrich static code analysis tools (code analyzers). We plan to develop a code-review supporting tool that detects problematic variable names and suggests better alternatives based on our survey dataset.

Acknowledgment. This work was supported by JSPS KAKENHI #20H04184, #21K11831, and #21K11833.

References

1. Eclipse Java development tools (JDT). https://www.eclipse.org/jdt/
2. Linux kernel coding style (2016). https://www.kernel.org/doc/html/v4.10/process/coding-style.html
3. Allamanis, M., Barr, E.T., Bird, C., Sutton, C.: Learning natural coding conventions. In: Proceedings of the 22nd ACM SIGSOFT International Symposium on Foundations of Software Engineering, pp. 281–293, November 2014
4. Aman, H., Amasaki, S., Sasaki, T., Kawahara, M.: Empirical analysis of change-proneness in methods having local variables with long names and comments. In: Proceedings of 9th International Symposium on Empirical Software Engineering and Measurement, pp. 50–53, October 2015
5. Aman, H., Amasaki, S., Yokogawa, T., Kawahara, M.: Local variables with compound names and comments as signs of fault-prone Java methods. In: Joint Proceedings of the 4th International Workshop on Quantitative Approaches to Software Quality and 1st International Workshop on Technical Debt Analytics, pp. 4–11, December 2016
6. Beniamini, G., Gingichashvili, S., Orbach, A.K., Feitelson, D.G.: Meaningful identifier names: the case of single-letter variables. In: Proceedings of the 25th International Conference on Program Comprehension, pp. 45–54, May 2017
7. Binkley, D., Lawrie, D., Maex, S., Morrell, C.: Identifier length and limited programmer memory. Sci. Comput. Program. **74**(7), 430–445 (2009)

8. Caprile, B., Tonella, P.: Restructuring program identifier names. In: Proceedings of the International Conference on Software Maintenance, pp. 97–107, October 2000

9. Ceccato, M., Di Penta, M., Falcarin, P., Ricca, F., Torchiano, M., Tonella, P.: A family of experiments to assess the effectiveness and efficiency of source code obfuscation techniques. Empir. Softw. Eng. **19**(4), 1040–1074 (2014)

10. Corazza, A., Martino, S.D., Maggio, V.: LINSEN: an efficient approach to split identifiers and expand abbreviations. In: Proceedings of the 28th International Conference on Software Maintenance, pp. 233–242, September 2012

11. Deissenboeck, F., Pizka, M.: Concise and consistent naming. Softw. Qual. J. **14**(3), 261–282 (2006)

12. Enslen, E., Hill, E., Pollock, L., Vijay-Shanker, K.: Mining source code to automatically split identifiers for software analysis. In: Proceedings of the 6th International Working Conference on Mining Software Repositories, pp. 71–80, May 2009

13. Gosling, J., Joy, B., Steele, G.L., Jr., Bracha, G., Buckley, A.: The Java Language Specification. Addison-Wesley, Boston (2014)

14. Hill, E., Binkley, D., Lawrie, D., Pollock, L., Vijay-Shanker, K.: An empirical study of identifier splitting techniques. Empir. Softw. Eng. **19**(6), 1754–1780 (2014)

15. Hofmeister, J., Siegmund, J., Holt, D.V.: Shorter identifier names take longer to comprehend. In: Proceedings of the 24th International Conference on Software Analysis, Evolution, and Reengineering, pp. 217–227, February 2017

16. Kernighan, B.W., Pike, R.: The Practice of Programming. Addison-Wesley Longman, Boston (1999)

17. Swidan, A., Serebrenik, A., Hermans, F.: How do scratch programmers name variables and procedures? In: Proceedings of the 17th International Working Conference on Source Code Analysis and Manipulation, pp. 51–60, September 2017

Quality in Cyber-physical Systems

KNN-Averaging for Noisy Multi-objective Optimisation

Stefan Klikovits$^{(\boxtimes)}$ ⓘ and Paolo Arcaini ⓘ

National Institute of Informatics, Tokyo, Japan
{klikovits,arcaini}@nii.ac.jp

Abstract. Multi-objective optimisation is a popular approach for finding solutions to complex problems with large search spaces that reliably yields good optimisation results. However, with the rise of cyber-physical systems, emerges a new challenge of noisy fitness functions, whose objective value for a given configuration is non-deterministic, producing varying results on each execution. This leads to an optimisation process that is based on stochastically sampled information, ultimately favouring solutions with fitness values that have co-incidentally high outlier noise. In turn, the results are unfaithful due to their large discrepancies between sampled and expectable objective values. Motivated by our work on noisy automated driving systems, we present the results of our ongoing research to counteract the effect of noisy fitness functions without requiring repeated executions of each solution. Our method *kNN-Avg* identifies the k-nearest neighbours of a solution point and uses the weighted average value as a surrogate for its actually sampled fitness. We demonstrate the viability of kNN-Avg on common benchmark problems and show that it produces comparably good solutions whose fitness values are closer to the expected value.

Keywords: Multi-objective optimisation · Noisy fitness functions · Genetic algorithms · k-nearest neighbours · Cyber-physical systems

1 Introduction

In the past, multi-objective optimisation (MOO) has proven to be a robust and reliable means in the software engineering toolbox. Through iterative modifications of existing problem solutions, the algorithms try to approach optimal valuations. A *fitness function* evaluates the quality of each individual solution in one generation so that the best individuals can be used to guide the next generation. After reaching a target fitness or a given number of generations, the algorithm terminates and yields the best solutions found.

The authors are supported by ERATO HASUO Metamathematics for Systems Design Project (No. JPMJER1603), JST. Funding reference number: 10.13039/501100009024 ERATO. S. Klikovits is also supported by Grant-in-Aid for Research Activity Start-up 20K23334, JSPS.

A. C. R. Paiva et al. (Eds.): QUATIC 2021, CCIS 1439, pp. 503–518, 2021.
https://doi.org/10.1007/978-3-030-85347-1_36

MOO algorithms such as genetic algorithms (GAs) have been successfully applied to various optimisation problems, ranging from evolutionary design [3], biological and chemical modelling [6], to artificial intelligence [14]. MOO are particularly well-suited for modern cyber-physical systems (CPSs) and internet of things (IoT) applications, given the high-dimensional search space, where combinatorial testing and exhaustive verification reach their limits. When applied to CPSs, however, a new difficulty arises. Many such systems suffer from sensor errors and measurement noise. Similarly, with growing component numbers, inter-process communication causes non-deterministic behaviour due to message delays and synchronisation time variations. As the messages' processing times differ at runtime, noisy behaviour emerges [1]. Due to the noise, the reported fitness and the actually expected value (the mean over several evaluations) might vastly differ, leading to distrust of the method.

One of our lines of work is to identify problematic behaviour in automated driving systems (ADSs) by creating driving scenarios through map design changes (e.g. road shape), altering traffic participants (vehicles and pedestrians) and driving behaviour (e.g. aggressiveness). However, due to noisy inter-process communication, repeated executions of the same scenario can lead to differing observations, s.t. the distance between two cars may vary up to several meters. In other words, in our search for consistent collision scenarios, outliers for typical non-crash scenarios might be identified as crash scenarios. This leads to volatile test scenarios, non-reproducible crash reports, and otherwise inconsistent scenario design.

Evidently, a naive fix is to repeatedly run each configuration and select the mean or median fitness value to check for robustness. However, in our setting this is not possible, as a typical simulation takes 1 to 2 min. Assuming 1000 total optimisation steps, re-evaluating every run five more times adds some 80 to 160 h of simulation time to each individual scenario search, rendering this method infeasible for broad application.

In this paper, we introduce kNN-averaging to overcome the problem of lacking fitness robustness and outliers in noisy optimisation problems and provide our advances on common, theoretical benchmark problems. Our method *kNN-Avg* uses the k-nearest neighbours (kNN) (k being a hyper-parameter) to compute the fitness value and thereby reduce the noise. We show that in a typical setting without noise mitigation, GAs tend to predict outlier values and that kNN-Avg helps to overcome this problem, making the found solutions more robust. To evaluate our approach, we adapt three well-known MOO benchmarks to noisy environments and quantify our results using common quality indicators (QIs).

2   Multi-objective Optimisation and Genetic Algorithms

Multi-objective optimisation problems are a family of problems that aim to optimise multiple function values. Formally, the goal is to find the minimum parameter (a.k.a. *variable*) values $x \in \mathbb{X}$ such that the function values of a vector of *objective* functions f are minimised. $\mathbb{X} \subseteq \mathbb{R}^n$ represents the *solution space*, i.e. the input to f, and relates to the scenario parameters that we defined above. $\boldsymbol{x}$ is called a *solution*.

$$\min_{\boldsymbol{x} \in \mathbb{X}} f(\boldsymbol{x}) = \{f_1(x), \ldots, f_m(x)\}, \forall i \in \{1, \ldots, m\}, f_i : \mathbb{X} \to \mathbb{R} \qquad (1)$$

The output $f(\boldsymbol{x}) \in \mathbb{Y}$ is called the *objective* value of $\boldsymbol{x}$; $\mathbb{Y} \subseteq \mathbb{R}^m$ being the *objective space*. An optimisation problem is called *multi-objective* if $m > 1$.[1]

While for single-objective optimisation problems, a solution leading to a smaller objective value than another is considered better (*dominant*), this notion is not as clear in the MOO setting. Here, given two solutions $\boldsymbol{x}_a, \boldsymbol{x}_b \in \mathbb{X}$, we say that $\boldsymbol{x}_a$ dominates $\boldsymbol{x}_b$ ($\boldsymbol{x}_a \prec \boldsymbol{x}_b$) iff $\forall i \in \{1, \ldots, n\}, f_i(\boldsymbol{x}_a) \leqslant f_i(\boldsymbol{x}_b) \wedge \exists j \in \{1, \ldots, n\}: f_j(\boldsymbol{x}_a) < f_j(\boldsymbol{x}_b)$.

A solution is *Pareto optimal* iff there is no other solution that dominates it. A Pareto set $PS^* \in \mathbb{X}$ is the set of all Pareto optimal solutions, a Pareto-front PF^* is the image of the Pareto set in the objective space. Roughly speaking, PS^* is the set of solutions where we cannot optimise one f_i-dimension without having to reduce optimality in another one. This means, however, that there might be numerous Pareto optimal solutions for some problems. Figure 1a shows a solution set for the benchmark problem ZDT1 [17] alongside its Pareto front PF^*. Note that each value of the solution set is Pareto optimal.

Quality Indicators (QI). QIs allow an estimation of a MOO's performance. Numerous QIs have been proposed [13]. In this paper, we focus on two of the most common ones.

Hypervolume (HV) It calculates the hypervolume between a given reference point in the objective space and each of the solutions' objective values. Typically, it uses a reference that is worse than all expected objective values. Thus, the HV increases as the solutions approach the Pareto-optimality.

Inverse generational distance (IGD) IGD calculates the average Euclidean distance from each PF^*-point to its closest solution. IGD decreases when approaching PF^*.

Genetic algorithms (GAs). GAs [7] are a subfamily of evolutionary algorithms (EAs) whose working principle is based on the iterative creation of *populations* (sets of solutions, a.k.a. *generations*). An initial population can be created from random samples, and all following generations are based on the best candidates from their predecessors. This is achieved by ranking the solutions according to their fitness values $f(\boldsymbol{x})$ and applying *operators* to the best ones: *selection* keeps the good ones, *crossover* produces new solutions by "mating" two others, and *mutation* creates a slightly altered version of an existing one.

---

[1] In this paper, we consider *unconstrained* MOO problems, meaning that $f(\boldsymbol{x})$ always produces feasible output. For an introduction on constrained MOO see [8].

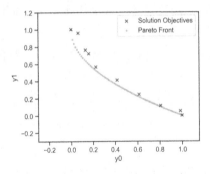

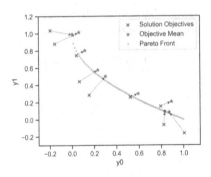

(a) A solution set for the MOO problem ZDT1 and optimal Pareto front PF*

(b) Noisy ZDT1$_{\sigma=0.1}$ objectives after optimisation, and the solutions' mean objectives.

Fig. 1. Left: search problem without noise; Right: noisy search problem

3   Noisy MOO and K-Nearest-Neighbour Averaging

We use the term *noisy MOO* to refer to problems whose fitness function $f(x)$ is non-deterministic. The formal problem statement, introduced in Eq. 1, can be updated to

$$\min_{x \in X} f(x) = \{f_1(x) + \delta_1, \ldots, f_m(x) + \delta_m\} \qquad (2)$$

where each δ_i is a noise value sampled from a distribution. In many real-world systems, as well as common benchmark studies, the noise in the system is Gaussian-distributed [11]. To make our results comparable, we follow this lead, and therefore, for the rest of this paper, we fix that δ_i is sampled from a normal distribution with mean $\mu = 0$ and a standard deviation σ. We use σ as a variable and alter it depending on the particular benchmark. For noisy systems, we indicate the problem's noise σ-parameter as subscript, e.g. ZDT1$_{\sigma=0.1}$, as in Fig. 1b.

Noise Effect. When introducing noise into an optimisation problem, the effect is that PF* no longer represents the optimal objective values but instead marks the mean objective values for PS*. Given a solution $s \in PS*$ and high enough repetitions, the mean value should be placed near the solution's expected (non-noisy) objective.

Interestingly though, when executing a GA on such a problem, the typical result (see also [10]) is that the algorithm computes a set of solutions that approaches PS*, but predicts objective values with high negative noise, falsely indicating extraordinarily good fitness values. Thus, in the final solution set S, the GA "pushes" the reported fitness value far beyond PF*, as can be seen in Fig. 1b. The result is that the objective values do not match the actual distributions of the solutions' expected mean objective values, and in fact over-estimate the quality of the S. Figure 1b displays both the sampled solutions' objective values as well as these solutions' mean objective values. S was obtained by running 100 iterations of the GA-optimisation of the noisy $\text{ZDT1}_{\sigma=0.1}$ problem. In the figure, we can observe several properties:

1. The objective values of the found non-dominated solution set S (marked by crosses) actually significantly surpass PF*.
2. By evaluating $s \in S$ repeatedly (or by removing the noise), we reveal the actual mean objective values, i.e. the centre points of the noisy objective distributions (marked by asterisks).
3. Some of the mean objective values are clearly dominated by others. Thus, evaluating $s \in S$ will likely lead to non-dominated solutions.
4. The observed objective values are typically based on large noise values, i.e. they are outliers.
5. On average, the distance between observed objectives and the mean objectives (indicated by the arrows) is rather large—even exceeding σ. Thus, the obtained solutions' fitness is misleading.
6. Even though the solutions' objective values do not match the mean objective values, the solutions' mean objective values approach PF*. This means that while we cannot expect fitness values to be as good as predicted by the optimisation process, on average the solution values will still be good.
7. It appears that the noise causes the search to stop further improvement, since outlier noise suggests the greatest possible fitness was already reached.

Ideally, the solutions' mean objectives would align with PF*, s.t. this result would produce the best fitness on average.

Research Goal. Indeed, in Fig. 1 where we know that the noise (induced by σ) is constant throughout the search space and as we know PF*, we can easily see the offset. However, for unknown problems, problems with potentially fluctuating noise magnitudes or similar situations, we should aim to produce solutions whose sampled objective values are close to the mean objective values. This way, we know that the individuals' objectives are reliable and the obtained values representative. In other words, our goal is to push the crosses in Fig. 1b closer towards the asterisks, while keeping the asterisks close to the ideal Pareto front PF*.

Mean Offset. Δf We introduce a new measure Δf to calculate the mean Euclidean distance between S's reported objective values $f(s), s \in S$—as obtained by the search—and the mean expected objective values $\tilde{f}(s)$—obtained e.g. by taking the mean of repeated invocations of f on s. Δf thus measures the average length of the arrows in Fig. 1b. The rest of this section describe our method which leverages the weighted average of the k-nearest neighbours to robustify the sampling process and reduce Δf.

$$\Delta f = \frac{\sum_{s \in S} \sqrt{(f(s) - \tilde{f}(s))^2}}{|S|} \tag{3}$$

3.1 KNN-Averaging

Theoretically, inputs to noisy fitness functions can be repeatedly evaluated and the sampled values averaged. Given high enough repetition frequency, this mean objective value should approach the actual expectation value. The problem of this method is the cost involved in the re-sampling of values, which can be significant for complex systems such as automated driving simulators, even rendering the search effectively infeasible.

Our novel approach *kNN-Avg* aims to approximate the re-sampling process and decrease the objective values noise, without actually performing the costly repeated sampling. Our concept is based on the hypothesis that solutions that are close to one another in the solution space will produce similarly distributed objective values. Thus, the goal is to identify previously evaluated solutions close to the currently sampled point and use their fitness values to help decrease the impact of outliers.

Standardised Euclidean Distance. Euclidean distance (ED) is one of the go-to distance measures when it comes to evaluating the proximity of multi-dimensional data points, providing the "shortest direct distance" between two points. On closer inspection, however, we notice that often the values depend on the individual dimensions' units. Thus, the Euclidean distance of values expressed in kilometres is vastly different than the one in metres. Moreover, the measure is not robust against large magnitude differences. When one dimension expresses vehicle size in metres, but the other travelled distances in kilometres, the second dimension will probably dominate the measure.

Our goal is thus to use a measure that normalises over the actually used search space to avoid such tilting of the distance measure. We therefore use the standardised Euclidean distance (SED), which normalises the values by relating the value difference to the dimension's variance within the total set of values in that dimension.

Definition 1 (Standardised Euclidean distance). *The standardised Euclidean distance (SED) of two vectors is the square-root of the sum of the squared element-wise difference divided by the dimension's variance σ_i^2:*

$$sed(\boldsymbol{x}_1, \boldsymbol{x}_2) = \sqrt{\sum_{i=1}^{N} \frac{(x_{1,i} - x_{2,i})^2}{\sigma_i^2}}, \tag{4}$$

Note that the difference to the "common" Euclidean distance, i.e. the division by the dimension's variance σ_i^2, places each dimension in relation to the global value spread. This robustifies standardised Euclidean distance (SED) against magnitude changes in the solution space and we can—in theory—even change, e.g. the units from km to m.

3.2   Hyper-parameters of kNN-Avg

Next to the choice of distance measure, the kNN-Avg algorithm offers several other configuration parameters. Here, we will briefly outline some of the questions that have to be answered before executing the algorithm.

How big should k be? Intuitively, we might want to include as many neighbours as possible to minimise the noise factor. The problem is, however, that higher k-values take more distant neighbours into account, which are less similar to the solution under investigation. Typically, the answer also depends on the shape of the search space and the standard deviation of the noise.

When does a neighbour stop being "near"? Especially at the beginning of the search when the sampling history is still sparse, a kNN algorithm without a *cutoff* limit might select rather distant neighbours for the averaging. To avoid this, we use a *maximum distance* MD to limit the kNN search to the local neighbourhood.

Should close neighbours weigh more? By default, our hypothesis is that close neighbours produce more similar value distributions than those further away. Based on an informal initial exploration, our algorithm uses the squared SED to decrease a neighbours impact weight. Nonetheless, this raises the question as to how those weights are shaped in general. We leave this more general question as future works.

We performed an upfront literature search, but it did not reveal conclusive answers or best practices for good choices on these hyper-parameter values. Thus, k and maximum distance MD are left variable. The experiments section explores the relationship between these hyper-parameter values and the performance of the MOO process. The weight measure on the other hand was fixed as the inverse-square of the SED. Before choosing squared, we also experimented with *linear* and *uniform* distance weights, but did not observe as good results.

3.3   Algorithm

Based on the kNN-Avg approach and the identified hyper-parameters we implemented the algorithm, as displayed in Listing 1.1. The algorithm is presented in a Python-like pseudo-language and makes references to "mock" functions such as `get_variances`. The actual implementation uses common Python libraries such as `numpy` and `pandas`.

The listing's `knn_evaluate`-function is meant to replace the native `evaluate`-function of a GA implementation. It is called once per generation and takes as input a list of solutions, as well as the KNN and MAX_DIST hyper-parameters. The output is a list of `Solution` objects, each containing variables and kNN-averaged objective values. Specifically, each population cycles through the following steps:

1. The algorithm first invokes the (noisy) default `evaluate` method (L 6). This can be e.g. the triggering of a simulator.

Listing 1.1. KNN-Evaluation algorithm in (Python-ish) pseudo-code

```
1   """Store the solutions with actually sampled values."""
2   HISTORY = list()  # global store of solutions
3   """Calculate KNN-averaged objectives for a list of solutions."""
4   def knn_evaluate(population: List[Solution], KNN: int, MAX_DIST:
        float) -> List[Solution]:
5       # standard evaluation of each solution; add results to the history
6       sampled = [evaluate(solution) for solution in population]
7       HISTORY.extend(sampled)
8       # calculates the list of variance (one per variable dimension)
9       variances = get_variances(HISTORY)
10      # calculate solutions with KNN-averaged objectives
11      knn_solutions = list()
12      for solution in population:
13          # store a map of solution-to-SED
14          distances={other:SED(solution, other, variances) for other in
            HISTORY}
15          # remove those that are larger than MAX_DISTANCE
16          knn = {sol: val for sol, val in knn.items() if val <= MAX_DIST}
17          # sort by distance and limit to KNN values
18          knn = distances.sort(by=distances.values())[:KNN]
19          # calculate the weights as the square of distance values;
20          # negate and add MAX_DIST so sol itself is largest
21          weights = math.square(knn.values()) * -1 + MAX_DIST
22          objs = [sol.objs for sol in knn]
23          avgs = weighted_mean(objs, weights, column=True)
24          # append to the list of returned solutions
25          knn_solutions.append(Solution(solution.vars, avgs))
26      return knn_solutions
27
28  """Data-class for solutions and corresponding objective values."""
29  class Solution(object):
30      vars = list()  # variables will be filled by the GA
31      objs = list()  # objectives are filled by us
```

2. After this evaluation, the solutions (now containing the sampling results) are added to the global HISTORY (L 2 and L 7).
3. In the next step, the variances are calculated for each solution dimension separately (L 9). The variances are later used to calculate the SED.
4. Then, each solution iterates through the following steps:
   (a) Calculate the solution's SEDs to each other solution in the global history—including itself and all other newly generated solutions (L 14).
   (b) Select all solutions closer than MAX_DIST (L 16).
   (c) Sort solutions by the SED and only keep the k-nearest neighbours (L 18).
   (d) Calculate the weights of each knn as the negative square of its SED (L 21). Then add MAX_DIST to make all values positive.
   (e) Calculate the objective values as the weighted mean values. Note that since objectives is a two-dimensional list, we have to specify column-wise aggregation, such that each dimension is averaged separately (L 22–23). The solution variables and averaged objectives are used to append a new Solution to the list that will be returned to the algorithm.

kNN-Avg Effect. The effect of the algorithm is visualised in Fig. 2. It shows the kNN-Avg approach at the evaluation of the 25th generation of a search problem. The evaluation history is shown as coloured crosses. Red dots display the sampled objective values, arrows indicate the corresponding objective values after kNN-Avg (red crosses).

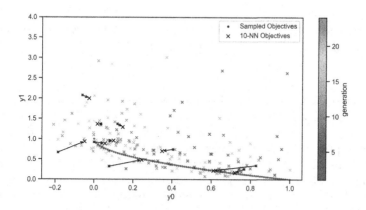

Fig. 2. 10-NN averaging at generation #25 for ZDT1$_{\sigma=0.1}$. Arrows connect sampled and respective 10-NN-averaged objective values. (Color figure online)

4   Evaluation

This section describes the experiments and analyses we performed to answer the following research questions (RQs):

- **RQ1:** Can kNN-Avg mitigate the outlier-effect of noisy MOO and bring the reported and mean objective values closer together (i.e. reduce Δf)?
- **RQ2:** How do the solutions of kNN-Avg compare to those of the baseline in terms of optimality (measured by quality indicators (QIs))?
- **RQ3:** Does the level of noise have an impact on whether kNN-Avg is able to produce good results?
- **RQ4:** What influence does the choice of hyper-parameters have on the efficiency of the approach?

Experimental Setup. To evaluate the kNN-Avg method, we implemented a set of noisy benchmarks. The implementation is based on the `pymoo` Python library [4], which provides a flexible framework for evaluation of MOO problems and algorithms.

For the kNN-Avg evaluation, we developed a `KNNAvgMixin`-wrapper that we can dynamically add to existing `pymoo` problems. The wrapper serves two purposes: First, it modifies the wrapped problem and artificially injects noise into

Table 1. Configurations of benchmarks and search algorithms

Label	Values	Comment
Problem	ZDT1, ZDT2, ZDT3	*Benchmark name*
Num variables	2, 4, 10	*Benchmark configuration*
σ (noise std. dev.)	0.00, 0.05, 0.10, 0.25, 0.50	*Benchmark noise*
Population size	10, 20	*GA setting*
k (num neighbours)	10, 25, 50, 100, 1000	*kNN-Avg hyper-parameter*
MD maximum distance	0.25, 0.5, 1.0, 2.0, 4.0	*kNN-Avg hyper-parameter*

the evaluated solutions. Second, it implements the kNN-Avg algorithm to counteract the effects of the noise. The wrapper also stores the full evaluation history
and adds data logging for our analysis. It can be flexibly added to existing
benchmark problems, e.g. those already available in pymoo.

Using this class, we ran experiments on three benchmark problems: ZDT1,
ZDT2 and ZDT3 [17]. These artificial MOO benchmarks aim to minimise two-
function objectives, based on a variable number of up to 30 inputs. In total,
we selected six individual settings with multiple values each, to avoid biasing
our algorithm and also obtain an overview of the influence of various hyper-
parameters (RQ4). Following guidelines [2], we executed 30 repetitions in each
setting to avoid statistical fluctuations and gain enough data for our later analysis. Table 1 displays the experiment settings and the values that each one may
take. The total number of experimental settings is given by the Cartesian product of the settings' values. In total, we executed 67,500 individual optimisation
runs.

As MOO method we use NSGA-II, configured with a random initial population, simulated binary crossover (probability 0.9) and polynomial mutation
(probability 1.0). The search was run for 100 generations using population size
10 or 20 (see Table 1).

4.1   Experimental Results

In order to evaluate the effectiveness of the approach, we proceeded as follows.

For each experiment, we took the set of optimised solutions S as computed by
the GA; then for each solution $s \in S$, we computed its "mean" objective value
$\tilde{s}$; all solutions $\tilde{s}$ constitute the "adjusted" solution set $\widetilde{S}$. Based thereon, we
computed the following metrics: (i) Δf, the average error in estimation between
the objective values of solutions in S and the adjusted ones in $\widetilde{S}$ (see Eq. (3));
(ii) $\widetilde{HV}$ and $\widetilde{IGD}$, the hypervolume and IGD (see Sect. 2) of the mean objectives
$\tilde{s} \in \widetilde{S}$.

As an example, Fig. 3 shows $\widetilde{HV}$, $\widetilde{IGD}$, and Δf for the ZDT1$_{\sigma=0.1}$ experiment with 2 variables, grouped by k and maximum distance MD, i.e. by the

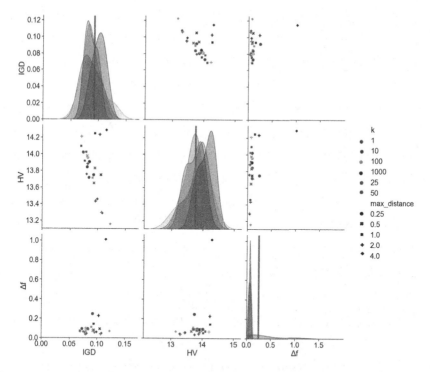

Fig. 3. Pairplot of average QI and Δf of 30 runs for ZDT1$_{\sigma=0.1}$. Diagonal plots show kernel density estimates. Baseline B($k = 1$; no averaging) is shown as a vertical line. (Color figure online)

hyper-parameters we want to evaluate[2]. The plots show the mean results of 30 individual NSGA-II optimisation runs after 100 generations with population size 10. The individual plots show two metrics plotted against each other, while the diagonal plots display the kernel density estimate[3] by k value. Roughly speaking, this is a distribution of where the individual metrics (grouped by k) are along the x-axis. Thus, for $\widetilde{IGD}$ and Δf, lower (left) is better, while for $\widetilde{HV}$ higher (right) is advantageous. Further, a flat, wide density shows a spread of values along the axis, while a short, high curve signifies a concentrated values. The baseline represents the standard (non-averaging) noisy MOO, where only the sampled value is chosen without any neighbours(i.e. $k = 1$). It is is drawn as vertical blue line. Note, that a comparison to other solution approaches to noisy MOO is left as future work.

We see from the positions of the data points, as well as from the density plots, that for most k values (except k=1000) the $\widetilde{IGD}$ is lower than B(blue line). For

---

[2] The implementation of our algorithm and the plots of all other experimental settings are available online https://github.com/ERATOMMSD/QUATIC2021-KNN-Averaging.).

[3] https://www.mvstat.net/tduong/research/seminars/seminar-2001-05.

Table 2. Comparison between the kNN-based settings $\texttt{KNN}_k^{MD}$ and the baseline B.

(a) No noise				(b) $\sigma = 0.05$				(c) $\sigma = 0.1$				(d) $\sigma = 0.25$				(e) $\sigma = 0.5$				(f) All			
App.	$\widetilde{HV}$	$\widetilde{IGD}$	Δf	App.	$\widetilde{HV}$	$\widetilde{IGD}$	Δf	App.	$\widetilde{HV}$	$\widetilde{IGD}$	Δf	App.	$\widetilde{HV}$	$\widetilde{IGD}$	Δf	App.	$\widetilde{HV}$	$\widetilde{IGD}$	Δf	App.	$\widetilde{HV}$	$\widetilde{IGD}$	Δf
$\texttt{KNN}_{10}^{0.25}$	≡	✗	✗	$\texttt{KNN}_{10}^{0.25}$	✗	≡	✓	$\texttt{KNN}_{10}^{0.25}$	≡	✓	✓	$\texttt{KNN}_{10}^{0.25}$	≡	≡	✓	$\texttt{KNN}_{10}^{0.25}$	≡	≡	✓	$\texttt{KNN}_{10}^{0.25}$	≡	✓	✓
$\texttt{KNN}_{10}^{0.5}$	✗	✗	✗	$\texttt{KNN}_{10}^{0.5}$	≡	≡	✓	$\texttt{KNN}_{10}^{0.5}$	≡	≡	✓	$\texttt{KNN}_{10}^{0.5}$	≡	≡	✓	$\texttt{KNN}_{10}^{0.5}$	≡	≡	✓	$\texttt{KNN}_{10}^{0.5}$	≡	✓	✓
$\texttt{KNN}_{10}^{1.0}$	✗	✗	✗	$\texttt{KNN}_{10}^{1.0}$	✗	✗	✓	$\texttt{KNN}_{10}^{1.0}$	≡	≡	✓	$\texttt{KNN}_{10}^{1.0}$	≡	≡	✓	$\texttt{KNN}_{10}^{1.0}$	≡	≡	✓	$\texttt{KNN}_{10}^{1.0}$	✗	≡	✓
$\texttt{KNN}_{10}^{2.0}$	✗	✗	✗	$\texttt{KNN}_{10}^{2.0}$	✗	✗	✓	$\texttt{KNN}_{10}^{2.0}$	✗	✗	✓	$\texttt{KNN}_{10}^{2.0}$	≡	≡	✓	$\texttt{KNN}_{10}^{2.0}$	≡	≡	✓	$\texttt{KNN}_{10}^{2.0}$	✗	≡	✓
$\texttt{KNN}_{10}^{4.0}$	✗	✗	✗	$\texttt{KNN}_{10}^{4.0}$	✗	✗	✓	$\texttt{KNN}_{10}^{4.0}$	✗	✗	✓	$\texttt{KNN}_{10}^{4.0}$	✗	≡	✓	$\texttt{KNN}_{10}^{4.0}$	≡	≡	✓	$\texttt{KNN}_{10}^{4.0}$	✗	✗	✓
$\texttt{KNN}_{25}^{0.25}$	✗	✗	✗	$\texttt{KNN}_{25}^{0.25}$	≡	≡	✓	$\texttt{KNN}_{25}^{0.25}$	≡	✓	✓	$\texttt{KNN}_{25}^{0.25}$	≡	≡	✓	$\texttt{KNN}_{25}^{0.25}$	≡	≡	✓	$\texttt{KNN}_{25}^{0.25}$	≡	✓	✓
$\texttt{KNN}_{25}^{0.5}$	✗	✗	✗	$\texttt{KNN}_{25}^{0.5}$	✗	✗	✓	$\texttt{KNN}_{25}^{0.5}$	≡	≡	✓	$\texttt{KNN}_{25}^{0.5}$	≡	≡	✓	$\texttt{KNN}_{25}^{0.5}$	≡	✓	✓	$\texttt{KNN}_{25}^{0.5}$	≡	≡	✓
$\texttt{KNN}_{25}^{1.0}$	✗	✗	✗	$\texttt{KNN}_{25}^{1.0}$	✗	✗	✓	$\texttt{KNN}_{25}^{1.0}$	✗	≡	✓	$\texttt{KNN}_{25}^{1.0}$	≡	✓	✓	$\texttt{KNN}_{25}^{1.0}$	≡	✓	✓	$\texttt{KNN}_{25}^{1.0}$	✗	≡	✓
$\texttt{KNN}_{25}^{2.0}$	✗	✗	✗	$\texttt{KNN}_{25}^{2.0}$	✗	✗	✓	$\texttt{KNN}_{25}^{2.0}$	✗	✗	✓	$\texttt{KNN}_{25}^{2.0}$	✗	≡	✓	$\texttt{KNN}_{25}^{2.0}$	≡	✓	✓	$\texttt{KNN}_{25}^{2.0}$	✗	✗	✓
$\texttt{KNN}_{25}^{4.0}$	✗	✗	✗	$\texttt{KNN}_{25}^{4.0}$	✗	✗	✓	$\texttt{KNN}_{25}^{4.0}$	✗	✗	✓	$\texttt{KNN}_{25}^{4.0}$	✗	≡	✓	$\texttt{KNN}_{25}^{4.0}$	≡	✓	✓	$\texttt{KNN}_{25}^{4.0}$	✗	✗	✓
$\texttt{KNN}_{50}^{0.25}$	✗	✗	✗	$\texttt{KNN}_{50}^{0.25}$	≡	≡	✓	$\texttt{KNN}_{50}^{0.25}$	≡	≡	✓	$\texttt{KNN}_{50}^{0.25}$	✓	✓	✓	$\texttt{KNN}_{50}^{0.25}$	≡	≡	✓	$\texttt{KNN}_{50}^{0.25}$	≡	✓	✓
$\texttt{KNN}_{50}^{0.5}$	✗	✗	✗	$\texttt{KNN}_{50}^{0.5}$	≡	≡	✓	$\texttt{KNN}_{50}^{0.5}$	≡	≡	✓	$\texttt{KNN}_{50}^{0.5}$	≡	≡	✓	$\texttt{KNN}_{50}^{0.5}$	≡	≡	✓	$\texttt{KNN}_{50}^{0.5}$	≡	≡	✓
$\texttt{KNN}_{50}^{1.0}$	✗	✗	✗	$\texttt{KNN}_{50}^{1.0}$	✗	✗	≡	$\texttt{KNN}_{50}^{1.0}$	✗	≡	✓	$\texttt{KNN}_{50}^{1.0}$	≡	≡	✓	$\texttt{KNN}_{50}^{1.0}$	≡	≡	✓	$\texttt{KNN}_{50}^{1.0}$	✗	≡	✓
$\texttt{KNN}_{50}^{2.0}$	✗	✗	✗	$\texttt{KNN}_{50}^{2.0}$	✗	✗	✗	$\texttt{KNN}_{50}^{2.0}$	✗	✗	✓	$\texttt{KNN}_{50}^{2.0}$	✗	≡	✓	$\texttt{KNN}_{50}^{2.0}$	≡	✓	✓	$\texttt{KNN}_{50}^{2.0}$	✗	✗	✓
$\texttt{KNN}_{50}^{4.0}$	✗	✗	✗	$\texttt{KNN}_{50}^{4.0}$	✗	✗	✗	$\texttt{KNN}_{50}^{4.0}$	✗	✗	✓	$\texttt{KNN}_{50}^{4.0}$	✗	≡	✓	$\texttt{KNN}_{50}^{4.0}$	≡	✓	✓	$\texttt{KNN}_{50}^{4.0}$	✗	✗	✓
$\texttt{KNN}_{100}^{0.25}$	✗	✗	✗	$\texttt{KNN}_{100}^{0.25}$	≡	≡	✗	$\texttt{KNN}_{100}^{0.25}$	≡	≡	✓	$\texttt{KNN}_{100}^{0.25}$	≡	≡	✓	$\texttt{KNN}_{100}^{0.25}$	≡	≡	✓	$\texttt{KNN}_{100}^{0.25}$	≡	≡	✓
$\texttt{KNN}_{100}^{0.5}$	✗	✗	✗	$\texttt{KNN}_{100}^{0.5}$	✗	✗	≡	$\texttt{KNN}_{100}^{0.5}$	≡	≡	✓	$\texttt{KNN}_{100}^{0.5}$	≡	≡	✓	$\texttt{KNN}_{100}^{0.5}$	≡	≡	✓	$\texttt{KNN}_{100}^{0.5}$	✗	≡	✓
$\texttt{KNN}_{100}^{1.0}$	✗	✗	✗	$\texttt{KNN}_{100}^{1.0}$	✗	✗	≡	$\texttt{KNN}_{100}^{1.0}$	✗	≡	✓	$\texttt{KNN}_{100}^{1.0}$	≡	✓	✓	$\texttt{KNN}_{100}^{1.0}$	≡	≡	✓	$\texttt{KNN}_{100}^{1.0}$	✗	≡	✓
$\texttt{KNN}_{100}^{2.0}$	✗	✗	✗	$\texttt{KNN}_{100}^{2.0}$	✗	✗	✗	$\texttt{KNN}_{100}^{2.0}$	✗	✗	✓	$\texttt{KNN}_{100}^{2.0}$	✗	≡	✓	$\texttt{KNN}_{100}^{2.0}$	≡	✓	✓	$\texttt{KNN}_{100}^{2.0}$	✗	✗	✓
$\texttt{KNN}_{100}^{4.0}$	✗	✗	✗	$\texttt{KNN}_{100}^{4.0}$	✗	✗	✗	$\texttt{KNN}_{100}^{4.0}$	✗	✗	✓	$\texttt{KNN}_{100}^{4.0}$	✗	≡	✓	$\texttt{KNN}_{100}^{4.0}$	≡	≡	✓	$\texttt{KNN}_{100}^{4.0}$	✗	✗	✓
$\texttt{KNN}_{1000}^{0.25}$	✗	✗	✗	$\texttt{KNN}_{1000}^{0.25}$	≡	≡	✗	$\texttt{KNN}_{1000}^{0.25}$	≡	≡	✓	$\texttt{KNN}_{1000}^{0.25}$	≡	≡	✓	$\texttt{KNN}_{1000}^{0.25}$	≡	≡	✓	$\texttt{KNN}_{1000}^{0.25}$	≡	✓	✓
$\texttt{KNN}_{1000}^{0.5}$	✗	✗	✗	$\texttt{KNN}_{1000}^{0.5}$	≡	≡	≡	$\texttt{KNN}_{1000}^{0.5}$	≡	≡	✓	$\texttt{KNN}_{1000}^{0.5}$	≡	≡	✓	$\texttt{KNN}_{1000}^{0.5}$	≡	≡	✓	$\texttt{KNN}_{1000}^{0.5}$	≡	≡	✓
$\texttt{KNN}_{1000}^{1.0}$	✗	✗	✗	$\texttt{KNN}_{1000}^{1.0}$	✗	✗	≡	$\texttt{KNN}_{1000}^{1.0}$	≡	≡	✓	$\texttt{KNN}_{1000}^{1.0}$	≡	≡	✓	$\texttt{KNN}_{1000}^{1.0}$	≡	≡	✓	$\texttt{KNN}_{1000}^{1.0}$	≡	≡	✓
$\texttt{KNN}_{1000}^{2.0}$	✗	✗	✗	$\texttt{KNN}_{1000}^{2.0}$	✗	✗	✗	$\texttt{KNN}_{1000}^{2.0}$	✗	✗	≡	$\texttt{KNN}_{1000}^{2.0}$	✗	≡	✓	$\texttt{KNN}_{1000}^{2.0}$	≡	✓	✓	$\texttt{KNN}_{1000}^{2.0}$	✗	≡	✓
$\texttt{KNN}_{1000}^{4.0}$	✗	✗	✗	$\texttt{KNN}_{1000}^{4.0}$	✗	✗	✗	$\texttt{KNN}_{1000}^{4.0}$	✗	✗	≡	$\texttt{KNN}_{1000}^{4.0}$	✗	≡	✓	$\texttt{KNN}_{1000}^{4.0}$	≡	✓	✓	$\texttt{KNN}_{1000}^{4.0}$	✗	✗	≡

Legend: ≡: there is no statistically significant difference between $\texttt{KNN}_k^{MD}$ and B.
✓: $\texttt{KNN}_k^{MD}$ is statistically significantly better.   ✗: B is statistically significantly better.

$\widetilde{HV}$ the value is higher, except $k=25$. Of particular interest is Δf, which shows a significant discrepancy between the kNN-Avg evaluations and B, in favour of kNN-Avg.

Thus, we conclude that for this particular benchmark, the kNN-Avg approach produces better results on average than B. We report in the online repository[2] the detailed analyses of all the 45 benchmarks. In the following, we perform an overall analysis to assess how the proposed approach performs in general.

We calculated the experiments results' average (grouped by k and MD) and compared them with the results of the baseline B, across all experiment configurations (all combinations of *Problem, Num Variables, σ,* and *Population size*). By following guidelines for conducting experiments with randomised algorithms [2], we compared them using the Wilcoxon signed rank test for the statistical significance (at significance level $\alpha = 0.05$), and the Vargha-Delaney's $\hat{A}_{12}$ as effect size. Table 2 reports the results of the statistical tests, displaying whether kNN-Avg's performance is statistically significantly better, equal, or worse than the B's. Table 2a reports the results for the benchmarks with no noise, Table 2b–2e the results for the benchmarks having a specific noise level $\sigma = a$, and Table 2f the results by benchmarks with any level of noise.

4.2   Evaluation

RQ1: Can kNN-Avg mitigate the outlier-effect of noisy MOO and bring the reported and mean objective values closer together? From

Table 2a, it is clear there is no advantage in using kNN-Avg for non-noisy systems. Indeed, the approach computes approximated fitness values, although the sampled ones are already precise. Instead, for any noise level (Table 2b–2e) and most experimental settings, statistically, kNN-Avg outperforms Bin terms of Δf. This clearly shows that kNN-Avg succeeds in producing solutions whose sampled objective values are closer to their mean values.

RQ2: How do the solutions of kNN-Avg compare to those of Bin terms of optimality (i.e. in terms of quality indicators)? For non-noisy benchmarks (Table 2a), kNN-Avg is worse than Bin term of solution quality; this effect is expected, as the approach perturbates the fitness value when it is not needed. Nonetheless, for any noise level (Table 2b–2e), we observe that there are several hyper-parameter configurations where kNN-Avg produces equal or better results for both HV and IGD.

RQ3: Does the level of noise have an impact on whether kNN-Avg is able to produce good results? With increasing noise level, kNN-Avg's results improve. For noise $\sigma = 0.5$ (Table 2e), none of the settings of kNN-Avg produces worse solutions. This shows that our approach is particularly efficient for highly noisy systems.

RQ4: Which is the influence of the method hyper-parameters on the efficiency of the approach? kNN-Avg is initialised with two parameters, the number of neighbours k, and the maximum distance MD. The results suggest that there is no big influence of the used k. For MD on the other hand, lower values usually provide better results across noise levels. This is reasonable, as smaller values of MD make the approach more conservative and avoid averaging too different values.

4.3   Threats to Validity

The validity of kNN-Avg could be affected by some threats. We discuss them in terms of *construct, conclusion, internal,* and *external validity.*

Construct Validity. One threat is that the evaluation metrics may not reflect the object of the investigation, that is, the ability of kNN-Avg to produce solutions with low Δf and still have a good quality in terms of the objective functions. Furthermore, it may be that the newly introduced measure Δf is not a faithful measure for robustness in this context. As different QIs may give different results (in terms of solution ranking), we used two distinct ones [13] to avoid biasing; of course, many more indicators could have been used. We further applied this result on several benchmarks to judge the results.

Conclusion Validity. Different factors can affect the ability to draw definitive conclusions; one of these is the random behaviour of the search algorithms. To mitigate such a threat, we executed each experiment 30 times, as suggested in a guideline on conducting experiments with randomised algorithms [2]. Still following [2], we compared the results of different versions of kNN-Avg and of the baseline approach by using suitable tests that account both for statistical significance and effect size.

Internal Validity. One threat could be to wrongly identify a causal relationship between the usage of kNN-Avg and the improvement in Δf. To mitigate, we carefully tested the implementation, and we make it available for inspection and experiments reproduction.

External Validity. kNN-Avg has been experimented on 45 benchmark models, varying in objective functions, variable numbers, and noise. The benchmarks are commonly used in the MOO community to assess search algorithms. However, more experiments are needed to claim the generability of the approach, possibly using more complex CPSs affected by noise, such as ADSs. This is left as future work.

5   Related Works

Other approaches have been proposed for handling noise in multi-objective optimisation; see [11] for a survey. Early works [9] suggest performing multiple evaluations of the fitness functions and try to understand the sufficient number of evaluations; such approaches may not be applicable in practice when evaluating the fitness functions is expensive (e.g. using ADS simulators).

Park and Ryu [15] propose to handle the noise by performing multiple evaluations of the solutions over several different generations. The approach differs from ours, as we rely on the average fitness values of the kNN, while they calculate the average of multiple re-executions of the same solution.

Other methods [12,16], instead, propose to modify the ranking method to take the system noise into account. The main problem of these works is that they make prior assumptions on the distribution of objective function values; kNN-Avg, instead, makes no assumption on the noise distribution and tries to discover it at runtime.

The closest approach to ours is proposed by Branke [5]. It considers averaging as one of the 10 possible ways to estimate fitness. However, the approach differs in several ways: (i) the approach only applies to single-objective problems; (ii) the distance function does not consider the different dimensions (as we do with SED, see Sect. 3.1); (iii) it takes the whole population into account, instead of limiting the averaging to the kNN.

6   Conclusion and Future Works

This paper presents a novel approach to multi-objective optimisation (MOO) of noisy fitness functions. In such settings, MOO methods such as genetic algorithms tend to wrongly rely on outlier values to guide the optimisation. This results in the problem that the fitness of the reported solutions differs significantly from the expected fitness values obtained by re-running the solutions, which harms trustworthiness. A naive fix would be to repeatedly sample a solution and calculate the mean of observed values, which can easily become very costly for more complex systems.

We present an approach for reducing the noise while avoiding re-sampling. Our *kNN-Avg* algorithm works by keeping the history of all evaluated solutions and calculates the weighted mean of the k-nearest neighbours (kNN). We show the details of our implementation and provide an experimental evaluation based on three common benchmark problems, modified with different noise levels. The results indicate that our kNN-Avg method indeed succeeds in reducing the discrepancy between the solution's fitness and the actual target fitness, thereby increasing the trustworthiness of results.

In future, we plan to extend our approach in several directions. First, we plan on applying kNN-Avg to more benchmark problems, including constrained ones, and evaluate its performance on different types of noise. Next, we are in the process of evaluating the method in a scenario generation setting for an automated driving system. Finally, we want to investigate the algorithm's hyper-parameters and test if any correlations between problem, noise level and algorithm configuration exist.

References

1. Afzal, A., Goues, C.L., Hilton, M., Timperley, C.S.: A study on challenges of testing robotic systems. In: 2020 IEEE 13th International Conference on Software Testing, Validation and Verification (ICST), pp. 96–107 (2020)
2. Arcuri, A., Briand, L.: A practical guide for using statistical tests to assess randomized algorithms in software engineering. In: Proceedings of the 33rd International Conference on Software Engineering, ICSE 2011, pp. 1–10. ACM, New York (2011)
3. Bentley, P.J., Wakefield, J.P.: Generic evolutionary design. In: Chawdhry, P.K., Roy, R., Pant, R.K. (eds.) Soft Computing in Engineering Design and Manufacturing, pp. 289–298. Springer, London (1998). https://doi.org/10.1007/978-1-4471-0427-8_31
4. Blank, J., Deb, K.: Pymoo: multi-objective optimization in Python. IEEE Access **8**, 89497–89509 (2020)
5. Branke, J.: Creating robust solutions by means of evolutionary algorithms. In: Eiben, A.E., Bäck, T., Schoenauer, M., Schwefel, H.-P. (eds.) PPSN 1998. LNCS, vol. 1498, pp. 119–128. Springer, Heidelberg (1998). https://doi.org/10.1007/BFb0056855
6. Carroll, D.L.: Chemical laser modeling with genetic algorithms. AIAA J. **34**(2), 338–346 (1996)
7. Eiben, A.E., Smith, J.E.: Introduction to Evolutionary Computing, 2nd edn. Springer, Heidelberg (2015). https://doi.org/10.1007/978-3-662-44874-8
8. Fan, Z., Fang, Y., Li, W., Lu, J., Cai, X., Wei, C.: A comparative study of constrained multi-objective evolutionary algorithms on constrained multi-objective optimization problems. In: 2017 IEEE Congress on Evolutionary Computation (CEC), pp. 209–216. IEEE (2017)
9. Fitzpatrick, J.M., Grefenstette, J.J.: Genetic algorithms in noisy environments. Mach. Learn. **3**(2–3), 101–120 (1988)

518   S. Klikovits and P. Arcaini

10. Goh, C.K., Tan, K.C.: An investigation on noisy environments in evolutionary multiobjective optimization. IEEE Trans. Evol. Comput. **11**(3), 354–381 (2007)
11. Goh, C.K., Tan, K.C.: Evolutionary Multi-objective Optimization in Uncertain Environments, vol. 186. Springer, Heidelberg (2009). https://doi.org/10.1007/978-3-540-95976-2
12. Hughes, E.J.: Evolutionary multi-objective ranking with uncertainty and noise. In: Zitzler, E., Thiele, L., Deb, K., Coello Coello, C.A., Corne, D. (eds.) EMO 2001. LNCS, vol. 1993, pp. 329–343. Springer, Heidelberg (2001). https://doi.org/10.1007/3-540-44719-9_23
13. Li, M., Yao, X.: Quality evaluation of solution sets in multiobjective optimisation: a survey. ACM Comput. Surv. (CSUR) **52**(2), 1–38 (2019)
14. Mirjalili, S.: Genetic Algorithm. In: Mirjalili, S. (ed.) Evolutionary Algorithms and Neural Networks. Studies in Computational Intelligence, vol. 780, pp. 43–55. Springer, Cham (2019). https://doi.org/10.1007/978-3-319-93025-1_4
15. Park, T., Ryu, K.R.: Accumulative sampling for noisy evolutionary multi-objective optimization. In: Proceedings of the 13th Annual Conference on Genetic and Evolutionary Computation, GECCO 2011, pp. 793–800. Association for Computing Machinery, New York (2011)
16. Teich, J.: Pareto-front exploration with uncertain objectives. In: Zitzler, E., Thiele, L., Deb, K., Coello Coello, C.A., Corne, D. (eds.) EMO 2001. LNCS, vol. 1993, pp. 314–328. Springer, Heidelberg (2001). https://doi.org/10.1007/3-540-44719-9_22
17. Zitzler, E., Deb, K., Thiele, L.: Comparison of multiobjective evolutionary algorithms: empirical results. Evol. Comput. **8**(2), 173–195 (2000)

Software Quality Education and Training

Exercise Perceptions: Experience Report from a Secure Software Development Course

Akond Rahman[1]([⊠])(iD), Shahriar Hossain[2], and Dibyendu Brinto Bose[3]

[1] Tennessee Technological University, Cookeville, TN, USA
arahman@tntech.edu
[2] Kennessaw State University, Kennessaw, GA, USA
[3] Reeve Systems, Dhaka, Bangladesh

Abstract. The ubiquitous use of software in critical systems necessitates integrating cybersecurity concepts into the software engineering curriculum so that students studying software engineering have adequate knowledge to securely develop software projects, which could potentially secure critical systems. An experience report of developing and conducting a course can help educators to gain an understanding of student preferences on topics related to secure software development. We provide an experience report related to the 'Secure Software Development' course conducted at Tennessee Technological University. We discuss student motivations, as well as positive and negative perceptions of students towards exercises. Based on our findings, we recommend educators to integrate real-world exercises into a secure software development course with careful consideration of tool documentation, balance in exercise diversity, and student background.

Keywords: Devsecops · Education · Experience report · Secure software

1 Introduction

With the emergence of the fourth industrial revolution[1] the use of software is becoming pervasive in critical systems, such as energy, health care, and transportation [4]. Security weaknesses in software used in critical systems can create serious consequences, such as creating large-scale outages, as it happened for Americold, a U.S.-based cold storage company[2]. Examples of cybersecurity attacks similar to that of Americold, highlight the need of educating software developers about cybersecurity concepts. Educators have also acknowledged to

---

[1] https://jia.sipa.columbia.edu/fourth-industrial-revolution-shaping-new-era.
[2] https://threatpost.com/food-supply-americold-cyberattack/161402/.

Partially funded by the U.S. National Science Foundation (NSF) award # 2026869. Special thanks to the PASER group at TnTU for their feedback.

A. C. R. Paiva et al. (Eds.): QUATIC 2021, CCIS 1439, pp. 521–535, 2021.
https://doi.org/10.1007/978-3-030-85347-1_37

bring in cybersecurity research concepts into the curriculum of software engineering so that students gain knowledge about the cybersecurity concepts [18].

To strengthen the computer science curriculum at Tennessee Technological University (TnTU), a faculty at the Department of Computer Science (CS) introduced the 'Secure Software Development' course in Fall 2020. The purpose of this graduate-level course was to provide students with fundamental knowledge and training on secure software development. The course focused on using a hands-on approach where students will learn about cybersecurity and software engineering concepts via class lectures as well as by solving programming exercises.

We present an experience report of the exercises that were conducted as part of the 'Secure Software Development' course. Our reported experience related to exercises can be helpful for other educators who want to adopt secure software development as a course into their CS curriculum. Furthermore, our experience report can provide clues for researchers on how to better integrate cybersecurity into software engineering.

We answer the following research questions:

- **RQ1:** *What are students' motivations for enrolling in the 'Secure Software Development' course? Based on student feedback, which components of the 'Secure Software Development' are aligned with student motivations?*
- **RQ2:** *What is the performance of students in exercises conducted as part of the 'Secure Software Development' course?*
- **RQ3:** *What are the positive perceptions of exercises conducted as part of the 'Secure Software Development' course?*
- **RQ4:** *What are the negative perceptions of exercises conducted as part of the 'Secure Software Development' course?*

We answer the research questions by analyzing grade books and survey results collected from a graduate course titled 'Secure Software Development', which was introduced for the first time at TnTU. To synthesize students' positive and negative perceptions we apply open coding [17], a qualitative analysis technique to generate high-level categories from text input. Prior to conducting the survey and analysis we obtain Internal Review Board (IRB) approval from TnTU (IRB#2316).

Our contributions are listed as follows:

- A list of positive perceptions expressed by students regarding exercises conducted in the 'Secure Software Development' course;
- A list of negative perceptions expressed by students regarding exercises conducted in the 'Secure Software Development' course;
- A list of students' motivations to enroll in the 'Secure Software Development' course; and
- A publicly-available repository of materials used to conduct exercises in the 'Secure Software Development' course [2].

2   Overview of the Course and Exercises

The course is titled 'Secure Software Development', which was introduced in the graduate curriculum in the Department of Computer Science (CS) at TnTU for the first time. The pre-requisite of this course for students was to be enrolled as a graduate student in the Department of CS at TnTU. Prior to conducting the course, the syllabus of the course was shared amongst all graduate students through e-mails in April 2020. A total of 12 students enrolled in the course. The instructor of the course conducted an initial survey of students' experience in software engineering and cybersecurity. The students' reported academic and professional experience in software engineering and cybersecurity is presented in Table 1. The course included three components: class lectures, exercises, and a semester long project assigned individually to each student.

Table 1. Students' experience in cybersecurity and software engineering

Experience	Cybersecurity	Soft. engg.
<1 year	8	4
1–2 years	2	1
3–4 years	2	4
>4 years	0	3

The course included eight exercises that discussed eight topics related to secure software development. Before assigning each exercise necessary theoretical concepts were covered by the instructor. Each of the exercises maps to a knowledge unit (KU) recommended by the U.S. National Center of Academic Excellence in Cyber Defense Education (CAE-CD) [13]. KUs are CS-related topics deemed essential or recommended by the U.S. National Center of Academic Excellence to develop a curriculum related to cyber defense education. We describe each of the exercises below:

Exercise#1 - Git Hooks for Automated Security Static Analysis: The purpose of this exercise was to help students learn how to integrate security using a single example of Git hook[3]. Automated security static analysis is considered as a good practice to integrate security into software development workflows. If a software repository uses Git, then using Git-based utilities, such as Git Hooks, automated security static analysis can be performed. As part of this exercise, students were asked to learn about Git hooks, and how to create a Git hook so that upon committing a file, a security static analysis tool can run and scan all files in the repository. To perform security static analysis the students used cppcheck, a security static analysis tool for C/C++ code[4].

---

[3] https://git-scm.com/book/en/v2/Customizing-Git-Git-Hooks.
[4] http://cppcheck.sourceforge.net/.

Exercise#2 - Logging Location: The purpose of this exercise was to identify locations where logging needs to be enabled for machine learning projects. In this exercise the students were asked to inspect machine learning code implementation in Python and identify locations where logging needs to be enabled but is not. Before assigning this exercise the students were exposed to concepts related to security-related logging provided by prior work [5, 9].

Exercise#3 - Privacy Violations in Software Projects: The purpose of this exercise was to make students aware of how implementation of a software project can violate privacy properties of individuals using the software. As part of this exercise, *first*, the students read a scientific paper [15] and identified personally identifiable identifiers (PIIs), i.e., what utilities of the Android development kit are susceptible to leaking information that can identify an individual. Examples of PIIs include permissions used in Android, such as ACCESS_FINE_LOCATION and GET_ACCOUNTS. *Second*, the students had to identify if these permissions are used in a set of 50 Android applications. *Finally*, the students were required to report which of the identified permissions from the first step were used in the source code of the collected Android applications.

Exercise#4 - Security Requirements Validation: The purpose of this exercise was to help students understand how security requirements can be translated to test cases and observe if a given piece of software satisfy the specified requirements. Security requirements are a specific sub-category of software requirements that are related to ensuring confidentially, integrity, or availability [7]. As part of this exercise the students conducted test driven development, where they *first* wrote test cases for a simple calculator to satisfy the following requirements: (i) the calculator must be able to multiply and divide, (ii) all methods related to mathematical operations should sanitize input, (iii) all methods related to mathematical operations should handle division-by-zero exceptions, and (iv) all methods related to mathematical operations should be fast. *Second*, following the practice of test-driven development, the students were required to write code so that the test cases written in the first step are satisfied.

Exercise#5 - Security Smells: The purpose of this exercise was to allow students to apply their knowledge related to security smells gathered in the lecture and apply it to SaltStack[5] scripts. Security smells are recurring coding patterns that are indicative of security weaknesses [16]. SaltStack scripts are used to implement the practice of infrastructure as code (IaC), the practice of managing system configuration automatically using dedicated programming languages and by applying recommended software engineering best practices [16]. As part of this exercise the students were asked to perform two tasks: *first*, the students were asked to manually inspect three SaltStack scripts to identify security smells. *Second*, the students were asked to build an automated program to detect the identified security smell instances.

Exercise#6 - Security Static Analysis for Adversarial Machine Learning: The purpose of this exercise was to help students learn about how security

---

[5] https://www.saltstack.com/.

static analysis can be conducted for machine learning projects at scale. Adversarial machine learning focuses on securing implementation of machine learning projects to protect against adversaries. Practitioners consider application of security static analysis as an important practice to protect machine learning projects against adversarial attacks [10]. As part of the exercise, *first*, the students were asked to use `bandit`, a static analysis tool for Python[6], and apply it automatically for 175 machine learning projects collected from the ModelZoo repository[7]. *Second*, the students were asked to automatically filter static analysis results that are of 'low' severity as reported by Bandit.

Exercise#7 - Taint Analysis: The purpose of this exercise was to give students hands-on experience about taint analysis. Taint analysis is the technique of tracking a potential security weakness in the source code for the software of interest [8]. Taint analysis can help to reduce false positives during security static analysis and also help understand which parts of the software are affected by the security weaknesses. As part of this exercise, the students had to inspect one Python file and perform two tasks: *first*, they had to report the complete flow of a taint, i.e., hard-coded password in the Python file. *Second*, they had to mine abstract syntax tree of the Python file to automatically report the complete flow of the taint.

Exercise#8 - White-box Fuzzing: The purpose of this exercise was to help students get hands-on experience on white box fuzzing and understand how white box fuzzing can help find faults in software. White-box fuzzing is the technique of providing malicious input by inspecting the source code of software artifacts and identify faults within the software [1]. In this exercise the students were asked to craft malicious input semi-automatically for an Ansible script. Ansible is a tool to implement the practice of IaC [16], which compiles and executes Ansible scripts to automatically provision cloud computing resources.

3   RQ1: Student Motivations

In this section we provide the methodology and findings for **RQ1: *What are students' motivations for enrolling in the 'Secure Software Development' course? Based on student feedback, which components of the 'Secure Software Development' are aligned with student motivations?***

3.1   Methodology to Answer RQ1

We collect student responses through an online survey that was deployed at the beginning of the semester. The purpose of this survey was to understand the experience level of students with software engineering and cybersecurity. As part of the survey we asked: *"What were your motivations to enroll in the 'Secure Software Development' course"*? The question was open-ended.

---

[6] https://bandit.readthedocs.io/en/latest/.
[7] https://modelzoo.co/.

We apply a qualitative analysis technique called open coding [17] to generate categories from the text responses to the question. The derived categories of student perceptions are susceptible to rater bias as the categories are all derived by the first author. We mitigate this limitation by allocating another rater who is the last author of the paper. The last author provided a mapping for the obtained responses to the identified categories. The agreement rate is 100% with a Cohen's Kappa [6] of 1.0.

3.2   Answer to RQ1

We identify three motivation categories for enrolling in the 'Secure Software Development' course. We describe these categories below. The name of each category related to student motivations is followed by the count of students who mentioned the identified category:

Motivation#1 - Academic Requirements (2 out of 12): Two students enrolled in the course to satisfy course requirements: *"this class will be helpful for my masters thesis and professional career"*.

Motivation#2 - Career Development (7 out of 12): Students were motivated by the fact that the content of the course could help in their career pursuits. As reported in Table 1, the enrolled students' experience in software engineering and cybersecurity varied, yet majority of the students perceived the course content to advance their professional career. One student stated *"I will be pursuing a cybersecurity related position, but I think that it [the course] will be something that will serve me well whether I choose to stay in a government position, go into private industry, or in academia"*. Strengthening software engineering skills was also a motivating factor as one student stated *"software development is not my strong suit and I want to gain knowledge on how I can develop software applications in a more robust way considering security"*.

Motivation#3 - Gain Research Background (3 out of 12): Students mentioned the focus and the content of the course may help them to conduct their research projects. One student mentioned *"I enjoy working in software security and I will be doing my course project consistent with my research work"*.

We also asked students about which course component helped them to satisfy their motivations. The question was presented as a survey and all students participated. As shown in Table 2 we observe students to perceive exercises to be most aligned with their motivations to enroll in the course, followed by the semester-long project.

Table 2. Exercises are perceived to be best suited with enrollment motivations

Experience	Respondent count
Exercise	11
Semester-long project	9
Lectures	8

4 RQ2: Student Performance in Exercises

In this section, we provide the methodology and results for **RQ2: *What is the performance of students in exercises conducted as part of the 'Secure Software Development' course?***

4.1 Methodology to Answer RQ2

We answer RQ2 by using information related to percentage of task completed obtained from the course gradebook. Once the deadline for each exercise passed the instructor inspected and graded the submission materials. Grades were assigned based on the amount completed and correctness of the provided solution.

4.2 Answer to RQ2

We answer RQ2 by reporting summary statistics for grades obtained for each exercise. The summary statistics for grades is provided in Table 3. From the statistics presented in Table 3, we observe students to perform the worst for taint analysis. Students performed the best for security requirements validation.

Table 3. Summary statistics of grades for eight exercises

Exercise name	Stats (min., median, max.)
Git hooks for automated security static analysis	(30%, 100%, 100%)
Logging location	(71%, 100%, 100%)
Privacy violations in software projects	(50%, 95%, 100%)
Security requirements validation	(85%, 100%, 100%)
Security smells	(45%, 65%, 100%)
Security static analysis for adversarial machine learning	(80%, 100%, 100%)
Taint analysis	(20%, 30%, 70%)
White-box fuzzing	(45%, 100%, 100%)

5   RQ3: Positive Perceptions of Exercises

In this section we provide the methodology and results for **RQ3**: *What are the positive perceptions of exercises conducted as part of the 'Secure Software Development' course?*

5.1   Methodology to Answer RQ3

For each exercise the students were required to participate in a survey that asked two questions: *(i) Survey_Q1: What are the positive aspects of the exercise?*, and *(ii) Survey_Q2: What are the negative aspects of the exercise?* We use the answers provided by the students for Survey_Q1 to answer RQ3. We apply open coding [17] to determine categories that express positive aspects of the students for each exercise. Our process of applying open coding was similar to that of deriving student motivations described in Sect. 3.1. Similar to RQ1, we conduct rater verification, where the last author provided a mapping for the obtained responses to the identified categories related to positive perceptions of students. The agreement rate between the first and last author for the obtained responses is 65% with a Cohen's Kappa [6] of 0.53.

5.2   Answer to RQ3

We identify six categories of positive perceptions. A mapping between each identified category and each exercise is presented in Table 4. The number of students who have reported the category for an exercise is presented in parenthesis. For example according to Table 4, skill set development was mentioned by six students for the exercise related to security smell detection. We describe each identified category related to positive perception below:

Positive Perception#1 - Lecture Reinforcement: The conducted exercises provided students the opportunity to get a better understanding of what was being taught in the class lectures. The exercises complemented the class lectures by providing students clarity, as noticed by one student for the security smell exercise *"[it] was nice to actually use what we learned in class and reinforce the material"*. For the logging-related exercise one student stated *"I got to actually implement some of the concepts discussed in class which can be beneficial to future work I will perform"*. One student found the exercises to be a better medium for learning the concepts taught as part of the lecture *"I always learn better from assignments that involve coding rather reading/studying the subject"*.

Positive Perception#2 - Practicality: All exercises were perceived as practical by the students. For the exercise related to privacy violation one student stated *"practical knowledge of identifying personally identifiable information (PII) in Android project source code"*. For the exercise related to security requirements validation one student stated *"I had been introduced to TDD before theoretically, and the process did not really make sense to me. With this [exercise] and actually going through the process with a practical, hands-on example*

Table 4. Positive perceptions and corresponding exercises.

Exercise topic	Reported positive perception
Git hooks for automated security static analysis	Skill set development (8), Practicality (7)
Logging location	Skill Set Development (4), Lecture reinforcement (4), Program comprehension (1), Practicality (4)
Privacy violations in software projects	Skill set development (7), Practicality (4)
Security requirements validation	Skill set development (4), Practicality (3)
Security smells	Skill set development (6), Lecture reinforcement (3), Practicality (5), Sense of accomplishment (1)
Security static analysis for adversarial machine learning	Practicality (4)
Taint analysis	Skill Set Development (5), Program comprehension (3), Practicality (2), Self evaluation (1)
White-box fuzzing	Skill set development (6), Lecture reinforcement (2), Practicality (7), Sense of accomplishment (2), Self evaluation (1)

was very helpful in understanding how it works and the usefulness of the practice; practical knowledge gain".

Positive Perception#3 - Program Comprehension: For exercises related to logging location, security smell detection, and taint analysis, students were required to inspect source code. As part of the assignment students navigated source code files written in Python and SaltStack, which helped them to better navigate source code. The exercises helped students to get better at program comprehension. For example, in the case of taint analysis one student stated *"The exercise of manually going through the code to track the tainted paths was a valuable and helpful exercise"*.

Positive Perception#4 - Self Evaluation: Students mentioned how the exercises helped them to self-evaluate their programming skills. The exercise related to taint analysis required programming using the 'ast' library[8], which helped students to assess what they knew. One student stated that the exercises are helpful because: *"they are highly applicable and from my personal point of view they exposing my shortcomings in programming"*.

---

[8] https://docs.python.org/3/library/ast.html.

Positive Perception#5 - Sense of Accomplishment: The exercises helped students to gain a sense of accomplishment. For the white-box fuzzing exercise one student was able to find a bug in the Ansible compiler, which the student perceived as an accomplishment: *"Being able to use fuzzing to test a production application and being able to cause a crash in that application"*.

Positive Perception#6 - Skill Set Development: For multiple exercises the students mentioned that the assigned exercises help them to learn new tools and techniques needed in software engineering. For the security smell exercise one student stated exercises of this nature *"is highly appreciated as it helps to get a diverse skill set"*. Completion of the fuzzing-related exercise required students to learn on how to parse YAML files, which one student perceived positively and stated *"it was cool to use pyyaml, I haven't done that before"*. About the exercise that involved security requirement validation a student stated: *"I've never used the python unit test module, and I believe this [exercise] gave me exposure and a hands on experience on performing/creating unit tests in Python"*. The idea of using Git hooks for secure software development came as a pleasant surprise for one student *"Very cool to learn about git hooks and realize how useful it could be for software projects. I was not aware that git provided this feature prior"*.

6   RQ4: Negative Perceptions of Exercises

In this section, we provide the methodology and results for **RQ4: *What are the negative perceptions of exercises conducted as part of the 'Secure Software Development' course?***

6.1   Methodology to Answer RQ4

We use the answers provided by the students for Survey_Q2 ('What are the negative aspects of the exercise?') included in our survey to answer RQ4. We apply open coding [17] to determine categories that express negative perceptions of students for each exercise. Our process of applying open coding was similar to that of RQ1 and RQ3. We also conduct rater verification, where the last author provided a mapping for the obtained responses to the identified categories related to negative perceptions of students. The agreement rate between the first and last author for the obtained responses is 83% with a Cohen's Kappa [6] of 0.62.

6.2   Answer to RQ4

We identify three categories of negative perceptions expressed by students for exercises. A complete mapping between the identified categories and the applicable exercise is provided in Table 5. In Table 5, the 'Reported Negative Perception' column states the negative perception category names and the count of students who stated the category enclosed within parenthesis. 'None' indicates that no negative perceptions were reported by students for a certain exercise. We describe each of the categories below:

Negative Perception#1 - Artifact Management: All artifacts i.e., datasets and scripts for each exercise was shared using a Docker image. The Docker image was available using the instructor's DockerHub account, which included all necessary dependencies to run certain programs needed to complete each exercise. While downloading the Docker images one student commented: *"seems unnecessary to download a docker image of some 800+ MB to work on a small python file".* Transfer of files back and forth between the Docker image and the development environment also created negative experience for one student: *"dev environment is in Windows ... Docker is in a virtual machine ... passing files back and forth is tedious".*

Negative Perception#2 - Lack of Background: Despite detailed written instructions, we observe students to express a lack of background for each of the eight exercises. For example, while identifying and detecting security smells in SaltStack scripts one student found comprehension of SaltStack scripts to be difficult: *"I think SaltStack scripts are hard to look through especially if your not familiar ... I spent a lot of time trying to look up and research how to get the scripts to parse".* For the logging-related exercise, one student was not familiar with machine learning, and stated *"I cannot really think of any negatives other than my limited experience with machine learning and zero experience with the Keras library. I struggled to know exactly what the code was doing in the* `doDeepLearning` *function.".* Even though the instructions on how to use the Docker image were given for each exercise, the students faced challenges: *"I didn't know that 'exiting' from the shell will destroy the running image, and when I rerun the Docker image all my work was gone".*

Negative Perception#3 - Limiting Documentation: Students expressed negative perceptions while following the instructions provided in the documentation of software libraries. For the taint analysis exercise one student found the documentation of the Python-based 'ast' library: *"Need to use the python library AST, which is difficult to understand from the documentation".* Such views were expressed by multiple students for the Python-based 'javalang' library that was needed to complete the exercise related to privacy: *"Struggled to find good resources for the javalang library beyond the basic examples and just ran out of time to try to get it to work".* Another student stated *"Couldn't find good documentation for javalang. Figuring out how to use the package was mostly trial and error with the* `dir()` *function and interactive python console to learn how to get the needed information".*

Table 5. Negative perceptions and corresponding exercises.

Exercise topic	Reported negative perception
Git hooks for automated security static analysis	None
Logging location	Lack of background (2), Artifact management (1)
Privacy violations in software projects	Limiting documentation (4)
Security requirements validation	None
Security smells	Lack of background (2), Artifact management (1)
Security static analysis for adversarial machine learning	Artifact management (1)
Taint analysis	Limiting documentation (2), Artifact management (1)
White-box fuzzing	Artifact management (3)

7 Discussion

We discuss the lessons that we learned from our findings as follows:

Students Prefer Real-world Exercises: We observe students to positively perceive exercises that involve code snippets collected from real-world open source projects and usage of real-world tools that are well-known in industry. Based on our findings, we advocate cybersecurity educators to design exercises and exams using real-world projects for a secure software development course.

The Good and the Bad of Exercise Diversity: Topic-wise exercises in the 'Secure Software Development' course are diverse, which involved a diverse set of technologies, such as SaltStack, Ansible, Python-based TDD, Android applications, Git hooks, and machine learning code developed in Python. On one side we have observed positive aspects of such diversity, for example, students being exposed to a diverse set of tools and techniques that enhance their skill set. On the other hand, students face challenges as they do not have necessary background. Based on our experience, we urge educators to be aware of the possible and negative aspects for introducing a diverse set of exercises, and find a balance that is adequate for a secure software development course.

Documentation and Tool Challenges: For multiple exercises students mentioned existing documentation to be limiting. For example, while completing the exercise related to taint analysis the documentation for 'ast' was hard to comprehend. Similarly, for the privacy violation exercise, students found the 'javalang' documentation to be hard to follow. Our findings show that students face documentation-related challenges while completing exercises. We urge software engineering researchers to systematically investigate the pervasiveness of the reported documentation-related challenges and identify techniques to miti-gate such challenges.

From our reported findings in Sect. 6.2, we observe that use of Docker image may be inappropriate for exercises as it incurs overhead with respect to com-putation time and storage. We urge CS education researchers to synthesize the best practices on sharing artifacts for students, which will ensure that necessary dependencies of a software artifact is installed with limited overhead.

The Curious Case of Taint Analysis: From Table 3, we observe majority of the students to not complete the exercise related to taint analysis. Even though the students expressed positive perceptions about the exercise itself, we observe a disconnect between their perceptions and their ability to complete the exercise. One possible explanation can be attributed to the documentation of ast, which students found lacking. Another possible explanation is that students were not previously exposed to compiler-related courses, which hindered the students to conduct the exercise. Till date, TnTU does not offer compiler-related course, which could have exposed students to concepts, such as parse trees and abstract syntax trees. The instructor used one class lecture to expose students to concepts, such as parse trees, liveness of variables, and recursion, but that may not have been sufficient to mitigate the deficiency of the students. The lesson learned from conducting the taint analysis exercise is that (i) not all graduate students may not be proficient in parse tree mining and/or recursion, and (ii) before assigning taint analysis exercises instructors should dedicate multiple lectures on program analysis and recursion.

Limitations of the Paper: Our derived categories related to perceptions are susceptible to rater bias, as they were derived by the first author. We mitigate this limitation by assigning another rater who mapped student response to the identified categories. We also acknowledge the identified findings are limited to the sample size: our findings may not be generalizable to other courses related to secure software development that are conducted at other universities. Further-more, our findings are derived from a course that was conducted once.

8   Related Work

Our paper is closely related with prior publications related to cybersecurity edu-cation. Beach [3] surveyed 129 education institutions that offer cybersecurity programs and reported 62% of the surveyed institutions do not consider human factors while developing their cybersecurity curriculum. Wood and Raj [20] described how key-logger exercises can be integrated into cybersecurity education curriculum. Lukowiak et al. [11] reported that presenting the course materials in an incremental manner helped students to reinforce the content provided in class lectures. Veneruso et al. [19] described their experience of using 'CyberVR', a game that uses visual reality, to teach cybersecurity concepts to students. Mountrouidou et al. [12] described their experience in integrating cybersecu-rity concepts into the general curriculum of a liberal arts degree and reported that if cybersecurity modules are flexible, then they can be incorporated into a general education curriculum. Olano et al. [14] reported their experience of introducing 'SecurityEmpire' in an undergraduate course to teach cybersecurity concepts to students. They [14] reported SecurityEmpire to help increase awareness and engagement about cybersecurity amongst students. Veneruso et al. [19] reported CyberVR to be equally effective, but more engaging in teaching cybersecurity-related concepts, compared to that of textbook-based methods. Theisen et al. [18] documented their experience of conducting a massively online open course (MOOC) related to secure software development, and observed on-campus students to have higher quiz scores than that of MOOC students.

The above-mentioned description shows the prevalence of experience reports related to a wide range of cybersecurity education concepts, such as hardware device, gaming, MOOCs, virtual reality, and industrial control systems. However, we observe a lack of research that discusses the experience of conducting a course related to secure software development, which we address in this paper.

9 Conclusion

We have reported our experience in conducting a secure software development course for the first time at TnTU. We document multiple types of perceptions that express students' positive attitude towards the assigned exercises, such as self evaluation, skill set development, and practicality. Students reported three categories of negative perceptions too, namely, lack of background, limiting documentation, and artifact management. Based on our findings, we recommend educators to integrate real-world exercises into a secure software development course with careful consideration of tool documentation, balance in exercise diversity, and student background.

References

1. Ammann, P., Offutt, J.: Introduction to Software Testing. Cambridge University Press, Cambridge (2016)
2. Anonymous: Materials for the Secure Software Development Course, December 2020. https://figshare.com/s/f40c6df28ab2a2b55165
3. Beach, S.K.: Usable cybersecurity: human factors in cybersecurity education curricula. Nat. Cybersecur. Inst. J. 1(1), 5–15 (2014)
4. Bures, T., et al.: Software engineering for smart cyber-physical systems: challenges and promising solutions. ACM SIGSOFT Softw. Eng. Notes 42(2), 19–24 (2017)
5. Chuvakin, A., Peterson, G.: How to do application logging right. IEEE Secur. Priv. 8(4), 82–85 (2010). https://doi.org/10.1109/MSP.2010.127
6. Cohen, J.: A coefficient of agreement for nominal scales. Educ. Psychol. Measur. 20(1), 37–46 (1960). https://doi.org/10.1177/001316446002000104
7. Firesmith, D., et al.: Engineering security requirements. J. Object Technol. 2(1), 53–68 (2003)

8. Gupta, M.K., Govil, M.C., Singh, G.: Static analysis approaches to detect SQL injection and cross site scripting vulnerabilities in web applications: a survey. In: International Conference on Recent Advances and Innovations in Engineering (ICRAIE-2014), pp. 1–5 (2014). https://doi.org/10.1109/ICRAIE.2014.6909173

9. King, J., Pandita, R., Williams, L.: Enabling forensics by proposing heuristics to identify mandatory log events. In: Proceedings of the 2015 Symposium and Bootcamp on the Science of Security, HotSoS 2015, Association for Computing Machinery, New York (2015). https://doi.org/10.1145/2746194.2746200

10. Kumar, R.S.S., et al.: Adversarial machine learning-industry perspectives. arXiv preprint arXiv:2002.05646 (2020)

11. Lukowiak, M., Radziszowski, S., Vallino, J., Wood, C.: Cybersecurity education: bridging the gap between hardware and software domains. ACM Trans. Comput. Educ. **14**(1), 1–20 (2014). https://doi.org/10.1145/2538029

12. Mountrouidou, X., Li, X., Burke, Q.: Cybersecurity in liberal arts general education curriculum. In: Proceedings of the 23rd Annual ACM Conference on Innovation and Technology in Computer Science Education, ITiCSE 2018, pp. 182–187. Association for Computing Machinery, New York (2018). https://doi.org/10.1145/3197091.3197110

13. NIETP: NIETP About CAE Program (2020). https://www.iad.gov/nietp/CAERequirements.cfm. Accessed 18 Dec 2020

14. Olano, M., et al.: SecurityEmpire: development and evaluation of a digital game to promote cybersecurity education. In: 2014 USENIX Summit on Gaming, Games, and Gamification in Security Education (3GSE 14). USENIX Association, San Diego, August 2014. https://www.usenix.org/conference/3gse14/summit-program/presentation/olano

15. Onik, M.M.H., Kim, C.S., Lee, N.Y., Yang, J.: Personal information classification on aggregated android application's permissions. Appl. Sci. **9**(19), 3997 (2019)

16. Rahman, A., Rahman, M.R., Parnin, C., Williams, L.: Security smells in ansible and chef scripts: a replication study. ACM Trans. Softw. Eng. Methodol. **30**(1), 1–31 (2021). https://doi.org/10.1145/3408897

17. Saldana, J.: The Coding Manual for Qualitative Researchers. Sage (2015)

18. Theisen, C., Williams, L., Oliver, K., Murphy-Hill, E.: Software security education at scale. In: Proceedings of the 38th International Conference on Software Engineering Companion, pp. 346–355 (2016)

19. Veneruso, S.V., Ferro, L.S., Marrella, A., Mecella, M., Catarci, T.: CyberVR: an interactive learning experience in virtual reality for cybersecurity related issues. In: Proceedings of the International Conference on Advanced Visual Interfaces, AVI 2020, Association for Computing Machinery, New York (2020). https://doi.org/10.1145/3399715.3399860

20. Wood, C., Raj, R.: Keyloggers in cybersecurity education. In: Security and Management, pp. 293–299. Citeseer (2010)

A Software Quality Course: The Breadth Approach

Luigia Petre[(✉)] [iD]

Åbo Akademi University, Turku, Finland
lpetre@abo.fi

Abstract. We present a Software Quality course taught in a MSc program in Computer Science and Engineering. The course takes an overview ('breadth') approach, reviewing the most important topics that contribute to the quality of software. The course has been taught traditionally as well as online; we discuss the advantages and disadvantages of both styles and point out what should be kept from the online experience. We also discuss the students' evaluation and feedback.

Keywords: Software quality · Requirements · Formal methods · Software architectures · Software metrics · Online teaching · Learning journals · Polls

1 Introduction

The hiring policies in software industry differ substantially from other domains. A person who has not graduated the heavy medical education programs will never be hired as a doctor in a respectable hospital, nor would anyone hire lawyers who have not passed their bar exam. A software company does not follow the same protocol. The candidates to hire are certainly scrutinised by their prospective future companies, maybe subjected to coding interviews and/or other methods, but a diploma is not necessarily a requirement [8] for working as a software engineer. Persons deemed intelligent and malleable enough can be hired by a company, who then trains them in developing specific skills in demand. This practice has an immediate consequence: many students drop from their university programs once they find suitable employment, with their education only partially completed. Given the ubiquity of software in our society, this situation is rather alarming: are these software engineers able to ensure the quality of the software running our lives?

Even more worrisome, the existing university curricula do not offer much in terms of software quality education. While students are offered a rather wide selection of programming languages and paradigms to choose from, the quality of their code is not much emphasised. Some curricula can have courses on algorithmic complexity, requirements, or software architecture, but they are not as common as the programming courses. Formal methods courses are often left

A. C. R. Paiva et al. (Eds.): QUATIC 2021, CCIS 1439, pp. 536–552, 2021.
https://doi.org/10.1007/978-3-030-85347-1_38

out completely, as are the software metrics courses. In this context, even the students who do graduate their respective programs, are not well prepared to analyse how 'good' certain software is or how to build software of good quality.

In this paper we present a course entitled 'Software Quality', taught in a MSc program in Computer Science and Engineering. After taking this course, the students should be able to:

- Identify and experiment with four pillars of quality software: **requirements, analysis (formal methods), software architecture**, and **software metrics**
- Devise a **requirements document**
- Perform **basic software analysis** with formal methods
- **Distinguish several software architectures** with their advantages and disadvantages for quality
- Recognize and evaluate **different software metrics**
- Enumerate and apply different **quality management techniques**

While this is surely not the first time a course on Software Quality was taught, the novelty of our approach consists in recognising the complex nature of software quality and, hence, investigating a wide array of topics that contribute to it. For instance, formal methods are not typically considered an essential topic for software quality, unless formal methods researchers are involved. Still, formal methods are the only way to capture software 'blueprints' and to provide qualitative assessment of various software properties. It is also important to recognise that formal methods do not (cannot) tell the whole story of software quality, one reason being scalability.

We argue that, for students completing their software engineering education, a course like this one is beneficial, as it offers the big picture of what good software is about. Depending on the topic they will specialise and be employed in, they can later focus on certain aspects, be that requirements, formal analysis, software architecture and/or software metrics. Moreover, for students not completing their software engineering degrees, working with a skilled software quality manager may be instrumental. These no-degree employees are the stereotypical intelligent programmers, more than able to assimilate and eventually master needed topics. Knowledgeable software quality managers can pinpoint exactly the techniques needed in their particular jobs, be that requirements elicitation, feature verification, unit testing, documentation readability, etc.

In addition to the content, we also explain the teaching methods we used in the course. They essentially boil down to the Roman 'repetitio mater studiorum' proverb, meaning that repetition is the mother of learning. We use various techniques for this, such as weekly learning journals and regular polls and quizzes to enforce repetition. The feedback from students has been positive; apparently they are engaged by these methods rather that overwhelmed.

The online teaching aspect is also discussed. We compare the results of teaching this course traditionally vs online and point out what we believe should be kept from the online experience.

We proceed as follows. In Sect. 2, we present the main tenets of the course and we overview its structure. Section 3 reviews the teaching of the four pillars: requirements, formal methods, software architectures and software metrics, respectively. Section 4 explains the quality management topic. In Sect. 5 we explore the evaluation of students throughout the course and in Sect. 6 their feedback. Conclusions are presented in Sect. 7.

2 Basic Concepts and the Particulars of the Course

As with many concepts related to software, terminology can be vague and mean many things. The notion of Software Quality is no exception. Expectations of a 'good' software may include code 'cleverly' built - whatever that might mean, fast software, or a good user interface, to name a few. This is the starting point for the course, exploring the terms of software, quality, and software quality for a whole 1.5-h lecture.

Software. We begin with the idea that software is eating the world [2]. Software is a wonderful human development, which has increased our quality of life tremendously. It has revolutionised entire industries, with businesses replaced almost completely by software, such as in music and photography, to businesses where their products' value comes increasingly more from software, such as in the car manufacturing. It has created an immense work space and continues to be employed in aiding or solving a huge array of problems, leading to its increased complexity: it is harder to pinpoint exactly all it does. This leads to the concept of software crisis, where methods for developing small software systems kept being applied for their large counterparts, leading to famous software failures. For avoiding the latter, we need to better understand the definition and nature of software, which we do by investigating a classical reference [5].

Quality. To grasp what is meant by quality, in general, we delve into a bit of history, recognising notable personalities with an influence on quality, such as Frederick Winslow Taylor (1910s), Henry Ford (1863–1947), Walter Shewhart (1920s), and W. Edwards Deming (1950s). Often, we only present the technical aspect of our topics (to save time), but explanations about the people who led to particular developments (and why) are motivating the students. We distinguish between quality assurance and quality control, explaining that quality assurance allows a shift to the 'left': we take care of this earlier in the product lifecycle.

Software Quality. With an adequate understanding of the concepts of software and quality, we move on to explore what is usually understood by the concept of software quality. Based on a classical source [5], we first underline the four main software characteristics contributing to the challenge of ensuring its quality: complexity, conformity to other interfaces, changeability, and invisibility. We then emphasize four partial solutions to software quality, namely the 'buy vs build' solution, the refinement of requirements and rapid prototyping, the incremental development, and the contribution of great designers. We analyse these in some detail and emphasize how they keep being valid more than three decades after they were suggested.

We then move on to more concrete terms and topics we will explore in some detail during the course. We first distinguish between functional (what the system should do) and structural quality (how the system should do it). The concepts of fault, error and failure are also defined and placed in the context of quality assurance vs control. We point to some bodies whose mission is, in a form or another, software quality and explain their main role in quality management, hence their treatment in that module of the course. We end this part by explaining the four pillars of the course, namely Requirements Engineering, Formal Methods, Software Architectures, and Software Metrics. We also show how they correspond to the classical principles proposed by Turing award recipient Fred Brooks [5].

It always seems to be a surprise to the students to learn that a software of good quality is the one implementing its requirements (functional and structural), nothing more and nothing less.

2.1   Structure and Teaching Methods

This course has been taught several times, always in an 8-week period, both typically, in a classroom, as well as online. The components of the course are: (1) Lectures (with polls), (2) Learning Journals (mandatory), (3) Quizzes, (4) Discussion Seminars, and (5) Exam (mandatory). The components are distributed as follows during the 8 weeks:

- Lect. 1 (week 1) → The concepts of software, quality, and software quality
- Lect. 2 (week 1) → Requirements - types and elicitation
- Lect. 3 (week 2) → Requirements - specification, validation, evolution
- Discussion seminar 1 (week 2) → we exercise requirements
- Lect. 4 (week 3) → Models and TLA+: the case of Amazon Web Services
- Lect. 5 (week 3) → The case of the French metro and modelling in Event-B
- Lect. 6 (week 4) → Program verification, the case of Dafny
- Discussion seminar 2 (week 4) → we discuss examples of specifications in TLA+, Event-B and Dafny
- Lect. 7 (week 5) → Model checking, SAT and SMT solvers run our provers
- Lect. 8 (week 5) → Software Architecture is key
- Lect. 9 (week 6) → More software architecture fundamentals for quality and how could measurement and metrics for software help us
- Discussion seminar 3 (week 6) → we discuss logical properties, we ponder about some architecture questions and reflect on testing, bugs and correctness
- Lect. 10 (week 7) → Software metrics for internal product attributes (mostly size)
- Lect. 11 (week 7) → Software metrics for internal and external product attributes (structure, usability, maintainability, security)

- Lect. 12 (week 8) → Quality Management - planning, standards, ISO 9001, reviews and inspections
- Invited lecture (week 8) → Quality in Space Software

The optional components of the course are the lectures, the quizzes, and the discussion seminars. There are typically 12 regular lectures and one invited lecture at the end of the course, to exemplify how software quality is ensured in space software. There are three discussion seminars, where we typically explore the concepts of the previous lectures in more depth. During every lecture, the teacher poses several online and anonymous polls checking whether some explained concepts have been well understood. Each poll consists in 1–2 multi-choice questions relating to a concept or methodology just explained by the teacher. After the students reply online (they are given a minute usually), the teacher displays the proportion of answers on each option and discusses what is the correct answer. Since not all the students can (nor have they to) participate in the lectures, these polls are then posted as quizzes to be - optionally - taken at any time during the course. Each taken quiz is worth max one point (out of 100 for maximum grade of the course).

The only mandatory components of the course are the learning journals and the exam. Every week, the student has to fill in a learning journal entry, of half a page to one page (or longer if desired). In each entry, they should explain what are the main concepts they learned during that week, give some definitions and examples, and discuss the topics in any way they see fit. They are encouraged to also ask questions, to point out what topics were new to them or were seen before, as well as what they enjoyed and what they did not. The teacher then reads each entry and replies to questions, comments on the entry and awards maximum 2.5 points per lecture. In a week with two lectures, this means the learning journal can earn maximum 5 points, and in a week with one lecture and one discussion seminar - maximum 2.5 points. Hence, the learning journals can bring up to 30% of the grade. The remaining 70% is to be obtained from the exam, which reviews the concepts learned during the course.

As seen, the maximum grade can be obtained only from the mandatory components (learning journals and exam), but additional points can be obtained from quizzes (max 12 points in total).

3   Content of the Course

The four main pillars of the software quality that we explore in the course are requirements, formal methods, software architecture, and software metrics. In the following we shortly overview our approach in teaching them.

3.1   Requirements

Getting the requirements wrong, even partially, is the single most devastating reason for software problems, be them only faults or errors, or full blown failures.

Although many universities (including ours) have at least one course dedicated to (functional) requirements, we dedicate two lectures to requirements in this course and emphasize their role in software quality. There were some students (up to 10%) who remarked that they knew all about this topic, but the vast majority appreciated the overview, especially in light of the 'surprising' definition of software quality - implementation of requirements. Below we discuss the topics we cover with respect to requirements.

Requirements Definition and Types. Given the vast diversity of software, understanding what a requirement is, who formulates it and how is of high relevance. There are several ways of classifying requirements, the most important of which are descriptive vs prescriptive, user vs system, and functional vs non-functional. We discuss these in some details, with the help of examples. Understanding the levels of abstraction implicit to classes of stakeholders, the immutability of some requirements, or the necessary measurability of non-functional requirements are topics that contribute to the quality of software we develop.

Requirements Engineering. Getting the requirements into a requirements document is referred to as requirement engineering. This is an iterative process, well described in standard software engineering books [12]. We investigate the following topics:

- **Requirements Elicitation.** We start with the extreme approaches of business geniuses such as Steve Jobs' opinion that customers do not know what they want or Henry Ford's observation that, if queried, customers would have desired faster horses (not cars). Obtaining the requirements from customers is a complex process, involving often contradictory, incomplete or changing requirements. Several methods of elicitation are analysed, such as interviews, ethnography and stories.
- **Requirements Specification.** There are several alternatives to formulating requirements, in natural language, in some structured or tabular forms, or as use cases. We review all these with examples, and then ponder on the sections of the requirements document and its users.
- **Requirements Feasibility and Validation.** Not all systems can or should be built; in feasibility studies we focus on asking the right questions to determine if it is worth to develop a software. Once we determine it is, validating the requirements with the stakeholders is very useful.
- **Requirements Change.** Software is infinitely malleable, as debated in the initial lecture, hence changing it and its requirements is to be accounted for. Traceability is one essential aspect that, if not handled properly, can threaten software quality. For that, we explore traceability methods especially.

3.2 Formal Methods

A formal method allows to analyse a model of the software or even the software itself, to verify it respects certain properties.

Why Formal Methods. Formal Methods are not a mainstream teaching subject in today's universities. Their promoters are the researchers and, more recently, some industrial giants: Amazon [6,9], Facebook [10], and Google [11].

Software is embedded almost in all aspects of the society, so it is necessary to be able to guarantee what it does before deploying it. This is particularly essential in critical software, such as air transportation, army, nuclear plants, medicine, etc. Mass software construction does not rely on formal methods, but on simulation and testing. While these techniques have their uses, we argue for them being insufficient: clear analysis of models is needed, and we discuss models to understand their role in formal methods.

When Formal Methods. The software lifecycle with respect to quality is four-stepped: (1) we collect the relevant (user and system, functional and non-functional) requirements, (2) we draw the software architecture of the system, (3) we apply formal methods to the modules identified via software architecture, and (4) we evaluate our results with software metrics. The effective implementation of the software takes place during steps (2)–(3).

In this course we treat formal methods before software architectures, because they address the analysis of functional requirements; software architecture deals with analysing the non-functional requirements. In addition, formal methods require a special mindset that is likelier to be present in the first half of the course.

Three Formal Methods. We assume we have a correct set of requirements: how do we transform them into software and how do we guarantee that all the requirements and nothing more is implemented? We explore this with three formal methods: TLA+, Event-B, and Dafny.

- **TLA+** TLA+ is reviewed with two case studies: its adoption at Amazon [9] and by following its inventor, Turing award laureate Leslie Lamport, teaching the modeling and verification of a famous logical problem: the water jug riddle. This was part of the quest in the Bruce Willis and Samuel Jackson movie Die Hard 3. At some point, the heroes need precisely 4 gallons of water and they have two jugs, a 3-gallon one and a 5-gallon one, that they can fill with water from a tap. Model checking is employed to verify properties, i.e., all states of the modeled system are explored for these properties. In particular, model checking is used to verify that there is no possible sequence of actions that can end up with the bigger jug having exactly 4 gallons of water; the TLA+ model checker returns a counterexample, meaning it found a particular sequence of actions that achieves that.
- **Event-B** Event-B is motivated by its active use at Siemens, to develop the software on driverless trains [4]. Event-B comes with a tool for proving: we first write the model and the tool verifies its correct syntax; nothing out of ordinary so far. But then, we also formulate properties that we would like our model (the future software) to respect: the tool verifies if these properties

hold for the model. Moreover, we can start from a simple model capturing just the essence of the software, and then add details. The tool keeps checking if the more complex version still respects the properties and if it is indeed a correct development of the simpler model. This development strategy is called refinement.
- **Dafny** Dafny is two languages into one: an imperative language, with an executable core and a functional, specification language for annotations. Annotations describe what a program should do, and Dafny generates proofs that the annotations match the code; if it cannot, then it asks for proof hints, which might be given or might suggest a problem t0 resolve. Amazon Web Services (AWS) use Dafny and other formal tools [6] and claim that this is one of the main reasons why people move to AWS: they want formal guarantees that their data is stored correctly.

How Formal Methods Prove. An extra lecture delving into the proving techniques in formal methods is necessary at this point. We investigate mainly model checking and satisfiability (SAT and SMT) checkers. With this, the students are shown the breadth of the topic of formal methods as well as the richness of its aspects. It equips the students with knowledge that - given the scarcity of higher education in this field - can offer them a big advantage compared to their peers. The relatively brief excursion into formal methods (4 lectures) is not exhaustive by far, but with it, the students know the main coordinates as well as where to look for more.

3.3   Software Architectures

We now address non-functional requirements, after the treatment of functionality with formal methods. Non-functional requirements are a direct consequence of the unavoidable complexity of software, hence the overall structure of the software system becomes relevant. In software architecture, we refer to non-functional requirements as **software qualities** and to design decisions for achieving them as **tactics**.

- **Software Qualities.** We focus on availability, modifiability, performance and security. Availability is concerned with failures, modifiability with changes, performance with timing, while security combines availability (providing services to legitimate users) with resisting unauthorised users.
- **Tactics.** For each quality, there are tactics that favour it and tactics that do not. This is one of the cornerstones of understanding software architecture: there are many ways to implement a certain functionality, some better for certain goals. It is impossible to satisfy all possible qualities, hence defining the most important ones for a system allows a trade-off with the various stakeholders [3].
- **Architectural styles.** A collection of tactics forms a particular software architecture. People have devised generic styles that promote or inhibit certain software qualities. We analyse several styles and focus on cloud architectures, since the concepts are familiar to students; they have an easier time to

depict the main architectural issues of interest and then to generalise them to other styles [12].

- **Views and Documentation.** Another aspect of complexity inherent to software is that we can decompose a system based on various criteria: functionality, concurrency, physical allocation, etc. These are structures of a system that can be viewed in different ways, for instance in certain templates or diagrams. This is important for building the system, but also for documenting it.

3.4   Software Metrics

In this module we describe how we can measure the quality of software [7].

- **Software measurement.** We start by clarifying what we want to measure, for instance the likelihood of product failure or delay, of losing key personnel, of bankruptcy, etc. In general, the ideal is of getting a 'big picture' indicator of software 'goodness' during development or maintenance. We clarify that there are several entities we can measure, such as products, processes, or resources, and for each we can have several attributes we are interested in, both internal (say, size for code) or external (say, reliability for code). The problem in software measurement is that we want to control external attributes such as reliability of code (a product), productivity for personnel (a resource), or cost-effectiveness for design (a process). However, we can only measure internal attributes, for instance code, team or design size.
- **Software size.** Size is an interesting internal attribute that is used widely to predict many other measures. We learn to express size in the number of lines of code, differentiating between more and less important lines; Halstead's length, vocabulary and volume; the number of function points. We learn to use size to normalize measures of other attributes, quantify the amount of reuse, and measure attributes related to software testing.
- **Software structure.** Software structure manifests as structure of data (trail of data items as created or handled by the program) and structure of control (sequence in which instructions are executed in a program). This can indicate issues impossible to see with the number of lines of code, for instance, the iterative and looping nature of the program. Since there is a link between structure and quality of software, we investigate structure in some detail. Structure is usually detected by studying flowgraphs, so we quickly review them. We discuss structured programming, prime decomposition, cyclomatic complexity, and as an example, their applicability in testing. Flowgraphs illustrate the inner structure of software modules, but there are also attributes for measuring the overall structure of a software system and its inter-module relations. We study here modularity, morphology, tree impurity and internal reuse.
- **External attributes.** We are interested in measuring the quality of software code, especially its external attributes that depend on users. What we can measure, however, are the internal attributes, that can well be predictors

of external attributes and that are available for measurement early in the software lifecycle. In contrast, the external attributes depend on the user's interaction with the (ready) system, so much later in the software lifecycle. We discuss in some detail the measuring of defects, usability, maintainability and security.

4   Quality Management

Should software quality be the job of the software engineers, should some administrators take care of it, or both? We argue for the last option and explain what it means to have both a software engineering and a software quality team [12].

Quality Processes and Culture. While small and large software projects have different quality assurance processes, we can apply a quality process to any software project. A specific quality management team (different from the software engineering team) needs to ensure the realisation of such a process. The expectation is that a 'good' process will lead to a 'good' software. The quality and the project managers can agree on a particular quality assurance process, with a certain number of milestones. The process can follow standards for quality that are specific to the organisation and/or to the specific product being developed. The quality manager should report to higher management, while the project manager should have the freedom to ratify what quality procedures are relevant to the current project.

Standards. Software standards are important for several reasons. They can be a reservoir of best practices, used to avoid past mistakes; they can clarify the organisation's view on quality or even the user expectations; they can provide for smooth adaptation and/or continuity for new employees, who understand the organisation through the prism of its standards. The quality and project managers can define both process and product standards. Both types should avoid being over-prescriptive and requiring excessive clerical work. A method of convincing software engineers on the worth of following standards is to include them in the process of devising them. There are numerous international and national standards as well, and certain companies require to work only with other companies who have followed particular software standards (e.g., ISO 9001). However, such standards typically confirm the presence of a particular process that has been followed in creating certain products; the quality of said products is a totally different issue.

Reviews and Inspections. The most typical type of quality 'assurance' in companies is that of organising reviews and inspections. The reviews can 'sign off' a certain product, to move into the next phase and should be organised with several participants well in advance. Program inspections can be simpler, such as peer reviews where the most common mistakes are checked, e.g., 'have all variables been initialised?' or 'is each loop certain to terminate?' or 'has space been allocated correctly?', etc. The existence of a quality culture in the organisation is of utmost interest here, since blame pointing is really unhelpful and can lead to people hiding and refusing to share their code.

5   Course Evaluation

As can be seen from the described course content, the topics are modular and we delve into each of them only to some level of detail. Ideally, a university should have more courses to offer on each of the topics (requirements, formal methods, software architectures, software metrics, and quality management). In a software quality course we can only have an overview (breadth-approach) of these topics and study how they contribute to improving the software products.

Fig. 1. Some software quality slides

This breadth-approach required a certain approach to teaching, based on repetition, to better cement the certainly new concepts. First off, the lectures were made as interesting as possible, with each slide well-thought of in terms of content and pictures. Some examples of slides are shown in Fig. 1. Then, to interrupt the monotony of the teacher talking, we introduced several polls per lecture. These polls are very easy to implement in Zoom, for instance, but can be certainly kept when returning to traditional teaching. One thing we can safely assume about our students is that they all have a mobile device with them, and so they can type some tiny-url addresses that can take them to the anonymous polls. DirectPoll [1] is one such resource. The results of their voting can be then shown on the big screen. This feature is entertaining both for teachers and

Poll 5:Why FM@Amazon   1 question   Yes

1. Why did Amazon AWS people started to look for formal methods? (Multiple Choice)

> Answer 1: Because Microsoft, Facebook and Google already used them, and they did not want to be left behind.
>
> Answer 2: Because of the complexity of their algorithms and code
>
> Answer 3: Because of subtle bugs in designs
>
> Answer 4: Because they wanted to replace the standard verification techniques in industry (design reviews, code reviews, stress testing, fault injection, etc) with formal methods.
>
> Answer 5: Because they are in a critical business domain.

Fig. 2. A poll

Why did Amazon AWS people started to look for formal methods?

a. Because they wanted to replace the standard verification techniques in industry (design reviews, code reviews, stress testing, fault injection, etc) with formal methods.

b. Because they are in a critical business domain.

c. Because Microsoft, Facebook and Google already used them, and they did not want to be left behind.

d. Because of the complexity of their algorithms and code

e. Because of subtle bugs in designs

Fig. 3. A quiz question

students, makes the students more willing to focus on what is taught, knowing there will be a check-up very soon, and contributes to the repetition of concepts, as argued in Sect. 1. It is also very friendly: it is anonymous, the teacher explains the correct choice immediately after, and can also discuss the probable reasons some other options were chosen as well as why they were not correct. If some students really do not have a mobile device with them, then the polls are available as quizzes during the whole duration of the course; this also helps people who do not take part in the lectures. An example of a poll is shown in Fig. 2 and its quiz counterpart in Fig. 3.

The second way of implementing repetition to favour learning is by using weekly learning journals. They are rather modern and many courses implement them; the difference from the approaches in many other courses is that, in the presented course, the teacher really reads all entries and provides feedback, even if short. While a student listens to a lecture, certain questions and comments arise, but they are maybe unexpressed due to a variety of reasons (shyness, not wanting to interrupt the teacher, what will other people think if I ask this, etc.). The learning journals are the place to ask everything; they offer regular slices of personalised teaching, each learning journal entry being a private discussion between the teacher and the student. It is in fact very enriching for both parties. Comments like 'more polls', 'less slides', 'go slower', 'can we study cloud architectures too?' are only some examples of feedback to the teaching style. The most interesting and thought provoking questions and comments are those

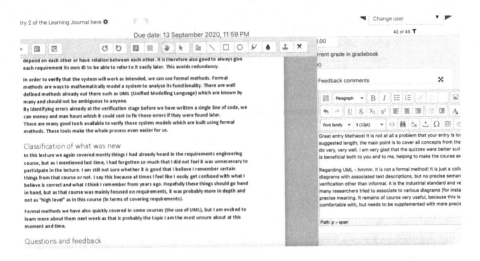

Fig. 4. A learning journal entry

related to content, because the students understand the material in their own unique way, influenced also by their background and sometimes work experience. An example of a learning journal entry is shown in Fig. 4.

The third way of implementing repetition is by introducing three discussion seminars, paced throughout the course, one after three lectures. There we discuss ideally all that students would like to delve deeper into. In practice, students are again shy and expect the teacher to come up with topics of discussion. We set up little problems and exercises (sometimes posed a few days before the seminar) to sparkle up the discussion. This works better in the traditional setting than online, but overall, people like to be poked and prodded a little and asked to explain their opinion.

All in all, these three methods (polls, learning journals and discussion seminars) contribute to exercise all the topics we discuss about in the lectures. They reinforce the concepts, clarify them, and keep the students engaged and interested. The most rewarding aspect is that the students appreciate the effort (for instance to read and reply to the learning journals questions) and so it all seems like a good idea worth continuing with.

6   Students' Feedback

In our university, the students' feedback is not mandatory nor recompensed, hence we have rather low rates of participation, about 30%. With this is mind, we explored the following questions for student feedback:

1. "I believe that the content of the course was, overall, according to its learning objectives." (4)
2. "The structure of the course helped me to achieve its learning objectives" (4)

3. "The course materials helped me achieve its learning objectives." (3.93)
4. "The teacher's pedagogical skills supported my learning." (3.73)
5. "I have actively participated in the course activities." (3.47)
6. "I feel that the course supported my education and/or future work." (3.8)
7. "I feel that the course has worked well in digital form." (4)
8. "Free comments on questions 1–7 and the course in general. What worked well and what less well?"
9. "The experience of writing a learning journal helped." (4)
10. "Could you please explain in a few words how was your experience of learning the whole course online? Was it lonely? Was it better? Did you miss anything?"
11. "Do you feel like you understand software quality better after this course?"

For questions 1.–7. and 9., students must choose between grades 1–4, 4 representing 'totally of the same opinion' and 1 meaning 'totally of the opposite opinion'. The scores obtained are indicated in parentheses. The comments for question 8. are below:

1. "Some lectures had a tad too much info, otherwise the format was good".
2. "Great material and engaging polls during the lectures".
3. "The course was quite interesting and thanks to the teacher, she never made the course boring".
4. "It was a very helpful course. The only thing which was quite hard for me is size of lecture slides, in my opinion there were too many slides".
5. "I feel good about the course content and the teaching method. Big thank to the lecturer!"
6. "For a remote course all went really well in my opinion"
7. "There's been only one issue with the course. I think it would have been better if students were expected to gain a certain number of points from their learning journal entries instead of having to submit all of them. Otherwise the course was very informative and the streaming format worked very well. I'm also glad that the teacher provided feedback to our learning journal".
8. "Very thorough course. I learned several concepts during this course. I like that it is in digital form".
9. "The course is designed, structured and executed well".

The answers to question 10. are below:

1. "Was better for me as i work besides school so was nice that the lectures were recorded so I could watch them later".
2. "It was well planned and went smoothly for me. In fact, online course is better than the traditional one as learning at own pace and own comfort zone is easier".
3. "It was ok, no problems".
4. "Face-to-face courses are always better in my opinion, but the teacher handled the distance courses very well. Being able to watch again the lectures is a big plus".

5. "It was great, easier to focus".
6. "I missed the face to face interaction with fellow students, but also the teacher. I can't speak to if the course was "better" when it was held online this year. But I can say that the course lectures did not suffer because of it. Maybe even better, because of the Zoom polls".
7. "Specifically for this software quality, it was quite good, not lonely at all. I like it".
8. "It worked perfectly with my situation at the moment, online studies and work are a perfect fit, almost"
9. "My online learning experience is good in general. Some major benefits: I can arrange my time to watch the recorded lessons later. I can target the interesting parts of the course. I can skip some parts that I already knew".
10. "For me remote learning is preferred, since I have to actively work. I could tackle immediate work tasks when needed (once during this course) without losing time to move around the campus".
11. "I actually prefer it to normal lectures, because I can always go back to recorded videos. I can also watch materials whenever it fits my schedule. I can manage my time more efficiently and so I learn better. Distant learning has been a bit lonely, but I think it works well with courses that consist mostly of lectures".
12. "My experience of this course is very good. I was learning it in my own time and I didn't feel much pressure".
13. "It was challenging to always try to keep focused when you are at home with so many distractions".
14. "I am used to the online mode of learning now, and it was designed engagingly with the discussion seminars and quizzes".

The replies to question 11. were different shades of 'yes'; one answer stood out: "Even if I have years of experience working as a programmer, the course is still very helpful to connect and fulfil my understanding of software quality, especially regarding the software quality practices from big companies".

7   Conclusions

Given freedom in the job of teaching a course whose content is not totally standard, there is a big temptation to choose one's favourite topic related to the course name. In the present case, formal methods were briefly considered to form the (only) body of the course, also given their relative under-representation in Computer Science and Engineering curricula. But formal methods require a certain background and a certain openness in the local industry - not everyone lives in Seattle to be hired by Amazon. More importantly, they do not tell the whole story of Software Quality. Getting the requirements well is certainly the starting point. The huge complexity of contemporary software makes formal methods inapplicable on the whole system in all details, requiring software architecture techniques to reach modules of functionality. Finally, we need a way to measure what we produce; logical properties again do not tell the whole story and need to be supplemented by measuring a variety of attributes (e.g., structure).

We taught this course in both settings - traditional and online. The traditional setting has the advantage of 'reading' the students much better. Compare discussing our topics with and in front of our students and getting immediate body language feedback on the quality of our discourses with looking at cameras and talking in front of our laptops, with tens of black rectangles representing the students, neither seen nor heard. The online setting has made it possible for more students to take the course (51 compared to 19), since the barriers of being in the classroom were eliminated. We recorded the lectures and saved the videos in the Moodle page of the course; we (a digital assistant) even split each main video of a lecture into several smaller videos addressing certain topics and saved those too in the Moodle page. These are likely to remain useful regardless of the teaching style. A hybrid style is in fact very probable, in which the traditional teaching is resumed, but the lectures are still recorded for those who cannot make it to class.

Finally, we found especially the learning journals and the polls to be extremely useful for learning. They seemed to also be entertaining for both teachers and students, and so learning becomes almost a game. These ideas can certainly be re-purposed for other courses as well, especially those courses with abstract and harder to grasp topics.

References

1. Direct poll. https://www.directpoll.com. Accessed 20 Apr 2021
2. Andreessen, M.: Why software is eating the world. Wall Street J. (2011). Accessed 9 Apr 2021
3. Bass, L., Clements, P., Kazman, R.: Software Architecture in Practice, 3rd edn. Addison-Wesley, Boston (2013)
4. Behm, P., Benoit, P., Faivre, A., Meynadier, J.-M.: Météor: a successful application of B in a large project. In: Wing, J.M., Woodcock, J., Davies, J. (eds.) FM 1999. LNCS, vol. 1708, pp. 369–387. Springer, Heidelberg (1999). https://doi.org/10.1007/3-540-48119-2_22
5. Brooks, F.P.: No silver bullet - essence and accident in software engineering. Comput. J. **20**(4), 10–19 (1987). Accessed 9 Apr 2021
6. Cook, B.: Formal reasoning about the security of Amazon web services. In: Chockler, H., Weissenbacher, G. (eds.) CAV 2018. LNCS, vol. 10981, pp. 38–47. Springer, Cham (2018). https://doi.org/10.1007/978-3-319-96145-3_3
7. Fenton, N., Bieman, J.: Software Metrics: A Rigorous and Practical Approach, 3rd edn. CRC Press, Boca Raton (2015)
8. Milord, J.: No degree? No problem. Here are the jobs at top companies you can land without one. LinkedInNews, 8 April 2019. Accessed 20 Apr 2021
9. Newcombe, C., Rath, T., Zhang, F., Munteanu, B., Brooker, M., Deardeuff, M.: How Amazon web services uses formal methods. CACM **58**(4), 66–73 (2015)
10. O'Hearn, P.: Continuous reasoning: scaling the impact of formal methods. In: Logic in Computer Science, pp. 13–25. ACM (2018)

11. Sadowski, C., van Gogh, J., Jaspan, C., Söderberg, E., Winter, C.: Tricorder: building a program analysis ecosystem. In: International Conference on Software Engineering, pp. 598–608. IEEE (2015)
12. Sommerville, I.: Software Engineering, 10th edn. Pearson Education, London (2016). Accessed 20 Apr 2021

Students Projects' Source Code Changes Impact on Software Quality Through Static Analysis

Sivana Hamer[(✉)], Christian Quesada-López, and Marcelo Jenkins

University of Costa Rica, San José, Costa Rica
{sivana.hamer,cristian.quesadalopez,marcelo.jenkins}@ucr.ac.cr

Abstract. Monitoring and examining source code and quality metrics is an essential task in software development projects. Still, it is challenging to evaluate for educational projects due to the time and effort required by instructors, and constant change during the software project evolution. In this paper, we used an automated approach to analyze source code and quality metrics' evolution and impact in software engineering projects using static code analysis on each software change (commits and merges). We examined five undergraduate software engineering projects' changed modules, compilability, and source code and quality metrics (size, complexity, duplication, maintainability, and security). In total, we assessed 12,103 changes from 103 students contributing to the projects. Our approach allowed us to identify students' project trends in the impact of the source code changes, providing insights into behaviors such as technology knowledge deficiencies, issues in continuous integration practices, and software quality degradation. We believe that the early, constant feedback on student software engineering project quality can help instructors improve their courses and students enhance their development practices. Tracking of source code evolution could be done via static analysis and instructors could use the analysis results for teaching.

Keywords: Change analysis · Quality metrics · Project based learning · Software engineering education · Mining software repositories

1 Introduction

Software development emphasizes the importance of delivering functionality, but it is also vital to focus on software quality [1]. Quality is essential for the reliability and effectiveness of the software products [2]. Software engineering education requires more attention in improving quality skills, among others, as there is a gap for early career software engineering graduates between what they know and what the industry requires [3]. This gap has lead to a paradigm shift in education towards project-based learning to help students acquire skills needed in their professional careers [4]. Still, there are several challenges in assessing students' skills

© Springer Nature Switzerland AG 2021
A. C. R. Paiva et al. (Eds.): QUATIC 2021, CCIS 1439, pp. 553–564, 2021.
https://doi.org/10.1007/978-3-030-85347-1_39

as it evolves, consumes considerable time and effort, lacks objective and widely accepted metrics, and requires timely feedback [5,6]. Therefore, instructors and students require early, constant, and real-time feedback in software engineering projects with tools that automatically extract software metrics.

To gather insights into the evolution of quality in student projects, measurements can be used to assess the status of projects and products [7]. Specifically, source code metrics allow us to gain insights into software attributes measured, including code quality measurements [8]. Recent approaches have focused on not only analyzing the quality of different software versions and their evolution, but also the impact of each change in a project using Distributed Version Control Systems, such as Git [9], that save every source code change [1]. Automating the collection of metrics can help instructors identify trends gaining insights into students' behavior, and students improve their development practices.

In this paper, we applied an automated approach [10] to analyze the evolution and impact [1] of source code and quality attributes in software engineering projects. Our goal was to gain insights in students' development practices and software quality trends and behaviors by analyzing the source code changes. We analyzed how changes impact the source code and quality of different aspects of software engineering projects using a static code analyzer. We examined five undergraduate software development projects' changed modules, compilability and software quality based on attributes for size, complexity, duplication, maintainability and security. With the recollected data, we found several improvement opportunities for software engineering practices in software courses. This work investigated the following research questions:

RQ1. To what extent do students commit impactful changes?
RQ2. To what extent impactful changes affect software quality attributes?

This is a work in progress evaluating our approach in five students' projects to determine the feasibility of the tool. For future work, we plan on gathering both instructors' and students' feedback on our approach to study the benefits in the learning process. The remainder of the paper is organized as follows. Section 2 details related work. Section 3 presents the methodology. Section 4 details the results. Finally, Sect. 5 details the conclusions and future work.

2 Related Work

Several approaches have focused on measuring student projects. Mierle et al. [11] determine indicators for student performance using behavior, work habits, and code quality measures. Robles and González-Barbona [12] automatically evaluate students' assignments using code quality, software metrics, and work metrics. Bai et al. [6] developed an online-offline approach that provides an automatic customized assessment and feedback tool, measuring aspects for the issues, commits, branches, test coverage, and code quality. Koetter et al. [5] examined, at the end of the life cycle of a software project, maintainability metrics, and code history. Hamer et al. [13] analyzed Git contributions and their distribution of contributions for students, teams, and projects. Recent approaches have also focused on incorporating software quality assurance practices in development courses. Gomes et al. [14] propose a tool and an approach for software quality assurance, finding that the tool provided support in understanding source code quality. Raibulet and Fontana [15] found that students were enthusiastic about developing a software project using GitHub, SonarQube, and Microsoft Project. Lu et al. [16] incorporated a continuous inspection tool in students' software development projects and evaluated how it affects software quality. Plösch and Neumüller [17] studied the impact of using static analysis tools on students' software quality. We extend our previous work by creating a tool and analyzing four additional projects, focusing on the instructors' point of view [10].

3   Empirical Study

3.1   Measurement Approach and Change-Impact Analysis

Our approach was based on the work of Behnamghader et al. [1]. For the application of our automated measurement procedure, the modules were obtained from the changes metadata in the repository, the compilability by executing each change in the project, and the source code, and quality metrics by analyzing each version of the source code (snapshot) using the static code analyzer SonarQube (version 8.4 with default settings). These metrics were used to determine the impact of a change (commit and merges), and the difference between the current and previous snapshot. The tool maintains the link between each change, and the students or teams who contributed to the change to provide real-time feedback about these metrics.

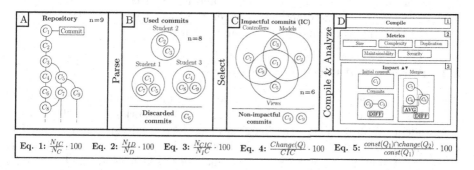

$$\text{Eq. 1: } \frac{N_{IC}}{N_C} \cdot 100 \qquad \text{Eq. 2: } \frac{N_{ID}}{N_D} \cdot 100 \qquad \text{Eq. 3: } \frac{N_{CIC}}{N_{IC}} \cdot 100 \qquad \text{Eq. 4: } \frac{Change(Q)}{CIC} \cdot 100 \qquad \text{Eq. 5: } \frac{const(Q_1) \cap change(Q_2)}{const(Q_1)} \cdot 100$$

Fig. 1. Automated measurement approach. Adapted from [10].

Figure 1 shows the stages of the automated measurement approach. In *Stage A* the project repository is selected and the changes extracted. Then, in *Stage B*, the changes are parsed, where students with multiple identities are grouped up into one account using mailmaps. From our analysis we excluded students who withdrew from a course. Next, in *Stage C*, we selected the changes that impacted the main modules. The main modules were the modules that save the majority of the source code [1]. In our case, as the web applications were developed in ASP.NET MVC, the main modules were the folders of Controllers (application logic), Models (data entities), and Views (user-interface). The database project files (DB) and the testing project files were also considered for the analysis (but as non-main modules). The testing project files includes test cases for Unit & Integration testing (U&I tests) and User Interface testing (UI tests). Finally, in *Stage D* the snapshot for each impactful change is compiled and built, and the metrics for the compilable changes are extracted using the static analysis tool. We considered five groups of metrics provided by the tool[1]: size, complexity, duplication, maintainability, and security. Size represents the magnitude, measured in lines of code (LC), number of functions (FN), number of classes including nested classes, interfaces, enums and annotations (CS), and commented lines of code (CL). Complexity is measured in cyclomatic complexity (CX) and cognitive complexity (CC). Cyclomatic complexity is calculated based on the number of paths through the code [18]. Cognitive complexity measures how hard it is to understand the code's control flow [19]. It is calculated based on ignoring structures with multiple statements into only one, the linear code flow and nested structures [20]. Duplication refers to duplicated source code. Duplicated lines (DL) are the number of lines repeated, while duplicate files (DF) are the number of files with duplicated lines. Maintainability refers to the ease of maintenance, measured in number of code smells (SM), and minutes of technical debt (TD). Finally, security references how protected a software system is, measured in the number of vulnerabilities (VL). The formula to calculate the impact of the metrics on the changes depends on the type of change. The impact of the initial change is the value of each software attribute, for changes with one parent (i.e., commit) is the difference between the current software attribute and the preceding change (parent change), and for changes with more than one parent (i.e., merge) is the difference between the current software attribute and the average of the preceding changes (parent changes).

3.2 Projects and Git Repositories

The student projects were developed in a third-year undergraduate course offered at the University of Costa Rica, with 16 to 25 students working on each project. The students applied agile methodologies (mostly scrum) divided into teams of 4 to 7 members using scrums of scums. Each project developed one web application with a relational database. The main technologies used were ASP.NET MVC, Visual Studio, SQL Server, C#, JavaScript, HTML, CSS, and Git. All projects planned were in the same domain (transnational information systems), and they were comparable in size and complexity to the teams size that developed them. Examples of the developed projects include assessment systems for teachers and classroom reservation systems. Table 1 summarizes the projects, including the number of student, teams, changes (commits and merges), impactful changes (IC), and cumulative size in lines of code (LC). In total, we analyzed 12,103 changes from 103 students contributing to the projects.

---

[1] https://docs.sonarqube.org/latest/user-guide/metric-definitions/.

4   Results

In this section, we answer each research question. The results and visualizations for the projects are available at https://tinyurl.com/dve55xae.

4.1   Changes' Impact on the Software (RQ1)

We calculate the percentage of impactful changes (Fig. 1 Eq. 1) using the number of changes (N_C) and impactful changes (N_{IC}). We also determine the percentage of students with impactful changes (Fig. 1 Eq. 2) with the number of students changes (N_D) and the students who performed impactful changes (N_{ID}). Table 2 shows, per each main module, the number of changes (Changes, n), the impactful changes and percentage of changes (Changes, Impactful), the number of students (Students, n), and students contributing to impactful changes and percentage of students (Students, Impactful). We also calculated the percentage of compilable impactful changes (Fig. 1 Eq. 3) with the number of impactful changes ($N_I C$) and compilable impactful changes ($N_C IC$). Table 2 shows the number and percentage of compiled impactful changes (Changes, Compilability).

In total there are $7,983$ commits and $4,120$ merges. Thus, there are 1.94 commits per merge. This allows us to identify continuous integration practices during the project. This allowed us to identify continuous integration practices during the project which seemed to be high. Still, if students had difficulties merging code this could increase this metric, thus more training should be conducted to improve this practice. On average 84% of the changes impacted the main modules with an emphasis on changing Views (64%). Therefore students' primary focus was the main module, specifically focusing on the front-end. The module with the most change variation was Models, ranging from 34% to 54%. There are differences in behavior between commits and merges. Merges are more likely to be impactful than commits, as 97% of the merges and 78% of the commits are impactful. Impactful commits always have as the most to least contributed modules Views, Controllers and Models.

Figure 2 shows the number of changes that impacted each module set. Subfigure 2a shows the main modules impacted by changes. Out of the $10,130$ impactful changes in the main module, $4,323$ (43%) change only one, $2,613$ (26%) change

Table 1. Student projects

Project	Students	Teams	Changes	IC	LOC
SE1	25	5	3,477	2,789	27,726
SE2	21	4	1,656	1,452	7,123
SE3	20	4	2,253	1,820	16,881
SE4	21	4	2,464	2,094	21,006
SE5	16	3	2,253	1,975	11,527
$\sum$	103	20	12,103	10,130	84,263

Table 2. Average percentages of impactful changes, students, and compilable impactful changes

Module	Changes			Students			Changes	
	A	IMP	%	A	IMP	%	COM	%
Controllers		1,363	57		21	100	1,168	86
Models	2,421	951	41	21	21	100	778	83
Views		1,513	63		21	100	1,324	88
All		2,026	84		21	100	1,766	88
St. dev	593	438	3	3	3	0	286	7

two and 3,194 (31%) change all three of the main modules. Hence, changes tend to cover multiple development layers. Views is the module that is significantly most likely to be contributed without changes to other modules, with 29% of the changes only affecting this module. When students contributed to two modules, they tended to focus on changes to adjacent development layers (i.e., between the Controllers and Views, or Controllers and Models). Subfigure 2 shows all the projects modules impact of changes. Other modules were also highly contributed, with 5,401 changes (44% out of the 12,103 changes). Only 1,298 (10%) changes affected only other modules. The most to least changed non-main modules are DB with 4,418, U&I tests with 2,109 and UI tests 397. Non-main modules also are more likely to have cross-functional changes. There are 675 changes that are not included in any of these six modules, including changes to the files for configuring git, JavaScript source code, and project configuration.

The percentage of students with impactful changes shows that all students contribute to at least one impactful change and merge in the main modules across every project. Meanwhile, impactful commits were not always contributed. All students contributed to a change in DB and U&I test modules. But, 18% of the students did not contribute to UI tests. Furthermore, this problem in non-main modules contributions is very widespread. The number of students who did not commit to the DB, U&I test and UI test is 5%, 11% and 50%, respectively. Specifically, in UI tests, SE1 and SE2 commit participation ranges from 67% to 84% of students not participating. Still, even the project with the highest participation in commits for UI tests, SE4, has 19% of the students not-contributing.

The percentage of compilable impactful changes results indicate that, on average, 88% of the impactful changes compile. Merges are less compilable (83%) than commits (91%) across all projects. The most compilable module for all the projects is Views (88%), followed by Controllers (86%) and lastly Models (83%). The compilable changes drastically varied from projects ranging from 69% to 94%, with all projects having compilability issues. Furthermore, merges are still considerably less compilable than commits across all projects.

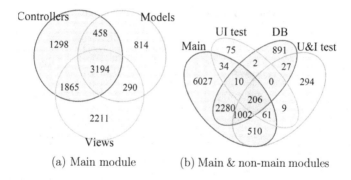

(a) Main module   (b) Main & non-main modules

Fig. 2. Modules impacted by changes

We also analyzed for the non-compilable changes how many errors were there, who produced them, which modules caused the errors, what compilability issues were raised, and why the errors were produced. Out of the 1,302 non-compilable impactful changes, we found 8,782 errors were 97%, 75%, and 93% of the students participated in non-compilable changes, commits and merges, respectively. Compilability errors were widespread for all students, with more errors while merging. Errors originated from changes to the Controllers, Models, application and session events, packages, configurations, and binaries. Compilability problems originated from the Version Control Systems while merging and configuring Git files. Changes may have compiled locally but due to modifications to the configuration files, files were missing when changes were integrated. Students also had issues with the project's Models and configuration.

Results show that not all students are contributing to all the modules, though all of them do seem to contribute to the main module. Hence, further attention must be given to the projects to verify if students are actually developing full-stack development skills, specially related with testing practices. Students faced several difficulties with Git and the development framework. Therefore, students require further training with the development technologies with workshops or laboratories. Furthermore, good development practices such as compiling the code before integrating branches and following pull request procedures need to be further emphasized with stricter protocols.

4.2 Changes' Impact on Quality Metrics (RQ2)

We analyze how changes impacted each quality attribute (percentage of impactful changes). The percentage of impactful changes (Fig. 1 Eq. 4) is calculated with the impactful changes with compilable parents CIC and compilable impactful changes that either increased or decreased the quality attribute $change(Q_y)$. Table 3 shows the average percentage of change that impacted the source code metrics (P), changes which increased the metrics (▲) and changes which decreased the metrics (▼). We also examine how the changes evolve and impact

Table 3. Source code metrics changes

Module	LC			FN			CS			CL			CX			CC			DL			DF			SM			TD			VL		
	P	▲	▼	P	▲	▼	P	▲	▼	P	▲	▼	P	▲	▼	P	▲	▼	P	▲	▼	P	▲	▼	P	▲	▼	P	▲	▼	P	▲	▼
Controllers	84	70	14	52	45	7	19	17	2	65	49	16	69	59	10	60	51	9	22	13	9	11	8	2	64	46	18	67	45	21	2	1	1
Models	34	31	3	30	27	3	20	19	2	15	13	2	30	27	3	5	5	0	2	2	0	2	2	0	25	22	3	26	21	4	0	0	0
Views	80	62	17	0	0	0	0	0	0	30	22	8	28	23	5	0	0	0	36	21	15	23	15	7	21	17	4	22	17	5	0	0	0
All	78	63	16	38	32	5	17	15	2	51	38	13	50	43	7	40	34	6	33	19	14	20	14	6	48	35	13	49	34	15	1	1	0
St. dev	7	6	2	6	6	0	5	5	1	2	2	1	7	6	1	6	5	2	7	4	3	3	3	2	6	4	2	4	3	2	2	2	1

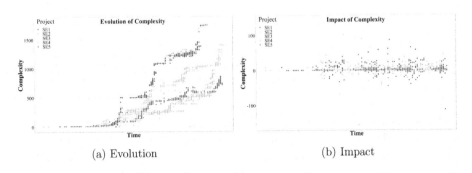

(a) Evolution   (b) Impact

Fig. 3. Cyclomatic complexity evolution and impact by project

the quality attributes. For example, Fig. 3 shows the evolution of the Cyclomatic Complexity metric for each project with the accumulative changes and the impact of the changes. The Y-axis represents the values of the analyzed attribute, and the X-axis the evolution during the project.

For the size metrics, LC changes in 78% and increases in 63%. The Models is the module that changes this metric the least and also has the highest variation between projects. Hence, the contributions to Models vary by project. Furthermore, this metric increases around deadlines mostly in a step-like pattern. This step like increase can be seen for all metrics except VL across all projects. The average impact of a commit is 18 LC. Furthermore, FN changes in 38% and increases in 30% of the changes. For the Views, the metrics FN, CS and CC had a 0% percentage of change, hence were mostly not detected in the case of our technology. Models also have 15% of variation between projects. On average, a commit impacts in 1 FN. CS change percentage is 17%, with a 15% of increase. The LC per CS shows that the size of classes varies greatly between projects. This shows that students add code more frequently than they comment it. Furthermore, as the size metrics can be separated by module the languages used could be further analyzed.

For complexity metrics, we found that the CX percentage of change is 50%, increasing in 43% of the changes. On average, commits impact 0 CX and changes impact 5 CX. We found that the relationship between LC and CX is not linear in some projects. Most of the projects have the percentage of change for the Models near 0%. In the case of these MVC projects, this indicates that the students follow the instructions to implement business rules in the business layer.

DL changes in 33% of the changes, increasing in 19% of the changes. The average impact of a commit is 4 DL. Therefore, DL seems to be quite prevalent in student projects. Views is the module that has the most changes in DL, increasing the metric in 21% of the changes. The DL per LC, for all projects except SE2, is around 4, hence DL is very prevalent in the projects. DF changes in 20% of the changes and increases in 14% of the changes. The module with the most DF is also Views. DL and DF have a step-like behavior but also dips a bit around deadlines. Thus students are considerably reducing duplicate code.

SM changes on average in 48% of the changes, increasing in 35% of the changes. On average, a commit impacts in 1 SM. The Controllers module has the highest percentage of change of SM. Furthermore, SE3 has the highest SM, by a considerable margin, out of all the projects even though it is not the biggest project in LC. Thus, SM does not also follow a linear relationship with LC. The SM per CS ranges between 5 to 11. TD percentage of change is 49%, and percentage of change increase is 34%. On average, a commit impacts, for the metric TD, is 2 minutes. Also, the module with the most changes for TD is Controllers. The technical debt varies considerably between projects, ranging from 1,432 to 3,647 minutes. The relationship between TD and LC is also not linear, as SE3 and SE4 have a higher TD per LC (10) than SE5 (8).

Lastly, the metric of VL detected at most 10 VL in the Controllers and Views. For this metric, future work is addressed to identify the types of vulnerabilities to analyze their impact on projects from a security perspective.

We also examined why impactful changes occurred by analyzing 10 commits across all projects, whose impact is the farthest away from the average for each metric. In total, this generated 62 commits, as some commits were impacted by multiple metrics. We found 8 commits that either commented or uncommented code due to problems generated by changes in the Models, impacting the size, complexity and maintainability of the software significantly. In 5 commits, we found refactoring efforts reducing considerably at least a complexity metric and generally the maintainability. Also, we found in 7 commits that removed old code, considerably reducing the size, complexity and maintainability metrics. CS changes were affected in 4 commits by changing the Models metadata or creating a Model manually. In 8 commits, a View was either added or updated that severely increased the duplication and LC metrics. Lastly, we found 8 cases were most or all a feature was added, usually from end-to-end, always increasing the complexity and LC metrics.

Students had difficulties in producing high quality software with degradation over time, thus a bigger focus should be given to training students in producing quality software. Specifically, we found evidence that students contribute a lot of duplicate code to the Views, while the Controllers module requires the most attention with regards to complexity and maintainability. Therefore, quality assurance activities should be followed throughout the project using the metrics to determine the quality deficiencies and improve the product. Instructors should also consider the complexity and effort required by each module in their analysis.

5 Conclusions

Analyzing source code changes can offer useful insights about software development practices and courses improvement opportunities for student projects. The results show the feasibility of our approach to collect data about the changes, changed modules, developers, compilability, and software quality. Our findings give instructors' information for multiple improvement opportunities for students' software projects. Our approach helps to determine patterns in students' changes that include software modules students are contributing to, who is contributing to each of the modules, what are the trends in the compilability errors, why students produce compilability errors, and what effects (evolution and impact) do changes have on software attributes (size, complexity, duplication, maintainability, and security). The results could be used to identify recurring problems in projects, such as lack of technology competency, continuous integration deficiencies and evidence that software quality degration. We believe our approach can be applied in any project where instructors desire to improve students' software development practices and competencies, providing constant, early and real-time data to instructors and students alike.

Instructors can gain data-driven insights into how impactful changes affect different facets of the software projects, specifically, the changed modules, compilability and software quality. This helps instructors understand what is happening in software projects, and plan how to improve the courses and instructions. Furthermore, as the approach can be automated instructors can focus on tackling didactic issues from the collected data. We recommend instructors to consider the data in real-time to determine improvement opportunities in courses, such as additional activities or protocols, and aid in grade assignment. Students benefit from gaining timely and objective feedback on their development skills, particularly in creating high-quality software. This helps students understand how their changes affect software attributes and identify future areas for improvement that they can focus on, becoming more marketable to employers. These benefits are not limited to students but also include software development professionals.

As future work, we plan to analyze in more depth the causes, types, and patterns of code smells, vulnerabilities, and technical debt of changes for students and teams to determine expected and outlier behavior. As we only included metrics available from SonarQube, we also plan to include other tools to gather more metrics. Furthermore, the changes impact could be further analyzed to determine patterns between the different metrics. Finally, we plan on applying the approach in an online student project, and gather both instructors' and students' perceptions of the tool to reveal the real value of the approach.

Acknowledgments. This research was partially funded by Universidad de Costa Rica, project No. 834-C1-011.

References

1. Behnamghader, P., Alfayez, R., Srisopha, K., Boehm, B.: Towards better understanding of software quality evolution through commit-impact analysis. In: 2017 IEEE International Conference on Software Quality, Reliability and Security (QRS), pp. 251–262. IEEE (2017)
2. Gillies, A.: Software Quality: Theory and Management. Lulu. com (2011)
3. Garousi, V., Giray, G., Tuzun, E., Catal, C., Felderer, M.: Closing the gap between software engineering education and industrial needs, IEEE Software (2019)
4. Quesada-López, C., Martínez, A.: Implementation of project based learning: lessons learned. In: XLV Latin American Computing Conference (CLEI), pp. 1–10. IEEE (2019)
5. Koetter, F., Kochanowski, M., Kintz, M., Kersjes, B., Bogicevic, I., Wagner, S.: Assessing software quality of agile student projects by data-mining software repositories. In: Proceedings of the 11th International Conference on Computer Supported Education-Volume 2: CSEDU, INSTICC. SciTePress, 2019, pp. 244–251 (2019)
6. Bai, X., Li, M., Pei, D., Li, S., Ye, D.: Continuous delivery of personalized assessment and feedback in agile software engineering projects. In: Proceedings of the 40th International Conference on Software Engineering: Software Engineering Education and Training, 2018, pp. 58–67 (2018)
7. Fenton, N., Bieman, J.: Software Metrics: A Rigorous and Practical Approach, Third edn. CRC Press, Boca Raton (Oct 2014)
8. Nuñez-Varela, A.S., Pérez-Gonzalez, H.G., Martínez-Perez, F.E., Soubervielle-Montalvo, C.: Source code metrics: a systematic mapping study. J. Syst. Softw. **128**, 164–197 (2017)
9. Chacon, S., Straub, B.: Pro git. Apress (2014)
10. Hamer, S., Quesada-López, C., Martínez, A., Jenkins, M.: Measuring students' source code quality in software development projects through commit-impact analysis. In: Rocha, Á., Ferrás, C., López-López, P.C., Guarda, T. (eds.) ICITS 2021. AISC, vol. 1331, pp. 100–109. Springer, Cham (2021). https://doi.org/10.1007/978-3-030-68418-1_11
11. Mierle, K., Laven, K., Roweis, S., Wilson, G.: Mining student CVS repositories for performance indicators. ACM SIGSOFT Softw. Eng. Notes **30**(4), 1–5 (2005)
12. Robles, G., Gonzalez-Barahona, J.M.: Mining student repositories to gain learning analytics. In: IEEE Global Engineering Education Conference (EDUCON), pp. 1249–1254. IEEE (2013)
13. Hamer, S., Quesada-López, C., Martínez, A., Jenkins, M.: Measuring students' contributions in software development projects using git metrics. In: 2020 XLVI Latin American Computing Conference (CLEI). IEEE (2020)
14. de Andrade Gomes, P.H., Garcia, R.E., Spadon, G., Eler, D.M., Olivete, C., Correia, R.C.M.: Teaching software quality via source code inspection tool. In: 2017 IEEE Frontiers in Education Conference (FIE), pp. 1–8 (Oct 2017)
15. Raibulet, C., Arcelli Fontana, F.: Collaborative and teamwork software development in an undergraduate software engineering course. J. Syst. Softw. **144**, 409–422 (2018)
16. Lu, Y., Mao, X., Wang, T., Yin, G., Li, Z.: Improving students' programming quality with the continuous inspection process: a social coding perspective. Front. Comput. Sci. **14**(5), 145205 (2020)

17. Plösch, R., Neumüller, C.: Does static analysis help software engineering students? In: Proceedings of the 2020 9th International Conference on Educational and Information Technology, ser. ICEIT 2020. New York, NY, USA: Association for Computing Machinery, pp. 247–253 (Feb 2020)
18. McCabe, T.J.: A complexity measure. IEEE Trans. Softw. Eng. **4**, 308–320 (1976)
19. Barón, M.M., Wyrich, M., Wagner, S.: An empirical validation of cognitive complexity as a measure of source code understandability. In: Proceedings of the 20: ACM / IEEE International Symposium on Empirical Software Engineering and Measurement (ESEM). IEEE Computer Society Press, 2020, pp. 1–12 (2020)
20. Campbell, G.A.: Cognitive complexity-a new way of measuring understandability, SonarSource SA, p. 10 (2018)

Author Index

Printed in the United States
by Baker & Taylor Publisher Services